Sources of World History

Readings for World Civilization

Sources of World History

Readings for World Civilization

Volume I

FIFTH EDITION

MARK A. KISHLANSKY
Harvard University

WADSWORTH
CENGAGE Learning™

Australia • Brazil • Japan • Korea • Mexico • Singapore • Spain • United Kingdom • United States

WADSWORTH
CENGAGE Learning

Sources of World History: Readings for World Civilization, Volume I, Fifth Edition

Mark A. Kishlansky

Senior Publisher: Suzanne Jeans

Acquisitions Editor: Nancy Blaine

Development Manager: Jeff Greene

Development Editor: Larry Goldberg

Editorial Assistant: Emma Goehring

Senior Media Editor: Lisa Ciccolo

Content Project Management: PreMediaGlobal

Senior Marketing Manager: Katherine Bates

Marketing Coordinator: Lorreen Pelletier

Marketing Communications Manager: Caitlin Green

Senior Art Director: Cate Rickard Barr

Print Buyer: Sandee Milewski

Senior Rights Acquisition Specialist, Text: Katie Huha

Rights Acquisition Specialist, Image: Jennifer Meyer Dare

Production Service: PreMediaGlobal

Cover Designer: Lori Leahy, Mighty Quinn Graphics

Cover Image: Ando Hiroshige (Utawaga Hiroshige) (1797–1858). *Evening Snow at Asakusa,* from the series Eight Views of Edo. Color print from woodblocks. Japan, c.1843–47. Victoria and Albert Museum, London, Great BritainPhoto Credit: V&A Images, London/Art Resource, NY

Compositor: PreMediaGlobal

For product information and technology assistance, contact us at **Cengage Learning Customer & Sales Support, 1-800-354-9706**

For permission to use material from this text or product, submit all requests online at **www.cengage.com/permissions** Further permissions questions can be emailed to **permissionrequest@cengage.com**

Library of Congress Control Number: 2010939316

ISBN-13: 978-0-495-91317-7

ISBN-10: 0-495-91317-0

Wadsworth
20 Channel Center Street
Boston, MA 02210
USA

Cengage Learning is a leading provider of customized learning solutions with office locations around the globe, including Singapore, the United Kingdom, Australia, Mexico, Brazil and Japan. Locate your local office at **international.cengage.com/region**

Cengage Learning products are represented in Canada by Nelson Education, Ltd.

For your course and learning solutions, visit **www.cengage.com**

Purchase any of our products at your local college store or at our preferred online store **www.cengagebrain.com**

Instructors: Please visit **login.cengage.com** and log in to access instructor-specific resources.

Printed in the United States of America
1 2 3 4 5 6 7 15 14 13 12 11

Contents

PART I   Ancient Societies   1

Origin Stories   1

The Cradle of Civilization   24

Contents by Region

Middle East

Chronological Contents

Preface

Sources of World History is a collection of documents designed to supplement textbook and lectures in the teaching of world civilization. The use of primary materials is an essential component of the study of history. By hearing the voices of the past, students come to realize both the similarities and differences between their society and previous ones. In witnessing others ponder the same questions that rouse their own curiosity, students feel a connection between the past and the present.

Moreover, by observing the ways in which such questions and experiences are worked out and described, students come to an understanding and respect for the integrity of other cultures. In confronting the materials of the past, students exercise an historical imagination that is at the heart of the teaching and learning of history.

Historical sources are the building blocks from which instructor and textbook writer have ultimately constructed their accounts and their explanations of world historical development. It is essential that even beginning students learn that the past does not come to us prepackaged but is formed by historians who exercise their own imaginations on primary materials. Historical thinking involves examining the ideas of others, understanding past experiences on others' terms, and recognizing other points of view. This is a process that makes everyone, student and instructor alike, an historian.

I have observed a number of principles in selecting the materials for this collection, which is designed for beginning-level college students. I believe strongly in the value of primary materials and feel that they should be made as accessible to contemporary students as possible. Thus, I have preferred to use up-to-date translations of many texts despite the costliness of acquiring their rights. Many of the late-nineteenth-century translations that are commonly used in source books present texts that are syntactically too complex for modern students to comprehend easily. I have also chosen to present longer selections than is usual in books of this type.

Unlike works that contain snippets of hundreds of documents, *Sources of World History* presents a sizable amount of a small number of sources. It therefore allows students to gain a deeper feeling for authors and texts and to concentrate their energies and resources. No selection is so long that it cannot be easily read at a sitting, and none is so short as to defy recall. Each selection raises a significant issue around which classroom discussion can take place or to which lectures can refer. Some may even stimulate students to seek out the complete original works.

Two other principles lie behind the selections I have made. The first is that a steady diet of even the world's greatest thinkers is unpalatable without other varieties of social and cultural materials. For this reason, I have tried to leaven the mass of intellectual history with materials that draw on social conditions or common experiences in past eras. Not only should these aid students in making connections between past and present, but they should also introduce them to the varieties of materials from which history is re-created. Secondly, I have been especially concerned to recover the voices or highlight the experiences of those who are not always adequately represented in surveys of world civilization. The explosion of work in social history, in the history of the family, and in the history of women has made possible the inclusion of materials here that were barely discovered a generation ago. Although this effort can be clearly seen in the materials chosen for the modern sections, it is also apparent in the selections made from earlier documents.

By providing longer selections and by expanding the scope of the materials to be incorporated, I have necessarily been compelled to make some hard choices. There exists a superabundance of materials that demand inclusion in a collection such as this. I have tried to find representative examples of the works of each of the major civilization complexes—Asia, Africa, Latin America, and the Islamic world as well as the central works of Western civilization. This poses very difficult problems of balance, equity, and accessibility. Because early African and Latin American civilizations were oral cultures, they have necessarily left fewer documentary artifacts, despite the richness of their cultures. Much of what is known comes to us through the eyes of travelers or through the memory of later representatives of these cultures. I have included many such documents along with cautions about how to use them. I have also included Western views of Asia in an effort to raise questions of a comparative and cross-cultural nature. Having so few documents for so many civilizations necessarily raises questions of selection. It is my conviction that it is the experience of using primary materials—rather than the primary materials that are used—that is vital.

Thus, I have tried to provide a balance among constitutional documents, political theory, philosophy, imaginative literature, and social description. In all cases, I have made the pedagogical value of the specific texts the prime consideration, selecting for significance, readability, and variety.

The feature "How to Read a Document" is designed to introduce students to a disciplined approach of working with primary sources and to encourage them to use their imaginations in their historical studies. No brief introduction pretends to be authoritative, and many other strategies and questions can be adopted in training students to become critical readers. It is hoped that this introduction will remove some of the barriers that usually exist between student and source by walking students through a single exercise with a document in front of them. Any disciplined approach to source materials will sensitize students to the construction of historical documents, their content and meaning, and the ways in which they relate to modern experience. Individual instructors will easily be able to improve upon the example offered here.

The feature "How to Read a Visual Image" reminds students that not all historical remains are literary. Images form an important part of modern historical reconstructions and students should gain proficiency in decoding them through careful and disciplined examination. This feature guides them through that process.

A number of individuals helped to stimulate my thinking about the selection of sources in the original edition of this work. I would especially like to thank Eric McGeer, R. Bin Wong, Ann Waltner, Leroy Vail, and Mark Wasserman. My greatest debt was to Susan Lindsey Lively for her assistance in compiling these texts. Her discipline helped keep me going as we sifted through hundreds of possible selections, and her common sense tempered our final choices. Thomas Cogswell, of the University of California at Riverside, and Monica Poole made substantial contributions to the revision of earlier editions.

In this fifth edition to *Sources of World History,* I have attempted to expand the coverage of non-Western societies as well as to offer more in the way of comparative perspectives by including sections of cultural encounters, particularly in the earlier periods. On the advice of users of the book I have eliminated some texts that students found confusing and added new ones that give fresher perspectives on conventional subjects. As always, my thanks are due to the many users of *Sources of World History* who have taken the time to send me suggestions, corrections, and encouragement. I am always amazed by how many students take time to e-mail me with suggestions. I am particularly grateful to the following reviewers who made many helpful suggestions and helped to shape the fifth edition: David Burden, Indiana Wesleyan University; Greg Culver, Austin Peay State University; Jennifer Edwards, Manhattan College; Jeffrey Hamilton, Baylor University; John Hosler, Morgan State University; David Rands, Frostburg State University; Jonathan Reid, East Carolina University; and Pamela Vaughan Knaus, Colorado State University.

For this revision Rena Lauer did all of the hard work of locating and copying new selections and her knowledge of the Middle Ages in all parts of the world was of invaluable assistance in improving coverage in this edition.

Finally, my thanks go to Larry Goldberg, developmental editor and Dewanshu Ranjan, Project Manager at PreMediaGlobal.

Mark A. Kishlansky
Cambridge MA

How to Read a Document

Do you remember the first time you ever used a road map? After struggling to unfold it and get the right side up and the right way around, you were then confronted by an astonishing amount of information. You could calculate the distance between places, from towns to cities, or cities to cities, even the distance between exits on the toll roads. You could observe relative population density and categorize large and small places. You could even judge the quality of roads. But most likely, you used that map to help you figure out how to get from one place to another, how to find the best route for the trip you were taking.

To make the map tell you that, you had to know how to ask the right questions. It all seems so obvious now—you put one finger on the place where you were and another on the place to which you wanted to go, and then you found the best and most direct route between them. In doing something as simple as this, you made a lot of assumptions about the map. First, you assumed that the map is directionally oriented, with north at the top, east to the right, south and west opposite. Second, you assumed that the map is to scale, that the distances between places on the map are proportional to their distances in reality. Third, you assumed that intersections on the map were intersections on the ground, that the two roads that appear to cross on paper actually do cross in reality. These assumptions make possible the answer to your initial question. Of course, if any of them were not true, you would have found out soon enough.

Learning to read an historical document is much like learning to read a map. It is important to ask the right questions and to make the right assumptions. But unlike the real voyage that the map makes possible, the voyage made with an historical document is one of the imagination. You will have to learn to test your assumptions and to sharpen your ability to ask questions before you can have any confidence that you are on the right road. Like anything else, this is a matter of concentration and practice.

You will have to discipline yourself to ask and answer questions about the document on the first level before you pose questions on higher levels. At the beginning, you will be asking questions that you can answer directly; by the end, you will be asking questions that will give full play to your imagination and your skills as an historian. Let us consider an example. Read the following selection slowly and carefully.

1   Ye emperors, kings, dukes, marquises, earls, and knights, and all other people
2   desirous of knowing the diversities of the races of mankind, as well as the
3   diversities of kingdoms, provinces, and regions of all parts of the East, read
4   through this book, and ye will find in it the greatest and most marvellous char-
5   acteristics of the peoples especially of Armenia, Persia, India, and Tartary, as
6   they are severally related in the present work by Marco Polo, a wise and
7   learned citizen of Venice, who states distinctly what things he saw and what
8   things he heard from others. For this book will be a truthful one.
9   Kublai, who is styled grand khan, or lord of lords, is of the middle stature, that
10 is, neither tall nor short; his limbs are well formed, and in his whole figure
11 there is a just proportion. His complexion is fair, and occasionally suffused
12 with red, like the bright tint of the rose, which adds much grace to his coun-
13 tenance. His eyes are black and handsome, his nose is well shaped and promi-
14 nent. He has four wives of the first rank, who are esteemed legitimate, and the
15 eldest born son of any one of these succeeds to the empire, upon the decease
16 of the grand khan. They bear equally the title of empress, and have their sep-
17 arate courts. None of them have fewer than three hundred young female
18 attendants of great beauty, together with a multitude of youths as pages, and
19 other eunuchs, as well as ladies of the bedchamber; so that the number of per-
20 sons belonging to each of their respective courts amounts to ten thousand.
21 Besides these, he has many concubines provided for his use, from a province
22 of Tartary named Ungut, having a city of the same name, the inhabitants of
23 which are distinguished for beauty of features and fairness of complexion.
24 Thither the grand khan sends his officers every second year, or oftener, as it
25 may happen to be his pleasure, who collect for him, to the number of four or
26 five hundred, or more, of the handsomest of the young women, according to
27 the estimation of beauty communicated to them in their instructions....
28 Upon their arrival in his presence, he causes a new examination to be made by
29 a different set of inspectors, and from amongst them a further selection takes
30 place, when thirty or forty are retained for his own chamber.... These, in the
31 first instance, are committed separately to the care of the wives of certain of
32 the nobles, whose duty it is to observe them attentively during the course of
33 the night, in order to ascertain that they have not any concealed imperfec-
34 tions, that they sleep tranquilly, do not snore, have sweet breath, and are free

35 from unpleasant scent in any part of the body. Having undergone this rigor-
36 ous scrutiny, they are divided into parties of five, one of which parties attends
37 during three days and three nights, in his majesty's interior apartment, where
38 they are to perform every service that is required of them, and he does with
39 them as he likes. The remainder of them, whose value had been estimated at
40 an inferior rate, are assigned to the different lords of the household…. In this
41 manner he provides for them all amongst his nobility. It may be asked whether
42 the people of the province do not feel themselves aggrieved in having their
43 daughters thus forcibly taken from them by the sovereign? Certainly not; but,
44 on the contrary, they regard it as a favour and an honour done to them; and
45 those who are the fathers of handsome children feel highly gratified by his
46 condescending to make choice of their daughters.
47 The grand khan usually resides during three months of the year, namely,
48 December, January, and February, in the great city of Kanbalu, situated towards
49 the north-eastern extremity of the province of Cathay; and here, on the south-
50 ern side of the new city, is the site of his vast palace, the form and dimensions
51 of which are as follows. In the first place is a square enclosed with a wall and
52 deep ditch; each side of the square being eight miles in length, and having at
53 an equal distance from each extremity an entrance-gate, for the concourse of
54 people resorting thither from all quarters. Within this enclosure there is, on
55 the four sides, an open space one mile in breadth, where the troops are sta-
56 tioned; and this is bounded by a second wall, enclosing a square of six miles,
57 having three gates on the south side, and three on the north, the middle por-
58 tal of each being larger than the other two, and always kept shut, excepting on
59 the occasions of the emperor's entrance or departure…. Within these walls,
60 which constitute the boundary of four miles, stands the palace of the grand
61 khan, the most extensive that has ever yet been known. It reaches from the
62 northern to the southern wall, leaving only a vacant space (or court), where
63 persons of rank and the military guards pass and repass. It has no upper floor,
64 but the roof is very lofty. The paved foundation or platform on which it stands
65 is raised ten spans above the level of the ground, and a wall of marble, two paces
66 wide, is built on all sides, to the level of this pavement, within the line of which
67 the palace is erected; so that the wall, extending beyond the ground plan of the
68 building, and encompassing the whole, serves as a terrace, where those who
69 walk on it are visible from without. Along the exterior edge of the wall is a
70 handsome balustrade, with pillars, which the people are allowed to approach.
71 The sides of the great halls and the apartments are ornamented with dragons in

72 carved work and gilt, figures of warriors, of birds, and of beasts, with represen-
73 tations of battles. The inside of the roof is contrived in such a manner that
74 nothing besides gilding and painting presents itself to the eye. On each of the
75 four sides of the palace there is a grand flight of marble steps, by which you
76 ascend from the level of the ground to the wall of marble which surrounds the
77 building, and which constitute the approach to the palace itself. The grand hall
78 is extremely long and wide, and admits of dinners being there served to great
79 multitudes of people. The palace contains a number of separate chambers, all
80 highly beautiful, and so admirably disposed that it seems impossible to suggest
81 any improvement to the system of their arrangement. The exterior of the roof
82 is adorned with a variety of colours, red, green, azure, and violet, and the sort
83 of covering is so strong as to last for many years. The glazing of the windows is
84 so well wrought and so delicate as to have the transparency of crystal. In the
85 rear of the body of the palace there are large buildings containing several
86 apartments, where is deposited the private property of the monarch, or his
87 treasure in gold and silver bullion, precious stones, and pearls, and also his
88 vessels of gold and silver plate. Here are likewise the apartments of his wives
89 and concubines; and in this retired situation he despatches business with
90 convenience, being free from every kind of interruption.

Now what sense can we make out of all of that? You have just read a historical document, a selection from *The Travels of Marco Polo: The Venetian*. It was written in 1298, while Marco Polo was in prison, and was based on his own observations during seventeen years of travel in Asia. Marco Polo was born into a Venetian merchant family. His father and elder brothers had made an earlier trip into Asia, where they had met the Grand Khan. Marco accompanied his brothers on their return trip. During his stay he was favored with free passage throughout the khan's dominions, and on his return to Venice he was required to tell and retell the stories of his journey. After commanding a ship in an unsuccessful war against Genoa, Marco Polo was captured and imprisoned. It was during this time that he sorted through the many notations that he had made in Asia and composed the tale of his travels.

To understand this document, we will need to ask and answer a series of questions about it. Let us start at the beginning with some questions that we might designate as Level One questions.

LEVEL ONE

The first set of questions that need to be addressed are those for which you should be able to find concrete answers. The answers to these questions will give you the basic information you need to begin the process of interpretation. Although Level One questions are seemingly straightforward, they contain important implications for deeper interpretation. If you do not consciously ask these questions, you will deprive yourself of some of the most important evidence there is for understanding documents. Train yourself to underline or highlight the information that will allow you to answer the following questions.

1. Who Wrote This Document?

In the first place, we need to know how this document came to be created. In the case of *The Travels of Marco Polo: The Venetian,* we know that the document was written by Marco Polo **(line 6),** who was an Italian merchant. This document is thus the work of a single author written from his own point of view. What is especially important to remember is that Marco Polo was an outsider, describing a society that was not his own. His account of China in the thirteenth century was an account of a European's impressions of China. We will need to learn as much as we can about the "author" of a document to help us answer more complicated questions.

2. Who Is the Intended Audience?

The audience of a document will tell us much about the document's language, about the amount of knowledge that the writer is assuming, even sometimes about the best form for the document to take. There can be more than one audience intended by the writer. *The Travels of Marco Polo: The Venetian* was written in the thirteenth century, and therefore it was not written for "publication" in the conventional sense of the word. In fact, *The Travels* was not published for centuries after its composition. But Marco Polo obviously intended his work to be read by others, and it was circulated in manuscript and repeated orally. His preface was addressed to "emperors, kings, dukes, marquises, earls, and knights" **(line 1),** a rather distinguished audience. But his real audience was his own countrymen, to whom he was describing a foreign place in terms they would understand. Notice, for example, how he describes the khan's complexion, "like the bright tint of the rose" **(line 12).**

3. What Is the Story Line?

The final Level One question has to do with the content of the document. We now know enough about it in a general way to pay attention to what it actually says. To answer this question, you might want to take some notes while you are reading or underline the important parts in your text. The story here seems to be simple. Marco Polo is impressed with the splendor of the court of the grand khan and especially with the way in which he finds his wives and concubines. Polygamy is interesting to a European viewing a non-Western society, and Marco Polo describes it in a way that will titillate his anticipated audience. He also makes it believable, explaining why parents would volunteer their daughters **(lines 44–45).** He is also impressed with the size of everything that surrounds the Grand Khan. If each of his wives had a retinue of 10,000 **(line 20),** their courts alone would be more populous than the entire city of Venice.

LEVEL TWO

If Level One questions allow you to identify the nature of the document and its author, Level Two questions allow you to probe behind the essential facts. Now that you know who wrote the document, to whom it is addressed, and what it is about, you can begin trying to understand it. Since your goal is to learn what this document means, first in its historical context and then in your current context, you now want to study it from a more detached point of view, to be less accepting of "facts" and more critical in the questions you pose. At the first level, the document controlled you; at the second level, you will begin to control the document.

1. Why Was This Document Written?

Understanding the purpose of an historical document is critical to analyzing the strategies that the author employs within it. A document intended to convince will employ logic; a document intended to entertain will employ fancy; a document attempting to motivate will employ emotional appeals. To find these strategies, we must first know what purpose the document was intended to serve. Travelers' tales generally have two interrelated purposes: first, to impress upon one culture the differences to be found in another; and second, to show people their own culture in a new light. Marco Polo is genuinely impressed with the opulence and power of the khan; but he is also impressed by the way that the khan provides for his nobles, how he rewarded those who have been faithful to him **(lines 40–41).** As the member of an elite merchant family, Marco Polo was concerned that the Venetian doge rewarded those faithful to him, especially those who might be temporarily imprisoned.

2. What Type of Document Is This?

The form of a document is vital to its purpose. We would expect a telephone book to be alphabetized, a conventional poem to be in meter, and a work of philosophy to be in prose. Here we have a traveler's account, and its style and language are employed to create wonder and admiration in its readers. To do this the author needs to provide detailed description that is visually arresting yet sufficiently concrete to be persuasive. This is especially difficult when describing customs as alien to Venetians as those practiced at the court of the grand khan. In order to be believed, the traveler has to overcome the natural skepticism of his audience. During his lifetime, Marco Polo was nicknamed "Marco Millione" (Marco Millions) because people thought he exaggerated the numbers of the Chinese population and the extent of the khan's wealth.

3. What Are the Basic Assumptions Made in This Document?

All documents make assumptions that are bound up—with their intended audience, with the form in which they are written, and with their purpose. Some of the assumptions that are at work in this selection from *The Travels of Marco Polo: The Venetian* relate to the way in which a state is ruled. Marco Polo describes the khan and his court as if government in China were organized in the same way that government in Italy was. Thus the khan can be understood as a sort of pope or doge. Similarly, Marco Polo assumes that his readers will admire great wealth and large quantities of things. He takes pains to describe things as beautiful, great, wide, and large **(lines 52–81)**.

LEVEL THREE

So far, you have been asking questions of your document that the document itself can answer. Sometimes it is more difficult to know who composed a document or who was the intended audience than it has been with *The Travels of Marco Polo: The Venetian* Sometimes you have to guess at the purpose of the document, but essentially Level One and Level Two questions have direct answers. Once you have learned to ask them, you will have a great deal of information about the historical document at your disposal. You will then be able to think historically, that is, to pose your own questions about the past and to use the material the document presents to you in order to find answers. In Level Three you will exercise your critical imagination, probing the material and developing your own assessment of its value. Level Three questions will not always have definite answers; in fact, they are the kind of questions that arouse disagreement and debate and that make for lively classroom discussion.

1. Can I Believe This Document?

If they are successful, documents designed to persuade, to recount events, or to motivate people to act must be believable to their audience. But for the critical historical reader, it is that very believability that must be in question. Every author has a point of view, and exposing the assumptions of the document is an essential task for the reader. We must treat all claims skeptically (even while admiring audacity, rhetorical tricks, and clever comparisons). One question we certainly want to ask is, "Is this a likely story?" Do the parents of daughters destined for concubinage at court really believe that it is a sign of good fortune? Do all officers sent by the khan really perform their duties speedily and efficiently? Is there really a wall 8 miles square around the city that contains the khan's palace **(line 52)**? Testing the credibility of a document means looking at it from the other side. What would most impress a subject of the khan about his own society? What would most impress him about Venice?

2. What Can I Learn About the Society
That Produced This Document?

All documents unintentionally reveal things about their authors and about their age. It is the things that are embedded in the very language, structure, and assumptions of the document that can tell us the most about the historical period or event that we are studying. This is centrally important in studying a travel account. We must ask ourselves both what we can learn about China in the late thirteenth century and what we can learn about Venice. Marco Polo is acting as a double filter, running Chinese customs through his own European expectations and then explaining them to Europeans through his expectation of what they will believe and what they will reject. He is also telling us, indirectly, about the things that Venetians would find unusual and wonderful and therefore by contrast what they would find commonplace.

We can learn many things about both Chinese and Venetian society by reading into this document rather than by simply reading it.

3. What Does This Document Mean to Me?

So what? What does *The Travels of Marco Polo: The Venetian,* written almost seven hundred years ago, have to do with you? Other than the practical problem of passing your exams and getting your degree, why should you be concerned with historical documents and what can you learn from them? Only you can answer that question. But you will not be able to answer it until you have asked it. You should demand to know the meaning of each document you read. What it meant to the historical actors—authors, audience, and society—and what it means to our own society. In light of *The Travels of Marco Polo: The Venetian*, how would you go about describing an alien society to your generation? How would you go about appreciating an alien culture? Look around your classroom and ask yourself how often you represent yourself to members of other cultures and how often you have to understand the assumptions of other cultures to understand your classmates.

Now that you have seen how to unfold the map of a historical document, you must get used to asking these questions by yourself. The temptation will be great to jump from Level One to Level Three, to start in the middle, or to pose the questions in no sequence at all. After all, you probably have a ready-made answer to the question, "What does this document mean to me?" If you develop the discipline of asking all your questions in the proper order, however, you will soon find that you are able to gain command of a document on a single reading and that the complicated names and facts that ordinarily would confuse you will easily settle into a pattern around one or another of your questions. After a few weeks, reread these pages and ask yourself how careful you have been to maintain the discipline of posing historical questions. Think also about how much more comfortable you now feel about reading and discussing historical documents.

How to Read a Visual

You will notice that this reader includes a number of visuals that relate to the readings and eras covered. Many of them are paintings; a few are sculptures or photographs of pieces of architecture, the latter two intended to illustrate important aspects of time, place, and custom rather than solely to be works of art.

This art stretches across a span of 4,000 or so years and encompasses many styles and subjects. If you are an artist or have a strong background in art history, you will feel right at home. If not, here are the main aspects of art to examine:

- *Line* gives shape to the objects in a picture.
- *Color* has a primary appeal to the senses and can be very effective at stimulating emotions.
- *Light,* specifically the use of lighter and darker areas, can direct attention to certain areas and can also stimulate emotions.
- *Composition* refers to the size and placement of objects.
- *Meaning* is the message or mood the artist sought to convey.

The captions that accompany the visuals in this reader are intended to help you interpret each illustration in light of the era and topic of the reading within which it appears. You might also scrutinize the piece and ask yourself:

- Who was the artist? From what social class did he or she spring? What does this tell you about the work of art?
- From what social classes do the subjects of the piece appear to come? What does this tell you about the society?
- How do the clothing, hairstyles, and body shapes compare with those of today in Western society?
- What activities are depicted in the work?

- If the piece is a religious object, what would you infer about the nature of the religion?
- With architecture, what might be the motivation of rulers for creating such monuments?

Benin Brass Oba Plaque

Look at this image. It is one of a series of brass plaques commissioned during the sixteenth and seventeenth centuries by the oba, or kings of Benin, one of the largest and most prosperous kingdoms in Africa. The plaques were created over generations to commemorate the power of the oba, whom the Edo people believed were divinely endowed as kings. The first thing to notice about the plaque is that it has holes in it at the top where it was nailed to specially designated posts within the royal palace. There were at least nine hundred of these royal plaques, and it is believed that they were ordered in some pattern that has now been lost. These works were designed for public display, both to commemorate the lives of individual obas and to symbolize their royal power. Thus they served the dual purposes of portraiture and of history. The plaques were made of brass rather than any other material, because brass did not tarnish and therefore the image of each oba would survive perpetually. It is thought that the technique of brass casting was brought to Africa by the Portuguese but then adapted by the skills of Edo sculptors. The small figures at the bottom have the qualities associated with woodcarving. Asking questions about the purpose of a work of art and the materials used to create it opens up a wealth of information about the society from which it came.

Look next at the composition. Six figures are represented, but they are not presented in balance. Observe that the oba is by far the largest of the figures, and his head and body dominate the work. He dwarfs his own subjects, who are depicted at the bottom. They are shown in postures of subservience, and the one carrying the oba's sword is naked. The oba's military power is demonstrated by his spear and shield, his wealth by the coral necklace that he wears wrapped around his face. The heads of all of the Edo depicted here seem too large for their bodies. That is because the Edo believed that the spirit of a person resided in their head; this was one of the reasons they preserved peoples' heads after they died. Although the compositional relationship between the oba and his subjects is not surprising, there are two other figures on this plaque. They are African renditions of Portuguese traders, the first Europeans that the Benin peoples encountered. One can easily see that the traders' heads are shaped differently than the heads of the Edo, undoubtedly a statement of the differences the Edo saw in the spirit of Europeans. The Portuguese are portrayed in profile, hovering in midair at each ear of the oba. This symbolized the fact that only the oba had the power to deal with Europeans and to bring to his people the new wealth that came in trade. That the Portuguese were given no legs and no place to stand suggests that they were without roots in Benin culture or society. All of these meanings can be learned by careful study of the composition of the plaque and by wondering why things are presented in a particular manner.

Finally, we should attempt to discover the reasons for the production of this particular work of art by this particular society. Though artists work through their own skill and individual genius, art is produced within a social and political context. In the case of the oba plaques we can readily see that these are works designed to commemorate a political structure, to celebrate particular events, and to define the relationship between natives and foreigners. The fact that the plaques were publicly displayed in the royal palace confirms their role in asserting the power of oba over those who came to trade with them. The plaques also reinforced the distance between rulers and subjects and the military might of the Benin regime. They were a pictorial representation of power in an African state as it confronted the challenge of the first European encounters.

PART I ✳ Ancient Societies

Origin Stories

Mesopotamian cylinder of the Shar-Kali Sham.

1

The Ancestors of the People Called Indians

(The Huarochirí Manuscript) (ca. 1598–1608 C.E.)

Among the oral testimonies recorded by Spanish missionaries in South America, the Huarochirí Manuscript is the most important account of pre-Columbian religious beliefs amongst the native Andean peoples. It contains an account of the formation of the world, of the gods and superhumans who once populated it, and of their continued relationship with contemporary Andean peoples. The Checas tribes lived in the Andean province of Huarochirí in what is now Peru. They had been conquered by the Incas before the arrival of the Spaniards in the sixteenth century who resettled them. Spanish missionaries took an especial interest in the religious beliefs of the Checas in their own efforts to convert them to Christianity. It was in this context that the Huarochirí Manuscript, written in Quechua and Spanish, was produced, probably at the end of the sixteenth century. It contains annotations by the Spanish priest Francisco de Avila, whose special interest was in suppressing native "heresies." Its authorship was a complex mixture of Checas oral history seen through the prism of Spanish Roman Catholicism, and while its compilers were Spaniards, one feels the presence of the authentic voice of the Checas in numerous places within the text.

This selection from the Huarochirí Manuscript tells the story of the original huacas, *or ancestor beings, of the Checas, and of* villcas, *or demigod humans whom the* huacas *protected. Among the most important of these* huacas *was Cuni Raya, god of irrigation and water, and Paria Caca, a figure associated with the twin-capped mountains that dominated the Checas landscape. Both play an important role in the selection that follows.*

[PREFACE]

If the ancestors of the people called Indians had
    known writing in earlier times, then the lives
    they lived would not have faded from view
    until now.
As the mighty past of the Spanish Vira
    Cochas is visible until now, so, too, would
    theirs be.
But since things are as they are, and since
    nothing has been written until now,
I set forth here the lives of the ancestors of the
    Huaro Cheri people, who all descend from
    one forefather:

What faith they held, how they live up until
    now, those things and more;
Village by village it will be written down: how
    they lived from their dawning age onward.

CHAPTER 1

How the Idols of Old Were, and How They Warred Among Themselves, and How the Natives Existed at That Time

In very ancient times, there were huacas
named Yana ñamca and Tuta ñamca.

2

Later on another huaca named Huallallo
  Caruincho defeated them.
After he defeated them, he ordered the people
  to bear two children and no more.
He would eat one of them himself.
The parents would raise the other, whichever
  one was loved best.
Although people did die in those times,
  they came back to life on the fifth day
  exactly.
And as for their foodstuffs, they ripened
  exactly five days after being planted.
These villages and all the others like them
  were full of Yunca.

When a great number of people had filled the
  land, they lived really miserably, scratching
  and digging the rock faces and ledges to
  make terraced fields.
These fields, some small, others large, are still
  visible today on all the rocky heights.
And all the birds of that age were perfectly
  beautiful, parrots and toucans all yellow and
  red.

Later, at the time when another huaca named
  Paria Caca appeared, these beings and all
  their works were cast out to the hot Anti
  lands by Paria Caca's actions.
Further on we'll speak of Paria Caca's
  emergence and of his victories.
Also, as we know, there was another huaca
  named Cuni Raya.
Regarding him, we're not sure whether he
  existed before Paria Caca or maybe after
  him.
However, Cuni Raya's essential nature almost
  matches Vira Cocha's. For when people
  worshiped this huaca, they would invoke
  him, saying,

  Cuni Raya Vira Cocha,
  You who animate mankind,
  Who charge the world with being,
  All things are yours!
  Yours the fields and yours the people.

And so, long ago, when beginning anything
  difficult, the ancients, even though they
couldn't see Vira Cocha, used to throw coca
  leaves to the ground, talk to him, and
  worship him before all others, saying,

  Help me remember how,
  Help me work it out,
  Cuni Raya Vira Cocha!

And the master weaver would worship and
  call on him whenever it was hard for him to
  weave.
For that reason, we'll write first about this
  huaca and about his life, and later on about
  Paria Caca.

CHAPTER 2

How Cuni Raya Vira Cocha Acted in His Own Age. The Life of Cuni Raya Vira Cocha. How Caui Llaca Gave Birth to His child, and What Followed

A long, long time ago, Cuni Raya Vira
  Cocha used to go around posing as a
  miserably poor and friendless man, with
  his cloak and tunic all ripped and tattered.
  Some people who didn't recognize him for
  who he was yelled, "You poor lousy
  wretch!"
Yet it was this man who fashioned all the
  villages. Just by speaking he made the fields,
  and finished the terraces with walls of fine
  masonry. As for the irrigation canals, he
  channeled them out from their sources just
  by tossing down the flower of a reed called
  pupuna.
After that, he went around performing all
  kinds of wonders, putting some of the local
  huacas to shame with his cleverness.
Once there was a female huaca named Caui
  Llaca.
Caui Llaca had always remained a virgin. Since
  she was very beautiful, every one of the
  huacas and villcas longed for her. "I've got
  to sleep with her!" they thought.
But she never consented.

Once this woman, who had never allowed any male to fondle her, was weaving beneath a lúcuma tree.

Cuni Raya, in his cleverness, turned himself into a bird and climbed into the lúcuma.

He put his semen into a fruit that had ripened there and dropped it next to the woman.

The woman swallowed it down delightedly.

Thus she got pregnant even though she remained untouched by man.

In her ninth month, virgin though she was, she gave birth just as other women give birth.

And so, too, for one year she nursed her child at her breast, wondering, "Whose child could this be?"

In the fullness of the year, when the youngster was crawling around on all fours, she summoned all the huacas and villcas to find out who was the child's father.

When the huacas heard the message, they were overjoyed, and they all came dressed in their best clothes, each saying to himself, "It's me!" "It's me she'll love!"

This gathering took place at Anchi Cocha, where the woman lived.

When all the huacas and villcas had taken their seats there, that woman addressed them:

"Behold, gentlemen and lords. Acknowledge this child. Which of you made me pregnant?" One by one she asked each of them:

"Was it you?"

"Was it you?"

But nobody answered, "The child is mine."

The one called Cuni Raya Vira Cocha had taken his seat at the edge of the gathering. Since he looked like a friendless beggar sitting there, and since so many handsome men were present, she spurned him and didn't question him. She thought, "How could my baby possibly be the child of that beggar?"

Since no one had said, "The child is mine," she first warned the huacas, "If the baby is yours, it'll crawl up to you," and then addressed the child:

"Go, identify your father yourself!"

The child began at one end of the group and crawled along on all fours without climbing up on anyone, until reaching the other end, where its father sat.

On reaching him, the baby instantly brightened up and climbed onto its father's knee.

When its mother saw this, she got all indignant: "Atatay, what a disgrace! How could I have given birth to the child of a beggar like that?" she said. And taking along only her child, she headed straight for the ocean.

And then, while all the local huacas stood in awe, Cuni Raya Vira Cocha put on his golden garment. He started to chase her at once, thinking to himself, "She'll be overcome by sudden desire for me."

"Sister Caui Llaca!" he called after her. "Here, look at me! Now I'm really beautiful!" he said, and he stood there making his garment glitter.

Caui Llaca didn't even turn her face back to him.

"Because I've given birth to the child of such a ruffian, such a mangy beggar, I'll just disappear into the ocean," she said. She headed straight out into the deep sea near Pacha Camac, out there where even now two stones that clearly look like people stand.

And when she arrived at what is today her dwelling, she turned to stone.

Yet Cuni Raya Vira Cocha thought, "She'll see me anyway, she'll come to look at me!" He followed her at a distance, shouting and calling to her over and over.

First, he met up with a condor.

"Brother, where did you run into that woman?" he asked him.

"Right near here. Soon you'll find her," replied the condor.

Cuni Raya Vira Cocha spoke to him and said,

"You'll live a long life. You alone will eat any dead animal from the wild mountain slopes, both guanacos and vicuñas, of any kind and in any number. And if anybody should kill you, he'll die himself, too."

Farther on, he met up with a skunk.

"Sister, where did you meet that woman?" he asked.

"You'll never find her now. She's gone way far away," replied the skunk.

When she said this, he cursed her very hatefully, saying,

"As for you, because of what you've just told me, you'll never go around in the daytime. You'll only walk at night, stinking disgustingly. People will be revolted by you."

Next he met up with a puma.

"She just passed this way. She's still nearby. You'll soon reach her," the puma told him.

Cuni Raya Vira Cocha spoke to him, saying,

"You'll be well loved. You'll eat llamas, especially the llamas of people who bear guilt. Although people may kill you, they'll wear you on their heads during a great festival and set you to dancing. And then when they bring you out annually, they'll sacrifice a llama first and then set you to dancing."

Then he met up with a fox.

"She's already gone way far away. You'll never find her now," that fox told him.

When the fox said this, he replied,

"As for you, even when you skulk around keeping your distance, people will thoroughly despise you and say, 'That fox is a sneak thief.' When they kill you, they'll just carelessly throw you away, and your skin, too."

Likewise he met up with a falcon.

"She's just passed this way. You'll soon find her," said the falcon.

He replied,

"You're greatly blessed. When you eat, you'll eat the hummingbird first, then all the other birds. When people kill you, the man who has slain you will have you mourned with the sacrifice of a llama. And when they dance, they'll put you on their heads so you can sit there shining with beauty."

And then he met up with some parakeets.

"She's already gone way far away. You'll never find her now," the parakeets told him.

"As for you, you'll travel around shrieking raucously," replied Cuni Raya Vira Cocha. "Although you may say, 'I'll spoil your crops!' when people hear your screaming they'll chase you away at once. You'll live in great misery amidst the hatred of humans."

And so he traveled on. Whenever he met anyone who gave him good news, he conferred on him good fortune. But he went along viciously cursing those who gave him bad news.

When he reached the seashore, [crossed out in original manuscript: he went straight over it. Today people say, "He was headed for Castile," but in the old days people said, "He went to another land."] he turned back toward Pacha Camac.

He arrived at the place where Pacha Camac's two daughters lived, guarded by a snake.

Just before this, the two girls' mother had gone into the deep sea to visit Caui Llaca. Her name was Urpay Huachac.

While Urpay Huachac was away, Cuni Raya Vira Cocha seduced one girl, her older daughter.

When he sought to sleep with the other sister, she turned into a dove and darted away.

That's why her mother's name means "Gives Birth to Doves."

At that time there wasn't a single fish in the ocean.

Only Urpay Huachac used to breed them, at her home, in a small pond.

It was these fish, all of them, that Cuni Raya angrily scattered into the ocean, saying, "For what did she go off and visit Caui Llaca, the woman of the ocean depths?"

Ever since then, fish have filled the sea.

Then Cuni Raya Vira Cocha fled along the seashore.

When Urpay Huachac's daughters told her
   how he'd seduced them, she got furious and
   chased him.
As she followed him, calling him again and
   again, he waited for her and said, "Yes?"
"Cuni, I'm just going to remove your lice,"
   she said, and she picked them off.
While she picked his lice, she caused a huge
   abyss to open up next to him, thinking to
   herself, "I'll knock Cuni Raya down into it."
But Cuni Raya in his cleverness realized this;
   just by saying, "Sister, I've got to go off for a
   moment to relieve myself," he made his
   getaway to these villages.
He traveled around this area for a long, long
   time, tricking lots of local huacas and
   people, too.

CHAPTER 3

What Happened to the Indians in Ancient Times When the Ocean Overflowed

Now we'll return to what is said of very early
   people.
The story goes like this.
In ancient times, this world wanted to come
   to an end.
A llama buck, aware that the ocean was about
   to overflow, was behaving like somebody
   who's deep in sadness. Even though its
   [father] owner let it rest in a patch of
   excellent pasture, it cried and said, "In, in,"
   and wouldn't eat.
The llama's [father] owner got really angry,
   and he threw the cob from some maize he
   had just eaten at the llama.
"Eat, dog! This is some fine grass I'm letting
   you rest in!" he said.
Then the llama began speaking like a human
   being.
"You simpleton, whatever could you be
   thinking about? Soon, in five days, the
   ocean will overflow. It's a certainty. And the
   whole world will come to an end," it said.

The man got good and scared. "What's going
   to happen to us? Where can we go to save
   ourselves?" he said.
The llama replied, "Let's go to Villca Coto
   mountain.
There we'll be saved. Take along five days'
   food for yourself."
So the man went out from there in a great
   hurry, and himself carried both the llama
   buck and its load.
When they arrived at Villca Coto mountain,
   all sorts of animals had already filled it up:
   pumas, foxes, guanacos, condors, all kinds
   of animals in great numbers.
And as soon as that man had arrived there, the
   ocean overflowed.
They stayed there huddling tightly together.
The waters covered all those mountains and it
   was only Villca Coto mountain, or rather its
   very peak, that was not covered by water.
Water soaked the fox's tail.
That's how it turned black.
Five days later, the waters descended and
   began to dry up.
The drying waters caused the ocean to retreat
   all the way down again and exterminate all
   the people.
Afterward, that man began to multiply once
   more.
That's the reason there are people until today.
Regarding this story, we Christians believe it
   refers to the time of the Flood.
But they believe it was Villca Coto mountain
   that saved them.

CHAPTER 4

How the Sun Disappeared for Five Days. In What Follows We Shall Tell the Story About the Death of the Sun

In ancient times the Sun died.
Because of his death it was night for five days.
Rocks banged against each other.
Mortars and grindstones began to eat people.

Buck llamas started to drive men.
Here's what we Christians think about it: We think these stories tell of the darkness following the death of Our Lord Jesus Christ.
Maybe that's what it was.

CHAPTER 5

How in Ancient Times Paria Caca Appeared on a Mountain Named Condor Coto in the Form of Five Eggs, and What Followed. Here Will Begin the Account of Paria Caca's Emergence

In the four preceding chapters we have already recounted the lives lived in ancient times.

Nevertheless, we don't know the origins of the people of those days, nor where it was they emerged from.

These people, the ones who lived in that era, used to spend their lives warring on each other and conquering each other. For their leaders, they recognized only the strong and the rich.

We speak of them as the Purum Runa, "people of desolation."

It was at this time that the one called Paria Caca was born in the form of five eggs on Condor Coto mountain.

A certain man, and a poor friendless one at that, was the first to see and know the fact of his birth; he was called Huatya Curi, but was also known as Paria Caca's son.

Now we'll speak of this discovery of his, and of the many wonders he performed....

FOCUS QUESTIONS

1. How did the original huacas exercise their domination? What softened its rigors?
2. Why would the story of Cuni Raya and Caui Llaca appeal to the Spanish?
3. What is the significance of animals for the Checas?
4. Can you find parallels in the crucial events of Checas prehistory with those of Christian prehistory? What do these similarities tell you about the composition of the text?

2

The Creation Epic (ca. 2000 B.C.E.)

Mesopotamian civilization emerged in a land that knew little continuity or order. Both climate and geography made life hazardous and unpredictable. In contrast to life in ancient Egypt, where the seasonal flooding of the Nile and the relative isolation of the country fostered a sense of regularity, Mesopotamians lived with uncertainty. The religion of the people reflects these environmental conditions. Faced by a world in which change was often rapid and violent, Mesopotamians sought an explanation for their social reality through a belief in the capriciousness of the gods.

The Creation Epic describes a bitter conflict between the gods Marduk and Tiamat that led to the creation of the world that the Mesopotamians knew. Tiamat was the oldest of the gods, but she was also the patron of the primeval chaos. Marduk was the warrior god whose purpose was to institute order. The world that emerged from this battle maintained precarious stability—subject always to the whims of inexplicable divinity.

TABLET I

When on high, heaven was not named;
Below, dry land was not named.
Apsu, their first begetter,
Mummu (and) Tiamat, the mother of all of them.
Their waters combined together.
Field was not marked off, sprout had not come forth.
When none of the gods had yet come forth
Had not borne a name,
No destinies had been fixed;
Then gods were created in the midst of heaven.
Lakhmu and Lakhamu came forth
Ages increased …
Anshar and Kishar were created.
After many days had passed by there came forth …
Anu, their son …
Anshar and Anu …
Anu …
Nudimmud whom his father, his mother, …
Of large intelligence, knowing (wise),
Exceeding strong …
Without a rival …
Then were established….
Then Apsu, the begetter of the great gods,
Cried out, to Mummu, to his messenger, he spoke:
"Oh Mummu, joy of my liver,
Come, unto Tiamat let us go."
They went, and before Tiamat they crouched,
Hatching a plan with regard to the gods …
Apsu opened his mouth and spoke,
Unto Tiamat, the splendid one addressed a word:

"… their course against me
By day I have no rest, at night I cannot lie down, I wish to destroy their course,
So that clamor cease and we may again lie down to sleep."
When Tiamat (heard) this,
She raged and shrieked for (revenge?),
She herself became furiously enraged.
Evil she conceived in her heart.
"All that we have made let us destroy,
That their course may be full of misery so that we may have release."
Mummu answered and counselled Apsu,
Hostile was the counsel of Mummu.
"Come, their course is strong, destroy it!
Then by day thou wilt have rest,
At night thou wilt lie down."
Apsu (hearkened), and his face shone;
Evil he planned against the gods, his sons….
They uttered curses and at the side of Tiamat advanced.
In fury and rage they devised plans ceaselessly night and day.
They rushed to the conflict, raging and furious.
They grouped themselves and ranged the battle array.
Ummu-Khubar, creator of all things,
Gathering invincible weapons, she brought forth huge monsters,
Sharp of tooth and merciless of fang.
With poison instead of blood she filled their bodies.
She clothed with terror the terrible dragons,
Decking them with brilliancy, giving them a lofty stature,
So that whoever beheld them would be overcome with terror.

With their bodies reared up, none could
  withstand their attack.
She brought forth great serpents, dragons and
  the Lakhami,
Hurricanes, raging dogs and scorpion men,
Mighty tempests, fish men, and rams,
Bearing cruel weapons, fearless in combat,
Mighty in command, irresistible.
In all eleven monsters of this kind she made.
Among the gods, the first born who formed
  the assembly,
She exalted Kingu, giving him high rank in
  their midst;
To march in advance and to direct the host;
To be foremost in arming for the attack,
To direct the fight in supreme control,
To his hand she confided. She decked him out
  in costly garments:
"I have uttered thy magic formula, in the
  assembly of the gods I have exalted thee."
The dominion over all the gods was entrusted
  unto his hands:
"Be thou exalted, my one and only husband;
May the Anunnaki exalt thy name above all
  the gods!"
She gave him the tablets of fate, to his breast
  she attached them.
"Oh, thou, thy command will be irresistible!
Firmly established be the utterance of thy
  mouth!
Now Kingu is exalted, endowed with the
  power of Anu;
Among the gods, his children, he fixes
  destinies.
By the word of thy mouth fire will be
  quenched;
The strong in battle will be increased in
  strength."

TABLET II

Tiamat finished her work.
(The evil that) she contrived against the gods
  her offspring,
To avenge Apsu, Tiamat planned evil.

When she had equipped her army, it was
  revealed to Ea;
Ea heard the words,
And was grievously afflicted, and over-
  whelmed with grief.
Days passed by and his anger was appeased.
To Anshar, his father, he took the way.
To Father Anshar who begot him he went.
All that Tiamat had planned he repeated to
  him.
"Tiamat our mother has taken a dislike for us,
She has assembled a host, she rages furiously.
All the gods are gathered to her,
Aye, even those whom thou hast created,
  march at her side."
[Anshar asks his son Marduk to fight Tiamat]
"Thou art my son of strong courage, ... draw
  nigh to the battle!
... at sight of thee there shall be peace."
The Lord rejoiced at the word of his father.
He drew nigh and stood in front of Anshar;
Anshar saw him and his heart was full of joy.
He kissed him on the mouth, and fear
  departed from him.
"(Oh my father), may the words of thy lips
  not be taken back,
May I go and accomplish the desire of thy
  heart"
"Oh, my son, full of all knowledge,
Quiet Tiamat with thy supreme incantation;
Quickly proceed (on thy way)!
Thy blood will not be poured out, thou shalt
  surely return."
The lord rejoiced at the word of his father,
His heart exulted and he spoke to his father.
"Oh Lord of the gods, (who fixes) the fate of
  the great gods,
If I become thy avenger,
Conquering Tiamat, and giving life to thee,
Call an assembly and proclaim the preemi-
  nence of my lot!
That when in Upshukkinaku thou joyfully
  seatest thyself,
My command in place of thine should fix
  fates.
What I do should be unaltered,

The word of my lips be never changed or
   annulled."

TABLET III

Then they gathered and went,
The great gods, all of them, who fix fates,
Came into the presence of Anshar, they filled
   (the assembly hall),
Embracing one another in the assembly (hall),
They prepared themselves to feast at the
   banquet.
They ate bread, they mixed the wine,
The sweet mead confused (their senses).
Drunk, their bodies filled with drink,
They shouted aloud, with their spirits exalted,
For Marduk, their avenger, they fixed the
   destiny.

TABLET IV

They prepared for him a royal chamber,
In the presence of his fathers as ruler he stood
"Thou art the weightiest among the great
   gods.
Thy (power of decreeing) fate is unrivalled,
   thy command is (like that of) Anu.
Oh Marduk, thou art mightiest among the
   great gods!
Thy power of decreeing fate unrivalled, thy
   word is like that of Anu!
From now on thy decree will not be altered,
Thine it shall be to raise up and to bring low,
Thy utterance be established, against thy
   command no rebellion!
None among the gods will transgress the limit
   (set by thee).
Abundance is pleasing to the shrines of the gods,
The place of their worship will be established
   as thy place.
Oh Marduk, thou art our avenger!
We give thee kingship over the entire
   universe,
Take thy seat in the assembly, thy word be
   exalted;

Thy weapon be not overcome, may it crush
   thy enemies.
Oh lord, the life of him who trusts in thee will
   be spared,
But pour out the life of the god who has
   planned evil." …
He sent forth the winds which he had created,
   the seven of them;
To trouble the spirit of Tiamat, they followed
   behind him.
Then the lord raised on high the Deluge, his
   mighty weapon.
He mounted the storm chariot, unequalled in
   power.
He harnessed and attached to it four horses,
Merciless, overwhelming, swiftly flying.
(Sharp of) teeth, bearing poison….
Then the lord drew nigh, piercing Tiamat
   with his glance;
He saw the purpose of Kingu, her spouse,
As he (i.e., Marduk) gazed, he (i.e., Kingu)
   tottered in his gait. His mind was destroyed,
   his action upset,
And the gods, his helpers, marching at his
   side,
Saw (the terror of) the hero and leader.
But Tiamat (uttered a cry) and did not turn
   her back
From her lips there gushed forth rebellious
   words
… "coming to thee as lord of the gods,
As in their own sanctuaries they are gathered
   in thy sanctuary."
Then the lord raised on high the Deluge, the
   great weapon
And against Tiamat, who was foaming with
   wrath, thus sent forth (his answer).
"Great art thou! Thou hast exalted thyself
   greatly.
Thy heart hath prompted thee to arrange for
   battle….
Thou hast (exalted) Kingu to be thy husband,
(Thou hast given him power to issue) the
   decrees of Anu.
(Against the gods, my fathers), thou hast
   planned evil;

Against the gods, my fathers, thou hast planned evil.
Let thy army be equipped, thy weapons be girded on;
Stand; I and thou, let us join in battle."
When Tiamat heard this,
She was beside herself, she lost her reason.
Tiamat shouted in a paroxysm of fury,
Trembling to the root, shaking in her foundations.
She uttered an incantation, she pronounced a magic formula.
The gods of battle, appeal to their weapons.
Then stepped forth Tiamat and the leader of the gods, Marduk.
To the fight they advanced, to the battle they drew nigh.
The lord spread his net and encompassed her,
The evil wind stationed behind him he drove into her face.
Tiamat opened her mouth to its full extent.
He drove in the evil wind before she could close her lips.
The terrible winds filled her belly,
Her heart was seized, and she held her mouth wide open.
He drove in the spear and burst open her belly,
Cutting into her entrails, he slit her heart.
He overcame her and destroyed her life;
He cast down her carcass and stood upon it.
When he had thus subjected Tiamat, the leader,
Her host was scattered, her assembly was dissolved;
And the gods, her helpers, who marched beside her,
In fear and trembling turned about,
Taking to flight to save their lives.
But they were surrounded and could not escape.
He captured them and smashed their weapons,
They were cast into the net, and brought into the snare; ...
After he (i.e., Marduk) had bound and cast down his enemies,

Had battered down the arrogant foe,
Had completely gained the victory of Anshar over the enemy,
The hero Marduk had attained the aim of Nudimmud,
He strengthened his hold over the captive gods.
To Tiamat, whom he had bound, he came back,
And the lord trampled under foot the foundation of Tiamat.
With his merciless weapon he smashed her skull,
He cut the channels of her blood,
And made the north wind carry them to secret places.
His fathers beheld and rejoiced exceeding glad,
Presents and gifts they brought to him.
Then the lord rested and looked at the carcass.
He divided the flesh of the monster, and created marvellous things.
He split her like a fish flattened into two halves;
One half he took and made it a covering for heaven.
He drew a bolt, he stationed a watchman,
Enjoining that the waters be not permitted to flow out.
He passed over the heavens, inspecting the regions (thereof),
And over against the Apsu, he set the dwelling of Nudimmud.
The lord measured the structure of the Deep.
He established E-sharra as a palace corresponding to it.
The palace E-sharra which he created as heaven,
He caused Anu, Enlil and Ea to inhabit their districts.

TABLET V

He made stations for the great gods,
The stars, their counterparts, the twin stars he fixed.

He fixed the year and divided it into divisions.
For the twelve months he fixed three stars.
Also for the days of the year (he had fashioned)
   pictures....

TABLET VI

Upon (Marduk's) hearing the word of the
   gods,
His heart led him to create (marvellous things)
He opened his mouth and (spoke) to Ea

(What) he had conceived in his heart he
   imparted to him;
"My blood I will take and bone I will (form).
I will set up man that man ...
I will create man to inhabit (the earth),
That the worship of the gods be fixed, that
   they may have shrines.
But I will alter the ways of the gods, I will
   change ...
They shall be joined in concert, unto evil shall
   they" ...
Ea answered him and spoke.

FOCUS QUESTIONS

1. Conflict seems to be a major theme of this
   creation epic. What, in practical terms, does
   war among gods mean for mere mortals?

2. Mortals play little part in the struggles of the
   gods. Why? What assumptions about
   humanity and its relations to the gods are
   revealed in the epic?

3. Who won the battle between Marduk and
   Tiamat? What followed the end of that war?

4. Extreme violence marks much of the creation
   epic. What lessons might you draw from
   this about the nature of Mesopotamian
   society?

3

The Book of Genesis (ca. 10th–6th century B.C.E.)

The Book of Genesis is the first book of the Old Testament as well as the first book of the Hebrew Torah. It was probably composed between the tenth and sixth century B.C.E. Genesis tells the Judeo-Christian story of creation and the early history of the Hebrew people. The Judeo-Christian creation was the work of a single God who formed the environment for the life of humans. The story is anthropocentric; that is, it revolves around the deeds of men and women from their creation through the expulsion from the Garden of Eden to their corruption of the earth. God cleanses this corruption with a mighty flood of water that eliminates all but one human family, that of Noah.

The story told in Genesis is so well known that it is difficult to attempt to read it critically as an historical document. Because it is the best known of all the creation epics, there is a temptation to regard it as the unique story of the origins of humanity and the universe. It is most fruitfully read in comparison with other stories of creation.

CHAPTER 1

In the beginning God created the heaven and the earth.

And the earth was without form, and void; and darkness *was* upon the face of the deep. And the Spirit of God moved upon the face of the waters.

And God said, Let there be light: and there was light.

And God saw the light, that it *was* good: and God divided the light from the darkness.

And God called the light Day, and the darkness he called Night.

And the evening and the morning were the first day.

And God said, Let there be a firmament in the midst of the waters, and let it divide the waters from the waters.

And God made the firmament, and divided the waters which *were* under the firmament from the waters which *were* above the firmament: and it was so.

And God called the firmament Heaven. And the evening and the morning were the second day.

And God said, Let the waters under the heaven be gathered together unto one place, and let the dry *land* appear: and it was so.

And God called the dry *land* Earth; and the gathering together of the waters called he Seas: and God saw that *it was* good.

And God said, Let the earth bring forth grass, the herb yielding seed, *and* the fruit tree yielding fruit after his kind, whose seed *is* in itself, upon the earth: and it was so.

And the earth brought forth grass, and herb yielding seed after his kind, and the tree yielding fruit, whose seed *was* in itself, after his kind: and God saw that *it was* good.

And the evening and the morning were the third day.

And God said, Let there be lights in the firmament of the heaven to divide the day from the night; and let them be for signs, and for seasons, and for days, and years:

And let them be for lights in the firmament of the heaven to give light upon the earth: and it was so.

And God made two great lights; the greater light to rule the day, and the lesser light to rule the night: *he made* the stars also.

And God set them in the firmament of the heaven to give light upon the earth,

And to rule over the day and over the night, and to divide the light from the darkness: and God saw that *it was* good.

And the evening and the morning were the fourth day.

And God said, Let the waters bring forth abundantly the moving creature that hath life, and fowl *that* may fly above the earth in the open firmament of heaven.

And God created great whales, and every living creature that moveth, which the waters brought forth abundantly, after their kind, and every winged fowl after his kind: and God saw that *it was* good.

And God blessed them, saying, Be fruitful, and multiply, and fill the waters in the seas, and let fowl multiply in the earth.

And the evening and the morning were the fifth day.

And God said, Let the earth bring forth the living creature after his kind, cattle, and creeping thing, and beast of the earth after his kind: and it was so.

And God made the beast of the earth after his kind, and cattle after their kind, and every thing that creepeth upon the earth, after his kind: and God saw that *it was* good.

Scala/Art Resource, NY

Michelangelo, Creation of Adam. In 1508, Pope Julius II recalled Michelangelo to Rome and commissioned him to decorate the ceiling of the Sistine Chapel. This colossal project was not completed until 1512. Michelangelo attempted to tell the story of the Fall of Man by depicting nine scenes from the biblical book of Genesis. In this scene, the well-proportioned figure of Adam, meant by Michelangelo to be a reflection of divine beauty, awaits the divine spark.

And God said, Let us make man in our image, after our likeness: and let them have dominion over the fish of the sea, and over the fowl of the air, and over the cattle, and over all the earth, and over every creeping thing that creepeth upon the earth.

So God created man in his *own* image, in the image of God created he him; male and female created he them.

And God blessed them, and God said unto them, Be fruitful, and multiply, and replenish the earth, and subdue it: and have dominion over the fish of the sea, and over the fowl of the air, and over every living thing that moveth upon the earth.

And God said, Behold, I have given you every herb bearing seed, which *is* upon the face of all the earth, and every tree, in the which *is* the fruit of a tree yielding seed; to you it shall be for meat.

And to every beast of the earth, and to every fowl of the air, and to every thing that creepeth upon the earth, wherein *there* is life, *I have given* every green herb for meat: and it was so.

And God saw every thing that he had made, and, behold, *it was* very good. And the evening and the morning were the sixth day.

CHAPTER 2

Thus the heavens and the earth were finished, and all the host of them.

And on the seventh day God ended his work which he had made; and he rested on the seventh day from all his work which he had made.

And God blessed the seventh day, and sanctified it: because that in it he had rested from all his work which God created and made.

These *are* the generations of the heavens and of the earth when they were created, in the day that the LORD God made the earth and the heavens,

And every plant of the field before it was in the earth, and every herb of the field before it grew: for the LORD God had not caused it to rain upon the earth, and *there was* not a man to till the ground.

But there went up a mist from the earth, and watered the whole face of the ground.

And the LORD God formed man *of* the dust of the ground, and breathed into his nostrils the breath of life; and man became a living soul.

And the LORD God planted a garden eastward in Eden; and there he put the man whom he had formed.

And out of the ground made the LORD God to grow every tree that is pleasant to the sight, and good for food; the tree of life also in the midst of the garden, and the tree of knowledge of good and evil.

And a river went out of Eden to water the garden; and from thence it was parted, and became into four heads.

The name of the first *is* Pi'son: that *is* it which compasseth the whole land of Hav'i-lah, where *there is* gold;

And the gold of that land *is* good: there *is* bdellium and the onyx stone.

And the name of the second river *is* Gi'hon: the same *is* it that compasseth the whole land of E-thi-o'pi-a.

And the name of the third river *is* Hid'dekel: that *is* it which goeth toward the east of Ass-yr'i-a. And the fourth river *is* Euphra'tes.

And the LORD God took the man, and put him into the garden of Eden to dress it and to keep it.

And the LORD God commanded the man, saying, Of every tree of the garden thou mayest freely eat:

But of the tree of the knowledge of good and evil, thou shalt not eat of it: for in the day that thou eatest thereof thou shalt surely die.

And the LORD God said, *It is* not good that the man should be alone; I will make him an help meet for him.

And out of the ground the LORD God formed every beast of the field, and every fowl of the air; would call *them* unto Adam to see what he would call them; and whatsoever Adam called every living creature, that *was* the name thereof. And Adam gave names to all cattle, and to the fowl of the air, and to every beast of the field; but for Adam there was not found an help meet for him.

And the LORD God caused a deep sleep to fall upon Adam, and he slept: and he took one of his ribs, and closed up the flesh instead thereof;

And the rib, which the LORD God had taken from man, made he a woman, and brought her unto the man.

And Adam said, This *is* now bone of my bones, and flesh of my flesh: she shall be called Woman, because she was taken out of Man.

Therefore shall a man leave his father and his mother, and shall cleave unto his wife: and they shall be one flesh.

And they were both naked, the man and his wife, and were not ashamed.

CHAPTER 3

Now the serpent was more subtil than any beast of the field which the LORD God had made.

And he said unto the woman, Yea, hath God said, Ye shall not eat of every tree of the garden?

And the woman said unto the serpent, We may eat of the fruit of the trees of the garden:

But of the fruit of the tree which *is* in the midst of the garden, God hath said, Ye shall not eat of it, neither shall ye touch it, lest ye die.

And the serpent said unto the woman, Ye shall not surely die:

For God doth know that in the day ye eat thereof, then your eyes shall be opened, and ye shall be as gods, knowing good and evil.

And when the woman saw that the tree *was* good for food, and that it *was* pleasant to the eyes, and a tree to be desired to make *one* wise, she took of the fruit thereof, and did eat, and gave also unto her husband with her; and he did eat.

And the eyes of them both were opened, and they knew that they *were* naked; and they sewed fig leaves together, and made themselves aprons.

And they heard the voice of the LORD God walking in the garden in the cool of the day: and Adam and his wife hid themselves from the presence of the LORD God amongst the trees of the garden.

And the LORD God called unto Adam, and said unto him, Where *art* thou?

And he said, I heard thy voice in the garden, and I was afraid, because I *was* naked; and I hid myself.

And he said, Who told thee that thou *wast* naked? Hast thou eaten of the tree, whereof I commanded thee that thou shouldest not eat?

And the man said, The woman whom thou gavest *to be* with me, she gave me of the tree, and I did eat.

And the LORD God said unto the woman, What *is* this *that* thou hast done? And the woman said, The serpent beguiled me, and I did eat.

And the LORD God said unto the serpent, Because thou hast done this, thou *art* cursed above all cattle, and above every beast of the field; upon thy belly shalt thou go, and dust shalt thou eat all the days of thy life:

And I will put enmity between thee and the woman, and between thy seed and her seed; it shall bruise thy head, and thou shalt bruise his heel.

Unto the woman he said, I will greatly multiply thy sorrow and thy conception; in sorrow thou shalt bring forth children; and thy desire *shall be* to thy husband, and he shall rule over thee.

And unto Adam he said, Because thou hast hearkened unto the voice of thy wife, and hast eaten of the tree, of which I commanded thee, saying, Thou shalt not eat of it: cursed *is* the ground for thy sake; in sorrow shalt thou eat *of* it all the days of thy life;

Thorns also and thistles shall it bring forth to thee; and thou shalt eat the herb of the field;

In the sweat of thy face shalt thou eat bread, till thou return unto the ground; for out of it wast thou taken: for dust thou *art,* and unto dust shalt thou return.

And Adam called his wife's name Eve; because she was the mother of all living.

Unto Adam also and to his wife did the LORD God make coats of skins, and clothed them.

And the LORD God said, Behold, the man is become as one of us, to know good and evil: and now, lest he put forth his hand, and take also of the tree of life, and eat, and live for ever:

Therefore the LORD God sent him forth from the garden of Eden, to till the ground from whence he was taken.

So he drove out the man; and he placed at the east of the garden of Eden Cher'u-bims, and a flaming sword which turned every way, to keep the way of the tree of life.

CHAPTER 4

And Adam knew Eve his wife; and she conceived, and bare Cain, and said, I have gotten a man from the Lord.

And she again bare his brother Abel. And Abel was a keeper of sheep, and Cain was a tiller of the ground.

And in process of time it came to pass, that Cain brought of the fruit of the ground an offering unto the LORD.

And Abel, he also brought of the firstlings of his flock and of the fat thereof. And the LORD had respect unto Abel and to his offering:

But unto Cain and to his offering he had not respect. And Cain was very wroth, and his countenance fell.

And the LORD said unto Cain, Why art thou wroth? and why is thy countenance fallen?

If thou doest well, shalt thou not be accepted? and if thou doest not well, sin lieth at the door. And unto thee *shall be* his desire, and thou shalt rule over him.

And Cain talked with Abel his brother: and it came to pass, when they were in the field, that Cain rose up against Abel his brother, and slew him.

And the LORD said unto Cain, Where *is* Abel thy brother? And he said, I know not: *Am* I my brother's keeper?

And he said, What hast thou done? the voice of thy brother's blood crieth unto me from the ground.

And now *art* thou cursed from the earth, which hath opened her mouth to receive thy brother's blood from thy hand;

When thou tillest the ground, it shall not henceforth yield unto thee her strength; a fugitive and a vagabond shalt thou be in the earth.

And Cain said unto the LORD, My punishment *is* greater than I can bear.

Behold, thou hast driven me out this day from the face of the earth; and from thy face shall I be hid; and I shall be a fugitive and a vagabond in the earth; and it shall come to pass, *that* every one that findeth me shall slay me.

And the LORD said unto him, Therefore whosoever slayeth Cain, vengeance shall be taken on him sevenfold. And the LORD set a mark upon Cain, lest any finding him should kill him.

And Cain went out from the presence of the LORD, and dwelt in the land of Nod, on the east of Eden.

And Cain knew his wife; and she conceived, and bare E'noch: and he builded a city, and called the name of the city, after the name of his son, E'noch.

And unto E'noch was born I'rad: and I'rad begat Me-hu'ja-el: and Me-hu'ja-el begat Me-thu'sa-el: and Me-thu'sa-el begat La'mech.

And La'mech took unto him two wives: the name of the one *was* Adah, and the name of the other Zil'lah.

And Adah bare Ja'bal: he was the father of such as dwell in tents, and *of such as have* cattle.

And his brother's name *was* Ju'bal: he was the father of all such as handle the harp and organ.

And Zil'lah, she also bare Tu'bal-cain, an instructer of every artificer in brass and iron: and the sister of Tu'bal-cain *was* Na'a-mah.

And La'mech said unto his wives, Adah and Zil'lah, Hear my voice; ye wives of La'mech, hearken unto my speech: for I have slain a man to my wounding, and a young man to my hurt.

If Cain shall be avenged sevenfold, truly La'mech seventy and sevenfold.

And Adam knew his wife again; and she bare a son, and called his name Seth: For God, *said she*, hath appointed me another seed instead of Abel, whom Cain slew.

And to Seth, to him also there was bore a son; and he called his name E'nos: then began men to call upon the name of the LORD.

. . .

CHAPTER 5

And it came to pass, when men began to multiply on the face of the earth, and daughters were born unto them,

That the sons of God saw the daughters of men that they *were* fair; and they took them wives of all which they chose.

And the LORD said, My spirit shall not always strive with man, for that he also *is* flesh: yet his days shall be an hundred and twenty years.

There were giants in the earth in those days; and also after that, when the sons of God came in unto the daughters of men, and they bare *children* to them, the same *became* mighty men which *were* of old, men of renown.

And GOD saw that the wickedness of man was great in the earth, and *that* every imagination of the thoughts of his heart *was* only evil continually.

And it repented the LORD that he had made man on the earth, and it grieved him at his heart.

And the LORD said, I will destroy man whom I have created from the face of the earth; both man, and beast, and the creeping thing, and the fowls of the air; for it repenteth me that I have made them.

But Noah found grace in the eyes of the LORD.

These *are* the generations of Noah: Noah was a just man *and* perfect in his generations, *and* Noah walked with God.

And Noah begat three sons, Shem, Ham, and Ja'pheth.

The earth also was corrupt before God, and the earth was filled with violence.

And God looked upon the earth, and, behold, it was corrupt; for all flesh had corrupted his way upon the earth.

And God said unto Noah, The end of all flesh is come before me; for the earth is filled with violence through them; and behold, I will destroy them with the earth.

Make thee an ark of gopher wood; rooms shalt thou make in the ark, and shalt pitch it within and without with pitch.

And this *is the fashion* which thou shalt make it *of*. The length of the ark *shall be* three hundred cubits, the breadth of it fifty cubits, and the height of it thirty cubits.

A window shalt thou make to the ark, and in a cubit shalt thou finish it above; and the door of the ark shalt thou set in the side thereof; *with* lower, second, and third *stories* shalt thou make it.

And, behold, I, even I, do bring a flood of waters upon the earth, to destroy all flesh, wherein *is* the breath of life, from under heaven; *and* every thing that *is* in the earth shall die.

But with thee will I establish my covenant; and thou shalt come into the ark, thou, and thy sons, and thy wife, and thy sons' wives with thee.

And of every living thing of all flesh, two of every *sort* shalt thou bring into the ark, to keep *them* alive with thee; they shall be male and female.

Of fowls after their kind, and of cattle after their kind, of every creeping thing of the earth after his kind, two of every *sort* shall come unto thee, to keep *them* alive.

And take thou unto thee of all food that is eaten, and thou shalt gather *it* to thee; and it shall be for food for thee, and for them.

Thus did Noah; according to all that God commanded him, so did he.

CHAPTER 6

And the LORD said unto Noah, Come thou and all thy house into the ark; for thee have I seen righteous before me in this generation.

Of every clean beast thou shalt take to thee by sevens, the male and his female: and of beasts that *are* not clean by two, the male and his female.

Of fowls also of the air by sevens, the male and female; to keep seed alive upon the face of all the earth.

For yet seven days, and I will cause it to rain upon the earth forty days and forty nights; and every living substance that I have made will I destroy from off the face of the earth.

And Noah did according unto all that the LORD commanded him.

And Noah *was* six hundred years old when the flood of waters was upon the earth.

And Noah went in, and his sons, and his wife, and his sons' wives with him, into the ark, because of the waters of the flood.

Of clean beasts, and of beasts that *are* not clean, and of fowls, and of every thing that creepeth upon the earth.

They went in two and two unto Noah into the ark, the male and the female, as God had commanded Noah.

And it came to pass after seven days, that the waters of the flood were upon the earth.

In the six hundredth year of Noah's life, in the second month, the seventeenth day of the month, the same day were all the fountains of the great deep broken up, and the windows of heaven were opened.

And the rain was upon the earth forty days and forty nights.

In the selfsame day entered Noah, and Shem, and Ham, and Ja'pheth, the sons of Noah, and Noah's wife, and the three wives of his sons with them, into the ark;

They, and every beast after his kind, and all the cattle after their kind, and every creeping thing that creepeth upon the earth after his kind, and every fowl after his kind, every bird of every sort.

And they went in unto Noah into the ark, two and two of all flesh, wherein *is* the breath of life.

And they that went in, went in male and female of all flesh, as God had commanded him: and the LORD shut him in.

And the flood was forty days upon the earth; and the waters increased, and bare up the ark, and it was lift up above the earth.

And the waters prevailed, and were increased greatly upon the earth; and the ark went upon the face of the waters.

And the waters prevailed exceedingly upon the earth; and all the high hills, that *were* under the whole heaven, were covered.

Fifteen cubits upward did the waters prevail; and the mountains were covered.

And all flesh died that moved upon the earth, both of fowl, and of cattle, and of beast, and of every creeping thing that creepeth upon the earth, and every man:

All in whose nostrils *was* the breath of life, of all that *was* in the dry *land,* died.

And every living substance was destroyed which was upon the face of the ground, both man, and cattle, and the creeping things, and the fowl of the heaven; and they were destroyed from the earth: and Noah only remained *alive,* and they that *were* with him in the ark.

And the waters prevailed upon the earth an hundred and fifty days.

FOCUS QUESTIONS

1. Why is it significant that God created man in his own image?

2. What is the relationship between humans and animals?

3. What is the position of women in Genesis?

4. What is the significance of the story of the flood?

4

The Kojiki (712 C.E.)

The Kojiki, *which means "Records of Ancient Matters," is the oldest surviving book written in Japanese. Its subject is even older, the myths and legends about the creation of Japan. It was compiled in 712 C.E. under the direction of Opo nö Yasumarö to glorify the Imperial line and to preserve an account of Japan's leading families. Earlier efforts to achieve the same goal were incorporated into the Kojiki that has come down to us; it is impossible to determine which parts were composed when. The impetus for a systematic compilation of ancient genealogical and historical materials was the Chinese that threatened the position of native Japanese families. The Kojiki is composed of three parts or volumes, the first consisting of legends of gods and goddesses and of the creation of the Japanese Islands. The succeeding volumes concern the reigns of ancient emperors and empresses, until the story merges into the contemporary history of the Emperor Temmu. Though the Kojiki, in its historical sections, is not regarded as a reliable account of early Japanese politics, it preserves the flavor of the spoken and sung traditions that celebrated the divine nature of the Imperial dynasty.*

The work is in a variety of forms, genealogical lists, lyrical poems, and songs which make it likely that some of its parts were intended to be sung, despite the centuries-old literary tradition at the Japanese court.

In this selection from the first book of the Kojiki, the original formation of Japan is narrated. The history of the two deities, Izanagi and Izanami, is recounted along with the story of their marriage and divorce.

CHAPTER 1

The Five Separate Heavenly Deities Come into Existence

At the time of the beginning of heaven and earth, there came into existence in Takama-nö-para a deity named Amë-nö-mi-naka-nusi-nö-kamï; next, Takami-musubi-nö-kamï; next, Kamï-musubi-nö-kamï. These three deities all came into existence as single deities, and their forms were not visible.

Next, when the land was young, resembling floating oil and drift-like a jellyfish, there sprouted forth something like reed-shoots. From these came into existence the deity Umasi-asi-kabï-piko-dinö-kamï; next, Amë-nö-tökö-tati-nö-kamï. These two deities also came into existence as single deities, and their forms were not visible.

The five deities in the above section are the Separate Heavenly Deities....

...

CHAPTER 2

Izanagi and Izanami are Commanded to Solidify the Land. They Create Onögörö Island

At this time the heavenly deities, all with one command, said to the two deities Izanagi-nö-mikötö and Izanami-nö-mikötö:

"Complete and solidify this drifting land!"

Giving them the Heavenly Jeweled Spear, they entrusted the mission to them.

Thereupon, the two deities stood on the Heavenly Floating Bridge and, lowering the jeweled spear, stirred with it. They stirred the brine with a churning-churning sound, and when they lifted up [the spear] again, the brine dripping down from the tip of the spear piled up and became an island. This was the island Onögörö.

CHAPTER 3

Izanagi and Izanami Marry and Bear their First Offspring

Descending from the heavens to this island, they erected a heavenly pillar and a spacious palace.

At this time [Izanagi-nö-mikötö] asked his spouse Izanami-nö-mikötö, saying:

"How is your body formed?"

She replied, saying:

"My body, formed though it be formed, has one place which is formed insufficiently."

Then Izanagi-nö-mikötö said:

"My body, formed though it be formed, has one place which is formed to excess. Therefore, I would like to take that place in my body which is formed to excess and insert it into that place in your body which is formed insufficiently, and [thus] give birth to the land. How would this be?"

Izanami-nö-mikötö replied, saying:

"That will be good."

Then Izanagi-nö-mikötö said:

"Then let us, you and me, walk in a circle around this heavenly pillar and meet and have conjugal intercourse."

After thus agreeing, [Izanagi-nö-mikötö] then said:

"You walk around from the right, and I will walk around from the left and meet you."

After having agreed to this, they circled around; then Izanami-nö-mikötö said first:

"*Ana-ni-yasi,* how good a lad!"

Afterwards, Izanagi-nö-mikötö said:

"*Ana-ni-yasi,* how good a maiden!"

After each had finished speaking, [Izanagi-nö-mikötö] said to his spouse:

"It is not proper that the woman speak first."

Nevertheless, they commenced procreation and gave birth to a leech-child. They placed this child into a boat made of reeds and floated it away.

Next, they gave birth to the island of Apa. This also is not reckoned as one of their children.

CHAPTER 4

Izanagi and Izanami, Learning the Reason for Their Failure, Repeat the Marriage Ritual

Then the two deities consulted together and said:

"The child which we have just borne is not good. It is best to report [this matter] before the heavenly deities."

Then they ascended together and sought the will of the heavenly deities. The heavenly deities thereupon performed a grand divination and said:

"Because the woman spoke first, [the child] was not good. Descend once more and say it again."

Then they descended again and walked once more in a circle around the heavenly pillar as [they had done] before.

Then Izanagi-nö-mikötö said first:

"*Ana-ni-yasi,* how good a maiden!"

Afterwards, his spouse Izanami-nö-mikötö said:

"*Ana-ni-yasi,* how good a lad!"

CHAPTER 5

Izanagi and Izanami Give Birth to Numerous Islands

After they had finished saying this, they were united and bore as a child [the island] Apadi-nö-po-nö-sa-wakë-nö-sima....

CHAPTER 6

Izanagi and Izanami Give Birth to Numerous Deities. Izanami Dies After Bearing the Fire-Deity

After they had finished bearing the land, they went on to bear deities….

At this time Izanagi-nö-mikötö said:

"Alas, I have given my beloved spouse in exchange for a mere child!"

Then he crawled around her head and around her feet, weeping.

At this time in his tears there came into existence the deity who dwells at the foot of the trees in the foothills of Mount Kagu, named Naki-sapa-menö-kamï.

Then he buried the departed Izanami-nö-kamï on Mount Piba, the border between the land of Idumo and the land of Papaki.

CHAPTER 7

Izanagi Kills the Fire-Deity. Various Deities Come into Existence

Then Izanagi-nö-mikötö unsheathed the sword ten hands long which he was wearing at his side and cut off the head of his child Kagu-tuti-nö-kamï.

Hereupon the blood adhering to the tip of the sword gushed forth onto the massed rocks; the deity who came into existence therefrom was Ipasaku-nö-kamï; next, Ne-saku-nö-kamï; next, Ipatutu-nö-wo-nö-kamï. (Three deities)

Next, the blood adhering to the sword-guard of the sword also gushed forth onto the massed rocks; the deity who came into existence therefrom was Mika-paya-pi-nö-kamï; next, Pi-paya-pi-nö-kamï; next, Take-mika-duti-nö-wo-nö-kamï, also named Take-putu-nö-kamï, and also named Töyö-putu-nö-kamï. (Three deities)

Next, the blood collected at the hilt of the sword dripped through his fingers; the deity who came into existence therefrom was Kura-okaminö-kamï; next, Kura-mitu-pa-nö-kamï.

The deities in the above section, altogether eight in number from Ipa-saku-nö-kamï through Kuramitu-pa-nö-kamï, are deities born by the sword….

CHAPTER 8

Izanagi Visits Izanami in the Land of Yömï. Breaking the Taboo, He Looks Upon Her Corpse

At this time, [Izanagi-nö-mikötö], wishing to meet again his spouse Izanami-nö-mikötö, went after her to the land of Yömï.

When she came forth out of the door of the hall to greet him, Izanagi-nö-mikötö said:

"O, my beloved spouse, the lands which you and I were making have not yet been completed; you must come back!"

Then Izanami-nö-mikötö replied, saying:

"How I regret that you did not come sooner. I have eaten at the hearth of Yömï. But, O my beloved husband, how awesome it is that you have entered here! Therefore I will go and discuss for a while with the gods of Yömï my desire to return. Pray do not look upon me!"

Thus saying, she went back into the hall, but her absence was so long that [Izanagi-nö-mikötö] could no longer wait.

Thereupon he broke off one of the large end-teeth of the comb he was wearing in his left hair-bunch, lit [it as] one fire, and entered in to see.

At this time, maggots were squirming and roaring [in the corpse of Izanami-nö-mikötö].

In her head was Great-Thunder;
In her breast was Fire-Thunder;
In her belly was Black-Thunder;
In her genitals was Crack-Thunder;
In her left hand was Young-Thunder;
In her right hand was Earth-Thunder;
In her left foot was Sounding-Thunder;
In her right foot was Reclining-Thunder;
Altogether there were eight thunder-deities.

CHAPTER 9

Izanagi Flees and Eludes His Pursuers. Izanagi and Izanami Break their Troth

Hereupon, Izanagi-nö-mikötö, seeing this, was afraid, and he turned and fled.

At this time his spouse Izanami-nö-mikötö said:

"He has shamed me!"

Thereupon she dispatched the hags of Yömï to pursue him.

Then Izanagi-nö-mikötö undid the black vine securing his hair and flung it down; immediately it bore grapes. While [the hags] were picking and eating [the grapes], he fled.

When again they pursued him, he next pulled out the comb he was wearing in his right hair-bunch and flung it down; immediately bamboo shoots sprouted forth. While [the hags] were pulling up and eating [the bamboo shoots], he fled.

Later, [Izanami-nö-mikötö dispatched] the eight thunder-deities and a horde of warriors of Yömï to pursue him.

Then [Izanagi-nö-mikötö] unsheathed the sword ten hands long which he was wearing at his side and fled while waving it behind him.

The pursuit continued, and when [Izanagi-nö-mikötö] had arrived at the foot of [the pass] Yömö-tu-pira-saka, he took three peaches which were there and, waiting for [his pursuers], attacked [them with the peaches]. They all turned and fled.

Then Izanagi-nö-mikötö said to the peaches:

"Just as you have saved me, when, in the Central Land of the Reed Plains, any of the race of mortal men fall into painful straits and suffer in anguish, then do you save them also."

He bestowed [upon the peaches] the name Opo-kamu-du-mi-nö-mikötö.

Finally, his spouse Izanami-nö-mikötö herself came in pursuit of him. Then he pulled a tremendous boulder and closed [the pass] Yömö-tu-pirasaka with it.

They stood facing each other, one on each side of the boulder, and broke their troth.

At this time Izanami-nö-mikötö said:

"O my beloved husband, if you do thus, I will each day strangle to death one thousand of the populace of your country."

To this Izanagi-nö-mikötö said:

"O my beloved spouse, if you do thus, I will each day build one thousand five hundred parturition huts."

This is the reason why one thousand people inevitably die and one thousand five hundred people are inevitably born every day.

Izanami-nö-kamï is also called Yömö-tu-opokamï. Also, because she joined in the pursuit, she is called Ti-siki-nö-opo-kamï.

The boulder which closed [the pass] Yömö-tu-pira-saka is called Ti-gapesi-nö-opo-kamï; it is also called Sayari-masu-yömï-do-nö-opo-kamï.

The so-called Yömö-tu-pira-saka is now called the pass Ipuya-zaka in the land of Idumo.

FOCUS QUESTIONS

1. How were the original Japanese islands created?
2. What views did the gods have concerning gender?
3. Are the Japanese deities mortal or immortal?
4. How did Izanagi shame Izanami? What does this tell us of the values of the deities?
5. Why do you think there is so much violence in this creation myth?

The Cradle of Civilization

The Great Pyramids of Giza.

5

The Epic of Gilgamesh (ca. 2000 B.C.E.)

The Epic of Gilgamesh, *the best known of the Mesopotamian myths, is one of the world's oldest surviving pieces of literature. Only incomplete versions have come down to us, the longest of which is a copy written on 12 tablets found in the Royal Library of Nineveh. The epic tells the story of the wanderings of Gilgamesh, the part-human, part-divine king of Uruk. Around 2000 B.C.E., Uruk, one of the most important of the Mesopotamian city-states, was ruled by a King Gilgamesh, but it is impossible to be certain that the events recounted in the epic derive from his reign.*

The peoples of the ancient Near East lived precariously, always at the mercy of nature. Flood and drought were the most common natural disasters, and The Epic of Gilgamesh *contains echoes of the great flood narrated in the Bible. Gilgamesh's travels are motivated by a search for the survivors of this great flood, who supposedly know the secret of everlasting life. The twin themes of the unpredictability of the gods and the inevitability of death dominate the epic.*

Siduri, she the divine cup-bearer,
Sits there by the rim of the sea.
Sits there and looks afar off ...
She is wrapped in a shawl ...
Gilgamesh ran thither and drew nigh unto her.
He is clad in skins,
His shape is awesome,
His body godlike,
Woe is in his heart.
He is like a wanderer of far ways.
The face of her, the cup-bearer, looks afar off,
She talks to herself and says the word,
Takes counsel in her heart:
"Is he yonder one who deviseth ill?
Whither is he going in the wrath of his heart?"
As Siduri saw him, she locked her gate,
Locked her portal, locked her chamber....

Gilgamesh says to her, to the cup-bearer:
"Cup-bearer, what ails thee,
That thou lockest thy gate,
Lockest thy portal,
Lockest thy chamber?
I will crash the door, I will break the lock." ...

The cup-bearer says to him, to Gilgamesh:
"Why are thy cheeks so wasted,
Thy visage so sunken,
Thy heart so sad,
Thy shape so undone?
Why is woe in thy heart?
Why art thou like a wanderer of far ways?
Why is thy countenance
So destroyed with grief and pain?
Why hast thou from wide-away
Made haste over the steppes?"

Gilgamesh says to her, to the cup-bearer:
"Why should my cheeks not be so wasted,
My visage so sunken,
My heart so sad,
My shape so undone?
How should woe not be in my heart?
Why should I not be like
A wanderer of far ways?
Why should not my countenance
Be destroyed with grief and pain?
Why should I not to the far-away
Make haste over the steppes?

My beloved friend, the panther of the steppes,
Engidu, my beloved friend,
The panther of the steppes who could do all
    things,
So that we climbed the mountain,
Overthrew Khumbaba,
Who housed in the cedar-forest,
So that we seized and slew the bull-of-heaven,
So that we laid lions low
In the ravines of the mountain,
My friend,
Who with me ranged through all hardships,
Engidu, my friend, who killed lions with me,
Who with me ranged through all hardships,
Him hath the fate of mankind overtaken.
Six days and six nights have I wept over him,
Until the seventh day
Would I not have him buried.
Then I began to be afraid …
Fear of death seized upon me.
Therefore I make away over the steppes.
The fate of my friend weighs me down.
Therefore I make haste
On a far way over the steppes.
The fate of Engidu, my friend,
Weigheth me down.
Therefore I make haste on a long road over
    the steppes.
Why should I be silent thereon?
Why should I not cry it forth?
My friend, whom I love,
Hath turned into earth.
Must not I too, as he,
Lay me down
And rise not up again
For ever and for ever?—
Ever since he is gone, I cannot find Life,
And rove, like a hunter, round over the fields.
Cup-bearer, now I behold thy face;
But Death, whom I fear, I would not behold."

The cup-bearer, she says to him, to
    Gilgamesh:
"Gilgamesh, whither runnest thou?
Life, which thou seekest, thou wilt not find.
When the gods created mankind,
They allotted to mankind Death,
But Life they withheld in their hands.
So, Gilgamesh, fill thy body,
Make merry by day and night,
Keep each day a feast of rejoicing!
Day and night leap and have thy delight!
Put on clean raiment,
Wash thy head and bathe thee in water,
Look cheerily at the child who holdeth thy
    hand,
And may thy wife have joy in thy arms!"

Gilgamesh says again to her, to the
    cup-bearer:
"Go to, cup-bearer!
Where is the way to Utnapishtim?
What is his sign? Give it to me!
If it can be done,
I will pass over the sea;
If it cannot be done,
I will make away over the steppes."
Ur-Shanabi says to him, to Gilgamesh:
"What is thy name? Say forth!
I am Ur-Shanabi,
Man-servant of Utnapishtim, the far one."

Gilgamesh speaks to him, to Ur-Shanabi:
"My name is Gilgamesh,
I have come from long away …
At last, Ur-Shanabi, I behold thy face.
Let me look on Utnapishtim, the far one."

Ur-Shanabi says to him, to Gilgamesh:
"Why are thy cheeks so wasted,
Thy visage so sunken,
Thy heart so sad,
Thy shape so undone?
Why is woe in thy heart?
Why art thou like a wanderer of far ways?
Why is thy countenance
So destroyed with grief and pain?
Why hast thou from long away
Come ahaste over the steppes?"

Gilgamesh says to him,
To Ur-Shanabi, the shipman:
"Why should my cheeks not be so wasted,
My visage so sunken,

My heart so sad,
My shape so undone?"
Gilgamesh and Ur-Shanabi boarded the ship,
They headed the ship into the flood
And sailed forth,
A way of one month and fifteen days.
As he took his bearings on the third day,
Ur-Shanabi had reached the water of death.
Ur-Shanabi says to him, to Gilgamesh:
"Quick, Gilgamesh, take a pole!
For thy hands must not touch
The waters of death."

Utnapishtim descrieth his face afar;
Talks to himself and saith the word,
Takes counsel in his heart:
"Why are the stone-coffers
Of the ship all to-broken?
And one who belongs not to me
Sails in the ship!
He who comes yonder, he cannot be man! ...
I gaze thither, but I understand it not.
I gaze thither, but I grasp it not." ...

Utnapishtim says to him, to Gilgamesh:
"What is thy name? Say forth!
I am Utnapishtim who hath found Life."
Gilgamesh says to him, to Utnapishtim:
"My name is Gilgamesh.
I have come from wide-away ...
Now I behold thee, Utnapishtim, thou far one."
Gilgamesh says again to him, to
   Utnapishtim:
"Methought, I will go and see
Utnapishtim, of whom men tell.
So I betook me through all lands to and fro,
So I betook me over the mountains
That are hard to cross over,
So I fared over all seas.
With good have I not been glutted ...
I filled my body with pain;
Ere ever I got to Siduri, the cup-bearer,
Was my clothing gone ...
I had to hunt all the wild of the fields,
Lions and panthers,
Hyenas, and deer, and ibex.
Their flesh do I eat,

With their skins do I clothe me." ...
And whilst Gilgamesh sits there in a posture of
   rest,
Sleep bloweth upon him like a stormwind.
Utnapishtim says to her, to his wife:
"Look at the strong one
Who longed after Life
Like a stormwind, sleep bloweth against him!"
His wife speaks to him, to Utnapishtim,
To the far one:
"Touch him, that the man may wake up!
Let him, on the way whence he came,
Safe and sound return home.
Through the gate, through which he went,
May he return back to his land!"
Utnapishtim says to her, to his wife:
"Oh, thou hast pity upon the man!
Go to, bake loaves for him,
And lay them at his head!
And the days which he sleeps

Do thou mark on the house-wall."
She baked loaves for him and laid them at his
   head.
And the days which he slept she marked on
   the wall.
Utnapishtim announced to him:
"One is dry, a loaf for him,
A second is kneaded, a third damp,
A fourth is become white, a roasted loaf for
   him,
A fifth is become old,
A sixth is baked, a seventh—"
Then of a sudden he touched him,
And the man awoke.
Gilgamesh says to him,
To Utnapishtim, the far one:
I was benumbed by the sleep that fell on me.
Then didst thou touch me quick and awaken
   me."
Utnapishtim says to him, to Gilgamesh:
"Go to, Gilgamesh, thy loaves are counted ...
One was dry, a loaf for thee,
A second was kneaded, a third damp,
A fourth was become white, a roasted loaf for
   thee,

A fifth was become old,
A sixth was baked, a seventh—
Then of a sudden I touched,
And thou awokest!"
Gilgamesh says to him,
To Utnapishtim, the far one:
"What shall I do, Utnapishtim?
Whither shall I go,
Now that the Snatcher hath laid hold on my
    body?
In my sleeping-chamber dwells Death,
And whithersoever I flee, is he, is Death, there."

Utnapishtim says to him,
To Ur-Shanabi, the shipman:
"Ur-Shanabi, the landing-place
Shall no more desire thee;
The crossing-spot shall hate thee …
The man whom thou leddest hither,
Whose body filth covers,
From whom beast-skins have taken
The beauty of the body,
Escort him, Ur-Shanabi,
And bring him to the bathing-place;
Let him wash clean as snow
His filth in the water!
Let him cast off his skins
That the sea bear them away!
His body shall again show beautiful!
Be the band round his head made new!
Let him be clad in a robe,
In a shirt for his nakedness!
Until he comes again to his city,
Until he gets to his journey's end,
The robe shall not grow old,
Shall always be made new."

Gilgamesh and Ur-Shanabi boarded the ship,
They headed the ship into the flood,
And sailed away.
Then said his wife to him,
To Utnapishtim, the far one:
"Gilgamesh hath set forth;
He hath worn himself out, and suffered
    torments.
What wilt thou give him,
That with it he may reach his homeland?"

And Gilgamesh has already lifted the pole,
And brings the ship again near the shore:
Utnapishtim says to him, to Gilgamesh:
"Gilgamesh, thou hast set forth;
Thou hast worn thyself out, and suffered
    torments.
What shall I give thee
That with it thou reachest thy homeland?
I will lay open before thee
Knowledge deep-hidden;
About a plant of life will I tell thee.
The plant looks like the prick-thorn …
Its thorn like the thorn of the rose
Can prick the hand hard.
When thou gettest this plant in thy hands,
Eat thereof and thou wilt live."

When Gilgamesh learned of this …
He bound heavy stones on his feet;
These drew him down deep in the sea. He
    himself took the plant,
And it pricked his hand hard.
He cut off the heavy stones …
And laid the plant beside him.
Gilgamesh says to him,
To Ur-Shanabi, the shipman:
"Ur-Shanabi, this plant
Is a plant-of-promise,
Whereby a man obtains his desire.
I will bring it to ramparted Uruk;
I will make the warriors eat thereof …
Its name is: 'The-old-man-becomes-young-
    again.'
I myself will eat thereof,
And return back to my youth."

After twenty miles they took a little food,
After thirty miles they rested for the night.
Then Gilgamesh saw a pit with cool water;
He stepped into it and bathed in the water.
Then a serpent savoured the smell of the plant;
She crept along and took the plant …

When he returned, he shrieked out a curse.
Gilgamesh sat himself down and weeps,
His tears run over his face.
He speaks and says to Ur-Shanabi, the
    shipman:

"For whom, Ur-Shanabi,
Have my arms worn themselves out?
For whom hath been spent the blood of my
   heart?
I worked good not for myself—
For the worm of the earth have I wrought
   good...."
After twenty miles they took a little food,
After thirty miles they rested for the night.

At last they reached ramparted Uruk.
Gilgamesh says to him,
To Ur-Shanabi, the shipman:
"Mount up, Ur-Shanabi,
Go up along the walls of ramparted Uruk,
Observe the bricks, behold the groundwork,
4. If the bricks are not firm and lasting,
And if the foundations were not
Laid by the seven wise-men...."

FOCUS QUESTIONS

1. What does Gilgamesh run from, and what is he searching for?

2. Life in Mesopotamia was very hazardous. Describe some of the dangers Gilgamesh faced.

3. How do gods such as Siduri and Utnapishtim intervene in the lives of mortals?

4. What can you say about the Mesopotamian view of life as illustrated by the epic? What answers to the problems of survival does it offer?

Live your life to the fullest

6

Code of Hammurabi
(early 18th century B.C.E.)

Hammurabi (d. 1750 B.C.E.) was a ruler of the Old Babylonian or Amorite dynasty from 1792 to 1750 B.C.E. His principal achievement was unifying his Mesopotamian kingdom by controlling the Euphrates River. Though little is known about either his family life or the events of his reign, Hammurabi's military achievements are undoubted.

Discovered in the early twentieth century, the Code of Hammurabi was hailed as the first law code in Western history. Its severe punishments for criminal offenses and its explicit statement of the doctrine of "an eye for an eye" also led to its connection with the Mosaic code. It is now clear that Hammurabi's Code is a compendium of earlier laws rather than an innovation of this Babylonian ruler. Its influence on Hebrew law is also less direct than was once thought. What remains significant about Hammurabi's Code, however, is what it tells us about the importance of writing and literacy among the elites of Babylonian society and about their well-developed notions of law and justice.

THE LAWS

(noble)

If a seignior accused a(nother) seignior and brought a charge of murder against him, but has not proved it, his accuser shall be put to death.

If a seignior brought a charge of sorcery against a(nother) seignior, but has not proved it, the one against whom the charge of sorcery was brought, upon going to the river, shall throw himself into the river, and if the river has then overpowered him, his accuser shall take over his estate; if the river has shown that seignior to be innocent and he has accordingly come forth safe, the one who brought the charge of sorcery against him shall be put to death, while the one who threw himself into the river shall take over the estate of his accuser.

If a seignior came forward with false testimony in a case, and has not proved the word which he spoke, if that case was a case involving life, that seignior shall be put to death.

If he came forward with (false) testimony concerning grain or money, he shall bear the penalty of that case.

If a seignior stole the property of church or state, that seignior shall be put to death; also the one who received the stolen goods from his hand shall be put to death.

If a seignior has purchased or has received for safekeeping either silver or gold or a male slave or a female slave or an ox or a sheep or an ass or any sort of thing from the hand of a seignior's son or a seignior's slave without witnesses and contracts, since that seignior is a thief, he shall be put to death.

If a seignior stole either an ox or a sheep or an ass or a pig or a boat, if it belonged to the church (or) if it belonged to the state, he shall make thirty-fold restitution; if it belonged to a private citizen, he shall make good tenfold. If the thief does not have sufficient to make restitution, he shall be put to death.

If a seignior has stolen the young son of a(nother) seignior, he shall be put to death.

If a seignior has helped either a male slave of the state or a female slave of the state or a male slave of a private citizen or a female slave of a private citizen to escape through the city-gate, he shall be put to death.

If a seignior has harbored in his house either a fugitive male or female slave belonging to the state or to a private citizen and has not brought him forth at the summons of the police, that householder shall be put to death.

If a seignior committed robbery and has been caught, that seignior shall be put to death.

If the robber has not been caught, the robbed seignior shall set forth the particulars regarding his lost property in the presence of god, and the city and governor, in whose territory and district the robbery was committed, shall make good to him his lost property.

If either a sergeant or a captain has obtained a soldier by conscription or he accepted and has sent a hired substitute for a campaign of the king, that sergeant or captain shall be put to death.

If either a sergeant or a captain has appropriated the household goods of a soldier, has wronged a soldier, has let a soldier for hire, has abandoned a soldier to a superior in a lawsuit, has appropriated the grant which the king gave to a soldier, that sergeant or captain shall be put to death.

If a seignior has bought from the hand of a soldier the cattle or sheep which the king gave to the soldier, he shall forfeit his money.

When a seignior borrowed money from a merchant and pledged to the merchant a field prepared for grain or sesame, if he said to him, "Cultivate the field, then harvest (and) take the grain or sesame that is produced," if the tenant has produced grain or sesame in the field, the owner of the field at harvest-time shall himself take the grain or sesame that was produced in the field and he shall give to the merchant grain for his money, which he borrowed from the merchant, together with its interest, and also for the cost of cultivation.

If he pledged a field planted with (grain) or a field planted with sesame, the owner of the field shall himself take the grain or sesame that was produced in the field and he shall pay back the money with its interest to the merchant.

If he does not have the money to pay back, (grain or) sesame at their market value in accordance with the ratio fixed by the king he shall give to the merchant for his money, which he borrowed from the merchant, together with its interest.

If the tenant has not produced grain or sesame in the field, he may not change his contract.

If a seignior was too lazy to make [the dike of] his field strong and did not make his dike strong and a break has opened up in his dike and he has accordingly let the water ravage the farmland, the seignior in whose dike the break was opened shall make good the grain that he let get destroyed.

If he is not able to make good the grain, they shall sell him and his goods, and the farmers whose grain the water carried off shall divide (the proceeds).

If a seignior, upon opening his canal for irrigation, became so lazy that he has let the water ravage a field adjoining his, he shall measure out grain on the basis of those adjoining his.

If a seignior pointed the finger at a nun or the wife of a(nother) seignior, but has proved nothing, they shall drag that seignior into the presence of the judges and also cut off half his (hair).

If a seignior acquired a wife, but did not draw up the contracts for her, that woman is no wife.

If the wife of a seignior has been caught while lying with another man, they shall bind them and throw them into the water. If the husband of the woman wishes to spare his wife, then the king in turn may spare his subject.

If a seignior bound the (betrothed) wife of a (nother) seignior, who had had no intercourse with a male and was still living in her father's house, and he has lain in her bosom and they have caught him, that seignior shall be put to death, while that woman shall go free.

If a seignior's wife was accused by her husband, but she was not caught while lying with another man, she shall make affirmation by god and return to her house.

If the finger was pointed at the wife of a seignior because of another man, but she has not been caught while lying with the other man, she shall throw herself into the river for the sake of her husband.

If a seignior was taken captive, but there was sufficient to live on in his house, his wife [shall not leave her house, but she shall take care of her person by not] entering [the house of another].

If that woman did not take care of her person, but has entered the house of another, they shall prove it against that woman and throw her into the water.

If the seignior was taken captive and there was not sufficient to live on in his house, his wife may enter the house of another, with that woman incurring no blame at all.

If, when a seignior was taken captive and there was not sufficient to live on in his house, his wife has then entered the house of another before his (return) and has borne children, (and) later her husband has returned and has reached his city, that woman shall return to her first husband, while the children shall go with their father.

If, when a seignior deserted his city and then ran away, his wife has entered the house of another after his (departure), if that seignior has returned and wishes to take back his wife, the wife of the fugitive shall not return to her husband because he scorned his city and ran away.

If a seignior wishes to divorce his wife who did not bear him children, he shall give her money to the full amount of her marriage-price and he shall also make good to her the dowry which she brought from her father's house and then he may divorce her.

If there was no marriage-price, he shall give her one mina of silver as the divorce-settlement.

If he is a peasant, he shall give her one-third mina of silver.

If a seignior's wife, who was living in the house of the seignior, has made up her mind to leave in order that she may engage in business, thus neglecting her house (and) humiliating her husband, they shall prove it against her; and if her husband has then decided on her divorce, he may divorce her, with nothing to be given her as her divorce-settlement upon her departure. If her husband has not decided on her divorce, her husband may marry another woman, with the former woman living in the house of her husband like a maidservant.

If a woman so hated her husband that she has declared, "You may not have me," her record shall be investigated at her city council, and if she was careful and was not at fault, even though her husband has been going out and disparaging her greatly, that woman, without incurring any blame at all, may take her dowry and go off to her father's house.

If she was not careful, but was a gadabout, thus neglecting her house (and) humiliating her husband, they shall throw that woman into the water.

If a seignior's wife has brought about the death of her husband because of another man, they shall impale that woman on stakes.

If a seignior has had intercourse with his daughter, they shall make that seignior leave the city.

If a seignior chose a bride for his son and his son had intercourse with her, but later he himself has lain in her bosom and they have caught him, they shall bind that seignior and throw him into the water.

If a seignior chose a bride for his son and his son did not have intercourse with her, but he himself has lain in her bosom, he shall pay to her one-half mina of silver and he shall also make good to her whatever she brought from her father's house in order that the man of her choice may marry her.

If a seignior has lain in the bosom of his mother after (the death of) his father, they shall burn both of them.

If a son has struck his father, they shall cut off his hand.

If a seignior has destroyed the eye of a member of the aristocracy, they shall destroy his eye.

If he has broken a(nother) seignior's bone, they shall break his bone.

If he has destroyed the eye of a commoner or broken the bone of a commoner, he shall pay one mina of silver.

If he has destroyed the eye of a seignior's slave or broken the bone of a seignior's slave, he shall pay one-half his value.

see social status.

FOCUS QUESTIONS

1. Many ancient law codes were transmitted orally, through memorization. What are some advantages of a written legal code? Can you think of some disadvantages?

2. The areas of society that are regulated often indicate something about what is important to those who make the laws. What seem to be the main concerns of this law code?

3. Does the code make distinctions among people? Are some more important than others? How are people of different status dealt with under the law?

4. The penalties for breaking the law in Babylon were often very harsh. Why do you think the code was so severe?

7

The Book of the Dead (ca. 16th century B.C.E.)

The Book of the Dead is a collection of spells and prayers that the Egyptians believed were crucial to well-being in the afterlife. Composed of some two hundred chapters, it contains charms from as early as 2400 B.C.E. as well as more recent incantations. Sometime in the sixteenth century B.C.E. anonymous priests and scribes collected the chapters into a single volume. Many copies of the book have been found in tombs and burial chambers, where they were presumably placed for the use of the dead. They were copied on papyrus rolls, and some of the surviving ones are elaborately illustrated.

The following selection is an incantation meant to prepare the deceased for the judgment of the gods. The chant provides much direct evidence of the manners and values of everyday life in ancient Egypt.

THE PROTESTATION OF GUILTLESSNESS

What is said on reaching the Broad-Hall of the Two Justices, absolving X of every sin which he has committed, and seeing the faces of the gods:

Hail to thee, O great god, lord of the Two Justices! I have come to thee, my lord, I have been brought that I might see thy beauty. I know thee; I know thy name and the names of the forty-two gods who are with thee in the Broad-Hall of the Two Justices, who live on them who preserve evil and who drink their blood on that day of reckoning up character in the presence of Wenofer. Behold, "Sati-mertifi, Lord of Justice," is thy name. I have come to thee; I have brought thee justice; I have expelled deceit for thee.

I have not committed evil against men.
I have not mistreated cattle.
I have not blasphemed a god.
I have not done violence to a poor man.
I have not done that which the gods abominate.
I have not defamed a slave to his superior.
I have not made (anyone) sick.
I have not made (anyone) weep.

I have not killed.
I have given no order to a killer.
I have not caused anyone suffering.
I have not cut down on the food-(income) in the temples.
I have not damaged the bread of the gods.
I have not taken the loaves of the blessed (dead).
I have not had sexual relations with a boy.
I have not defiled myself.
I have neither increased or diminished the grain-measure.
I have not taken milk from the mouths of children.
I have not driven cattle away from their pasturage.
I have not snared the birds of the gods.
I have not caught fish in their marshes.
I have not held up the water in its season.
I have not built a dam against running water.
I have not driven away the cattle of the god's property.
I have not stopped a god on his procession.

I am pure! My purity is the purity of the great benu-bird which is in Herakleopolis, because I am really that nose of the Lord of Breath, who makes

Egyptian Female Musicians. This New Kingdom tomb painting shows a group of musicians in graceful poses. The three women are carefully individualized and supple in rendition. Their hand gestures and head positions lend a distinct expressiveness to the whole composition.

all men to live, on that day of filling out the Eye (of Horus) in Heliopolis, in the second month of the second season, the last day, in the presence of the lord of this land. I am the one who has seen the filling out of the Eye in Heliopolis. Evil will never happen to me in this land or in this Broad-Hall of the Two Justices, because I know the names of these gods who are in it, the followers of the great god.

O Wide-of-Stride, who comes forth from Heliopolis. I have not committed evil.

O Embracer-of-Fire, who comes forth from Babylon, I have not stolen.

O Nosey, who comes forth from Hermopolis, I have not been covetous.

O Swallower-of-Shadows, who comes forth from the pit, I have not robbed.

O Dangerous-of-Face, who came forth from Rostau, I have not killed men.

O Ruti, who comes forth from heaven, I have not damaged the grain-measure.

O Flamer, who comes forth backward, I have not stolen the property of a god.

O Breaker-of-Bones, who comes forth from Herakleopolis, I have not told lies.

O Commander-of-Fire, who comes forth from Memphis, I have not taken away food.

O Dweller-in-the-Pit, who comes forth from the west, I have not been contentious.

O White-of-Teeth, who comes forth from the Faiyum, I have not trespassed.

O Eater-of-Blood, who comes forth from the execution-block, I have not slain the cattle of the god.

O Eater-of-Entrails, who comes forth from the Thirty, I have not practised usury.

O Lord-of-Justice, who comes forth from Ma'ati, I have not stolen the bread-ration.

O Wanderer, who comes forth from Bubastis, I have not gossiped.

O Djudju-serpent, who comes forth from Busiris, I have not argued with some one summoned because of his property.

O Wamemti-serpent, who comes forth from the place of judgment, I have not committed adultery.

O Superior-of-the-Nobles, who comes forth from Imau, I have not caused terror.

O Wrecker, who comes forth from the Saite Nome, I have not trespassed.

O Mischief-Maker, who comes forth from the sanctuary, I have not been (over) heated.

O Child, who comes forth from the Heliopolitan Nome, I have not been unresponsive to a matter of justice.

O Ser-kheru, who comes forth from Wensi, I have not been quarrelsome.

O Dark-One, who comes forth from the darkness, I have not been abusive.

O Bringer-of-His-Peace, who comes forth from Sais, I have not been (over)-energetic.

O Lord-of-Faces, who comes forth from the Heroonpolite Nome, my heart has not been hasty.

O Tern-sep, who comes forth from Busiris, I have not been abusive against a king.

O Acting-with-His-Heart, who comes forth from Tjebu, I have not waded in water.

O Flowing-One, who comes forth from Nun, my voice has not been loud.

O Commander-of-the-People, who comes forth from his shrine, I have not been abusive against a god.

O In-af serpent, who comes forth from the cemetery, I have not blasphemed against my local god.

Words to be spoken by *X:*

Hail to you, ye gods who are in this Broad-Hall of the Two Justices! I know you; I know your names. I shall not fall for dread of you. Ye have not reported guilt of mine up to this god in whose retinue ye are; no deed of mine has come from you. Ye have spoken truth about me in the presence of the All-Lord, because I acted justly in Egypt.

Hail to you who are in the Broad-Hall of the Two Justices, who have no deceit in your bodies, who live on truth and who eat of truth in the presence of Horus, who is in his sun disc. May ye rescue me from Babi, who lives on the entrails of elders on that day of the great reckoning. Behold me—I have come to you without sin, without guilt, without evil, without a witness (against me), without one against whom I have taken action. I live on truth, and I eat of truth. I have done that which men said and that with which gods are content. I have satisfied a god with that which he desires. I have given bread to the hungry, water to the thirsty, clothing to the naked, and a ferry-boat to him who was marooned. I have provided divine offerings for the gods and mortuary offerings for the dead. (So) rescue me,

you; protect me, you. Ye will not make report against me in the presence [of the great god.] I am one pure of mouth and pure of hands, one to whom "Welcome, welcome, in peace!" is said by those who see him. I am one who has a concern for the gods, who knows the nature of their bodies. I have come here to testify to justice and to bring the scales to their (proper) position in the cemetery.

O thou who art high upon his standard, Lord of the Atef-Crown, whose name has been made "Lord of Breath," mayest thou rescue me from thy messengers who give forth uncleanliness and create destruction, who have no covering up of their faces, because I have effected justice for the Lord of Justice, being pure—my front is pure, my rear is clean, my middle is in the flowing water of justice; there is no part of me free of justice....

INSTRUCTIONS FOR THE USE OF THE SPELL

To be done in conformance with what takes place in this Broad-Hall of the Two Justices. This spell is to be recited when one is clean and pure, clothed in (fresh) garments, shod with white sandals, painted with stibium, and anointed with myrrh, to whom cattle, fowl, incense, bread, beer, vegetables have been offered. Then make thou this text in writing on a clean pavement with ochre smeared with earth upon which pigs and (other) small cattle have not trodden. As for him on whose behalf this book is made, he shall be prosperous and his children shall be prosperous, without greed, because he shall be a trusted man of the king and his courtiers. Loaves, jars, bread, and joints of meat shall be given to him from the altar of the great god. He cannot be held back at any door of the west, (but) he shall be ushered in with the Kings of Upper and Lower Egypt, and he shall be in the retinue of Osiris.

Right and true a million times.

FOCUS QUESTIONS

1. Passing into the afterlife was not easy. What hurdles did the dead face before reaching safety?

2. Egyptian society obviously had a very well-developed sense of right and wrong. What kinds of things should a righteous person do? What are some of the sins a person might commit?

3. In what ways do Egyptian ideas of right and wrong resemble our own? How are they different?

4. *The Book of the Dead* was clearly thought to be a very important means to everlasting life by contemporary Egyptians, who often brought it with them to the tomb. How could it also have been useful for the living?

8

Instructions in Letter Writing by an Egyptian Scribe (ca.1200 B.C.E.)

ANONYMOUS

We now know so much about ancient Egypt because the Egyptians developed a system of writing, which they used for personal and public business as well as for religious purposes. They also discovered an ideal medium for recording their thoughts, for the marsh grass that surrounded them could be processed into papyrus, a relatively inexpensive and quite durable form of paper. These developments made the Egyptians place particular emphasis on scribes.

Gaining the necessary skills and education for this profession, however, was not easy, because it required years of assiduous training. In the following selection from a surviving papyrus, a teacher rebukes a promising student for failing to take his studies seriously. In addition to outlining the inherent merits of being a scribe, the teacher reviews the other possible professions that the failing student might be forced to adopt if he is not fortunate enough to enjoy the lifestyle of a scribe.

Young fellow, how conceited you are! You do not listen when I speak. Your heart is denser than a great obelisk, a hundred cubits high, ten cubits thick.

But though I beat you with every kind of stick, you do not listen. If I knew another way of doing it, I would do it for you, that you might listen. You are a person fit for writing, though you have not yet known a woman. Your heart discerns, your fingers are skilled, your mouth is apt for reciting.

You are worse than the goose of the shore, that is busy with mischief. It spends the summer destroying the dates, the winter destroying the seed-grain. It spends the balance of the year in pursuit of the cultivators.

You are worse than the desert antelope that lives by running. It spends no day in plowing. Never at all does it tread on the threshing-floor. It lives on the oxen's labor, without entering among them. But though I spend the day telling you "Write," it seems like a plague to you. Writing is very pleasant!

See for yourself with your own eye. The occupations lie before you.

The washerman's day is going up, going down. All his limbs are weak, <from> whitening his neighbors' clothes every day, from washing their linen.

The maker of pots is smeared with soil, like one whose relations have died. His hands, his feet are full of clay; he is like one who lives in the bog.

The cobbler mingles with vats. His odor is penetrating. His hands are red with madder, like one who is smeared with blood. He looks behind him for the kite, like one whose flesh is exposed.

The watchman prepares garlands and polishes vase-stands. He spends a night of toil just as one on whom the sun shines.

The merchants travel downstream and upstream. They are as busy as can be, carrying goods from one town to another. They supply him who has wants. But the tax collectors carry off the gold, that most precious of metals.

The ships' crews from every house (of commerce), they receive their loads. They depart from Egypt for Syria, and each man's god is with him. (But) not one of them says: "We shall see Egypt again!"

The carpenter who is in the shipyard carries the timber and stacks it. If he gives today the output of yesterday, woe to his limbs! The shipwright stands behind him to tell him evil things.

His outworker who is in the fields, his is the toughest of all the jobs. He spends the day loaded with his tools, tied to his tool-box. When he returns home at night, he is loaded with the tool-box and the timbers, his drinking mug, and his whetstones.

The scribe, he alone, records the output of all of them. Take note of it!

Let me also expound to you the situation of the peasant, that other tough occupation. [Comes] the inundation and soaks him—, he attends to his equipment. By day he cuts his farming tools; by night he twists rope. Even his midday hour he spends on farm labor. He equips himself to go to the field as if he were a warrior. The dried field lies before him; he goes out to get his team. When he has been after the herdsman for many days, he gets his team and comes back with it. He makes for it a place in the field. Comes dawn, he goes to make a start and does not find it in its place. He spends three days searching for it; he finds it in the bog. He finds no hides on them; the jackals have chewed them. He comes out, his garment in his hand, to beg for himself a team.

When he reaches his field he finds <it> 'broken up.' He spends time cultivating, and the snake is after him. It finishes off the seed as it is cast to the ground. He does not see a green blade. He does three plowings with borrowed grain. His wife has gone down to the merchants and found nothing for 'barter.' Now the scribe lands on the shore. He surveys the harvest. Attendants are behind him with staffs, Nubians with clubs. One says (to him): "Give grain." "There is none." He is beaten savagely. He is bound, thrown in the well, submerged head down. His wife is bound in his presence. His children are in fetters. His neighbors abandon them and flee. When it's over, there's no grain.

If you have any sense, be a scribe. If you have learned about the peasant, you will not be able to be one. Take note of it!

The scribe of the army and commander of the cattle of the house of Amun, Nebmarenakht, speaks to the scribe Wenemdiamun, as follows. Be a scribe! Your body will be sleek; your hand will be soft. You will not flicker like a flame, like one whose body is feeble. For there is not the bone of a man in you. You are tall and thin. If you lifted a load to carry it, you would stagger, your legs would tremble. You are lacking in strength; you are weak in all your limbs; you are poor in body.

Set your sight on being a scribe; a fine profession that suits you. You call for one; a thousand answer you. You stride freely on the road. You will not be like a hired ox. You are in front of others.

I spend the day instructing you. You do not listen! Your heart is like an <empty> room. My teachings are not in it. Take their ('meaning') to yourself

The marsh thicket is before you each day, as a nestling is after its mother. You follow the path of pleasure; you make friends with revellers. You have made your home in the brewery, as one who thirsts for beer. You sit in the parlor with an idler. You hold the writings in contempt. You visit the whore. Do not do these things! What are they for? They are of no use. Take note of it!

Furthermore. Look, I instruct you to make you sound; to make you hold the palette freely. To make you become one whom the king trusts; to make you gain entrance to treasury and granary. To make you receive the ship-load at the gate of the granary. To make you issue the offerings on feast days. You are dressed in fine clothes; you own horses. Your boat is on the river; you are supplied with attendants. You stride about inspecting. A mansion is built in your town. You have a powerful office, given you by the king. Male and female slaves are about you. Those who are in the fields grasp your hand, on plots that you have made. Look, I make you into a staff of life! Put the writings in your heart, and you will be protected from all kinds of toil. You will become a worthy official.

Do you not recall the (fate of) the unskilled man? His name is not known. He is ever burdened <like an ass carrying> in front of the scribe who knows what he is about.

Come, <let me tell you> the woes of the soldier, and how many are his superiors: the general, the troop-commander, the officer who leads, the standard-bearer, the lieutenant, the scribe, the commander of fifty, and the garrison-captain. They go in and out in the halls of the palace, saying: "Get laborers!" He is awakened at any hour. One is after him as (after) a donkey. He toils until the Aten sets in his darkness of night. He is hungry, his belly hurts; he is dead while yet alive. When he receives the grain-ration, having been released from duty, it is not good for grinding.

He is called up for Syria. He may not rest. There are no clothes, no sandals. The weapons of war are assembled at the fortress of Sile. His march is uphill through mountains. He drinks water every third day; it is smelly and tastes of salt. His body is ravaged by illness. The enemy comes, surrounds him with missiles, and life recedes from him. He is told: "Quick, forward, valiant soldier! Win for yourself a good name!" He does not know what he is about. His body is weak, his legs fail him. When victory is won, the captives are handed over to his majesty, to be taken to Egypt. The foreign woman faints on the march; she hangs herself <on> the soldier's neck. His knapsack drops, another grabs it while he is burdened with the woman. His wife and children are in their village; he dies and does not reach it. If he comes out alive, he is worn out from marching. Be he at large, be he detained, the soldier suffers. If he leaps and joins the deserters, all his people are imprisoned. He dies on the edge of the desert, and there is none to perpetuate his name. He suffers in death as in life. A big sack is brought for him; he does not know his resting place.

Be a scribe, and be spared from soldiering! You call and one says: "Here I am." You are safe from torments. Every man seeks to raise himself up. Take note of it!

FOCUS QUESTIONS

1. What were the material rewards of an ancient Egyptian scribe?

2. What are the drawbacks of attempting to win fame and fortune on the battlefield?

3. Use this discussion of different professions to describe the ancient Egyptian economy and its social structure.

4. Compose a modern version of this teacher's exhortation.

9

The Book of Exodus
(ca. 10th–6th century B.C.E.)

The Book of Exodus is the second book of the Old Testament as well as the second book of the Hebrew Torah. It was probably composed between the tenth and sixth centuries B.C.E. Exodus tells the story of the enslavement of the Hebrew people at the hands of the Egyptians, of their liberation under the leadership of Moses, and of their journey into the promised land. The central actions are the confrontation between Moses and the pharaoh and God's deliverance of the Hebrews across the Red Sea. Much of the story takes place during the 40 years when the Hebrews wandered in the desert and when a nation was forged through tribulation. On Mount Sinai, Moses received the Ten Commandments, the foundation of Judeo-Christian ethics.

On the third new moon after the people of Israel had gone forth out of the land of Egypt, on that day they came into the wilderness of Sinai.

And when they set out from Rephidim and came into the wilderness of Sinai, they encamped in the wilderness; and there Israel encamped before the mountain. And Moses went up to God, and the Lord called to him out of the mountain, saying, "Thus you shall say to the house of Jacob, and tell the people of Israel; You have seen what I did to the Egyptians, and how I bore you on eagles' wings and brought you to myself. Now therefore, if you will obey my voice and keep my covenant, you shall be my own possession among all peoples; for all the earth is mine, and you shall be to me a kingdom of priests and a holy nation. These are the words which you shall speak to the children of Israel."

So Moses came and called the elders of the people, and set before them all these words which the Lord had commanded him. And all the people answered together and said, "All that the Lord has spoken we will do." And Moses reported the words of the people to the Lord. And the Lord said to Moses, "Lo, I am coming to you in a thick cloud, that the people may hear when I speak with you, and may also believe you for ever."

On the morning of the third day there were thunders and lightnings, and a thick cloud upon the mountain, and a very loud trumpet blast, so that all the people who were in the camp trembled. Then Moses brought the people out of the camp to meet God; and they took their stand at the foot of the mountain. And Mount Sinai was wrapped in smoke, because the Lord descended upon it in fire; and the smoke of it went up like the smoke of a kiln, and the whole mountain quaked greatly. And as the sound of the trumpet grew louder and louder, Moses spoke, and God answered him in thunder. And the Lord came down upon Mount Sinai, to the top of the mountain; and the Lord called Moses to the top of the mountain, and Moses went up. And the Lord said to Moses, "Go down and warn the people, lest they break through to the Lord to gaze and many of them perish. And also let the priests who come near to the Lord consecrate themselves, lest the Lord break out upon them."

And Moses said to the Lord, "The people cannot come up to Mount Sinai; for thou thyself didst charge us, saying, 'Set bounds about the mountain, and consecrate it.'" And the Lord said to him, "Go down, and come up bringing Aaron with you; but do not let the priests and the people break through to come up to the Lord, lest he break out against them." So Moses went down to the people and told them.

And God spoke all these words, saying,

"I am the Lord your God, who brought you out of the land of Egypt, out of the house of bondage.

"You shall have no other gods before me.

"You shall not make for yourself a graven image, or any likeness of anything that is in heaven above, or that is in the earth beneath, or that is in the water under the earth; you shall not bow down to them or serve them; for I the Lord your God am a jealous God, visiting the iniquity of the fathers upon the children to the third and the fourth generation of those who hate me, but showing steadfast love to thousands of those who love me and keep my commandments.

"You shall not take the name of the Lord your God in vain; for the Lord will not hold him guiltless who takes his name in vain.

"Remember the sabbath day, to keep it holy. Six days you shall labor, and do all your work; but the seventh day is a sabbath to the Lord your God; in it you shall not do any work, you, or your son, or your daughter, your manservant, or your maidservant, or your cattle, or the sojourner who is within your gates; for in six days the Lord made heaven and earth, the sea, and all that is in them, and rested the seventh day; therefore the Lord blessed the sabbath day and hallowed it.

"Honor your father and your mother, that your days may be long in the land which the Lord your God gives you.

"You shall not kill.

"You shall not commit adultery.

"You shall not steal.

"You shall not bear false witness against your neighbor.

"You shall not covet your neighbor's house; you shall not covet your neighbor's wife, or his manservant, or his maidservant, or his ox, or his ass, or anything that is your neighbor's."

Now when all the people perceived the thunderings and the lightnings and the sound of the trumpet and the mountain smoking, the people were afraid and trembled; and they stood afar off, and said to Moses, "You speak to us, and we will hear; but let not God speak to us, lest we die." And Moses said to the people, "Do not fear; for God has come to prove you, and that the fear of him may be before your eyes, that you may not sin."

And the people stood afar off, while Moses drew near to the thick darkness where God was. And the Lord said to Moses, "Thus you shall say to the people of Israel: 'You have seen for yourselves that I have talked with you from heaven. You shall not make gods of silver to be with me, nor shall you make for yourselves gods of gold.'"

When the people saw that Moses delayed to come down from the mountain, the people gathered themselves together to Aaron, and said to him, "Up, make us gods, who shall go before us; as for this Moses, the man who brought us up out of the land of Egypt, we do not know what has become of him." And Aaron said to them, "Take off the rings of gold which are in the ears of your wives, your sons, and your daughters, and bring them to me." So all the people took off the rings of gold which were in their ears, and brought them to Aaron. And he received the gold at their hand, and fashioned it with a graving tool, and made a molten calf; and they said, "These are your gods, O Israel, who brought you up out of the land of Egypt!" When Aaron saw this, he built an altar before it; and Aaron made proclamation and said, "Tomorrow shall be a feast to the Lord."

And they rose up early on the morrow, and offered burnt offerings and brought peace offerings; and the people sat down to eat and drink, and rose up to play.

And the Lord said to Moses, "Go down; for your people, whom you brought up out of the land of Egypt, have corrupted themselves; they have turned aside quickly out of the way which I commanded them; they have made for themselves a molten calf, and have worshiped it and sacrificed to it, and said, 'These are your gods, O Israel, who brought you up out of the land of Egypt!'" And the Lord said to Moses, "I have seen this people, and behold, it is a stiffnecked people; now therefore let me alone, that my wrath may burn hot against them and I may consume them; but of you I will make a great nation."

But Moses besought the Lord his God, and said, "O Lord, why does thy wrath burn hot against thy people, whom thou has brought forth out of the land of Egypt with great power and with a mighty hand? Why should the Egyptians say, 'With evil intent did he bring them forth, to slay them in the mountains, and to consume them from the face of the earth?' Turn from thy fierce wrath, and repent of this evil against thy people. Remember Abraham, Isaac, and Israel, thy servants, to whom thou didst swear by thine own self, and didst say to them, 'I will multiply your descendants as the stars of heaven, and all this land that I have promised I will give to your descendants, and they shall inherit it for ever.'" And the Lord repented of the evil which he thought to do to his people.

And Moses turned, and went down from the mountain with the two tables of the testimony in his hands, tables that were written on both sides; on the one side and on the other were they written. And the tables were the work of God, and the writing was the writing of God, graven upon the tables.

When Joshua heard the noise of the people as they shouted, he said to Moses, "There is a noise of war in the camp." But he said, "It is not the sound of shouting for victory, or the sound of the cry of defeat, but the sound of singing that I hear." And as soon as he came near the camp and saw the calf and the dancing, Moses' anger burned hot, and he threw the tables out of his hands and broke them at the foot of the mountain. And he took the calf which they had made, and burnt it with fire, and ground it to powder, and scattered it upon the water, and made the people of Israel drink it.

On the morrow Moses said to the people, "You have sinned a great sin. And now I will go up to the Lord; perhaps I can make atonement for your sin." So Moses returned to the Lord and said, "Alas, this people have sinned a great sin; they have made for themselves gods of gold. But now, if thou wilt forgive their sin and if not, blot me, I pray thee, out of thy book which thou hast written." But the Lord said to Moses, "Whoever has sinned against me, him will I blot out of my book. But now go, lead the people to the place of which I have spoken to you; behold, my angel shall go before you. Nevertheless, in the day when I visit, I will visit their sin upon them."

And the Lord sent a plague upon the people, because they made the calf which Aaron made.

The Lord said to Moses, "Depart, go up hence, you and the people whom you have brought up out of the land of Egypt, to the land of which I swore to Abraham, Isaac, and Jacob, saying, 'To your descendants I will give it.' And I will send an angel before you, and I will drive out the Canaanites, the Amorites, the Hittites, the Per'izzites, the Hivites, and the Jeb'usites. Go up to a land flowing with milk and honey; but I will not go up among you, lest I consume you in the way, for you are a stiff-necked people."

When the people heard these evil tidings, they mourned; and no man put on his ornaments. For the Lord had said to Moses, "Say to the people of Israel, 'You are a stiff-necked people; if for a single moment I should go up among you, I would consume you. So now put off your ornaments from you, that I may know what to do with you.'" Therefore the people of Israel stripped themselves of their ornaments, from Mount Horeb onward.

Now Moses used to take the tent and pitch it outside the camp, far off from the camp; and he called it the tent of meeting. And every one who sought the Lord would go out to the tent of meeting, which was outside the camp. Whenever Moses went out to the tent, all the people rose up, and every man stood at his tent door, and looked after Moses, until he had gone into the tent. When Moses entered the tent, the pillar of cloud would descend and stand at the door of the tent, and the Lord would speak with Moses. And when all the people saw the pillar of cloud standing at the door of the tent, all the people would rise up and worship, every man at his tent door. Thus the Lord used to speak to Moses face to face, as a man speaks to his friend.

FOCUS QUESTIONS

1. In the Book of Exodus, Moses is the main intermediary between God and the Hebrew people. How does he manage his task? What problems does he face?

2. What is the relationship between God and the Hebrews like? Is it a smooth one?

3. The Ten Commandments were the basis of Hebrew law and later were incorporated into Christian thought. They also had contemporary utility. In what ways could they be useful to a tribe of nomads?

4. How does the story told in Exodus create a sense of identity and purpose for the Hebrews?

5. How different is the Hebrews' view of their God from those of other Near Eastern cultures, such as the Mesopotamians or Egyptians? Do you see any similarities?

Archaic and Classical Greece

The Parthenon, Athens. This famous temple was built to house a 40-foot statue of Athena, the goddess after whom the city was named. The ivory-and-gold statue has been gone for many centuries.

FOCUS QUESTIONS

1. The Parthenon was built as a temple to Athena, Greek goddess of wisdom and war. Does the structure of the temple reflect Athena's qualities?

2. The temple had two rooms. One housed a statue of Athena, the other was used as a treasury. Why would the Greeks have wanted a treasury in their temple?

3. The Parthenon was built at a time of great prosperity for the City of Athens. What about the temple reflects this?

4. A contemporary author described the Athenians as exceptionally religious, using the grandeur of the Parthenon to support his statement. Do you agree that the greatness of the Parthenon indicates a heightened religiosity?

10

The Iliad (9th–8th century B.C.E.)

HOMER

Homer is the name given to the composer of the two greatest epic poems in the Western tradition, The Iliad *and* The Odyssey. *It appears that Homer lived in either the ninth or eighth century* B.C.E., *if evidence from the epics can be used to date the life of their author. The Homeric poems formed part of an oral tradition, sung by troubadours and passed from generation to generation, changed in the process of retelling. The characteristic meter of the verses undoubtedly aided memory. Homer, reputed to have been a blind poet, is credited with the composition of* The Iliad *and with being the inspiration behind* The Odyssey, *the story of the travels of the Greek warrior Odysseus. Both works were committed to written form and codified during the Hellenistic period of Greek history.*

*   The Iliad *tells the story of the Greek siege of Troy (Ilion in Greek) after the abduction of Helen, wife of Menelaus, the king of Sparta. The central actors in the story are Achilles and Hector, the greatest Greek and Trojan warriors, respectively. The war serves as a backdrop for their personal confrontation, and the story ends with the resolution of their conflict. The values of Greek and Trojan society are readily identifiable in the final meeting between the two warriors, which the following excerpt describes.*

The aged monarch Priam was the first
To see him as he scoured the plain, and shone
Like to the star which in the autumn time
Rises and glows among the lights of heaven
With eminent lustre at the dead of night—
Orion's Hound they call it—bright indeed,
And yet of baleful omen, for it brings
Distressing heat to miserable men.
So shone the brass upon the warrior's breast
As on he flew. The aged Priam groaned,
And smote his head with lifted hands,
    and called
Aloud, imploring his beloved son,
Who eagerly before the city gate
Waited his foe Achilles. Priam thus,
With outstretched hands, besought him
    piteously:
"O wait not, Hector, my beloved son,

To combat with Pelides thus alone
And far from succor, lest thou meet thy
    death,
Slain by his hand, for he is mightier far
Than thou art. Would that he, the cruel one,
Were but as much the favorite of the gods
As he is mine! then should the birds of prey
And dogs devour his carcass, and the grief
That weighs upon my spirit would depart.
Come within the walls,
My son, that thou mayst still be the defence
Of Ilium's sons and daughters, nor increase
The glory of Pelides with the loss
Of thine own life. Have pity upon me,
Who only live to suffer—whom the son
Of Saturn, on the threshold of my age,
Hath destined to endure a thousand griefs,
And then to be destroyed—to see my sons

Slain by the sword, my daughters dragged
  away
Into captivity, their chambers made
A spoil, our infants dashed against the ground
By cruel hands, the consorts of my sons
Borne off by the ferocious Greeks...."
So the old monarch spake, and with his hands
Tore his gray hair, but moved not Hector
  thus.
Then came, with lamentations and in tears,
The warrior's mother forward. One hand laid
Her bosom bare; she pressed the other hand
Beneath it, sobbed, and spake these winged
  words—
"Revere this bosom, Hector, and on me
Have pity. If when thou wert but a babe
I ever on this bosom stilled thy cries,
Think of it now, beloved child; avoid
That dreadful chief; withdraw within the
  walls,
Nor madly think to encounter him alone,
Son of my love and of my womb! If he
Should slay thee, I shall not lament thy death
Above thy bier—I, nor thy noble wife—
But far from us the greedy dogs will throng
To mangle thee beside the Grecian fleet."
Thus weeping bitterly, the aged pair
Entreated their dear son, yet moved him not.
He stood and waited for his mighty foe
Achilles, as a serpent at his den,
Fed on the poisons of the wild, awaits
The traveller, and, fierce with hate of man,
And glaring fearfully, lies coiled within.
So waited Hector with a resolute heart,
And kept his ground, and, leaning his bright
  shield
Against a tower that jutted from the walls,
Conferred with his great soul impatiently:
"Ah me! if I should pass within the walls,
Then will Polydamas be first to cast
Reproach upon me; for he counselled me
To lead the Trojans back into the town
That fatal night which saw Achilles rise
To join the war again. I yielded not
To his advice; far better if I had.
Now, since my fatal stubbornness has brought

This ruin on my people, I most dread
The censure of the men and long-robed
  dames
Of Ilium. Men less brave than I will say,
'Foolhardy Hector in his pride has thrown
His people's lives away.' So they will speak,
And better were it for me to return,
Achilles slain, or, slain myself by him,
To perish for my country gloriously.
But should I lay aside this bossy shield
And this stout helm, and lean against the wall
This spear, and go to meet the gallant son
Of Peleus, with a promise to restore
Helen and all the treasure brought with her
To Troy by Paris, in his roomy ships—
All that the war was waged for—that the sons
Of Atreus may convey it hence, besides
Wealth drawn from all the hoards within the
  town,
And to be shared among the Greeks; for I
Would bind the Trojans by a solemn oath
To keep back nothing, but divide the
  whole—
Whate'er of riches this fair town contains
Into two parts. But why should I waste
  thought
On plans like these? I must not act the part
Of suppliant to a man who may not show
Regard or mercy, but may hew me down
Defenceless, with my armor laid aside
As if I were a woman. Not with him
May I hold parley from a tree or rock,
As youths and maidens with each other hold
Light converse. Better 't were to rush at once
To combat, and the sooner learn to whom
Olympian Jove decrees the victory."
Such were his thoughts. Achilles now drew
  near.
Like crested Mars, the warrior-god, he came.
On his right shoulder quivered fearfully
The Pelian ash, and from his burnished mail
There streamed a light as of a blazing fire,
Or of the rising sun. When Hector saw,
He trembled, nor could venture to remain,
But left the gates and fled away in fear.
Pelides, trusting to his rapid feet,

Pursued him. As, among the mountain wilds,
A falcon, fleetest of the birds of air,
Darts toward a timid dove that wheels away
To shun him by a sidelong flight, while he
Springs after her again and yet again,
And screaming follows, certain of his prey,
Thus onward flew Achilles, while as fast
Fled Hector in dismay, with hurrying feet,
Beside the wall; … one fled, and one pursued,
A brave man fled, a braver followed close,
And swiftly both. Not for a common prize,
A victim from the herd, a bullock's hide,
Such as reward the fleet of foot, they ran—
The race was for the knightly Hector's life.
As firm-paced coursers, that are wont to win,
Fly toward the goal, when some magnificent
     prize,
A tripod or a damsel, is proposed
In honor of some hero's obsequies.
So these flew thrice on rapid feet around
The city of Priam. All the gods of heaven
Looked on, and thus the Almighty Father
     spake:
"Alas! I see a hero dear to me
Pursued around the wall. My heart is grieved
For Hector, who has brought so many thighs
Of bullocks to my altar on the side
Of Ida ploughed with glens, or on the heights
Of Ilium. The renowned Achilles now
Is chasing him with rapid feet around
The city of Priam. Now bethink yourselves,
And answer. Shall we rescue him from death?
Or shall we doom him, valiant as he is,
To perish by the hand of Peleus' son?"
When the twain had come
For the fourth time beside Scamander's
     springs,
The All-Father raised the golden balance
     high,
And, placing in the scales two lots which bring
Death's long dark sleep—one lot for Peleus'
     son,
And one for knightly Hector—by the midst
He poised the balance. Hector's fate sank
     down
To Hades, and Apollo left the field.

And when the advancing-chiefs stood face to
     face,
The crested hero, Hector, thus began:
"No longer I avoid thee as of late,
O son of Peleus! Thrice around the walls
Of Priam's mighty city have I fled,
Nor dared to wait thy coming. Now my heart
Bids me encounter thee; my time is come
To slay or be slain. Now let us call
The gods to witness, who attest and guard
The covenants of men. Should Jove bestow
On me the victory, and I take thy life,
Thou shalt meet no dishonor at my hands;
But, stripping off the armor, I will send
The Greeks thy body. Do the like by me."
The swift Achilles answered with a frown:
"Accursed Hector, never talk to me
Of covenants. Men and lions plight no faith,
Nor wolves agree with lambs, but each must
     plan
Evil against the other. So between
Thyself and me no compact can exist,
Or understood intent. First, one of us
Must fall and yield his life-blood to the god
Of battles. Summon all thy valor now.
A skilful spearman thou hast need to be,
And a bold warrior. There is no escape,
For now doth Pallas doom thee to be slain
By my good spear. Thou shalt repay to me
The evil thou hast done my countrymen,
My friends whom thou hast slaughtered in thy
     rage."
He spake, and, brandishing his massive spear,
Hurled it at Hector, who beheld its aim
From where he stood. He stooped, and over
     him
The brazen weapon passed, and plunged to
     earth.
Unseen by royal Hector, Pallas went
And plucked it from the ground, and brought
     it back
And gave it to the hands of Peleus' son,
While Hector said to his illustrious foe:
"Godlike Achilles, thou hast missed thy mark;
Nor hast thou learned my doom from Jupiter,
As thou pretendest. Thou art glib of tongue,

And cunningly thou orderest thy speech.
In hope that I who hear thee may forget
My might and valor. Think not I shall flee,
That thou mayst pierce my back; for thou
     shalt send
Thy spear, if God permit thee, through my
     breast
As I rush on thee. Now avoid in turn
My brazen weapon. Would that it might pass
Clean through thee, all its length! The tasks
     of war
For us of Troy were lighter for thy death,
Thou pest and deadly foe of all our race!"
He spake, and brandishing his massive spear,
Hurled it, nor missed, but in the centre smote
The buckler of Pelides. Far away
It bounded from the brass, and he was vexed
To see that the swift weapon from his hand
Had flown in vain. He stood perplexed
     and sad;
No second spear had he. He called aloud
On the white-bucklered chief, Deiphobus,
To bring another: but that chief was far,
And Hector saw that it was so, and said:—
"Ah me! the gods have summoned me to die.
My hour at last is come;
Yet not ingloriously or passively
I die, but first will do some valiant deed,
Of which mankind shall hear in after time."
He spake, and drew the keen-edged sword
     that hung,
Massive and finely tempered, at his side,
And sprang—as when an eagle high in heaven,
Through the thick cloud, darts downward to
     the plain
To clutch some tender lamb or timid hare,
So Hector, brandishing that keen-edged
     sword,
Sprang forward, while Achilles opposite
Leaped toward him, all on fire with savage
     hate,
And holding his bright buckler, nobly
     wrought,
Before him. On his shining helmet waved
The fourfold crest; there tossed the golden
     tufts

With which the hand of Vulcan lavishly
Had decked it. As in the still hours of night
Hesper goes forth among the host of stars,
The fairest light of heaven, so brightly shone,
Brandished in the right hand of Peleus' son,
The spear's keen blade, as, confident to slay
The noble Hector, o'er his glorious form
His quick eye ran, exploring where to plant
The surest wound. The glittering mail of brass
Won from the slain Patroclus, guarded well
Each part, save only where the collar-bones
Divide the shoulder from the neck, and there
Appeared the throat, the spot where life is
     most
In peril. Through that part the noble son
Of Peleus drave his spear; it went quite
     through
The tender neck, and yet the brazen blade
Cleft not the windpipe, and the power to
     speak
Remained. The Trojan fell amid the dust,
And thus Achilles boasted o'er his fall:
"Hector, when from the slain Patroclus thou
Didst strip his armor, little didst thou think
Of danger. Thou hadst then no fear of me,
Who was not near thee to avenge his death.
Fool! there was left within the roomy ships
A mightier one than he, who should come
     forth,
The avenger of his blood, to take thy life.
Foul dogs and birds of prey shall tear thy flesh;
The Greeks shall honor him with funeral
     rites."
And then the crested Hector faintly said:
"I pray thee by thy life, and by thy knees,
And by thy parents, suffer not the dogs
To tear me at the galleys of the Greeks.
Accept abundant store of brass and gold,
Which gladly will my father and the queen,
My mother, give in ransom. Send to them
My body, that the warriors and the dames
Of Troy may light for me the funeral pile."
The swift Achilles answered with a frown:
"Nay, by my knees entreat me not, thou cur,
Nor by my parents. I could even wish
My fury prompted me to cut thy flesh

In fragments, and devour it, such the wrong
That I have had from thee. There will be none
To drive away the dogs about thy head,
Not though thy Trojan friends should bring
   to me
Tenfold and twenty-fold the offered gifts,
And promise others, not though Priam,
   sprung
From Dardanus, should send thy weight in
   gold.
Thy mother shall not lay thee on thy bier,
To sorrow over thee whom she brought forth;
But dogs and birds of prey shall mangle thee."

And then the crested Hector, dying, said:
"I know thee, and too clearly I foresaw
I should not move thee, for thou hast a heart
Of iron. Yet reflect that for my sake
The anger of the gods may fall on thee,
When Paris and Apollo strike thee down,
Strong as thou art, before the Scaean gates."
Thus Hector spake, and straightway o'er him
   closed
The night of death; the soul forsook his limbs,
And flew to Hades, grieving for its fate—
So soon divorced from youth and youthful
   might.

FOCUS QUESTIONS

1. What does *The Iliad* tell us about the Greek style of warfare?

2. What does *The Iliad* suggest to be the nature of the relations between city-states in Homer's time?

3. What role do the gods play in the lives of mortals? How closely involved are they in the

outcome of the struggle between Hector and Achilles?

4. Judging from the story Homer tells, what might you say about the ideals of the Greek warrior? How do warriors behave?

11

Description of Africa (450 B.C.E.)

HERODOTUS

Herodotus (ca. 484–430 or 420 B.C.E.) was the first narrative historian. Born at Halicarnassus, the intersection of the mighty Persian Empire and the Greek city-states in Asia Minor, he took as his principal subject the long conflict between the two. The details of Herodotus's life are obscure, and very little is known about him aside from what he reveals about himself in his own work. He appears to have lived for a time on the island of Samos and perhaps in Athens as well. His great history was probably composed in the Italian town of Thurii. In addition to his detailed accounts of the war against Persia,

Herodotus was a great traveler, making journeys that lasted years and that carried him to Egypt, throughout the Persian Empire, to the Balkans, and even into territory that is today part of Russia. Much of his account of the peoples he encountered became accepted knowledge for centuries.

In this section of the History, *Herodotus describes the North African tribes he calls Libyans. His first interest is their geographical relationship to each other, an issue in assessing their political and military relations. He has a sharp eye for social customs that differ between the Libyan tribes as well as those that differ from Greek practices.*

Now the Libyans have their dwelling as follows:— Beginning from Egypt, first of the Libyans are settled the Adyrmachidai, who practise for the most part the same customs as the Egyptians, but wear clothing similar to that of the other Libyans. Their women wear a bronze ring upon each leg, and they have long hair on their heads, and when they catch their lice, each one bites her own in retaliation and then throws them away. These are the only people of the Libyans who do this; and they alone display to the king their maidens when they are about to be married, and whosoever of them proves to be pleasing to the king is deflowered by him. These Adyrmachidai extend along the coast from Egypt as far as the port which is called Plynos.... Next after these ... towards the West come the Nasamonians, a numerous race, who in the summer leave their flocks behind by the sea and go up to the region of Augila to gather the fruit of the date-palms, which grow in great numbers and very large and are all fruit-bearing: these hunt the wingless locusts, and they dry them in the sun and then pound them up, and after that they sprinkle them upon milk and drink them. Their custom is for each man to have many wives, and they make their intercourse with them common in nearly the same manner as the Massagetai, that is they set up a staff in front of the door and so have intercourse. When a Nasamonian man marries his first wife, the custom is for the bride on the first night to go through the whole number of the guests having intercourse with them, and each man when he has lain with her gives a gift, whatsoever he has brought with him from his house. The forms of oath and of divination which they use are as follows:—they swear by the men among themselves who are reported to have been the most righteous and brave, by these, I say,

laying hands upon their tombs; and they divine by visiting the sepulchral mounds of their ancestors and lying down to sleep upon them after having prayed; and whatsoever thing the man sees in his dream, this he accepts. They practise also the exchange of pledges in the following manner, that is to say, one gives the other to drink from his hand, and drinks himself from the hand of the other; and if they have no liquid, they take of the dust from the ground and lick it.

Adjoining the Nasamonians is the country of the Psylloi. These have perished utterly in the following manner:—The South Wind blowing upon them dried up all their cisterns of water, and their land was waterless, lying all within the Syrtis. They then having taken a resolve by common consent, marched in arms against the South Wind (I report that which is reported by the Libyans), and when they had arrived at the sandy tract, the South Wind blew and buried them in the sand. These then having utterly perished, the Nasamonians from that time forward possess their land. Above these towards the South Wind in the region of wild beasts dwell the Garamantians, who fly from every man and avoid the company of all; and they neither possess any weapon of war, nor know how to defend themselves against enemies. These dwell above the Nasamonians; and next to the Nasamonians along the sea coast towards the West come the Macai, who shave their hair so as to leave tufts, letting the middle of their hair grow long, but round this on all sides shaving it close to the skin; and for fighting they carry shields made of ostrich skins. Through their land the river Kinyps runs out into the sea, flowing from a hill called the "Hill of the Charites." This Hill of the Charites is overgrown thickly with wood, while the rest of Libya which has been spoken of before is bare of trees; and the distance from the sea to this hill is two hundred furlongs. Next to these Macai are the Gindanes, whose women wear each of them a number of anklets made of the skins of animals, for the following reason, as it is said:—for every man who has commerce with her she binds on an anklet, and the woman who has most is esteemed the best, since she has been loved by the greatest number of men. In a peninsula which stands out into the sea from the land of these Gindanes dwell the Lotophagoi, who live by eating the fruit of the *lotos* only. Now the fruit of the lotos is in size like that of the mastrich-tree, and in flavour it resembles that of the date-palm. Of this fruit the Lotophagoi even make for themselves wine. Next after the Lotophagoi along the sea-coast are the Machlyans, who also make use of the lotos, but less than those above mentioned. These extend to a great river named the river Triton, and this runs out into a great lake called Tritonis, in which there is an island named Phla. About this island they say there was an oracle given to the Lacedemonians that they should make a settlement in it. The following story moreover is also told, namely that Jason, when the Argo had been completed by him under Mount Pelion, put into it a hecatomb and with it also a tripod of bronze, and sailed round Peloponnese, desiring to come to Delphi; and when in sailing he got near Malea, a North Wind seized his ship and carried it off to Libya, and before he caught sight of land he had come to be in the shoals of the lake Tritonis. Then as he was at a loss how he should bring his ship forth, the story goes that Triton appeared to him and bade Jason give him the tripod, saying that he would show them the right course and let them go away without hurt: and when Jason consented to it, then Triton showed them the passage out between the shoals and set the tripod in his own temple, after having first uttered a prophecy over the tripod and having declared to Jason and his company the whole matter, namely that whensoever one of the descendants of those who sailed with him in the Argo should carry away this tripod, then it was determined by fate that a hundred cities of Hellenes

should be established about the lake Tritonis. Having heard this the native Libyans concealed the tripod.

Next to these Machlyans are the Auseans. These and the Machlyans dwell round the lake Tritonis, and the river Triton is the boundary between them: and while the Machlyans grow their hair long at the back of the head, the Auseans do so in front. At a yearly festival of Athenē their maidens take their stand in two parties and fight against one another with stones and staves, and they say that in doing so they are fulfilling the rites handed down by their fathers for the divinity who was sprung from that land, whom we call Athenē: and those of the maidens who die of the wounds received they call "false-maidens." But before they let them begin the fight they do this:—all join together and equip the maiden who is judged to be fairest on each occasion, with a Corinthian helmet and with full Hellenic armour, and then causing her to go up into a chariot they conduct her round about the lake. Now I cannot tell with what they equipped the maidens in old time, before the Hellenes were settled near them; but I suppose that they used to be equipped with Egyptian armour, for it is from Egypt that both the shield and the helmet have come to the Hellenes, as I affirm. They say moreover that Athenē is the daughter of Poseidon and of the lake Tritonis, and that she had some cause of complaint against her father and therefore gave herself to Zeus, and Zeus made her his own daughter. Such is the story which these tell; and they have their intercourse with women in common, not marrying but having intercourse like cattle: and when the child of any woman has grown big, he is brought before a meeting of the men held within three months of that time, and whomsoever of the men the child resembles, his son he is accounted to be.

Thus then have been mentioned those nomad Libyans who live along the sea-coast: and above these inland is the region of Libya which has wild beasts; and above the wild-beast region there stretches a raised belt of sand, extending from Thebes of the Egyptians to the Pillars of Heracles. In this belt at intervals of about ten days' journey there are fragments of salt in great lumps forming hills, and at the top of each hill there shoots up from the middle of the salt a spring of water cold and sweet; and about the spring dwell men, at the furthest limit towards the desert, and above the wild-beast region. First, at a distance of ten days' journey from Thebes, are the Ammonians, whose temple is derived from that of the Theban Zeus, for the image of Zeus in Thebes also, as I have said before, has the head of a ram. These, as it chances, have also other water of a spring, which in the early morning is warm; at the time when the market fills, cooler; when midday comes, it is quite cold, and then they water their gardens; but as the day declines, it abates from its coldness, until at last, when the sun sets, the water is warm; and it continues to increase in heat still more until it reaches midnight, when it boils and throws up bubbles; and when midnight passes, it becomes cooler gradually till dawn of day. This spring is called the fountain of the Sun....

I have said that from Egypt as far as the lake Tritonis Libyans dwell who are nomads, eating flesh and drinking milk; and these do not taste at all of the flesh of cows, for the same reason as the Egyptians also abstain from it, nor do they keep swine. Moreover the women of the Kyrenians too think it not right to eat cows' flesh, because of the Egyptian Isis, and they even keep fasts and celebrate festivals for her; and the women of Barca, in addition to abstaining from cows' flesh, do not taste of swine either. Thus it is with these matters: but in the region to the West of lake Tritonis the Libyans cease to be nomads, and they do not practise the same customs, nor do to their children anything like that which the nomads are wont to do; for the nomad Libyans, whether all of them I cannot say for certain, but many of them, do as follows:— when their children are four years old, they burn with a greasy piece of sheep's wool the veins in the crowns of their heads, and some of them burn the veins of the temples, so that for all their lives to come the cold humour may not run down from their heads and do them hurt: and for this reason it is (they say) that they are so healthy; for the Libyans are in truth the most healthy of all races concerning which we

have knowledge, whether for this reason or not I cannot say for certain, but the most healthy they certainly are: and if, when they burn the children, a convulsion comes on, they have found out a remedy for this; for they pour upon them the water of a he-goat and so save them. I report that which is reported by the Libyans themselves.

The following is the manner of sacrifice which the nomads have:—they cut off a part of the animal's ear as a first offering and throw it over the house, and having done this they twist its neck. They sacrifice only to the Sun and the Moon; that is to say, to these all the Libyans sacrifice, but those who dwell round the lake Tritonis sacrifice most of all to Athenē, and next to Triton and Poseidon. It would appear also that the Hellenes made the dress and the *aigis* of the images of Athenē after the model of the Libyan women; for except that the dress of the Libyan women is of leather, and the tassels which hang from their *aigis* are not formed of serpents but of leather thongs, in all other respects Athenē is dressed like them. Moreover the name too declares that the dress of the figures of Pallas has come from Libya, for the Libyan women wear over their other garments bare goatskins (*aigeas*) with tasselled fringes and coloured over with red madder, and from the name of these goat-skins the Hellenes formed the name *aigis*. I think also that in these regions first arose the practice of crying aloud during the performance of sacred rites, for the Libyan women do this very well. The Hellenes have learnt from the Libyans also the yoking together of four horses. The nomads bury those who die just in the same manner as the Hellenes, except only the Nasamonians: these bury bodies in a sitting posture, taking care at the moment when the man expires to place him sitting and not to let him die lying down on his back. They have dwellings composed of the stems of asphodel entwined with rushes, and so made that they can be carried about. Such are the customs followed by these tribes....

The Carthaginians say also this, namely that there is a place in Libya and men dwelling there, outside the Pillars of Heracles, to whom when they have come and have taken the merchandise forth from their ships, they set it in order along the beach and embark again in their ships, and after that they raise a smoke; and the natives of the country seeing the smoke come to the sea, and then they lay down gold as an equivalent for the merchandise and retire to a distance away from the merchandise. The Carthaginians upon that disembark and examine it, and if the gold is in their opinion sufficient for the value of the merchandise, they take it up and go their way; but if not, they embark again in their ships and sit there; and the others approach and straightway add more gold to the former, until they satisfy them: and they say that neither party wrongs the other; for neither do the Carthaginians lay hands on the gold until it is made equal to the value of their merchandise, nor do the others lay hands on the merchandise until the Carthaginians have taken the gold.

FOCUS QUESTIONS

1. How do the Nasamonians toast each other?
2. Do the Libyans share myths with the Greeks?
3. How do the Libyans distinguish their people one from the other?

4. From where does Herodotus obtain his information, and how does he evaluate its veracity?

12

The Apology (399 B.C.E.)

PLATO

The Apology recounts Socrates' trial for heresy and corrupting the morals of the youth of Athens. Socrates (469–399 B.C.E.) lived his entire life as an Athenian. He served as an armored soldier in the Peloponnesian Wars but did not enter state service as might have been expected of one of his intellectual skills. Rather he took to walking throughout Athens, questioning those who followed him about the things they saw and delving for the underlying principles of human life. He took particular delight in showing that individuals reputed to be wise or honorable were nothing of the sort. Although Socrates was not officially a teacher—that is, he received no fees and worked in no fixed school—he instructed hundreds of Athenians in the technique of critical questioning that we now call the Socratic method. Among his pupils was Plato, a devoted follower who was present at the trial and who went into self-imposed exile after Socrates' death. The Apology, which means defense rather than retraction, relates to the speech that Socrates made to the jury at his trial, both before and after a verdict was reached by the 501 Athenian citizens who heard the evidence against him. Socrates was 70 at the time, and the imposition of the death penalty came as a shock to many of his admirers. The death of Socrates is narrated in another work of Plato's, The Phaedo.

How you have felt, O men of Athens, at hearing the speeches of my accusers, I cannot tell; but I know that their persuasive words almost made me forget who I was—such was the effect of them; and yet they have hardly spoken a word of truth. But many as their falsehoods were, there was one of them which quite amazed me—I mean when they told you to be upon your guard, and not to let yourselves be deceived by the force of my eloquence. They ought to have been ashamed of saying this, because they were sure to be detected as soon as I opened my lips and displayed my deficiency: they certainly did appear to be most shameless in saying this, unless by the force of eloquence they mean the force of truth; for then I do indeed admit that I am eloquent. But in how different a way from theirs! I must beg of you to grant me one favor, which is this—If you hear me using the same words in my defence which I have been in the habit of using, and which most of you may have heard in the agora, and at the tables of the money-changers, or anywhere else, I would ask you not to be surprised at this, and not to interrupt me. For I am more than seventy years of age, and this is the first time that I have ever appeared in a court of law, and I am quite a stranger to the ways of the place; and therefore I would have you regard me as if I were really a stranger, whom you would excuse if he spoke in his native tongue, and after the fashion of his country; that I think is not an unfair request. Never mind the manner, which may or may not be good; but think only of the justice of my cause, and give heed to that: let the judge decide justly and the speaker speak truly.

And first, I have to reply to the older charges and to my first accusers, and then I will go on to the later ones. For I have had many accusers, who accused me of old, and their false charges have continued during many years; and I am more afraid of them than of Anytus and his associates, who are dangerous, too, in their own way. But far more dangerous are these, who began when you were children,

and took possession of your minds with their falsehoods, telling of one Socrates, a wise man, who speculated about the heaven above, and searched into the earth beneath, and made the worse appear the better cause. These are the accusers whom I dread; for they are the circulators of this rumor, and their hearers are too apt to fancy that speculators of this sort do not believe in the gods.

There is another thing: young men of the richer classes, who have not much to do, come about me of their own accord; they like to hear the pretenders examined, and they often imitate me, and examine others themselves; there are plenty of persons, as they soon enough discover, who think that they know something, but really know little or nothing; and then those who are examined by them instead of being angry with themselves are angry with me: This confounded Socrates, they say; this villainous misleader of youth!—and then if somebody asks them, Why, what evil does he practice or teach? they do not know, and cannot tell; but in order that they may not appear to be at a loss, they repeat the ready-made charges which are used against all philosophers about teaching things up in the clouds and under the earth, and having no gods, and making the worse appear the better cause; for they do not like to confess that their pretence of knowledge has been detected—which is the truth; and as they are numerous and ambitious and energetic, and are all in battle array and have persuasive tongues, they have filled your ears with their loud and inveterate calumnies.

Some one will say: And are you not ashamed, Socrates, of a course of life which is likely to bring you to an untimely end? To him I may fairly answer: There you are mistaken: a man who is good for anything ought not to calculate the chance of living or dying; he ought only to consider whether in doing anything he is doing right or wrong—acting the part of a good man or of a bad. For this fear of death is indeed the pretence of wisdom, and not real wisdom, being the appearance of knowing the unknown; since no one knows whether death, which they in their fear apprehend to be the greatest evil, may not be the greatest good. Is there not here conceit of knowledge, which is a disgraceful sort of ignorance? And this is the point in which, as I think, I am superior to men in general, and in which I might perhaps fancy myself wiser than other men,—that whereas I know but little of the world below, I do not suppose that I know; but I do know that injustice and disobedience to a better, whether God or man, is evil and dishonorable, and I will never fear or avoid a possible good rather than a certain evil. If you say to me, Socrates, this time we will let you off, but upon one condition, that you are not to inquire and speculate in this way anymore, and that if you are caught doing this again you shall die—if this was the condition on which you let me go, I should reply: Men of Athens, I honor and love you; but I shall obey God rather than you, and while I have life and strength I shall never cease from the practice and teaching of philosophy, exhorting any one whom I meet after my manner, and convincing him, saying: O my friend, why do you, who are a citizen of the great and mighty and wise city of Athens, care so much about laying up the greatest amount of money and honor and reputation, and so little about wisdom and truth and the greatest improvement of the soul, which you never regard or heed at all? Are you not ashamed of this? And if the person with whom I am arguing, says: Yes, but I do care; I do not depart or let him go at once; I interrogate and examine and cross-examine him, and if I think that he has no virtue, but only says that he has, I reproach him with undervaluing the greater, and overvaluing the less. And this I should say to every one whom I meet, young and old, citizen and alien, but especially to the citizens, inasmuch as they are my brethren. For this is the command to God, as I would have you know; and I believe that to this day no greater good has ever happened in the state than my service to the God. For I do nothing but go about persuading you all, old and young alike, not to take thought for your persons or your properties, but first and chiefly to care about the greatest improvement of the soul. I tell you that virtue is not given by money, but that from virtue come money and every other good of man, public as well as private. This is my teaching, and if this is the doctrine which corrupts the youth, my influence is ruinous indeed. But if any one says that this is not my teaching, he is speaking an untruth. Wherefore, O men of Athens, I say to you, do as Anytus bids or not as Anytus bids, and either acquit me or not; but whatever you do, know that I shall never alter my ways, not even if I have to die many times.

And now, Athenians, I am not going to argue for my own sake, as you may think, but for yours, that you may not sin against the God, or lightly reject his boon by condemning me. For if you kill me you will not easily find another like me, who, if I may use such a ludicrous figure of speech, am a sort of gadfly, given to the state by the God; and the state is like a great and noble steed who is tardy in his motions owing to his very size, and requires to be stirred into life. I am that gadfly which God has given the state, and all day long and in all places am always fastening upon you, arousing and persuading and reproaching you. And as you will not easily find another like me, I would advise you to spare me. I dare say that you may feel irritated at being suddenly awakened when you are caught napping; and you may think that if you were to strike me dead, which you easily might, then you would sleep on for the remainder of your lives, unless God in his care of you gives you another gadfly. And that I am given to you by God is proved by this: that if I had been like other men, I should not have neglected all my own concerns or patiently seen the neglect of them during all these years, and have been doing yours, coming to you individually like a father or elder brother, exhorting you to regard virtue; this, I say, would not be like human nature. And had I gained anything, or if my exhortations had been paid, there would have been some sense in that; but now, as you will perceive, not even the impudence of my accusers dares to say that I have ever exacted or sought pay of any one; they have no witness of that. And I have a witness of the truth of what I say; my poverty is a sufficient witness.

There are many reasons why I am not grieved, O men of Athens, at the vote of condemnation. I expected this, and am only surprised that the votes

Scala/Art Resource, NY

The School of Athens. In this painting the Renaissance master Raphael presented his version of the humanist ideal of classical antiquity. Many Greek and Roman cultural heroes are depicted in the dress of sixteenth-century Italians in a setting of Renaissance architecture and sculpture. At the center of the composition, framed by the arch, Plato and Aristotle are deep in discussion.

are so nearly equal; for I had thought that the majority against me would have been far larger; but now, had thirty votes gone over to the other side, I should have been acquitted.

And so [the death penalty is proposed]. And what shall I propose on my part, O men of Athens? Clearly that which is my due. And what is that which I ought to pay or to receive? What shall be done to the man who has never had the wit to be idle during his whole life; but has been careless of what the many care about—wealth, and family interests, and military offices, and speaking in the assembly, and magistracies, and plots, and parties. Reflecting that I was really too honest a man to follow in this way and live, I did not go where I could do no good to you or to myself; but where I could do the greatest good privately to every one of you, thither I went, and sought to persuade every man among you, that he must look to himself, and seek virtue and wisdom before he looks to his private interests, and look to the state before he looks to the interests of the state; and that this should be the order which he observes in all his actions. What shall be done to such an one? Doubtless some good thing, O men of Athens, if he has his reward; and the good should be of a kind suitable to him. What would be a reward suitable to a poor man who is your benefactor, who desires leisure that he may instruct you? There can be no more fitting reward than maintenance in the Prytaneum, O men of Athens, a reward which he deserves far more than the citizen who has won the prize at Olympia in the horse or chariot race, whether the chariots were drawn by two horses or by many. For I am in want, and he has enough; and he only gives you the appearance of happiness, and I give you the reality. And if I am to estimate the penalty justly, I say that maintenance in the Prytaneum is the just return.

Not much time will be gained, O Athenians, in return for the evil name which you will get from the detractors of the city, who will say that you killed Socrates, a wise man; for they will call me wise even although I am not wise when they want to reproach you. If you had waited a little while, your desire would have been fulfilled in the course of nature. For I am far advanced in years, as you may perceive, and not far from death. I am speaking now only to those of you who have condemned me to death. And I have another thing to say to them: You think that I was convicted through deficiency of words—I mean, that if I had thought fit to leave nothing undone, nothing unsaid, I might have gained an acquittal. Not so: the deficiency which led to my conviction was not of words—certainly not. But I had not the boldness or impudence or inclination to address you as you would have liked me to address you, weeping and wailing and lamenting, and saying and doing many things which you have been accustomed to hear from others, and which, as I say, are unworthy of me. But I thought that I ought not to do anything common or mean in the hour of danger: nor do I now repent of the manner of my defence, and I would rather die having spoken after my manner, than speak in your manner and live. For neither in war nor yet at law ought any man to use every way of escaping death. For often in battle there is no doubt that if a man will throw away his arms, and fall on his knees before his pursuers, he may escape death; and in other dangers there are other ways of escaping death, if a man is willing to say and do anything. The difficulty, my friends, is not in avoiding death, but in avoiding

unrighteousness; for that runs faster than death. I am old and move slowly, and the slower runner has overtaken me, and my accusers are keen and quick, and the faster runner, who is unrighteousness, has overtaken them. And now I depart hence condemned by you to, suffer the penalty of death, and they too go their ways condemned by the truth to suffer the penalty of villainy and wrong; and I must abide by my award—let them abide by theirs. I suppose that these things may be regarded as fated,—and I think that they are well.

And now, O men who have condemned me, I would fain prophesy to you; for I am about to die, and that is the hour in which men are gifted with prophetic power. And I prophesy to you who are my murderers, that immediately after my death punishment far heavier than you have inflicted on me will surely await you. Me you have killed because you wanted to escape the accuser, and not to give an account of your lives. But that will not be as you suppose: far otherwise. For I say that there will be more accusers of you than there are now; accusers whom hitherto I have restrained: and as they are younger they will be more severe with you, and you will be more offended at them. For if you think that by killing men you can avoid the accuser censuring your lives, you are mistaken; that is not a way of escape which is either possible or honorable; the easiest and the noblest way is not to be crushing others but to be improving yourselves. This is the prophecy which I utter before my departure to the judges who have condemned me.

Wherefore, O judges, be of good cheer about death, and know this of a truth—that no evil can happen to a good man, either in life or after death. He and his are not neglected by the gods; nor has my own approaching end happened by mere chance. But I see clearly that to die and be released was better for me; and therefore the oracle gave no sign. For which reason, also, I am not angry with my accusers or my condemners; they have done me no harm, although neither of them meant to do me any good; and for this I may gently blame them.

Still I have a favor to ask of them. When my sons are grown up, I would ask you, O my friends, to punish them; and I would have you trouble them, as I have troubled you, if they seem to care about riches, or anything, more than about virtue; or if they pretend to be something when they are really nothing, then reprove them, as I have reproved you, for not caring about that for which they ought to care, and thinking that they are something when they are really nothing. And if you do this, I and my sons will have received justice at your hands.

The hour of departure has arrived, and we go our ways—I to die, and you to live. Which is better God only knows.

FOCUS QUESTIONS

1. What impressions do you get of Socrates from *The Apology?*

2. Socrates considers himself to be a philosopher. What does that mean? What does a philosopher do?

3. What, according to Socrates, was Athens losing by condemning him to death? What will be the consequences for the city?

4. Why did many Athenians think Socrates was such a dangerous man?

5. What fate did Socrates predict for those who condemned him?

6. *The Apology* presents a very sympathetic view of Socrates. If you were one of his accusers, how might you have put your case?

13

The Republic (ca. 327 B.C.E.)

PLATO

Plato (428–347 B.C.E.), a member of an aristocratic Athenian family, studied under Socrates, whose ideas and methods of teaching he was later to immortalize. Plato trained for a career in politics, but the turbulent events of the late fifth century B.C.E. turned him against the ruling regime. After the death of Socrates in 399 B.C.E., Plato began to travel and remained away from Athens for over a decade. He returned as a teacher and philosopher, spreading the views that had been taught to him by his master. In keeping with his idea that the state should be ruled by philosopher-kings, Plato founded his Academy for philosophical and political study. During this time he wrote extensively, producing his famous Dialogues. *His philosophy centered on the belief that a fixed reality existed beyond the experience of the senses. Although a polytheist, Plato believed in a single, universal Good.*

The Republic, *one of the most important philosophical tracts in Western history, takes the form of a dialogue about the composition of a perfect society ruled by a philosopher-king who always strives to achieve the Good. In the selection reprinted here, the dialogue between Socrates and Glaucon presents Plato's ideas about the proper education of women in the republic.*

I suppose that I must retrace my steps and say what I perhaps ought to have said before in the proper place. The part of the men has been played out, and now properly enough comes the turn of the women. Of them I will proceed to speak, and the more readily since I am invited by you.

For men born and educated like our citizens, the only way, in my opinion, of arriving at a right conclusion about the possession and use of women and children is to follow the path on which we originally started, when we said that the men were to be the guardians and watchdogs of the herd.

True.

Let us further suppose the birth and education of our women to be subject to similar or nearly similar regulations; then we shall see whether the result accords with our design.

What do you mean?

What I mean may be put into the form of a question, I said: Are dogs divided into hes and shes, or do they both share equally in hunting and in keeping watch and in the other duties of dogs? or do we entrust to the males the entire and exclusive care of the flocks, while we leave the females at home, under the idea that the bearing and suckling of their puppies is labour enough for them?

No, he said, they share alike; the only difference between them is that the males are stronger and the females weaker.

But can you use different animals for the same purpose, unless they are bred and fed in the same way?

You cannot.

Then, if women are to have the same duties as men, they must have the same nurture and education?

Yes.

The education which was assigned to the men and music and gymnastic.

Yes.

Then women must be taught music and gymnastic and also the art of war, which they must practise like the men?

That is the inference, I suppose.

I should rather expect, I said, that several of our proposals, if they are carried out, being unusual, may appear ridiculous.

No doubt of it.

Yes, and the most ridiculous thing of all will be the sight of women naked in the palaestra, exercising with the men, especially when they are no longer young; they certainly will not be a vision of beauty, any more than the enthusiastic old men who in spite of wrinkles and ugliness continue to frequent the gymnasia.

Yes, indeed, he said: according to present notions the proposal would be thought ridiculous.

But then, I said, as we have determined to speak our minds, we must not fear the jests of the wits which will be directed against this sort of innovation; how they will talk of women's attainments both in music and gymnastic, and above all about their wearing armour and riding upon horseback!

Very true, he replied.

First, then, whether the question is to be put in jest or in earnest, let us come to an understanding about the nature of woman: Is she capable of sharing either wholly or partially in the actions of men, or not at all? And is the art of war one of those arts in which she can or cannot share? That will be the best way of commencing the enquiry, and will probably lead to the fairest conclusion.

That will be much the best way.

Shall we take the other side first and begin by arguing against ourselves; in this manner the adversary's position will not be undefended.

Why not? he said.

Then let us put a speech into the mouths of our opponents. They will say: "Socrates and Glaucon, no adversary need convict you, for you yourselves, at the first foundation of the State, admitted the principle that everybody was to do the one work suited to his own nature." And certainly, if I am not mistaken, such an admission was made by us. "And do not the natures of men and women differ very much indeed?" And we shall reply: Of course they do. Then we shall be asked, "Whether the tasks assigned to men and to women should not be different, and such as are agreeable to their different natures?" Certainly they should. "But if so, have you not fallen into a serious inconsistency in saying that men and women, whose natures are so entirely different, ought to perform the same actions?"—What defence will you make for us my good Sir, against any one who offers these objections?

That is not an easy question to answer when asked suddenly; and I shall and I do beg of you to draw out the case on our side.

These are the objections, Glaucon, and there are many others of a like kind, which I foresaw long ago; they made me afraid and reluctant to take in hand any law about the possession and nurture of women and children.

By Zeus, he said, the problem to be solved is anything but easy.

Why yes, I said, but the fact is that when a man is out of his depth, whether he has fallen into a little swimming bath or into mid ocean, he has to swim all the same.

Very true.

And must not we swim and try to reach the shore: we will hope that Arion's dolphin or some other miraculous help may save us?

I suppose so, he said.

Well then, let us see if any way of escape can be found. We acknowledged—did we not? that different natures ought to have different pursuits, and that men's and women's natures are different. And now what are we saying?—that different natures ought to have the same pursuits, this is the inconsistency which is charged upon us.

Precisely.

Verily, Glaucon, I said, glorious is the power of the art of contradiction!

Why do you say so?

Because I think that many a man falls into the practice against his will. When he thinks that he is reasoning he is really disputing, just because he cannot define and divide, and so know that of which

he is speaking; and he will pursue a merely verbal opposition in the spirit of contention and not of fair discussion.

Yes, he replied, such is very often the case; but what has that to do with us and our argument?

A great deal; for there is certainly a danger of our getting unintentionally into a verbal opposition.

In what way?

Why we valiantly and pugnaciously insist upon the verbal truth, that different natures ought to have different pursuits, but we never considered at all what was the meaning of sameness or difference of nature, or why we distinguished them when we assigned different pursuits to different natures and the same to the same natures.

Why, no, he said, that was never considered by us.

I said: Suppose that by way of illustration we were to ask the question whether there is not an opposition in nature between bald men and hairy men; and if this is admitted by us, then, if bald men are cobblers, we should forbid the hairy men to be cobblers, and conversely?

That would be a jest, he said.

Yes, I said, a jest; and why? because we never meant when we constructed the State, that the opposition of natures should extend to every difference, but only to those differences which affected the pursuit in which the individual is engaged; we should have argued, for example, that a physician and one who is in mind a physician may be said to have the same nature.

True.

Whereas the physician and the carpenter have different natures?

Certainly.

And if, I said, the male and female sex appear to differ in their fitness for any art or pursuit, we should say that such pursuit or art should be assigned to one or the other of them; but if the difference consists only in women bearing and men begetting children, this does not amount to a proof that a woman differs from a man in respect of the sort of education she should receive; and we shall therefore continue to maintain that our guardians and their wives ought to have the same pursuits.

Very true, he said.

Next, we shall ask our opponent how, in reference to any of the pursuits or arts of civic life, the nature of a woman differs from that of a man?

That will be quite fair.

And perhaps he, like yourself, will reply that to give a sufficient answer on the instant is most easy; but after a little reflection there is no difficulty.

Yes, perhaps.

Suppose then that we invite him to accompany us in the argument, and then we may hope to show him that there is nothing peculiar in the constitution of women which would affect them in the administration of the State.

By all means.

Let us say to him: Come now, and we will ask you a question—when you spoke of a nature gifted or not gifted in any respect, did you mean to say that one man will acquire a thing easily, another with difficulty; a little learning will lead the one to discover a great deal; whereas the other, after much study and application, no sooner learns than he forgets; or again, did you mean, that the one has a body which is a good servant to his mind, while the body of the other is a hindrance to him? Would not these be the sort of differences which distinguish the man gifted by nature from the one who is ungifted?

No one will deny that.

And can you mention any pursuit of mankind in which the male sex has not all these gifts and qualities in a higher degree than the female? Need I waste time in speaking of the art of weaving, and the management of pancakes and preserves, in which womankind does really appear to be great, and in which for her to be beaten by a man is of all things the most absurd?

You are quite right, he replied, in maintaining the general inferiority of the female sex: although many women are in many things superior to men, yet on the whole what you say is true.

And if so, my friend, I said, there is no special faculty of administration in a state which a woman has because she is a woman, or which a man has by virtue of his sex, but the gifts of nature are alike diffused in both; all the pursuits of men are the pursuits of women also, but in all of them a woman is inferior to a man.

Very true.

Then are we to impose all our enactments on men and none of them on women?

That will never do.

One woman has a gift of healing, another not; one is a musician, and another has no music in her nature?

Very true.

And one woman has a turn for gymnastic and military exercises, and another is unwarlike and hates gymnastics?

Certainly.

And one woman is a philosopher, and another is an enemy of philosophy; one has spirit, and another is without spirit?

That is also true.

Then one woman will have the temper of a guardian, and another not. Was not the selection of the male guardians determined by differences of this sort?

Yes.

Men and women alike possess the qualities which make a guardian; they differ only in their comparative strength or weakness.

Obviously.

And those women who have such qualities are to be selected as the companions and colleagues of men who have similar qualities and whom they resemble in capacity and in character?

Very true.

And ought not the same natures to have the same pursuits?

They ought.

Then, as we were saying before, there is nothing unnatural in assigning music and gymnastic to the wives of the guardians—to that point we come round again.

Certainly not.

The law which we then enacted was agreeable to nature, and therefore not an impossibility or mere aspiration; and the contrary practice, which prevails at present, is in reality a violation of nature.

That appears to be true.

We had to consider, first, whether our proposals were possible, and secondly whether they were the most beneficial?

Yes.

And the possibility has been acknowledged?

Yes.

The very great benefit has next to be established?

Quite so.

You will admit that the same education which makes a man a good guardian will make a woman a good guardian; for their original nature is the same?

Yes.

I should like to ask you a question.

What is it?

Would you say that all men are equal in excellence, or is one man better than another?

The latter.

And in the commonwealth which we were founding do you conceive the guardians who have been brought up on our model system to be more perfect men, or the cobblers whose education has been cobbling?

What a ridiculous question!

You have answered me, I replied: Well, and may we not further say that our guardians are the best of our citizens?

By far the best.

And will not their wives be the best women?

Yes, by far the best.

And can there be anything better for the interests of the State than that of the men and women of a State should be as good as possible?

There can be nothing better.

And this is what the art of music and gymnastic, when present in such manner as we have described, will accomplish?

Certainly.

Then we have made an enactment not only possible but in the highest degree beneficial to the State?

True.

Then let the wives of our guardians strip, for their virtue will be their robe, and let them share in the toils of war and the defence of their country; only in the distribution of labours the lighter are to be assigned to the women, who are the weaker natures, but in other respects their duties are to be the same. And as for the man who laughs at naked women exercising their bodies from the best of motives, in his laughter he is plucking "A fruit of unripe wisdom," and he himself is ignorant of what he is laughing at, or what he is about; for that is, and ever will be, the best of sayings, *That the useful is the noble and the hurtful is the base.*

FOCUS QUESTIONS

1. Does Plato believe that the perfect society should be bound by tradition or convention?

2. Why, according to the conventional argument, should women be kept to their own "separate sphere"? Does Plato seem to agree?

3. Are men and women equal in Plato's *Republic?* What are the differences between them?

4. How should the state educate women? How does Plato's plan differ from the Greek reality?

5. What do you think Plato means when he says, "the useful is the noble and the hurtful is the base"?

14

Politics (4th century B.C.E.)

ARISTOTLE

Aristotle (384–322 B.C.E.) was the third of the great Greek philosophers and was arguably the most influential of all. The son of a physician, Aristotle was taught medicine and biology from an early age. He was sent to Athens specifically to be educated at Plato's Academy and there he imbibed the wisdom of Socrates as well. Aristotle's original philosophical achievements are nearly beyond comprehension. His scientific works include major treatises on astronomy, botany, physics, and zoology. His philosophical works include discourses on cosmology, ethics, logic, poetry, and politics. Like Plato, Aristotle founded a school in Athens, the Lyceum, but he taught by lecture rather than by Socratic cross-questioning. Aristotle's works were neither written nor published during his lifetime. They consisted mostly of lecture notes taken by his students and brought together into treatises. Thirty such works survive today, although it is believed that nearly two hundred existed in ancient times.

Politics was an attempt to establish principles of government along scientific lines. Aristotle was the first philosopher to explore the basic forms of government and to discuss their inherent strengths and weaknesses.

As what has already been said finishes the preface of this subject, and as we have considered at large the nature of all other states, it now remains that I should first say what ought to be the form laid down as that of the state which is in accordance with our idea; for no good state can exist without a proportionate supply of what is necessary. Many things therefore ought to be previously laid down as objects desirable, but none of them such as are impossible; I mean, relative to the number of citizens, and the extent of the territory. For as other artificers, such as the weaver and the shipwright, ought to have such materials as are fit for their work, so also ought the legislator and politician to endeavour to procure proper materials for the business they have in hand. Now the first and principal instrument of the politician is the number of people; he should therefore know how many and what they naturally ought to be; in like manner as to the country, how large and of what kind it ought to be. Most persons think that it is necessary for a city to be large in order to be happy; but even should this be true, still they cannot tell what is a large one and what a small one. For they estimate its greatness according to the multitude of its inhabitants, but they ought rather to look to its strengths than to its numbers. But even if it were proper to determine the strength of the city from the number of its inhabitants, it should never be inferred from the multitude in general who may happen to be in it—(for in a city there must necessarily be many slaves, sojourners, and foreigners)—but from those who are really part of the state, and properly constitute the members of it. A multitude of these is indeed a proof that the city is large, but where a large number of mechanics dwell, and but few soldiers, such a state cannot be great; for a great city and a populous one are not the same thing. This too is evident from the fact that it is very difficult, if not impossible, properly to govern a very numerous body of men; for of all the states which appear well governed, we find not one where the rights of a citizen are laid open to the entire multitude. And this is also made evident by proof from the nature of the thing; for as law is a certain order, so good law is of course a certain good order; but too large a multitude is incapable of this. For this is in very truth the prerogative of that Divine Power which comprehends the universe. Not but that, as quantity and greatness are usually essential to beauty, the perfection of a city consists in its being large, if only consistent with that order already mentioned. But still there is a determinate size to all cities, as well as everything else, whether animals, plants, or machines; for each of these have their proper powers, if they are neither too little nor too large; but when they have not their due growth, or are badly constructed, so it is with a city. One that is too small has not in itself the power of self-defence, but this power is essential to a city; one that is too large is capable of self-defence in what is necessary, in the same way as a nation, but then it is not a city; for it will be difficult to find a form of government for it. The first thing therefore necessary is, that a city should consist of the lowest numbers which will be sufficient to enable the inhabitants to live happily in their political community. And it follows, that the more the inhabitants exceed that necessary number, the greater will the city be. But, as we have already said, this must not be without bounds; but what is the proper limit of the excess, experience will easily show, and this experience is to be collected from the actions both of the governors and the governed. Now, as it belongs to the first to direct the inferior magistrates and to act as judges, it follows that they can neither determine causes with justice, nor issue their orders with propriety, without they know the characters of their fellow-citizens: so that whenever this happens to be impossible in these two particulars, the state must of necessity be badly managed; for in both of them it is unjust to determine too hastily, and without proper knowledge, which must evidently be the case where the number of the citizens is too many. Besides, it is more easy for strangers and sojourners to assume the rights of citizens, as they will easily escape detection owing to the greatness of the multitude. It is evident then, that the best boundary for a city is that wherein the numbers are the greatest possible, that they may be the better able to be sufficient in themselves, while they are not too large to be under the eye of the magistrates. And thus let us determine the extent of a city.

As to the extent of a country, it should be such as may enable the inhabitants to live at their ease with freedom and temperance. What the situation of the country should be, is not difficult to determine; but in some particulars respecting this point, we ought to be advised by those who are skilful in military affairs. It should be difficult of access to an enemy, but easy of egress to the inhabitants; and, as we said that the number of inhabitants ought to be such as can come under the eye of the magistrate, so should it be with the country; for by that means the country is easily defended. As to the position of the city, if one could place it to one's wish, it ought to lie well both for sea and land. One situation which it ought to have has been already mentioned; for it should be so placed as easily to give assistance to all parts, and also to receive the necessaries of life from every quarter; as also it should be accessible for the carriage of wood, or any other materials of the like kind which may happen to be in the country.

We now proceed to a point out of what natural disposition the citizens ought to be: but this surely any one would easily perceive who casts his eye over those states of Greece which bear a high repute, and indeed over all the habitable world, as it is divided among the nations. Those who live in cold countries, as the north of Europe, are full of courage, but wanting in understanding and in art; therefore they remain free for a long time; but, not being versed in the political science, they cannot reduce their neighbours under their power. But the Asiatics, whose understandings are quick, and who are conversant in the arts, are deficient in courage; and therefore they continue to be always conquered, and the slaves of others. But the Greeks, placed as it were between these two parts, partake of the nature of both, so as to be at the same time both courageous and intellectual; for which reason Greece continues free, and governed in the best manner possible, and capable of commanding the whole world, could it be combined into one system of policy. The races of the Greeks have the very same difference among themselves: for part of them possess but one of these qualities, whereas in the other they are both happily blended together. Hence it is evident, that those persons ought to be both intelligent and courageous who will be readily obedient to a legislator, whose object is virtue.

We are now to consider what those things are without which a city cannot possibly exist; for what we call parts of the city must of necessity be inherent in it. And this we shall more plainly understand, if we know the number of things necessary to a city. First, the inhabitants must have food: secondly, arts, for many instruments are necessary in life: thirdly, arms, for it is necessary that the community should have an armed force within themselves, both to support their government against the disaffected of themselves, and also to defend it from those who seek to attack it from without: fourthly, a certain revenue, as well for the internal necessities of the state, as for the business of war: fifthly, and indeed chief of all, the care of the service of gods: sixthly in order, but most necessary of all, a court to determine both civil and criminal causes. These things are matters which are absolutely required, so to speak, in every state: for a city is a number of people, not accidentally met together, but with a purpose of insuring to themselves sufficient independency and self-protection; and if anything necessary for these purposes is wanting, it is impossible that in such a situation these ends can be obtained. It is necessary therefore that a city should be composed with reference to these various trades; for this purpose a proper number of husbandmen are necessary to procure food; as also artificers and soldiers, and rich men, and priests, and judges, to determine what is necessary and beneficial.

Since we are inquiring what is the best government possible, and as it is admitted to be that in which the citizens are happy, and that, as we have already said, it is impossible to obtain happiness without virtue; it follows, that in the best governed states, where the citizens are really men of intrinsic and not relative goodness, none of them should be permitted to exercise any low mechanical employment or traffic, as being ignoble and destructive to virtue: neither should they who are destined for office be husbandmen; for leisure is necessary in order to improve in virtue, and to perform the duty which they owe to the state.

It is necessary that the citizens should be rich, and these are the men proper for citizens; for no low mechanic ought to be admitted to the rights of a citizen, nor any other sort of people, whose employment is not productive of virtue.

FOCUS QUESTIONS

1. Why is size an important consideration in the construction of a state? What are the advantages and disadvantages of large and small cities? What is the best size?

2. By using *Politics* as a guide, what seems to be the ideal physical setting for a city-state? Could you make some broader generalization about Greek city-states with this knowledge?

3. Why does Aristotle feel that the Greeks are more successful than other peoples in the ancient world?

4. What does a city-state require to survive?

5. Who is excluded from citizenship in the state? Why?

The Religions of the East

Buddha and Followers. This relief from northwestern India shows the influence of the art of Greece and Rome. The development of devotional Buddhism led to the large-scale production of Buddha images.

FOCUS QUESTIONS

1. The Buddha advised a life halfway between asceticism and indulgence, seeking peace by quelling desire and suffering. Do the followers depicted here make such a life look appealing?

2. Buddhism flourished in India thanks to the conversion and patronage of the Maurya rulers. Why might the Buddha's teachings have appealed to a king?

3. What made Buddhism "Indian"?

4. Devotional art like this depicting the Buddha and his followers was responsible for the spread of Buddhism over most of South and East Asia. Why do you think art like this was such an effective tool of conversion?

15

The Upanishads (ca. 600–500 B.C.E.)

The Upanishads are compilations from the teachings of late Vedic philosophers. They were composed during the seventh and sixth centuries B.C.E., although the Sanskrit texts that have survived are from later periods. They take the form of dialogues between teachers and pupils, in which a single great question is pondered, frequently through the use of allegory and paradox. Unlike earlier Vedic writings, they are introspective and seek to illuminate an inner spirit. The texts, over a hundred of which survive, are regarded as the crowning intellectual achievement of the Vedic age, introducing the concepts of karma and reincarnation into Indian thought.

Upanishad can be translated roughly as meaning "at the feet of a teacher"; or in the case of the selection chosen here from the Kaushîtake-Upanishad, *"at the couch of the Brahman." The Upanishads center upon the most basic of all philosophical questions: the nature of divinity and humanity and the relationships among sense, reason, and faith. They show elements of spiritualism and mysticism and are meant to be contemplated deeply.*

THE COUCH OF BRAHMAN

And Kitra said: "All who depart from this world go to the moon. In the former, the bright half, the moon delights in their spirits; in the other, the dark half, the moon sends them on to be born again. Verily, the moon is the door of the Svarga, i.e., the heavenly world. Now, if a man objects to the moon and is not satisfied with life there, the moon sets him free. But if a man does not object, then the moon sends him down as rain upon this earth. And according to his deeds and according to his knowledge he is born again here as a worm, or as an insect, or as a fish, or as a bird, or as a lion, or as a boar, or as a serpent, or as a tiger, or as a man, or as something else in different places. When he has thus returned to the earth, someone, a sage, asks: 'Who art thou?' And he should answer: 'From the wise moon, who orders the seasons, when it is born consisting of fifteen parts, from the moon who is the home of our ancestors, the seed was brought. This seed, even me, they, the

gods, mentioned in the Pañkâgnividyâ, gathered up in an active man, and through an active man they brought me to a mother. Then I, growing up to be born, a being living by months, whether twelve or thirteen, was together with my father, who also lived by years of twelve or thirteen months, that I might either know the true Brahman or not know it. Therefore, O ye seasons, grant that I may attain immortality, i.e., knowledge of Brahman. By this my true saying, by this my toil, beginning with the dwelling in the moon and ending with my birth on earth, I am like a season, and the child of the seasons.' 'Who art thou?' the sage asks again. 'I am thou,' he replies. Then he sets him free to proceed onward.

"He, at the time of death … approaches the couch Amitaugas. That is Prâna, i.e., speech. The past and the future are its eastern feet; prosperity and earth its western feet…. On this couch sits Brahman, and he who knows himself one with Brahman, sitting on the couch, mounts it first with one foot only. Then Brahman says to him: 'Who art thou?' and he shall answer: 'I am like a season, and the child of the seasons, sprung from the womb of endless space, from the light, from the luminous Brahman. The light, the origin of the year, which is the past, which is the present, which is all living things, and all elements, is the Self. Thou art the Self. What thou art, that am I.' Brahman says to him: 'Who am I?' He shall answer: 'That which is, the true.' Brahman asks: 'What is the true?' He says to him: 'What is different from the gods and from the senses that is Sat, but the gods and the senses are Tyam. Therefore, by that name Sattya, or true, is called all this whatever there is. All this thou art.' This is also declared by a verse: 'This great Rishi, whose belly is the Yagus, the head the Sâman, the form the Rik, is to be known as being imperishable, as being Brahman.'

"Brahman says to him: 'How dost thou obtain my male names?' He should answer: 'By breath.' Brahman asks: 'How my female names?' He should answer: 'By speech.' Brahman asks: 'How my neuter names?' He should answer: 'By mind.' 'How smells?' 'By the nose.' 'How forms?' 'By the eye.' 'How sounds?' 'By the ear.' 'How flavors of food?' 'By the tongue.' 'How actions?' 'By the hands.' 'How pleasures and pain?' 'By the body.' 'How joy, delight, and offspring?' 'By the organ.' 'How journeyings?' 'By the feet.' 'How thoughts, and what is to be known and desired?' 'By knowledge alone.'

"Brahman says to him: 'Water indeed is this my world, the whole Brahman world, and it is thine.'

'Whatever victory, whatever might belongs to Brahman, that victory and that might he obtains who knows this, yea, who knows this."

KNOWLEDGE OF THE LIVING SPIRIT

"Prâna, or breath, is Brahman," thus says Kaushitaki. "Of this prâna, which is Brahman, the mind is the messenger, speech the housekeeper, the eye the guard, the ear the informant. He who knows mind as the messenger of prâna, which is Brahman, becomes possessed of the messenger. He who knows speech as the housekeeper, becomes possessed of the housekeeper. He who knows the eye as the guard, becomes

possessed of the guard. He who knows the ear as the informant, becomes possessed of the informant.

"Now to that prâna, which is Brahman, all these deities, mind, speech, eye, ear, bring an offering, though he asks not for it, and thus to him who knows this all creatures bring an offering, though he asks not for it. For him who knows this, there is this Upanishad, or secret vow, 'Beg not!' As a man who has begged through a village and got nothing sits down and says, 'I shall never eat anything given by those people,' and as then those who formerly refused him press him to accept their alms, thus is the rule for him who begs not, but the charitable will press him and say, 'Let us give to thee.'"

LIFE AND CONSCIOUSNESS

Pratardana, the son of Divodâsa, King of Kâsî, came by means of fighting and strength to the beloved abode of Indra. Indra said to him: "Pratardana, let me give you a boon to choose." And Pratardana answered: "Do you yourself choose that boon for me which you deem most beneficial for a man." Indra said to him: "No one who chooses, chooses for another; choose thyself." Then Pratardana replied: "Then that boon to choose is no boon for me."

Then, however, Indra did not swerve from the truth, for Indra is truth. Indra said to him: "Know me only; that is what I deem most beneficial for man, that he should know me. I slew the three-headed son of Tvashtri; I delivered the Arunmukhas, the devotees, to the wolves; breaking many treaties, I killed the people of Prahlâda in heaven, the people of Puloma in the sky, the people of Kâlakañga on earth. And not one hair of me was harmed there. And he who knows me thus, by no deed of his is his life harmed: not by the murder of his mother, not by the murder of his father, not by theft, not by the killing of a Brahman. If he is going to commit a sin, the bloom does not depart from his face. I am prâna, meditate on me as the conscious self, as life, as immortality. Life is prâna, prâna is life. Immortality is prâna, prâna is immortality. As long as prâna dwells in this body, so long surely there is life.

By prâna he obtains immortality in the other world, by knowledge true conception. He who meditates on me as life and immortality, gains his full life in this world, and obtains in the Svarga world immortality and indestructibility."

Pratardana said: "Some maintain here, that the prânas become one, for otherwise no one could at the same time make known a name by speech, see a form with the eye, hear a sound with the ear, think a thought with the mind. After having become one, the prânas perceive all these together, one by one. While speech speaks, all prânas speak after it. While the eye sees, all prânas see after it. While the ear hears, all prânas hear after it. While the mind thinks, all prânas think after it. While the prâna breathes, all prânas breathe after it."

"Thus it is indeed," said Indra, "but nevertheless there is a preeminence among the prânas. Man lives deprived of speech, for we see dumb people. Man lives deprived of sight, for we see blind people. Man lives deprived of hearing, for we see deaf people. Man lives deprived of mind, for we see infants. Man lives deprived of his arms, deprived of his legs, for we see it thus. But prâna alone is the conscious self, and having laid hold of this body, it makes it rise up. Therefore it is said, 'Let man worship it alone as uktha.' What is prâna, that is pragñâ, or self-consciousness; what is pragñâ (self-consciousness), that is prâna, for together they live in this body, and together they go out of it. Of that, this is the evidence, this is the understanding. When a man, being thus asleep, sees no dream whatever, he becomes one with that prâna alone. Then speech goes to him, when he is absorbed in prâna, with all names, the eye with all forms, the ear with all sounds, the mind with all thoughts. And when he awakes, then, as from a burning fire sparks proceed in all directions; thus from that self the prânas, proceed, each towards its place: from the prânas the gods, from the gods the worlds.

"Of this, this is the proof, this is the understanding. When a man is thus sick, going to die, falling into weakness and faintness, they say: 'His thought has departed, he hears not, he sees not, he speaks not, he thinks not.' Then he becomes one with that prâna alone. Then speech goes to him who is absorbed in prâna, with all names, the eye with all forms, the ear with all sounds, the mind with all thoughts. And when he departs from this body, he departs together with all these.

"Let no man try to find out what speech is, let him know the speaker. Let no man try to find out what odor is, let him know him who smells. Let no man try to find out what form is, let him know the seer. Let no man try to find out what sound is, let him know the hearer. Let no man try to find out the tastes of food, let him know the knower of tastes. Let no man try to find out what action is, let him know the agent. Let no man try to find out what pleasure and pain are, let him know the knower of pleasure and pain. Let no man try to find out what happiness, joy, and offspring are, let him know the knower of happiness, joy, and offspring. Let no man try to find out what movement is, let him know the mover. Let no man try to find out what mind is, let him know the thinker. These ten objects (what is spoken, smelled, seen, felt) have reference to self-consciousness; the ten subjects (speech, the senses, mind) have reference to objects. If there were no objects, there would be no subjects; and if there were no subjects, there would be no objects. For on either side alone nothing could be achieved. But the self of pragñâ, consciousness, and prâna, life, is not many, but one. For as in a cart the circumference of a wheel is placed on the spokes, and the spokes on the nave, thus are these objects, as a circumference, placed on the subjects as spokes, and the subjects on the prâna. And that prâna, the living and breathing power, indeed is the self of pragñâ, the self-conscious self: blessed, imperishable, immortal. He does not increase by a good action, nor decrease by a bad action. For the self of prâna and pragñâ makes him, whom he wishes to lead up from these worlds, do a good deed; and the same makes him, whom he wishes to lead down from these worlds, do a bad deed. And he is the guardian of the world, he is the king of the world, he is the lord of the universe—and he is my (Indra's) self thus let it be known, yea, thus let it be known!

FOCUS QUESTIONS

1. What is prâna?
2. What role do the five senses (taste, hearing, sight, smell, and touch) play in the Upanishads?
3. What is the worldview embraced in the Upanishads? How does its vision of immortality differ from the older Vedic Aryan idea of life after death in either heaven or hell?

4. Numerous people, including many warrior-nobles, abandoned their class distinctions and ritualistic religious practices in order to seek Upanishadic truth. These people became hermits or wanderers seeking an ascetic existence. What effect, potentially, would this have on their society?

16

Sermons and Teachings (6th century B.C.E.)

THE BUDDHA

Siddhartha Gautama (ca. 563–483 B.C.E.) was the son of the king of a small Indian state. Legend holds that it was foretold at his birth that he would either be a great monarch or a great Buddha (literally, "an enlightened one"). His father, hoping for the former, raised Siddhartha in luxury. But at the age of 29 Siddhartha experienced a vision of human suffering that led him to renounce his worldly status and goods and take to the road as a wandering ascetic. He joined at least two ascetic sects, whose philosophies he quickly mastered; but neither allowed him to achieve the highest truth. He finally attained this goal one night while meditating, when he was able to comprehend his past and future lives. Siddhartha determined to teach the truths he had realized; he gathered disciples and preached a middle way between worldliness and asceticism. His teachings swept throughout East Asia, becoming the foundation for one of the world's great religions. Buddhist traditions flourished in both India and China, although they developed separately.

The teachings of the Buddha were recorded by his students and then codified over the next five hundred years. The Buddha's sermons are regarded by scholars as largely authentic, and part of his first sermon, the Sermon at Benares, is reproduced here. The selection following that is a disquisition on the concept of Nirvana.

THE SERMON AT BENARES

On seeing their old teacher approach, the five bhikkhus agreed among themselves not to salute him, nor to address him as a master, but by his name only. "For," so they said, "he has broken his vow and has abandoned holiness. He is no bhikkhu but Gotama, and Gotama has become a man who lives in abundance and indulges in the pleasures of worldliness."

But when the Blessed One approached in a dignified manner, they involuntarily rose from their seats and greeted him in spite of their resolution. Still they called him by his name and addressed him as "friend Gotama."

When they had thus received the Blessed One, he said: "Do not call the Tathagata by his name nor address him as 'friend,' for he is the Buddha, the Holy One. The Buddha looks with a kind heart equally on all living beings, and they therefore call him 'Father.' To disrespect a father is wrong; to despise him, is wicked.

"The Tathagata," the Buddha continued, "does not seek salvation in austerities, but neither does he for that reason indulge in worldly pleasures, nor live in abundance. The Tathagata has found the middle path.

"There are two extremes, O bhikkhus, which the man who has given up the world ought not to follow—the habitual practice, on the one hand, of self-indulgence which is unworthy, vain and fit only for the worldly-minded—and the habitual practice, on the other hand, of self-mortification, which is painful, useless and unprofitable.

"Neither abstinence from fish or flesh, nor going naked, nor shaving the head, nor wearing matted hair, nor dressing in a rough garment, nor covering oneself with dirt, nor sacrificing to Agni, will cleanse a man who is not free from delusions.

"Reading the Vedas, making offerings to priests, or sacrifices to the gods, self-mortification by heat or cold, and many such penances performed for the sake of immortality, these do not cleanse the man who is not free from delusions.

"Anger, drunkenness, obstinacy, bigotry, deception, envy, self-praise, disparaging others, superciliousness and evil intentions constitute uncleanness; not verily the eating of flesh.

"A middle path, O bhikkhus, avoiding the two extremes, has been discovered by the Tathagata—a path which opens the eyes, and bestows understanding, which leads to peace of mind, to the higher wisdom, to full enlightenment, to Nirvana!

"What is that middle path, O bhikkhus, avoiding these two extremes, discovered by the Tathagata— that path which opens the eyes, and bestows understanding, which leads to peace of mind, to the higher wisdom, to full enlightenment, to Nirvana?

"Let me teach you, O bhikkhus, the middle path, which keeps aloof from both extremes. By suffering, the emaciated devotee produces confusion and sickly thoughts in his mind. Mortification is not conducive even to worldly knowledge; how much less to a triumph over the senses!

"He who fills his lamp with water will not dispel the darkness, and he who tries to light a fire with rotten wood will fail. And how can anyone be free from self by leading a wretched life, if he does not succeed in quenching the fires of lust, if he still hankers after either worldly or heavenly pleasures. But he in whom self has become extinct is free from lust; he will desire neither worldly nor heavenly pleasures, and the satisfaction of his natural wants will not defile him. However, let him be moderate, let him eat and drink according to the needs of the body.

"Sensuality is enervating; the self-indulgent man is a slave to his passions, and pleasure-seeking is degrading and vulgar.

"But to satisfy the necessities of life is not evil. To keep the body in good health is a duty, for otherwise we shall not be able to trim the lamp of wisdom, and keep our mind strong and clear. Water surrounds the lotus-flower, but does not wet its petals.

"This is the middle path, O bhikkhus, that keeps aloof from both extremes."

And the Blessed One spoke kindly to his disciples, pitying them for their errors, and pointing out the uselessness of their endeavors, and the ice of ill-will that chilled their hearts melted away under the gentle warmth of the Master's persuasion.

Now the Blessed One set the wheel of the most excellent law rolling, and he began to preach to the five bhikkhus, opening to them the gate of immortality, and showing them the bliss of Nirvana.

The Buddha said:

"The spokes of the wheel are the rules of pure conduct: justice is the uniformity of their length; wisdom is the tire; modesty and thoughtfulness are the hub in which the immovable axle of truth is fixed.

4 noble truths:

"He who recognizes the existence of suffering, its cause, its remedy, and its cessation has fathomed the four noble truths. He will walk in the right path.

"Right views will be the torch to light his way. Right aspirations will be his guide. Right speech will be his dwelling-place on the road. His gait will be straight, for it is right behavior. His refreshments will be the right way of earning his livelihood. Right efforts will be his steps: right thoughts his breath; and right contemplation will give him the peace that follows in his footprints.

"Now, this, O bhikkhus, is the noble truth concerning suffering:

"Birth is attended with pain, decay is painful, disease is painful, death is painful. Union with the unpleasant is painful, painful is separation from the pleasant; and any craving that is unsatisfied, that too is painful. In brief, bodily conditions which spring from attachment are painful.

"This, then, O bhikkhus, is the noble truth concerning suffering.

"Now this, O bhikkhus, is the noble truth concerning the origin of suffering:

"Verily, it is that craving which causes the renewal of existence, accompanied by sensual delight, seeking satisfaction now here, now there, the craving for the gratification of the passions, the craving for a future life, and the craving for happiness in this life.

"This, then, O bhikkhus, is the noble truth concerning the origin of suffering.

"Now this, O bhikkhus, is the noble truth concerning the destruction of suffering:

"Verily, it is the destruction, in which no passion remains, of this very thirst; it, is the laying aside of, the being free from, the dwelling no longer upon this thirst.

"This, then, O bhikkhus, is the noble truth concerning the destruction of suffering.

"Now this, O bhikkhus, is the noble truth concerning the way which leads to the destruction of sorrow. Verily! it is this noble eightfold path; that is to say:

"Right views; right aspirations; right speech; right behavior; right livelihood; right effort; right thoughts; and right contemplation.

"This, then, O bhikkhus, is the noble truth concerning the destruction of sorrow.

"By the practice of lovingkindness I have attained liberation of heart, and thus I am assured that I shall never return in renewed births. I have even now attained Nirvana."

And when the Blessed One had thus set the royal chariot wheel of truth rolling onward, a rapture thrilled through all the universes.

The devas left their heavenly abodes to listen to the sweetness of the truth; the saints that had parted from life crowded around the great teacher to receive the glad tidings; even the animals of the earth felt the bliss that rested upon the words of the Tathagata: and all the creatures of the host of sentient beings, gods, men, and beasts, hearing the message of deliverance, received and understood it in their own language.

And when the doctrine was propounded, the venerable Kondanna, the oldest one among the five bhikkhus, discerned the truth with his mental eye, and he said: "Truly, O Buddha, our Lord, thou hast found the truth!" Then the other bhikkhus too, joined him and exclaimed: "Truly, thou art the Buddha, thou has found the truth."

And the devas and saints and all the good spirits of the departed generations that had listened to the sermon of the Tathagata, joyfully received the doctrine and shouted: "Truly, the Blessed One has founded the kingdom of righteousness. The Blessed One has moved the earth; he has set the wheel of Truth rolling, which by no one in the universe, be he god or man, can ever be turned back. The kingdom of Truth will be preached upon earth; it will spread; and righteousness, good-will, and peace will reign among mankind."

WHAT IS NIRVANA?

"Revered Nagasena, things produced of karma are seen in the world, things produced of cause are seen, things produced of nature are seen. Tell me what in the world is born not of karma, not of cause, not of nature."

"These two, sire, in the world are born not of karma, not of cause, not of nature. Which two? Ether, sire, and Nirvana."

"Do not, revered Nagasena, corrupt the Conqueror's words and answer the question ignorantly."

"What did I say, sire, that you speak thus to me?"

"Revered Nagasena, what you said about ether—that it is born not of karma nor of cause nor of nature—is right. But with many a hundred reasons did the Lord, revered Nagasena, point out to disciples the Way to the realization of Nirvana—and then *you* speak thus: 'Nirvana is born of no cause.'"

"It is true, sire, that with many a hundred reasons did the Lord point out to disciples the Way to the realization of Nirvana; but he did not point out a cause for the production of Nirvana."

"Well then, sire, attend carefully, listen closely, and I will tell the reason as to this. Would a man, sire, with his natural strength be able to go from here up a high Himalayan mountain?"

"Yes, revered Nagasena."

"But would that man, sire, with his natural strength be able to bring a high Himalayan mountain here?"

"Certainly not, revered sir."

"Even so, sire, it is possible to point out the Way for the realization of Nirvana, but impossible to show a cause for the production of Nirvana. Would it be possible, sire, for a man who, with his natural strength, has crossed over the great sea in a boat to reach the farther shore?"

"Yes, revered sir."

"But would it be possible, sire, for that man, with his natural strength, to bring the farther shore of the great sea here?"

"Certainly not, revered sir."

"Even so, sire, it is possible to point out the Way to the realization of Nirvana, but impossible to show a cause for the production of Nirvana. For what reason? It is because of the uncompounded nature of the thing."

"Revered Nagasena, is Nirvana uncompounded?"

"Yes, sire, Nirvana is uncompounded; it is made by nothing at all. Sire, one cannot say of Nirvana that it arises or that it does not arise or that it is to be produced or that it is past or future or present, or that it is cognizable by the eye, ear, nose, tongue or body."

"If, revered Nagasena, Nirvana neither arises nor does not arise and so on, as you say, well then, revered Nagasena, you indicate Nirvana as a thing that is not: Nirvana is not."

"Sire, Nirvana is; Nirvana is cognizable by mind; an ariyan-disciple, faring along rightly with a mind that is purified, lofty, straight, without obstructions, without temporal desires, sees Nirvana."

"But what, revered sir, is that Nirvana like that can be illustrated by similes? Convince me with reasons according to which a thing that is can be illustrated by similes."

"Is there, sire, what is called wind?"

"Yes, revered sir."

"Please, sire, show the wind by its colour or configuration or as thin or thick or long or short."

"But it is not possible, revered Nagasena, for the wind to be shown; for the wind cannot be grasped in the hand or touched; but yet there is the wind."

"If, sire, it is not possible for the wind to be shown, well then, there is no wind."

"I, revered Nagasena, know that there is wind, I am convinced of it, but I am not able to show the wind."

"Even so, sire, there is Nirvana; but it is not possible to show Nirvana by colour or configuration."

"Very good, revered Nagasena, well shown is the simile, well seen the reason; thus it is and I accept it as you say: There is Nirvana."

FOCUS QUESTIONS

1. What were some of the personal characteristics of the Buddha?

2. Why, when the five bhikkhus in the Sermon at Benares saw the Buddha, did they decide to

ignore him? What made them change their minds?

3. In the Sermon at Benares, the Buddha laid out the basic tenets of Buddhism. What are the four noble truths? What is the worldview espoused by these beliefs?

4. According to the Buddha, what is Nirvana? What role does Nirvana play in Buddhism?

5. The Buddhist movement fostered participation at different levels. Many followers sought the "ordinary" norm; one of their duties was to support those who sought the "extra-ordinary" norm and became monks and nuns. What effect would this dual community of believers have on their society?

17

Bhagavad-Gita (ca. 200 B.C.E.)

The Bhagavad-Gita (The Lord's Song) *is the most famous work of the Hindu tradition. Like many other epics, it was transmitted orally for centuries before being put in writing around 200 B.C.E. The* Bhagavad-Gita *is only one part of a larger epic known as the* Mahabharata, *the story of two branches of the same family who struggle for worldly power against each other. In it, the Hindu gods mix with humans to provide strategy and advice. The* Bhagavad-Gita *is a long interlude during which Arjuna, the warrior chieftain of one branch of the family, searches his soul for the ethical foundations of the battle he is about to fight. He cannot reconcile his worldly ambitions with the slaughter of his own kin. He is answered by Krishna, the highest Hindu deity, who reveals himself as Arjuna's charioteer and offers him a foundation for his actions. The* Bhagavad-Gita *remains a tract of philosophical power and literary beauty and continues to be the most influential work of Hinduism.*

Arjuna spake:—

"As I look, O Krishna, upon these kinsfolk meeting for battle, my limbs fail and my face withers.

Trembling comes upon my body, and upstanding of the hair;

Gandiva falls from my hand, and my skin burns. I cannot stand in my place; my mind is as if awhirl.

Contrary are the omens that I behold, O Long-Haired One. I see no blessing from slaying of kinsfolk in strife;

I desire not victory, O Krishna, nor kingship, nor delights. What shall avail me kingship, O Lord of the Herds, or pleasures, or life?

They for whose sake I desired kingship, pleasures, and delights stand here in battle array, offering up their lives and substance—teachers, fathers, sons, likewise grandsires, uncles, fathers-in-law, grandsons, brothers-in-law, kinsmen also.

· These though they smite me I would not smite, O Madhu-Slayer, even for the sake of empire over the Three Worlds, much less for the sake of the earth.

What pleasure can there be to us, O Troubler of the Folk, from slaughter of Dhritarashtra's folk? Guilt in sooth will lodge with us for doing these to death with armed hand.

Therefore it is not meet that we slay Dhritarashtra's folk, our kinsmen; for if we do to death our own kith how can we walk in joy, O Lord of Madhu?

Albeit they, whose wits are stopped by greed, mark not the guilt of destroying a stock and the sin of treason to friends, yet how, O Troubler of the Folk, shall not we with clear sight see the sin of destroying a stock, so that we be stayed from this guilt?

In the destruction of a stock perish the ancient Laws of the stock; when Law perishes, Lawlessness falls upon the whole stock.

When Lawlessness comes upon it, O Krishna, the women of the stock fall to sin; and from the women's sinning, O thou of Vrishni's race, castes become confounded.

Confounding of caste brings to hell alike the stock's slayers and the stock; for their Fathers fall when the offerings of the cake and the water to them fail.

By this guilt of the destroyers of a stock, which makes castes to be confounded, the everlasting Laws of race and Laws of stock are overthrown.

For men the Laws of whose stock are overthrown, O Troubler of the Folk, a dwelling is ordained in hell; thus have we heard.

Ah me! a heavy sin have we resolved to do, that we strive to slay our kin from lust after the sweets of kingship!

It were more comfortable to me if Dhritarashtra's folk with armed hand should slay me in the strife unresisting and weaponless."

Sanjaya spake:—

So spake Arjuna, and sate down on the seat of his chariot in the field of war; and he let fall his bow and arrows, for his heart was heavy with sorrow.

Sanjaya spake:—

So was he stricken by compassion and despair, with clouded eyes full of tears; and the Slayer of Madhu spake to him this word.

The Lord spake:—

"Wherefore, O Arjuna, hath come upon thee in thy straits this defilement, such as is felt by the ignoble, making not for heaven, begetting dishonour?

Fall not into unmanliness, O Pritha's son; it is unmeet for thee. Cease from this base faintness of heart and rise up, O affrighter of the foe!"

Arjuna spake:

"O Madhu's Slayer, how shall I contend in the strife with my arrows against Bhishma and Drona, who are meet for honour, O smiter of foes?

Verily it were more blest to eat even the food of beggary in this world, without slaughter of noble masters; were I to slay my masters, I should enjoy here but wealth and loves—delights sullied with blood.

We know not which is the better for us, whether we should overcome them or they overcome us; before us stand arrayed Dhritarashtra's folk, whom if we slay we shall have no wish for life.

My soul stricken with the stain of unmanliness, my mind all unsure of the Law, I ask thee—tell me clearly what will be the more blest way. I am thy disciple; teach me, who am come to thee for refuge.

I behold naught that can cast out the sorrow that makes my limbs to wither, though I win to wide lordship without rival on earth and even to empire over the gods."

So spake to the High-Haired One the Wearer of the Hair-Knot, affrighter of foes; "I will not war," he said to the Lord of the Herds, and made an end of speaking.

And as he sat despairing between the two hosts, O thou of Bharata's race, the High-Haired One with seeming smile spake to him this word.

The Lord spake:—

"Thou hast grieved over them for whom grief is unmeet, though thou speakest words of understanding. The learned grieve not for them whose lives are fled nor for them whose lives are not fled.

Never have I not been, never hast thou and never have these princes of men not been; and never shall time yet come when we shall not all be.

As the Body's Tenant goes through childhood and manhood and old age in this body, so does it pass to other bodies; the wise man is not confounded therein.

It is the touchings of the senses' instruments, O Kunti's son, that beget cold and heat, pleasure and pain; it is they that come and go, that abide not; bear with them, O thou of Bharata's race.

Verily the man whom these disturb not, indifferent alike to pain and to pleasure, and wise, is meet for immortality, O chief of men.

Of what is not there cannot be being; of what is there cannot be aught but being. The bounds of these twain have been beheld by them that behold the Verity.

But know that That which pervades this universe is imperishable; there is none can make to perish that changeless being.

It is these bodies of the everlasting, unperishing, incomprehensible Body-Dweller that have an end, as it is said. Therefore fight, O thou of Bharata's race.

He who deems This to be a slayer, and he who thinks This to be slain, are alike without discernment; This slays not, neither is it slain.

This never is born, and never dies, nor may it after being come again to be not; this unborn, everlasting, abiding Ancient is not slain when the body is slain.

Knowing This to be imperishable, everlasting, unborn, changeless, O son of Pritha, how and whom can a man make to be slain, or slay?

As a man lays aside outworn garments and takes others that are new, so the Body-Dweller puts away outworn bodies and goes to others that are new.

Weapons cleave not This, fire burns not This, waters wet not This, wind dries it not.

Not to be cleft is This, not to be burned, nor to be wetted, nor likewise to be dried; everlasting is This, dwelling in all things, firm, motionless, ancient of days.

Unshown is This called, unthinkable This, unalterable This; therefore, knowing it in this wise, thou dost not well to grieve.

So though thou deemest it everlastingly to pass through births and everlastingly through deaths, nevertheless, O strong of arm, thou shouldst not grieve thus.

For to the born sure is death, to the dead sure is birth; so for an issue that may not be escaped thou dost not well to sorrow.

Born beings have for their beginning the unshown state, for their midway the shown, O thou of Bharata's race, and for their ending the unshown; what lament is there for this?

As a marvel one looks upon This; as a marvel another tells thereof; and as a marvel another hears of it; but though he hear of This none knows it.

This Body's Tenant for all time may not be wounded, O thou of Bharata's stock, in the bodies of any beings. Therefore thou dost not well to sorrow for any born beings.

Looking likewise on thine own Law, thou shouldst not be dismayed; for to a knight there is no thing more blest than a lawful strife.

Happy the knights, O son of Pritha, who find such a strife coming unsought to them as an open door to Paradise.

But if thou wilt not wage this lawful battle, then wilt thou fail thine own Law and thine honour, and get sin.

Also born beings will tell of thee a tale of unchanging dishonour; and to a man of repute dishonour is more than death.

The lords of great chariots will deem thee to have held back from the strife through fear; and thou wilt come to be lightly esteemed of those by whom thou wert erstwhile deemed of much worth.

They that seek thy hurt will say many words of ill speech, crying out upon thee for thy faintness; now what is more grievous than this?

If thou be slain, thou wilt win Paradise; if thou conquer, thou wilt have the joys of the earth; therefore rise up resolute for the fray, O son of Kunti.

Holding in indifference alike pleasure and pain, gain and loss, conquest and defeat, so make thyself ready for the fight; thus shalt thou get no sin....

Into a godlike nature, O son of Pritha, enter great-hearted men who worship Me with undivided mind, knowing Me to be the Beginning of born beings, the unchanging;

Ever singing My praises, labouring firm in their vows, devoutly doing homage, everlastingly under the Rule, men wait on Me.

Others again there are that wait on Me, offering the Sacrifice of Knowledge, according to My unity, or My severalty, or My manifold aspects that face all ways.

The sacrifice am I, the offering am I, the Fathers' oblation am I, the herb am I, the spell am

I, the butter-libation am I, the fire am I, the rite of oblation am I;

father of this universe am I, mother, ordainer, grandsire, the thing that is known and the being that makes clean, the word *Om*, the Rik, the Sama, and the Yajus;

the way, the supporter, the lord, the witness, the dwelling, the refuge, the friend, the origin, the dissolution, the abiding-place, the house of ward, the changeless seed.

I give heat; I arrest and let loose the rain; I am likewise power of immortality and death, Being and No-Being, O Arjuna.

Men of the Threefold Lore that drink the *soma* and are cleansed of sin, worshipping me with sacrifices, pray for the way to paradise; winning as meed of righteousness the world of the Lord of Gods, they taste in heaven the heavenly delights of the gods.

When they have enjoyed that wide world of paradise and their wage of righteousness is spent, they enter into the world of mortals; thus the lovers of loves who follow the Law of the Three Books win but a going and a coming.

But to the men everlastingly under the Rule, who in undivided service think and wait on Me, I bring power to win and to maintain.

They also who worship other gods and make offering to them with faith, O son of Kunti, do verily make offering to Me, though not according to ordinance.

For I am He that has enjoyment and lordship of all sacrifices; but they recognise Me not in verity, and therefore they fall.

They whose vows are to the gods go to the gods, they whose vows are to the Fathers go to the Fathers; they who offer to ghosts go to ghosts; but they that offer to Me go to Me.

If one of earnest spirit set before Me with devotion a leaf, a flower, fruit, or water, I enjoy this offering of devotion.

Whatever be thy work, thine eating, thy sacrifice, thy gift, thy mortification, make thou of it an offering to Me, O son of Kunti.

Thus shalt thou be released from the bonds of Works, fair or foul of fruit; thy spirit inspired by casting-off of Works and following the Rule, thou shalt be delivered and come unto Me.

I am indifferent to all born beings; there is none whom I hate, none whom I love. But they that worship Me with devotion dwell in Me, and I in them.

Even though he should be a doer of exceeding evil that worships Me with undivided worship, he shall be deemed good; for he is of right purpose.

Speedily he becomes righteous of soul, and comes to lasting peace. O son of Kunti, be assured that none who is devoted to Me is lost.

For even they that be born of sin, O son of Pritha,—women, traffickers, and serfs,—if they turn to Me, come to the supreme path;

how much more then shall righteous Brahmans and devout kingly sages? As thou has come into this unstable and joyless world, worship Me.

Have thy mind on Me, thy devotion toward Me, thy sacrifice to Me, do homage to Me. Thus guiding thyself, given over to Me, so to Me shalt thou come."

The Lord spake:—

"Again, O strong-armed one, hearken to My sublime tale, which in desire for thy weal I will recite to thy delighted ear.

The ranks of the gods and the saints know not My origin; for I am altogether the Beginning of gods and saints.

He who unbewildered knows Me to be the unborn, the one without beginning, great lord of worlds, is released from all sins amidst mortals.

Understanding, knowledge, unconfounded vision, patience, truth, restraint of sense and spirit, joy and sorrow, origination and not-being, fear and fearlessness, harmlessness, indifference, delight, mortification, almsgiving, fame, and infamy—these are the forms of born beings' existence severally dispensed by Me.

The seven Great Saints, the four Ancients, and the Manus had their spirit of Me, and were born of My mind; of them are these living creatures in the world.

He that knows in verity My power and rule is assuredly ruled by unwavering Rule.

I am the origin of the All; from Me the All proceeds; with this belief the enlightened, possessed of the spirit, pay worship to Me.

FOCUS QUESTIONS

1. What is Arjuna's dilemma?
2. What is Krishna's answer?
3. How does the philosophy espoused by Krishna complement India's caste system?

4. What does this passage tell us about Hindu beliefs regarding the soul?

18

Analects (ca. 500 B.C.E.)

CONFUCIUS

Confucius (ca. 551–479 B.C.E.), called Master K'ung in Chinese, was born in Shantung province; his family was probably of the knightly class, just below that of the aristocracy. He made his living teaching the sons of the nobility. Along with traditional subjects, Confucius taught his students his own philosophy of principled service to the state; many of his pupils went on to distinguished careers in government. Despite his teachings and ambition, however, Confucius himself was never called to serve in government.

Little is known for certain about his life, and none of his own writings survived. He seems to have been the head of a family and to have migrated within several regions of China. Wherever he went he attracted a following. After his death he was elevated to the status of Divine Sage, which made his pronouncements infallible.

The Analects *(which comes from the Greek word for the original Chinese, meaning roughly "selected sayings"—the origin of the phrase, "Confucius says") were preserved and handed down by his followers. They are therefore cast in the form of pithy sayings rather than treatises and have a strongly didactic flavor. Their underpinning is a moral rather than a religious philosophy that emphasizes education and self-sacrifice. Confucianism has been the most influential philosophy in world history.*

BOOK II

The Master said, He who rules by moral force is like the pole-star, which remains in its place while all the lesser stars do homage to it.

The Master said, If out of the three hundred *Songs* I had to take one phrase to cover all my teaching, I would say 'Let there be no evil in your thoughts.'

The Master said, Govern the people by regulations, keep order among them by chastisements, and they will flee from you, and lose all self-respect. Govern them by moral force, keep order among them by ritual and they will keep their self-respect and come to you of their own accord.

The Master said, At fifteen I set my heart upon learning. At thirty, I had planted my feet firm upon the ground. At forty, I no longer suffered from perplexities. At fifty, I knew what were the biddings of Heaven. At sixty, I heard them with docile ear. At seventy, I could follow the dictates of my own heart; for what I desired no longer overstepped the boundaries of right.

Mêng I Tzu asked about the treatment of parents. The Master said, Never disobey! When Fan Ch'ih was driving his carriage for him, the Master said, Mêng asked me about the treatment of parents and I said, Never disobey! Fan Ch'ih said, In what sense did you mean it? The Master said, While they are alive, serve them according to ritual. When they die, bury them according to ritual and sacrifice to them according to ritual.

Mêng Wu Po asked about the treatment of parents. The Master said, Behave in such a way that your father and mother have no anxiety about you, except concerning your health.

Tzu-yu asked about the treatment of parents. The Master said, 'Filial sons' nowadays are people who see to it that their parents get enough to eat. But even dogs and horses are cared for to that extent. If there is no feeling of respect, wherein lies the difference?

Tzu-hsia asked about the treatment of parents. The Master said, It is the demeanour that is difficult. Filial piety does not consist merely in young people undertaking the hard work, when anything has to be done, or serving their elders first with wine and food. It is something much more than that.

The Master said, Look closely into his aims, observe the means by which he pursues them, discover what brings him content—and can the man's real worth remain hidden from you, can it remain hidden from you?

The Master said, He who by reanimating the Old can gain knowledge of the New is fit to be a teacher.

The Master said, A gentleman is not an implement.

Tzu-kung asked about the true gentleman. The Master said, He does not preach what he practises till he has practised what he preaches.

The Master said, A gentleman can see a question from all sides without bias. The small man is biased and can see a question only from one side.

The Master said, 'He who learns but does not think, is lost.' He who thinks but does not learn is in great danger.

The Master said, He who sets to work upon a different strand destroys the whole fabric.

The Master said, Yu, shall I teach you what knowledge is? When you know a thing, to recognize that you know it, and when you do not know a thing, to recognize that you do not know it. That is knowledge.

The Master said, Hear much, but maintain silence as regards doubtful points and be cautious in speaking of the rest; then you will seldom get into trouble. See much, but ignore what it is dangerous to have seen, and be cautious in acting upon the rest; then you will seldom want to undo your acts. He who seldom gets into trouble about what he has said and seldom does anything that he afterwards wishes he had not done, will be sure incidentally to get his reward.

Duke Ai asked, What can I do in order to get the support of the common people? Master Kung replied, If you 'raise up the straight and set them on top of the crooked,' the commoners will support you. But if you raise the crooked and set them on top of the straight, the commoners will not support you.

Chi K'ang-tzu asked whether there were any form of encouragement by which he could induce the common people to be respectful and loyal. The Master said, Approach them with dignity, and they will respect you. Show piety towards your parents and kindness towards your children, and they will be loyal to you. Promote those who are worthy, train those who are incompetent; that is the best form of encouragement.

Someone, when talking to Master K'ung, said, How is it that you are not in the public service? The Master said, The Book says: 'Be filial, only be filial and friendly towards your brothers, and you will be contributing to government.' There are other sorts of service quite different from what you mean by 'service.'

The Master said, just as to sacrifice to ancestors other than one's own is presumption, so to see what is right and not do it is cowardice.

BOOK IV

The Master said, It is Goodness that gives to a neighbourhood its beauty. One who is free to choose, yet does not prefer to dwell among the Good—how can he be accorded the name of wise?

The Master said, Without Goodness a man

Cannot for long endure adversity,

Cannot for long enjoy prosperity.

The Good Man rests content with Goodness; he that is merely wise pursues Goodness in the belief that it pays to do so.

Of the adage 'Only a Good Man knows how to like people, knows how to dislike them,' the Master said, He whose heart is in the smallest degree set upon Goodness will dislike no one.

Wealth and rank are what every man desires; but if they can only be retained to the detriment of the Way he professes, he must relinquish them. Poverty and obscurity are what every man detests; but if they can only be avoided to the detriment of the Way he professes, he must accept them. The gentleman who ever parts company with Goodness does not fulfil that name. Never for a moment does a gentleman quit the way of Goodness. He is never so harried but that he cleaves to this; never so tottering but that he cleaves to this.

The Master said, I for my part have never yet seen one who really cared for Goodness, nor one who really abhorred wickedness. One who really cared for Goodness would never let any other consideration come first. One who abhorred wickedness would be so constantly doing Good that wickedness would never have a chance to get at him. Has anyone ever managed to do Good with his whole might even as long as the space of a single day? I think not. Yet I for my part have never seen anyone give up such an attempt because he had not the *strength* to go on. It may well have happened, but I for my part have never seen it.

The Master said, In the morning, hear the Way; in the evening, die content!

The Master said, If it is really possible to govern countries by ritual and yielding, there is no more to

Portrait of Confucius. This portrait of Confucius is by an unknown artist. It shows a serene old teacher.

Giraudon/Art Resource, NY

be said. But if it is not really possible, of what use is ritual?

The Master said, In the presence of a good man, think all the time how you may learn to equal him. In the presence of a bad man, turn your gaze within!

The Master said, In serving his father and mother a man may gently remonstrate with them. But if he sees that he has failed to change their opinion, he should resume an attitude of deference and not thwart them; he may feel discouraged, but not resentful.

The Master said, In old days a man kept a hold on his words, fearing the disgrace that would ensue should he himself fail to keep pace with them.

The Master said, Those who err on the side of strictness are few indeed!

The Master said, A gentleman covets the reputation of being slow in word but prompt in deed.

The Master said, Moral force never dwells in solitude; it will always bring neighbours.

FOCUS QUESTIONS

1. Who are the people in the text who ask the Master questions?

2. Why do the *Analects* take the form of short, pithy sayings? How would their form affect their reception by the general population?

3. What are some of the personal characteristics Confucius values most?

4. The five Confucian relationships are husband–wife, older brother–younger brother, friend–friend, ruler–subject, and father–son. How are some of these relationships illustrated in the text? Why was having such a well-ordered, hierarchical society important to Confucius?

19

Tao-Te Ching (ca. 500 B.C.E.)

LAO-TZU

There remains considerable doubt about whether the Tao-Te Ching was written by a single person known as Lao-tzu. Tradition has it that Lao-tzu (ca. 570–490 B.C.E.) was a scholar at the Chou court entrusted with the keeping of sacred texts. He is said to have met Confucius and chided him for his vanity and to have disappeared while traveling in the west. Both stories are probably fictitious, although they are found in a biography of Lao-tzu written in 100 B.C.E.

What is not in doubt is the importance of Taoism in Chinese philosophical thinking. The Tao-Te Ching is composed in two parts, the Tao, which means "the way," and the Te, which means "virtue." Its 81 chapters are written in few characters, a form that is best rendered into verse. Taoism is a wholistic philosophy, fundamentally materialistic, which nevertheless provides a practical guide to morality and government. The various texts of the Tao-Te Ching show changes made as late as the first century C.E. The oldest surviving text was discovered in 1973 and dates from before 168 B.C.E.

1

As for the Way, the Way that can be spoken of
  is not the constant Way;
As for names, the name that can be named is
  not the constant name.
The nameless is the beginning of the ten
  thousand things;
The named is the mother of the ten thousand
  things.
Therefore, those constantly without desires,
  by this means will perceive its subtlety.
Those constantly with desires, by this means
  will see only that which they yearn for and
  seek.

These two together emerge;
They have different names yet they're called
  the same;
That which is even more profound than the
  profound—
The gateway of all subtleties.

6

The valley spirit never dies;
We call it the mysterious female.
The gates of the mysterious female—
These we call the roots of Heaven and Earth.
Subtle yet everlasting! It seems to exist.
In being used, it is not exhausted.

14

We look at it but do not see it;
We name this "the minute."
We listen to it but do not hear it;
We name this "the rarefied."
We touch it but do not hold it;
We name this "the level and smooth."
These three cannot be examined to the limit.
Thus they merge together as one.
"One"—there is nothing more encompassing
  above it,
And nothing smaller below it.

Boundless, formless! It cannot be named,
And returns to the state of no-thing.

This is called the formless form,
The substanceless image.
This is called the subtle and indistinct.
Follow it and you won't see its back;
Greet it and you won't see its head.
Hold on to the Way of the present—
To manage the things of the present,
And to know the ancient beginning.
This is called the beginning of the thread of
  the Way.

16

Take emptiness to the limit;
Maintain tranquility in the center.
The ten thousand things—side-by-side they
  arise;
And by this I see their return.
Things come forth in great numbers;
Each one returns to its root.
This is called tranquility.
"Tranquility"—This means to return to your
  fate.
To return to your fate is to be constant;
To know the constant is to be wise.
Not to know the constant is to be reckless and
  wild;
If you're reckless and wild, your actions will
  lead to misfortune.
To know the constant is to be all-embracing;
To be all-embracing is to be impartial;
To be impartial is to be kingly;
To be kingly is to be like Heaven;
To be like Heaven is to be one with the Tao;
If you're one with the Tao, to the end of your
  days you'll suffer no harm.

25

There was something formed out of chaos,
That was born before Heaven and Earth.
Quiet and still! Pure and deep!

It stands on its own and doesn't change.
It can be regarded as the mother of Heaven
    and Earth.
I do not yet know its name:
I "style" it "the Way."
Were I forced to give it a name, I would call it
    "the Great."

"Great" means "to depart";
"To depart" means "to be far away";
And "to be far away" means "to return."

The Way is great;
Heaven is great;
Earth is great;
And the king is also great.
In the country there are four greats, and the
    king occupies one place among them.
Man models himself on the Earth;
The Earth models itself on Heaven;
Heaven models itself on the Way;
And the Way models itself on that which is so
    on its own.

34

The Way floats and drifts;
It can go left or right.
It accomplishes its tasks and completes its
    affairs, and yet for this it is not given a name.
The ten thousand things entrust their lives to
    it, and yet it does not act as their master.
Thus it is constantly without desires.

It can be named with the things that are small.
The ten thousand things entrust their lives to
    it, and yet it does not act as their master.
It can be named with the things that are great.
Therefore the Sage's ability to accomplish the
    great
Comes from his not playing the role of the
    great.
Therefore he is able to accomplish the great.

52

The world had a beginning,
Which can be considered the mother of the
    world.
Having attained the mother, in order to
    understand her children,
If you return and hold on to the mother, till
    the end of your life you'll suffer no harm.
Block up the holes;
Close the doors;
And till the end of your life you'll not labor.
Open the holes;
Meddle in affairs;
And till the end of your life you'll not be
    saved.

To perceive the small is called "discernment."
To hold on to the pliant is called "strength."
If you use the rays to return to the bright light,
You'll not abandon your life to peril.
This is called Following the Constant.

FOCUS QUESTIONS

1. What is "the Way"?

2. What is the role of the sage in Taoism?

3. The basis for Taoist political philosophy is *wu wei*, or "not doing." How is this illustrated in the text? What, according to Lao-tzu, is the consequence of *wu wei*?

4. It has been asserted that the Chinese were Confucian while in public office but Taoist in their private lives because Taoism allowed them to escape the burden of their social responsibilities. What characteristics of Taoism allowed them to think this?

China: War and Politics

The Great Wall of China.

FOCUS QUESTIONS

1. The first Chin emperor commissioned a life-size army of 8,000 to be sculpted in terra-cotta to be buried near his tomb. Why would the emperor have wanted to be attended in death by soldiers?

2. Why did the emperor want such a vast army?

3. The soldiers are in a variety of poses—some are charioteers, others standing infantry, others kneeling archers—and archaeologists believe that each figure's head is unique. What does this indicate about the military in Chin times?

4. The first Chin emperor spent his last years on two projects: searching for an elixir of immortality, and constructing a small city for a tomb, of which these soldiers are only one part. How were these two accomplishments related?

20

The Art of War (ca. 500 B.C.E.)

SUN-TZU

Although almost nothing is known of the life of Sun-tzu, his tract The Art of War *has been one of the most influential military handbooks in world history. Legend has it that he served the Wu dynasty after being challenged by the emperor to make an effective army out of his concubines. Sun-tzu placed the emperor's two favorites at the head of two different files of concubines, and when they failed to discipline their charges he cut their heads off despite the emperor's protests. After that the concubines drilled effectively. He became known as* Sun the Warrior *and is reputed never to have lost a battle.*

The Art of War is notable for its realistic assessment of the political constraints on warfare. It is part drill book, part tactical survey, and part political treatise. Its advice has been followed for centuries, and modern Chinese leaders continue to consult it.

LAYING PLANS

Sun-tzu said:

The art of war is of vital importance to the state. It is a matter of life and death, a road either to safety or to ruin. Hence under no circumstances can it be neglected.

The art of war is governed by five constant factors, all of which need to be taken into account. They are: the Moral Law; Heaven; Earth; the Commander; Method and discipline.

The Moral Law causes the people to be in complete accord with their ruler, so that they will follow him regardless of their lives, undismayed by any danger.

Heaven signifies night and day, cold and heat, times and seasons.

Earth comprises distances, great and small; danger and security; open ground and narrow passes; the chances of life and death.

The Commander stands for the virtues of wisdom, sincerity, benevolence, courage, and strictness.

By *Method and discipline* are to be understood the marshaling of the army in its proper subdivisions, the gradations of rank among the officers, the maintenance of roads by which supplies may reach the army, and the control of military expenditure.

These five factors should be familiar to every general. He who knows them will be victorious; he who knows them not will fail.

Therefore, when seeking to determine your military conditions, make your decisions on the basis of a comparison in this wise:

Which of the two sovereigns is imbued with the Moral Law? *Kings' Mandate of Heaven*

Which of the two generals has the most ability?

With whom lie the advantages derived from Heaven and Earth?

On which side is discipline most rigorously enforced?

Which army is the stronger?

On which side are officers and men more highly trained?

In which army is there the most absolute certainty that merit will be properly rewarded and misdeeds summarily punished?

By means of these seven considerations I can forecast victory or defeat.... But remember: While heeding the profit of my counsel, avail yourself also

A Terra-cotta Army. Ranks of life-size infantrymen, horses, and chariots made of pottery are drawn up in battle formation in underground pits that flank the tomb of the first emperor of the Chin. They were intended to protect him in death.

of any helpful circumstances over and beyond the ordinary rules and modify your plans accordingly.

All warfare is based on deception. Hence, when able to attack, we must seem unable; when using our forces, we must seem inactive; when we are near, we must make the enemy believe we are far away; when far away, we must make him believe we are near. Hold out baits to entice the enemy. Feign disorder, and crush him. If he is secure at all points, be prepared for him. If he is in superior strength, evade him. If your opponent is of choleric temper, seek to irritate him. Pretend to be weak, that he may grow arrogant. If he is taking his ease, give him no rest. If his forces are united, separate them. Attack him where he is unprepared, appear where you are not expected.

ON WAGING WAR

When you engage in actual fighting, if victory is long in coming, the men's weapons will grow dull and their ardor will be dampened. If you lay siege to a town, you will exhaust your strength, and if the campaign is protracted, the resources of the state will not be equal to the strain. Never forget: When your weapons are dulled, your ardor dampened, your strength exhausted, and your treasure spent, other chieftains will spring up to take advantage of your extremity. Then no man, however wise, will be able to avert the consequences that must ensue.

Thus, though we have heard of stupid haste in war, cleverness has never been seen associated with long delays. In all history, there is no instance of a country having benefited from prolonged warfare. Only one who knows the disastrous effects of a long war can realize the supreme importance of rapidity in bringing it to a close. It is only one who is thoroughly acquainted with the evils of war who can thoroughly understand the profitable way of carrying it on.

The skillful general does not raise a second levy, neither are his supply wagons loaded more than twice. Once war is declared, he will not waste precious time in waiting for reinforcements, nor will he turn his army back for fresh supplies, but crosses the enemy's frontier without delay. The value of time—that is, being a little ahead of your opponent—has counted for more than either numerical superiority or the nicest calculations with regard to commissariat.

In war, then, let your great object be victory, not lengthy campaigns. Thus it may be known that the leader of armies is the arbiter of the people's fate, the man on whom it depends whether the nation shall be in peace or in peril.

THE SHEATHED SWORD

To fight and conquer in all your battles is not supreme excellence; supreme excellence consists in breaking the enemy's resistance without fighting. In the practical art of war, the best thing of all is to take the enemy's country whole and intact; to shatter and destroy it is not so good. So, too, it is better to capture an army entire than to destroy it, to capture a regiment, a detachment, or a company entire than to destroy them.

Thus the highest form of generalship is to balk the enemy's plans; the next best is to prevent the junction of the enemy's forces; the next in order is to attack the enemy's army in the field; and the worst policy of all is to besiege walled cities, because the preparation of mantlets, movable shelters, and various implements of war will take up three whole months: and the piling up of mounds over against the walls will take three months more. The general, unable to control his irritation, will launch his men to the assault like swarming ants, with the result that one third of his men are slain, while the town still remains untaken. Such are the disastrous effects of a siege.

The skillful leader subdues the enemy's troops without any fighting; he captures their cities without laying siege to them; he overthrows their kingdom without lengthy operations in the field. With his forces intact he disputes the mastery of the empire, and thus, without losing a man, his triumph is complete.

This is the method of attacking by stratagem of using the sheathed sword.

It is the rule in war: If our forces are ten to the enemy's one, to surround him; if five to one, to attack him; if twice as numerous, to divide our army into two, one to meet the enemy in front, and one to fall upon his rear; if he replies to the frontal attack, he may be crushed from behind; if to the rearward attack, he may be crushed in front.

If equally matched, we can offer battle; if slightly inferior in numbers, we can avoid the enemy; if quite unequal in every way, we can flee from him. Though an obstinate fight may be made by a small force, in the end it must be captured by the larger force.

The general is the bulwark of the state: if the bulwark is strong at all points, the state will be strong; if the bulwark is defective, the state will be weak.

There are three ways in which a sovereign can bring misfortune upon his army:

By commanding the army to advance or to retreat, being ignorant of the fact that it cannot obey. This is called hobbling the army.

By attempting to govern an army in the same way as he administers a kingdom, being ignorant of the conditions that obtain in an army. This causes restlessness in the soldiers' minds. Humanity and justice are the principles on which to govern a state, but not an army; opportunism and flexibility, on the other hand, are military rather than civic virtues.

He will win who knows when to fight and when not to fight.

He will win who knows how to handle both superior and inferior forces.

He will win whose army is animated by the same spirit throughout all its ranks.

He will win who, prepared himself, waits to take the enemy unprepared.

He will win who has military capacity and is not interfered with by the sovereign.

If you know the enemy and know yourself, you need not fear the result of a hundred battles. If you know yourself but not the enemy, for every victory gained you will also suffer a defeat. If you know neither the enemy nor yourself, you will succumb in every battle.

TACTICS

The good fighters of old first put themselves beyond the possibility of defeat, and then waited for an opportunity of defeating the enemy.

To secure ourselves against defeat lies in our own hands, but the opportunity of defeating the enemy is provided by the enemy himself. Hence the saying: One may *know* how to conquer without being able to *do* it.

Security against defeat implies defensive tactics; ability to defeat the enemy means taking the offensive. Standing on the defensive indicates insufficient strength; attacking, a superabundance of strength.

The general who is skilled in defense hides in the most secret recesses of the earth; he who is skilled in attack flashes forth from the topmost heights of heaven. Thus, on the one hand, we have ability to protect ourselves; on the other, to gain a victory that is complete.

To see victory only when it is within the ken of the common herd is not the acme of excellence. Nor is it the acme of excellence if you fight and conquer and the whole empire says, "Well done!" True excellence is to plan secretly, to move surreptitiously, to foil the enemy's intentions and balk his schemes, so that at last the day may be won without shedding a drop of blood....

What the ancients called a clever fighter is one who not only wins, but excels in winning with ease. But his victories bring him neither reputation for wisdom nor credit for courage. For inasmuch as they are gained over circumstances that have not come to light, the world at large knows nothing of them, and he therefore wins no reputation for wisdom; and inasmuch as the hostile state submits before there has been any bloodshed, he receives no credit for courage.

He wins his battles by making no mistakes. Making no mistakes is what establishes the certainty of victory, for it means conquering an enemy that is already defeated.

Hence the skillful fighter puts himself into a position that makes defeat impossible and does not miss the moment for defeating the enemy. Thus it is that in war the victorious strategist only seeks battle after the victory has been won, whereas he who is destined to defeat first fights and afterward looks for victory. A victorious army opposed to a routed one is as a pound's weight placed in the scale against a single grain. The onrush of a conquering force is like the bursting of pent-up waters into a chasm a thousand fathoms deep.

The consummate leader cultivates the Moral Law and strictly adheres to method and discipline; thus it is in his power to control success.

FOCUS QUESTIONS

1. What is Sun-tzu's attitude toward war?

2. What does Sun-tzu see as the highest form of victory in a war? What does he think it takes in order to achieve victory?

3. *The Art of War* has been used to illustrate the creativity of Chou thought. Why?

4. What does *The Art of War* tell us about the society for which it was written? What were its values and view of human nature?

21

The Book of Songs (ca. 1200–1100 B.C.E.)

ANONYMOUS

One of the oldest collections of poems in any language, the Book of Songs *has long held a central place in Chinese culture. Indeed, thanks to Confucius's fondness for citing these verses, they became one of the Five Classics in Confucian literature, and they long served as a set text in the Chinese examination system. Equally important as their role in Confucian thought is their subject matter, which makes the* Book of Songs *as delightful and as accessible now as it was three thousand years ago. Although most of the early texts in world literature chronicled the deeds of gods and monarchs, the* Book of Songs *offers a poignant look at the daily routine of ordinary people in north China.*

The following poems illustrate the central themes of the collection. The first three underscore individuals' often difficult relationships with the state; two lament the rigors of military service (122 and 127), and the last one voices a local official's frustration (272). The next two deal with the common problems of a rural community: the first evokes the rhythm of agricultural life (159), and the second stresses the importance of clan unity (194). Finally, the last two, recording a wife's longing for an absent husband (100) and a lover's impatience (46), might have been written yesterday.

122 How few of us are left, how few!
Why do we not go back?
Were it not for our prince and his concern,
What should we be doing here in the dew?

How few of us are left, how few!
Why do we not go back?
Were it not for our prince own concerns,
What should we be doing here in the mud?

127 Minister of War,
We are the king's claws and fangs.
Why should you roll us on from misery to
misery,
Giving us no place to stop in or take rest?

Minister of War,
We are the king's claws and teeth.
Why should you roll us from misery to misery,
Giving us no place to come to and stay?

Minister of War,
Truly you are not wise.
Why should you roll us from misery to
misery?
We have Mothers who lack food.

272 I go out at the northern gate;
Deep is my grief
I am utterly poverty-stricken and destitute;
Yet no one heeds my misfortunes.
Well, all is over now.
No doubt it was Heaven's doing,
So what's the good of talking about it?

The king's business came my way;
Government business of every sort was put
upon me.
When I came in from outside
The people of the house all turned on me and
scolded me.
Well, it's over now.
No doubt it was Heaven's doing.
So what's the good of talking about it?

The king's business was all piled upon me;
Government business of every sort was put
upon me.
When I came in from outside
The people of the house all turned upon me
and abused me.

Well, it's over now
No doubt it was Heaven's doing,
So what's the good of talking about it?

159 In the seventh month the Fire ebbs;
In the ninth month I hand out the coats.
In the days of the First, sharp frosts;
In the days of the Second, keen winds.
Without coats, without serge,
How should they finish the year?
In the days of the Third they plough;
In the days of the Fourth out I step
With my wife and children,
Bringing hampers to the southern acre
Where the field-hands come to take good
cheer.

In the seventh month the Fire ebbs;
In the ninth month I hand out the coats.
But when the spring days grow warm
And the oriole sings
The girls take their deep baskets
And follow the path under the wall
To gather the soft mulberry-leaves:
'The spring days are drawing out;
They gather the white aster in crowds.
A girl's heart is sick and sad
Till with her lord she can go home.'

In the seventh month the Fire ebbs;
In the eighth month they pluck the rushes,
In the silk-worm month they gather the
mulberry-leaves,
Take that chopper and bill
To lop the far boughs and high,
Pull towards them the tender leaves.
In the seventh month the shrike cries;
In the eighth month they twist thread,
The black thread and the yellow:
'With my red dye so bright
I make a robe for my lord.'

In the fourth month the milkwort is in spike,
In the fifth month the cicada cries.
In the eighth month the harvest is gathered,
In the tenth month the boughs fall.
In the days of the First we hunt the raccoon,
And take those foxes and wild-cats

To make furs for our Lord.
In the days of the Second is the great Meet;
Practice for deeds of war.
The one-year-old [boar] we keep;
The three-year we offer to our Lord.
In the fifth month the locust moves its leg,
In the sixth month the grasshopper shakes its
    wing,
In the seventh month, out in the wilds:
In the eighth month, in the farm,
In the ninth month, at the door.
In the tenth month the cricket goes under my
    bed.
I stop up every hole to smoke out the rats,
Plugging the windows, burying the doors:
'Come, wife and children,
The change of the year is at hand.
Come and live in this house.'
In the sixth month we eat wild plums and
    cherries,
In the seventh month we boil mallows and
    beans.
In the eighth month we dry the dates,
In the tenth month we take the rice
To make with it the spring wine,
So that we may be granted long life.
In the seventh month we eat melons,
In the eighth month we cut the gourds,
In the ninth month we take the seeding
    hemp,
We gather bitter herbs, we cut the ailanto for
    firewood,
That our husbandmen may eat.

In the ninth month we make ready the
    stackyards,
In the tenth month we bring in the harvest,
Millet for wine, millet for cooking, the early
    and the late,
Paddy and hemp, beans and wheat.
Come, my husbandmen,
My harvesting is over,
Go up and begin your work in the house,
In the morning gather thatch-reeds,
In the evening twist rope;
Go quickly on to the roofs.
Soon you will be beginning to sow your
    many grains.

In the days of the Second they cut the rice
    with tingling blows;

In the days of the Third they bring it into the
    cold shed.
In the days of the Fourth very early
They offer lambs and garlic.
In the ninth month are shrewd frosts,
In the tenth month they clear the
    stackgrounds.
With twin pitchers they hold the village feast,
Killing for it a young lamb
Up they go into their lord's hall,
Raise the drinking-cup of buffalo-horn:
'Hurray for our lord; may he live for ever and
    ever!'

194 The flowers of the cherry-tree,
    Are they not truly splendid?
    Of men that now are,
    None equals a brother.

When death and mourning affright us
Brothers are very dear;
As 'upland' and 'lowland' form a pair,
So 'elder brother' and 'younger brother' go
    together.
There are wagtails on the plain;
When brothers are hard pressed
Even good friends
At the most do but heave a sigh.

Brothers may quarrel within the walls,
But outside they defend one another from
    insult;
Whereas even good friends
Pay but short heed.

But when the times of mourning or violence
    are over,
When all is calm and still,
Even brothers
Are not the equal of friends.

Set out your dishes and meat-stands,
Drink wine to your fill;
All you brothers are here together,
Peaceful, happy, and mild.

Your wives and children chime as well
As little zithern with big zithern.
You brothers are in concord,

Peaceful, merry, in great glee.

Thus you bring good to house and home,
Joy to wife and child.
I have deeply studied, I have pondered,
And truly it is so.

100 My lord is on service;
He did not know for how long.
Oh, when will he come?
The fowls are roosting in their holes,
Another day is ending,
The sheep and cows are coming down.
My lord is on service;
How can I not be sad?

My lord is on service;
Not a matter of days, nor months.
Oh, when will he be here again?
The fowls are roosting on their perches,

Another day is ending,
The sheep and cows have all come down.
My lord is on service;
Were I but sure that he gets drink and
    food!

46 Oh you with the blue collar,
On and on I think of you.
Even though I do not go to you,
You might surely send me news?

Oh, you with the blue collar,
Always and ever I long for you.
Even though I do not go to you,
You might surely sometimes come?

Here by the wall-gate
I pace to and fro.
One day when I do not see you
Is like three months.

FOCUS QUESTIONS

1. Using evidence from the poems, discuss the crops and farming techniques of an ancient Chinese village.

2. What picture do you form of the social hierarchy in these villages?

3. To what extent is the royal government able to intrude into the lives of ordinary people?

4. If these poems were applied to the rural society of late twentieth-century America, which themes would still apply? Which would not?

22

The Records of the Grand Historian of China (110–85 B.C.E.)

SSU-MA CH'IEN

Ssu-ma Ch'ien (ca. 145–85 B.C.E.) was an official at the Han court during its greatest era. His father had served in the office of Grand Historian, and Ssu-ma Ch'ien succeeded to it after his father's death in 110 B.C.E The Grand Historian was responsible both for establishing and maintaining the royal calendar (the method of numbering the years of the dynasty) and for composing a record of the principal events of the reign. Thus Ssu-ma Ch'ien had trained as an astronomer as well as an historian, and he was responsible for an important reorganization of the Chinese calendar.

His Records of the Grand Historian went far beyond the conventional listing of court appointments and events in the life of the Imperial family. Ssu-ma Ch'ien believed that with the accession of the Emperor Wu Ti, the Han dynasty had reached its apex; and he decided to write a history of the dynasty as a whole. He divided his work into a chronology, a description of Han government, and a long biographical section in which he recorded the lives and deeds of great men. Ssu-ma Ch'ien believed that history was a moral and didactic subject, that it should teach lessons and reveal the values of the society being remembered. This method is clearly seen in his biographical sketches, like those of Pu Shih and Chi An, which follow.

PU SHIH

The emperor, impressed by the words of a man named Pu Shih, summoned him to court and made him a palace attendant, giving him the honorary rank of *tso-shu-ch'ang* and presenting him with ten *ch'ing* of land. These rewards were announced throughout the empire so that everyone might know of Pu Shih's example.

Pu Shih was a native of Ho-nan, where his family made a living by farming and animal raising. When his parents died, Pu Shih left home, handing over the house, the lands, and all the family wealth to his younger brother, who by this time was full grown. For his own share he took only a hundred or so of the sheep they had been raising, which he led off into the mountains to pasture. In the course of ten years or so, Pu Shih's sheep had increased to over a thousand and he had bought his own house and fields. His younger brother in the meantime had failed completely in the management of the farm, but Pu Shih promptly handed over to him a share of his own wealth. This happened several times. Just at that time the Han was sending its generals at frequent intervals to attack the Hsiung-nu. Pu Shih journeyed to the capital and submitted a letter to the throne, offering to turn over half of his wealth to the district officials to help in the defense of the border. The emperor dispatched an envoy to ask if Pu Shih wanted a post in the government.

"From the time I was a child," Pu Shih replied, "I have been an animal raiser. I have had no experience at government service and would certainly not want such a position."

"Perhaps then your family has suffered some injustice that you would like to report?" inquired the envoy.

But Pu Shih answered, "I have never in my life had a quarrel with anyone. If there are poor men in my village, I lend them what they need, and if there are men who do not behave properly, I guide and counsel them. Where I live, everyone does as I say. Why should I suffer any injustice from others? There is nothing I want to report!"

"If that is the case," said the envoy, "then what is your objective in making this offer?"

Pu Shih replied, "The Son of Heaven has set out to punish the Hsiung-nu. In my humble opinion, every worthy man should be willing to fight to the death to defend the borders, and every person with wealth ought to contribute to the expense. If this were done, then the Hsiung-nu could be wiped out!"

The envoy made a complete record of Pu Shih's words and reported them to the emperor. The emperor discussed the matter with the chancellor Kung-sun Hung, but the latter said, "The proposal is simply not in accord with human nature! Such eccentric people are of no use in guiding the populace, but only throw the laws into confusion. I beg Your Majesty not to accept his offer!"

For this reason the emperor put off answering Pu Shih for a long time, and finally, after several years had passed, turned down the offer, whereupon Pu Shih went back to his fields and pastures.

A year or so later the armies marched off on several more expeditions, and the Hun-yeh king and his people surrendered to the Han. As a result the expenditures of the district officials increased greatly and the granaries and treasuries were soon empty. The following year a number of poor people were transferred to other regions, all of them depending upon the district officials for their support, and there were not enough supplies to go around. At this point Pu Shih took two hundred thousand cash of his own and turned the sum over to the governor of Ho-nan to assist the people who were emigrating to other regions. A list of the wealthy men of Honan who had contributed to the aid of the poor was sent to the emperor and he recognized Pu Shih's name. "This is the same man who once offered half his wealth to aid in the defense of the border!" he exclaimed, and presented Pu Shih with a sum of money equivalent to the amount necessary to buy off four hundred men from military duty. Pu Shih once more turned the entire sum over to the district officials. At this time the rich families were all scrambling to hide their wealth; only Pu Shih, unlike the others, had offered to contribute to the expenses of the government. The emperor decided that Pu Shih was really a man of exceptional worth after all, and therefore bestowed upon him the honors mentioned above in order to hint to the people that they might well follow his example.

At first Pu Shih was unwilling to become a palace attendant, but the emperor told him, "I have some sheep in the Shang-lin Park which I would like you to take care of." Pu Shih then accepted the post of palace attendant and, wearing a coarse robe and straw sandals, went off to tend the sheep. After a year or so, the sheep had grown fat and were reproducing at a fine rate. The emperor, when he visited the park and saw the flocks, commended Pu Shih on his work. "It is not only with sheep," Pu Shih commented. "Governing people is

the same way. Get them up at the right time, let them rest at the right time, and if there are any bad ones, pull them out at once before they have a chance to spoil the flock!"

The emperor, struck by his words, decided to give him a trial as magistrate of the district of Kou-shih. When his administration proved beneficial to the people of Kou-shih, the emperor transferred him to the post of magistrate of Ch'eng-kao and put him in charge of the transportation of supplies, where his record was also outstanding. Because of his simple, unspoiled ways and his deep loyalty, the emperor finally appointed him grand tutor to his son Liu Hung, the king of Ch'i.

CHI AN

Chi An, whose polite name was Chi Ch'ang-ju, was a native of P'u-yang. His ancestors won favor with the rulers of the state of Wei and for seven generations, down to the time of Chi An, served without break as high officials.

During the reign of Emperor Ching, Chi An, on the recommendation of his father, was appointed as a mounted guard to the heir apparent. Because of his stern bearing he was treated with deference. Later, when Emperor Ching passed away and the heir apparent ascended the throne, Chi An was appointed master of guests.

When the tribes of Eastern and Southern Yueh began to attack each other, the emperor dispatched Chi An to go to the area and observe the situation. He did not journey all the way, however, but went only as far as Wu and then turned around and came back to the capital to make his report. "The Yüeh people have always been in the habit of attacking each other," he said. "There is no reason for the Son of Heaven's envoy to trouble himself about such matters!"

When a great fire broke out in Ho-nei and destroyed over a thousand houses, the emperor once more sent Chi An to observe the situation. On his return he reported, "The roofs of the houses were so close together that the fire spread from one to another; that is why so many homes were burned. It is nothing to worry about. As I passed through Ho-nan on my way, however, I noted that the inhabitants were very poor, and over ten thousand families had suffered so greatly from floods and droughts that fathers and sons were reduced to eating each other. I therefore took it upon myself to use the imperial seals to open the granaries of Honan and relieve the distress of the people. I herewith return the seals and await punishment for overstep-ping my authority in this fashion."

The emperor, impressed with the wisdom he had shown, overlooked the irregularity of his action and transferred him to the post of governor of Ying-yang. Chi An, however, felt that he was unworthy of a governorship and, pleading illness, retired to his home in the country. When the emperor heard of this, he summoned him to court again and appointed him a palace counselor. But because he sharply criticized the emperor on several occasions, it proved impossible to keep him around the palace for long. The emperor therefore transferred him to the post of governor of Tung-hai.

Chi An studied the doctrines of the Yellow Emperor and Lao Tzu. In executing his duties and governing the people he valued honesty and serenity, selecting worthy assistants and secretaries and leaving them to do as they saw fit. In his administration he demanded only that the general spirit of his directives be carried out and never made a fuss over minor details. He was sick a great deal of the time, confined to his bed and unable to go out, and yet after only a year or so as governor of Tung-hai he had succeeded in setting the affairs of the province in perfect order and winning the acclaim of the people.

The emperor, hearing of his success, summoned him to court and appointed him master of titles chief commandant, promoting him to one of the nine highest offices in the government. In this post, as well, Chi An emphasized a policy of laissez-faire, interpreting his duties very broadly and not bothering with the letter of the law.

Chi An was by nature very haughty and ill-mannered. He could not tolerate the faults of others and would denounce people to their faces. Those who took his fancy he treated very well, but those who didn't he could not even bear to see. For this reason most men gave him a wide berth. On the other hand he was fond of learning and liked to travel about doing daring and generous things for others, and his conduct was always above reproach. He was also fond of outspoken criticism and his words frequently brought scowls to the emperor's face. His constant ambition was to be as direct and outspoken as the Liang general Fu Po and Emperor Ching's minister Yuan Ang.

The emperor at the time was busy summoning scholars and Confucians to court and telling them, "I want to do thus-and-so, I want to do thus-and-so." Commenting on this, Chi An said to the emperor, "On the surface Your Majesty is practicing benevolence and righteousness, but in your heart you have too many desires. How do you ever expect to imitate the rule of the sage emperors Yao and Shun in this way?"

The emperor sat in silence, his face flushed with anger, and then dismissed the court. The other high officials were all terrified of what would happen to Chi An. After the emperor had left the room, he turned to his attendants and said, "Incredible—the stupidity of that Chi An!"

Later, some of the officials reproached Chi An for his behavior, but he replied, "Since the Son of Heaven has gone to the trouble of appointing us as his officials and aides, what business have we in simply flattering his whims and agreeing with what-ever he says, deliberately leading him on to unrighteous deeds? Now that we occupy these posts, no matter how much we may value our own safety, we cannot allow the court to suffer disgrace, can we?"

"What sort of man is Chi An anyway?" the emperor asked, to which Chuang Chu replied, "As long as he is employed in some ordinary post as an official, he will do no better than the average person. But if he were called upon to assist a young ruler or to guard a city against attack, then no temptation could sway him from his duty, no amount of entreaty could make him abandon his post. Even the bravest men of antiquity, Meng Pen and Hsia Yu, could not shake his determination!"

"Yes," said the emperor. "In ancient times there were ministers who were deemed worthy to be called the guardians of the altars of the nation. And men like Chi An come near to deserving the same appellation."

FOCUS QUESTIONS

1. Why did the emperor's counselors think that Pu Shih was eccentric? What behavior did they think reasonable?

2. What were the values that make the shepherd Pu Shih suited to serve as grand tutor to the emperor's son?

3. Why did Chi An not bother to investigate the civil war in Yüeh but did bother to distribute grain in Ho-nan?

4. What did Chi An think was the role of a counselor to the emperor of China?

23

Memorials (ca. 230 B.C.E.)

HAN FEI TZU

In the turbulent period in Chinese history known as the Era of Warring States, the Han kingdom, both smaller and poorer than its chief rivals, struggled for survival. At the end of this chaotic era, one of the Han princes, Han Fei Tzu, wrote a series of memorials, advising the Han king about how to check the state's decline. Although the Han king refused to acknowledge the wisdom of Han Fei Tzu's counsel, a neighboring ruler did, and he attempted to secure the prince's services. Unfortunately for Han Fei Tzu, this led to charges of disloyalty and ultimately to his execution in 233 B.C.E.

Han Fei Tzu's Memorials *have remained one of the classics of ancient Chinese law and statecraft. In contrast to the more philosophical approaches to the problems of government, common to Buddhist and Confucian writers, Han Fei Tzu analyzes the problems of government in a practical and realistic manner. What follows is his discussion of how ruler and subjects alike could detect the warning signs of imminent disaster, what he called the "Portents of Ruin."*

1. As a rule, if the state of the lord of men is small but the fiefs of private families are big, or if the ruler's sceptre is insignificant but the ministers are powerful, then ruin is possible.

2. If the ruler neglects laws and prohibitions, indulges in plans and ideas, disregards the defence works within the boundaries and relies on foreign friendship and support, then ruin is possible.

3. If all officials indulge in studies, sons of the family are fond of debate, peddlers and shopkeepers hide money in foreign countries, and

poor people suffer miseries at home, then ruin is possible.

4. If the ruler is fond of palatial decorations, raised kiosks, and embanked pools, is immersed in pleasures of having chariots, clothes, and curios, and thereby tires out the hundred surnames and exhausts public wealth, then ruin is possible.

5. If the ruler believes in date-selecting, worships devils and deities, believes in divination and lot-casting, and likes fêtes and celebrations, then ruin is possible.

6. If the ruler takes advice only from ministers of high rank, refrains from comparing different opinions and testifying to the truth, and uses only one man as a channel of information, then ruin is possible.

7. If posts and offices can be sought through influential personages and rank and bounties can be obtained by means of bribes, then ruin is possible.

8. If the ruler, being easy-going, accomplishes nothing, being tender-hearted, lacking in decision, and, wavering between acceptance and rejection, has no settled opinion, then ruin is possible.

9. If the ruler is greedy, insatiable, attracted to profit, and fond of gain, then ruin is possible.

10. If the ruler enjoys inflicting unjust punishment and does not uphold the law, likes debate and persuasion but never sees to their practicability, and indulges in style and wordiness but never considers their effect, then ruin is possible.

11. If the ruler is shallow-brained and easily penetrated, reveals everything but conceals nothing, and cannot keep any secret but communicates the words of one minister to another, then ruin is possible.

12. If the ruler is stubborn-minded, uncompromising, and apt to dispute every remonstrance and fond of surpassing everybody else, and never thinks of the welfare of the Altar of the Spirits of Land and Grain but sticks to self-confidence without due consideration, then ruin is possible.

13. The ruler who relies on friendship and support from distant countries, makes light of his relations with close neighbours, counts on the aid from big powers, and provokes surrounding countries, is liable to ruin.

14. If foreign travellers and residents, whose property and families are abroad, take seats in the state council and interfere in civil affairs, then ruin is possible.

15. If the people have no confidence in the premier and the inferiors do not obey the superiors while the sovereign loves and trusts the premier and cannot depose him, then ruin is possible.

16. If the ruler does not take able men of the country into service but searches after foreign gentlemen, and if he does not make tests according to meritorious services but would appoint and dismiss officials according to their mere reputations till foreign residents are exalted and ennobled to surpass his old acquaintances, then ruin is possible.

17. If the ruler disregards the matter of legitimacy and lets bastards rival legitimate sons, or if the sovereign dies before he inaugurates the crown prince, then ruin is possible.

18. If the ruler is boastful but never regretful, makes much of himself despite the disorder prevailing in his country, and insults the neighbouring enemies without estimating the resources within the boundaries, then ruin is possible.

19. If the state is small but the ruler will not acquiesce in a humble status; if his forces are scanty but he never fears strong foes; if he has no manners and insults big neighbours; or if he is greedy and obstinate but unskilful in diplomacy; then ruin is possible.

20. If, after the inauguration of the crown prince, the ruler takes in a woman from a strong enemy state, the crown prince will be endangered and the ministers will be worried. Then ruin is possible.

21. If the ruler is timid and weak in self-defence and his mind is paralysed by the signs of future

events; or if he knows what to decide on but dare not take any drastic measure; then ruin is possible.

22. If the exiled ruler is abroad but the country sets up a new ruler, or if before the heir apparent taken abroad as hostage returns, the ruler changes his successor, then the state will divide. And the state divided against itself is liable to ruin.

23. If the ruler keeps near and dear to the chief vassals whom he has disheartened and disgraced or stands close by the petty men whom he has punished, then he will make them bear anger and feel shame. If he goes on doing this, rebels are bound to appear. When rebels appear, ruin is possible.

24. If chief vassals rival each other in power and uncles and brothers are many and powerful, and if they form juntas inside and receive support from abroad and thereby dispute state affairs and struggle for supreme influence, then ruin is possible.

25. If words of maids and concubines are followed and the wisdom of favourites is used, and the ruler repeats committing unlawful acts regardless of the grievances and resentments inside and outside the court, then ruin is possible.

26. If the ruler is contemptuous to chief vassals and impolite to uncles and brothers, overworks the hundred surnames, and slaughters innocent people, then ruin is possible.

27. If the ruler is fond of twisting laws by virtue of his wisdom, mixes public with private affairs from time to time, alters laws and prohibitions at random, and issues commands and orders frequently, then ruin is possible.

28. If the terrain has no stronghold, the city-walls are in bad repair, the state has no savings and hoardings, resources and provisions are scarce, and no preparations are made for defence and attack, but the ruler dares to attack and invade other countries imprudently, then ruin is possible.

29. If the royal seed is short-lived, new sovereigns succeed to each other continuously, babies become rulers, and chief vassals have all the ruling authority to themselves and recruit partisans from among foreign residents and maintain inter-state friendship by frequently ceding territories, then ruin is possible.

30. If the crown prince is esteemed and celebrated, has numerous dependents and protégés, develops friendships with big powers, and exercises his authority and influence from his early years, then ruin is possible.

31. If the ruler is narrow-minded, quick-tempered, imprudent, easily affected, and, when provoked, becomes blind with rage, then ruin is possible.

32. If the sovereign is easily provoked and fond of resorting to arms and neglects agricultural and military training but ventures warfare and invasion heedlessly, then ruin is possible.

33. If nobles are jealous of one another, chief vassals are prosperous, seeking support from enemy states and harassing the hundred surnames at home so as to attack their wrongdoers, but the lord of men never censures them, then ruin is possible.

34. If the ruler is unworthy but his half-brothers are worthy; if the heir apparent is powerless and the bastard surpasses him; or if the magistrates are weak and the people are fierce; then the state will be seized with a panic. And a panic-stricken state is liable to ruin.

35. If the ruler conceals his anger, which he would never reveal, suspends a criminal case, which he never would censure, and thereby makes the officials hate him in secret and increases their worries and fears, and if he never comes to know the situation even after a long time, then ruin is possible.

36. If the commander in the front line has too much power, the governor on the frontier has too much nobility, and if they have the ruling authority to themselves, issue orders at their own will and do just as they wish without asking permission of the ruler, then ruin is possible.

37. If the queen is adulterous, the sovereign's mother is corrupt, attendants inside and outside

the court intercommunicate, and male and female have no distinction, such a régime is called "bi-regal." Any country having two rulers is liable to ruin.

38. If the queen is humble but the concubine is noble, the heir apparent is low but the bastard is high, the prime minister is despised but the court usher is esteemed, then disobedience will appear in and out of the court. If disobedience appears in and out of the court, the state is liable to ruin.

39. If chief vassals are very powerful, have many strong partisans, obstruct the sovereign's decisions, and administer all state affairs on their own authority, then ruin is possible.

40. If vassals of private families are employed but descendants of military officers are rejected, men who do good to their village communities are promoted but those who render distinguished services to their official posts are discarded, self-seeking deeds are esteemed but public-spirited works are scorned, then ruin is possible.

41. If the state treasury is empty but the chief vassals have plenty of money, native subjects are poor but foreign residents are rich, farmers and warriors have hard times but people engaged in secondary professions are benefited, then ruin is possible.

42. The ruler who sees a great advantage but does not advance towards it, hears the outset of a calamity but does not provide against it, thus neglecting preparations for attack and defence and striving to embellish himself with the practice of benevolence and righteousness, is liable to ruin.

43. If the ruler does not practise the filial piety of the lord of men but yearns after the filial piety of the commoner, does not regard the welfare of the Altar of the Spirits of Land and Grain but obeys the orders of the dowager queen, and if he allows women to administer the state affairs and eunuchs to meddle with politics, then ruin is possible.

44. If words are eloquent but not legal, the mind is sagacious but not tactful, the sovereign is versatile but performs his duties not in accordance with laws and regulations, then ruin is possible.

45. If new ministers advance when old officials withdraw, the unworthy meddle with politics when the virtuous pass out of the limelight, and men of no merit are esteemed when hardworking people are disdained, then the people left behind will resent it. If the people left behind resent it, ruin is possible.

46. If the bounties and allowances of uncles and brothers exceed their merits, their badges and uniforms override their grades, and their residences and provisions are too extravagant, and if the lord of men never restrains them, then ministers will become insatiable. If ministers are insatiable, then ruin is possible.

47. If the ruler's sons-in-law and grandsons live behind the same hamlet gate with the commoners and behave unruly and arrogantly towards their neighbours, then ruin is possible.

Thus, portents of ruin do not imply certainty of ruin but liability to ruin.

FOCUS QUESTIONS

1. According to Han Fei Tzu, what is the ideal relationship between king and people?

2. Discuss the role of the nobility in Han Fei Tzu's *Memorials*.

3. What is the importance of the royal family to Han Fei Tzu?

4. Would a Buddhist or Confucian writer have approved of Han Fei Tzu's advice?

Ancient Rome

Scala/Art Resource, NY

Interior of the Colosseum of Rome. The Colosseum was a large amphitheater constructed under the Emperor Vespasian and his son Titus. The amphitheaters in which the gladiatorial contests were held varied in size throughout the empire. The Roman emperors understood that gladiatorial shows and other forms of entertainment helped to divert the poor and destitute from any political unrest.

24

On the Laws (ca. 52 B.C.E.)

CICERO

Marcus Tullius Cicero (106–43 B.C.E.) is remembered as the greatest orator and rhetorician of the ancient world. He was born in the Italian countryside to a well-off family, although not one of the highest social ranking. Cicero's family moved to Rome, where he received an exceptional education, especially in law. In 80 B.C.E. he spoke on his first legal case and was an immediate sensation. He embarked upon a political career that was helped at every step by his remarkable rhetorical skills. Most unusually, given his class background, Cicero was elected consul in 63 B.C.E. He served with honor and achieved much before he fell victim to the factious politics surrounding Julius Caesar's rise to power. Although he took no part in Caesar's assassination, Cicero was condemned by Mark Antony and murdered.

Cicero claimed no originality in his writings and was important chiefly for transmitting Greek philosophy throughout the Roman world. Nevertheless, his treatise on oratory was among the most important of the ancient texts, and his reflections upon political life were of central importance to the classical revival of the Renaissance. On the Laws *was begun in 52 B.C.E. but was not published until after its author's death. Written in dialogue form, it espouses a view of natural law.*

MARCUS. But the whole subject of universal law and jurisprudence must be comprehended in this discussion, in order that this which we call civil law, may be confined in some one small and narrow space of nature. For we shall have to explain the true nature of moral justice, which must be traced back from the nature of man. And laws will have to be considered by which all political states should be governed. And last of all, shall we have to speak of those laws and customs of nations, which are framed for the use and convenience of particular countries, (in which even our own people will not be omitted,) which are known by the title of civil laws.

QUINTUS. You take a noble view of the subject, my brother, and go to the fountainhead, in order to throw light on the subject of our consideration: and those who treat civil law in any other manner, are not so much pointing out the paths of justice as those of litigation.

MARCUS. That is not quite the case, my Quintus. It is not so much the science of law that produces litigation, as the ignorance of it. But more of this by and by. At present let us examine the first principles of Right.

Now, many learned men have maintained that it springs from law. I hardly know if their opinion be not correct, at least according to their own definition; for "law," say they, "is the highest reason implanted in nature, which prescribes those things which ought to be done, and forbids the contrary." And when this same reason is confirmed and established in men's minds, it is then law.

They therefore conceive that prudence is a law, whose operation is to urge us to good actions, and restrain us from evil ones. And they think, too, that the Greek name for law which is derived from "to distribute," implies the very nature of the thing, that is, to give every man his due. The Latin name, *lex,* conveys the idea of selection, a *legendo.* According to the Greeks, therefore, the name of law implies an equitable distribution: according to the Romans, an equitable selection. And, indeed, both characteristics belong peculiarly to law.

And if this be a correct statement, which it seems to me for the most part to be, then the origin of right is to be sought in the law. For this is the true energy of nature—this is the very soul and reason of a wise man, and the test of virtue and vice. But since all this discussion of ours relates to a subject, the terms of which are of frequent occurrence in the popular language of the citizens, we shall be sometimes obliged to use the same terms as the vulgar, and to call that law, which in its written enactments sanctions what it thinks fit by special commands or prohibitions.

Let us begin, then, to establish the principles of justice on that supreme law, which has existed from all ages before any legislative enactments were drawn up in writing, or any political governments constituted.

Do you then grant that the entire universe is regulated by the power of the immortal Gods, that by their nature, reason, energy, mind, divinity, or some other word of clearer signification, if there be such, all things are governed and directed? For if you will not grant me this, that is what I must begin by establishing.

This animal—prescient, sagacious, complex, acute, full of memory, reason, and counsel, which we call man—has been generated by the supreme God in a most transcendent condition. For he is the only creature among all the races and descriptions of animated beings who is indued with superior reasons and thought, in which the rest are deficient. And what is there, I do not say in man alone, but in all heaven and earth, more divine than reason, which, when it becomes right and perfect, is justly termed wisdom?

There exists, therefore, since nothing is better than reason, and since this is the common property of God and man, a certain aboriginal rational intercourse between divine and human natures. But where reason is common, there right reason must also be common to the same parties; and since this right reason is what we call law, God and men must be considered as associated by law. Again, there must also be a communion of right where there is a communion of law. And those who have law and right thus in common, must be considered members of the same commonwealth.

And if they are obedient to the same rule and the same authority, they are even much more so to this one celestial regency, this divine mind and omnipotent deity. So that the entire universe may be looked upon as forming one vast commonwealth of gods and men. And, as in earthly states certain ranks are distinguished with reference to the relationships of families, according to a certain principle which will be discussed in its proper place, that principle, in the nature of things, is far more magnificent and splendid by which men are connected with the Gods, as belonging to their kindred and nation.

Now, the law of virtue is the same in God and man, and in no other disposition besides them. This virtue is nothing else than a nature perfect in itself, and wrought up to the most consummate excellence. There exists, therefore, a similitude between God and man. And as this is the case, what connection can there be which concerns us more nearly, and is more certain?

Since, then, the Deity has been pleased to create and adorn man to be the chief and president of all terrestrial creatures, so it is evident, without further argument, that human nature has also made very great advances by its own intrinsic energy: that nature, which without any other instruction than her own, has developed the first rude principles of the understanding, and strengthened and perfected reason to all the appliances of science and art.

ATTICUS. Oh ye immortal Gods! to what a distance back are you tracing the principles of justice! However, you are discoursing in such a style that I will not show any impatience to hear what I expect you to say on the Civil Law. But I will listen patiently, even if you spend the whole day in this kind of discourse: for assuredly these, which perhaps you are embracing in your argument for the sake of others, are grander topics than even the subject for which they prepare the way.

MARCUS. You may well describe these topics as grand, which we are now briefly discussing. But of all the questions which are ever the subject of discussion among learned men, there is none which it is more important thoroughly to understand than this, that man is born for justice, and that law and equity have not been established by opinion, but by nature. This truth will become still more apparent if we investigate the nature of human association and society.

For there is no one thing so like or so equal to another, as in every instance man is to man. And if the corruption of customs, and the variation of opinions, did not induce an imbecility of minds, and turn them aside from the course of nature, no one would more nearly resemble himself than all men would resemble all men. Therefore, whatever definition we give of man, will be applicable to the whole human race. And this is a good argument that there is no dissimilarity of kind among men; because if this were the case, one definition could not include all men.

It follows, then, that nature made us just that we might share our goods with each other, and supply each other's wants. You observe in this discussion, whenever I speak of nature, I mean nature in its genuine purity, but that there is, in fact, such corruption engendered by evil customs, that the sparks, as it were, of virtue which have been given by nature are extinguished, and that antagonist vices arise around it and become strengthened.

But if, as nature prompts them to, men would with deliberate judgment, in the words of the poet, "being men, think nothing that concerns mankind indifferent to them," then would justice be cultivated equally by all. For to those to whom nature has given reason, she has also given right reason, and therefore also law, which is nothing else than right reason enjoining what is good, and forbidding what is evil. And if nature has given us law, she hath also given us right. But she has bestowed reason on all, therefore right has been bestowed on all.

It is therefore an absurd extravagance in some philosophers to assert, that all things are necessarily just which are established by the civil laws and the institutions of nations. Are then the laws of tyrants just, simply because they are laws? Suppose the thirty tyrants of Athens had imposed certain laws on the Athenians? Or, suppose again that these Athenians were delighted with these tyrannical laws, would these laws on that account have been considered just? For my own part, I do not think such laws deserve any greater estimation than that passed during our own interregnum, which ordained that the dictator should be empowered to put to death with impunity whatever citizens he pleased, without hearing them in their own defence.

For there is but one essential justice which cements society, and one law which establishes this justice. This law is right reason, which is the true rule of all commandments and prohibitions. Whoever neglects this law, whether written or unwritten, is necessarily unjust and wicked.

But if justice consists in submission to written laws and national customs, and if, as the same school affirms, everything must be measured by utility alone, he who thinks that such conduct will be advantageous to him will neglect the laws, and break them if it is in his power. And the consequence is, that real justice has really no existence if it have not one by nature, and if that which is established as such on account of utility is overturned by some other utility.

But if nature does not ratify law, then all the virtues may lose their sway. For what becomes of generosity, patriotism, or friendship? Where will the desire of benefitting our neighbours, or the gratitude that acknowledges kindness, be able to exist at all? For all these virtues proceed from our natural inclination to love mankind. And this is the true basis of justice, and without this not only the mutual charities of men, but the religious services of the Gods, would be at an end; for these are preserved as I imagine, rather by the natural sympathy which subsists between divine and human beings, than by mere fear and timidity.

It follows that I may now sum up the whole of this argument by asserting, as is plain to every one from these positions which have been already laid down, that all right and all that is honourable is to be sought for its own sake. In truth, all virtuous men love justice and equity for what they are in themselves; nor is it like a good man to make a mistake, and love that which does not deserve their affection. Right, therefore, is desirable and deserving to be cultivated for its own sake; and if this be true of right, it must be true also of justice. What then shall we say of liberality? Is it exercised gratuitously, or does it covet some reward and recompense? If a man does good without expecting any recompense for his kindness, then it is gratuitous: if he does expect compensation, it is a mere matter of traffic. Nor is there any doubt that he who truly deserves the reputation of a generous and kindhearted man, is thinking of his duty, not of his interest. In the same way the virtue of justice demands neither emolument nor salary, and therefore we desire it for its own sake. And the case of all the moral virtues is the same, and so is the opinion formed of them.

FOCUS QUESTIONS

1. What are these laws? Are they the work of legislators, or do they have less definite roots?

2. Cicero is remembered especially for transmitting the ideas of Greek philosophers and shaping those ideas for a Roman audience. Can you identify any Greek influence in *On the Laws?*

3. *On the Laws* dwells upon human nature. What is the Roman vision of the individual? With what qualities are individuals endowed?

4. What is the difference between natural law and the civil law made by mortals?

5. *On the Laws* was very widely read by generations of Romans. What do you think the popularity of *On the Laws* reveals about Roman society?

25

The Aeneid (30–19 B.C.E.)

VIRGIL

Publius Virgilius Maro, known as Virgil (70–19 B.C.E.), was born near Mantua to a peasant family. Remarkably, given his family background, he was able to receive an education, first at local schools and then in Rome. He was especially skilled in rhetoric and philosophy, the two central subjects of the time. Unlike most other distinguished Romans, Virgil never aspired to public life but devoted himself entirely to writing poetry. His early works were merely preparation for the creation of an epic, regarded as the highest form of poetic expression.

This work was The Aeneid, *Virgil's story of the founding of Rome and the fulfillment of its great destiny. Initially, the poem was meant to honor the emperor; in it, Augustus was compared favorably to the mythical founder of Rome, Aeneas, after whom the poem was named. Virgil worked on* The Aeneid *for over a decade, and it remained unfinished at his death. The following selection comes from the opening stanzas of the poem.*

Arms and the man I sing, who first made way,
Predestined exile, from the Trojan shore
To Italy, the blest Lavinian strand.
Smitten of storms he was on land and sea
By violence of Heaven, to satisfy
Stern Juno's sleepless wrath; and much in war
He suffered, seeking at the last to found
The city, and bring o'er his fathers' gods
To safe abode in Latium; whence arose
The Latin race, old Alba's reverend lords.
And from her hills wide-walled, imperial Rome.

O Muse, the causes tell! What sacrilege,
Or vengeful sorrow, moved the heavenly
     Queen
To thrust on dangers dark and endless toil
A man whose largest honor in men's eyes
Was serving Heaven? Can gods such anger
     feel?

In ages gone an ancient city stood—
Carthage, a Tyrian seat, which from afar
Made front on Italy and on the mouths
Of Tiber's stream: its wealth and revenues
Were vast, and ruthless was its quest of war.
'IT'is said that Juno, of all lands she loved,
Most cherished this—not Samos' self so dear.
Here were her arms, her chariot; even then
A throne of power o'er nations near and far,
If Fate opposed not, 'It was her darling hope
To 'stablish here; but anxiously she heard
That of the Trojan blood there was a breed
Then rising, which upon the destined day
Should utterly o'erwhelm her Tyrian towers;
A people of wide sway and conquest proud
Should compass Libya's doom; such was the
     web
The Fatal Sisters spun.
Aeneas' wave-worn crew now landward
     made,
And took the nearest passage, whither lay

The coast of Libya. A haven there
Walled in by bold sides of a rocky isle,
Offers a spacious and secure retreat,
Where every billow from the distant main
Breaks, and in many a rippling curve retires.
Huge crags and two confronted promontories
Frown heaven-high, beneath whose brows
     outspread
The silent, sheltered waters; on the heights
The bright and glimmering foliage seems to
     show
A woodland amphitheatre: and yet higher
Rises a straight-stemmed grove of dense, dark
     shade.
Fronting on these a grotto may be seen.
O'erhung by steep cliffs; from its inmost wall
Clear springs gush out; and shelving seats it has
Of unhewn stone, a place the wood-nymphs
     love.
In such a port, a weary ship rides free
Of weight of firm-fluked anchor or strong
     chain.
Hither Aeneas, of his scattered fleet
Saving but seven, into harbor sailed:
With passionate longing for the touch of land,
Forth leap the Trojans to the welcome shore,
And fling their dripping limbs along the
     ground.
Then good Achates smote a flinty stone.
Secured a flashing spark, heaped on light
     leaves,
And with dry branches nursed the mounting
     flame
Then Ceres' gift from the corrupting sea
They bring away; and wearied utterly
Ply Ceres' cunning on the rescued corn.
And parch in flames, and mill 'twixt two
     smooth stones.

"Companions mine, we have not failed to feel

Calamity till now. O, ye have borne
Far heavier sorrow: Jove will make an end
Also of this. Ye sailed a course hard by
Infuriate Scylla's howling cliffs and caves.
Ye knew the Cyclops' crags. Lift up your
    hearts!
No more complaint and fear! It well may be
Some happier hour will find this memory fair.
Through chance and change and hazard
    without end.
Our goal is Latium: where our destinies
Beckon to blest abodes, and have ordained
That Troy shall rise new-born! Have patience
    all!
And bide expectantly that golden day."
Such was his word, but vexed with grief and
    care.
Feigned hopes upon his forehead firm he wore,
And locked within his heart a hero's pain.

After these things were past, exalted Jove,
From his ethereal sky surveying clear
The seas all winged with sails, lands widely
    spread.
And nations populous from shore to shore,
Paused on the peak of heaven, and fixed his
    gaze
On Libya. But while he anxious mused,
Near him, her radiant eyes all dim with tears,
Nor smiling any more, Venus approached,
And thus complained: "O thou who dost
    control
Things human and divine by changeless laws,
Enthroned in awful thunder! What huge
    wrong
Could my Aeneas and his Trojans few
Achieve against thy power? For they have
    borne
Unnumbered deaths, and, failing Italy,
The gates of all the world again them close.
Hast thou not give us thy covenant
That hence the Romans when the rolling
    years
Have come full cycle, shall arise to power
From Troy's regenerate seed, and rule
    supreme

The unresisted lords of land and sea?
O sire, what swerves thy will? How oft have I
In Troy's most lamentable wreck and woe.
Consoled my heart with this, and balanced oft
Our destined good against our destined ill!
But the same stormful fortune still pursues
My band of heroes on their perilous way.
When shall these labors cease, O glorious
    King?
Antenor, though th' Achoeans pressed him
    sore,
Found his way forth, and entered unassailed
Ilyria's haven, and the guarded land
Of the Liburni. Straight up stream he sailed
Where like a swollen sea Timavus pours
A nine-fold flood from roaring mountain
    gorge,
And whelms with voiceful wave the fields
    below.
He built Patavium there, and fixed abodes
For Troy's far-exiled sons; he gave a name
To a new land and race; the Trojan arms
Were hung on temple walls; and, to this day,
Lying in perfect peace, the hero sleeps.
But we of thine own seed, to whom thou dost
A station in the arch of heaven assign,
Behold our navy vilely wrecked, because
A single god is angry; we endure
This treachery and violence, whereby
Wide seas divide us from th' Hesperian shore.
Is this what piety receives? Or thus
Doth Heaven's decree restore our fallen
    thrones?"
Smiling reply, the Sire of gods and men,
With such a look as clears the skies of storm,
Chastely his daughter kissed, and thus spake
    on:
"Let Cythera cast her fears away!
Irrevocably blest the fortunes be
Of thee and thine. Nor shalt thou fail to see
That City, and the proud predestined wall
Encompassing Lavinium. Thyself
Shall starward to the heights of heaven bear
Aeneas the great-hearted. Nothing swerves
My will once uttered. Since such carking cares
Consume thee, I this hour speak freely forth,

And leaf by leaf the book of fate unfold.
Thy son in Italy shall wage vast war
And quell its nations wild; his city-wall
And sacred laws shall be a mighty bond
About his gathered people. Summers three
Shall Latium call him king; and three times
    pass
The winter o'er Rutulia's vanquished hills.
His heir, Ascanius, now Ilus called
(Ilus it was while Ilium's kingdom stood),
Full thirty months shall reign, then move the
    throne
From the Lavinian citadel, and build
For Alba Longa its well-bastioned wall.
Here three full centuries shall Hector's race
Have kingly power; till a priestess queen,
By Mars conceiving, her twin offspring bear;
Then Romulus, wolf-nursed and proudly clad
In tawny wolf-skin mantle, shall receive
The sceptre of his race. He shall uprear
The war-god's citadel and lofty wall,
And on his Romans his own name bestow.
To these I give no bounded times or power,
But empire without end. Yea, even my
    Queen,
Juno, who now chastiseth land and sea
With her dread frown, will find a wiser way,
And at my sovereign side protect and bless
The Romans, masters of the whole round
    world,

Who, clad in peaceful toga, judge mankind.
Such my decree! In lapse of seasons due,
The heirs of Ilium's kings shall bind in chains
Mycenae's glory and Achilles' towers,
And over prostrate Argos sit supreme.
Of Trojan stock illustriously sprung,
Lo, Caesar comes! whose power the ocean
    bounds,
Whose fame, the skies. He shall receive the
    name
Ilus nobly bore, great Julius, he.
Him to the skies, in Orient trophies dight,
Thou shalt with smiles receive; and he, like us,
Shall hear at his own shrines the suppliant
    vow.
Then will the world grow mild; the
    battlesound
Will be forgot; for olden Honor then,
With spotless Vesta, and the brothers twain,
Remus and Romulus, at strife no more,
Will publish sacred laws. The dreadful gates
Whence issueth war, shall with close-jointed
    steel
Be barred impregnably; and prisoned there
The heaven-offending Fury, throned on
    swords,
And fettered by a hundred brazen chains,
Shall belch vain curses from his lips of gore."

FOCUS QUESTIONS

1. *The Aeneid* offered Romans an explanation of their origins. Why would such a myth have been useful? What purpose might it have served?

2. What is Rome's destiny as foretold in *The Aeneid?* What stands in the way of success?

3. Virgil gives us a glimpse of what the Romans thought they were like. What sort of people do the founders of Rome appear to be?

4. Why do you think Virgil chose to tell his story in the form of an epic poem?

5. The links between *The Aeneid* and the works of Homer seem very clear. Why did the Romans want to connect themselves so closely with Homeric legends?

26

The Life of Augustus (ca. 122 C.E.)

SUETONIUS

Gaius Suetonius Tranquillus (ca. 69–122 C.E.) gained fame for his biographies of the first twelve Roman emperors. Born into a knightly family, Suetonius studied but never practiced law. He saw military and diplomatic service before entering the government of the Emperor Hadrian. Suetonius's historical interests shaped his public career, and he soon became the imperial archivist, the director of the Roman libraries, and a cultural advisor to the emperor. In 121 Suetonius rose to the key position of imperial secretary but was dismissed from office for failing to abide by court etiquette. He spent the final year of his life writing biographies.

The Life of Augustus is one of the best known of The Lives of the Twelve Caesars. *It was Suetonius's purpose to provide both a vivid portrayal of his subject as well as an account of the social environment in which Augustus lived.*

In military affairs he made many alterations, introducing some practices entirely new, and reviving others, which had become obsolete. He maintained the strictest discipline among the troops; and would not allow even his lieutenants the liberty to visit their wives, except reluctantly, and in the winter season only. A Roman knight having cut off the thumbs of his two young sons, to render them incapable of serving in the wars, he exposed both him and his estate to public sale. But upon observing the farmers of the revenue very greedy for the purchase, he assigned him to a freedman of his own, that he might send him into the country, and suffer him to retain his freedom. The tenth legion becoming mutinous, he disbanded it with ignominy; and did the same by some others which petulantly demanded their discharge; withholding from them the rewards usually bestowed on those who had served their stated time in the wars. The cohorts which yielded their ground in time of action, he decimated, and fed with barley. Centurions, as well as common

sentinels, who deserted their posts when on guard, he punished with death. For other misdemeanors he inflicted upon them various kinds of disgrace; such as obliging them to stand all day before the praetorium, sometimes in their tunics only, and without their belts, some-times to carry poles ten feet long, or sods of turf.

He was advanced to public offices before the age at which he was legally qualified for them: and to some, also, of a new kind, and for life. He seized the consulship in the twentieth year of his age, quartering his legions in a threatening manner near the city, and sending deputies to demand it for him in the name of the army. When the senate demurred, a centurion, named Cornelius, who was at the head of the chief deputation, throwing back his cloak, and shewing the hilt of his sword, had the presumption to say in the senate-house, "This will make him consul, if ye will not." His second consulship he filled nine years afterwards; his third, after the interval of only one year, and held the same office every year successively until the eleventh. From this

Statue Depicting Augustus as Emperor.

He twice entertained thoughts of restoring the republic; first, immediately after he had crushed Antony, remembering that he had often charged him with being the obstacle to its restoration. The second time was in consequence of a long illness, when he sent for the magistrates and the senate to his own house, and delivered them a particular account of the state of the empire. But reflecting at the same time that it would be both hazardous to himself to return to the condition of a private person, and might be dangerous to the public to have the government placed again under the control of the people, he resolved to keep it in his own hands, whether with the better event or intention, is hard to say. His good intentions he often affirmed in private discourse, and also published an edict, in which it was declared in the following terms: "May it be permitted me to have the happiness of establishing the commonwealth on a safe and sound basis, and thus enjoy the reward of which I am ambitious, that of being celebrated for moulding it into the form best adapted to present circumstances; so that, on my leaving the world, I may carry with me the hope that the foundations which I have laid for its future government, will stand firm and stable."

The city, which was not built in a manner suitable to the grandeur of the empire, and was liable to inundations of the Tiber, as well as to fires, was so much improved under his administration, that he boasted, not without reason, that he "found it of brick, but left it of marble." He also rendered it secure for the time to come against such disasters, as far as could be effected by human foresight. A great number of public buildings were erected by him, the most considerable of which were a forum, containing the temple of Mars the Avenger, the temple of Apollo on the Palatine hill, and the temple of Jupiter Tonans in the capitol. The reason of his building a new forum was the vast increase in the population, and the number of cases to be tried in the courts, for which, the two already existing not affording sufficient space, it was thought necessary to have a third. It was therefore opened for public use before the temple of Mars was completely finished; and a law was passed, that cases

period, although the consulship was frequently offered him, he always declined it, until, after a long interval, not less than seventeen years, he voluntarily stood for the twelfth, and two years after that, for a thirteenth; that he might successively introduce into the forum, on their entering public life, his two sons, Caius and Lucius, while he was invested with the highest office in the state.

He accepted of the tribunitian power for life, but more than once chose a colleague in that office for ten years successively. He also had the supervision of morality and observance of the laws, for life, but without the title of censor; yet he thrice took a census of the people, the first and third time with a colleague, but the second by himself.

should be tried, and judges chosen by lot, in that place.

He corrected many ill practices, which, to the detriment of the public, had either survived the licentious habits of the late civil wars, or else originated in the long peace. Bands of robbers showed themselves openly, completely armed, under colour of self-defence; and in different parts of the country, travellers, freemen and slaves without distinction, were forcibly carried off, and kept to work in the houses of correction. Several associations were formed under the specious name of a new college, which banded together for the perpetration of all kinds of villainy. The bandits he quelled by establishing posts of soldiers in suitable stations for the purpose; the houses of correction were subjected to a strict superintendence; all associations, those only excepted which were of ancient standing, and recognised by the laws, were dissolved. He burnt all the notes of those who had been a long time in arrear with the treasury, as being the principal source of vexatious suits and prosecutions. Places in the city claimed by the public, where the right was doubtful, he adjudged to the actual possessors. He struck out of the list of criminals the names of those over whom prosecutions had been long impending, where nothing further was intended by the informers than to gratify their own malice, by seeing their enemies humiliated; laying it down as a rule, that if any one chose to renew a prosecution, he should incur the risk of the punishment which he sought to inflict. And that crimes might not escape punishment, nor business be neglected by delay, he ordered the courts to sit during the thirty days which were spent in celebrating honorary games.

He was desirous that his friends should be great and powerful in the state, but have no exclusive privileges, or be exempt from the laws which governed others. When Asprenas Nonius, an intimate friend of his, was tried upon a charge of administering poison at the instance of Cassius Severus, he consulted the senate for their opinion what was his duty under the circumstances: "For," said he, "I am afraid, lest, if I should stand by him in the cause, I may be supposed to screen a guilty man; and if I do not, to desert and prejudge a friend." With the unanimous concurrence, therefore, of the senate,

he took his seat amongst his advocates for several hours, but without giving him the benefit of speaking to character, as was usual. He likewise appeared for his clients; as on behalf of Scutarius, an old soldier of his, who brought an action for slander. He never relieved any one from prosecution but in a single instance, in the case of a man who had given information of the conspiracy of Muraena; and that he did only by prevailing upon the accuser, in open court, to drop his prosecution.

The whole body of the people, upon a sudden impulse, and with unanimous consent, offered him the title of Father of His Country. It was announced to him first at Antium, by a deputation from the people, and upon his declining the honour, they repeated their offer on his return to Rome, in a full theatre, when they were crowned with laurel. The senate soon afterwards adopted the proposal, not in the way of acclamation or decree, but by commissioning M. Messala, in an unanimous vote, to compliment him with it in the following terms: "With hearty wishes for the happiness and prosperity of yourself and your family, Caesar Augustus, (for we think we thus most effectually pray for the lasting welfare of the state), the senate, in agreement with the Roman people, salute you by the title of Father of Your Country." To this compliment Augustus replied, with tears in his eyes, in these words (for I give them exactly as I have done those of Messala): "Having now arrived at the summit of my wishes, O Conscript Fathers, what else have I to beg of the Immortal Gods, but the continuance of this your affection for me to the last moments of my life?"

In person he was handsome and graceful, through every period of his life. But he was negligent in his dress; and so careless about dressing his hair, that he usually had it done in great haste, by several barbers at a time. His beard he sometimes clipped, and sometimes shaved; and either read or wrote during the operation. His countenance, either when discoursing or silent, was so calm and serene, that a Gaul of the first rank declared amongst his friends, that he was so softened by it, as to be restrained from throwing him down a precipice, in his passage over the Alps, when he had been admitted to approach him, under pretence of conferring with him. His eyes were bright and piercing; and he was willing it should be thought that there was something of a divine vigour in them. He was likewise not a little pleased to see people, upon his looking stead-fastly at them, lower their countenances, as if the sun shone in their eyes. But in his old age, he saw very imperfectly with his left eye. His teeth were thin set, small and scaly, his hair a little curled, and inclining to a yellow colour. His eyebrows met; his ears were small, and he had an aquiline nose. His complexion was betwixt brown and fair; his stature but low; though Julius Marathus, his freedman, says he was five feet and nine inches in height. This, however, was so much concealed by the just proportion of his limbs, that it was only perceivable upon comparison with some taller person standing by him.

He expired in the same room in which his father Octavius had died, when the two Sextus's, Pompey and Apuleius, were consuls, upon the fourteenth of the calends of September [the 19th August], at the ninth hour of the day, being seventy-six years of age, wanting only thirty-five days. His remains were carried by the magistrates of the municipal towns and colonies, from Nola to Bovillae, and in the night-time, because of the season of the year. During the intervals, the body lay in some basilica, or great temple, of each town. At Bovillae it was met by the Equestrian Order, who carried it to the city, and deposited it in the vestibule of his own house. The senate proceeded with so much zeal in the arrangement of his funeral,

and paying honour to his memory, that, amongst several other proposals, some were for having the funeral procession made through the triumphal gate, preceded by the image of Victory which is in the senate-house, and the children of highest rank and of both sexes singing the funeral dirge. Others proposed, that on the day of the funeral, they should lay aside their gold rings, and wear rings of iron; and others, that his bones should be collected by the priests of the principal colleges. One likewise pro posed to transfer the name of August to September, because he was born in the latter, but died in the former. Another moved, that the whole period of time, from his birth to his death, should be called the Augustan age, and be inserted in the calendar under that title. But at last it was judged proper to be moderate in the honours paid to his memory. Two funeral orations were pronounced in his praise, one before the temple of Julius, by Tiberius; and the other before the rostra, under the old shops, by Drusus, Tiberius's son. The body was then carried upon the shoulders of senators into the Campus Martius, and there burnt. A man of praetorian rank affirmed upon oath, that he saw his spirit ascend from the funeral pile to heaven. The most distinguished persons of the equestrian order, bare-footed, and with their tunics loose, gathered up his relics, and deposited them in the mausoleum, which had been built in his sixth consulship between the Flaminian Way and the bank of the Tiber; at which time likewise he gave the groves and walks about it for the use of the people.

FOCUS QUESTIONS

1. What did Augustus accomplish as emperor?
2. How did Augustus attempt to avoid appearing as a dictator? Can you cite an example from Suetonius's *Life?*
3. Would an author such as Suetonius be limited in his freedom to write a biography of a Roman emperor? What factors might he have

considered in assessing Augustus's accomplishments?

4. What skills did Augustus need to manipulate the extremely complex Roman political system? How did he manage?
5. Was Augustus's regime appreciated? How did Rome show its gratitude toward the emperor?

saw his spirit from heaven

27

The Sermon on the Mount (ca. 28–35 C.E.)

The Sermon on the Mount was delivered by Jesus some time after the beginning of his ministry in 27 C.E. and was recorded by the Apostle Matthew. It is a classic example of Jesus's method of teaching, but more importantly, its message lies at the heart of the religion that he founded. Unlike most teachers and prophets of his day, Jesus did not teach in a synagogue; rather, he brought his message directly to the people by traveling to various centers of population, where he would preach in the open air. Thus the setting of the Sermon on the Mount, *while unusual in the context of his contemporaries, was typical of Jesus's style.*

The message in the Sermon *is set firmly within the Jewish tradition. Jesus urges his listeners to a commitment to righteousness, which he defines with poignant simplicity.*

Then Jesus was led up by the Spirit into the wilderness to be tempted by the devil. And he fasted forty days and forty nights, and afterward he was hungry. And the tempter came and said to him, "If you are the Son of God, command these stones to become loaves of bread." But he answered, "It is written,

'Man shall not live by bread alone, but by every word that proceeds from the mouth of God.'"

Then the devil took him to the holy city, and set him on the pinnacle of the temple, and said to him. "If you are the Son of God, throw yourself down; for it is written,

'He will give his angels charge of you,' and 'On their hands they will bear you up, lest you strike your foot against a stone.'"

Jesus said to him, "Again it is written, 'You shall not tempt the Lord your God.'" Again, the devil took him to a very high mountain, and showed him all the kingdoms of the world and the glory of them; and he said to him, "All these I will give you, if you will fall down and worship me." Then Jesus said to him, "Begone, Satan! for it is written,

'You shall worship the Lord your God and him only shall you serve.'"   *monotheistic*

Then the devil left him, and behold, angels came and ministered to him.

From that time Jesus began to preach, saying, "Repent, for the kingdom of heaven is at hand."

As he walked by the Sea of Galilee, he saw two brothers, Simon who is called Peter and Andrew his brother, casting a net into the sea; for they were fishermen. And he said to them, "Follow me, and I will make you fishers of men." Immediately they left their nets and followed him. And going on from there he saw two other brothers, James the son of Zebedee and John his brother, in the boat with Zebedee their father, mending their nets, and he called them. Immediately they left the boat and their father, and followed him.

And he went about all Galilee, teaching in their synagogues and preaching the gospel of the kingdom and healing every disease and every infirmity among the people. So his fame spread throughout all Syria, and they brought him all the sick, those afflicted with various diseases and pains, demoniacs, epileptics, and paralytics, and he healed them. And great crowds followed him from Galilee and the Decapolis and Jerusalem and Judea and from beyond the Jordan.

Seeing the crowds, he went up on the mountain, and when he sat down his disciples came to him. And he opened his mouth and taught them, saying:

"Blessed are the poor in spirit, for theirs is the kingdom of heaven.

"Blessed are those who mourn, for they shall be comforted.

"Blessed are the meek, for they shall inherit the earth. _leaders - show humility_

"Blessed are those who hunger and thirst for righteousness, for they shall be satisfied.

"Blessed are the merciful, for they shall obtain mercy.

"Blessed are the pure in heart, for they shall see God.

"Blessed are the peacemakers, for they shall be called sons of God.

"Blessed are those who are persecuted for righteousness' sake, for theirs is the kingdom of heaven.

"Blessed are you when men revile you and persecute you and utter all kinds of evil against you falsely on my account. Rejoice and be glad, for your reward is great in heaven, for so men persecuted the prophets who were before you.

"You are the salt of the earth; but if salt has lost its taste, how shall its saltness be restored? It is no longer good for anything except to be thrown out and trodden under foot by men. _leaders - treat the ppl better_

#2 "You are the light of the world. A city set on a hill cannot be hid. Nor do men light a lamp and put it under a bushel, but on a stand, and it gives light to all in the house. Let your light so shine before men, that they may see your good works and give glory to your Father who is in heaven.

"Think not that I have come to abolish the law and the prophets; I have come not to abolish them but to fulfill them. For truly, I say to you, till heaven and earth pass away, not an iota, not a dot, will pass from the law until all is accomplished. Whoever then relaxes one of the least of these commandments and teaches men so, shall be called least in the kingdom of heaven; but he who does them and teaches them shall be called great in the kingdom of heaven. For I tell you, unless your righteousness exceeds that of the scribes and Pharisees, you will never enter the kingdom of heaven.

"You have heard that it was said to the men of old, 'You shall not kill; and whoever kills shall be liable to judgment.' But I say to you that every one who is angry with his brother shall be liable to judgment; whoever insults his brother shall be liable to the council, and whoever says, 'You fool!' shall be liable to the hell of fire. So if you are offering your gift at the altar, and there remember that your brother has something against you, leave your gift there before the altar and go; first be reconciled to your brother, and then come and offer your gift. Make friends quickly with your accuser, while you are going with him to court, lest your accuser hand you over to the judge, and the judge to the guard, and you be put in prison; truly, I say to you, you will never get out till you have paid the last penny. _It is not just the action - the thought._

"You have heard that it was said, 'You shall not commit adultery.' But I say to you that every one #1 who looks at a woman lustfully has already committed adultery with her in his heart. _harder to do_

"If your right eye causes you to sin, pluck it out and throw it away; it is better that you lose one of your members than that your whole body be thrown into hell. And if your right hand causes you to sin, cut it off and throw it away; it is better that you lose one of your members than that your whole body go into hell.

"It was also said, 'Whoever divorces his wife, let him give her a certificate of divorce.' But I say to you that every one who divorces his wife, except on the ground of unchastity, makes her an adulteress; and whoever marries a divorced woman commits adultery.

"Again you have heard that it was said to the men of old, 'You shall not swear falsely, but shall perform to the Lord what you have sworn.' But I say to you, Do not swear at all, either by heaven, for it is the throne of God, or by the earth, for it is his footstool, or by Jerusalem, for it is the city of the great King. And do not swear by your head, for you cannot make one hair white or black. Let what you say be simply 'Yes' or 'No'; anything more than this comes from evil.

"You have heard that it was said, 'An eye for an eye and a tooth for a tooth.' But I say to you, Do not resist one who is evil. But if any one strikes you on the right cheek, turn to him the other also; and if any one would sue you and take your coat, let him have your cloak as well; and if any one forces you to go one mile, go with him two miles. Give to him who begs from you, and do not refuse him who would borrow from you.

"You have heard that it was said, 'You shall love your neighbor and hate your enemy.' But I say to you, Love your enemies and pray for those who persecute you, so that you may be sons of your Father who is in heaven; for he makes his sun rise on the evil and on the good, and sends rain on the just and on the unjust. For if you love those who love you, what reward have you? Do not even the tax collectors do the same? And if you salute only your brethren, what more are you doing than others? Do not even the Gentiles do the same? You, therefore, must be perfect, as your heavenly Father is perfect.

FOCUS QUESTIONS

1. The *Sermon on the Mount* was written down and preserved for later generations, but it had originally been delivered orally. How might the transformation of the spoken to the written word affect the impact of the original message?

2. How does the *Sermon* resemble earlier expressions of the Jewish moral tradition?

3. How does Jesus elaborate on the Hebrew law?

4. To whom is Jesus's message principally directed? Is it to the rich and powerful or the humble? What is his advice?

5. Jesus taught his message through sermons, but he also demonstrated special powers. How did he do this?

PART II ✳ Traditional Societies

Africa and the Muslim World

Mansa Musa. Mansa Musa (1312–1337), king of the West African state of Mali, was one of the richest and most powerful rulers of his day. During his famous pilgrimage to Mecca, he arrived in Cairo with a hundred camels laden with gold and gave away so much gold that its value depreciated there for several years. His fame spread to Europe as well, evidenced by this Spanish map of 1375, which depicts Mansa Musa seated on his throne in Mali, holding an impressive gold nugget.

FOCUS QUESTIONS

1. This fourteenth-century Spanish map depicts Mansa Musa, Muslim ruler of Mali. What about the illustration indicates Mansa Musa's greatness?

2. Like many early modern Muslim rulers, Mansa Musa tolerated a non-Muslim majority within the state. How did this affect foreign perceptions of the state?

3. Mansa Musa built mosques and Islamic universities, established Timbuktu as one of the greatest centers of learning in the fourteenth-century world, and made Mali famous by his opulent pilgrimage to Mecca. How was Mali's increased stature related to Mansa Musa's Islam?

4. In the fourteenth century, the Islamic and Arabic influences in Spain were waning. How does this map reflect the increasing Christianization and latinization of Spain?

28

Code (529–565 C.E.)

JUSTINIAN I

Justinian I (483–565) began life as a peasant, although his uncle Justin, born a swineherd, had already become a Byzantine general. Justin ultimately rose to become emperor in 518, and, as he had no children of his own, he brought his nephew Justinian to Constantinople to be groomed as his successor. Justinian was named emperor in 527 only a few months before his uncle died. Justinian's rule was characterized by his desire to expand the borders of his empire and to reform its civil administration, but he was more successful as a reformer than a conqueror. He undertook a series of governmental reforms, began a public works program, and finally codified Byzantine law.

The Justinian Code was compiled at the emperor's command between 529 and 565. The state of Roman and Byzantine law had grown increasingly chaotic over the centuries, with a vast accumulation of contradictory laws and statues. The Code was designed to remove these anomalies by examining every known law to reduce duplication and contradiction. Teams of lawyers worked for decades on the project, and the result surpassed even the most optimistic hopes of the emperor. The Code formed the basis of European law for centuries. The section reproduced here relates to family law and covers marriage, divorce, and the responsibilities of parents and children.

FORMATION OF MARRIAGE

Marriage is the union of a man and a woman, a partnership for life involving divine as well as human law.

Marriage cannot take place unless everyone involved consents, that is, those who are being united and those in whose power they are.

According to Pomponius, if I have a grandson by one son and a granddaughter by another who are both in my power, my authority alone will be enough to allow them to marry, and this is correct.

A girl who was less than twelve years old when she married will not be a lawful wife until she reaches that age while living with her husband.

Where a grandson marries, his father must also consent: but if a granddaughter gets married, the consent and authority of the grand-father will suffice. Insanity prevents marriage being contracted, because consent is required; but once validly contracted, it does not invalidate the marriage.

When the relationship of brother and sister arises because of adoption, it is an impediment to marriage while the adoption lasts. So I will be able to marry a girl whom my father adopted and then emancipated. Similarly, if she is kept in his power and I am emancipated, we can be married. It is advisable, then, for someone who wishes to adopt his son-in-law to emancipate his daughter-in-law and for someone who wished to adopt his daughter-in-law to emancipate his son. We are not allowed to marry our paternal or maternal aunts or paternal or maternal great-aunts although paternal and maternal great-aunts are related in the fourth degree. Again, we are not allowed to marry a paternal aunt or great-aunt, even though they are related to us by adoption.

People who wrongfully prevent children in their power from marrying, or who refuse to provide a dowry for them can be forced by proconsuls and provincial governors to arrange marriages and provide dowries for them. Those who do not try to arrange marriages are held to prevent them.

Where he marries someone because his father forces him to do so and he would not have married her if the choice had been his, the marriage will nevertheless be valid, because marriage cannot take place without the consent of the parties; he is held to have chosen this course of action.

The *lex Papia* provides that all freeborn men, apart from senators and their children, can marry freedwomen.

Living with a freewoman implies marriage, not concubinage, as long as she does not make money out of prostitution.

An emancipated son can marry without his father's consent, and any son he has will be his heir.

Women accused of adultery cannot marry during the lifetime of their husbands, even before conviction.

Women who live in a shameful way and make money out of prostitution, even where it is not done openly, are held in disgrace. If a woman lives as a concubine with anyone other than her patron, I would say that she lacks the character of the mother of a household.

As far as marriages are concerned, it is always necessary to consider not just what is lawful but also what is decent. If the daughter, granddaughter, or great-granddaughter of a senator marries a freedman or someone who was an actor, or whose father or mother were actors, the marriage will be void.

DIVORCES AND REPUDIATIONS

Marriage is dissolved by the divorce, death, captivity, or other kind of slavery of either of the parties.

The word "divorce" derives from either the diversity of views it involves or because people who dissolve their marriage go in different directions. Where repudiation, that is, renunciation, is involved, these words are used: "Keep your things to yourself": or "Look after your own things." It is agreed that in order to end betrothals a renunciation must be made. Here the established words are: "I do not accept your conditions." It makes no difference whether the repudiation is made in the presence of the other party.

A true divorce does not take place unless an intention to remain apart permanently is present. So things said or done in anger are not effective until the parties show by their persistence that they are an indication of their considered opinion. So where repudiation takes place in anger and the wife returns shortly afterward, she is not held to have divorced her husband.

Julian asks in the eighteenth book of his *Digest* whether an insane woman can repudiate her husband or be repudiated by him. He writes that an insane woman can be repudiated, because she is in the same position as a person who does not know of the repudiation. But she could not repudiate her husband because of her madness, and her curator cannot do this either but her father can repudiate for her. He would not have dealt with repudiation here unless it was established that the marriage was to continue. This opinion seems to me to be correct.

The wives of people who fall into enemy hands can still be considered married women only in that other men cannot marry them hastily. Generally, as long as it is certain that a husband who is in captivity is still alive, his wife does not have the right to contract another marriage, unless she herself has given some ground for repudiation. But if it is not certain whether the husband in captivity is alive or has died, then if five years have passed since his capture, his wife has the right to marry again so that the first marriage will be held to have been dissolved with the consent of the parties and each of the parties will have their rights withdrawn. The same rule applies where a husband stays at home and his wife is captured.

Where someone who has given the other party written notice of divorce regrets having done this and the notice is served in ignorance of the change of mind, the marriage is held to remain valid, unless the person who receives the notice is aware of the change of mind and wants to end the marriage himself. Then the marriage will be dissolved by the person who received the notice.

THE RECOGNITION OF CHILDREN

It is not just a person who smothers a child who is held to kill it but also the person who abandons it, denies it food, or puts it on show in public places to excite pity which he himself does not have.

If anyone asks his children to support him or children seek support from their father, a judge should look into the question. Should a father be forced to support only children in his power or should he also support children who have been emancipated or have become independent in some other way? I think it is better to say that even where children are not in power, they must be supported by their parents and they, on the other hand, must support their parents. Must we support only our fathers, our paternal grandfathers, paternal great-grandfathers, and other relatives of the male sex, or are we compelled to support our mothers and other relatives in the maternal line? It is better to say that in each case the judge should intervene so as to give relief to the necessities of some of them and the infirmity of others. Since this obligation is based on justice and affection between blood relations, the judge should balance the claims of each person involved. The same is true in the maintenance of children by their parents. So we force a mother to support her illegitimate children and them to support her. The deified Pius also says that a maternal grandfather is compelled to support his grandchildren. He also stated in a rescript that a father must support his daughter, if it is proved in court that he was really her father. But where a son can support himself, judges should decide not to compel the provision of maintenance for him. So the Emperor Pius stated: "The appropriate judges before whom you will appear must order you to be supported by your father according to his means, provided that where you claim you are a tradesman, it is your ill health which makes you incapable of supporting yourself by your own labor." If a father denies that the person seeking support is his son and so maintains that he need not provide it, or where a son denies that the person seeking support is his father, the judges must decide this summarily. If it is established that the person is a son or a father, they must order him to be supported. But if this is not proved, they should not award maintenance. Remember if the judges declare that support must be provided, this does not affect the truth of the matter; for they did not declare that the person was the man's son, but only that he must be supported. If anyone refuses to provide support, the judges must determine the maintenance according to his means. If he fails to provide this, he can be forced to comply with the judgment by the seizing of his property in execution and selling it. The judges must also decide whether a relative or a father has any good reason for not supporting his children.

CONCUBINES

Can a woman living in concubinage leave her patron against his will and either marry someone else or become his concubine? I think that a concubine should not be granted the right to marry if she leaves her patron without his consent, since it is more respectable for a freedwoman to be her patron's concubine rather than the mother of a family. I agree with the view of Atilicinus that it is only women who have not been debauched that can be kept as concubines without fear of committing a crime. Where a man keeps a woman who has been convicted of adultery as a concubine, I do not think the *lex Julia* on adultery will apply, although it will if he marries her. If a woman has been her patron's concubine and then becomes his son's or grandson's or vice versa, I do not think she is behaving properly, since a relationship of this kind is almost criminal. So this sort of bad behavior is prohibited. Clearly, a man can keep a concubine of any age unless she is less than twelve years old.

If a patron who has a freedwoman as his concubine becomes insane, it is more humane to say that she is still his concubine.

Another person's freedwoman can be kept as a concubine as well as a freeborn woman, especially where she is of low birth or has been a prostitute. But if a man would rather have a freeborn woman with respectable background as his concubine, he will not be allowed to do this unless he clearly states the position in front of witnesses. But it will be necessary for him to marry her, or if he refuses, to commit debauchery with her. A person does not commit adultery by having a concubine; for because concubinage exists because of statute law, it is not penalized by statute.

A man can have a concubine in the province where he holds office.

FOCUS QUESTIONS

1. What does the *Code* reveal about the status of women in Justinian's time?

2. Upon what grounds could a divorce be procured under the *Code?*

3. The law has a great deal to say about the parent-child relationship. Could you make some generalization about parents and children in Byzantium from the *Code?*

4. The *Code* talks about concubines and wives alike. How were they different? What rights did each have?

5. Judging from the *Code's* discussion of marriage, could you offer any generalizations about the institution in Justinian's time?

29

Secret History (ca. 560 C.E.)

PROCOPIUS

Procopius was a Byzantine civil servant and historian whose works provide important information about the reign of the Emperor Justinian. Procopius was probably born in Palestine sometime between 490 and 510. After his early education, he sought a career in civil service and migrated to Constantinople, then the center of the Roman Empire. He served on a general's staff and was thus able to travel to Persia, Italy, and Africa, so his experience of Byzantine administration was extensive and firsthand. He had apparently returned to Constantinople by 540, but there is no trace of him thereafter.

Procopius wrote several official histories during his career, of which the most important is an account of the military campaigns of Justinian's reign, entitled On the Wars. *He also left a description of Justinian's public works project called* The Buildings. *His most famous work, however, was published after his death. This was the* Secret History, *a highly personal account of Justinian and the Empress Theodora. Whether Procopius's point of view was unique or common among Byzantine civil servants remains an open question.*

I think this is as good a time as any to describe the personal appearance of the man. Now in physique he was neither tall nor short, but of average height; not thin, but moderately plump; his face was round, and not bad looking, for he had good color, even when he fasted for two days. To make a long description short, he much resembled Domitian, Vespasian's son.

Now such was Justinian in appearance; but his character was something I could not fully describe. For he was at once villainous and amenable; as people say colloquially, a moron. He was never truthful with anyone, but always guileful in what he said and did, yet easily hoodwinked by any who wanted to deceive him. His nature was an unnatural mixture of folly and wickedness. What in olden times a peripatetic philosopher said was also true of him, that opposite qualities combine in a man as in the mixing of colors. I will try to portray him, however, insofar as I can fathom his complexity.

This Emperor, then, was deceitful, devious, false, hypocritical, two-faced, cruel, skilled in dissembling his thought, never moved to tears by either joy or pain, though he could summon them artfully at will when the occasion demanded, a liar always, not only offhand, but in writing, and when he swore sacred oaths to his subjects in their very hearing. Then he would immediately break his agreements and pledges, like the vilest of slaves, whom indeed only the fear of torture drives to confess their perjury. A faithless friend, he was a treacherous enemy, insane for murder and plunder, quarrelsome and revolutionary, easily led to anything evil, but never willing to listen to good counsel, quick to plan mischief and carry it out, but finding even the hearing of anything good distasteful to his ears.

How could anyone put Justinian's ways into words? These and many even worse vices were disclosed in him as in no other mortal: nature seemed to have taken the wickedness of all other men combined and planted it in this man's soul. And besides this, he was too prone to listen to accusations; and too quick to punish. For he decided such cases without full examination, naming the punishment when he had heard only the accuser's side of the matter. Without hesitation he wrote decrees for the plundering of countries, sacking of cities, and slavery of whole nations, for no cause whatever. So that if one wished to take all the calamities which had befallen the Romans before this time and weigh them against his crimes, I think it would be found that more men had been murdered by this single man than in all previous history.

He had no scruples about appropriating other people's property, and did not even think any excuse necessary, legal or illegal, for confiscating what did not belong to him. And when it was his, he was more than ready to squander it in insane display, or give it as an unnecessary bribe to the barbarians. In short, he neither held on to any money himself nor let anyone else keep any: as if his reason were not avarice, but jealousy of those who had riches. Driving all wealth from the country of the Romans in this manner, he became the cause of universal poverty.

Now this was the character of Justinian, so far as I can portray it.

As soon as Justinian came into power he turned everything upside down. Whatever had before been forbidden by law he now introduced into the government, while he revoked all established customs: as if he had been given the robes of an Emperor on the condition he would turn everything topsy-turvy. Existing offices he abolished, and invented new ones for the management of public affairs. He did the same thing to the laws and to the regulations of the army; and his reason was not any improvement of justice or any advantage, but simply that everything might be new and named after himself. And whatever was beyond his power to abolish, he renamed after himself anyway.

Of the plundering of property or the murder of men, no weariness ever overtook him. As soon as he had looted all the houses of the wealthy, he looked around for others; meanwhile throwing away the spoils of his previous robberies in subsidies to barbarians or senseless building extravagances. And when he had ruined perhaps myriads in this mad looting, he immediately sat down to plan how he could do likewise to others in even greater number.

As the Romans were now at peace with all the world and he had no other means of satisfying his lust for slaughter, he set the barbarians all to fighting each other. And for no reason at all he sent for the Hun chieftains, and with idiotic magnanimity gave them large sums of money, alleging he did this to secure their friendship. These Huns, as soon as they had got this money, sent it together with their soldiers to others of their chieftains, with the word to make inroads into the land of the Emperor: so that they might collect further tribute from him, to buy them off in a second peace. Thus the Huns enslaved the Roman Empire, and were paid by the Emperor to keep on doing it.

This encouraged still others of them to rob the poor Romans; and after their pillaging, they too were further rewarded by the gracious Emperor. In this way all the Huns, for when it was not one tribe of them it was another, continuously overran and laid waste the Empire. For the barbarians were led by many different chieftains, and the war, thanks to Justinian's senseless generosity, was thus endlessly protracted. Consequently no place, mountain or cave, or any other spot in Roman territory, during this time remained uninjured; and many regions were pillaged more than five times.

These misfortunes, and those that were caused by the Medes, Saracens, Slavs, Antes, and the rest of the barbarians, I described in my previous works. But, as I said in the preface to this narrative, the real cause of these calamities remained to be told here.

Moreover, while he was encouraging civil strife and frontier warfare to confound the Romans, with only one thought in his mind, that the earth should run red with human blood and he might acquire more and more booty, he invented a new means of murdering his subjects. Now among the Christians in the entire Roman Empire, there are many with dissenting doctrines, which are called heresies by the established church: such as those of the Montanists and Sabbatians, and whatever others cause the minds of men to wander from the true path.

All of these beliefs he ordered to be abolished, and their place taken by the orthodox dogma: threatening, among the punishments for disobedience, loss of the heretic's right to will property to his children or other relatives.

Now the churches of these so-called heretics, especially those belonging to the Arian dissenters, were almost incredibly wealthy. Neither all the Senate put together nor the greatest other unit of the Roman Empire, had anything in property comparable to that of these churches. For their gold and silver treasures, and stores of precious stones, were beyond telling or numbering: they owned mansions and whole villages, land all over the world, and everything else that is counted as wealth among men.

As none of the previous Emperors had molested these churches, many men, even those of the orthodox faith, got their livelihood by working on their estates. But the Emperor Justinian, in confiscating these properties, at the same time took away what for many people had been their only means of earning a living.

Agents were sent everywhere to force whomever they chanced upon to renounce the faith of their fathers. This, which seemed impious to rustic people, caused them to rebel against those who gave them such an order. Thus many perished at the hands of the persecuting faction, and others did away with themselves, foolishly thinking this the holier course of two evils; but most of them by far quitted the land of their fathers, and fled the country. The Montanists, who dwelt in Phrygia, shut themselves up in their churches, set them on fire, and ascended to glory in the flames. And thenceforth the whole Roman Empire was a scene of massacre and flight.

A similar law was then passed against the Samaritans, which threw Palestine into an indescribable turmoil. Those, indeed, who lived in my own Caesarea and in the other cities, deciding it silly to suffer harsh treatment over a ridiculous trifle of dogma, took the name of Christians in exchange for the one they had borne before, by which precaution they were able to avoid the perils of the new law. The most reputable and better class of these citizens, once they had adopted this religion, decided to remain faithful to it; the majority, however, as if in spite for having not voluntarily, but by the compulsion of law, abandoned the belief of their fathers, soon slipped away into the Manichean sect and what is known as polytheism.

The country people!, however, banded together and determined to take arms against the Emperor: choosing as their candidate for the throne a bandit named Julian, son of Sabarus. And for a time they held their own against the imperial troops; but finally, defeated in battle, were cut down, together with their leader. Ten myriads of men are said to have perished in this engagement, and the most fertile country on earth thus became destitute of farmers. To the Christian owners of these lands, the affair brought great hardship: for while their profits from these properties were annihilated, they had to pay heavy annual taxes on them to the Emperor for the rest of their lives, and secured no remission of this burden.

Next he turned his attention to those called Gentiles, torturing their persons and plundering their lands. Of this group, those who decided to become nominal Christians saved themselves for the time being; but it was not long before these, too, were caught performing libations and sacrifices and other unholy rites. And how he treated the Christians shall be told hereafter.

After this he passed a law prohibiting pederasty: a law pointed not at offenses committed after this decree, but at those who could be convicted of having practised the vice in the past. The conduct of the prosecution was utterly illegal. Sentence was passed when there was no accuser: the word of one man or boy, and that perhaps a slave, compelled against his will to bear witness against his owner, was defined as sufficient evidence. Those who were convicted were castrated and then exhibited in a public parade. At the start, this persecution was directed only at those who were of the Green party, were reputed to be especially wealthy, or had otherwise aroused jealousy.

The Emperor's malice was also directed against the astrologer. Accordingly, magistrates appointed to punish thieves also abused the astrologers, for no other reason than that they belonged to this profession: whipping them on the back and parading them on camels throughout the city, though they were old men, and in every way respectable, with no reproach against them except that they studied the science of the stars while living in such a city.

Consequently there was a constant stream of emigration not only to the land of the barbarians but to places farthest remote from the Romans; and in every country and city one could see crowds of foreigners. For in order to escape persecution, each would lightly exchange his native land for another, as if his own country had been taken by an enemy.

FOCUS QUESTIONS

1. What are the emperor's principal failings, according to Procopius?

2. Do Justinian's character flaws affect his ability to rule?

3. Justinian is criticized for his reforms by Procopius, a professional civil servant. If the emperor were to speak in his own defense, how might he answer the charges?

4. Why does Justinian's foreign policy fail? What do you think he was trying to accomplish?

5. Procopius presents us with an extremely biased picture of Justinian. Can such an unfair portrayal teach us anything of value about Justinian?

6. What does Procopius's bias tell us about him? Could you say something about his own views, given the picture he gives us of Justinian?

30

The Koran (7th century C.E.)

The Koran is the Holy Book of Islam. Revealed by God to Muhammad (ca. 570–632) over the course of two decades beginning in 610, it is the foundation upon which Islam was built. Believers consider the book to be literally true in all respects and to be the final authority on all moral and legal questions.

Roughly the same length as the New Testament, the Koran contains many references to both the Jewish and Christian traditions. It recognizes the contribution of biblical figures such as Noah and Moses and the importance of Jesus as a prophet. Nevertheless, it contains much that is unique. The Koran emphasizes the singularity of God as well as His divine plan. It also includes a system of ritual laws and ethics. Each man, for example, is allowed to marry no more than four wives. Followers are presented with a strict moral and dietary code and are required to make a pilgrimage to Mecca, the center of Islam. They are also required to treat all persons, believers and infidels, with compassion.

In the name of God, the most merciful and compassionate.

Praise be to God, the Lord of the worlds;
The most merciful, the compassionate;
The king of the day of Judgment.
Thee do we worship, and of Thee do we beg
assistance.
Direct us on the right way,
The way of those to whom Thou has been gracious; not of those against whom Thou art angry, nor of those who go astray.

In the name of God, the most merciful and compassionate.

Praise the name of thy Lord, the Most High, Who hath created and completely formed His creatures: Who determineth them to various ends, and directeth them to attain the same, Who produceth the pastures for cattle, and afterwards rendereth the same dry stubble of a dusky hue.

God will enable thee to rehearse His revelations, and thou shalt not forget any part thereof, except what God shall please, for He knoweth that which is manifest, and that which is hidden. And God will facilitate unto thee the most easy way. Therefore admonish thy people, if thy admonition shall be profitable unto them.

Whosoever feareth God, he will be admonished: but the most wretched unbeliever will turn away from it; who shall be cast to be broiled in the greater fire of hell, wherein he shall not die, neither shall he live.

Now hath he attained felicity who is purified by faith, and who remembereth the name of his Lord, and prayeth. But ye prefer this present life: yet the life to come is better, and more durable.

Verily this is written in the ancient Books, the Books of Abraham and Moses.

God! There is no god but Him, the Living, the Self-subsisting: He hath sent down unto thee the Book of the Koran with truth, confirming that which was revealed before it; For He had formerly sent down the Law and the Gospel, a guidance unto men; and He had also sent down the Salvation.

Koran Cover with Decorative Writing. During Muhammed's lifetime, scribes were already collecting and transferring the suras, or chapters, of the Koran onto parchment. The caliph Umar was responsible for codifying these. This Koran cover dates from the thirteenth century and is an outstanding example of the fine Arabic calligraphy for which Islamic artists were renowned.

Verily those who believe not the signs of God shall suffer a grievous punishment; for God is mighty, able to revenge.

Surely nothing is hidden from God, of that which is on earth, or in the heavens; it is He who formeth you in the wombs, as He pleaseth; there is no God but Him, the Mighty, the Wise.

It is He who hath sent down unto thee the Book, wherein are some verses clear to be understood: they are the foundation of the Book; and others are parabolical. But they whose hearts are perverse will follow that which is parabolical therein, out of love of schism, and a desire of the interpretation thereof, yet none knoweth the interpretation thereof, except God. But they who are well grounded in knowledge say, We believe therein, the whole is from our Lord; and none will consider except the prudent.

THE DOCTRINE OF ONE GOD

God! There is no God but Him; the Living, the Self-subsisting: neither slumber nor sleep seizeth Him; to Him belongeth whatsoever is in the heavens, and on earth. Who is he that can intercede with Him, but through His good pleasure? He knoweth that which is past, and that which is to come unto them, and they shall not comprehend anything of His knowledge, but so far as He pleaseth. His throne is extended over the heavens and the earth; and the preservation of both is no burden unto Him. He is the High, the Mighty.

Let there be no compulsion in religion. Now is right direction manifestly distinguished from deceit: whoever therefore shall deny Tagut [Satan] and believe in God, he shall surely take hold on a strong handle, which shall not be broken; God is He who heareth and seeth.

God is the patron of those who believe; He shall lead them out of darkness into light; but as to those who believe not, their patrons are Tagut; they shall lead them from the light into darkness; they shall be the companions of hell fire, they shall remain therein forever.

ALMS TO THE POOR

Who is he that will lend unto God an acceptable loan? For God will double the same unto him, and he shall receive moreover an honorable reward.

Verily as to those who give alms, both men and women, and those who lend unto God an acceptable loan, He will double the same unto them; and they shall moreover receive an honorable reward.

And they who believe in God and His apostles, these are the men of veracity and the witnesses in the presence of their Lord: they shall have their reward and their light. But as to those who believe not, and lie about God's signs; they shall be the companions of hell.

Know ye that this present life is only a play and a vain amusement; and worldly pomp, and the affectation of glory among you, and the multiplying of riches and children, are as the plants nourished by the rain, the springing up whereof delighteth the husbandman; then they wither, so that thou seest the same turn yellow, and at length they become dry stubble. But in the life to come will be a severe punishment for those who covet worldly grandeur; and pardon from God, and favor for those who renounce it: for this present life is no other than a deceitful provision.

Hasten with emulation to obtain pardon from your Lord, and Paradise, the extent whereof equaleth the extent of heaven and earth, prepared for those who believe in God and His apostles. Such is the bounty of God; He will give the same unto whom He pleaseth: and God is endured with great bounty.

It is not righteousness that ye turn your faces in prayer towards the East and the West, but righteousness is of him who believeth in God and the last day, and the angels and the Scriptures, and the prophets; who giveth money for God's sake unto his kindred, and unto orphans, and the needy, and the wayfarer, and those who ask, and for the redemption of captives; who is constant in prayer, and giveth alms; and of those who perform their promises which they have made, and who behave themselves patiently in adversity, and hardships, and in time of violence: these are they who are true, and these are they who fear God.

The Devil threateneth you with poverty, and commandeth you filthy covetousness; but God promiseth you pardon from Himself and abundance: God is Bounteous and Wise. He giveth wisdom unto whom He pleaseth; and he unto whom wisdom is given, hath received much good: but none will consider it, except the wise of heart.

And whatever alms ye shall give, or whatever vow ye shall vow, verily God knoweth it; but the ungodly shall have none to help them. If ye make your alms to appear, it is well; but if ye conceal them, and give them unto the poor, this will be better for you, and will remove some of your sins: and God is well informed of that which ye do.

The guidance of them belongeth not unto thee [O Apostle]; but God guideth whom He pleaseth. The good that ye shall give in alms shall redound unto yourselves; and ye shall not give unless out of desire of seeing the face of God. And what good thing ye shall give in alms, it shall be repaid you, and ye shall not be treated unjustly.

Alms unto the poor who are wholly employed in fighting for the religion of God, and cannot freely travel in the land; the ignorant man thinketh them rich, because of their modesty: thou shalt know them by this mark, they ask not men with importunity; and what good ye shall give them in alms, verily God knoweth it.

They who distribute alms of their substance night and day, in private and in public, shall have their reward with the Lord; on them shall no fear come, neither shall they be grieved.

WINE AND GAMBLING

O true believers! surely wine, and gambling and images, and divining arrows, are an abomination of the work of Satan; therefore avoid them, that ye may prosper.

Satan seeketh to sow dissension and hatred among you, by means of wine and gambling, and to divert you from remembering God, and from prayer; will ye not therefore abstain from them?

Obey God, and obey the Apostle, and take heed to yourselves; but if ye turn back, know that the duty of God's Apostle is only to preach publicly.

On those who believe and do good works, it is no sin that they have tasted wine or gambled before they were forbidden; if they fear God, and believe, and do good works, and shall for the future fear God, and believe, and shall persevere to fear him, and to do good, for God loveth those who do good.

PARADISE

The description of Paradise, which is promised unto the pious: therein are rivers of incorruptible water; and rivers of milk, the taste whereof changeth not; and rivers of wine, pleasant unto those who drink; and rivers of clarified honey. And therein shall they have plenty of all kinds of fruits; and pardon from their Lord. Shall the man for whom these things are prepared, be as they who must dwell forever in hell fire, and will have the boiling water given them to drink, which shall burst their bowels?

They [the righteous] shall repose on couches, the linings thereof shall be of thick silk interwoven with gold: and the fruit of the two gardens shall be near at hand to gather.

Which, therefore, of your Lord's benefits will ye ungratefully deny?

Therein shall be damsels, remaining their eyes from beholding any besides their spouses: whom no man or Jinni shall have touched before them,

Which, therefore, of your Lord's benefits will ye ungratefully deny?

Having complexions like rubies and pearls.

Which, therefore, of your Lord's benefits will ye ungratefully deny?

Shall the reward of good works be any other than good?

Which, therefore, of your Lord's benefits will ye ungratefully deny?

And besides these there shall be two other gardens.

Which, therefore, of your Lord's benefits will ye ungratefully deny?

Of a dark green color.

Which, therefore, of your Lord's benefits will ye ungratefully deny?

In each of them shall be two fountains pouring forth plenty of water.

Which, therefore, of your Lord's benefits will ye ungratefully deny?

In each of them shall be fruits, and palm trees, and pomegranates.

Which, therefore, of your Lord's benefits will ye ungratefully deny?

Therein shall be agreeable and beauteous damsels.

Which, therefore, of your Lord's benefits will ye ungratefully deny?

Having fine black eyes; and kept in pavilions from public view.

Which, therefore, of your Lord's benefits will ye ungratefully deny?

Whom no man shall have touched before their destined spouses, nor any Jinni.

Which, therefore, of your Lord's benefits will ye ungratefully deny?

Therein shall they delight themselves, lying on green cushions and beautiful carpets.

Which, therefore, of your Lord's benefits will ye ungratefully deny?

Blessed be the name of thy Lord, possessed of Glory and Honor!

FOCUS QUESTIONS

1. What are some of the characteristics shared by Islam, Christianity, and Judaism?

2. What is the responsibility of the believer toward the poor?

3. In what way is the Koran a code of conduct for everyday life?

4. What does the Koran teach should be done to the nonbeliever?

5. What does paradise look like? Why do you think the Koran portrays it as it does?

31

The Life of Muhammad (after 733 c.e.)

IBN ISHAQ

Ibn Ishaq (c.704–767 C.E.) was born in Medina, now in Saudi Arabia, at the beginning of the eighth century. His father and uncles were all Islamic scholars who collected information about the life of the prophet Muhammad, especially during his time in Medina. Ibn Ishaq followed in the family tradition, becoming expert on Muhammad's military campaigns. Little is known about his life except that he studied in Alexandria and sometime after 733 moved to Iraq, finally settling in Baghdad. It was during his travels that he collected information on the life of Muhammad, particularly upon his military campaigns and his establishment of Islam in Medina. As Ibn Ishaq lived nearly a century after his subject, nearly all of the stories he collected were second- and third-hand accounts handed down from generation to generation. He was particularly careful to identify the source of the stories he recounted though he has been criticized for his uncritical acceptance of them.

The Life of Muhammad, also called the Sirah, is an account of the Prophet's early life, his military campaigns, and his establishment of the religion of Islam. It was never finished as a complete literary work, and only two manuscript copies were left at Ibn Ishaq's death. It was ultimately edited by Ibn Hisham and presumably reordered into a biographical form. The following section is drawn from Ibn Ishaq's description of the revelation to Muhammad that he was the Prophet of Allah.

THE REVELATION

Like the Jews and Christians, the Arab soothsayers also spoke coming of the coming of an apostle, but their people paid no heed until Allah actually sent him, when, the prophecies made by the soothsayers having been fulfilled, the people became aware of their significance. Whereas the Jews and Christians culled their Prophecies from scripture, the Arab soothsayers received their foreknowledge of most events from the djinns, spirits of the air who stole information by listening close to heaven. But when the coming of the apostle was close at hand meteors from heaven were hurled at all the djinns and they were driven away from the places where they used to sit and listen; and they realized that this was by the command of Allah.

The first Arabs to be struck with fear at the sight of the shooting stars—for that was how the meteors thrown at the djinns appeared on earth—went to the wisest man of their tribe and said, "Have you seen what happened in the sky and the falling of some of the stars?" He replied, "If the stars thrown down were those which serve as signs and guides by land and sea, those by which the seasons of summer and winter are defined and by which the various affairs of mankind are regulated, then by Allah the world has come to an end with all the people thereof; but if those stars remain in their places and it is others which have been hurled down, then Allah has a different intention and does not mean to destroy creation."

Afterwards, the apostle of Allah asked some men of Medina what had been said there about the falling stars and was told: "We said, 'A king has died or has begun to reign; a child has been born, or has died.'" The apostle of Allah replied: "It was not so. When Allah reaches any decision concerning His people He is heard by the bearers of His throne, who praise Him; and this praise is taken up by the angels below them, and by others

still further below; and the praise continues to descend until it reaches the sky of this world, where other angels also praise. Then these ask each other why they praise, and the question ascends gradually till it reaches the bearers of the throne. They then, tell of the decree of Allah concerning His people, and the news travels down by degrees until it reaches the heaven of this world, where the angels discuss it. But the evil djinns, who used to listen to such discussions by stealth, sometimes misheard, and what they retailed to soothsayers on earth was sometimes true and sometimes false. The soothsayers also conversed about these matters, some giving true and some false accounts. So, when the coming of the apostle was being discussed by the angels, Allah foiled the evil djinns by hurling meteors, and from that time onwards an end was made to soothsayers."

When Muhammad was forty years old Allah sent him as a prophet of mercy to the people of the visible and of the invisible worlds, and to all mankind. With every prophet whom Allah had sent before the time of Muhammad, He had made a covenant, binding each of them to the coming of Muhammad, to declare him a true apostle, to aid him against every opponent, and to testify to every man who believed in the truth of their own prophetic missions that the mission of Muhammad was still to come. They complied, according to His command, and spread the covenant of Allah to all who believed in them, so that many men who believed in the Old or the New Testament believed also in the truth of this covenant.

According to his wife, the first prophetic sign shown by the apostle of Allah—after Allah determined to honor him and, through him, to show mercy to His servants—took the form of true visions. That is to say, the apostle of Allah never had a vision in his sleep; instead, it came like the break of day. She also said that Allah made him love solitude, so that he loved nothing more than to be alone.

When Allah had determined on the coming of the apostle of Allah, Muhammad went out on some business at such a distance that he left human habitation behind and came to deep valleys. He did not pass by a stone or a tree but it said "Salutation to thee, o apostle of Allah!" The apostle turned to his right, to his left, and looked behind, but saw nothing except trees and stones. Thus he remained for some time looking and listening, till Gabriel came to him with that revelation which the grace of Allah was to bestow upon him when he was at Hira during the month of Ramadan.

Every year the apostle of Allah spent a month praying at Hira and fed the poor who came to him; and when he returned to Mecca he walked round the Kaba seven or more times, as it pleased Allah, before entering his own house. In the month of Ramadan, in the year when Allah designed to bestow grace upon him, the apostle of Allah went to Hira as usual, and his family accompanied him. In the night the angel Gabriel came with the command of Allah. The apostle of Allah later said, "He came while I was asleep, with a cloth of brocade whereon there was writing, and he said, 'Read.' I replied, 'I cannot read it.' Then he pressed the cloth on me till I thought I was dying; he released his hold and said, 'Read.' I replied, 'I cannot read it.' And he pressed me again with it, till I thought I was dying. Then he loosed his hold of me and said, 'Read.' I replied, 'I cannot read it.' Once more he pressed me and said, 'Read.' Then I asked, 'What shall I read?' And I said this because I feared he would press me again. Then he said, 'Read in the name of the Lord thy creator; who created man from a drop of blood. Read, thy Lord is the most bountiful, who taught by means of the pen, taught man what he knew not.' Accordingly I read these words, and he had finished his task and departed from me. I awoke from my sleep, and felt as if words had been graven on my heart."

Afterwards I went out, and when I was on the centre of the mountain, I heard a voice from heaven, saying, "O Muhammad! Thou art the prophet of Allah, and I am Gabriel." I raised my head to look at the sky, and lo! I beheld Gabriel in the shape of a man with extended wings, standing in the firmament, with his feet touching the ground. And he said again, "O Muhammad! Thou art the apostle of Allah, and I am Gabriel." I continued to gaze at him, neither advancing nor retreating. Then I turned my face away from him to other parts of the sky, but in whatever direction I looked I saw him in the same form. I remained thus neither advancing nor retreating, and Khadija sent messengers to search for me. They went as far as the highest part of Mecca and again returned to her, while I remained standing on the same spot, until the angel departed from me and I returned to my family.

When I came to Khadija I narrated to her what I had seen, and she said, "Be of good cheer and comfort thyself ! I swear by him whose hand the life of Khadija is, that I hope thou wilt be the prophet of this nation!" Then she rose, collected her garments around her and departed to Waraqa. She described to him what the apostle of Allah had seen and heard, and Waraqa exclaimed, "Holy! Holy! I swear to Him in whose hands the life of Waraqa is that the Law of Moses has been bestowed on him and he is the prophet of this nation! Tell him to stand firm." Khadija then returned to the apostle of Allah and informed him of what Waraqa had said.

When the apostle of Allah ended his sojourn at Hira he departed to Mecca and went first round the Kaba, as was his habit. And he was met by Waraqa, who said, "Thou wilt be accused of falsehood, thou wilt be persecuted, exiled, and attacked." Then Waraqa bent his head towards the apostle and kissed him on the crown of the head, and the apostle of Allah departed to his house.

But the revelations were not continued and the apostle became much downcast, until Gabriel came to him with a message from Allah saying that He had not abandoned Muhammad; "By brightness, and by the night when it is dark, thy Lord has not forsaken nor hated thee, and the next life will be better for thee than the first. The Lord will give thee victory in this world and reward in the next. Did He not find thee an orphan and procure thee shelter? He found thee erring and guided thee; He found thee needy and enriched thee." The message to Muhammad continued: "Declare the goodness of thy Lord; declare what has come to thee from Allah, and declare His bounty and grace in thy mission; mention it, record it, and pray for manifestations of it." Accordingly the apostle of Allah began, at first in secret to those of his family whom he trusted, to promulgate the gospel bestowed by Allah on him, and on mankind through his agency.

Prayer was made an ordinance to Muhammad, and accordingly he prayed. The apostle of Allah was first commanded to make two prayer-flexions [prostrations] for every prayer, but later Allah commanded four prayer-flexions for those who were at home, although He confirmed the first ordinance of two prayer-flexions for those who were on a journey.

When prayer was made obligatory to the apostle of Allah, Gabriel came to him when he was in the highest part of Mecca, and spurred his heel into the ground towards the valley; a spring gushed forth and Gabriel performed religious ablutions. The apostle of Allah observed how purification for prayers was to be made, and washed himself likewise. Then Gabriel rose and prayed, and the apostle of Allah did so after him, and then Gabriel departed. When the apostle of Allah came to Khadija he performed the religious ablution in her presence to show her how purity was attained, just as Gabriel had done. And she, too, washed as she had been shown. Then the apostle prayed as Gabriel had prayed, and Khadija prayed after him.

Then Gabriel came to him and held noon-prayers when the sun passed the zenith; and prayed the afternoon prayers with him when his shadow was the same length as his own body. Then he prayed the sunset prayers when the sun disappeared, and the last evening prayer when the twilight disappeared. Next day he held morning prayers with the apostle at dawn; then the midday prayers when the shadow was one with him; and the afternoon prayers when it was twice as long as he; then the sunset orisons when the sun disappeared, as on the preceding day. Then he prayed with him the last

evening prayers when the first third of the night had elapsed, and lastly the morning prayers, when the morning dawned but the sun had not yet risen. Then he said, 'O Muhammad! The time of prayer is between thy prayers of yesterday and today.' ...

When the season of pilgrimage was at hand, the Quraysh assembled to agree on the attitude they should display about the apostle. They asked, "Shall we call him a soothsayer?" but al-Walid, the chief, replied, "He is not a soothsayer. We have seen soothsayers; he does not murmur and rhyme as they do." They continued, "Then we shall say that he is possessed by djinns." He replied, "He is not possessed. We have seen lunatics and know them. He does not gasp, nor roll his eyes, nor mutter." They said, "Then we shall say that he is a poet." Al-Walid replied, "He is not a poet. We know all the poets and their styles. He is not a poet." They asked, "Then what shall we say?" Al-Walid replied, "You cannot say any of these things, for it will be known that they are false. The best will be to say that he is a sorcerer, because he has come with words which are sorcery and which separate a man from his father or from his brother, or from his wife, or from his family."

When the season of the pilgrimage arrived, the Quraysh sat by the roadside and allowed no man to pass without warning about Muhammad. And the Arab pilgrims carried away from Mecca news of the apostle of Allah, so that his fame spread over the whole country.

When Islam began to spread in Mecca, the Quraysh imprisoned its believers or sought to turn them away from Islam. The nobles sent for Muhammad in order to justify themselves, and the apostle of Allah hastened to them in the hope that they had conceived a favorable opinion of what he had told them. But they only accused him once more of seeking riches and power. This he denied, and reaffirmed his mission from Allah. Then they said, "You know that no people are in greater want of land, of and of food than we are. Ask the Lord who has sent you to take away these mountains which confine us and to level out the country, to cause rivers to gush forth like the rivers of Syria, resurrect our ancestors that we may ask them whether what you say is true or false. If they declare you to be truthful and if you do what we have asked, we shall believe you and shall know that Allah has sent you to be an apostle." He replied, "I have not been sent to you with this, but I have brought to you from Allah the revelation He has sent. If you reject it, I appeal in this affair to Allah, that He decide between me and you."

They continued, "Ask, then, your Lord to send an angel to bear witness to your veracity. Ask Him to give you gardens, and treasures of gold and silver to enrich you; we know you go now to the markets to procure food as we procure it. Then we shall know your rank and station with Allah." The apostle of Allah said, "I shall not do this, nor ask for this. I was not sent to you for this; but Allah has sent me as a bearer of glad tidings and a preacher."

FOCUS QUESTIONS

1. What persuaded Muhammad that he was the prophet sent by Allah?

2. What was the significance of water for the Apostle?

3. Where did Muhammad find his first convert?

4. What were Muhammad's tribulations?

32

The Book of Contemplation (ca. 1183)

USAMA IBN MUNQIDH

Usama ibn Munqidh (1095-1188 CE) was a Syrian Muslim aristocratic who witnessed firsthand the first two Crusades and their aftermaths. From him we are able to get a unique point of view: the Crusades through Muslim eyes. Usama travelled throughout the Middle East as a soldier fighting with the Turko-Muslim warrior Zengi against the Byzantines, again other Muslim armies, and against Crusaders. Born into a noble family, Usama was able to ingratiate himself at Muslim caliphal (royal) courts and lived as a courtier in Damascus and Cairo, where he sometimes acted as an advisor to the caliphs presiding there. As a courtier he spent his time instigating political plots while also writing poetry and anthologies.

When not fighting against Crusaders, he often found them to be useful allies and entertaining companions. It appears that he had regular contact with Christians in the Crusader Kingdom of Jerusalem. His experiences interacting with these "Franks" (as he calls all Crusaders) form the basis of his most famous book, The Book of Contemplation. *Written in Arabic for a Muslim audience, this book is both a memoir and a guide for exemplary living. In this selection, Usama recounts some of the stranger behaviors of the Franks he has met.*

NEWLY ARRIVED FRANKS ARE
THE ROUGHEST

Anyone who is recently arrived from the Frankish lands is rougher in character than those who have become acclimated and have frequented the company of Muslims. Here is an instance of their rough character (may God abominate them!):

Whenever I went to visit the holy sites in Jerusalem, I would go in and make my way up to the al-Aqsa Mosque, beside which stood a small mosque that the Franks had converted into a church. When I went into the al-Aqsa Mosque—where the Templars, who are my friends, were—[135] they would clear out that little mosque so that I could pray in it. One day, I went into the little mosque, recited the opening formula 'God is great!' and stood up in prayer. At this, one of the Franks rushed at me and grabbed me and turned my face towards the east, saying, 'Pray like *this!*'

A group of Templars hurried towards him, took hold of the Frank and took him away from me. I then returned to my prayers. The Frank, that very same one, took advantage of their inattention and returned, rushing upon me and turning my face to the east, saying, 'Pray like *this!*'

So the Templars came in again, grabbed him and threw him out. They apologized to me, saying, 'This man is a stranger, just arrived from the Frankish lands sometime in the past few days. He has never before seen anyone who did not pray towards the east.'

'I think I've prayed quite enough,' I said and left. I used to marvel at that devil, the change of his expression, the way he trembled and what he must have made of seeing someone praying towards Mecca.

WHEN GOD WAS YOUNG

I saw one of the Franks come up to the amir Mu'in al-Din (may God have mercy upon him) while he was in the Dome of the Rock, and say, 'Would you like to see God when He was young?'

'Why yes,' Mu'in al-Din replied.

So this Frank walked in front of us until he brought us to an icon of Mary and the Messiah (Peace be upon him) when he was a child, sitting in her lap. 'This is God when He was young,' he said.

May God be exalted far beyond what the infidels say!

FRANKS HAVE NO HONOUR
OR PROPRIETY

The Franks possess nothing in the way of regard for honour or propriety. One of them might be walking along with his wife and run into another man. This other man might then take his wife to one side and chat with her, while the husband just stands there waiting for her to finish her conversation. And if she takes too long, he'll just leave her alone with her conversation partner and walk away!

[136] Here is an example that I myself witnessed. Whenever I went to Nablus, I used to stay at the home of a man called Mu'izz, whose home was the lodging-house for Muslims. The house had windows that opened onto the road and, across from it on the other side of the road, there was a house belonging to a Frankish man who sold wine for the merchants. He would take some wine in a bottle and go around advertising it, saying, 'So-and-So the merchant has just opened a cask of this wine. Whoever wishes to buy some can find it at such-and-such a place.' And the fee he charged for making that announcement was the wine in the bottle. So one day, he came back home and discovered a man in bed with his wife. The Frank said to the man, 'What business brings you here to my wife?'

'I got tired,' the man replied, 'so I came in to rest.'

'But how did you get into my bed?' asked the Frank.

'I found a bed that was all made up, so I went to sleep in it,' he replied.

'While my wife was sleeping there with you?' the Frank pursued.

'Well, it's her bed,' the man offered. 'Who am I to keep her out of it?'

'By the truth of my religion,' the Frank said, 'if you do this again, we'll have an argument, you and I!'

And that was all the disapproval he would muster and the extent of his sense of propriety!

Here is another example. We had with us a bath-keeper called Salim, who was originally an inhabitant of Ma'arra, and who served in the bath-house of my father (may God have mercy upon him). He told me:

I once opened a bath-house in Ma'arra to earn my living. Once, one of their knights came in. Now, they don't take to people wearing a towel about their waist in the bath, so this knight stretched out his hand, pulled off my towel from my waist and threw it down. He looked at me—I had recently shaved my pubic hair—and said, 'Salim!' Then he moved in closer to me. He then stretched his hand over my groin, saying, 'Salim! Good! By the truth of my religion, do that to me too!'

He then lay down on his back: he had it thick as a beard down in that place! So I shaved him and he passed his hand over it and, finding it smooth to the touch, said, 'Salim, by the truth of your religion, do it to Madame!'—*madame* in their language means 'the lady', meaning his wife. He then told one of his attendants, 'Tell Madame to come here.'

The attendant went and brought her and showed her in. She lay down on her back and the knight said, 'Do her like you did me!' So I shaved her [137] hair there as her husband stood watching me. He then thanked me and paid me my due for the service.

Now, consider this great contradiction! They have no sense of propriety or honour, yet they have immense courage. Yet what is courage but a product of honour and disdain for ill repute?

Here is an example close to that one. I once went to the baths in the city of Tyre and took a seat in a secluded room there. While I was there, one of my attendants in the bath said to me, 'There are women here with us!' When I went outside, I sat down on the benches and, sure enough, the woman who was in the bath had come out and was standing with her father directly across from me, having put her garments on again. But I couldn't be sure if she was a woman. So I said to one of my companions, 'By God, go have a look at this one—is she a woman?' What I meant was for him to go and ask about her. But instead he went—as I watched—and lifted her hem and pulled it up. At this, her father turned to me and explained, 'This is my daughter. Her mother died, and so she has no one who will wash her hair. I brought her into the bath with me so that I might wash her hair.'

'That's a kind thing you're doing,' I assured him. 'This will bring you heavenly reward.'

ANOTHER EXAMPLE OF THEIR MEDICINE

Another example of their wondrous medicine was related to us by William de Bures, lord of Tiberias and a man with some standing among the Franks. It happened that he travelled with the amir Mu'in al-Din (may God have mercy upon him) from Acre to Tiberias, and I accompanied him. On the way, he related to us the following story:

In our land there was a highly esteemed knight who took ill and was on the point of death. We went to one of our notable priests and asked him, 'Will you come with us and have a look at Sir So-and-So?' 'Yes,' he replied and walked back with us. We were certain now that if only he would lay his hands upon him, he would recover. When the priest saw the knight he said, 'Bring me some wax.' So we brought him a bit of wax, which he softened and shaped like a knuckle-bone. Then he inserted one in each nostril and the knight died. [138] 'He's dead!' we remarked. 'Yes,' the priest replied. 'He was in great pain, so I closed up his nose so that he could die and find relief.'

TWO OLD WOMEN RACE

Let this go and bring the conversation back to Harim.

And let us stop discussing their medical practices and move on to something else.

I was present in Tiberias during one of their feast-days. The knights had gone out to practise fighting with spears, and two decrepit old women went out with them. They positioned the two women at one end of the practice-field and at the other end they left a pig, which they had roasted and laid on a rock. They then made the two old women race one another, each one accompanied by a detachment of horsemen who cheered her on. At every step, the old women would fall down but then get up again as the audience laughed, until one of them overtook the other and took away the pig as her prize.

EXAMPLES OF FRANKISH
JURISPRUDENCE

I was an eyewitness one day in Nablus when two men came forward to fight a duel. The reason behind it was that some Muslim bandits took one of the villages of Nablus by surprise, and one of the peasants there was accused of complicity. They said, 'He guided the bandits to the village!' So he fled.

But the king sent men to arrest the peasant's sons, so the man came back before the king and said, 'Grant me justice. I challenge to a duel the

man who said that I guided the bandits to the village.'

The king said to the lord of the village, its fief-holder, 'Bring before me the man whom he has challenged.'

So the lord went off to his village, where a blacksmith lived, and took him, telling him, 'You will fight in a duel.' This was the fief-holder's way of making sure that none of his peasants [139] would be killed and his farming ruined as a result.

I saw that blacksmith. He was a strong young man, but lacking resolve: he would walk a bit, then sit down and order something to drink. Whereas the other man, who had demanded the duel, was an old man but strong-willed: he would shout taunts as if he had no fears about the duel. Then the *vicomte* came—he is the governor of the town—and gave each one of the duellists a staff and a shield and arranged the people around them in a circle.

The two men met. The old man would press the blacksmith back until he pushed him away as far as the circle of people, then he would return to the centre. They continued exchanging blows until the two of them stood there looking like pillars spattered with blood. The whole affair was going on too long and the *vicomte* began to urge them to hurry, saying, 'Be quick about it!'

The blacksmith benefited from the fact that he was used to swinging a hammer, but the old man was worn out. The blacksmith hit him and he collapsed, his staff falling underneath his back. The blacksmith then crouched on top of him and tried to stick his fingers in the old man's eyes, but couldn't do it because of all the blood. So he stood up and beat the man's head in with his staff until he had killed him. In a flash, they tied a rope round the old man's neck, dragged him off and strung him up. The blacksmith's lord now came and bestowed his own mantle upon him, let him mount behind him on his horse and rode away with him.

And that was but a taste of their jurisprudence and their legal procedure, may God curse them!

On one occasion, I went with the amir Mu'in al-Din (may God have mercy upon him) to Jerusalem, and we stopped at Nablus. While there, a blind man—a young man wearing fine clothes, a Muslim—came out to the amir with some fruit and asked him for permission to be admitted into his service in Damascus. The amir did so. I asked about him and I was told that his mother had been married to a Frank, whom she had killed. Her son used to attempt various ruses on their pilgrims, and he and his mother used to work together to kill them. They finally brought charges against him for that and made him subject to the legal procedure of the Franks, to wit:

They set up a huge cask and filled it with water and stretched a plank of wood across it. Then they bound the arms of the accused, tied a rope around his shoulders and threw him into the cask. If he were innocent, then he would sink in the water and they would then pull him up by that rope so he wouldn't die in the water; if he were guilty, then he would not sink in the water. That man tried [140] eagerly to sink into the water when they threw him in, but he couldn't do it. So he had to submit to their judgment—may God curse them—and they did some work on his eyes.

The man later arrived in Damascus, so the amir Mu'in al-Din (may God have mercy upon him) assigned him a stipend to meet all his needs and said to one of his attendants, 'Take him to Burhan al-Din ibn al-Balkhi (may God have mercy upon him) and tell him to order someone to teach the Qur'an and some jurisprudence to this man.'

At this the blind man said, 'Victory and mastery be yours! This wasn't what I was thinking!'

'Then what were you thinking I would do?' asked the amir.

'That you would give me a horse, a mule and weapons, and make a horseman out of me!' the man answered.

The amir then said, 'I never thought that a blind man would join the ranks of our cavalry.'

FOCUS QUESTIONS

1. How does Usama characterize Christian women?

2. Why does Usama disapprove of Frankish jurisprudence?

3. What are the personality traits and behaviors which Usama ascribes to the Christians in this selection? What does this tell us about the traits and behaviors approved of in Usama's own Muslim society?

4. What do you think this reading tells us about the relationship between Christians and Muslims during and after the Second Crusade? Is this what you expected?

5. Why would Usama call all Crusaders Franks? What insight might that offer about Muslim views of Crusaders?

33

Book of the Maghrib (13th century C.E.)

IBN SAID

Ibn Said (ca. 1204–1274) was a North African Muslim. Although the events of his life are shrouded in mystery, some of his historical works have survived. The best known is the Book of the Maghrib. *Said was fascinated by life in Spain, and it is possible that he settled there during the Muslim occupation. The* Book of the Maghrib *tells of the Muslim conquest and occupation of Iberia. Writing from the point of view of the Muslim occupiers, Ibn Said nevertheless uncovers the divisions within Muslim rule, thus foretelling the eventual Christian reconquest of Spain.*

The greatest importance of the Book of the Maghrib *lies in its description of the rich Moorish culture that developed in Muslim Spain. The art and science of the Moors far surpassed the achievements of the Spanish, and Said celebrates the work of Muslim poets and writers. His book leaves an unforgettable impression of a new society in Europe.*

Andalus [the Iberian Peninsula], which was conquered in the year 92 of the Hijra, continued for many years to be a dependency of the Eastern Khalifate, until it was snatched away from their hands by one of the surviving members of the family of Umeyyah (Umayyad), who, crossing over from Barbary, subdued the country, and formed therein an independent kingdom, which he transmitted to his posterity. During three centuries and a half, Andalus, governed by the princes of this dynasty, reached the utmost degree of power and prosperity, until civil war breaking out among its inhabitants, the Muslims, weakened by internal discord, became every where the prey of the artful Christians, and the territory of Islam was considerably reduced, so much so that at the present moment the worshippers of the crucified hold the greatest part of Andalus in their hands, and their country is divided into various powerful kingdoms, whose rulers assist each other whenever the Muslims attack their territories.

This brings to my recollection the words of an eastern geographer who visited Andalus in the fourth century of the Hijra (tenth century A.D.), and during the prosperous times of the Cordovan Khalifate, I mean Ibnu Haukal Annassibi, who, describing Andalus, speaks in very unfavourable terms of its inhabitants. As his words require refutation I shall transcribe here the whole of the passage. "Andalus," he says, "is an extensive island, a little less than a month's march in length, and twenty and odd days in width. It abounds in rivers and springs, is covered with trees and plants of every description, and is amply provided with every article which adds to the comforts of life; slaves are very fine, and may be procured for a small price on account of their abundance; owing, too, to the fertility of the land, which yields all sorts of grain, vegetables, and fruit, as well as to the number and goodness of its pastures in which innumerable flocks of cattle graze, food is exceedingly abundant and cheap, and the inhabitants are thereby plunged into indolence and sloth, letting mechanics and men of the lowest ranks of society overpower them and conduct their affairs. Owing to this it is really astonishing how the Island (i.e., peninsula) of Andalus still remains in the hands of the Muslims, being, as they are, people of vicious habits and low inclinations, narrow-minded, and entirely devoid of fortitude, courage, and the military accomplishments necessary to meet face to face the formidable nations of Christians who surround them on every side, and by whom they are continually assailed."

Such are the words of Ibnu Haukal; but, if truth be told, I am at a loss to guess to whom they are applied. To my countrymen they certainly are not; or, if so, it is a horrible calumny, for if any people on the earth are famous for their courage, their noble qualities, and good habits, it is the Muslims of Andalus; and indeed their readiness to fight the common enemy, their constancy in upholding the holy tenets of their religion, and their endurance of the hardships and privations of war, have become almost proverbial. So, as far as this goes, Ibnu Haukal is decidedly in error, for as the proverb says, "the tongue of stammering is at times more eloquent than the tongue of eloquence." As to the other imputation, namely, their being devoid of all senses, wisdom, and talent, either in the field or in administration, would to God that the author's judgment were correct, for then the ambition of the chiefs would not have been raised, and the Muslims would not have turned against each other's breasts and dipped in each other's blood those very weapons which God Almighty put into their hands for the destruction and annihilation of the infidel Christian. But, as it is, we ask— were those Sultans and Khalifs wanting in prudence and talents who governed this country for upwards of five hundred years, and who administered its affairs in the midst of foreign war and civil discord? Were those fearless warriors deficient in courage and military science who withstood on the frontiers of the Muslim empire the frightful shock of the innumerable infidel nations who dwell within and out of Andalus, whose extensive territories cover a surface of three months' march, and all of whom ran to arms at a moment's notice to defend the religion of the crucified? And if it be true that at the moment I write the Muslims have been visited by the wrath of heaven, and that the Almighty has sent down defeat and shame to their arms, are we to wonder at it at a time when the Christians, proud of their success, have carried their arms as far as Syria and Mesopotamia, have invaded the districts contiguous to the country which is the meeting-place of the Muslims, and the cupola of Islam, committed all sorts of ravages and depredations, and conquered the city of Haleb (Aleppo) and its environs, and done other deeds which are sufficiently declared in the histories of the time? No, it is by no means to be wondered at, especially when proper attention is paid to the manner in which the Andalusian Muslims have come to their present state of weakness and degradation. The process is this: the Christians will rush down from their mountains, or across the plain, and make an incursion into the Muslim territory; there they will pounce upon a castle and seize it: they will ravage the neighbouring country, take the inhabitants captive, and then retire to their country with all the plunder they have collected, leaving, nevertheless, strong garrisons in the castles and towers captured by them. In the meanwhile the Muslim king in whose dominions the inroad has been made, instead of attending to his own interests and stopping the disease by applying cauterization, will be waging war against his neighbours of the Muslims; and these, instead of defending the common cause, the cause of religion and truth,—instead of assisting their brother, will confederate and ally to deprive him of whatever dominions still remain in his hands. So, from a trifling evil at first, it will grow into an irreparable calamity, and the Christians will advance farther and farther until they subdue the whole of that country exposed to their inroads, where, once established and fortified, they will direct their attacks to another part of the Muslim territories, and carry on the same war of havoc and destruction. Nothing of this, however, existed at the time when Ibnu Haukal visited Andalus; for although we are told by Ibnu Hayyan and other writers that the Christians began as early as the reign of 'Abdu-r-rahman II (912-961) to grow powerful, and to annoy the Muslims on the frontiers, yet it is evident that until the breaking out of the civil wars, which raged with uncommon violence throughout Andalus, the encroachments of the barbarians on the extensive and unprotected frontiers of the Muslim empire were but of little consequence.

But to return to our subject. During the first years after the conquest the government of Andalus was vested in the hands of military commanders appointed by the Viceroys of Africa, who were themselves named by the Khalifs of Damascus. These governors united in their hands the command of the armies and the civil power, but, being either removed as soon as named, or deposed by military insurrections, much confusion and disorder reigned at all times in the state, and the establishment and consolidation of the Muslim power in Andalus were thwarted in their progress at the very onset. It was not until the arrival of the Bení Umeyyah in Andalus that the fabric of Islam may be said to have rested on a solid foundation. When 'Abdu-r-rahman Ibn Mu'awiyeh had conquered the country, when every rebel had submitted to him, when all his opponents had sworn allegiance to him, and his authority had been universally acknowledged, then his importance increased, his ambition spread wider, and both he and his successors displayed the greatest magnificence in their court, and about their persons and retinue, as likewise in the number of officers and great functionaries of the state. At first they contented themselves with the title of *Bentú-l-khaháyif* (sons of the Khalifs), but in process of time, when the limits of their empire had been considerably extended by their conquests on the opposite land of Africa, they took the appellation of Khalifs and *Omará-l-mumenín* (Princes of the believers). It is generally known that the strength and solidity of their empire consisted principally in the policy

pursued by these princes, the magnificence and splendour with which they surrounded their court, the reverential awe with which they inspired their subjects, the inexorable rigour with which they chastised every aggression on their rights, the impartiality of their judgments, their anxious solicitude in the observance of the civil law, their regard and attention to the learned, whose opinions they respected and followed, calling them to their sittings and admitting them to their councils, and many other brilliant qualities; in proof of which frequent anecdotes occur in the works of Ibnu Hayyan and other writers; as, for instance, that whenever a judge summoned the Khalif, his son, or any of his most beloved favourites, to appear in his presence as a witness in a judicial case, whoever was the individual summoned would attend in person—if the Khalif, out of respect for the law—and if a subject, for fear of incurring his master's displeasure.

But when this salutary awe and impartial justice had vanished, the decay of their empire began, and it was followed by a complete ruin. I have already observed that the princes of that dynasty were formerly styled *Omará-bná-l-kho-lafá* (Amirs, sons of the Khalifs), but that in latter times they assumed the title of *Omará-l-múmenín* (Princes of the believers). This continued until the disastrous times of the civil war, when the surviving members of the royal family hated each other, and when those who had neither the nobility nor the qualities required to honour the Khalifate pretended to it and wished for it; when the governors of provinces and the generals of armies declared themselves independent and rose every where in their governments, taking the title of *Molúku-t-tawáyif* (Kings of small estates), and when confusion and disorder were at their highest pitch. These petty sovereigns, of whom some read the *khotbah* for the Khalifs of the house of Merwan—in whose hands no power whatsoever remained—while others proclaimed the Abbasside Sultans, and acknowledged their Imam, all began to exercise the powers and to use the appendages of royalty, assuming even the titles and names of former Khalifs, and imitating in every thing the bearing and splendour of the most powerful sovereigns,—a thing which they were enabled to accomplish from the great resources of the countries over which they ruled,—for although Andalus was divided into sundry petty kingdoms, yet such was the fertility of the land, and the amount of taxes collected from it, that the chief of a limited state could at times display at his court a greater magnificence than the ruler of extensive dominions. However, the greatest among them did not hesitate to assume, as I have already observed, the names and tides of the most famous Eastern Khalifs; for instance, Ibnu Rashik Al-kairwání says that 'Abbád Ibn Mohammed Ibn 'Abbád took the surname of Al-mu'atadhed, and imitated in all things the mode of life and bearing of the Abbaseside Khalif Al-mu'atadhed-billah; his son, Mohammed Ibn'Abbád, was styled Almu'atamed; both reigned in Seville, to which kingdom they in process of time added Cordova and other extensive territories in the southern and western parts of Andalus, as will hereafter be shown.

As long as the dynasty of Umeyyah occupied the throne of Cordova, the successors of 'Abdurrahmán contrived to inspire their subjects with love of their persons, mixed with reverential awe; this they accomplished by surrounding their courts with splendour, by displaying the greatest magnificence whenever they appeared in public, and by employing other means which I have already hinted at, and deem it not necessary to repeat: they continued thus until the times of the civil war, when, having lost the affections of the people, their subjects began to look with an evil eye at their prodigal expense, and the extravagant pomp with which they surrounded their persons. Then came the Bení Hamúd, the descendants of Idrís, of the progeny of 'Ali Ibn Abí Tálib, who, having snatched the Khalifate from the hands of the Bení Merwán, ruled for some time over the greatest part of Andalus. These princes showed also great ostentation, and, assuming the same titles that the Abbasside Khalifs had borne, they followed their steps in every thing concerning the arrangements of their courts and persons; for instance, whenever a *mun-*

shid wanted to extemporize some verses in praise of his sovereign, or any subject wished to address him on particular business, the poet or the petitioner was introduced to the presence of the Khalif, who sat behind a curtain and spoke without showing himself, the *Hájib* or curtain-drawer standing all the time by his side to communicate to the party the words or intentions of the Khalif. So when Ibnu Mokéná Al-lishbóni (from Lisbon), the poet, appeared in presence of the Hájib of Idrís Ibn Yahya Al-hamúdí, who was proclaimed Khalif of Malaga, to recite the *kassídah* of his which is so well known and rhymes in *min*, when he came to that part which runs thus—

> The countenance of Idrís, son of Yahya, son of Alí, son of Hamúd, prince of the believers, is like a rising sun; it dazzles the eyes of those who look at it—
> Let us see it, let us seize the rays of yonder light, for it is the light of the master of the worlds—

The Sultan himself drew the curtain which concealed him, and said to the poet—"Look, then," and showed great affability to Ibn Mokéná, and rewarded him very handsomely.

But when, through the civil war, the country was broken up into sundry petty sovereignties, the new monarchs followed quite a different line of politics; for, wishing to become popular, they treated their subjects with greater familiarity, and had a more frequent intercourse with all classes of society; they often reviewed their troops, and visited their provinces; they invited to their presence the doctors and poets, and wished to be held from the beginning of their reign as the patrons of science and literature: but even this contributed to the depression of the royal authority, which thus became every day less dreaded; besides, the arms of the Muslims being employed during the long civil wars against one another, the inhabitants of the different provinces began to look on each other with an evil eye; the ties by which they were united became loose, and a number of independent states were formed, the government of which passed from father to son in the same manner as the empire of Cordova had been transmitted to the sons and heirs of the Khalifs. Thus separated from each other, the Muslims began to consider themselves as members of different nations, and it became every day more difficult for them to unite in the common cause; and owing to their divisions, and to their mutual enmity, as well as to the sordid interest and extravagant ambition of some of their kings, the Christians were enabled to attack them in detail, and subdue them one after the other. However, by the arrival of the Bení 'Abdu-l-múmen all those little states were again blended into one, and the whole of Andalus acknowledged their sway, and continued for many years to be ruled by their successors, until, civil war breaking out again, Ibn Húd, surnamed Almutawákel, revolted, and finding the people of Andalus ill-disposed against the Almohades, and anxious to shake off their yoke, he easily made himself master of the country. Ibn Húd, however, followed the policy of his predecessors (the kings of the small states); he even surpassed them in folly and ignorance of the rules of good government, for he used to walk about the streets and markets, conversing and laughing with the lowest people, asking them questions, and doing acts unsuitable to his high station, and which no subject ever saw a Sultan do before, so much so that it was said, not without foundation, that he looked more like a performer of legerdemain than a king. Fools, and the ignorant vulgar seemed, it is true, to gaze with astonishment and pleasure at this, familiarity, but as the poet has said—

> These are things to make the fools laugh, but the consequences of which prudent people are taught to fear.

These symptoms went on increasing until populous cities and extensive districts became the prey of the Christians, and whole kingdoms were snatched from the hands of the Muslims. Another very aggravating circumstance added its weight to the general calamity, namely, the facility with which the power changed hands. Whoever has read attentively what we have just said about the mode of attaining and using the royal power in Andalus, must be convinced that nothing was so easy, especially in latter times, as to arrive at it. The process is this: whenever a knight is known to surpass his countrymen in courage, generosity, or any of those qualities which make a man dear to the vulgar, the people cling to him, follow his party, and soon after proclaim him their king, without paying the least regard to his ascendancy, or stopping to consider whether he is of royal blood or not. The new king then transmits the state as an inheritance to his son or nearest relative, and thus a new dynasty is formed. I may, in proof of this, quote a case which has just taken place among us: a certain captain made himself famous by his exploits, and the victories he won over the enemy, as likewise by his generous and liberal disposition towards the citizens and the army; all of a sudden his friends and partisans resolved to raise him to the throne, and regardless of their own safety, as well as that of their families, friends, and clients residing at court, and whose lives were by their imprudence put in great jeopardy, they rose in a castle, and proclaimed him king; and they never ceased toiling, calling people to their ranks, and fighting their opponents, until their object was accomplished, and their friend solidly established on his throne. Now Eastern people are more cautious about altering the succession, and changing the reigning dynasty; they will on the contrary avoid it by all possible means, and do their best to leave the power in the hands of the reigning family, rather than let discord and civil dissensions sap the foundations of the state, and introduce dissolution and corruption into the social body.

Among us the change of dynasty is a thing of frequent occurrence, and the present ruler of Andalus, Ibnu-l-ahmar, is another instance of what I have advanced. He was a good soldier, and had been very successful in some expeditions against the Christians, whose territories he was continually invading, sallying out at the head of his followers from a castle called *Hisn-Arjónah* (Arjona), where he generally resided. Being a shrewd man, and versed in all the stratagems of war, he seldom went out on an expedition without returning victorious, and laden with plunder, owing to which he amassed great riches, and the number of his partisans and followers were considerably increased. At last, being prompted by ambition to aspire to the royal power, he at first caused his troops to proclaim him king; then sallying out of his stronghold he got possession of Cordova, marched against Seville, took it, and killed its king Al-bájí. After this he subdued Jaen, the strongest and most important city in all Andalus, owing to its walls and the position it occupies, conquered likewise Malaga, Granada, and their districts, and assumed the title of *Amíru-l-moslemín* (Prince of the Muslims); and at the moment I write he is obeyed all over Andalus, and every one looks to him for advice and protection.

FOCUS QUESTIONS

1. For most Christians, the Muslim world was monolithic. Is this generalization borne out by Ibn Said?

2. What seems to be the Muslim view of Christians?

3. How do political leaders establish themselves in Muslim Spain?

4. How might Muslims defend themselves from Christian aggression? Why have they been unsuccessful?

5. What characterizes warfare between Christians and Muslims?

34

The Muqaddimah (1377 C.E.)

IBN KHALDÛN

Ibn Khaldûn (1332–1406) was born into an aristocratic family in the Muslim city of Tunis. Both his grandfather and father were prominent intellectuals and political advisors, and Ibn Khaldûn was trained to follow in their footsteps. He was tutored in Arabic, studied the Koran (Qur'ân) with churchmen, and was groomed for political office, which he first achieved at the age of 20. Ibn Khaldûn soon moved to Fez, one of the great intellectual centers of Northern Africa. For the next decade he served as a political advisor to a series of Moorish rulers, traveling to both Granada and Seville on diplomatic missions. In the unstable world of the mid-fourteenth century, his political life propelled him into high offices and low dungeons. After his second period of incarceration, Ibn Khaldûn briefly retired from public life and entered a monastery to concentrate upon scholarly activities. Ultimately he found the time to compose the Muqaddimah *(introduction) to what he planned would be a universal history.*

The Muqaddimah *is unique in its period for being both a chronicle of historical events and a presentation of Ibn Khaldûn's view of the process of history. He believed that the historical process displayed a rational pattern, that it was dominated by humans, and that it had both purpose and meaning. Thus he spent much of his "introduction" describing the origin and rationale for institutions. In the excerpted section he recounts the history of the office of the imam.*

The position of imam is a necessary one. The consensus of the men around Muhammad and the men of the second generation shows that (the imamate) is necessary according to the religious law. At the death of the Prophet, the men around him proceeded to render the oath of allegiance to Abû Bakr and to entrust him with the supervision of their affairs. And so it was at all subsequent periods. In no period were the people left in a state of anarchy. This was so by general consensus, which proves that the position of imam is a necessary one.

Some people have expressed the opinion that the necessity of the imamate is apparent for rational reasons, and that the consensus which happens to exist merely confirms the authority of the intellect in this respect. As they say, what makes (the imam rationally) necessary is the need of human beings for social organization and the impossibility of their living and existing by themselves. One of the necessary consequences of social organization is disagreement, because of the pressure of cross-purposes. As long as there is no ruler who exercises a restraining influence, this leads to trouble which, in turn, may lead to the destruction and uprooting of mankind. Now, the preservation of the species is one of the necessary intentions of the religious law.

This very idea is the one the philosophers had in mind when they considered prophethood as something (intellectually) necessary for mankind. We have already shown the incorrectness of their reasoning. One of its premises is that the restraining influence comes into being only through a religious law from God, to which the mass submits as a matter of belief and religious creed. This premise is not acceptable. The restraining influence comes into being as the result of the impetus of royal authority and the forcefulness of the mighty, even if there is no religious law. This was the case among heathens and other nations who had no scriptures and had not been reached by a prophetic mission.

Or, we might say: In order to remove disagreement, it is sufficient that every individual should know that injustice is forbidden him by the authority of the intellect. Then, their claim that the removal of disagreement takes place only through the existence of the religious law in one case, and the position of the imam in another case, is not correct. It may (be removed) as well through the existence of powerful leaders, or through the people refraining from disagreement and mutual injustice, as through the position of the imam. Thus, the intellectual proof based upon that premise does not stand up. This shows that the necessity of (an imam) is indicated by the religious law, that is, by the consensus, as we have stated before.

Some people have taken the exceptional position of stating that the position of imam is not necessary at all, neither according to the intellect nor according to the religious law. People who have held that opinion include the Mu'tazilah al-Asamm and certain Khârijites, among others. They think that it is necessary only to observe the religious laws. When Muslims agree upon (the practice of) justice and observance of the divine laws, no imam is needed, and the imamate is not necessary. Those (who so argue) are refuted by the consensus. They adopted such an opinion because they were (attempting to) escape the royal authority and its overbearing, domineering, and worldly ways. They had seen that the religious law was full of censure and blame for such things and for the people who practised them, and that it encouraged the desire to abolish them.

The religious law does not censure royal authority as such and does not forbid its exercise. It merely censures the evils resulting from it, such as tyranny, injustice, and pleasure-seeking. Here, no doubt, we have forbidden evils. They are the concomitants of royal authority. The religious law praises justice, fairness, the fulfilment of religious duties, and the defence of religion. It states that these things will of necessity find their reward (in the other world). Now, all these things are concomitants of royal authority, too. Thus, censure attaches to royal authority only on account of some of its qualities and conditions, not others. (The religious law) does not censure royal authority as such, nor does it seek to suppress it entirely. It also censures concupiscence and wrathfulness in responsible persons, but it does not want to see either of these qualities relinquished altogether, because necessity calls for their existence. It merely wants to see that proper use is made of them. David and Solomon possessed royal authority such as no one else ever possessed, yet they were divine prophets and belonged, in God's eyes, among the noblest human beings that ever existed.

Furthermore, we say to them: The (attempt to) dispense with royal authority by (assuming) that the institution (of the imamate) is not necessary does not help you at all. You agree that observance of the religious laws is a necessary thing. Now, that is achieved only through group feeling and power, and group feeling, by its very nature, requires royal authority. Thus, there will be royal authority, even if no imam is set up. Now, that is just what you (wanted to) dispense with.

If it has been established that the institution (of the imamate) is necessary by the consensus, (it must be added that this institution) is a community duty and is left to the discretion of all competent Muslims. It is their obligation to see to it that (the imamate) is set up, and everybody has to obey (the imam) in accordance with the verse of the Qur'ân, "Obey God, and obey the apostle and the people in authority among you."

It is not possible to appoint two men to the position (of imam) at the same time. Religious scholars generally are of this opinion, on the basis of certain traditions.

Others hold that (the prohibition against two imams) applies only to two imams in one locality, or where they would be close to each other. When there are great distances and the imam is unable to control the farther region, it is permissible to set up another imam there to take care of public interests....

The pre-requisites governing the institution of (the imamate) are four: (1) knowledge, (2) probity, (3) competence, and (4) freedom of the senses and limbs from any defect that might affect judgment and action. There is a difference of opinion concerning a fifth prerequisite, that is, (5) Qurashite descent.

1. The necessity of knowledge as a prerequisite is obvious. The imam can execute the divine laws only if he knows them. Those he does not know, he cannot properly present. His knowledge is satisfactory only if he is able to make independent decisions. Blind acceptance of tradition is a shortcoming, and the imamate requires perfection in all qualities and conditions.

2. Probity is required because (the imamate) is a religious institution and supervises all the other institutions that require (this quality). There is no difference of opinion as to the fact that his probity is nullified by the actual commission of forbidden acts and the like. But there is a difference of opinion on the question of whether it is nullified by innovations in dogma.

3. Competence means that he is willing to carry out the punishments fixed by law and to go to war. He must understand warfare and be able to assume responsibility for getting the people to fight. He also must know about group feeling and the fine points (of diplomacy). He must be strong enough to take care of political duties. All of which is to enable him to fulfil his functions of protecting religion, leading in the holy war against the enemy, maintaining the (religious) laws, and administering the (public) interests.

4. Freedom of the senses and limbs from defects or disabilities such as insanity, blindness, muteness, or deafness, and from any loss of limbs affecting (the imam's) ability to act, such as missing hands, feet, or testicles, is a prerequisite of the imamate, because all

such defects affect his full ability to act and to fulfil his duties. Even in the case of a defect that merely disfigures the appearance, as, for instance, loss of one limb, the condition of freedom from defects (remains in force as a condition in the sense that it) aims at his perfection.

Lack of freedom of action is connected with loss of limbs. Such a lack may be of two kinds. One is forced (inaction) and complete inability to act through imprisonment or the like. (Absence of any restriction upon freedom of action) is as necessary a condition (of the imamate) as freedom from bodily defects. The other kind is in a different category. (This lack of freedom of action implies that) some of (the imam's) men may gain power over him, although no disobedience or disagreement may be involved, and keep him in seclusion. Then, the problem is shifted to the person who has gained power. If he acts in accordance with Islam and justice and praiseworthy policies, it is permissible to acknowledge (him). If not, Muslims must look for help from persons who will restrain him and eliminate the unhealthy situation created by him, until the caliph's power of action is reestablished.

5. The pre-requisite of a Qurashite origin is based upon the consensus on this point that obtained in the men around Muhammad on the day of Abû Bakr's elevation to the caliphate....

Among those who deny that Qurashite descent is a condition of the imamate is judge Abû Bakr al-Bâqillânî. The Qurashite group feeling had come to disappear and dissolve (in his day), and non-Arab rulers controlled the caliphs. Therefore, when he saw what the condition of the caliphs was in his day, he dropped the pre-requisite of a Qurashite origin.

Scholars in general, however, retain Qurashite descent as a condition (of the imamate). (They maintain that) the imamate rightly belongs to a Qurashite, even if he is too weak to handle the affairs of the Muslims. Against them is the fact that this involves dropping the pre-requisite of competence, which requires that he have the power to discharge his duties. If his strength has gone with the disappearance of group feeling, his competence, too, is gone. And if

the condition of competence be eliminated, that will reflect further upon knowledge and religion. (In this case, then, all) the conditions governing the institution would no longer be considered, and this would be contrary to the consensus....

When one considers what God meant the caliphate to be, nothing more needs (to be said) about it. God made the caliph his substitute to handle the affairs of His servants. He is to make them do the things that are good for them and forbid them to do those that are harmful. He has been directly told so. A person who lacks the power to do a thing is never told directly to do it. The religious leader, Ibn al-Khatîb, said that most religious laws apply to women as they do to men. However, women are not directly told (to follow the religious laws) by express reference to them in the text, but, in (Ibn al-Khatîb's) opinion, they are included only by way of analogical reasoning. That is because women have no power whatever. Men control their (actions), except in as far as the duties of divine worship are concerned, where everyone controls his own. Therefore, women are directly told (to fulfil the duties of divine worship) by express reference to them in the text, and not (merely) by way of analogical reasoning.

Furthermore, (the world of) existence attests to (the necessity of group feeling for the caliphate). Only he who has gained superiority over a nation or a race is able to handle its affairs. The religious law would hardly ever make a requirement in contradiction to the requirements of existence....

26 THE TRANSFORMATION OF THE CALIPHATE INTO ROYAL AUTHORITY

Royal authority is the natural goal of group feeling. It results from group feeling, not by choice but through (inherent) necessity and the order of existence, as we have stated before. All religious laws and practices and everything that the masses are expected to do requires group feeling. Only with the help of group feeling can a claim be successfully pressed, as we have stated before.

Group feeling is necessary to the Muslim community. Its existence enables (the community) to fulfil what God expects of it. Still, we find that Muhammad censured group feeling and urged us to reject it and to leave it alone. He said: "God removed from you the arrogance of pre-Islamic times and its pride in ancestry. You are the children of Adam, and Adam was made of dust." God said: "Most noble among you in God's eyes is he who fears God most."

We also find that Muhammad censured royal authority and its representatives. He blamed them because of their enjoyment of good fortune, their senseless waste, and their deviations from the path of God. He enjoined friendship among all Muslims and warned against discord and dissension.

It should be known that in Muhammad's opinion, all of this world is a vehicle for transport to the other world. He who loses the vehicle can go nowhere. When Muhammad forbids or censures certain human activities or urges their omission, he does not want them to be neglected altogether. Nor does he want them to be completely eradicated, or the powers from which they result to remain altogether unused. He wants those powers to be employed as much as possible for the right aims. Every intention should thus eventually become the right one and the direction of all human activities one and the same.

Muhammad did not censure wrathfulness with the intention of eradicating it as a human quality. If the power of wrathfulness were no longer to exist in man, he would lose the ability to help the truth become victorious. There would no longer be holy war or glorification of the word of God. Muhammad censured the wrathfulness that is in the service of Satan and reprehensible purposes, but the wrathfulness that is one in God and in the service of God deserves praise. Such praiseworthy wrathfulness was one of the qualities of Muhammad.

Likewise, when he censures the desires, he does not want them to be abolished altogether, for a complete abolition of concupiscence in a person would make him defective and inferior. He wants the desires to be used for permissible purposes to serve the public interests, so that man becomes an active servant of God who willingly obeys the divine commands.

Likewise, when the religious law censures group feeling and says: "Neither your blood relatives nor your children will be of use to you (on the Day of Resurrection)," (such a statement) is directed against a group feeling that is used for worthless purposes, as was the case in pre-Islamic times. It is also directed against a group feeling that makes a person proud and superior. For an intelligent person to take such an attitude is considered a gratuitous action, which is of no use for the other world, the world of eternity. On the other hand, a group feeling that is working for the truth and for fulfilment of the divine commands is something desirable. If it were gone, religious laws would no longer be, because they materialize only through group feeling, as we have stated before.

Likewise, when Muhammad censures royal authority, he does not censure it for gaining superiority through truth, for forcing the great mass to accept the faith, nor for looking after the (public) interests. He censures royal authority for achieving superiority through worthless means and for employing human beings for indulgence in (selfish) purposes and desires, as we have stated. If royal authority would sincerely exercise its superiority over men for the sake of God and so as to cause those men to worship God and to wage war against His enemies, there would not be anything reprehensible in it....

When the Messenger of God was about to die, he appointed Abû Bakr as his representative to (lead the) prayers, since (prayer) was the most important religious activity. People were, thus, content to accept him as caliph, that is, as the person who causes the great mass to act according to the religious laws. No mention was made of royal authority, because royal authority was suspected of being worthless, and because at that time it was the prerogative of unbelievers and enemies of Islam. Abû Bakr discharged the duties of his office in a manner pleasing to God, following the traditions of his master. He fought against apostates until all the Arabs were united in Islam. He then appointed 'Umar his successor. 'Umar followed Abû Bakr's example and fought against (foreign) nations. He defeated them and permitted the Arabs to appropriate their worldly possessions and their royal authority, and the Arabs did that.

Al-Mas'ûdî says: "In the days of 'Uthmân, the men around Muhammad acquired estates and money. On the day 'Uthmân was killed, 150,000 dinars and 1,000,000 dirhams were in the hands of his treasurer. The value of his estates in Wâdai l-Qurâ and Hunayn and other places was 200,000 dinars. He also left many camels and horses. The eighth part of the estate of az-Zubayr after his death amounted to 50,000 dinars. He also left 1,000 horses and 1,000 female servants. Talhah's income from the 'Irâq was 1,000 dinars a day, and his income from the region of ash-Sharâh was more than that. The stable of 'Abd-ar-Rahmân b. 'Awf contained 1,000 horses. He also had 1,000 camels and 10,000 sheep. One-fourth of his estate after his death amounted to 84,000. Zayd b. Thâbit left silver and gold that was broken into pieces with pickaxes, in addition to the (other) property and estates that he left, in the value of 100,000 dinars. Az-Zubayr built himself a residence in al-Basrah and other residences in Egypt and al-Kûfah and Alexandria. Talhah built one in al-Kûfah and had his residence in Medina improved. He used plaster, bricks, and teakwood. Sa'd b. Abî Waqqâs built himself a residence in al-'Aqîq suburb of Medina). He made it high and spacious, and had balustrades put on top of it. Al-Miqdâd built his residence in Medina and had it plastered inside and out. Ya'lâ, b. Munyah left 50,000 dinars and estates and other things the value of which amounted to 300,000 dirharms." End of the quotation from al-Mas'ûdi.

Such were the gains people made. Their religion did not blame them for (amassing so much), because, as booty, it was lawful property. They did not employ their property wastefully but in a planned way in all their conditions, as we have stated. Amassing worldly property is reprehensible, but it did not reflect upon them, because blame attaches only to waste and lack of planning, as we have indicated. Since their expenditure followed a plan and served the truth and its ways, amassing (so much property) helped them along on the path of truth and served the purpose of attaining the other world.

Soon, the desert attitude of the Arabs and their low standard of living approached its ends. The nature of royal authority—which is the necessary consequence of group feeling as we have stated—showed itself, and with it, there came superiority and force. Royal authority, as (the early Muslims) saw it, belonged in the same category as luxury and amassed property. They did not apply their superiority to worthless things, and they did not abandon the intentions of their religion or the ways of truth.

When trouble arose between 'Ali and Mu'âwiyah as a necessary consequence of group feeling, they were guided in their dissensions by the truth and by independent judgment. They did not fight for any worldly purpose or over preferences of no value, or for reasons of personal enmity. This might be suspected, and heretics might like to think so. However, what caused their difference was their independent judgment as to where the truth lay. It was on this matter that each side opposed the point of view of the other. Even though 'Ali was in the fight, Mu'âwiyah's intentions were not evil. He wanted the truth, but missed it. Each was right in so far as his intentions were concerned. Now, the nature of royal authority requires that one person claim all the glory for himself and appropriate it to himself. It was not for Mu'âwiyah to deny (the natural requirement of royal authority) to himself and his people. (Royal authority) was a natural thing that group feeling, by its very nature, brought in its train. Even the Umayyads and those of their followers who were not after the truth like Mu'âwiyah felt that. They banded together around him and were willing to die for him. Had Mu'âwiyah tried to lead them on another course of action, had he opposed them and not claimed all the power for (himself and them), it would have meant the dissolution of the whole thing that he had consolidated. It was more important to him to keep it together than to bother about a course of action that could not entail much criticism.

When royal authority is obtained and we assume that one person has it all for himself, no objection can be raised if he uses it for the various ways and aspects of the truth. Solomon and his father David had the royal authority of the Israelites for themselves, as the nature of royal authority requires, and it is well known how great a share in prophecy and truth they possessed.

Likewise, Mu'âwiyah appointed Yazîd as his successor, because he was afraid of the dissolution of the whole thing, inasmuch as the Umayyads did not like to see the power handed over to any outsider. Had Mu'âwiyah appointed anyone else his successor, the Umayyads would have been against him. Moreover, they had a good opinion of Yazîd. Mu'âwiyah would not have been the man to appoint Yazîd his successor, had he believed him to be really so wicked. Such an assumption must be absolutely excluded in Mu'âwiyah's case.

The same applies to Marwân b. al-Hakam and his sons. Even though they were kings, their royal ways were not those of worthless men and oppressors. They complied with the intentions of the truth with all their energy, except when necessity caused them to do something (unworthy). Such (a necessity existed) when there was fear that the whole thing might face dissolution. (To avoid that) was more important to them than any (other) intention. That this was (their attitude) is attested by the fact that they followed and imitated (the early Muslims).

Then came the later Umayyads. As far as their worldly purposes and intentions were concerned, they acted as the nature of royal authority required. They forgot the deliberate planning and the reliance upon the truth that had guided the activities of their predecessors. This caused the people to censure their actions and to accept the 'Abbâsid propaganda in the place of the Umayyads'. Thus, the 'Abbâsids took over the government. The probity of the 'Abbasids was outstanding. They used their royal authority to further, as far as possible, the different aspects and ways of the truth. (The early 'Abbâsids) eventually were succeeded by the descendants of ar-Rashîd. Among them there were good and bad men. Later on, when the power passed to their descendants, they gave royal authority and luxury their due. They became enmeshed in worldly affairs of no value and turned their backs on Islam. Therefore, God permitted them to be ruined, and the Arabs to be completely deprived of their power, which He gave to others. Whoever considers the biographies of these caliphs and their different approaches to truth and worthlessness knows that what we have stated is correct....

It has thus become clear how the caliphate was transformed into royal authority. The form of government in the beginning was a caliphate. Everybody had his restraining influence in himself, that is, (the restraining influence of) Islam. They preferred (Islam) to their worldly affairs, even if (the neglect of worldly affairs) led to their own destruction.

When 'Uthmân was besieged in his house, al-Hasan, al-Husayn, 'Abdallâh b. 'Umar, Ibn Ja'far, and others came and offered to defend him. But he refused and did not permit swords to be drawn among Muslims. He feared a split and wanted to preserve the harmony that would keep the whole thing intact, even if it could be done only at the cost of his own destruction.

At the beginning of his (term of) office, 'Ali himself was advised by al-Mughîrah to leave az-Zubayr, Mu'âwiyah, and Talhah in their positions, until the people had agreed to render the oath of allegiance to him and the whole thing was consolidated. After that, he might do what he wanted. That was good power politics. 'Ali, however, refused. He wanted to avoid deceit, because deceit is forbidden by Islam. Al-Mughîrah came back to him the following morning and said: "I gave you that advice yesterday, but then I reconsidered it and realized that it was neither right nor good advice. You were right." 'Alî replied: "Indeed, no. I know that the advice you gave me yesterday was good advice and that you are deceiving me today. However, regard for the truth prevented me from following your good advice." To such a degree were these early Muslims concerned with improving their religion at the expense of their worldly affairs.

It has thus been shown how the form of government came to be royal authority. However, there remained the traits that were characteristic of the caliphate, namely, preference for Islam and its ways, and adherence to the path of truth. A change became apparent only in the restraining influence that had been Islam and now came to be group feeling and the sword. That was the situation in the time of Mu'âwiyah, Marwân, his son 'Abd-al-Malik, and the first 'Abbâsid caliphs down to ar-Rashîd and some of his sons. Then, the characteristic traits of the caliphate disappeared, and only its name remained. The form of government came to be royal authority pure and simple. Superiority attained the limits of its nature and was employed for particular (worthless) purposes, such as the use of force and the arbitrary gratification of desires and for pleasure.

This was the case with the successors of the sons of 'Abd-al-Malik and the 'Abbâsids after al-Mu'tasim and al-Mutawakkil. They remained caliphs in name, because the Arab group feeling continued to exist. In these two stages caliphate and royal authority existed side by side. Then, with the disappearance of Arab group feeling and the annihilation of the race and complete destruction of (Arabism), the caliphate lost its identity. The form of government remained royal authority pure and simple.

This was the case, for instance, with the non-Arab rulers in the East. They showed obedience to the caliph in order to enjoy the blessings (involved in that), but royal authority belonged to them with all its titles and attributes. The caliph had no share in it.

It is thus clear that the caliphate at first existed without royal authority. Then, the characteristic traits of the caliphate became mixed up and confused. Finally, when its group feeling had separated from the group feeling of the caliphate, royal authority came to exist alone.

27 THE MEANING OF THE OATH OF ALLEGIANCE

It should be known that the *bay'ah* (oath of allegiance) is a contract to render obedience. It is as though the person who renders the oath of allegiance made a contract with his amir, to the effect that he surrenders supervision of his own affairs and those of the Muslims to him and that he will not contest his authority and that he will obey him by (executing) all the duties with which he might be charged, whether agreeable or disagreeable.

When people rendered the oath of allegiance to the amir and concluded the contract, they put their hands into his hand to confirm the contract. This was considered to be something like the action of buyer and seller (after concluding a bargain). Therefore, the oath of allegiance was called *bay'ah,* the infinitive of *ba'a* to sell (or buy). The *bay'ah* was a handshake. Such is its meaning in customary linguistic terminology and the accepted usage of the religious law.

The oath of allegiance that is common at present is the Persian custom of greeting kings by kissing the earth, or their hand, their foot, or the lower hem of their garment. The term *bay'ah,* which means a contract to render obedience, was used metaphorically to denote this, since such an abject form of greeting and politeness is one of the consequences and concomitants of obedience. (The practice) has become so general that it has become customary and has replaced the handshake which was originally used, because shaking hands with everybody meant that the ruler lowered himself and made himself cheap, things that are detrimental to leadership and the dignity of the royal position. However, (the handshake is practised) by a very few rulers who want to show themselves humble and who, therefore, themselves shake hands with their nobles and with famous divines among their subjects.

This customary meaning of the oath of allegiance should be understood. A person must know it, because it imposes upon him certain duties toward his ruler and imam. His actions will thus not be frivolous or gratuitous. This should be taken into consideration in one's dealings with rulers.

FOCUS QUESTIONS

1. What is the relationship between religious law and royal authority?

2. Why is the prerequisite that the Imam be of Qurashite origins disputed?

3. How do religious laws affect women?

4. What does Ibn Khaldûn mean by "group feeling"? What effect does group feeling have on Islamic society?

35

Travels in Africa (1364 C.E.)

IBN BATTUTA

Muhammad Ibn Abdullah Ibn Battuta (1304–1377) spent most of his long life traveling in Asia and Africa. He was born in Tangier and made the first of his four pilgrimages to Mecca at the age of 25. After performing his religious obligations, Ibn Battuta kept traveling for 24 years. He visited all of the Muslim states of the Middle East as well as Sri Lanka, India, and China. Ibn Battuta remains one of the central sources of knowledge about African and Muslim civilization in this early period.

His journey to the empire of Mali, the subject of these selections, began in 1352. He has left a vivid picture of the desert crossing, describing in detail his adventures as he traveled by camel on a traditional caravan route. Much of the information that he provides is unique, but all of it is shaped by his own background, religion, and sense of cultural superiority.

Then I set off at the beginning of ... February 1352 with a caravan whose leader was Abu Muhammad Yandakan al-Masufi, may God have mercy on him. In the caravan was a company of merchants of Sijilmasa and others. After 25 days we arrived at Taghaza. This is a village with nothing good about it. One of its marvels is that its houses and mosque are of rock salt and its roofs of camel skins. It has no trees, but is nothing but sand with a salt mine. They dig in the earth for the salt, which is found in great slabs lying one upon the other as though they have been shaped and placed underground. A camel carries two slabs of it. Nobody lives there except the slaves of the Masufa who dig for the salt. They live on the dates imported to them from Dar'a and Sijilmasa, on camel-meat, and on anili imported from the land of the Sudan. The Sudan come to them from their land and carry the salt away. One load of it is sold at Iwalatan for eight or ten mithqals, and at the city of Mali for 30 or twenty mithqals. It has sometimes fetched 40 mithqals.

The Sudân use salt for currency as gold and silver is used. They cut it into pieces and use it for their transactions. Despite the meanness of the village of Taghaza they deal with *qintar* upon *qintar* of gold there.

We stayed there for ten days, under strain because the water there is brackish. It is the most fly-ridden of places.

Water is taken on there for entering the wilderness which comes after it. This is a distance of ten days without water except rarely. As for us, we found plenty of water there in pools left by the rain. On one day we found a pool between two rocky hillocks with sweet water in it, so we renewed our water supplies and washed our clothes.

There are many truffles in that wilderness and lice are so numerous that people suspend cords round their necks with mercury in them, which kills them.

In those days we used to go on ahead of the caravan and whenever we found a place suitable for grazing we pastured the beasts there. This we continued to do till a man named Ibn Ziri became lost in the desert. After that we neither went on ahead nor lagged behind. Strife and the exchange of insults had taken place between Ibn Ziri and his maternal cousin, named Ibn 'Adi, so that he fell behind the caravan and lost the way, and when the people encamped there was no news of him. I advised his cousin to hire one of the Masufa to follow his track in the hope of finding him, but he refused. Next day one of the Masufa undertook, without pay, to look for him. He found his traces, which sometimes followed the beaten track and sometimes left it, but could get no news of him. We met a caravan on our way, and they told us that some men had become separated from them. We found one of them dead, with his clothes on him and a whip in hand, under a little tree of the kind that grows in the sand. There was water a mile or so away from him.

Takshif is the name for any man of the Masufa who is hired by the people of the caravan to go on ahead to Iwalatan with people's letters to their associates there, so that they may rent houses for them and come out to meet them with water for a distance of four days' travel. Anyone who has no associate at Iwalatan writes to one of the merchants there who is known for his honesty and he acts as his partner in the matter. Sometimes the *takshif* perishes in that wilderness so that the people of Iwalatan do not know about the caravan and all or many of its people perish.

There are many demons in this wilderness. If the *takshif* is alone they play with him and seduce him so that he becomes diverted from his purpose and perishes since there is no clear road or track. There is nothing but sand blown about by the wind so that you see mountains of sand in one place then you see them transported to another. The guide there is the one who has been many times to and fro and is sagacious. I thought it remarkable that our guide was blind in one eye and diseased in the other and yet knew the way better than anyone.

There was in the caravan a merchant of Tlemcen called al-Hajj Zayyan. He had a habit of seizing snakes and playing with them. I used to forbid him but he would not desist. One day he put his hand into the hole of a lizard to pull it out and found in its place a snake, which he took in his hand. He was about to mount when it stung him on the index finger of the right hand. He suffered great pain so his hand was cauterized, but during the evening the pain increased. He therefore slaughtered a camel and put his hand into its stomach and left it like that for the night, whereupon the flesh of his finger fell off piece by piece, so he cut it off at the root. The people of the Masufa told us that the snake had drunk water before stinging him; if it had not drunk it would have killed him.

When those who had come out to meet us with water arrived our horses drank and we entered an exceedingly hot wilderness unlike those we have been accustomed to. We used to set off after the afternoon prayer and travel for the whole night and encamp in the morning. Men of the Masufa and Bardama and others used to come with loads of water for sale.

Then we reached the town of Iwalatan at the beginning of the month of Rabi' al-awwal after a journey from Sijilmasa of two whole months.... When we arrived there the merchants placed their belongings in an open space, where the Sudan took over the guard of them while they went to the *farba*. He was sitting on a carpet under a *saqif* with his assistants in front of him with lances and bows in their hands and the chief men of the Masufa behind him. The merchants stood before him while he addressed them, in spite of their proximity to him, through an interpreter, out of contempt for them. At this I repented at having come to their country because of their ill manners and their contempt for white men. I made for the house of Ibn Badda', a respectable man of Sala to whom I had written to rent a house for me. He had done so. Then the *mushrif* of Iwalatan, invited those who had come with the caravan to receive his reception-gift (*diyafa*). I declined to go but my companions entreated me urgently, so I went with those who went. Then the *diyafa* was brought. It was *anili* meal mixed with a little honey and yoghourt (*laban*) which they had placed in half a gourd made into a kind of bowl. Those present drank and went away. I said to them: "Was it to this that the black man invited us?" They said: "Yes, for them this is a great banquet." Then I knew for certain that no good was to be expected from them and I wished to depart with the pilgrims of Iwalatan. But then I thought it better to go to see the seat of their king.

My stay in Iwalatan lasted about 50 days. Its inhabitants did me honour and made me their guest. Among them was the qadi of the place Muhammad b. 'Abd Allah b. Yanumur and his brother the faqih and teacher Yahya. The town of Iwalatan is extremely hot. There are a few little palm trees there in the shade of which they sow water melons. Their water comes from *ahsa* there. Mutton is abundant there and the people's clothes are of Egyptian cloth, of good quality. Most of the inhabitants there belong to the Masufa, whose women are of surpassing beauty and have a higher status than the men.

These people have remarkable and strange ways. As for their men, they feel no jealousy. None of them traces his descent through his father, but from his maternal uncle, and a man's heirs are the sons of his sister only, to the exclusion of his own sons. This is something that I have seen nowhere in the world except among the Indian infidels in the land of Mulaybar, whereas these are Muslims who observe the prayer and study fiqih and memorize the Koran. As for their women, they have no modesty in the presence of men and do not veil themselves in spite of their assiduity in prayer. If anybody wishes to marry one of them he may do so, but they do not travel with the husband, and if one of them wished to do so her family would prevent her.

The women there have friends and companions among the foreign men, just as the men have companions from among the foreign women. One of them may enter his house and find his wife with her man friend without making any objection.

One day I went into the presence of the qadi of Iwalatan, after asking his permission to enter, and found with him a young and remarkably beautiful woman. When I saw her I hesitated and wished to withdraw, but she laughed at me and experienced no shyness. The qadi said to me: "Why are you turning back? She is my friend." I was amazed at their behaviour, for he was a faqih and a pilgrim. I was informed that he had asked the sultan's permission to make the Pilgrimage that year with his lady friend (I do not know whether it was this one or not) but he had not allowed him.

One day I went into the presence of Abu Muhammad Yandakan al-Masufi in whose company we had come and found him sitting on a carpet. In the courtyard of his house there was a canopied couch with a woman on it conversing with a man seated. I said to him: "Who is this woman?" He said: "She is my wife." I said: "What connection has the man with her?" He replied: "He is her friend." I said to him: "Do you acquiese in this when you have lived in our country and become acquainted with the precepts of the Shar'?" He replied: "The association of women with men is agreeable to us, and a part of good conduct, to which no suspicion attaches. They are not like the women of your country." I was astonished at his laxity. I left him, and did not return thereafter. He invited me several times but I did not accept.

WHAT I APPROVED OF AND WHAT I DISAPPROVED OF AMONG THE ACTS OF THE SUDAN

One of their good features is their lack of oppression. They are the farthest removed of people from it and their sultan does not permit anyone to practise it. Another is the security embracing the whole country, so that neither traveller there nor dweller has anything to fear from thief or usurper. Another is that they do not interfere with the wealth of any white man who dies among them. They simply leave it in the hands of a trustworthy white man until the one to whom it is due takes it. Another is their assiduity in prayer and their persistence in performing it in congregation and beating their children to make them perform it. If it is a Friday and a man does not go early to the mosque he will not find anywhere to pray because of the press of the people. It is their habit that every man sends his servant with his prayer-mat to spread it for him in a place which he thereby has a right to until he goes to the mosque. Their prayer-carpets are made from the fronds of the tree resembling the palm which has no fruit. Another of their good features is their dressing in fine white clothes on Friday. If any one of them possesses nothing but a ragged shirt he washes it and cleanses it and attends the Friday prayer in it. Another is their eagerness to memorize the great Koran. They place fetters on their children if there appears on their part a failure to memorize it and they are not undone until they memorize it.

I went into the house of the qadi on the day of the festival and his children were fettered so I said to him: "Aren't you going to let them go?" He replied: "I shan't do so until they've got the Koran by heart!" One day I passed by a youth of theirs, of good appearance and dressed in fine clothes, with a heavy fetter on his leg. I said to those who were with me: "What has this boy done? Has he killed somebody?" The lad understood what I had said and laughed, and they said to me: "He's only been fettered so that he'll learn the Koran!"

One of their disapproved acts is that their female servants and slave girls and little girls appear before men naked, with their privy parts uncovered. During Ramadan I saw many of them in this state, for it is the custom of the *farariyya* to break their fast in the house of the sultan, and each one brings his food carried by twenty or more of his slave girls, they all being naked. Another is that their women go into the sultan's presence naked and uncovered, and that his daughters go naked. On the night of 25 Ramadan I saw about 200 slave girls bringing out food from his palace naked, having with them two of his daughters with rounded breasts having no covering upon them. Another is their sprinkling dust and ashes on their heads out of good manners. Another is what I mentioned in connection with the comic anecdote about the poets' recitation. Another is that many of them eat carrion, and dogs, and donkeys.

FOCUS QUESTIONS

1. What was it like to travel in western Africa in the fourteenth century?

2. How was Ibn Battuta treated by the people of Mali? How do you think Ibn Battuta treated them?

3. What did Ibn Battuta find unusual about the customs of the people with whom he came

into contact? What do his observations tell us about his own culture?

4. What role did religion play in the life of Ibn Battuta? What role did it play in the lives of the people of Mali?

36

Ethiopia Oriental (1609 C.E.)

JOAO DOS SANTOS

Joao dos Santos was a Dominican friar of Portuguese extraction. Little is known about his life before he was sent with a group of priests to east Africa and ultimately India. He spent nearly a decade along the east African coast between 1585 and 1597. There he joined other Portuguese missionaries and soldiers and was eyewitness to a number of ferocious battles between African tribes. He also witnessed several massacres by cannibalistic tribes.

Dos Santos's Ethiopia Oriental *provides a horrifying account of the brutality of life in Africa. Warring tribes and Portuguese adventurers proved an explosive mixture. Christian missionaries were spared neither the rigors of the environment nor the danger of capture and annihilation.*

About Tete are eleven Towns of Cafres which have each their Encosse, or Cafar Captayne, all Vassels, and subject to the jurisdiction of the Captayne of Tete. The Manamotapa having conquered those parts, distributed to diverse divers governments, and these to the Captayne of Tete and his Successors, to whom they are subject as to their King, asking his license when they will sow their rounds; the Encosses comming accompanied with some of his Cafres, and a Present, when they petition him. Before Tete, on the otherside of the River within Land to the East and North-East, are two kinds of Maneating Cafres, the Mumbos and Zimbas or Muzimbas, who eate those they take in warre, and their slaves also when they are past labour, and sell it as Beefe or Mutton. The Captayne of Tete with his eleven Encosses, and their Companies slue six hundred of the Mumbos in a Battell, not leaving one alive, and carried away their Wives and Children Captives. This was at Chicoronga a Mumbos Towne, in which was a slaughter-house, where every day they butchered their Captives; neere which the Portugals found many Negroes, men and women, bound hand and foot, destined to the slaughter for the next dayes food, whom with many others they freed. They undertooke this Expedition in behalfe of a friend of theirs, against whom these Mumbos led by their Captayne Quizura made warre. All the ground before Quizuras Gate was paved with mens Skuls, which he had killed in that war, upon which they must passe which went in or out; a thing in his conceit of great Majestie. But now he lost himselfe and all his. These Cafres about Tete are prone to warres, saying, If they dye their troubles are ended; if they live, they shall enjoy spoyles. Whiles I was there, the Captayne Pero Fernandez de Chaves, wanting Timber for a Church Doores and Porch, pretended warre, and summoned these eleven Encosses, which came willingly, but were diverted to this Timber businesses.

Whiles I was at Sena, the Muzimbas warred on some of the Portugals friends, and did eate many of them, who besought helpe of Andre de Santiago, Captayne of Sena; who went and set upon them in their Fort, which they had fortified round with a wall of Wood, with wings (revezes) and port-holes, and a deepe wide ditch, insomuch, that he was forced to send to Chaves for his best helpe, who came with above one hundred Portugals and Misticos, and those eleven Encosses. The Muzimbas by their Espials had Intelligence of their comming on the other-side the River without order, and therefore stole out of the Fort by night, and Embuscadoed themselves, and set upon the Portugals (which marched halfe a league before the Cafres) suddenly and furiously; killed them every one, and cut off their armes and legges, which with their armes they carried privily to their Fortresse. The Cafres arriving at the Wood, and seeing the slaughter returned home to Tete, and related the late Tragedie. These Zimbas worship no God, nor Idol, but their King, who (they say) is God of the Earth: and if it rains when hee would not, they shoot their Arrowes at the Skie for not obeying him; and he only eates not mans flesh. These are talle, bigge, strong; and have for Armes, small Hatchets, Arrowes, Azagaies, great Bucklers, with which they cover their whole bodies of light wood, lined with wild beasts skinnes. They eate those which they kill in warre and drink, in their skuls. If any of their own Cafres be sicke or wounded, to save labour of cure they kill and eate them.

They feasted with great jollities that day of their Victorie, and the night following; and the next morning early sallied out of their Fortresse, the Captayne arrayed in a Dominicans Casula, or Massing Vestment (Nicolas de Rosario, whom they had taken with the Portugals, and carried with them, and put to a cruell death) with a gilt Chalice in his left hand, and an Azagay in his right; and all the other Zimbas with the quarters of the Portugals at their backes, and the Captaynes head on the point of a long Lance; and drumming on the Drumme which they had taken, they presented themselves with great cryes to Santiago, and the Portugals, and after this muster returned to their Fort, saying, they must goe eate their Tete friends, Santiago, and his Portugals (which stayed wayting for Chaves, and knew nothing) now terrified with this Spectacle, resolved (if feare be capable of that word) to haste away as soone as night came, and passing over the River was perceived by the Muzimbas, who issued out upon them with great

force and slue many on the banke, and amongst others Santiago. Thus of Tete and Sena were one hundred and thirtie Portugals and Misticos, with their two valiant Captaines slayne, with little losse on their part, comming on them with sudden advantage: this was done An. 1592. Don Pedro de Sousa, Captaine of Mozambique, the next yeere, with two hundred Portugals, and fifteene hundred Cafres passed the River Zambeze, pitched his tents where Santiago had done, battered the walls of their Fort with his Artillery; but to no purpose, because they were of grosse wood, having on the inside much earth of that which was taken out of the ditch. Whereupon he resolved to stop up part of the ditch, which with much labour and perill, and some losse, he effected; some passed with hatchets to the foot of the trench, and began to cut; but the Zimbas from the walls scalded them with hot water and Oyle, specially the naked Cafres, so that none durst approach againe, as well for scalding, as for long Iron hookes which they put out of the portholes, wherewith they wounded the assaylants, and held them fast, pulling them to the holes, and killing them: so that they were forced to retire to their Tents. The next day hee caused rods to be gathered, and great baskets thereof to be made as high as their trenches, which were carried thither, and filled with earth, for the Souldiers to stand and fight upon them, that the Zimbas might not issue with their scalding liquors. Two moneths were spent in this warre, when some of the Inhabitants of that River (which liked their living by wares better than to endanger dying by warres) fained Letters from Sena, written from their wives, pretending great danger from a Cafer, which came to robbe them in the Portugals absence; which Sousa believing to bee true, brake up the siege, and passing the River by night was perceived by the Zimbas; who sallied forth with a great Crie, assayled the Campe, killed some which were behind, tooke the most of the spoiles with the Artillerie. Thus returned the Portugals with disgrace, and the Zimbas grew prouder, and after made peace with them notwithstanding.

One of these Zimbas ambitious of that honour, which they place in killing and eating of men, to get himselfe a name, adjoyned others of his Nation to him, and went Eastward, killing and eating every living thing, Men, Women, Children, Dogs, Cats, Rats, Snakes, Lizards, sparing nothing but such Cafres as adjoyned themselves to their companie in that designer. And thus five thousand of them were assembled, and went before the Ile of Quiloa; where the Sea prohibiting their passage, a traiterous Moore came and offered his service to guide them over at the low ebbes of spring tides, upon condition to spare his kindred, and to divide the spoyles with him. The Zimba accepted it, and effected his cruell purpose, slaying and taking (for future dainties to eate at leasure) three thousand Moores, and tooke the Citie Quiloa, with great riches, the people escaping by hiding themselves in the wildernesse till the Zimbas were gone; then returning to their Citie (antiently the royall Seat of the Kings of that Coast) and to this day are seene the ruines of their sumptuous Mezquites and Houses. Now, for the reward of the Traytor, he sentenced him with all his kindred to be cast into the Sea, bound hand and foot, to bee food for the fishes; saying, it was not meet that one should remayne of so wicked a generation, nor would he eate their flesh, which could not but be venomous.

After this he passed along the Coast, till he came against the Ile of Mombaza; which foure Turkish Galleyes of the Red Sea defended, and slue many of them with their Artillery: but Thome de Sousa arriving with a fleet from India tooke the Turkes, and withall destroyed Mombaza in the sight of the Muzimbas. The Captaine said that the Portugals were the Gods of the Sea, and hee of the Land; and sent an Ambassadour to Sousa, professing friendship to them, and requesting that seeing they had honourably ended their enterprise, he might beginne his, namely, to kill and eate every living thing in the Iland, which by their consent he did accordingly, burning the Palme-trees and Woods where many men were hidden, whom hee tooke and eate with all hee could get.

Thence he returned to the Coast, and went to Melinde, where Mathew Mendez with thirty Portugals ayded the King, and three thousand warlike Cafres, called Mossegueios, came also to his succour, which came suddenly on their backes when they had gotten up the wall, and were almost possessed of the Bulwarke, and chased them with such a furie, that only the Captaine with above one hundred others escaped; having found none in three hundred leagues march, which durst encounter them. And thus much of the Zimbas....

[There follows a brief description of the coast of Mozambique and the islands off it, which were under the jurisdiction of the Captain, or Governor, of Mozambique. He then turns to the part of the coast which was under the jurisdiction of the Captain of Mombasa.]

From this last Cape [Cape Delgado] to the Line [of the Equator] is the Coast of Melinde, which is of the jurisdiction of the Captaine of Mombaça. The firme Land is inhabited by Cafres, differing in Language and Customes, agreeing in barbarousnesse. Along the Kingdome of Mongallo runnes to the North the Kingdome of Munimugi, a great Cafte which confines on the South with the Lands of Mauraca and of Embeoe, and on the North with the Abyssine. The principall Iland of this Coast, Quiloa, hath beene in times past the Seat Royall, the King of the whole Coast residing there, who is now a Pety Prince; and Mombaça is the chiefe Ile and Citie, where the Portugals have a Fort, the residence of the Captaine of the Coast of Melinde. Pemba is an Iland about eight leagues from the Shoare, and ten long, plentifull of Rice and Kine, Fruits and Wood: sometime subject to the Portugalls till the pride and lazinesse of some made the people rebell, and could never after be regayned. In the Ile of Pate are Pate, Sio and Ampaza, three Cities governed by so many Kings, tributarie to Portugal. Ampaza hath been best builded of any Citie in those parts, but destroyed by the Portugals, the Citie sacked and burnt with eight thousand Palme-Trees, which grew about it, cut downe. The Ile of Lamo hath great Asses, but of little service. This Island was chastised when Ampaza was destroyed, and Mombaça also, by Martin Alfonso de Mello. The King of Ampaza was slaine, and his head carried on a Pole at Goa in triumph. When he was gone, Mirale Beque [Amir Ali Bey] the Turks came with foure Galleys out of the Red Sea, and infested that Coast, till the Zimbas and the Portugalls ended the businesse with a new Armada, the Portugals captiving and spoyling, the Zimbas eating the Turkes and Inhabitants. The King of Lamo for betraying the Portugals to the Turkes were beheaded. The Ile and Citie of Mandra [? Manda] which had denyed the Portugals to land, saying, the Sunne onely might enter there, was sacked and two thousand Palme-trees cut down. In the Coast of Melinde they are great Witches. The Mossegueyos live of their Kine, which they oft let blond both to prevent the garget, and to make therewith a kinds of pottage with milke and fresh dung of the same Kine, which mixed together and heat at the fire they drinke, saying, it makes them strong. The Boyes of seven or eight yeeres weare Clay fastened on the hayre of the head, and still renewed with new Clay, weighing sometimes five or six pounds. Nor may they be free hereof till the Warre or lawfull fight hee hath killed a man, and show to the Captaine some tokens of that fact; which only makes them free and Knights of their cast. Hereupon they grow audacious, and prove dreadfull to others.

Brava is a small Citie but strong, inhabited with Moores, Friends and Vassals to the Portugals. It is in one Degree North, and very hot. Magadoxo is in 3° 30°. Within the land are the Maracatos, which have a custome to sew up their Females, specially their Slaves being young to make them unable for conception, which makes these Slaves sell dearer both for their chastitie, and for better confidence which their Masters put in them. They cut also their Boyes and make them Eunuches.

In the Ile of Zanzibar dwelt one Chande a great Sorcerer, which caused his Pangayo *pan-gaia, small dhow],* which the Factor had taken against his will, to stand still as it were in defiance of the Winde, till the Factor had satisfied him, and then to flye forth the River after her fellowes at his words. Hee made that a Portugall which had angred him, could never open his mouth to speake, but a Cock crowed in his belly, till he had reconciled himselfe: with other like odious sorceries.

From Magadoxo to Sacotora [Socotra] one hundred and fifty leagues is a desart Coast, and dishabited without Rivers. In which Desarts breed the great birds, called Emas, which breed on the Sands, and have but two young ones, as Pigeons. Their stomacks will consume Iron and Stones, and flye not but touch the ground with their feet, running with their wings spread, as lightly as other Birds flye. They are white, ash-coloured; their egges white, holding almost three pints.

FOCUS QUESTIONS

1. What was the attitude of the Mumbos toward life and death? Does it relate to their cannibalism?

2. What is Joao dos Santos's reaction to the cannibalism of the Mumbos? To their slaughter?

3. What were the symbols of the Zimbas' monarchy? How did they sustain the king's power?

4. What was the nature of warfare as practiced by the Portuguese against Ampaza?

Asian Cultures

Réunion des Musées Nationaux/Art Resource, NY

Palace Scene. This thirteenth-century painting is an illustration from *The Tale of Genji*, Japan's most famous novel, depicting domestic life within the palace.

FOCUS QUESTIONS

1. What do these scenes indicate about medieval Japanese courtly love?

2. *The Tale of Genji* shaped aristocratic behavior more than it reflected it. Do these illustrations from it indicate an idealized portrait of domestic conduct?

3. What do the constant presence and changing character of the barriers (a screen in the first panel, the woman's back in the second, a bench in the third) indicate about *The Tale of Genji*?

4. *The Tale of Genji* was written by a woman. Do these illustrations inspired by the novel reflect its female authorship?

37

Lessons for Women (ca. 99 C.E.)

PAN CHAO

Pan Chao (ca. 45–116 C.E.) was born into an important Chinese literary family that had, for generations, served at the courts of Chinese rulers. Her father was a renowned scholar, but it was her mother who educated and trained her for literary pursuits. She was widely regarded as the leading woman of learning at the court of the Emperor Han Ho-ti (88–105) and she served as tutor to his wives and daughters. Pan's brother was the official historian of the Han court; and when he died with his major work unfinished, it was Pan Chao who was appointed to complete it. Although as a woman she could not hold the rank of Imperial historian, she finished the Book of Han, *one of the most important sources for the study of the Han dynasty. Pan Chao also composed poetry and took a special interest in works relating to women, writing a commentary on the* Lives of Admirable Women *by Liu Hsiang. It was that work which may have inspired her own brief treatise, Nü Chieh, or* Lessons for Women.*

Lessons for Women *is a brief tract that mostly espoused traditional Confucian views but was presented in a practical, guidebook form. The work was probably written for the instruction of her own daughters, although its literary form suggests that Pan Chao hoped it might reach a wider audience.*

LESSONS FOR WOMEN: INSTRUCTIONS IN SEVEN CHAPTERS FOR A WOMAN'S ORDINARY WAY OF LIFE IN THE FIRST CENTURY A.D.

Introduction

I, the unworthy writer, am unsophisticated, unenlightened, and by nature unintelligent, but I am fortunate both to have received not a little favor from my scholarly father, and to have had a (cultured) mother and instructresses upon whom to rely for a literary education as well as for training in good manners. More than forty years have passed since at the age of fourteen I took up the dustpan and the broom in the Ts'ao family. During this time with trembling heart I feared constantly that I might disgrace my parents, and that I might multiply difficulties for both the women and the men (of my husband's family). Day and night I was distressed in heart, (but) I labored without confessing weariness. Now and hereafter, however, I know how to escape (from such fears).

Being careless, and by nature stupid, I taught and trained (my children) without system. Consequently I fear that my son Ku may bring disgrace upon the Imperial Dynasty by whose Holy Grace he has unprecedentedly received the extraordinary privilege of wearing the Gold and the Purple, a privilege for the attainment of which (by my son, I) a humble subject never even hoped. Nevertheless, now that he is a man and able to plan his own life,

I need not again have concern for him. But I do grieve that you, my daughters, just now at the age for marriage, have not at this time had gradual training and advice; that you still have not learned the proper customs for married women. I fear that by failure in good manners in other families you will humiliate both your ancestors and your clan. I am now seriously ill, life is uncertain. As I have thought of you all in so untrained a state, I have been uneasy many a time for you. At hours of leisure I have composed in seven chapters these instructions under the title, "Lessons for Women." In order that you may have something wherewith to benefit your persons, I wish every one of you, my daughters, each to write out a copy for yourself.

From this time on every one of you strive to practise these (lessons).

CHAPTER I

Humility

On the third day after the birth of a girl the ancients observed three customs: (first) to place the baby below the bed; (second) to give her a potsherd with which to play; and (third) to announce her birth to her ancestors by an offering. Now to lay the baby below the bed plainly indicated that she is lowly and weak, and should regard it as her primary duty to humble herself before others. To give her potsherds with which to play indubitably signified that she should practise labor and consider it her primary duty to be industrious. To announce her birth before her ancestors clearly meant that she ought to esteem as her primary duty the continuation of the observance of worship in the home.

These three ancient customs epitomize a woman's ordinary way of life and the teachings of the traditional ceremonial rites and regulations. Let a woman modestly yield to others; let her respect others; let her put others first, herself last. Should she do something good, let her not mention it; should she do something bad, let her not deny it. Let her bear disgrace; let her even endure when others speak or do evil to her. Always let her

seem to tremble and to fear. (When a woman follows maxims such as these,) then she may be said to humble herself before others.

Let a woman retire late to bed, but rise early to duties; let her not dread tasks by day or by night. Let her not refuse to perform domestic duties whether easy or difficult. That which must be done, let her finish completely, tidily, and systematically. (When a woman follows such rules as these,) then she may be said to be industrious.

Let a woman be correct in manner and upright in character in order to serve her husband. Let her live in purity and quietness (of spirit), and attend to her own affairs. Let her love not gossip and silly laughter. Let her cleanse and purify and arrange in order the wine and the food for the offerings to the ancestors. (When a woman observes such principles as these,) then she may be said to continue ancestral worship.

No woman who observes these three (fundamentals of life) has ever had a bad reputation or has fallen into disgrace. If a woman fail to observe them, how can her name be honored; how can she but bring disgrace upon herself?

CHAPTER II

Husband and Wife

The Way of husband and wife is intimately connected with *Yin* and *Yang*, and relates the individual to gods and ancestors. Truly it is the great principle of Heaven and Earth, and the great basis of human relationships. Therefore the "Rites" honor union of man and woman; and in the "Book of Poetry" the "First Ode" manifests the principle of marriage. For these reasons the relationship cannot but be an important one.

If a husband be unworthy then he possesses nothing by which to control his wife. If a wife be unworthy, then she possesses nothing with which to serve her husband. If a husband does not control his wife, then the rules of conduct manifesting his authority are abandoned and broken. If a wife does not serve her husband, then the proper relationship

Art Resource, NY

The Emperor's Favorite. Lady Yang was a favorite concubine of the T'ang ruler Ming-huang and was blamed for luring him from his official duties.

(between men and women) and the natural order of things are neglected and destroyed. As a matter of fact the purpose of these two (the controlling of women by men, and the serving of men by women) is the same.

Now examine the gentlemen of the present age. They only know that wives must be controlled, and that the husband's rules of conduct manifesting his authority must be established. They therefore teach their boys to read books and (study) histories. But they do not in the least understand that husbands and masters must (also) be served, and that the proper relationship and the rites should be maintained.

Yet only to teach men and not to teach women,—is that not ignoring the essential relation between them? According to the "Rites," it is the rule to begin to teach children to read at the age of eight years, and by the age of fifteen years they ought then to be ready for cultural training. Only why should it not be (that girls' education as well as boys' be) according to this principle?

CHAPTER III

Respect and Caution

As *Yin* and *Yang* are not of the same nature, so man and woman have different characteristics. The distinctive quality of the *Yang* is rigidity; the function of the *Yin* is yielding. Man is honored for strength; a woman is beautiful on account of her gentleness. Hence there arose the common saying: "A man though born like a wolf may, it is feared, become a weak monstrosity; a woman though born like a mouse may, it is feared, become a tiger."

Now for self-culture nothing equals respect for others. To counteract firmness nothing equals compliance. Consequently it can be said that the Way of respect and acquiescence is woman's most important principle of conduct. So respect may be defined as nothing other than holding on to that which is permanent; and acquiescence nothing other than being liberal and generous. Those who are steadfast in devotion know that they should stay in their proper places; those who are liberal and generous esteem others, and honor and serve (them).

If husband and wife have the habit of staying together, never leaving one another, and following each other around within the limited space of their own rooms, then they will lust after and take liberties with one another. From such action improper language will arise between the two. This kind of discussion may lead to licentiousness. Out of licentiousness will be born a heart of disrespect to the husband. Such a result comes from not knowing that one should stay in one's proper place.

Furthermore, affairs may be either crooked or straight; words may be either right or wrong. Straightforwardness cannot but lead to quarreling; crookedness cannot but lead to accusation. If there are really accusations and quarrels, then undoubtedly there will be angry affairs. Such a result comes from not esteeming others, and not honoring and serving (them).

(If wives) suppress not contempt for husbands, then it follows (that such wives) rebuke and scold (their husbands). (If husbands) stop not short of anger, then they are certain to beat (their wives). The correct relationship between husband and wife is based upon harmony and intimacy, and (conjugal) love is grounded in proper union. Should actual blows be dealt, how could matrimonial relationship be preserved? Should sharp words be spoken, how could (conjugal) love exist? If love and proper relationship both be destroyed, then husband and wife are divided.

CHAPTER IV

Womanly Qualifications

A woman (ought to) have four qualifications: (1) womanly virtue; (2) womanly words; (3) womanly bearing; and (4) womanly work. Now what is called womanly virtue need not be brilliant ability, exceptionally different from others. Womanly words need be neither clever in debate nor keen in conversation. Womanly appearance requires

neither a pretty nor a perfect face and form. Womanly work need not be work done more skilfully than that of others.

To guard carefully her chastity; to control circumspectly her behavior; in every motion to exhibit modesty; and to model each act on the best usage, this is womanly virtue.

To choose her words with care; to avoid vulgar language; to speak at appropriate times; and not to weary others (with much conversation), may be called the characteristics of womanly words.

To wash and scrub filth away; to keep clothes and ornaments fresh and clean; to wash the head and bathe the body regularly, and to keep the person free from disgraceful filth, may be called the characteristics of womanly bearing.

With whole-hearted devotion to sew and to weave; to love not gossip and silly laughter; in cleanliness and order (to prepare) the wine and food for serving guests, may be called the characteristics of womanly work.

These four qualifications characterize the greatest virtue of a woman. No woman can afford to be without them. In fact they are very easy to possess if a woman only treasure them in her heart. The ancients had a saying: "Is Love afar off? If I desire love, then love is at hand!" So can it be said of these qualifications.

CHAPTER V

Whole-Hearted Devotion

Now in the "Rites" is written the principle that a husband may marry again, but there is no Canon that authorizes a woman to be married the second time. Therefore it is said of husbands as of Heaven, that as certainly as people cannot run away from Heaven, so surely a wife cannot leave (a husband's) home).

If people in action or character disobey the spirits of Heaven and of Earth, then Heaven punishes them. Likewise if a woman errs in the rites and in the proper mode of conduct, then her husba[?] esteems her lightly. The ancient book, "A P[?]

for Women," says: "To obtain the love of one man is the crown of a woman's life; to lose the love of one man is to miss the aim in woman's life." For these reasons a woman cannot but seek to win her husband's heart. Nevertheless, the beseeching wife need not use flattery, coaxing words, and cheap methods to gain intimacy.

Decidedly nothing is better (to gain the heart of a husband) than whole-hearted devotion and correct manners. In accordance with the rites and the proper mode of conduct, (let a woman) live a pure life. Let her have ears that hear not licentiousness; and eyes that see not depravity. When she goes outside her own home, let her not be conspicuous in dress and manners. When at home let her not neglect her dress. Women should not assemble in groups, nor gather together, (for gossip and silly laughter). They should not stand watching in the gateways. (If a woman follows) these rules, she may be said to have whole-hearted devotion and correct manners.

If, in all her actions, she is frivolous, she sees and hears (only) that which pleases herself. At home her hair is dishevelled, and her dress is slovenly. Outside the home she emphasizes her femininity to attract attention; she says what ought not to be said; and she looks at what ought not to be seen. (If a woman does such as) these, (she may be) said to be without whole-hearted devotion and correct manners.

CHAPTER VI

Implicit Obedience

Now "to win the love of one man is the crown of a woman's life; to lose the love of one man is her eternal disgrace." This saying advises a fixed will and a whole-hearted devotion for a woman. Ought she then to lose the hearts of her father- and mother-in-law?

There are times when love may lead to differences of opinion (between individuals); there are times when duty may lead to disagreement. Even should the husband say that he loves something, when the parents-in-law say "no," this is called a

case of duty leading to disagreement. This being so, then what about the hearts of the parents-in-law? Nothing is better than an obedience which sacrifices personal opinion.

Whenever the mother-in-law says, "Do not do that," and if what she says is right, unquestionably the daughter-in-law obeys. Whenever the mother-in-law says, "Do that," even if what she says is wrong, still the daughter-in-law submits unfailingly to the command.

Let a woman not act contrary to the wishes and the opinions of parents-in-law about right and wrong; let her not dispute with them what is straight and what is crooked. Such (docility) may be called obedience which sacrifices personal opinion. Therefore the ancient book, "A Pattern for Women," says: "If a daughter-in-law (who follows the wishes of her parents-in-law) is like an echo and a shadow, how could she not be praised?"

CHAPTER VII

Harmony with Younger Brothers- and Sisters-in-Law

In order for a wife to gain the love of her husband, she must win for herself the love of her parents-in-law. To win for herself the love of her parents-in-law, she must secure for herself the good will of younger brothers- and sisters-in-law. For these reasons the right and the wrong, the praise and the blame of a woman alike depend upon younger brothers- and sisters-in-law. Consequently it will not do for a woman to lose their affection.

They are stupid both who know not that they must not lose (the hearts of) younger brothers- and sisters-in-law, and who cannot be in harmony with them in order to be intimate with them. Excepting only the Holy Men, few are able to be faultless. Now Yen Tzû's greatest virtue was that he was able to reform. Confucius praised him (for not committing a misdeed) the second time. (In comparison with him) a woman is the more likely (to make mistakes).

Although a woman possesses a worthy woman's qualifications, and is wise and discerning by nature, is she able to be perfect? Yet if a woman live in harmony with her immediate family, unfavorable criticism will be silenced (within the home. But) if a man and woman disagree, then this evil will be noised abroad. Such consequences are inevitable. The "Book of Change" says:

"Should two hearts harmonize,
The united strength can cut gold.
Words from hearts which agree,
Give forth fragrance like the orchid."

This saying may be applied to (harmony in the home).

Though a daughter-in-law and her younger sisters-in-law are equal in rank, nevertheless (they should) respect (each other); though love (between them may be) sparse, their proper relationship should be intimate. Only the virtuous, the beautiful, the modest, and the respectful (young women) can accordingly rely upon the sense of duty to make their affection sincere, and magnify love to bind their relationships firmly.

Then the excellence and the beauty of such a daughter-in-law becomes generally known. Moreover, any flaws and mistakes are hidden and unrevealed. Parents-in-law boast of her good deeds; her husband is satisfied with her. Praise of her radiates, making her illustrious in district and in neighborhood; and her brightness reaches to her own father and mother.

But a stupid and foolish person as an elder sister-in-law uses her rank to exalt herself; as a younger sister-in-law, because of parents' favor, she becomes filled with arrogance. If arrogant, how can a woman live in harmony with others? If love and proper relationships be perverted, how can praise be secured? In such instances the wife's good is hidden, and her faults are declared. The mother-in-law will be angry, and the husband will be indignant. Blame will reverberate and spread in and outside the home. Disgrace will gather upon the daughter-in-law's person, on the one hand to add humiliation to her own father and mother, and on the other to increase the difficulties of her husband.

Such then is the basis for both honor and disgrace; the foundation for reputation or for ill-repute. Can a woman be too cautious? Consequently to seek the hearts of young brothers- and sisters-in-law decidedly nothing can be esteemed better than modesty and acquiescence.

Modesty is virtue's handle; acquiescence is the wife's (most refined) characteristic. All who possess these two have sufficient for harmony with others. In the "Book of Poetry" it is written that "here is no evil; there is no dart." So it may be said of (these two, modesty and acquiescence).

FOCUS QUESTIONS

1. What are the responsibilities of a woman to her family in Han China?

2. Are the precepts of humility a practical or an ideal guide for the life of a woman?

3. How do the concepts of yin and yang govern relations between the sexes?

4. Why does Pan Chao believe in the importance of education for women?

38

A Record of Buddhistic Kingdoms (399–414 C.E.)

FA-HSIEN

Fa-hsien (also Fa-hien), which means "illustrious master of the law," was a Chinese Buddhist monk. Orphaned at an early age, Fa-hsien decided to continue the religious life planned for him by his father rather than to be incorporated into the family of his uncle. Little is known of his novitiate, though one legend tells of how he shamed a band of thieves from stealing the grain of his monastery. At the age of 25, Fa-hsien began a quest to learn about Buddhist traditions in India and to discover authentic Buddhist writings. His travels in Sumatra, Ceylon, India, and Tibet coincided with a general curiosity of Chinese Buddhists about the practice of their religion abroad. Fa-hsien recovered a large quantity of Buddhist writings and returned to China, where he devoted the rest of his life to translating them from Sanskrit. It is recorded that he died at the age of 88.

A Record of Buddhistic Kingdoms (394–414) is an account of the journey of Fa-hsien and his companions, mostly in India. They visited as many of the Buddhist sacred shrines as they could, especially those associated with the presence of the Buddha. The selections presented here show the reasons for the establishment of these shrines, the legends that surrounded them, and the ways in which they were maintained.

Buddha's alms-bowl is in this country. Formerly, a king of Yüeh-she raised a large force and invaded this country, wishing to carry the bowl away. Having subdued the kingdom, as he and his captains were sincere believers in the Law of Buddha, and wished to carry off the bowl, they proceeded to present their offerings on a great scale. When they had done so to the Three Precious Ones, he made a large elephant be grandly caparisoned, and placed the bowl upon it. But the elephant knelt down on the ground, and was unable to go forward. Again he caused a four-wheeled waggon to be prepared in which the bowl was put to be conveyed away. Eight elephants were then yoked to it, and dragged it with their united strength; but neither were they able to go forward. [The] king knew that the time for an association [between] himself and the bowl had not yet arrived, and was sad and deeply ashamed of himself. Forthwith he built a tope at the place and a monastery, and left a guard to watch (the bowl), making all sorts of contributions.

There may be there more than seven hundred monks. When it is near midday, they bring out the bowl, and, along with the common people, make their various offerings to it, after which they take their midday meal. In the evening, at the time of incense, they bring the bowl out again. It may contain rather more than two pecks, and is of various colours, black predominating, with the seams that show its fourfold composition distinctly marked. Its thickness is about the fifth of an inch, and it has a bright and glossy lustre. When poor people throw into it a few flowers, it becomes immediately full, while some very rich people, wishing to make offering of many flowers, might not stop till they had thrown in hundreds, thousands, and myriads of bushels, and yet would not be able to fill it.

Going west for sixteen yojanas, Fa-hsien came to the city He-lo in the borders of the country of Nagâra, where there is the flat-bone of Buddha's skull, deposited in a vihâra adorned all over with gold-leaf and the seven sacred substances. The king of the country, revering and honouring the bone, and anxious lest it should be stolen away, has selected eight individuals, representing the great families in the kingdom, and committed to each a seal, with which he should seal (its shrine) and guard (the relic). At early dawn these eight men come, and after each has inspected his seal, they open the door. This done, they wash their hands with scented water and bring out the bone, which they place outside the vihâra, on a lofty platform, where it is supported on a round pedestal of the seven precious substances, and covered with a bell of lapis lazuli, both adorned with rows of pearls. Its colour is of a yellowish white, and it forms an imperfect circle twelve inches round, curving upwards to the centre. Every day, after it has been brought forth, the keepers of the vihâra ascend a high gallery, where they beat great drums, blow conchs, and clash their copper cymbals. When the king hears them, he goes to the vihâra, and makes his offerings of flowers and incense. When he has done this, he (and his attendants) in order, one after another, (raise the bone), place it (for a moment) on the top of their heads, and then depart, going out by the door on the west as they had entered by that on the east. The king every morning makes his offerings and performs his worship, and afterwards gives audience on the business of his government. The chiefs of the Vaisyas also make their offerings before they attend to their family affairs. Every day it is so, and there is no remissness in the observance of the custom. When all the offerings are over, they replace the bone in the vihâra, where there is a vimoksha tope, of the seven precious substances, and rather more than five cubits high, sometimes open, sometimes shut, to contain it. In front of the door of the vihâra, there are parties who every morning sell flowers and incense, and those who wish to make offerings buy some of all kinds.

The kings of various countries are also constantly sending messengers with offerings. The vihâra stands in a square of thirty paces, and though heaven should shake and earth be rent, this place would not move.

From this place they travelled south-east, passing by a succession of very many monasteries, with a multitude of monks, who might be counted by myriads. After passing all these places, they came to a country named Muttra. They still followed the course of the P'oo-na river, on the banks of which, left and right, there were twenty monasteries, which might contain three thousand monks; and (here) the Law of Buddha was still more flourishing. Everywhere, from the Sandy Desert, in all the countries of India, the kings had been firm believers in that Law. When they make their offerings to a community of monks, they take off their royal caps, and along with their relatives and ministers, supply them with food with their own hands. That done, (the king) has a carpet spread for himself on the ground, and sits down on it in front of the chairman;—they dare not presume to sit on couches in front of the community. The laws and ways, according to which the kings presented their offerings when Buddha was in the world, have been handed down to the present day.

All south from this is named the Middle Kingdom. In it the cold and heat are finely tempered, and there is neither hoarfrost nor snow. The people are numerous and happy; they have not to register their households, or attend to any magistrates and their rules; only those who cultivate the royal land have to pay (a portion of) the gain from it. If they want to go, they go; if they want to stay on, they stay. The king governs without decapitation or (other) corporal punishments. Criminals are simply fined, lightly or heavily, according to the circumstances (of each case). Even in cases of repeated attempts at wicked rebellion, they only have their right hands cut off. The king's body-guards and attendants all have salaries. Throughout the whole country the people do not kill any living creature, nor drink intoxicating liquor, nor eat onions or garlic. The only exception is that of the Chandâlas. That is the name for those who are (held to be) wicked men, and live apart from others. When they enter the gate of a city or a market-place, they strike a piece of wood to make themselves known, so that men know and avoid them, and do not come into contact with them. In that country they do not keep pigs and fowls, and do not sell live cattle; in the markets there are no butchers' shops and no dealers in intoxicating drink…. Only the Chandâlas are fishermen and hunters, and sell flesh meat. At the places where Buddha, when he was in the world, cut his hair and nails, topes are erected; and where the three Buddhas that preceded Sâkyamuni Buddha and he himself sat; where they walked, and where images of their persons were made. At all these places topes were made, and are still existing. At the place where 'Sakra, Ruler of the Devas, and the king of the Brahmaloka followed Buddha down (from the Trayastrimsas heaven) they have also raised a tope.

At this place the monks and nuns may be a thousand, who all receive their food from the common store, and pursue their studies, some of the mahâyâna and some of the hînayâna. Where they live, there is a white-eared dragon, which acts the part of patron to the community of these monks, causing abundant harvests in the country, and the enriching rains to come in season, without the occurrence of any calamities, so that the monks enjoy their repose and ease. In gratitude for its kindness, they have made for it a dragon-house, with a carpet for it to sit on, and appointed for it a diet of blessing, which they present for its nourishment. Every day they set apart three of their number to go to its house, and eat there. Whenever the summer retreat is ended, the dragon straightway changes its form, and appears as a small snake, with white spots at the side of its ears. As soon as the monks recognise it, they fill a copper vessel with cream, into which they put the creature, and then carry it round from the one who has the highest seat (at their tables) to him who has the lowest, when it appears as if saluting them. When it has been taken round, immediately it disappears; and every year it thus comes forth once. The country is very productive, and the people are prosperous, and happy beyond comparison. When people of other countries come to it, they are exceedingly attentive to them all, and supply them with what they need.

When Fa-hsien and Tâo-ching first arrived at the Jetavana monastery, and thought how the World-honoured one had formerly resided there for twenty-five years, painful reflections arose in their minds. Born in a border-land, along with their like-minded friends, they had travelled through so many kingdoms; some of those friends had returned (to their own land), and some had (died), proving the impermanence and uncertainty of life; and to-day they saw the place where Buddha had lived now unoccupied by him. They were melancholy through their pain of heart, and the crowd of monks came out, and asked them from what kingdom they were come. "We are come," they replied, "from the land of Han." "Strange," said the monks with a sigh, "that men of a border country should be able to come here in search of our Law!" Then they said to one another, "During all the time that we, preceptors and monks, have succeeded to one another, we have never seen men of Han, followers of our system, arrive here."

To each of the great residences for the monks at the Jetavana vihâra there were two gates, one facing the east and the other facing the north. The park (containing the whole) was the space of ground which the (Vaisya) head Sudatta purchased by covering it with gold coins. The vihâra was exactly in the centre. Here Buddha lived for a longer time than at any other place, preaching his Law and converting men. At the places where he walked and sat they also (subsequently) reared topes, each having its particular name; and here was the place where Sundari murdered a person and then falsely charged Buddha (with the crime). Outside the east gate of the Jetavana, at a distance of seventy paces to the north, on the west of the road, Buddha held a discussion with the (advocates of the) ninety-six schemes of erroneous doctrine, when the king and his great officers, the householders, and people were all assembled in crowds to hear it. Then a woman belonging to one of the erroneous systems, by name Chañchamana, prompted by the envious hatred in her heart, and having put on (extra) clothes in front of her person, so as to give her the appearance of being with child, falsely accused Buddha before all the assembly of having acted unlawfully (towards her). On this, 'Sakra, Ruler of

Devas, changed himself and some devas into white mice, which bit through the strings about her waist; and when this was done, the (extra) clothes which she wore dropt down on the ground. The earth at the same time was rent, and she went (down) alive into hell.

FOCUS QUESTIONS

1. Why do Fa-hsien and the monks he meets at Jetavana think of China as a borderland?

2. What is the relationship between the relic of the Buddha's skull and the community in which it is kept?

3. What form of government does Fa-hsien most admire? How is order kept?

4. What is the significance of the dragon/snake to the monks?

5. What conclusions do you draw from the accusations made against the Buddha?

39

The Seventeen Article Constitution (640 C.E.)

PRINCE SHOTOKU

Developments in Chinese culture have often had a profound impact on neighboring states. Beginning in the sixth century, for example, Japan became interested in all things Chinese. First, Japan adopted the Chinese variety of Buddhism, and this religious change in turn led to a general transformation of traditional Japanese society. Consequently, a culture, long dominated by powerful clans and by customary Shinto rituals, became one with a strong emperor and central bureaucracy, governing according to Confucian and Buddhist ideals.

This transformation can clearly be seen in The Seventeen Article Constitution, *which Prince Shotoku instituted in 604 during his regency, which lasted from 593 to 622. Not so much a formal legal document as a string of moral precepts, liberally borrowed from Chinese sources, the* Constitution *guided the Taika reforms later in the century, which greatly enhanced the authority of the central government at the expense of the clans.*

THE SEVENTEEN ARTICLE CONSTITUTION, 604 A.D.

Summer, 4th month, 3rd day [12th year of Empress Suiko, 604 A.D.] The Crown Prince personally drafted and promulgated a constitution consisting of seventeen articles, which are as follows:

I. Harmony is to be cherished, and opposition for opposition's sake must be avoided as a matter of principle. Men are often influenced by partisan feelings, except a few sagacious ones. Hence there are some who disobey their lords and fathers, or who dispute with their neighboring villages. If those above are harmonious and those below are cordial, their discussion will be guided by a spirit of conciliation, and reason shall naturally prevail. There will be nothing that cannot be accomplished.

II. With all our heart, revere the three treasures. The three treasures, consisting of Buddha, the Doctrine, and the Monastic Order, are the final refuge of the four generated beings, and are the supreme objects of worship in all countries. Can any man in any age ever fail to respect these teachings? Few men are utterly devoid of goodness, and men can be taught to follow the teachings. Unless they take refuge in the three treasures, there is no way of rectifying their misdeeds.

III. When an imperial command is given, obey it with reverence. The sovereign is likened to heaven, and his subjects are likened to earth. With heaven providing the cover and earth supporting it, the four seasons proceed in orderly fashion, giving sustenance to all that which is in nature. If earth attempts to overtake the functions of heaven, it destroys everything. Therefore when the sovereign speaks, his subjects must listen; when the superiors acts, the inferior must follow his examples. When an imperial command is given, carry it out with diligence. If there is no reverence shown to the imperial command ruin will automatically result.

IV. The ministers and functionaries must act on the basis of decorum, for the basis of governing the people consists in decorum. If the superiors do not behave with decorum, offenses will ensue. If the ministers behave with decorum, there will be no confusion about ranks. If the people behave with decorum, the nation will be governed well of its own.

V. Cast away your ravenous desire for food and abandon your covetousness for material possessions. If a suit is brought before you, render a clear-cut judgment.... Nowadays, those who are in the position of pronouncing judgment are motivated by making private gains, and as a rule, receive bribes. Thus the plaints of the rich are like a stone flung into water, while those of the poor are like water poured over a stone. Under these circumstances, the poor will be denied recourses to justice, which constitutes a dereliction of duty of the minister.

VI. Punish that which is evil and encourage that which is good. This is an excellent rule from antiquity. Do not conceal the good qualities of others, and always correct that which is evil which comes to your attention. Consider those flatterers and tricksters as constituting a superb weapon for the overthrow of the state, and a sharp sword for the destruction of people. Smooth-tongued adulators love to report to their superiors the errors of their inferiors; and to their inferiors, castigate the errors of their superiors. Men of this type lack loyalty to the sovereign and have no compassion for the people. They are the ones who can cause great civil disorders.

VII. Every man must be given his clearly delineated responsibility. If a wise man is entrusted with office, the sound of praise arises. If a wicked man holds office, disturbances become frequent.... In all things, great or small, find the right man, and the country will be well governed. On all occasions, in an emergency or otherwise, seek out a wise man, which in itself is an enriching experience. In this manner, the state will be lasting and its sacerdotal functions will be free from danger. Therefore did the sage kings of old seek the man to fill the office, not the office for the sake of the man.

VIII. The ministers and functionaries must attend the court early in the morning and retire late. The business of the state must not be taken lightly. A full day is hardly enough to complete work, and if the attendance is late, emergencies cannot be met. If the officials retire early, the work cannot be completed.

IX. Good faith is the foundation of righteousness, and everything must be guided by faith. The key to the success of the good and the failure of the bad can also be found in good faith. If the officials observe good faith with one another, everything can be accomplished. If they do not observe good faith, everything is bound to fail.

X. Discard wrath and anger from your heart and from your looks. Do not be offended when others differ with you. Everyone has his own mind, and each mind has its own leanings. Thus what is right with him is wrong with us, and what is right with us is wrong with him. We are not necessarily sages, and he is not necessarily a fool. We are all simply ordinary men, and none of us can set up a rule to determine the right from wrong…. Therefore, instead of giving way to anger as others do, let us fear our own mistakes. Even though we may have a point, let us follow the multitude and act like them.

XI. Observe clearly merit and demerit and assign reward and punishment accordingly. Nowadays, rewards are given in the absence of meritorious work, punishments without corresponding crimes. The ministers, who are in charge of public affairs, must therefore take upon themselves the task of administering a clear-cut system of rewards and punishments.

XII. Provincial authorities or local nobles are not permitted to levy exactions on the people. A country cannot have two sovereigns, nor the people two masters. The people of the whole country must have the sovereign as their only master. The officials who are given certain functions are all his subjects. Being the subjects of the sovereign, these officials have no more right than others to levy exactions on the people.

XIII. All persons entrusted with office must attend equally to their functions. If absent from work due to illness or being sent on missions, and work for that period is neglected, on their return, they must perform their duties conscientiously by taking into account that which transpired before and during their absence. Do not permit lack of knowledge of the intervening period as an excuse to hinder effective performance of public affairs.

XIV. Ministers and functionaries are asked not to be envious of others. If we envy others, they in turn will envy us, and there is no limit to the evil that envy can cause us. We resent others when their intelligence is superior to ours, and we envy those who surpass us in talent. This is the reason why it takes five hundred years before we can meet a wise man, and in a thousand years it is still difficult to find one sage. If we cannot find wise men and sages, how can the country be governed?

XV. The way of a minister is to turn away from private motives and to uphold public good. Private motives breed resentment, and resentful feelings cause a man to act discordantly. If he fails to act in accord with others, he sacrifices the public interests for the sake of his private feelings. When resentment arises, it goes counter to the existing order and breaks the law. Therefore it is said in the first article that superiors and inferiors must act in harmony. The purport is the same.

XVI. The people may be employed in forced labor only at seasonable times. This is an excellent rule from antiquity. Employ the people in the winter months when they are at leisure. However, from spring to autumn, when they are engaged in agriculture or sericulture, do not employ them. Without their agricultural endeavor, there is no food, and without their sericulture, there is no clothing.

XVII. Major decisions must not be made by one person alone, but must be deliberated with many. On the other hand, it is not necessary to consult many people on minor questions. If important matters are not discussed fully, there may always be a fear of committing mistakes. A thorough discussion with many can prevent it and bring about a reasonable solution.

FOCUS QUESTIONS

1. What is the role that Shotoku assigns to the emperor?

2. From the evidence of the *Constitution,* what kind of economy did Japan have in the seventh century?

3. How does Shotoku incorporate Buddhist ideals into the *Constitution?*

4. What do you think of the *Constitution* as a practical document for governance?

40

The Examination System During the T'ang Dynasty (8th century C.E.)

As the first T'ang emperors had themselves been bureaucrats, it is not surprising that after they seized power they initiated a series of reforms designed to centralize power. A hierarchy of the departments of state was created with power ascending to the emperor's three central councils. T'ang reforms began with a stiffening of the examination system by which government servants were chosen. The tests became harder to pass and more difficult to corrupt. Aspirants, even from noble families, thus had to devote their teenage years to study if they were to rise to high levels of imperial service. Those who passed were honored and brought honor to their villages and regions. Even those who failed were respected for making the attempt.

The importance of the examination system in identifying the future governors of China inevitably led to snobbery and hypocrisy. Stories of abuses became a part of folk culture and served both as warnings and instruction for succeeding generations. The following is a selection of such tales.

Hsiao Ying-shih passed the imperial examination in 735. Proud of his talent, he was unequaled in conceit and arrogance. He often took a pot of wine and went out to visit rural scenic areas. Once during such an outing, he stayed at an inn, drinking and chanting poetry by himself. Suddenly a storm arose, and an old man dressed in a purple robe came in with a page boy to take shelter. Because of their informality, Hsiao Ying-shih treated them rather insolently. In a short while, the storm was over, the rain stopped, carriages and retinues came, and the old man was escorted away. Flustered, Hsiao Ying-shih inquired about the old man's identity, and the people around him said, "That was the Minister of the Board of Civil Office."

Now, Hsiao Ying-shih had gone to see the Minister many times, yet had not been received. When he heard that the old man was none other than the Minister himself, he was flabbergasted.

The next day, Hsiao brought a long letter with him and went to the Minister's residence to apologize. The Minister had him brought into the hallway and scolded him severely. "I regret that I am not related to you in any way, otherwise I would like to give you some good 'family discipline,'" said the Minister. "You are reputed to be a literary talent, yet your arrogance and poor manners are such that it is perhaps better for you to remain a mere chin-shih (presented scholar)."

Hsiao Ying-shih never got anywhere in officialdom, dying as a Chief Clerk in Yang prefecture. Lu Chao was from I-ch'un of Yüan-chou. He and Huang P'o, also from the same prefecture, were equally famous. When they were young, Huang P'o was wealthy, but Lu Chao was very poor. When they were ready for the imperial examination, the two of them decided to set out on the trip together. The Prefect gave a farewell dinner at the Pavilion of Departure, but Huang P'o alone was invited. When the party was at its peak, with lots of wine and music, Lu Chao passed by the Pavilion, riding on an old, weak horse. He traveled some ten li out of the city limits, then stopped to wait for Huang P'o to join him.

The next year, Lu Chao came back to his hometown, having been awarded the title of chuang-yüan [number one]. All the officials from the Regional Commander on down came out to welcome him, and the Prefect of Yüan-chou was greatly embarrassed.

Once when the Prefect invited him to watch the Dragon Boat Race, Lu Chao composed a poem during the banquet which read:

> "It is a dragon," I told you.
> But you had refused to believe.
> Now it returns with the trophy,
> Much in the way I predicted.

Lu Hui's mother's brother was Cheng Yü. As his parents died when he was small, Lu Hui was brought up in his mother's family, and Cheng Yü often encouraged him to take the imperial examination and become a chin-shih. Lu Hui was recommended for the examinations for the "widely brilliant" in the early part of 870, but in 880, bandits encroached on the capital, forcing him to flee to the south. At that same time Cheng Yü's son Hsü was stationed in Nanhai as a Regional Commander. Lu Hui and Cheng Hsü had gone to school together, but when Hsü was already a county official, Hui was still a commoner. The two of them, however, equally enjoyed the favor of Cheng Yü.

During the ten years in which Cheng Hsü rose to become a Governor-General, Lu Hui remained a destitute scholar. Once again he managed to escape an uprising and came to Cheng Hsü, carrying but one sack of personal belongings. Cheng Hsü still treated him kindly. At this time, the Emperor was on the expedition to Shu, and the whole country was in turmoil. Cheng Hsü encouraged Lu Hui to seize the opportunity to advance himself. "How long can a man live?" he said to Lu Hui. "If there is a shortcut to riches and fame, why insist on going through the examination?"

But Lu Hui was adamant. Cheng Hsü asked his friends and assistants to try to persuade Lu Hui to give up the exams; he even left the seat on his right-hand side vacant for Lu Hui to occupy. Lu Hui therefore said to him, "Our great nation has established the examination system for the outstanding and the talented. I do not have the ability and dare not dream of such honors. However, when he was alive, my uncle again and again encouraged me to take the examinations. Now his study is empty and quiet, but I cannot bring myself to break our agreement. If I have to die as a mere student, it is my fate. But I will not change my mind for the sake of wealth. I would sooner die."

When Cheng Hsü saw Lu Hui's determination, he respected him even more than before. Another ten years passed before Lu Hui finally passed the examination under the Lord of Hung-nung, and he died as one of the highest officials in the whole empire.

Liu Hsü-po and Lord P'ei of T'ai-ping had once sat close to each other during the imperial examination. When Lord P'ei became the administrator of the imperial examinations, Liu was still only a candidate for the examination. On the day when the examinees were tested on their "miscellaneous essays," Liu presented a poem to the chief examiner, his old classmate:

> I remember evenings like this twenty years
>   ago:
> The candles were the same, so was the breeze.
> How many more years will I have, I wonder,
> To wear this gunny robe,
> And to wait to reach you.

The Chief Minister Wang Ch'i was appointed chief examiner in the imperial examinations during the Ch'ang-ch'ing period (821–824). He had Po Min-chung in mind as the candidate for the chuang-yüan [number one] but was displeased with Min-chung's close association with Ho Pa-chi, a talented but eccentric man. Therefore, Wang Ch'i had a confidant reveal his displeasure to Min-chung, hinting to him to break off his friendship.

This messenger went to see Po Min-chung and told him the Chief Minister's intentions. "I will do as you say," Min-chung readily agreed.

In a little while Ho Pa-chi came to visit, as usual, and the servants lied to him, saying that

Min-chung was not home. He waited a little, then left without saying a word. A moment later, Po Min-chung rushed out and ordered the servants to send for Ho. When he arrived, Min-Cheng told him everything, and then said, "I can be a chin-shih under any examiner. I can't, however, wrong my best friend for this reason." The two of them then merrily drank wine and took a nap.

This whole sequence took place right before the eyes of the messenger from the Chief Minister, and he left in a fury. When he returned to the Chief Minister, he told him the story and thought this was the end of Po Min-chung. But Wang Ch'i said instead, "I only thought of taking Po Min-chung; now I should also consider Ho Pa-chi."

Hsü T'ang was from Ching county of Hsüan-chou and had been taking the examinations since he was young. In the same village there was a man named Wang Tsun, who had served as a minor government clerk when young. After Hsü T'ang had taken the examination, Hsü T'ang treated him with contempt, still but a low functionary in the government. Yet Wang Tsun wrote good poetry, although no one knew about it because he kept it a secret.

One day, Wang Tsun resigned from his post and set out for the capital to take the imperial examination. As he was approaching the capital, he met Hsü T'ang, who was seeing some friends off at the outskirts of the city.

"Eh," Hsü T'ang asked him, "what are you doing here in the capital?"

"I have come to take the imperial examination," answered the former functionary.

Upon hearing this, Hsü T'ang angrily declared, "How insolent you are, you lowly clerk!" Although they were now fellow candidates for the imperial examination, Hsü T'ang treated him with contempt. But in the end, Wang Tsun passed the examination and became very famous. HsüT'ang did not pass until five years later.

P'eng K'an and Chan Pi were both from I-ch'un of Yüan-chou, and their wives were sisters. P'eng K'an passed the imperial examination and became a chin-shih, whereas Chan Pi remained a mere functionary in the county.

At the celebration banquet given by P'eng K'an's in-laws, all the guests were either high officials or renowned scholars. P'eng K'an was seated at the head of the table, and the whole company was enchanted by his exuberant character. When Chan Pi arrived at the banquet, he was told to eat his food in the back room.

Seeing that Chan Pi was not even disturbed by this, his wife scolded him severely: "You are a man, yet you cannot push yourself ahead. Now that you are so humiliated where is your sense of shame?" These words stimulated Chan Pi, and he began to study very hard. Within a few years, he also passed the imperial examination.

Previously, P'eng K'an used to insult Chan Pi. On the day when the results of the imperial examination were announced, P'eng K'an was out in the countryside, donkey riding for pleasure. Suddenly a servant boy came running and reported to him the good news about Chan Pi. P'eng K'an was so shocked that he fell off his saddle.

This is the origin of the lampoon that spread throughout Yüan-chou:

When Chan Pi the exams did pass,
P'eng K'an fell off his ass.

Chang Shu and Ts'ui Chao-wei were both sent up from Hsi-ch'uan to take the examination in the early years of Chung-ho [881–884]. While there the two of them went together to have their fortunes told.

At the time, Chang Shu was reputed for his literary talent, and was generally known as the "number-one-to-be." Even Ts'ui Chao-wei was regarded as inferior to him. However, the fortune-teller hardly paid any attention to Chang Shu but looked Ts'ui Chao-wei over and told him, "You will definitely pass the imperial examination and come out on top." Then, seeing that Chang Shu was annoyed, the fortune-teller said to him, "As to you, sir, you will also pass, but not until Mr. Ts'ui here becomes the Minister and you pay homage to him."

When they were taking the examination that year, Chang Shu had a death in the family and had to withdraw while Ts'ui Chao-wei turned out to be the "number one." Frustrated, Chang Shu vented his indignation in writing lines such as "I had followed you a thousand miles but only lost your tail during the morning's storm." Naturally, Ts'ui Chao-wei was very disturbed. At a drinking party, Ts'ui Chao-wei toasted Chang Shu, asking him to drink a huge horn-shaped goblet of wine. When Chang declined, Ts'ui said to him, "Just drink it, and when I become the Chief Minister, I will let you be the number-one." Chang walked out in a fury, and the two of them became foes.

Seven years later, Ts'ui was appointed Chief Minister by the Emperor, and Chang Shu later passed the examination under the chief-examiner Lord P'ei. As predicted, Chang had to pay homage to Ts'ui.

FOCUS QUESTIONS

1. What values do these tales hold to be more important than passing the civil service examination?

2. What do the aspirants hope to gain by passing the examinations?

3. What do these passages tell us about the structure of Chinese government in the eighth and ninth centuries?

4. What was the role of status and deference in this society?

41

The Lotus of the Wonderful Law (806 C.E.)

In the eighth century, a new form of Buddhism spread from China to Japan. It was known as the Tendai sect, and it derived its inspiration from a series of Sanskrit texts that focused on the Lotus Sutra, regarded by the Tendai as the final and most authentic teaching of the Buddha. The Tendai sect was established in Japan by Siacho (767–822), who had made several missions to China and was permitted to remain there in search of Buddhist texts On his return, Siacho was given imperial permission to found a new Buddhist sect on Mt. Hiei based on the teaching of the Lotus Sutra.

Using parables was a favorite method of Tendai teaching. "The Parable of the Burning House," which is a part of the Lotus of the Wonderful Law*, is designed to show the superiority of the single sutra (that of the Lotus) over traditional Buddhist teaching of the equal power of the three sutras. Tendai Buddhists believed that all humans could be redeemed and reach universal enlightenment.*

A PARABLE

OF THE BURNING HOUSE

Let us suppose the following case, Sariputra.... There was a certain housekeeper, old, aged, decrepit, very advanced in years, rich, wealthy, opulent; he had a great house, high, spacious, built a long time ago and old, inhabited by some two, three, four, or five hundred living beings. The house had but one door, and a thatch; its terraces were tottering, the bases of its pillars rotten, the coverings and plaster of the walls loose. On a sudden the whole house was from every side put in conflagration by a mass of fire. Let us suppose that the man had many little boys, say five, or ten, or even twenty, and that he himself had come out of the house.

Now, Sariputra, that man, on seeing the house from every side wrapt in a blaze by a great mass of fire, got afraid, and … calls to the boys: "Come, my children; the house is burning with a mass of fire; come, lest you be burnt in the mass fire, and come to grief and disaster." But the ignorant boys do not heed the words of him who is their well-wisher; they are not afraid … nor know the purport of the word "burning"; they run hither and thither, walk about, and repeatedly look at their father; all, because they are so ignorant.

… The man has a clear perception of their inclinations. Now these boys happen to have many and manifold toys to play with, pretty, nice, pleasant, dear, amusing, and precious. The man, knowing the disposition of the boys, says to them: "My children, your toys, which you are so loath to miss, which are so various and multifarious, [such as] bullock-carts, goat-carts, deer-carts, which are so pretty, nice, dear, and precious to you, have all been put by me outside the house-door for you to play with. Come, run out, leave the house; to each of you I shall give what he wants. Come soon, come out for the sake of these toys." And the boys, on hearing the names mentioned of such playthings as they like and desire, quickly rush out from the burning house, with eager effort and great alacrity, one having no time to wait for the other, and pushing each other on with the cry of "Who shall arrive first, the very first?"

The man, seeing that his children have safely and happily escaped, goes and sits down in the open air on the square of the village, his heart is filled with joy and delight. The boys go up to the place where their father is sitting, and say: "Father, give us those toys to play with, those bullock-carts, and deer-carts." Then, Sariputra, the man gives to his sons, who run swift as the wind, bullock-carts only, made of seven precious substances, provided with benches, hung with a multitude of small bells, lofty, adorned with rare and wonderful jewels, embellished with jewel wreaths, decorated with garlands of flowers, carpeted with cotton mattresses and woolen coverlets, covered with white cloth and silk, having on both sides rosy cushions, yoked with white, very fair and fleet bullocks, led by a multitude of men. To each of his children he gives several bullock-carst of one appearance and one kind, provided with flags, and swift as wind. That man does so, Sariputra, because being rich, … he rightly thinks: "Why should I give these boys inferior carts, all these boys being my own children, dear and precious? I have such great vehicles, and ought to treat all the boys equally and without partiality. As I won many treasures and granaries, I could give such great vehicles to all beings, how much more then to my own children." Meanwhile the boys are mounting the vehicles with feelings of astonishment and wonder. Now, Sariputra, what is thy opinion? Has that man made himself guilty of a falsehood by first holding out to his children the prospect of three vehicles and afterwards giving to each of them the greatest vehicles only, the most magnificent vehicle?

Sariputra answered: By no means, Lord. That is not sufficient to qualify the man as a speaker of falsehood, since it only was a skilful device to persuade his children to go out of the burning house and save their lives. Nay, besides recovering their very bodies, O Lord, they have received all those toys. If that man, O Lord, had given no single cart, even then he would not have been a speaker of falsehood, for he had previously been meditating on saving the little boys from a great mass of pain by some able device….

The venerable Sariputra having thus spoken, the Lord said to him: Very well, Sariputra, quite so; it is even as you say. So too, Sariputra, the Tathagata is free from all dangers, wholly exempt from all misfortune, despondency, calamity, pain, grief, the thick enveloping dark mists of ignorance. He, the Tathagata, endowed with Buddha-knowledge, forces, absence of hesitation, uncommon properties, and mighty by magical power, is the father of the world, who has reached the highest perfection in the knowledge of skillful means, who is most merciful, long-suffering, benevolent, compassionate. He appears in this triple world, which is like a house the roof and shelter whereof are decayed, [a house] burning by a mass of misery, … Once born, he sees how the creatures are burnt, tormented, vexed, distressed by birth, old age, disease, death, grief, wailing, pain, melancholy, despondency; how for the sake of enjoyment, and prompted by sensual desires, they severally suffer various pains. In consequence both of what in this world they are seeking and what they have acquired, they will in a future state suffer various pains, in hell, in the brute creation, in the realm of Yamaraja (king of the dead); suffer such pains as poverty in the world of gods or men, union with hateful persons or things, and separation from the beloved ones. And while incessantly whirling in that mass of evils they are sporting, playing, diverting themselves; they do not fear, nor dread, nor are they seized with terror; they do not know, nor mind; they are not startled, do not try to escape, but are enjoying themselves in that triple world which is like unto a burning house, and run hither and thither. Though overwhelmed by that mass of evil, they do not conceive the idea that they must beware of it.

Under such circumstances, Sariputra, the Tathagata reflects thus: "Verify, I am the father of these beings; I must save them from this mass of evil, and bestow on them the immense, inconceivable bliss of Buddha-knowledge, wherewith they shall sport, play, and divert themselves, wherein they shall find their rest. If, in the conviction of my possessing the power of knowledge and magical faculties, I manifest to these beings the knowledge, forces, and absence of hesitation of the Tathagata, without availing myself of some device, these beings will not escape. For they are attached to the pleasures of the five senses, to worldly pleasures; they will not be freed from birth, old age, disease, death, grief, wailing, pain, melancholy, despondency, by which they are burnt, tormented, vexed, distressed. Unless they are forced to leave the triple world which is like a house the shelter and roof whereof is in a blaze, how are they to get acquainted with Buddha-knowledge?"

Now, Sariputra, even as that man with powerful arms, without using the strength of his arms, attracts his children out of the burning house by an able device, and afterwards gives them magnificent, great carts, so Sariputra, the Tathagata possessed of knowledge and freedom from all hesitation, without using them, in order to attract the creatures out of the triple world which is like a burning house with decayed roof and shelter, shows, by his knowledge of able devices, three vehicles, viz. the vehicle of the disciples, the vehicle of the pratyeka-buddhas, and the vehicle of the bodhisattvas. By means of these three vehicles he attracts the creatures and speaks to them thus: "Do not delight in this triple world, which is like a burning house, in these miserable forms, sounds, odors, flavors, and contacts. For in delighting in this triple world you are burnt, heated, inflamed with the thirst inseparable from the pleasures of the five senses. Fly from this triple world; betake yourselves to the three vehicles…. I give you my pledge for it, that I shall give you these three vehicles, make an effort to run out of this triple world. And to attract them I say: "These vehicles are grand, praised by the Aryas, and provided with most pleasant things; with such you are to sport, play, and divert yourselves in a noble manner. You will feel the great delight of the faculties, powers, constituents of Bodhi, meditations, the eight degrees of emancipation, self-concentration, and the results of self-concentration, and you will become greatly happy and cheerful."

FOCUS QUESTIONS

1. Why did Sariputra have to bribe the boys with toys to get them out of the burning house?

2. With what dilemma is Sariputra faced once the boys escaped?

3. What is the Lord's answer?

4. How does the parable prove the superiority of the single sutra?

42

The Tale of Genji (ca. 1000 C.E.)

LADY MURASAKI

Lady Murasaki Shikibu (ca. 978–1026) spent most of her life at the Heian court. Her father was a government official and, in keeping with tradition, she was called by his office rather than her own name, which has not survived. Lady Murasaki was a success at court because she had learned Chinese and was able to teach it to one of the imperial princesses. She married a lieutenant in the imperial guard but was soon widowed. It was after her husband's death that she began to compose The Tale of Genji, *which was written over many years and remained unfinished at her death.*

The Tale of Genji *is the world's first surviving novel. It is a loosely woven account of the life of Genji ("the shining one"), a fictitious imperial prince who lived in the eighth century. The depiction of courtly love became a model for aristocratic behavior. The tale was immediately popular and remains the best loved of all Japanese novels.*

YUGAO

He had come in a plain coach with no outriders. No one could possibly guess who he was, and feeling quite at his ease he leant forward and deliberately examined the house. The gate, also made of a kind of trellis-work, stood ajar, and he could see enough of the interior to realize that it was a very humble and poorly furnished dwelling. For a moment he pitied those who lived in such a place, but then he remembered the song "Seek not in the wide world to find a home; but where you chance to rest, call that your house"; and again, "Monarchs may keep their palaces of jade, for in a leafy cottage two can sleep."

There was a wattled fence over which some ivy-like creeper spread its cool green leaves, and among the leaves were white flowers with petals half unfolded like the lips of people smiling at their own thoughts. "They are called Yugao, 'Evening Faces'," one of his servants told him; "how strange to find so lovely a crowd clustering on this deserted wall!" And indeed it was a most strange and delightful thing to see how on the narrow tenement in a poor quarter of the town they had clambered over rickety eaves and gables and spread wherever there was room for them to grow. He sent one of his servants to pick some. The man entered at the half-opened door, and had begun to pluck the flowers, when a little servant girl in a long yellow tunic came through a quite genteel sliding door, and holding out towards Genji's servant a white fan heavily perfumed with incense, she said to him "Would you like something to put them on? I am afraid you have chosen a wretched-looking bunch," and she handed him the fan…. He looked at the fan upon which the white flowers had been laid. He now saw that there was writing on it, a poem carelessly but elegantly scribbled: "The flower that puzzled you was but the *Yugao,* strange beyond knowing in its dress of shining dew." It was written with a deliberate negligence which seemed to aim at concealing the writer's status and identity. But for all that the hand showed a breeding and distinction which agreeably surprised him.

He had never … been interested in anyone of quite the common classes. But now … he had explored (so it seemed to him) every corner of society, including in his survey even those categories which his friends had passed over as utterly remote and improbable. He thought of the lady who had, so to speak, been thrown into his life as an extra.

Genji never asked her by what name he was to call her, nor did he reveal his own identity. He came very poorly dressed and—what was most unusual for him—on foot. But Koremitsu regarded this as too great a tribute to so unimportant a lady, and insisted upon Genji riding his horse, while he walked by his side. In doing so he sacrificed his own feelings; for he too had reasons for wishing to create a good impression in the house, and he knew that by arriving in this rather undignified way he would sink in the estimation of the inhabitants. Fortunately his discomfiture was almost unwitnessed, for Genji took with him only the one attendant who had on the first occasion plucked the flowers—a boy whom no one was likely to recognize; and lest suspicions should be aroused, he did not even take advantage of his presence in the neighbourhood to call at his foster-nurse's house.

The lady was very much mystified by all these precautions and made great efforts to discover something more about him. She even sent someone after him to see where he went to when he left her at day-break; but he succeeded in throwing his pursuer off the scent and she was no wiser than before. He was now growing far too fond of her. He was miserable if anything interfered with his visits; and though he utterly disapproved of his own conduct and worried a great deal about it, he soon found that he was spending most of his time at her house.

He knew that at some time or another in their lives even the soberest people lose their heads in this way; but hitherto he had never really lost his, or done anything which could possibly have been considered very wrong. Now to his astonishment and dismay he discovered that even the few morning hours during which he was separated from her were becoming unendurable. 'What is it in her that makes me behave like a madman?' he kept on asking himself. She was astonishingly gentle and unassuming, to the point even of seeming rather apathetic, rather deficient perhaps in depth of character and emotion; and though she had a certain air of girlish inexperience, it was clear that he was not by any means her first lover; and certainly she was rather plebeian. What was it exactly that so fascinated him? He asked himself the question again and again, but found no answer.

She for her part was very uneasy to see him come to her thus in shabby old hunting-clothes, trying always to hide his face, leaving while it was still dark and everyone was asleep. He seemed like some demon-lover in an old ghost-tale, and she was half-afraid. But his smallest gesture showed that he was someone out of the ordinary, and she began to suspect that he was a person of high rank, who had used Koremitsu as his go-between. But Koremitsu obstinately pretended to know nothing at all about his companion, and continued to amuse himself by frequenting the house on his own account.

What could it mean? She was dismayed at this strange love-making with—she knew not whom. But about her too there was something fugitive, insubstantial. Genji was obsessed by the idea that, just as she had hidden herself in this place, so one day she would once more vanish and hide, and he would never be able to find her again. There was every sign that her residence here was quite temporary. He was sure that when the time came to move she would not tell him where she was going. Of course her running away would be proof that she was not worth bothering about any more, and he ought, thankful for the pleasure they had had together, simply to leave the matter at that. But he knew that this was the last thing he would be likely to do.

"I am going to take you somewhere very nice where no one will disturb us" he said at last. "No, No" she cried; "your ways are so strange, I should be frightened to go with you." She spoke in a tone of childish terror, and Genji answered smiling: "One or the other of us must be a fox-in-disguise. Here is a chance to find out which it is!" He spoke very kindly, and suddenly, in a tone of absolute submission, she consented to do whatever he thought best. He could not but be touched at her willingness to follow him in what must appear to her to be the most hazardous and bizarre adventure.

Their room was in the front of the house. Genji got up and opened the long, sliding shutters. They stood together looking out. In the courtyard near them was a clump of fine Chinese bamboos; dew lay thick on the borders, glittering here no less brightly than in the great gardens to which Genji was better accustomed. There was a confused buzzing of insects. Crickets were chirping in the wall. He had often listened to them, but always at a distance; now, singing so close to him, they made a music which was unfamiliar and indeed seemed far lovelier than that with which he was acquainted. But then, everything in this place where one thing was so much to his liking, seemed despite all drawbacks to take on a new tinge of interest and beauty. She was wearing a white bodice with a soft, grey cloak over it. It was a poor dress, but she looked charming and almost distinguished; even so, there was nothing very striking in her appearance—only a certain fragile grace and elegance. It was when she was speaking that she looked really beautiful, there was such pathos, such earnestness in her manner. If only she had a little more spirit! But even as she was he found her irresistible and longed to take her to some place where no one could disturb them: "I am going to take you somewhere not at all far away where we shall be able to pass the rest of the night in peace. We cannot go on like this, parting always at break of day." "Why have you suddenly come to that conclusion?" she asked, but she spoke submissively. He vowed to her that she should be his love in this and in all future lives and she answered so passionately that she seemed utterly transformed from the listless creature he had known, and it was hard to believe that such vows were no novelty to her.

They drove to an untenanted mansion which was not far off. While he waited for the steward to come out Genji noticed that the gates were crumbling away; dense shinobu-grass grew around them. So sombre an entrance he had never seen. There was a thick mist and the dew was so heavy that when he raised the carriage-blind his sleeve was drenched. "Never yet has such an adventure as this befallen me" said Genji; "so I am, as you may imagine, rather excited," and he made a poem in which he said that though love's folly had existed since the beginning of the world, never could man have set out more rashly at the break of day into a land unknown. "But to you this is no great novelty?" She blushed and in her turn made a poem: "I am as the moon that walks the sky not knowing what menace the cruel hills may hold in store; high though she sweeps, her light may suddenly be blotted out."

FOCUS QUESTIONS

1. Why was it significant to Genji that his lover was of the common class?

2. What were some of the different signs of class in Heian Japan?

3. How are women portrayed in this passage? Is it surprising to realize that a woman wrote *The Tale of Genji*?

4. What does this passage tell us about the importance of manners and appearance in Heian Japan?

5. How does Lady Murasaki portray the relationship between love and nature?

43

Precepts for Social Life (1178 C.E.)

YÜAN TS'AI

Though we know few actual details of his early life, we do know that Yüan Ts'ai (ca. 1140–1195) came from a family of educated property holders. He attended Hangchow University in order to prepare for the rigorous civil service examinations, which he passed in 1163. He served as a provincial magistrate in four different jurisdictions before finally gaining a high office in the capital toward the end of his life. He wrote a number of political treatises but showed little interest in the more characteristic intellectual pursuits of philosophy or poetry.

Precepts for Social Life was written as a conduct book. As such it is difficult to tell how much of Yüan Ts'ai's observations are descriptive, showing how things were, and how much prescriptive, showing how things ought to be. The sections excerpted here focus on the role of women during the Sung Dynasty.

THE PROBLEMS OF WOMEN

Women Should Not Take Part in Affairs Outside the Home

Women do not take part in extra-familial affairs. The reason is that worthy husbands and sons take care of everything for them, while unworthy ones can always find ways to hide their deeds from the women.

Many men today indulge in pleasure and gambling; some end up mortgaging their lands, and even go so far as to mortgage their houses without their wives' knowledge. Therefore, when husbands are bad, even if wives try to handle outside matters, it is of no use. Sons must have their mothers' signatures to mortgage their family properties, but there are sons who falsify papers and forge signatures, sometimes borrowing money at high interest from people who would not hesitate to bring their claim to court. Other sons sell illicit tea and salt to get money, which, if discovered by the authorities, results in fines. Mothers have no control in such matters. Therefore, when sons are bad, it is useless for mothers to try to handle matters relating to the outside world.

For women, these are grave misfortunes, but what can they do? If husbands and sons could only remember that their wives and mothers are helpless and suddenly repent, would that not be best?

Women's Sympathies Should Be Indulged

Without going overboard, people should marry their daughters with dowries appropriate to their family's wealth. Rich families should not consider their daughters outsiders but should give them a share of the property. Sometimes people have incapable sons and so have to entrust their affairs to their daughters' families; even after their deaths, their burials and sacrifices are performed by their daughters. So how can people say that daughters are not as good as sons?

Generally speaking, a woman's heart is very sympathetic. If her parents' family is wealthy and her husband's family is poor, she wants to take her parents' wealth to help her husband's family prosper. If her husband's family is wealthy but her parents' family is poor, then she wants to take from her husband's family to enable her parents to prosper. Her parents and husband should be sympathetic toward her feelings and indulge some of her wishes. When her own sons and daughters are grown and married, if either her son's family or her daughter's family is wealthy while the other is poor, she wishes to take from the wealthy one to give to the poor one. Her sons and daughters should understand her feelings and be somewhat indulgent. But taking from the poor to make the rich richer is unacceptable, and no one should ever go along with it.

Orphaned Girls Should Have Their Marriages Arranged Early

When a widow remarries she sometimes has an orphaned daughter not yet engaged. In such cases she should try to get a respectable relative to arrange a marriage for her daughter. She should also seek to have her daughter reared in the house of her future in-laws, with the marriage to take place after the girl has grown up. If the girl were to go along with the mother to her step-father's house, she would not be able to clear herself if she were subjected to any humiliations.

For Women Old Age is Particularly Hard to Bear

People say that, though there may be a hundred years allotted to a person's life, only a few reach seventy, for time quickly runs out. But for those destined to be poor, old age is hard to endure. For them, until about the age of fifty, the passage of twenty years seems like only ten; but after that age, ten years can feel as long as twenty. For women who live a long life, old age is especially hard to bear, because most women must rely on others for their existence. Before a woman's marriage, a good father is even more important than a good grandfather; a good brother is even more

important than a good father; a good nephew is even more important than a good brother. After her marriage, a good husband is even more important than a good father-in-law; a good son is even more important than a good husband; and a good grandson is even more important than a good son. For this reason women often enjoy comfort in their youth but find their old age difficult to endure. It would be well for their relatives to keep this in mind.

It is Difficult for Widows to Entrust Their Financial Affairs to Others

Some wives with stupid husbands are able to manage the family's finances, calculating the outlays and receipts of money and grain, without being cheated by anyone. Of those with degenerate husbands, there are also some who are able to manage the finances with the help of their sons without ending in bankruptcy. Even among those whose husbands have died and whose sons are young, there are occasionally women able to raise and educate their sons, keep the affection of all their relatives, manage the family business, and even prosper. All of these are wise and worthy women. But the most remarkable are the women who manage a household after their husbands have died leaving them with young children. Such women could entrust their finances to their husbands' kinsmen or their own kinsmen, but not all relatives are honorable, and the honorable ones are not necessarily willing to look after other people's business.

When wives themselves can read and do arithmetic, and those they entrust with their affairs have some sense of fairness and duty with regard to food, clothing, and support, then things will usually work out all right. But in most of the rest of the cases, bankruptcy is what happens.

Beware of Future Difficulties in Taking in Female Relatives

You should take into your own house old aunts, sisters, or other female relatives whose children and grandchildren are unfilial and do not support them. However, take precautions. After a woman dies, her unfilial sons or grandsons might make outrageous accusations to the authorities, claiming that the woman died from hunger or cold or left valuables in trunks. When the authorities receive such complaints, they have to investigate and trouble is unavoidable. Thus, while the woman is alive, make it clear to the public and to the government that the woman is bringing nothing with her but herself. Generally, in performing charitable acts, it is best to make certain that they will entail no subsequent difficulties.

Before Buying a Servant Girl or Concubine, Make Sure of the Legality

When buying a female servant or concubine, inquire whether it is legal for her to be indentured or sold before closing the deal. If the girl is impoverished and has no one to rely on, then she should be brought before the authorities to give an account of her past. After guarantors have been secured and an investigation conducted, the transaction can be completed. But if she is not able to give an account of her past, then the agent who offered her for sale should be questioned. Temporarily she may be hired on a salaried basis. If she is ever recognized by her relatives, she should be returned to them.

Hired Women Should Be Sent Back When Their Period of Service is Over

If you hire a man's wife or daughter as a servant, you should return her to her husband or father on completion of her period of service. If she comes from another district, you should send her back to it after her term is over. These practices are the most humane and are widely carried out by the gentry in the Southeast. Yet there are people who do not return their hired women to their husbands but wed them to others instead; others do not return them to their parents but marry them off themselves. Such actions are the source of many lawsuits.

How can one not have sympathy for those separated from their relatives, removed from their hometowns, who stay in service for their entire lives with neither husbands nor sons? Even in death these women's spirits are left to wander all alone. How pitiful they are!

FOCUS QUESTIONS

1. What was the status of women in twelfth-century China?

2. What were the most important functions of women in this society? Could they step outside of their traditional roles?

3. What was the role of men in the lives of women?

4. How did the concept of honor regulate women's lives?

44

The Laws of Manu (before 200 C.E.)

ANONYMOUS

The Laws of Manu *is one of the oldest surviving legal codes in the world. Although the actual author of this text is unknown, it purports to record the teachings of Manu, the son of the Hindu god Brahma. This text was considered to have both divine origins and legal force, giving it especial authority. Though it has come down to us in Sanskrit, compiled in all likelihood in India sometime before 200 C.E., the* Laws of Manu *was created over many centuries as part of oral tradition. Because of its long gestation, the* Laws of Manu *reflects ancient Indian moral codes as well as the social values it was intended to preserve. Although it is more prescriptive than descriptive, the* Laws of Manu *reveals the ideals of Indian society. It contains two of the defining features of early South Asian life, belief in reincarnation and in a social caste system.*

In four main sections, it offers a creation story, tells of the sources of law, explains how the social classes should work, and then describes how an elite man should act. Within it are rules for personal hygiene, sexual conduct, and relations amongst the castes. This section deals with the place of the priest (the Brahmin) and others in Hindu society.

[87] But to protect this whole creation, the lustrous one made separate innate activities for those born of his mouth, arms, thighs, and feet. [88] For priests, he ordained teaching and learning, sacrificing for themselves and sacrificing for others, giving and receiving. [89] Protecting his subjects, giving, having sacrifices performed, studying, and remaining unaddicted to the sensory objects are, in summary, for a ruler. [90] Protecting his livestock, giving, having sacrifices performed, studying, trading, lending money, and farming the land are for a commoner. [91] The Lord assigned only one activity to a servant: serving these (other) classes without resentment.

[92] A man is said to be purer above the navel; therefore the Self-existent one said that his mouth was the purest part of him. [93] The priest is the Lord of this whole creation, according to the law, because he was born of the highest part of the body, because he is the eldest, and because he maintains the Veda. [94] The Self-existent one emitted him from his own mouth, first, when he had generated inner heat, to convey the offerings to the gods and the ancestors, and to guard this whole (creation). [95] What living being is greater than him? For it is through his mouth that those (gods) who live in the triple heaven always eat their offerings, and the ancestors (eat) their offerings. [96] The best of living beings are those that have the breath of life; and (the best) of those that have the breath of life are those that live by their intelligence; the best of those that have intelligence are men; and priests are traditionally regarded as (the best) of men. [97] Among priests, learned men (are the best); among learned men, those who understand their obligations; among those who understand their obligations, those who fulfill them; and among those who fulfill them, those who know the Veda.

[98] The very birth of a priest is the eternal physical form of religion; for he is born for the sake of religion and is fit to become one with ultimate reality. [99] For when a priest is born he is born at the top of the earth, as the lord of all living beings, to guard the treasure of religion. [100] All of this belongs to the priest, whatever there is in the universe; the priest deserves all of this because of his excellence and his high birth. [101] The priest eats only what is his own, he wears what is his own, and he gives what is his own; other people eat through the priest's mercy.

[102] To distinguish the (priest's) innate activity and those of the rest (of the classes) in their order, the wise Manu, son of the Self-existent, made this teaching. [103] A learned priest – but no one else – should study it carefully and explain it to his pupils properly. [104] A priest who studies this teaching and has fulfilled his vow is not constantly smeared with the faults of the effects of past actions born of mind-and-heart, speech, and body. [105] He purifies the rows for seven generations in the past and seven in the future; and he alone deserves this entire earth. [106] This (teaching) is the best support for wellbeing; it increases intelligence; it is conducive to fame long life, and the supreme good.

[107] This (teaching) describes religion in its entirety, as well as the virtues and vices of the effects of past actions and the eternal rule of conduct for the four classes. [108] The rule of conduct, the highest jaw, is described both in the revealed canon and in tradition; therefore a twice-born person who is self-possessed should always engage in it. [109] A priest who has slipped from (proper) conduct does not reap the fruit of the Veda; but one who is engaged in (proper) conduct is traditionally said to enjoy the full fruit. [110] When the hermits saw that the course of religion thus comes from (proper) conduct, they understood that (proper) conduct was the ultimate root of all inner heat.

[111] In this teaching, Manu has declared the origin of the universe and the rules for the transformative rituals, the carrying out of vows and attendance upon (a teacher) and the ultimate rule for the graduation bath; [112] the taking of a wife and the mark of (different kinds of) marriages, the regulations for the great sacrifices and the obligatory rule of the ceremonies for the dead; [113] the mark of the (various) means of livelihood, the vows of a Vedic graduate, what is to be eaten and not to be eaten, purification and the cleansing of things; [114] the application of the duties of women, the rules for the generation of inner heat, Freedom, and renunciation, all the duties of a king, and decision-making in lawsuits; [115] the regulations for questioning witnesses; the duties of husband and wife; the law for the division (of inheritances), gambling, and 'cleaning out thorns'; [116] attendance by commoners and servants, and the origin of confused classes; the religious duties of (all) classes in extremity, and the rules for restorations; [117] the threefold course of transmigration that arises from the effects of past actions; the supreme good, and the examination of the virtues and vices of the effects of past actions; [118] the obligatory duties of (particular) countries, castes, and families; and the duties of sects of heretics.

[119] Learn this teaching, all of you, from me today, just as Manu told it to me long ago when I asked him.

FOCUS QUESTIONS

1. Who is supposed to learn and teach the *Laws of Manu?*

2. Describe the social hierarchy developed in this text.

3. This excerpt from the *Laws of Manu* can be found in the sections on the origins of the world. Why do you think the author thought that this was an appropriate place for it? What might this tell us about how the author thought about the importance of order in society?

4. What is the relationship between government and religion in this text?

The Fall of Rome and the European Middle Ages

The Vikings Attack England. This illustration from an eleventh-century English manuscript depicts a band of armed Vikings invading England. Two ships have already reached the shore, and a few Vikings are shown walking down a long gangplank onto English soil.

FOCUS QUESTIONS

1. Why are two Vikings in the ship in the foreground talking?

2. What do the heads of animals carved into some of the ships signify? Is it relevant that some ships have animals' heads and others do not?

3. Notice the fish in the water. Why do you think the artist included them?

4. The two Vikings walking along the gangplanks are beardless. What might this mean?

45

The Germania (98 c.e.)

TACITUS

Cornelius Tacitus (ca. 56–120) was the greatest of the Roman historians. Little is known of his early life, but he must have come from comfortable surroundings, for he was trained for a public career. He practiced law and moved up the ranks of public service, benefiting from his marriage to the daughter of Julius Agricola, governor of Britain. Elected consul in 97, Tacitus distinguished himself by his oratory. It appears that soon after his election he retired from public life to devote himself to writing, although he served as proconsul of Asia in 112. Both a biographer and a scholar of recent Roman history, Tacitus prepared a life of his father-in-law as well as his History, *which ended just before his consulship.*

The Germania *(98) was one of Tacitus's earliest works, describing firsthand the customs and characteristics of the Germanic tribes living on the Roman frontier. It remains a principal source for understanding Roman attitudes toward other peoples and for re-creating early Germanic life.*

The people of Germany appear to me indigenous, and free from intermixture with foreigners, either as settlers or casual visitants. For the emigrants of former ages performed their expeditions not by land, but by water; and that immense, and, if I may so call it, hostile ocean, is rarely navigated by ships from our world. Then, besides the dangers of a boisterous and unknown sea, who would relinquish Asia, Africa, or Italy, for Germany, a land rude in its surface, rigorous in its climate, cheerless to every beholder and cultivator, except a native?

In the election of kings they have regard to birth; in that of generals, to valor. Their kings have not an absolute or unlimited power; and their generals command less through the force of authority than of example. If they are daring, adventurous, and conspicuous in action, they procure obedience from the admiration they inspire. None, however, but the priests are permitted to judge offenders, to inflict bonds or stripes; so that chastisement appears not as an act of military discipline, but as the instigation of the god whom they suppose present with warriors. They also carry with them to battle certain images and standards taken from the sacred groves.

Tradition relates that armies beginning to give way have been rallied by the females, through the earnestness of their supplications, the interposition of their bodies, and the pictures they have drawn of impending slavery, a calamity which these people bear with more impatience for their women than themselves; so that those states who have been obliged to give among their hostages the daughters of noble families, are the most effectually bound to fidelity. They even suppose somewhat of sanctity and prescience to be inherent in the female sex; and therefore neither despise their counsels, nor disregard their responses. We have beheld, in the reign of Vespasian, Veleda, long reverenced by many as a deity. Aurima, moreover, and several others, were formerly held in equal veneration, but not with a servile flattery, nor as though they made them goddesses.

No people are more addicted to divination by omens and lots. The latter is performed in the following simple manner. They cut a twig from a fruit-tree, and divide it into small pieces, which, distinguished by certain marks, are thrown promiscuously upon a white garment. Then, the priest of the canton, if the occasion be public; if private, the master of the family; after an invocation of the gods, with his eyes lifted up to heaven, thrice takes out each piece, and, as they come up, interprets their signification according to the marks fixed upon them. If the result prove unfavorable, there is no more consultation on the same affair that day; if propitious, a confirmation by omens is still required. In common with other nations, the Germans are acquainted with the practice of auguring from the notes and flight of birds; but it is peculiar to them to derive admonitions and presages from horses also. Certain of these animals, milk-white, and untouched by earthly labor, are pastured at the public expense in the sacred woods and groves. These, yoked to a consecrated chariot, are accompanied by the priest,

and king, or chief person of the community, who attentively observe their manner of neighing and snorting; and no kind of augury is more credited, not only among the populace, but among the nobles and priests. For the latter consider themselves as the ministers of the gods, and the horses, as privy to the divine will. Another kind of divination, by which they explore the event of momentous wars, is to oblige a prisoner, taken by any means whatsoever from the nation with whom they are at variance, to fight with a picked man of their own, each with his own country's arms; and, according as the victory falls, they presage success to the one or to the other party.

The Germans transact no business, public or private, without being armed: but it is not customary for any person to assume arms till the state has approved his ability to use them. Then, in the midst of the assembly, either one of the chiefs, or the father, or a relation, equips the youth with a shield and javelin. These are to them the manly gown; this is the first honor conferred on youth; before this they are considered as part of a household: afterward, of the state. The dignity of chieftain is bestowed even on mere lads, whose descent is eminently illustrious, or whose fathers have performed signal services to the public; they are associated, however, with those of mature strength, who have already been declared capable of service; nor do they blush to be seen in the rank of companions. For the state of companionship itself has its several degrees, determined by the judgment of him whom they follow; and there is a great emulation among the companions, which shall possess the highest place in the favor of their chief; and among the chiefs, which shall excel in the number and valor of his companions. It is their dignity, their strength, to be always surrounded with a large body of select youth, an ornament in peace, a bulwark in war. And not in his own country alone, but among the neighboring states, the fame and glory of each chief consists in being distinguished for the number and bravery of his companions. Such chiefs are courted by embassies; distinguished by presents; and often by their reputation alone decide a war.

In the field of battle, it is disgraceful for the chief to be surpassed in valor; it is disgraceful for the companions not to equal their chief, but it is reproach and infamy during a whole succeeding life to retreat from the field surviving him. To aid, to protect him; to place their own gallant actions to the account of his glory, is their first and most sacred engagement. The chiefs fight for victory; the companions for their chief. If their native country be long sunk in peace and inaction, many of the young nobles repair to some other state then engaged in war. For, besides that repose is unwelcome to their race, and toils and perils afford them a better opportunity of distinguishing themselves; they are unable, without war and violence, to maintain a large train of followers. The companion requires from the liberality of his chief, the warlike steed, the bloody and conquering spear; and in place of pay he expects to be supplied with a table, homely indeed, but plentiful. The funds for this munificence must be found in war and rapine; nor are they so easily persuaded to cultivate the earth, and await the produce of the seasons, as to challenge the foe, and expose themselves to wounds; nay, they even think it base and spiritless to earn by sweat what they might purchase with blood.

During the intervals of war, they pass their time less in hunting than in a sluggish repose, divided between sleep and the table. All the bravest of the warriors, committing the care of the house, the family affairs, and the lands, to the women, old men, and weaker part of the domestics, stupefy themselves in inaction: so wonderful is the contrast presented by nature, that the same persons love indolence, and hate tranquility! It is customary for the several states to present, by voluntary and individual contributions, cattle or grain to their chiefs; which are accepted as honorary gifts, while they serve as necessary supplies. They are peculiarly pleased with presents from neighboring nations, offered not only by individuals, but by the community at large; such as fine horses, heavy armor, rich housing, and gold chains. We have now taught them also to accept of money.

It is well known that none of the German nations inhabit cities, or even admit of contiguous settlements. They dwell scattered and separate, as a spring, a meadow, or a grove may chance to invite them. Their villages are laid out, not like ours in rows of adjoining buildings; but every one surrounds his house with a vacant space, either by way of security against fire, or through ignorance of the art of building. For, indeed, they are unacquainted with the use of mortar and tiles; and for every purpose employ rude unshapen timber, fashioned with no regard to pleasing the eye. They bestow more than ordinary pains in coating certain parts of their buildings with a kind of earth, so pure and shining that it gives the appearance of painting.

The dress of the women does not differ from that of the men; except that they more frequently wear linen, which they stain with purple, and do not lengthen their upper garment into sleeves, but leave exposed the whole arm, and part of the breast.

The matrimonial bond is, nevertheless, strict and severe among them; nor is there any thing in their manners more commendable than this. Almost singly among the barbarians, they content themselves with one wife; a very few of them excepted, who, not through incontinence, but because their alliance is solicited on account of their rank, practice polygamy. The wife does not bring a dowry to her husband, but receives one from him. The parents and relations assemble, and pass their approbation on the presents—presents not adapted to please a female taste, or decorate the bride; but oxen, a caparisoned steed, a shield, a spear, and sword. By virtue of these, the wife is espoused; and she in her turn makes a present of some arms to her husband. This they consider as the firmest bond of union; these, the sacred mysteries, the conjugal deities. That the woman may not think herself excused from exertions of fortitude, or exempt from the casualties of war, she is admonished by the very ceremonial of her marriage, that she comes to her husband as a partner in toils and dangers; to suffer and to dare equally with him, in peace and in war; this is indicated by the yoked oxen, the harnessed steed, the offered arms. Thus she is to live; thus to die. She receives what she is to return inviolate and honored to her children; what her daughters-in-law are to receive, and again transmit to her grandchildren.

They live, therefore, fenced around with chastity, corrupted by no seductive spectacles, no convivial

incitements. Men and women are alike unacquainted with Clandestine correspondence. Adultery is
extremely rare among so numerous a people. Its
punishment is instant, and at the pleasure of the
husband. He cuts off the hair of the offender, strips
her, and in presence of her relations expels her from
his house, and pursues her with stripes through the
whole village. Nor is any indulgence shown to a
prostitute. Neither beauty, youth, nor riches can
procure her a husband; for none there looks on
vice with a smile, or calls mutual seduction the

way of the world. Still more exemplary is the practice of those states in which none but virgins marry,
and the expectations and wishes of a wife are at
once brought to a period. Thus, they take one husband as one body and one life; that no thought, no
desire, may extend beyond him; and he may be
loved not only as their husband, but as their marriage. To limit the increase of children, or put to
death any of the later progeny, is accounted infamous: and good habits have there more influence
than good laws elsewhere.

FOCUS QUESTIONS

1. Tacitus's view of the Germans is that of an
   outsider looking in. How might his background affect his description?

2. How is German society organized? Who bears
   authority within it, and how do they achieve power?

3. Why is German society so warlike? What purpose
   does warfare serve among the Germanic tribes?

4. What is the family life of the Germans like?

5. Implicit in Tacitus's account of the morals of
   the Germans is a comment upon the Romans
   of his own time. What do you think he is
   trying to say?

46

The Burgundian Code (ca. 474 C.E.)

*The Burgundians were a Germanic tribe that moved westward across the Rhine River
until stopped by the Roman army. In the fourth century, they were incorporated into the
Roman Empire and settled north of Lake Geneva. During the reign of Gundobad
(474–516), one of the greatest Burgundian kings, the tribe occupied the largest amount of
territory in its history and became a major power in northwestern Europe, even defeating
the Franks. After his death, the kingdom contracted and was soon absorbed into the
Frankish empire.*

Gundobad's codification, known as The Burgundian Code, *was undoubtedly a
combination of older laws and those current in the late fifth century. As Romans and
Burgundians had been neighbors for over a century, procedures such as those outlined here
must have developed slowly.*

1. In the name of God in the second year of the reign of our lord the most glorious king Gundobad, this book concerning laws past and present, and to be preserved throughout all future time, has been issued on the fourth day before the Kalends of April (March 29) at Lyons.

2. For the love of justice, through which God is pleased and the power of earthly kingdoms acquired, we have obtained the consent of our counts and leaders, and have desired to establish such laws that the integrity and equity of those judging may exclude all rewards and corruptions from themselves.

3. Therefore all administrators and judges must judge from the present time on between Burgundians and Romans according to our laws which have been set forth and corrected by a common method, to the end that no one may hope or presume to receive anything by way of reward or emolument from any party as the result of the suits or decisions: but let him whose case is deserving obtain justice and let the integrity of the judge alone suffice to accomplish this.

4. We believe the condition of this law should be imposed on us that no one may presume to tempt our integrity in any kind of case with favors or rewards; first, since our zeal for equity repudiates from ourselves those things which we forbid to all judges under our rule, let our treasury accept nothing more than has been established in the laws concerning the payment of fines.

5. Therefore let all nobles, counsellors, bailiffs, mayors of our palace, chancellors, counts of the cities or villages, Burgundian as well as Roman, and all appointed judges and military judges know that nothing can be accepted in connection with those suits which have been acted upon or decided, and that nothing can be sought in the name of promise or reward from those litigating: nor can the parties (to the suit) be compelled by the judge to make a payment in order that they may receive anything (from their suit).

OF MURDERS

1. If anyone presumes with boldness or rashness bent on injury to kill a native freeman of our people of any nation or a servant of the king, in any case a man of barbarian tribe, let him make restitution for the committed crime not otherwise than by the shedding of his own blood.

2. We decree that this rule be added to the law by a reasonable provision, that if violence shall have been done by anyone to any person, so that he is injured by blows of lashes or by wounds, and if he pursues his persecutor and overcome by grief and indignation kills him, proof of the deed shall be afforded by the act itself or by suitable witnesses who can be believed. Then the guilty party shall be compelled to pay to the relatives of the person killed half his wergeld according to the status of the person: that is, if he shall have killed a noble of the highest class, we decree that the payment be set at one hundred fifty solidi, i.e., half his wergeld; if a person of middle class, one hundred solidi; if a person of the lowest class, seventy-five solidi.

3. If a slave unknown to his master presumes to kill a native freeman, let the slave be handed over to death, and let the master not be made liable for damages.

4. If the master knows of the deed, let both be handed over to death.

5. If the slave himself flees after the deed, let his master be compelled to pay thirty solidi to the relatives of the man killed for the value (wergeld) of the slave.

OF THE COMMISSION OF CRIMES
WHICH ARE CHARGED
AGAINST NATIVE FREEMAN

1. If a native freeman, either barbarian or Roman, is accused of a crime through suspicion, let him render oath, and let him swear with his wife and sons and twelve relatives: if indeed he does not have wife and sons and he has mother or father, let him complete the designated number with father and mother. But if he has neither father nor mother, let him complete the oath with twelve relatives.

2. But if he who must take oath wishes to take it with raised hand, and if those who are ordered to

hear the oath—those three whom we always command to be delegated by the judges for hearing an oath—before they enter the church declare they do not wish to receive the oath, then he who was about to take oath is not permitted to do so after this statement, but they (the judges) are hereby directed by us to commit the matter to the judgment of God (i.e., to ordeal).

3. If however, having received permission, he has taken the oath, and if he has been convicted after the oath, let him know that he must make restitution by a ninefold payment to those in whose presence the judge ordered him to give his oath.

4. But if they (those appointed to hear the oath) fail to come to the place on the appointed day, and, if they shall not have been detained by any illness or public duty, let them pay a fine of six solidi. But if they were detained by any illness or duty, let them make this known to the judge or send other persons in their place whom they can trust to receive the oath for them.

5. If moreover he who is about to take the oath does not come to the place, let the other party wait until the sixth hour of the day; but if he has not come by the sixth hour, let the case be dismissed without delay.

6. But if the other (the accusing party) does not come, let him who was about to take the oath depart without loss.

LET BURGUNDIANS AND ROMANS BE HELD UNDER THE SAME CONDITIONS IN THE MATTER OF KILLING SLAVES

1. If anyone kills a slave, barbarian by birth, a trained (select) house servant or messenger, let him compound sixty solidi; moreover, let the amount of the fine be twelve solidi. If anyone kills another's slave, Roman or barbarian, either ploughman or swine-herd, let him pay thirty solidi.

2. Whoever kills a skilled goldsmith, let him pay two hundred solidi.

3. Whoever kills a silversmith, let him pay one hundred solidi.

4. Whoever kills a blacksmith, let him pay fifty solidi.

5. Whoever kills a carpenter, let him pay forty solidi.

OF THE STEALING OF GIRLS

1. If anyone shall steal a girl, let him be compelled to pay the price set for such a girl ninefold, and let him pay a fine to the amount of twelve solidi.

2. If a girl who has been seized returns uncorrupted to her parents, let the abductor compound six times the wergeld of the girl; moreover, let the fine be set at twelve solidi.

3. But if the abductor does not have the means to make the above-mentioned payment, let him be given over to the parents of the girl that they may have the power of doing to him whatever they choose.

4. If indeed, the girl seeks the man of her own will and comes to his house, and he has intercourse with her, let him pay her marriage price threefold; if moreover, she returns uncorrupted to her home, let her return with all blame removed from him.

5. If indeed a Roman girl, without the consent or knowledge of her parents, unites in marriage with a Burgundian, let her know she will have none of the property of her parents.

OF SUCCESSION

1. Among Burgundians we wish it to be observed that if anyone does not leave a son, let a daughter succeed to the inheritance of the father and mother in place of the son.

2. If by chance the dead leave neither a son or daughter, let the inheritance go to the sisters or nearest relatives.

3. It is pleasing that it be contained in the present law that if a woman having a husband dies without children, the husband of the dead wife may not demand back the marriage price which had been given for her.

4. Likewise, let neither the woman nor the relatives of the woman seek back that which a woman pays when she comes to her husband if the husband dies without children.

5. Concerning those women who are vowed to God and remain in chastity, we order that if they have two brothers they receive a third portion of the inheritance of the father, that is, of that land which the father, possessing by the right of sors (allotment), left at the time of his death. Likewise, if she has four or five brothers, let her receive the portion due to her.

6. If moreover she has but one brother, let not a half, but a third part go to her on the condition that, after the death of her who is a woman and a nun, whatever she possesses in usufruct from her father's property shall go to the nearest relatives, and she will have no power of transferring anything therefrom, unless perhaps from her mother's goods, that is, from her clothing or things of the cell, or what she has acquired by her own labor.

7. We decree that this should be observed only by those whose fathers have not given them portions; but if they shall have received from their father a place where they can live, let them have full freedom of disposing of it at their will.

OF THOSE THINGS WHICH HAPPEN BY CHANCE

1. If any animal by chance, or if any dog by bite, causes death to a man, we order that among Burgundians the ancient rule of blame be removed henceforth: because what happens by chance ought not to conduce to the loss or discomfiture of man. So that if among animals, a horse kills a horse unexpectedly, or an ox gores an ox, or a dog gnaws a dog, so that it is crippled, let the owner hand over the animal or dog through which the loss is seen to have been committed to him who suffers the loss.

2. In truth, if a lance or any kind of weapon shall have been thrown upon the ground or set there without intent to do harm, and if by accident a man or animal impales himself thereupon, we order that he to whom the weapon belongs shall pay nothing unless by chance he held the weapon in his own hands in such a manner that it could cause harm to a man.

OF BURGUNDIAN WOMEN ENTERING A SECOND OR THIRD MARRIAGE

1. If any Burgundian woman, as is the custom, enters a second or third marriage after the death of her husband, and she has children by each husband, let her possess the marriage gift in usufruct while she lives; after her death, let what his father gave her be given to each son, with the further provision that the mother has the power neither of giving, selling, or transferring any of the things which she received in the marriage gift.

2. If by chance the woman has no children, after her death let her relatives receive half of whatever has come to her by way of marriage gift, and let the relatives of the dead husband who was the donor receive half.

3. But if perchance children shall have been born and they shall have died after the death of their father, we command that the inheritance of the husband or children belong wholly to the mother. Moreover, after the death of the mother, we decree that what she holds in usufruct by inheritance from her children shall belong to the legal heirs of her children. Also we command that she protect the property of her children dying intestate.

4. If any son has given his mother something by will or by gift, let the mother have the power of doing whatever she wishes therewith; if she dies intestate, let the relatives of the woman claim the inheritance as their possession.

5. If any Burgundian has sons (children?) to whom he has given their portions, let him have the power of giving or selling that which he has reserved for himself to whomever he wishes.

OF INJURIES WHICH ARE SUFFERED BY WOMEN

1. If any native freewoman has her hair cut off and is humiliated without cause (when innocent) by any native freeman in her home or on the road, and this can be proved with witnesses, let the doer of the deed pay her twelve solidi, and let the amount of the fine be twelve solidi.

2. If this was done to a freedwoman, let him pay her six solidi.

3. If this was done to a maidservant, let him pay her three solidi, and let the amount of the fine be three solidi.

4. If this injury (shame, disgrace) is inflicted by a slave on a native freewoman, let him receive two hundred blows; if a freedwoman, let him receive a hundred blows; if a maidservant, let him receive seventy-five blows.

5. If indeed the woman whose injury we have ordered to be punished in this manner commits fornication voluntarily (i.e., if she yields), let nothing be sought for the injury suffered.

OF DIVORCES

1. If any woman leaves (puts aside) her husband to whom she is legally married, let her be smothered in mire.

2. If anyone wishes to put away his wife without cause, let him give her another payment such as he gave for her marriage price, and let the amount of the fine be twelve solidi.

3. If by chance a man wishes to put away his wife, and is able to prove one of these three crimes against her, that is, adultery, witchcraft, or violation of graves, let him have full right to put her away: and let the judge pronounce the sentence of the law against her, just as should be done against criminals.

4. But if she admits none of these three crimes, let no man be permitted to put away his wife for any other crime. But if he chooses, he may go away from the home, leaving all household property behind, and his wife with their children may possess the property of her husband.

OF THE PUNISHMENT OF SLAVES WHO COMMIT A CRIMINAL ASSAULT ON FREEBORN WOMEN

1. If any slave does violence to a native freewoman, and if she complains and is clearly able to prove this, let the slave be killed for the crime committed.

2. If indeed a native free girl unites voluntarily with a slave, we order both to be killed.

3. But if the relatives of the girl do not wish to punish their own relative, let the girl be deprived of her free status and delivered into servitude to the king.

OF INCESTUOUS ADULTERY

If anyone has been taken in adultery with his relative or with his wife's sister, let him be compelled to pay her wergeld, according to her status, to him who is the nearest relative of the woman with whom he committed adultery; and let the amount of the fine be twelve solidi. Further, we order the adulteress to be placed in servitude to the king.

OF THE INHERITANCE OF THOSE WHO DIE WITHOUT CHILDREN

1. Although we have ordered many things in former laws concerning the inheritance of those who die without children, nevertheless after considering the matter thoroughly, we perceive it to be

just that some of those things which were ordered before should be corrected. Therefore we decree in the present constitution that if a woman whose husband has died without children has not taken her vows a second time, let her possess securely a third of all the property of her husband to the day of her death; with the further provision that after her death, all will revert to the legitimate heirs of her husband.

2. Let that remain in effect which has been stated previously concerning the mourning gift.

For if she wishes to marry within a year from the time of the death of her first husband, let her have full right to do so, but let her give up that third part of the property which she had been permitted to possess. However, if she wishes to take a husband after a year or two have passed, let her give up all as has been stated above which she received from her first husband, and let the heirs in whose portion the inheritance of her former husband belongs receive the price which must be paid for her (second) marriage.

FOCUS QUESTIONS

1. How free is Gundobad to make laws? What limits are there upon his authority as king?

2. How does the code distinguish between classes of peoples? Does social status matter?

3. What principles underlie the Burgundian view of crime and punishment? How do the Burgundians punish criminals, and how do they determine guilt?

4. The code says a great deal about women and family matters. What is the status of women in Burgundian society?

5. You have read several excerpts from legal codes in earlier parts of this book. What are the sorts of things that seem common to these codes in general? Can you think of ways in which *The Burgundian Code* is quite different?

47

The Life of Charlemagne (ca. 829–836 C.E.)

EINHARD

Einhard (ca. 770–840) was a prominent scholar and historian of the reign of Charlemagne. Little has been preserved concerning Einhard's youth, although it is supposed that he was born in Germany near the monastery of Fulda where he was educated. While at Fulda, he developed a reputation as a brilliant scholar, and he soon entered Charlemagne's court in the city of Aachen, which was renowned for its intellectual sophistication—despite the fact that the emperor himself was illiterate—and where many promising young scholars came to serve. Einhard took a position as a teacher in the school that trained the children of the nobility. Einhard grew to become one of the emperor's most trusted advisors.

The Life of Charlemagne was written during Einhard's retirement, between 829 and 836. It was produced as a token of gratitude to the emperor as well as to teach Charlemagne's children about the achievements of their father. Though it is based on classical models, The Life *was the first medieval biography of a layman. It became one of the most frequently copied works of the Middle Ages.*

PRIVATE LIFE AND CHARACTER OF CHARLEMAGNE

I have shown, then, how Charles protected and expanded his kingdom and also what splendour he gave to it. I shall now go on to speak of his mental endowments, of his steadiness of purpose under whatever circumstances of prosperity or adversity, and of all that concerns his private and domestic life.

In educating his children he determined to train them, both sons and daughters, in those liberal studies to which he himself paid great attention. Further, he made his sons, as soon as their age permitted it, learn to ride like true Franks, and practise the use of arms and hunting. He ordered his daughters to learn wool work and devote attention to the spindle and distaff, for the avoidance of idleness and lethargy, and to be trained to the adoption of high principles.

He bore the deaths of his two sons and of his daughters with less patience than might have been expected from his usual stoutness of heart, for his domestic affection, a quality for which he was as remarkable as for courage, forced him to shed tears. Moreover, when the death of Hadrian, the Roman Pontiff, whom he reckoned as the chief of his friends, was announced to him, he wept for him as though he had lost a brother or a very dear son. For he showed a very fine disposition in his friendships: he embraced them readily and maintained them faithfully, and he treated with the utmost respect all whom he had admitted into the circle of his friends.

He had such care of the upbringing of his sons and daughters that he never dined without them when he was at home, and never travelled without them. His sons rode along with him, and his daughters followed in the rear. Some of his guards, chosen for this very purpose, watched the end of the line of march where his daughters travelled. They were very beautiful, and much beloved by their father, and, therefore, it is strange that he would give them in marriage to no one, either among his own people or of a foreign state. But up to his death he kept them all at home, saying that he could not forego their society. And hence the good fortune that followed him in all other respects was here broken by the touch of scandal and failure. He shut his eyes, however, to everything, and acted as though no suspicion of anything amiss had reached him, or as if the rumour of it had been discredited.

He had a great love for foreigners, and took such pains to entertain them that their numbers were justly reckoned to be a burden not only to the palace but to the kingdom at large. But, with his usual loftiness of spirit, he took little note of such charges, for he found in the reputation of generosity and in the good fame that followed such actions a compensation even for grave inconveniences.

He paid the greatest attention to the liberal arts, and showed the greatest respect and bestowed high honours upon those who taught them. For his lessons in grammar he listened to the instruction of Deacon Peter of Pisa, an old man; but for all other subjects Albinus, called Alcuin, also a deacon, was his teacher—a man from Britain, of the Saxon race, and the most learned man of his time. Charles spent much time and labour in learning rhetoric and dialectic, and especially astronomy, from Alcuin. He learnt, too, the art of reckoning, and with close application scrutinised most carefully the course of the stars. He tried also to learn to write, and for this purpose used to carry with him and keep under the pillow of his couch tablets and

Bridgeman-Giraudon/Art Resource, NY

The Coronation of Charlemagne. This manuscript illustration shows Leo III placing a crown on Charlemagne's head.

writing-sheets that he might in his spare moments accustom himself to the formation of letters. But he made little advance in this strange task, which was begun too late in life.

He paid the most devout and pious regard to the Christian religion, in which he had been brought up from infancy. And, therefore, he built the great and most beautiful church at Aix, and decorated it with gold and silver and candelabras and with wicket-gates and doors of solid brass. And, since he could not procure marble columns elsewhere for the building of it, he had them brought from Rome and Ravenna. As long as his health permitted it he used diligently to attend the church both in the morning and evening, and during the night, and at the time of the Sacrifice. He took the greatest care to have all the services of the church performed with the utmost dignity, and constantly warned the keepers of the building not to allow anything improper or dirty either to be brought into or to remain in the building. He provided so great a quantity of gold and silver vessels, and so large a supply of priestly vestments, that at the religious services not even the doorkeepers, who form the lowest ecclesiastical order, had to officiate in their ordinary dress. He carefully reformed the manner of reading and singing; for he was thoroughly instructed in both, though he never read publicly himself, nor sang except in a low voice, and with the rest of the congregation.

He was most devout in relieving the poor and in those free gifts which the Greeks call alms. For he gave it his attention not only in his own country and in his own kingdom, but he also used to send money across the sea to Syria, to Egypt, to Africa—to Jerusalem, Alexandria, and Carthage—in compassion for the poverty of any Christians whose miserable condition in those countries came to his ears. It was for this reason chiefly that he cultivated the friendship of kings beyond the sea, hoping thereby to win for the Christians living beneath their sway some succour and relief.

Beyond all other sacred and venerable places, he loved the church of the holy Apostle Peter at Rome, and he poured into its treasury great wealth in silver and gold and precious stones. He sent innumerable gifts to the Pope; and during the whole course of his reign he strove with all his might (and, indeed, no object was nearer to his heart than this) to restore to the city of Rome her ancient authority, and not merely to defend the church of Saint Peter but to decorate and enrich it out of his resources above all other churches. But although he valued Rome so much, still during all the forty-seven years that he reigned, he only went there four times to pay his vows and offer up his prayers.

When he had taken the imperial title he noticed many defects in the legal systems of his people; for the Franks have two legal systems, differing in many points very widely from one another, and he, therefore, determined to add what was lacking, to reconcile the differences, and to amend anything that was wrong or wrongly expressed. He completed nothing of all his designs beyond adding a few capitularies, and those unfinished. But he gave orders that the laws and rules of all nations comprised within his dominions which were not already written out should be collected and committed to writing.

He also wrote out the barbarous and ancient songs, in which the acts of the kings and their wars were sung, and committed them to memory. He also began a grammar of his native language.

FOCUS QUESTIONS

1. What does Einhard's biography tell us about the education and upbringing of royal children? How does Charlemagne treat his children, and is he, by the standards of the time, a successful father?

2. Although Charlemagne was never literate, Einhard still counted him a learned man. How did the emperor qualify for this distinction?

3. In what ways was Charlemagne a model king?

4. Einhard based his work on the biographies of ancient rulers, such as Suetonius's *Life of Augustus*. Can you detect any similarities with such classical biographies?

5. What would you say is the message that Einhard is trying to put across with his work? How does he do it?

48

Magna Carta (1215 C.E.)

Magna Carta (the Great Charter) was a series of concessions made by King John of England to his rebellious barons in 1215. English participation in the Third Crusade had disastrous consequences for England's internal stability. Not only had the great barons of the realm been forced to pay for the army led by King Richard I, they were also faced with the expense of ransoming him back from Germany. Failures of English policy in France and a dispute between John and the Catholic Church added to the problems of this unpopular ruler. Finally, under the leadership of the Archbishop of Canterbury, a segment of the aristocracy rebelled and asserted the nobles' traditional rights against the monarchy. These were conceded in Magna Carta.

Magna Carta was not a bill of rights, nor did it institute any major reforms in the relationship between kings and their subjects. Its original purpose was to bind the king to respect the privileges of the barons, especially in matters of taxation. But its significance in constitutional history was that it formally defined these rights for posterity. Over the centuries, Magna Carta has been seen as the bedrock for the protection of the rights of subjects against arbitrary rule by the crown.

John, by the Grace of God, King of England, Lord of Ireland, Duke of Normandy and Acquitaine, and Earl of Anjou, to his Archbishops, Bishops, Abbots, Earls, Barons, Justiciaries, Foresters, Sheriffs, Governors, Officers, and to all Bailiffs, and his faithful subjects—Greeting. Know ye, that We, in the presence of God, and for the salvation of our own soul, and of the souls of all our ancestors, and of our heirs, to the honour of God, and the exaltation of the Holy Church and amendment of our Kingdom, by this our present Charter, have confirmed, for us and our heirs forever:

1. That the English Church shall be free, and shall have her whole rights and her liberties inviolable; and we will this to be observed in such a manner, that it may appear from thence, that the freedom of elections, which was reputed most requisite to the English Church, which we granted, and by our Charter confirmed, and obtained the Confirmation of the same, from our Lord Pope Innocent the Third, before the rupture between

us and our Barons, was of our own free will; which Charter we shall observe, and we will it to be observed with good faith, by our heirs forever.

We have also granted to all the freemen of our Kingdom, for us and our heirs forever, all the underwritten Liberties, to be enjoyed and held by them and by their heirs, from us and from our heirs.

2. If any of our Earls or Barons, or others who hold of us in chief by military service, shall die, and at his death his heir shall be of full age, and shall owe a relief; he shall have his inheritance by the ancient relief; that is to say, the heir or heirs of an Earl, a whole Earl's Baron, for one hundred pounds; the heir or heirs of a Baron, for a whole Barony, by one hundred pounds; the heir or heirs of a Knight, for a whole Knight's fee, by one hundred shillings at most; and he who owes less, shall give less, according to the ancient custom of fees.

3. But if the heir of any such be under age, and in wardship, when he comes to age he shall have his inheritance without relief and without fine.

4. The warden of the land of such heir who shall be under age, shall not take from the lands of the heir any but reasonable issues, and reasonable customs, and reasonable services, and that without destruction and waste of the men or goods....

6. Heirs shall be married without disparagement, so that before the marriage be contracted it shall be notified to the relations of the heir by consanguinity.

7. A widow after the death of her husband shall immediately, and without difficulty, have her marriage and her inheritance; nor shall she give anything for her dower, or for her marriage, or for her inheritance, which her husband and she held at the day of his death; and she may remain in her husband's house forty days after his death, within which time her dower shall be assigned.

8. No widow shall be distrained to marry herself, while she is willing to live without a husband; but yet she shall give security that she will not marry herself without our consent, if she hold of us, or without the consent of the lord of whom she does hold, if she hold of another....

...

12. No scutage nor aid shall be imposed in our kingdom, unless by the common council of our kingdom; excepting to redeem our person, to make our eldest son a knight, and once to many our eldest daughter, and not for these, unless a reasonable aid shall be demanded.

13. In like manner let it be concerning the aids of the City of London. And the City of London shall have all its ancient liberties, and its free customs, as well by land as by water. Furthermore, we will and grant that all other Cities, Burghs, and Towns, and Ports, should have all their liberties and free customs.

14. And also to have the common council of the kingdom, to assess and aid, otherwise than in the three cases aforesaid: and for the assessing of scutages, we will cause to be summoned the Archbishops, Bishops, Abbots, Earls, and great Barons, individually by our letters. And besides, we will cause to be summoned in general by our Sheriffs and Bailiffs, all those who hold of us in chief, at a certain day, that is to say at the distance of forty days (before their meeting), at the least, and to a certain place; and in all the letters of

summons, we will express the cause of the summons; and the summons being thus made, the business shall proceed on the day appointed, according to the counsel of those who shall be present, although all who have been summoned have not come....

...

27. If any free-man shall die intestate, his chattels shall be distributed by the hands of his nearest relations and friends, by the view of the Church, saving to every one the debts which the defunct owed.

28. No Constable nor other Bailiff of ours shall take the corn or other goods of any one without instantly paying money for them, unless he can obtain respite from the free-will of the seller.

29. No Constable (Governor of a Castle) shall distrain any Knight to give money for castle-guard, if he be willing to perform it in his own person, or by another able man, if he cannot perform it himself, for a reasonable cause; and if we have carried or sent him into the army he shall be excused from castle-guard, according to the time that he shall be in the army by our command.

30. No Sheriff nor Bailiff of ours, nor any other person shall take the horses or carts of any free-man for the purpose of carriage, without the consent of the said free-man.

31. Neither we, nor our Bailiffs, will take another man's wood, for our castles or other uses, unless by the consent of him to whom the wood belongs....

...

35. There shall be one measure of wine throughout all our kingdom, and one measure of ale, and one measure of corn, namely, the quarter of London; and one breadth of dyed cloth, and of russets, and of halberjects, namely, two ells within the lists. Also it shall be the same with weights as with measures....

39. No free-man shall be seized, or imprisoned, or dispossessed, or outlawed, or in any way destroyed; nor will we condemn him, nor will we commit him to prison, excepting by the legal judgment of his peers, or by the laws of the land.

40. To none will we sell, to none will we deny, to none will we delay right or justice.

41. All Merchants shall have safety and security in coming into England, and going out of England,

A Prospect of Carcassonne. The best-preserved walled medieval town in France, Carcassonne shows how important protection from enemy armies and marauders was in the Middle Ages. Most West European towns once possessed such walls but demolished them later in order to expand.

and in staying and in traveling through England, as well by land as by water, to buy and sell, without any unjust exactions, according to ancient and right customs, excepting in the time of war....

...

54. No man shall be apprehended or imprisoned on the appeal of a woman for the death of any other man than her husband....

...

61. But since we have granted all these things aforesaid, for God and for the amendment of our kingdom, and for the better extinguishing the discord which has arisen between us and our Barons, we being desirous that these things should possess entire and unshaken stability forever, give and grant to them the security underwritten, namely, that the Barons may elect twenty-five Barons of the kingdom, whom they please, who shall with their whole power, observe, keep, and cause to be observed, the peace and liberties which we have granted to them, and have confirmed by this, our present charter, in this manner; that is to say, if we, or our Justiciary, or our bailiffs or any of our officers, shall have injured any one in anything, or shall have violated any article of the peace or security, and the injury shall have been shown to four of the aforesaid twenty-five Barons, the said four Barons shall come to us, or to our Justiciary if we be out of the kingdom, and making known to us the excess committed, petition that we cause that excess to be redressed without delay. And if we shall not have redressed the excess, or, if we have been out of the kingdom, our Justiciary shall not have redressed it within the term of forty days, computing from the time when it shall

have been made known to us, or to our Justiciary, if we have been out of the kingdom, the aforesaid four Barons shall lay that cause before the residue of the twenty-five Barons; and they, the twenty-five Barons, with the community of the whole land, shall distress and harass us by all the ways in which they are able; that is to say, by the taking of our castles, lands and possessions, and by any other means in their power, until the excess shall have been redressed, according to their verdict, saving harmless our person and the persons of our Queen and children, and when it hath been redressed they shall behave to us as they have done before....

62. And we have fully remitted and pardoned to all men all the ill-will, rancour and resentments which have arisen between us and our subjects, both clergy and laity, from the commencement of the discord.

63. Wherefore our will is, and we firmly command that the Church of England be free, and that the men in our kingdom have and hold the aforesaid liberties, rights and concessions, well in peace, freely and quietly, fully and entirely, to them and their heirs, of us and our heirs, in all things and places for ever, as is aforesaid. It is also sworn, both on our part and on that of the Barons, that all the aforesaid shall be observed in good faith and without any evil intention. Witnessed by the above and many others. Given by our hand in the Meadow which is called Running-mead, between Windsor and Staines, this 15th day of June, in the 17th year of our reign.

FOCUS QUESTIONS

1. Who do you think the chief beneficiaries of the charter were?

2. What are the general issues that seem to concern the barons most? How has the king infringed upon the rights of the barons?

3. Some historians have said that the real importance of the charter is that it made the king subject to the laws. How does the charter do that, and why is this important?

4. Several important clauses in *Magna Carta* deal with the king's powers over the family lives of his nobility. What was the king's interest in these matters?

5. Do you think that the barons thought the king was trustworthy? How were the provisions of the charter to be enforced?

6. In what areas can you see *Magna Carta* as an ancestor of later views about individual freedom?

49

Njal's Saga (13th century C.E.)

ANONYMOUS

Njal's Saga is considered one of the finest examples of the Icelandic saga tradition. Though compiled in the thirteenth century, it purports to describe the nature of life in ninth-century Iceland, a society dominated by families and their feuds. It's hero is Njal, a wise and peaceful man who nevertheless is drawn into conflict and violence to uphold the values of his lineage. The story follows a blood feud into which he is drawn and reveals how feuds are maintained and escalated. In this rough world of an eye-for-an-eye, Njal's Saga *shows the extent and limits of primitive Icelandic law before the coming of Christianity. The island of Iceland had no king, but instead was surprisingly egalitarian; laws could be made by all free men who met at a parliament called the "Althing" but they were only binding if the community was willing to enforce them. Though written 800 years ago,* Njal's Saga *has the tempo and drama of a modern action movie.*

This was not a society that often resorted to courts and lawsuits. Most wrongs were righted through vengeance and feuds, but these had their own set of rules and concepts of justice. Although Icelandic women like Bergthora had limited power, since they could not join in at the Althing they had other ways of making their influence felt. The following selection portrays the dynamic of an Icelandic blood feud.

35 It was the custom between Gunnar and Njal, because of their close friendship, that every winter one of them would invite the other to his home for a winter feast. It was now Gunnar's turn to be Njal's guest at the winter feast, and so he and Hallgerd went to Bergthorshvol. Helgi and his wife were not there. Njal welcomed them, and when they had been there a while Helgi and his wife Thorhalla returned.

Bergthora went up to the cross-bench, together with Thorhalla, and spoke to Hallgerd: 'You must move aside for this woman.'

Hallgerd spoke: 'I'll not move aside for anyone, and I won't sit in the corner like a cast-off hag.'

'I decide things here,' said Bergthora.

After that Thorhalla sat down.

Bergthora came to the table with water for washing hands. Hallgerd took her hand and said, 'There's not much to choose between you and Njal – you have gnarled nails on every finger, and he's beardless.'

'That's true,' said Bergthora, 'and yet we don't hold it against each other. But your husband Thorvald was not beardless, and yet you had him killed.'

'There's little use to me in being married to the most manly man in Iceland,' said Hallgerd, 'if you don't avenge this, Gunnar.'

He sprang up and leaped across the table and spoke: 'I'm going home, and it would be best for you to pick quarrels with your servants, and not in the dwellings of others. I'm in debt to Njal for many honours, and I'm not going to be a cat's-paw for you.'

After that Gunnar and Hallgerd set off for home.

'Keep this in mind, Bergthora,' said Hallgerd, 'that we're not finished yet.'

Bergrhora said that Hallgerd would not be better off for that, Gunnar said nothing more and went home to Hlidarendi and was there all through the winter. Summer came, and the time For the Thing.

36 Gunnar got ready to ride to the Thing, and before he left he spoke to Hallgerd: 'Behave yourself while I'm away and don't show your bad temper where my friends are concerned.'

'The trolls take your friends,' she said.

Gunnar rode to the Thing, and saw that it was no good talking to her. Njal and all his Sons also rode to the Thing.

Now to tell what was happening at home: Gunnar and Njal together owned some woodland at Raudaskrid. They had not divided it up, and each of them was in the habit of cutting what he needed, without blame from the other.

Kol was the name of Haligerd's overseer. He had been with her a long time, and was the worst sort of person. A man named Svart was Njal and Bergthora's servant, and they were quite fond of him.

Bergthora spoke with Svart and told him to go to Raudaskrid and chop wood—'and I will send men to haul it home.'

He said he would do as she wished. He went up to Raudaskrid and started chopping, and was to stay there for a week.

Some poor men came to Hlidarendi from east of the Markarfljot and reported that Svart had been at Raudaskrid chopping wood, and working hard at it.

'It seems that Bergthora is out to rob me in a big way,' said Hallgerd, 'but I'll see to it that he won't chop any more.'

Rannveig, Gunnar's mother, overheard this and spoke: 'Housewives have been good here, even without plotting to kill men.'

The night passed, and in the morning Hallgerd said to Kol, 'I have thought of a job for you,' and she handed him a weapon. 'Go up to Raudaskrid. You'll find Svart there.'

'What am I to do with him?' he said.

'Do you need to ask that?' she said. 'You—the worst sort of person? Kill him!'

'I can do that,' he said, 'and yet it's likely to cost me my life.'

'Everything grows big in your eyes,' she said, 'and this is had of you after all the times I've spoken up for you. I'll find another man to do this if you don't dare.'

He took the axe and was very angry, and took a horse that Gunnar owned and rode until he came east to the Markarfljot. There he dismounted and waited in the woods until men had carried off the timber and Svart was left alone.

Kol charged towards him and said, 'More men than you know how to chop hard'—and he sank the axe into his head and struck him his death blow and then rode back and told Hallgerd of the slaying.

She said, 'I'll look after you so that no one will harm you.'

'That may be,' he said, 'but before I did the slaying I had a dream that pointed the other way.'

The men came back to the woods and found Svart dead and carried his body home.

Hallgerd sent a man to Gunnar at the Thing to tell him of the slaying. Gunnar did not find fault with Hallgerd in the presence of the messenger, and at first people did not know whether he thought well or ill of it. After a while he stood up and asked his men to come with him. They did, and went together to Njal's booth, and Gunnar sent a man to ask Njal to come outside, Njal came out at once, and he and Gunnar went apart to talk.

Gunnar spoke: 'I have a slaying to tell you of: my wife and my overseer Kol brought it about, and your servant Svart was the victim.'

Njal remained silent while Gunnar told him everything. Then he spoke: 'You must not let her have her way in everything.'

Gunnar said, 'You make the judgement yourself.'

Njal said, 'It's going to be hard for you to atone for all of Hallgerd's misdoings, and another time the effects will be greater than now, where just the two of us are involved—though this matter itself is far short of going well—and you and I will have to keep in mind the good things we've been saying to each other for a long time. I expect that you will do well, but you will be tested hard.'

Njal accepted self-judgement from Gunnar and said, 'I'm not going to push this too hard: pay me twelve ounces of silver. But I want to stipulate that if something happens from my side which you have to judge, you will not set harder terms than I have done.'

Gunnar paid the money readily and then rode home.

Njal and his sons returned from the Thing. Bergthora saw the money and said, 'This was moderately done—the same amount must be paid for Kol when the time comes.'

Gunnar returned from the Thing and reproached Hallgerd. She said that better men than Svart had died in many places without compensation.

Gunnar said she would decide her own actions—'but I shall decide how the cases are settled.'

Hallgerd frequently boasted of the slaying of Svart, and Bergthora did not like that at all.

FOCUS QUESTIONS

1. What sparked the feud between Hallgerd and Bergthora?

2. Why do you think Svart is the one who is killed if Hallgerd is upset at Bergthora?

3. Why does Gunnar pay Njal 12 ounces of silver? What is the money supposed to represent?

4. What can this feud tell us about the role of women in Icelandic society?

The Development
of Christianity

The Twenty-Fourth Psalm. This ninth-century European psalter retained artistic conventions of late antiquity in both textual presentation and illustration. Notice the arrangement of the handwritten Latin verses in three columns, and the situation of the title above the columns but below the illustration.

50

The City of God (413–426 C.E.)

AUGUSTINE OF HIPPO

Augustine of Hippo (354–430) was the most important Christian philosopher and theologian of late antiquity. Born in Roman North Africa, the son of a pagan father and a devoutly Christian mother, Augustine himself remained pagan until adulthood. Although his family was not rich, he was sent for schooling at Carthage, where he developed a taste and aptitude for philosophy. At the age of 32 he converted to Christianity and became a priest in 391. He recounted the story of his inner struggles in The Confessions *(ca. 400), one of the most famous of all Christian autobiographies. In 396 Augustine was consecrated Bishop of Hippo, a position he held until his death. There he combined pastoral duties with the writing of major theological and philosophical works. His great achievement was a synthesis of classical and Christian tradition. He died when Hippo was besieged by the Vandals in 430.*

The City of God (413–426) was Augustine's major work. It provides a summary of Christian thought at the moment when the Roman Empire was under siege. Augustine contrasts the world of corruption and sin inhabited by humans with God's world of blissful perfection.

OF THAT PART OF THE WORK WHEREIN THE DEMONSTRATION OF THE BEGINNINGS AND ENDS OF THE TWO CITIES, THE HEAVENLY AND THE EARTHLY, ARE DECLARED

We give the name of the city of God unto that society whereof that scripture bears witness, which has gained the most exalted authority and preeminence over all other works whatsoever, by the disposing of the divine providence, not the chance decisions of men's judgments. For there it is said: "Glorious things are spoken of thee, thou city of God": and in another place: "Great is the Lord, and greatly to be praised in the city of our God, even upon His holy mountain, increasing the joy of all the earth." And by and by in the same psalm: "As we have heard, so have we seen in the city of the Lord of Hosts, in the city of our God: God has established it for ever." And in another: "The rivers' streams shall make glad the city of God, the most High sanctified His tabernacle, God is in the midst of it unmoved." These testimonies, and thousands more, teach us that there is a city of God, whereof His inspired love makes us desire to be members. The earthly citizens prefer their gods before this heavenly city's holy Founder, knowing not that He is the God of gods, not of those false, wicked, and proud ones, (which lacking His light so universal and unchangeable, and being thereby reduced to a state of extreme need, each one follows his own state, as it were, and begs divine honours of his deluded servants), but of the godly and holy ones, who select their own submission to Him, rather than the world's to them, and love rather to worship Him their God, than to be worshipped for gods themselves. And now, knowing what is next expected of me, as my promise—viz. to dispute (as far as my poor talent allows) of the origin, progress, and consummation of the two cities that in this world lie confusedly together, by the assistance of the same God and King of ours, I set pen to paper, intending first to show the beginning of these two, arising from the difference between the angelical powers.

THE STATE OF THE TWO CITIES, THE HEAVENLY AND THE EARTHLY

Two loves therefore have given origin to these two cities, self-love in contempt of God unto the earthly, love of God in contempt of one's self to the heavenly. The first seeks the glory of men, and the latter desires God only as the testimony of the conscience, the greatest glory. That glories in itself, and this in God. That exalts itself in self-glory: this says to God: "My glory and the lifter up of my head." That boasts of the ambitious conquerors led by the lust of sovereignty: in this all serve each other in charity, both the rulers in counselling and the subjects in obeying. That loves worldly virtue in the potentates: this says unto God: "I will love thee, O Lord, my strength." And the wise men of that follow either the good things of the body, or mind, or both: living according to the flesh; and such as might know God; "honoured Him not as God, nor were thankful, but became vain in their own imaginations, and their foolish heart was darkened; for professing themselves to be wise, that is, extolling themselves proudly in their wisdom, they became fools; changing the glory of the incorruptible God to the likeness of the image of a corruptible man, and of birds and four-footed beasts and serpents": for they were the people's guides or followers unto all those idolatries, and served the creature more than the Creator who is blessed for ever. But in this other, this heavenly city, there is no wisdom of man, but only the piety that serves the true God and expects a reward in the society of the holy angels, and men, that God may be all in all.

OF THE TWO CONTRARY COURSES TAKEN BY THE HUMAN RACE FROM THE BEGINNING

Of the place and felicity of the local paradise, together with man's life and fall therein, there are many opinions, many assertions, and many books, as several men thought, spoke, and wrote. What we held hereof, or could gather out of holy scriptures, correspondent unto their truth and authority, we related in some of the foregoing books. If they be farther looked into, they will give birth to more questions and longer disputations than we have now room for. Our time is not so large as to permit us to argue scrupulously upon every question that may be asked by busy heads that are more curious of inquiry than capable of understanding. I think we have sufficiently discussed the doubts concerning the beginning of the world, the soul, and mankind; which last is divided into two sorts, such as live according to man, and such as live according to God. These we mystically call two cities or societies, the one predestined to being eternally with God, the other condemned in perpetual torment with the devil. This is their end, of which hereafter. Now seeing we have said sufficient concerning their origin, both in the angels whose number we know not, and in the two first parents of mankind. I think it fit to pass on to their progression from man's first offspring until he cease to beget anymore. All the time included between these two points, wherein the livers ever succeed the diers, is the progression of these two cities. Cain therefore was the first begotten of those two that were mankind's parents, and he belongs to the city of man; Abel was the later, and he belongs to the city of God. For as we see that in an individual man (as the apostle says) that which is spiritual is not first, but that which is natural first, and then the spiritual (whereupon all that comes from Adam's corrupted nature must needs be evil and carnal at first, and then if a man be regenerate by Christ, becomes good and spiritual afterward): so in the first propagation of man, and progression of the two cities of which we dispute, the carnal citizen was born first, and the pilgrim on earth or heavenly citizen afterwards, being by grace predestined, and by grace elected, by grace a pilgrim upon earth, and by grace a citizen in heaven. For as for his birth; it was out of the same corrupted mass that was condemned from the beginning; but God like a potter (for this simile the apostle himself uses) out of the same lump, made "one vessel to honour and another to reproach." The vessel of reproach was made first, and the vessel of honour afterwards. For in each individual, as I said, there is first reprobation, whence we must need begin (and wherein we need not remain), and afterwards goodness, to which we come by profiting, and coming thither therein make our abode. Whereupon it follows that no one can be good that has not first been evil, though all that be evil become not good; but the sooner a man betters himself the quicker does this name follow him, abolishing the memory of the other. Therefore, it is recorded of Cain that he built a city, but Abel was a pilgrim, and built none. For the city of the saints is above, though it have citizens here upon earth, wherein it lives as a pilgrim until the time of the kingdom come; and then it gathers all the citizens together in the resurrection of the body, and gives them a kingdom to reign in with their King for ever and ever.

OF THE SONS OF THE FLESH AND THE SONS OF PROMISE

The shadow and prophetical image of this city (not making it present but signifying it) served here upon earth, at the time when such a foreshadowing was needed; and was called the holy city, because it was a symbol of the city that was to be, though not the reality. Of this city serving as an image, and the free city herein prefigured, the apostle speaks thus unto the Galatians: "Tell me, ye that desire to be under the law, do ye not hear the law? For it is written that Abraham had two sons, one by a bond-woman, and the other by a free: but the son of the bondwoman was born of the flesh, and the son of the freewoman by promise. Which things are an allegory: for these are the two Testaments, the one given from Mount Sinai, begetting man in servitude, which is Hagar; for Sinai is a mountain in Arabia, joined to the Jerusalem on earth, for it serves with her children. But our mother the celestial Jerusalem is free, for it is written: 'Rejoice, thou barren that bearest not: break forth into joy, and cry out, thou that travailest not with child, for the desolate hath many more children than the married wife.' But we, brethren, are the sons of promise to Isaac. But as then he that was born of the flesh persecuted him that was born after the spirit, even so it is now. But what says the scripture? 'Cast out the bondwoman and her son, for the bondwoman's son shall not be heir with the freewoman's.' Then, brethren, we are not children of the bondwoman, but of the free." Thus the apostle authorizes us to conceive of the Old and New Testaments. For a part of the earthly city was made an image of the heavenly, not signifying itself but another, and therefore serving: for it was not ordained to signify itself but another, and itself was signified by another precedent type; for Hagar, Sarah's servant, and her son, were an image hereof. And because, when the light comes, the shadows must flee away, Sarah the freewoman signifying the free city (which that shadow of the earthly Jerusalem signified in another manner) said: "Cast out the bondwoman and her son: for the bondwoman's son shall not be heir with my son Isaac": whom the apostle calls the freewoman's son. Thus then we find this earthly city in two forms; the one presenting itself, and the other prefiguring the celestial city, and serving it. Our nature corrupted by sin produces citizens of earth; and grace freeing us from the sin of nature makes us citizens of heaven: the first are called the vessels of wrath, the last of mercy. And this was signified in the two sons of Abraham, the one of whom being born of the bondwoman was called Ishmael, being the son of the flesh; the other, the freewoman's, Isaac, the son of promise. Both were Abraham's sons; but natural custom begot the first, and gracious promise the latter. In the first was a demonstration of man's use, in the second was a revelation of God's goodness.

OF THE ETERNAL FELICITY OF THE CITY OF GOD, AND THE PERPETUAL SABBATH

How great shall that felicity be, where there shall be no evil thing, where no good thing shall lie hidden, where we shall have leisure to utter forth the praises of God, which shall be all things in all! There shall be true glory, where no man shall be praised for error or flattery. True honour, which shall be denied unto none which is worthy, shall be given unto none unworthy. But neither shall any unworthy person covet after it, where none is permitted to be but he who is worthy. There is true peace, where no man suffers anything which may molest him, either from himself or from any other. He Himself shall be reward of virtue, who has given virtue, and has promised Himself unto him, than whom nothing can be better and greater. For what other thing is that which He has said by the prophet: "I will be their God, and they shall be My people"; but "I will be whereby they shall be satisfied: I will be whatsoever is lawfully desired of men, life, health, food, abundance, glory, honour, peace, and all good things"? For so also is that rightly understood, which the apostle says: "That God may be all in all." He shall be the end of our desires, who shall be seen without end, who shall be loved without any disgust, and praised without any tediousness. This function, this affection, this action verily shall be unto all, as the eternal life shall be common to all. But who is sufficient to think, much less to utter, what degrees there shall also be of the rewards for merits, of the honours and glories? But we must not doubt but that there shall be degrees. And also that blessed city shall see this in itself—that no inferior shall envy his superior, even as now the other angels do not envy the archangels; as every one will not wish to be what he has not received, although he be bound in a most peaceable bond of concord with him who has received, even as the finger does not wish to be the eye in the body, since a peaceable conjunction and knitting together of the whole flesh contains both members. Therefore one shall so have a gift less than another has, that he also has this further gift that he does not wish to have any more. By Him being restored and perfected with a greater grace we shall rest for ever, seeing that He is God, with whom we shall be replenished, when He shall be all in all.

FOCUS QUESTIONS

1. How do you think that Augustine's background as an urban Roman affected his thought?

2. What is the difference between the city of God and the earthly city?

3. How, according to Augustine, do people become "residents" of the city of God?

4. Augustine does not envisage a community of social equals in the city of God. Would this, in Augustine's view, lead to conflict? Why or why not?

5. There are several clues in *The City of God* about the nature of society in late classical cities: Augustine makes assumptions about social status, for example. Judging from his work, what might you say about the real cities that Augustine knew?

51

The Rule (ca. 535–540 C.E.)

ST. BENEDICT OF NURSIA

Benedict of Nursia (ca. 480–547), the patron saint of Europe, played a key role in the foundation of Christian monasteries throughout the continent. Benedict came from a prosperous Italian family and was sent to Rome for his education. He grew up during a period of social and political disorder as the Roman world was fast vanishing. Benedict was shocked by the immorality and corruption that he witnessed in Rome, and in reaction he retreated to a cave outside of the city where he lived as a hermit for three years. During this time his reputation as a holy man spread, and he was persuaded to take charge of a local monastery. His attempts to reform this institution were not altogether successful, and Benedict narrowly escaped being poisoned there. He subsequently founded his own monastery at Monte Cassino, which became the model for the Benedictine order.

Benedict's Rule *was a system of regulations for a monastic order. It is a guide to life in a religious community and enjoins the residents to prayer, hard work, obedience, and hospitality. The* Rule *became the constitution of countless monasteries and nunneries in succeeding centuries.*

What are the Instruments of Good Works.—

1. First Instrument: in the first place to love the Lord God with all one's heart, all one's soul, and all one's strength.
2. Then, one's neighbour as oneself.
3. Then not to kill.
4. Not to commit adultery.
5. Not to steal.
6. Not to covet.
7. Not to bear false witness.
8. To honour all men.
9. Not to do to another what one would not have done to oneself.
10. To deny oneself, in order to follow Christ.
11. To chastise the body.
12. Not to seek after delicate living.
13. To love fasting.
14. To relieve the poor.
15. To clothe the naked.
16. To visit the sick.
17. To bury the dead.
18. To help in affliction.
19. To console the sorrowing.
20. To keep aloof from worldly actions.
21. To prefer nothing to the love of Christ.
22. Not to gratify anger.
23. Not to harbour a desire of revenge.
24. Not to foster guile in one's heart.
25. Not to make a feigned peace.
26. Not to forsake charity.
27. Not to swear, lest perchance, one forswear oneself.

28. To utter truth from heart and mouth.

29. Not to render evil for evil.

30. To do no wrong to anyone, yea, to bear, patiently wrong done to oneself.

31. To love one's enemies.

32. Not to render cursing for cursing, but rather blessing.

33. To bear persecution for justice's sake.

34. Not to be proud.

35. Not given to wine.

36. Not a glutton.

37. Not drowsy.

38. Not slothful.

39. Not a murmurer.

40. Not a detractor.

41. To put one's hope in God.

42. To attribute any good that one sees in oneself to God and not to oneself.

43. But to recognize and always impute to oneself the evil that one does.

44. To fear the Day of Judgement.

45. To be in dread of hell.

46. To desire with all spiritual longing everlasting life.

47. To keep death daily before one's eyes.

48. To keep guard at all times over the actions of one's life.

49. To know for certain that God sees one everywhere.

50. To dash down at the feet of Christ one's evil thoughts, the instant that they come into the heart.

51. And to lay them open to one's spiritual father.

52. To keep one's mouth from evil and wicked words.

53. Not to love much speaking.

54. Not to speak vain words or such as move to laughter.

55. Not to love much or excessive laughter.

56. To listen willingly to holy reading.

57. To apply oneself frequently to prayer.

58. Daily to confess in prayer one's past sins with tears and sighs to God, and to amend them for the time to come.

59. Not to fulfill the desires of the flesh: to hate one's own will.

60. To obey in all things the commands of the Abbot, even though he himself (which God forbid) should act otherwise; being mindful of that precept of the Lord: "What they say, do ye; but what they do, do ye not."

61. Not to wish to be called holy before one is so: but first to be holy, that one may be truly so called.

62. Daily to fulfill by one's deeds the commandments of God.

63. To love chastity.

64. To hate no man.

65. Not to be jealous, nor to give way to envy.

66. Not to love strife.

67. To fly from vainglory.

68. To reverence seniors.

69. To love juniors.

70. To pray for one's enemies in the love of Christ.

71. To make peace with an adversary before the setting of the sun.

72. And never to despair of God's mercy.

Behold, these are the tools of the spiritual craft, which, if they be constantly employed day and night, and duly given back on the Day of Judgment, will gain for us from the Lord that reward which He Himself has promised—"which eye hath not seen, nor ear heard; nor hath it entered into the heart of man to conceive what God hath prepared for them that love him." And the workshop where we are to labour diligently at all these things is the cloister of the monastery, and stability in the community.

OF OBEDIENCE

The first degree of humility is obedience without delay. This becomes those who hold nothing dearer to them than Christ, and who on account of the holy servitude which they have taken upon them, and for fear of hell, and for the glory of life everlasting, as soon as anything is ordered by the superior, just as if it had been commanded by God Himself, are unable to bear delay in doing it. It is of these that the Lord says: "At the hearing of the ear he hath obeyed me." And again, to teachers he saith: "He that heareth you heareth me."

THE SPIRIT OF SILENCE

Let us do as says the prophet: "I said, I will take heed to my ways, that I sin not with my tongue: I have placed a watch over my mouth; I became dumb, and was silent, and held my peace even from good things." Here the prophet shows that if we ought to refrain even from good words for the sake of silence, how much more ought we to abstain from evil words, on account of the punishment due to sin!

Therefore, on account of the importance of silence, let leave to speak be seldom granted even to perfect disciples, although their conversation be good and holy and tending to edification; because it is written: "In much speaking thou shalt not avoid sin"; and elsewhere: "Death and life are in the power of the tongue." For it becomes the master to speak and to teach, but it beseems the disciple to be silent and to listen.

And, therefore, if anything has to be asked of a superior, let it be done with all humility and subjection of reverence, lest he seem to say more than is expedient.

But as for buffoonery or silly words, such as move to laughter, we utterly condemn them in every place, nor do we allow the disciple to open his mouth in such discourse.

OF HUMILITY

The Holy Scripture cries out to us, brethren, saying: "Everyone that exalteth himself shall be humbled, and he that humbleth himself shall be exalted." In saying this, it teaches us that all exaltation is a kind of pride, against which the prophet shows himself to be on his guard when he says: "Lord, my heart is not exalted nor mine eyes lifted up: nor have I walked in great things, nor in wonders above me." And why? "If I did not think humbly, but exalted my soul: like a child that is weaned from his mother, so wilt thou requite my soul."

Whence, brethren, if we wish to arrive at the highest point of humility and speedily to reach that heavenly exaltation to which we can only ascend by the humility of this present life, we must by our ever-ascending actions erect such a ladder as that which Jacob beheld his dream, by which the angels appeared to him descending and ascending. This descent and ascent signify nothing else than that we descend by exaltation and ascend by humility. And the ladder thus erected is our life in the world, which, if the heart be humbled, is lifted up by the Lord to heaven. The sides of the same ladder we understand to be our body and soul, in which the call of God has placed various degrees of humility or discipline, which we must ascend.

HOW THE MONKS ARE TO SLEEP

Let them sleep each one in a separate bed, receiving bedding suitable to their manner of life, as the Abbot shall appoint.

If it be possible, let all sleep in one place; but if the number do not permit of this, let them repose by tens or twenties with the seniors who have charge of them. Let a candle burn constantly in the cell until morning.

Let them sleep clothed, and girded with belts or cords—but not with knives at their sides, lest perchance they wound themselves in their sleep—and thus be always ready, so that when the signal is given they rise without delay, and hasten each to forestall the other in going to the Work of God, yet with all gravity and modesty.

Let not the younger brethren have their beds by themselves, but among those of the seniors. And when they rise for the Work of God, let them gently encourage one another, because of the excuses of the drowsy.

OF THE DAILY MANUAL LABOUR

Idleness is the enemy of the soul. Therefore should the brethren be occupied at stated times in manual labour, and at other fixed hours in sacred reading.

We think, therefore, that the times for each may be disposed as follow: from Easter to the Calends of October, on coming out in the morning let them labour at whatever is necessary from the first until about the fourth hour. From the fourth hour until close upon the sixth let them apply themselves to reading. After the sixth hour, when they rise from table, let them rest on their beds in all silence; or if anyone chance to wish to read to himself, let him so read as not to disturb anyone else. Let None be said rather soon, at the middle of the eighth hour; and then let them again work at whatever has to be done until Vespers.

If, however, the needs of the place or poverty require them to labour themselves in gathering in the harvest, let them not grieve at that; for then are they truly monks when they live by the labour of their hands, as our Fathers and the Apostles did. But let all things be done in moderation for the sake of the faint-hearted.

From the Calends of October until the beginning of Lent let the brethren devote themselves to reading till the end of the second hour. At the second hour let Terce be said, after which they shall all labour at their appointed work until None. At the first signal for the hour of None all shall cease from their work, and be ready as soon as the second signal is sounded. After their meal let them occupy themselves in their reading or with the psalms.

OF THE RECEPTION OF GUESTS

Let all guests that come be received like Christ Himself, for He will say: "I was a stranger and ye took me in." And let fitting honour be shown to all, especially, however, to such as are of the household of the faith and to pilgrims.

FOCUS QUESTIONS

1. The creation of *The Rule* is a comment upon Benedict's view of the nature of humanity. What are people like, and what good is *The Rule?*

2. Benedict has taken great care to order the lives of his monks in great detail. What is their daily life like?

3. Why does Benedict have such a high regard for silence? Why is talk dangerous?

4. Monasteries that kept to Benedict's *Rule* could be very useful institutions. How?

5. Every monastery reflected something about the society of which it was a part. What does *The Rule* tell us about the social and economic structure of the time?

52

Admonitions (ca. 1220 C.E.)

ST. FRANCIS OF ASSISI

Francis of Assisi (1181 or 1182–1226) was one of the best-loved and most influential saints of the medieval Church. The son of an Italian cloth merchant, Francis was a typical youth. He was taught to read and write Latin as a boy, and as he grew up he became a popular figure in his hometown. Not especially religious in his youth, he was briefly a soldier, and a prisoner of war in 1202. In 1205 a vision turned his thoughts to religion and he renounced all of his material possessions, donned a hair shirt, and set out to preach to the unconverted. Francis's charm and magnetic personality quickly drew a large following. After receiving the pope's blessing, Francis became the leader of a new order of monks, the Franciscans. Unlike other monastic orders, the friars, as they were known, had no abbeys or property of any kind. They traveled the highways, first of Italy and later of all of Europe, preaching the gospel and living from the alms of the people. In his later years, Francis received the stigmata, or the imprint of the wounds of Christ, and suffered from a series of painful illnesses. His fame grew, as did his order. He was canonized only two years after his death, a measure of his popularity and holiness.

The Admonitions were probably written around the time of the foundation of the Franciscan order. They are a simple prescription for a Christian life, meant for his fellow Franciscans. In these instructions Francis emphasizes the virtues of humility, obedience, and poverty.

THE BLESSED SACRAMENT

Our Lord Jesus told his disciples, *I am the way, and the truth, and the life. No one comes to the Father but through me. If you had known me, you would also have known my Father.*

Sacred Scripture tells us that the Father dwells in *light inaccessible* and that *God is spirit*, and St. John adds, *No one at any time has seen God.* Because God is a spirit, he can be seen only in spirit; *It is the spirit that gives life; the flesh profits nothing.* But God the Son is equal to the Father and so he too can be seen only in the same way as the Father and the Holy Spirit. That is why all those were condemned who saw our Lord Jesus Christ in his humanity but did not see or believe in spirit in his divinity, that he

was the true Son of God. In the same way now, all those are damned who see the sacrament of the Body of Christ which is consecrated on the altar in the form of bread and wine by the words of our Lord in the hands of the priest, and do not see or believe in spirit and in God that this is really the most holy Body and Blood of our Lord Jesus Christ. It is the Most High himself who has told us, This is my Body and Blood *of the new covenant,* and, *He who eats my flesh and drinks my blood has life everlasting.*

And so it is really the Spirit of God who dwells in his faithful who receive the most holy Body and Blood of our Lord. Anyone who does not have this Spirit and presumes to receive him *eats and drinks judgement to himself.* And so we may ask in the words of Scripture, *Men of rank, how long will you be dull of heart?* Why do you refuse to recognize the truth *and believe in the Son of God?* Every day he humbles himself just as he did when he came from his *heavenly throne* into the Virgin's womb; every day he comes to us and lets us see him in abjection, when he descends from the bosom of the Father into the hands of the priest at the altar. He shows himself to us in this sacred bread just as he once appeared to his apostles in real flesh. With their own eyes they saw only his flesh, but they believed that he was God, because they contemplated him with the eyes of the spirit. We, too, with our own eyes, see only bread and wine, but we must see further and firmly believe that this is his most holy Body and Blood, living and true. In this way our Lord remains continually with his followers, as he promised, *Behold, I am with you all days, even unto the consummation of the world.*

PERFECT AND IMPERFECT OBEDIENCE

Our Lord tells us in the Gospel, *Everyone of you who does not renounce all that he possesses cannot be my disciple,* and, *He who would save his life will lose it.* A man takes leave of all that he possesses and loses both his body and his life when he gives himself up completely to obedience in the hands of his superior. Any good that he says or does which he knows is not against the will of his superior is true obedience. A subject may realize that there are many courses of action that would be better and more profitable to his soul than what his superior commands. In that case he should make an offering of his own will to God, and do his best to carry out what the superior has enjoined. This is true and loving obedience which is pleasing to God and one's neighbour.

If a superior commands his subject anything that is against his conscience, the subject should not spurn his authority, even though he cannot obey him. If anyone persecutes him because of this, he should love him all the more, for God's

sake. A religious who prefers to suffer persecution rather than be separated from his confrères certainly perseveres in true obedience, because he lays down his life for his brethren. There are many religious who under the pretext of doing something more perfect than what their superior commands look behind and go back to their own will that they have given up. People like that are murderers, and by their bad example they cause the loss of many souls.

NO ONE SHOULD CLAIM THE OFFICE OF SUPERIOR AS HIS OWN

I did *not come to be served but to serve,* our Lord tells us. Those who are put in charge of others should be no prouder of their office than if they had been appointed to wash the feet of their confrères. They should be no more upset at the loss of their authority than they would be if they were deprived of the task of washing feet. The more they are upset, the greater the risk they incur to their souls.

NO ONE SHOULD GIVE WAY TO PRIDE BUT BOAST ONLY IN THE CROSS OF THE LORD

Try to realize the dignity God has conferred on you. He created and formed your body in the image of his beloved Son, and your soul in his own likeness. And yet every creature under heaven serves and acknowledges and obeys its Creator in its own way better than you do. Even the devils were not solely responsible for crucifying him; it was you who crucified him with them and you continue to crucify him by taking pleasure in your vices and sins.

What have you to be proud of? If you were so clever and learned that you knew everything and could speak every language, so that the things of heaven were an open book to you, still you could not boast of that. Any of the devils knew more about the things of heaven, and knows more about the things of earth, than any human being, even one who might have received from God a special revelation of the highest wisdom. If you were the most handsome and the richest man in the world, and could work wonders and drive out devils, all that would be something extrinsic to you; it would not belong to you and you could not boast of it. But there is one thing of which we can all boast; we can boast of our humiliations and in taking up daily the holy cross of our Lord Jesus Christ.

THE IMITATION OF CHRIST

Look at the Good Shepherd, my brothers. To save his sheep he endured the agony of the cross. They followed him in trials and persecutions, in ignominy, hunger, and thirst, in humiliations and temptations, and so on. And for this God rewarded them with eternal life. We ought to be ashamed of ourselves; the saints endured all that, but we who are servants of God try to win honour and glory by recounting and making known what they have done.

GOOD WORKS MUST FOLLOW KNOWLEDGE

St. Paul tells us, *The letter kills, but the spirit gives life.* A man has been killed by the letter when he wants to know quotation only so that people will think he is very learned and he can make money to give to his relatives and friends. A religious has been killed by the letter when he has no desire to follow the spirit of Sacred Scripture, but wants to know what it says only so that he can explain it to others. On the other hand, those have received life from the spirit of Sacred Scripture who, by their words and example, refer to the most high God, to whom belongs all good, all that they know or wish to know, and

do not allow their knowledge to become a source of self-complacency.

BEWARE THE SIN OF ENVY

St. Paul tells us, *No one can say Jesus is Lord, except in the Holy Spirit* and, *There is none who does good, no, not even one.* And so when a man envies his brother the good God says or does through him, it is like committing a sin of blasphemy, because he is really envying God, who is the only source of every good.

CHARITY

Our Lord says in the Gospel, *Love your enemies.* A man really loves his enemy when he is not offended by the injury done to himself, but for love of God feels burning sorrow for the sin his enemy has brought on his own soul, and proves his love in a practical way.

NO ONE SHOULD BE SCANDALIZED AT ANOTHER'S FALL

Nothing should upset a religious except sin. And even then, no matter what kind of sin has been committed, if he is upset or angry for any other reason except charity, he is only drawing blame upon himself. A religious lives a good life and avoids sin when he is never angry or disturbed at anything. Blessed the man who keeps nothing for himself, but renders *to Caesar the things that are Caesar's, and to God the things that are God's.*

HOW TO KNOW THE SPIRIT OF GOD

We can be sure that a man is a true religious and has the spirit of God if his lower nature does not give way to pride when God accomplishes some good through him, and if he seems all the more worthless and inferior to others in his own eyes. Our lower nature is opposed to every good.

PATIENCE

We can never tell how patient or humble a person is when everything is going well with him. But when those who should co-operate with him do the exact opposite, then we can tell. A man has as much patience and humility as he has then, and no more.

POVERTY OF SPIRIT

Blessed are the poor in spirit, for theirs is the kingdom of heaven. There are many people who spend all their time at their prayers and other religious exercises and mortify themselves by long fasts and so on. But if anyone says as much as a word that implies a reflection on their self-esteem or takes something from them, they are immediately up in arms and annoyed. These people are not really poor in spirit. A person is really poor in spirit when he hates himself and loves those who strike him in the face.

THE HUMBLE RELIGIOUS

Blessed the religious who takes no more pride in the good that God says and does through him, than in that which he says and does through someone else. It is wrong for anyone to be anxious to receive more from his neighbour than he himself is willing to give to God.

COMPASSION FOR ONE'S NEIGHBOUR

Blessed the man who is patient with his neighbour's shortcomings as he would like him to be if he were in a similar position himself.

THE VIRTUOUS AND HUMBLE RELIGIOUS

Blessed the religious who has no more regard for himself when people praise him and make much of him than when they despise and revile him and say that he is ignorant. What a man is before God, that he is and no more. Woe to that religious who, after he has been put in a position of authority by others, is not anxious to leave it of his own free will. On the other hand, blessed is that religious who is elected to office against his will but always wants to be subject to others.

THE HAPPY AND THE SILLY RELIGIOUS

Blessed that religious who finds all his joy and happiness in the words and deeds of our Lord and uses them to make people love God gladly. Woe to the religious who amuses himself with silly gossip, trying to make people laugh.

THE TALKATIVE RELIGIOUS

Blessed that religious who never says anything just for what he can get out of it. He should never be *hasty in his words* or open his heart to everyone, but he should think hard before he speaks. Woe to that religious who does not keep the favours God has given him to himself; people should see them only through his good works, but he wants to tell everybody about them, hoping he will get something out of it. In this way he has received his reward, and it does not do his listeners any good.

TRUE CORRECTION

Blessed that religious who takes blame, accusation, or punishment from another as patiently as if it were coming from himself. Blessed the religious who obeys quietly when he is corrected, confesses his fault humbly and makes atonement cheerfully. Blessed the religious who is in no hurry to make excuses, but accepts the embarrassment and blame for some fault he did not commit.

TRUE LOVE

Blessed that friar who loves his brother as much when he is sick and can be of no use to him as when he is well and can be of use to him. Blessed that friar who loves and respects his brother as much when he is absent as when he is present and who would not say anything behind his back that he could not say charitably to his face.

RELIGIOUS SHOULD BE RESPECTFUL TOWARDS THE CLERGY

Blessed is that servant of God who has confidence in priests who live according to the laws of the holy Roman Church. Woe to those who despise them.

Even if they fall into sin, no one should pass judgement on them, for God has reserved judgement on them to himself. They are in a privileged position because they have charge of the Body and Blood of our Lord Jesus Christ, which they receive and which they alone administer to others, and so anyone who sins against them commits a greater crime than if he sinned against anyone else in the whole world.

VIRTUE AND VICE

Where there is Love and Wisdom,
there is neither Fear nor Ignorance.
Where there is Patience and Humility,
there is neither Anger nor Annoyance.
Where there is Poverty and Joy,
there is neither Cupidity nor Avarice.
Where there is Peace and Contemplation,
there is neither Care nor Restlessness.
Where there is the Fear of God to guard the
    dwelling,
there no enemy can enter.
Where there is Mercy and Prudence
there is neither Excess nor Harshness.

FOCUS QUESTIONS

1. Whom do you think St. Francis was addressing in his *Admonitions*? How might his message differ if it were meant for a different audience?

2. What qualities does Francis seem to admire most?

3. What seems to be Francis's opinion about material things?

4. Several of the sections of *Admonitions* deal with relationships between superiors and subordinates. What should these relationships be like?

5. Does Francis give clergymen and monks a special place in society? Are his expectations different for them?

53

Summa Theologica (1265–1273 C.E.)

ST. THOMAS AQUINAS

Thomas Aquinas (1225–1274) was born in Italy near the town of Aquino from which he took his name. His family was minor nobility, but Thomas was destined for a career in the Church from an early age. He was sent to a monastery to be trained as a monk, but his outstanding intellectual abilities led to further education. Aquinas studied first at the University of Naples and then, after he joined the newly formed Dominican order, at the University of Paris, where he studied philosophy and theology. His special interest was in ancient Greek thought, especially that of Aristotle, which he did much to popularize at the university. His reputation, however, was derived from his theological knowledge, which was unsurpassed within his generation. He was summoned to Rome in 1259 to become a theological advisor to the pope. He died in 1274 on his way to a Church council called to heal the split between the Roman and Eastern churches. Canonized in 1323, he is widely regarded as the most important philosopher of Catholicism.

Summa Theologica is a massive compilation of Aquinas's learning. It treats the entire range of subjects with which the Church dealt, from the existence of God to the definition of a just war. The Summa takes the form of questions and answers. The answer sections provide pros and cons of the views expressed by the Church and clarified by Aquinas. As its importance grew over the next four hundred years, it became the central work of Catholicism.

WHETHER IT CAN BE DEMONSTRATED THAT GOD EXISTS?

Objection 1. It seems that the existence of God cannot be demonstrated. For it is an article of faith that God exists. But what is of faith cannot be demonstrated, because a demonstration produces scientific knowledge; whereas faith is of the unseen. Therefore it cannot be demonstrated that God exists....

...

Obj. 3. Further, if the existence of God were demonstrated, this could only be from His effects. But His effects are not proportionate to Him, since He is infinite and His effects are finite; and between the finite and infinite there is no proportion. Therefore, since a cause cannot be demonstrated by an effect not proportionate to it, it seems that the existence of God cannot be demonstrated.

On the contrary, The Apostle says: *The invisible things of Him are clearly seen, being understood by the things that are made.* But this would not be unless the existence of God could be demonstrated through the things that are made; for the first thing we must know of anything is, whether it exists.

I answer that, Demonstration can be made in two ways: One is through the cause, and is called *a priori,* and this is to argue from what is prior absolutely. The other is through the effect, and is called a demonstration *a posteriori;* this is to argue from what is prior relatively only to us. When an effect is better known to us than its cause, from the effect we proceed to the knowledge of the cause. And from every effect the existence of its proper cause can be demonstrated, so long as its effects are better known to us; because since every effect depends upon its cause, if the effect exists, the cause must pre-exist. Hence the existence of God, in so far as it is not self-evident to us, can be demonstrated from those of His effects which are known to us.

Reply Obj. 1. The existence of God and other like truths about God, which can be known by natural reason, are not articles of faith, but are pre-ambles to the articles; for faith presupposes natural knowledge, even as grace presupposes nature, and perfection supposes something that can be per-fected. Nevertheless, there is nothing to prevent a man, who cannot grasp a proof, accepting, as a matter of faith, something which in itself is capable of being scientifically known and demonstrated....

...

Reply Obj. 3. From effects not proportionate to the cause no perfect knowledge of that cause can be obtained. Yet from every effect the existence of the cause can be clearly demonstrated, and so we can demonstrate the existence of God from His effects: though from them we cannot perfectly know God as He is in His essence.

We must now consider war, under which head there are four points of inquiry: Whether some kind of war is lawful? Whether it is lawful for clerics to fight? ... Whether it is lawful to fight on holy days?

WHETHER IT IS ALWAYS SINFUL TO WAGE WAR?

Objection 1. It would seem that it is always sinful to wage war. Because punishment is not inflicted except for sin. Now those who wage war are threatened by Our Lord with punishment, ac-cording to Matth. xxvi. 52: *All that take the sword shall perish with the sword.* Therefore all wars are unlawful.

Obj. 2. Further, whatever is contrary to a Divine precept is a sin. But war is contrary to a Divine pre-cept, for it is written: *But I say to you not to resist evil;* and: *Not revenging yourselves, my dearly beloved, but give place unto wrath.* Therefore war is always sinful.

Obj. 3. Further, nothing, except sin, is contrary to an act of virtue. But war is contrary to peace. Therefore war is always a sin.

Obj. 4. Further, the exercise of a lawful thing is itself lawful, as is evident in scientific exercises. But warlike exercises which take place in tournaments are forbidden by the Church, since those who are slain in these trials are deprived of ecclesiastical burial. Therefore it seems that war is a sin in itself.

On the contrary, Augustine says in a sermon on the son of the centurion: *If the Christian Religion forbade war altogether, those who sought salutary advice in the Gospel would rather have been counselled to cast aside their arms, and to give up soldiering altogether. On the contrary, they were told: "Do violence to no man; ... and be content with your pay." If he commanded them to be content with their pay, he did not forbid soldiering.*

I answer that, In order for a war to be just, three things are necessary. First, the authority of the sov-ereign by whose command the war is to be waged. For it is not the business of a private individual to declare war, because he can seek for redress of his rights from the tribunal of his superior. Moreover it is not the business of a private individual to sum-mon together the people, which has to be done in wartime. And as the care of the common weal is committed to those who are in authority, it is their business to watch over the common weal of the city, kingdom or province subject to them. And just as it is lawful for them to have recourse to the sword in defending that common weal against internal disturbances, when they punish evildoers, according to the words of the Apostle: *He beareth not the sword in vain: for he is God's minister, an avenger to execute wrath upon him that doth evil;* so too, it is their business to have recourse to the sword of war in defending the common weal against external enemies. Hence it is said to those who are in authority: *Rescue the poor and deliver the needy out of the hand of the sinner; and for this reason Augustine says:*

The natural order conducive to peace among mortals demands that the power to declare and counsel war should be in the hands of those who hold the supreme authority.

Secondly, a just cause is required, namely that those who are attacked, should be attacked because they deserve it on account of some fault. Wherefore Augustine says: *A just war is wont to be described as one that avenges wrongs, when a nation or state h be punished, for refusing to make amends for the wrongs inflicted by its subjects, or to restore what it has seized unjustly.*

Thirdly, it is necessary that the belligerents should have a rightful intention, so that they intend the advancement of good, or the avoidance of evil. Hence Augustine says: *True religion looks upon as peaceful those wars that are waged not for motives of aggrandizement, or cruelty, but with the object of securing peace, of punishing evil-doers, and of uplifting the good.* For it may happen that the war is declared by the legitimate authority, and for a just cause, and yet be rendered unlawful through a wicked intention. Hence Augustine says: *The passion for inflicting harm, the cruel thirst for vengeance an unpacific and relentless spirit, the fever of revolt*, the lust of power, and such like things, all these are rightly condemned in war.

Reply Obj. 1. As Augustine says: *To take the sword is to arm oneself in order to take the life of anyone, without the command or permission of superior or lawful authority.* On the other hand, to have recourse to the sword (as a private person) by the authority of the sovereign or judge, or (as a public person) through zeal for justice, and by the authority, so to speak, of God, is not to *take the sword*, but to use it as commissioned by another, wherefore it does not deserve punishment. And yet even those who make sinful use of the sword are not always slain with the sword, yet they always perish with their own sword, because, unless they repent, they are punished eternally for their sinful use of the sword.

Reply Obj. 2. Such like precepts, as Augustine observes should always be borne in readiness of mind, so that we be ready to obey them, and, if necessary, to refrain from resistance or self-defence. Nevertheless it is necessary sometimes for a man to act otherwise for the common good, or for the good of those with whom he is fighting. Hence Augustine says: *Those whom we have to punish with a kindly*

severity, it is necessary to handle in many ways against their will. For when we are stripping a man of the lawlessness of sin, it is good for him to be vanquished, since nothing is more hopeless than the happiness of sinners, whence arises a guilty impunity, and an evil will, like an internal enemy.

Reply Obj. 3. Those who wage war justly aim at peace, and so they are not opposed to peace, except to the evil peace, which Our Lord came not to send upon earth. Hence Augustine says: *We do not seek peace in order to be at war, but we go to war that we may have peace. Be peaceful, therefore, in warring, so that you may vanquish those whom you war against, and bring them to the prosperity of peace.*

Reply Obj. 4. Manly exercises in warlike feats of arms are not all forbidden, but those which are inordinate and perilous, and end in slaying or plundering. In olden times warlike exercises presented no such danger, and hence they were called *exercises of arms* or *bloodless wars*, as Jerome states in an an epistle.

WHETHER IT IS LAWFUL FOR CLERICS AND BISHOPS TO FIGHT?

Objection 1. It would seem lawful for clerics and bishops to fight. For, as stated above, wars are lawful and just in so far as they protect the poor and the entire common weal from suffering at the hands of the foe. Now this seems to be above all the duty of prelates, for Gregory says: *The wolf comes upon the sheep, when any unjust and rapacious man oppresses those who are faithful and humble. But he who was thought to be the shepherd, and was not, leaveth the sheep, and flieth, for he fears lest the wolf hurt him, and dares not stand up against his injustice.* Therefore it is lawful for prelates and clerics to fight.

Obj. 2. Further, Pope Leo IV writes: *As untoward tidings had frequently come from the Saracen side, some said that the Saracens would come to the port of Rome secretly and covertly; for which reason we commanded our people to gather together, and ordered them go down to the seashore.* Therefore it is lawful for bishops to fight.

Obj. 3. Further, apparently, it comes to the same whether a man does a thing himself, or consents to its being done by another, according to Rom. i. 32: *They who do such things, are worthy of death, and not only they that do them, but they also that consent to t that do them.* Now those, above all, seem to consent to a thing, who induce others to do it. But it is lawful for bishops and clerics to induce others to fight: for it is written that Charles went to war with the Lombards at the instance and entreaty of Adrian, bishop of Rome. Therefore they also are allowed to fight.

Obj. 4. Further, whatever is right and meritorious in itself, is lawful for prelates and clerics. Now it is sometimes right and meritorious to make war, for it is written that if *a man die for the true faith, or to save his country, or in defense of Christians, God will give him a heavenly reward.* Therefore it is lawful for bishops and clerics to fight.

On the contrary, It was said to Peter as representing bishops and clerics: *Put up again thy sword into the scabbard.* Therefore it is not lawful for them to fight.

I answer that, Several things are requisite for the good of a human society: and a number of things are done better and quicker by a number of persons than by one, as the Philosopher observes, while certain occupations are so inconsistent with one another, that they cannot be fittingly exercised at the same time; wherefore those who are deputed to important duties are forbidden to occupy themselves with things of small importance. Thus according to human laws, soldiers who are deputed to warlike pursuits are forbidden to engage in commerce.

Now warlike pursuits are altogether incompatible with the duties of a bishop and a cleric, for two reasons. The first reason is a general one, because, to wit, warlike pursuits are full of unrest, so that they hinder the mind very much from the contemplation of Divine things, the praise of God, and prayers for the people, which belong to the duties of a cleric. Wherefore just as commercial enterprises are forbidden to clerics, because they unsettle the mind too much, so too are warlike pursuits, according to 2 Tim. ii. 4: *No man being a soldier to God, entangleth himself with secular business.* The second reason is a special one, because, to wit, all the clerical Orders are directed to the ministry of the altar,

on which the Passion of Christ is represented sacramentally, according to 1 Cor. xi. 26: *As often as you shall eat this bread, and drink the chalice, e you shall show the death of the Lord, until He come.* Wherefore it is unbecoming for them to slay or shed blood, and it is more fitting that they should be ready to shed their own blood for Christ, so as to imitate in deed what they portray in their ministry. For this reason it has been decreed that those who shed blood, even without sin, become irregular. Now no man who has a certain duty to perform, can lawfully do that which renders him unfit for that duty. Wherefore it is altogether unlawful for clerics to fight, because war is directed to the shedding of blood.

Reply Obj. 1. Prelates ought to withstand not only the wolf who brings spiritual death upon the flock, but also the pillager and the oppressor who work bodily harm; not, however, by having recourse themselves to material arms, but by means of spiritual weapons, according to the saying of the Apostle: *The weapons of our warfare are not carnal, but mighty through God.* Such are salutary warnings, devout prayers, and, for those who are obstinate, the sentence of excommunication.

Reply Obj. 2. Prelates and clerics may, by the authority of their superiors, take part in wars, not indeed by taking up arms themselves, but by affording spiritual help to those who fight justly, by exhorting and absolving them, and by other like spiritual helps. Thus in the Old Testament the priests were commanded to sound the sacred trumpets in the battle. It was for this purpose that bishops or clerics were first allowed to go to the front: and it is an abuse of this permission, if any of them take up arms themselves.

Reply Obj. 3. As stated above every power, art or virtue that regards the end, has to dispose that which is directed to the end. Now, among the faithful, carnal wars should be considered as having for their end the Divine spiritual good to which clerics are deputed. Wherefore it is the duty of clerics to dispose and counsel other men to engage in just wars. For they are forbidden to take up arms, not as though it were a sin, but because such an occupation is unbecoming their personality.

Reply Obj. 4. Although it is meritorious to wage a just war, nevertheless it is rendered unlawful for clerics, by reason of their being deputed to works more meritorious still. Thus the marriage act may be meritorious; and yet it becomes reprehensible in those who have vowed virginity, because they are bound to a yet greater good....

WHETHER IT IS LAWFUL TO FIGHT ON HOLY DAYS?

Objection 1. It would seem unlawful to fight on holy days. For holy days are instituted that we may have our time to the things of God. Hence they are included in the keeping of the Sabbath prescribed in Exod. xx. 8: for *sabbath* is interpreted *rest*. But wars are full of unrest. Therefore by no means is it lawful to fight on holy days.

Obj. 2. Further, certain persons are reproached because on fast-days they exacted what was owing to them, were guilty of strife, and of smiting with the fist. Much more, therefore, is it unlawful to fight on holy days.

Obj. 3. Further, no ill deed should be done to avoid temporal harm. But fighting on a holy day seems in itself to be an ill deed. Therefore no one should fight on a holy day even through the need of avoiding temporal harm.

On the contrary, It is written: The Jews rightly determined ... saying: *Whosoever shall come up against us to fight on the Sabbath-day, we will fight against him.*

I answer that, The observance of holy days is no hindrance to those things which are ordained to man's safety, even that of his body. Hence Our Lord argued with the Jews, saying: *Are you angry at Me because I have healed the whole man on the Sabbath-day?* Hence physicians may lawfully attend to their patients on holy days. Now there is much more reason for safeguarding the common weal (whereby many are saved from being slain, and innumerable evils both temporal and spiritual prevented), than the bodily safety of an individual. Therefore, for the purpose of safeguarding the common weal of the faithful, it is lawful to carry on a war on holy days, provided there be need for doing so: because it would be to tempt God, if notwithstanding such a need, one were to choose to refrain from fighting.

However, as soon as the need ceases, it is no longer lawful to fight on a holy day, for the reasons given: wherefore this suffices for the *Replies* to the *Objections*.

FOCUS QUESTIONS

1. How does Aquinas prove the existence of God?

2. What are Aquinas's views about war? What is a just war?

3. War is, of course, a political act. What are the political assumptions Aquinas makes in his discussion of war?

4. How does Christianity limit war?

5. Whom do you think Aquinas was trying to persuade with his book? What kind of audience would have been best suited for this method of argument?

54

The Letters (12th century C.E.)

HELOISE

Heloise of Argenteuil (ca. 1100–1164) was an abbess (the head of a convent), but she is most famous for her illicit love affair with her tutor, the scholar Peter Abelard. As a young woman she was known as a brilliant scholar and (atypically for a woman) was therefore sent to study under one of the most famous teachers in Paris. This teacher, Peter Abelard, became her lover, and she bore him a son whom she named after the latest technology to arrive in western Europe: Astrolabe. Horrified by these events, Heloise's uncle attacked and castrated Abelard, after which both halves of the couple retired to monastic houses. They continued to write letters to one another, in which they discussed their past but also philosophical and religious questions.

Heloise's intellectual success was not the norm for women in the twelfth century. Attitudes towards women in medieval Europe were mixed. Some thought that women were all like Eve—temptresses and weak; others saw them through the lens of the Virgin Mary—pure and maternal. Here, Heloise addresses her view on being a woman.

What misery for me—born as I was to be the cause of such a crime! Is it the general lot of women to bring total ruin on great men? Hence the warning about women in Proverbs: 'But now, my son, listen to me, attend to what I say: do not let your heart entice you into her ways, do not stray down her paths; she has wounded and laid low so many, and the strongest have all been her victims. Her house is the way to hell, and leads down to the halls of death.' And in Ecclesiastes: 'I put all to the test … I find woman more bitter than death; she is a snare, her heart a net, her arms are chains. He who is pleasing to God eludes her, but the sinner is her captive.'

It was the first woman in the beginning who lured man from Paradise, and she who had been created by the Lord as his helpmate became the instrument of his total downfall. And that mighty man of the Lord, [Samson] the Nazirite whose conception was announced by an angel, Delilah alone overcame; betrayed to his enemies and robbed of his sight, he was driven by his suffering to destroy himself along with his enemies. Only the woman he had had sex with could infatuate Solomon, wisest of all men; she drove him to such a pitch of madness that although he was the man whom the Lord had chosen to build the temple in preference to his father David, who was a righteous man, she plunged him into idolatry until the end of his life, so that he abandoned the worship of God which he had preached and taught in word and writing. Job, holiest of men, fought his last and hardest battle against his wife, who urged him to curse God. The cunning arch-tempter well knew from repeated experience that men are most easily brought to ruin through their wives, and so he directed his usual malice against us too, and tempted you through marriage when he could not destroy you through fornication. Denied the power to do evil through evil, he effected evil through good.

At least I can thank God for this: the tempter did not prevail on me to do wrong of my own consent, like the women I have mentioned, though in the outcome he made me the instrument of his malice. But even if my conscience is clear through innocence, and no consent of mine makes me guilty of this crime, too many earlier sins were committed to allow me to be wholly free from guilt. I yielded long before to the pleasures of carnal desires, and merited then what I weep for now. The sequel is a fitting punishment for my former sins, and an evil beginning must be expected to come to a bad end. For this offence, above all, may I have strength to do proper penance, so that at least by long contrition I can make some amends for your pain from the wound inflicted on you; and what you suffered in the body for a time, I may suffer, as is right, throughout my life in contrition of mind, and thus make reparation to you at least, if not to God.

For if I truthfully admit to the weakness of my most wretched soul, I can find no penitence whereby to appease God, whom I always accuse of the greatest cruelty in regard to this outrage. By rebelling against his ordinance, I offend him more by my indignation than I placate him by making amends through penitence. How can it be called repentance for sins, however great the mortification of the flesh, if the mind still retains the will to sin and is on fire with its old desires? It is easy enough for anyone to confess his sins, to accuse himself, or even to mortify his body in outward show of penance, but it is very difficult to tear the heart away from hankering after its dearest pleasures. Quite rightly then, when the saintly Job said, 'I will speak out against myself,' that is, 'I will loose my tongue and open my mouth in confession to accuse myself of my sins,' he added at once, 'I will speak out in bitterness of soul.' St Gregory comments on this: 'There are some who confess their faults aloud but in doing so do not know how to groan over them—they speak cheerfully of what should be lamented. And so whoever hates his faults and confesses them must still confess them in bitterness of spirit, so that this bitterness may punish him for what his tongue, at his mind's bidding, accuses him.' But this bitterness of true repentance is very rare, as St Ambrose observes, when he says: 'I have more easily found men who have preserved their innocence than men who have known repentance.'

In my case, the pleasures of lovers which we shared have been too sweet—they cannot displease me, and can scarcely shift from my memory. Wherever I turn they are always there before my eyes, bringing with them awakened longings and fantasies which will not even let me sleep. Even during the celebration of the Mass, when our prayers should be purer, lewd visions of those pleasures take such a hold upon my unhappy soul that my thoughts are on their wantonness instead of on prayers. I should be groaning over the sins I have committed, but I can only sigh for what I have lost. Everything we did and also the times and places where we did it are stamped on my heart along with your image, so that I live through them all again with you. Even in sleep I know no respite. Sometimes my thoughts are betrayed in a movement of my body, or they break out in an unguarded word. In my utter wretchedness, that cry from a suffering soul could well be mine: 'Miserable creature that I am, who is there to rescue me out of the body doomed to this death?' Would that I could truthfully answer: 'The grace of God through Jesus Christ our Lord.' This grace, my dearest, came upon you unsought—a single wound of the body by freeing you from these torments has healed many wounds in your soul. Where God may seem to you an adversary, he has in fact proved himself kind: like an honest doctor who does not shrink from giving pain if it will bring about a cure. But for me, youth and passion and experience of pleasures which were so delightful intensify the torments of the flesh and longings of desire, and the assault is the more overwhelming as the nature they attack is the weaker.

Men call me chaste; they do not know the hypocrite I am. They consider purity of the flesh a virtue, though virtue belongs not to the body but to the soul. I can win praise in the eyes of men but deserve none before God, who searches our hearts and loins and sees in our darkness. I am judged religious at a time when there is little in religion which is not hypocrisy, when whoever does not offend the opinions of men receives the highest praise. And yet perhaps there is some merit and it seems somehow acceptable to God, if a person whatever her intention gives no offence to the Church in her outward behaviour, if the name of the Lord is not blasphemed among the infidels because of her nor if she does not disgrace the Order of her profession amongst the worldly. And this too is a gift of God's grace and comes through his bounty—not only to do good but to abstain from evil—though the latter is vain if the former does not follow from it, as it is written: 'Turn from evil and do good.' Both are vain if not done for love of God.

FOCUS QUESTIONS

1. Does Heloise feel guilty for her sexuality? Does she regret her actions?

2. What is the relationship between the physical and the spiritual in Heloise's mind?

3. Describe how Heloise uses examples from the Bible to express her feelings about being a woman.

4. How does Heloise treat the Christianity of her own time? What are the implications of this?

PART III ✳ Dynasties and Empires

Cultures in Collision

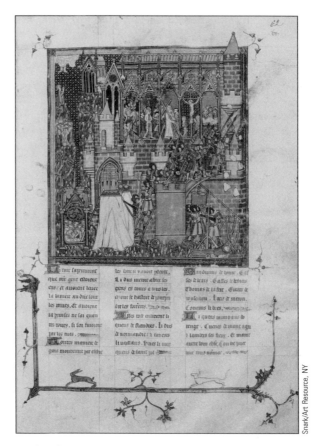

Shark/Art Resource, NY

Battle of Jerusalem. During the First Crusade, Europeans conquered sites in the Middle East and organized Christian kingdoms. This illustration from a twelfth-century manuscript depicts the Battle of Jerusalem, in which European crusaders conquered Jerusalem and established a latinized Christian community.

55

The Alexiad (1097 C.E.)

ANNA COMNENA

After the great Muslim victory at Manzikert in 1071, which enabled them to overrun central Asia Minor, the Byzantine emperor appealed to the Christian West for assistance. Only in 1095, after many delays, did Pope Urban II finally respond to this plea by launching the First Crusade with the exhortation, "God wills it!" Two years later, the "Frankish" leaders of the Crusade—Godfrey of Bouillon, Robert of Normandy, Baldwin of Flanders, Raymond of Toulouse, and Bohemund of Otranto—finally stood before Emperor Alexius I in his palace in Byzantium. Their audience was as awkward as it was momentous. The crusaders needed the emperor's assistance in ferrying their troops to Asia Minor, and Alexius first sought an oath of homage and fealty from these counts. Both sides were curious about each other.

Attending this audience was the emperor's learned daughter, Anna, who recorded the Byzantines' first reactions to the approach of the crusaders and then her impressions of the meetings in her later history of Alexius I's reign.

He [Alexius] heard a report of the approach of innumerable Frankish armies. Now he dreaded their arrival for he knew their irresistible manner of attack, their unstable and mobile character and all the peculiar natural and concomitant characteristics which the Frank retains throughout; and he also knew that they were always agape for money, and seemed to disregard their truces readily for any reason that cropped up. For he had always heard this reported of them, and found it very true. However, he did not lose heart, but prepared himself in every way so that, when the occasion called, he would be ready for battle. And indeed the actual facts were far greater and more terrible than rumour made them. For the whole of the West and all the barbarian tribes which dwell between the further side of the Adriatic and the pillars of Heracles, had all migrated in a body and were marching into Asia through the intervening Europe, and were making the journey with all their household.

After him [Count Raymond] came another innumerable, heterogeneous crowd collected from nearly all the Frankish countries, together with their leaders, kings, dukes, counts and even bishops. The Emperor sent men to receive them kindly and to convey promises of reasonable help, for he was always clever at providing for the future, and in grasping at a glance what was expedient for the moment. He also gave orders to men specially appointed for this purpose to supply them with victuals on their journey, so that they might not for any reason whatsoever have a handle for a quarrel against him. And they (the Crusaders) hastened on to the capital. One might have likened them to the stars of heaven or the sand poured out along the edge of the sea. For these men that hurried on to approach Constantinople were "as many as there are leaves and flowers in the spring time," as Homer says. Though I much desire to do so, I cannot detail the names of the leaders. For my speech is paralysed partly because I cannot articulate these strange names which are so unpronounceable, and partly because of the number of them. And, why indeed should we endeavour to recount the names of such a multitude, when even the men who were present were soon filled with indifference at the sight? When they finally reached the capital they disposed their armies at the Emperor's bidding close to the Monastery of Cosmidium and they extended right up to the Hieron. It was not nine heralds, as formerly in Greece, who controlled this army by their shouts, but a large number of brave hoplites who accompanied them and persuaded them to yield to the Emperor's orders. Now the Emperor was anxious to force them all to take the same oath as Godfrey had taken, so he invited them separately and conversed with them privately about his wishes, and made use of the more reasonable ones as intermediaries with the more recalcitrant. As they would not obey, for they were expecting Bohemund to arrive, but found various means of evasion by continually making some fresh demands, the Emperor very easily saw through their pretences and by harassing them in every possible way, he forced them to take Godfrey's oath, and sent for Godfrey from over the sea at Pelecanus that he might be present during the taking of the oath. Thus they all assembled, Godfrey amongst them, and after the oath had been taken by all the Counts, a certain venturesome noble sat down on the Emperor's seat. The Emperor put up with him and said not a word, knowing of old the Latins' haughty nature. But Count Baldwin stepped forward and taking him by the hand raised him up, rebuked him severely, and said, "It was wrong of you to do such a thing here, and that too when you have promised fealty to the Emperor; for it is not customary for the Roman Emperors to allow their subjects to sit beside them on the throne, and those who become his Majesty's sworn bondmen must observe the customs of the country." He made no reply to Baldwin, but darted a fierce glance at the Emperor and muttered some words to himself in his own language, saying, "Look at this rustic that keeps his seat, while such valiant captains are standing round him." The movement of the Latin's lips did not escape the Emperor, who called one of the interpreters of the Latin tongue and asked the purport of his words. When he heard what the remark was, he said nothing to the Latin for some time, but kept the saying in his heart. As they were all taking leave of the Emperor, he called that haughty-minded, audacious Latin, and enquired who he was and of what country and lineage. "I am a Frank of the purest nobility" he replied, "all that I know is that at the cross-roads in the country whence I come there stands an old sanctuary, to which everyone who desires to fight in single combat goes ready accoutred for single combat, and there prays to God for help while he waits in expectation of the man who will dare to fight him. At those cross-roads I too have often tarried, waiting and longing for an antagonist; but never has one appeared who dared to fight me." In reply to this the Emperor said, "If you did not find a fight when you sought for it then, now the time has come which will give you your fill of fighting. But I strongly advise you not to place yourself in the rear nor in the front of your line, but to stand in the centre for I have had a long experience of the Turkish method of fighting." It was not to this man only that he gave this advice, but to all the others he foretold the accidents likely to happen on their journey, and counselled them never to pursue the barbarians very far when God granted them a victory over them, for fear of being killed by falling into ambushes.

The Emperor sent for Bohemund and requested him to take the customary oath of the Latins. And he, mindful of his own position, namely, that he was not descended from illustrious ancestors, nor had a great supply of money, and for this reason not even many troops, but only a very limited number of Frankish retainers, and being moreover by nature ready to swear falsely, yielded readily to the Emperor's wish. Then the Emperor selected a room in the palace and had the floor strewn with every kind of riches, ... and so filled the chamber with garments and stamped gold and silver, and other materials of lesser value, that one could not even walk because of their quantity. And he told the man who was to show Bohemund these things, to throw open the doors suddenly. Bohemund was amazed at the sight and exclaimed, "If all these treasures were mine, I should have made myself master of many countries long ere this!" and the attendant replied, "The Emperor makes you a present of all these riches today." Bohemund was overjoyed and after thanking for the present he went away to rest in the house where he lodged. But when these treasures were brought to him, he who had admired them before had changed his mind and said, "Never did I imagine that the Emperor would inflict such dishonour on me. Take them away and give them back to him who sent them." But the Emperor, knowing the Latins' characteristic fickleness, quoted the popular proverb, "Let bad things return to their own master." When Bohemund heard of this and saw the porters carefully packing the presents up again, he changed his mind—he, who a minute before was sending them away and was annoyed at them, now gave the porters pleasant looks, just like a polypus that changes its form in an instant. For by nature the man was a rogue and ready for any eventualities; in roguery and courage he was far superior to all the Latins who came through then, as he was inferior to them in forces and money. But in spite of his surpassing all in superabundant activity in mischief, yet fickleness like some natural Latin appendage attended him too. So he who first rejected the presents, afterwards accepted them with great pleasure. For he was sad in mind as he had left his country a landless man, ostensibly to worship at the Holy Sepulchre, but in reality with the intent of gaining

a kingdom for himself, or rather, if it were possible, to follow his father's advice and seize the Roman Empire itself, and as he wanted to let out every reef, as the proverb has it, he required a great deal of money. But the Emperor, who understood his melancholy and ill-natured disposition, did his best cleverly to remove anything that would assist him in his secret plans. Therefore when Bohemund demanded the office of Great Domestic of the East, he did not gain his request, for he was trying to "out-Cretan a Cretan." For the Emperor feared that if he gained power he would make the other Counts his captives and bring them round afterwards to doing whatever he wished. Further, he did not want Bohemund to have the slightest suspicion that he was already detected, so he flattered him with fair hopes by saying, "The time for that has not come yet; but by your energy and reputation and above all by your fidelity it will come ere long." After this conversation and after bestowing gifts and honours of many kinds on them, the next day he took his seat on the imperial throne and summoned Bohemund and all the Counts. To them he discoursed of the things likely to befall them on their journey, and gave them useful advice; he also instructed them in the Turks' usual methods of warfare, and suggested the manner in which they should dispose the army and arrange their ranks, and advised them not to go far in pursuit of the Turks when they fled. And after he had in this way somewhat softened their savage behaviour by dint of money and advice, and had given them good counsel, he suggested their crossing into Asia.

FOCUS QUESTIONS

1. Considering that the crusaders had come to help battle the Moslems, why were the Byzantines so reserved about the arrival of the Franks?

2. What did the Byzantines think of the crusaders? What did they see as their strengths and weaknesses?

3. Emperor Alexius plainly treated Prince Bohemund differently from the rest of the crusading lords. What lay behind the emperor's attitude?

4. What did Anna mean when she said that Bohemund was trying to "out-Cretan a Cretan"? From this comment, can you deduce what the crusaders thought of the Byzantines?

56

The Journey of Louis VII to the East (1147 C.E.)

ODO OF DEUIL

Fifty years after the leaders of the First Crusade had appeared before Alexius I and Anna Comnena, those of the Second Crusade stood before Alexius's grandson, Emperor Manuel, in the same audience chamber.

This time, the crusaders were led by Emperor Conrad III and Louis VII of France. Again they requested Byzantine assistance in crossing into Asia, for which Emperor Manuel attempted to secure concessions. Because he had recently concluded a treaty with his Muslim neighbor, through which the crusaders would also have to pass, negotiations were difficult; and ultimately the Europeans were denied safe passage. Without Byzantine military support, the Second Crusade was unable to march overland to the Holy Land, and the crusaders suffered heavy losses in their attempt to pass through Asia Minor.

One of Louis VII's bishops, Odo of Deuil (d. 1162), recorded his impressions of the visit to Byzantium in his later history of Louis's involvement in the Second Crusade. Despite the bishop's repeated protestations of impartiality, his recollections were inevitably colored by the disasters, which were soon to overwhelm the expedition, all of which the French blamed on the Byzantines. The following passage begins just after Emperor Manuel has provided the crusaders with food and lodging.

This outcome would have satisfied the messengers if they had not judged one crime in the light of another; for they learned that the emperor had an agreement with the Turks and that the very man who had written to our king that he was going to accompany him in fighting the infidels and had won a recent and renowned victory over them had actually confirmed a twelve-year armistice with them. Also, his treachery was increased and made manifest by the fact that only a great number could get through his realm in safety; for the bishop of Langres and the count of Warenne and certain others, who had sent a few men ahead to Constantinople to provide arms and food for the journey, had suffered a considerable loss of possessions and were mourning their wounded and dead. And this did not happen just once; for from the time when we entered his territory we endured the robberies which his people perpetrated on us because our strength did not equal theirs. Perhaps this condition would have been bearable, and it could have been said that we deserved the evils which we suffered on account of the evils which we had committed, if blasphemy had not been added. For instance, if our priests celebrated mass on Greek altars, the Greeks afterwards purified them with propitiatory offerings and ablutions, as if they had been defiled. All the wealthy people have their own chapels, so adorned with paintings, marble and lamps that each magnate might justly say, "O Lord, I have cherished the beauty of Thy house," if the light of the true faith shone therein. But, O dreadful thing! we heard of an ill usage of theirs which should be expiated by death; namely, that every time they celebrate the marriage of one of our men, if he has been baptized in the Roman way, they rebaptize him before they make the pact. We know other heresies of theirs, both concerning their treatment of the Eucharist and concerning the procession of the Holy Ghost, but none of these matters would mar our page if not pertinent to our subject. Actually, it was for these reasons that the Greeks had incurred the hatred of our men, for their error had become known even among the lay people. Because of this they were judged not to be Christians, and the Franks considered killing them a matter of no importance and hence could with the more difficulty be restrained from pillage and plundering.

But let us return to the king, who, although he received new messengers from the emperor nearly every day, nevertheless complained about the delay of his own ambassadors, because he did not know what had happened to them. The Greeks always reported good news, but they never showed any proof of it, and they were the less believed because on every occasion all used the same prefatory flattery. The king accepted, but considered of slight value their *polychroniae* [lavish flattery] (for that is the name of the gestures of honor which they exhibit, not only toward kings, but even toward certain of their nobles, lowering the head and body humbly or kneeling on the ground or even prostrating themselves). Occasionally the empress wrote to the queen. And then the Greeks degenerated entirely into women; putting aside all manly vigor, both of words and of spirit, they lightly swore whatever they thought would please us, but they neither kept faith with us nor maintained respect for themselves. In general they really have the opinion that anything which is done for the holy empire cannot be considered perjury. Let no one think that I am taking vengeance on a race of men hateful to me and that because of my hatred I am inviting a Greek whom I have not seen. Whoever has known the Greeks will, if asked, say that when they are afraid they become despicable in their excessive

debasement and when they have the upper hand they are arrogant in their severe violence to those subjected to them. However, they toiled most zealously in advising the king to turn his route from Adrianople to St. George of Sestos and there to cross the sea the more swiftly and advantageously. But the king did not wish to undertake something which he had heard that the Franks had done. Thus, by the same paths, but not with the same omens, he followed the Germans who had preceded us, and when a day's journey from Constantinople met his own messengers, who told him the stories concerning the emperor which we have already related in part. There were those who then advised the king to retreat and to seize the exceedingly rich land with its castles and cities and meanwhile to write to King Roger [of Sicily], who was then vigorously attacking the emperor, and, aided by his fleet, to attack Constantinople itself. But, alas for us, nay, for all St. Peter's subjects, their words did not prevail! Therefore, we proceeded, and when we approached the city, lo, all its nobles and wealthy men, clerics as well as lay people, trooped out to meet the king and received him with due honor, humbly asking him to appear before the emperor and to fulfil the emperor's desire to see and talk with him. Now the king, taking pity on the emperor's fear and obeying his request, entered with a few of his men and received an imperial welcome in the portico of the palace. The two sovereigns were almost identical in age and stature, unlike only in dress and manners. After they had exchanged embraces and kisses, they went inside, where, when two chairs had been arranged, they both sat down. Surrounded by a circle of their men, they conversed with the help of an interpreter. The emperor asked about the king's present state and his wishes for the future, wishing for him the things which are God's to give and promising him those within his own power. Would it had been done as sincerely as it was gracefully! If his gestures, his liveliness of expression, and his words had been a true indication of his inner thoughts, those who stood nearby would have attested that he cherished the king with great affection; but such evidence is only plausible, not conclusive.

Afterwards they parted as if they were brothers, and the imperial nobles took the king away to the palace which had been designated as his lodging.

Conducted by the emperor, the king also visited the shrines and, after returning, when won over by the urgency of his host's requests, dined with him. That banquet afforded pleasure to ear, mouth, and eye with pomp as marvelous, viands as delicate, and pastimes as pleasant as the guests were illustrious. There many of the king's men feared for him; but he, who had entrusted the care of himself to God, feared nothing at all, since he had faith and courage; for one who is not inclined to do harm does not easily believe that anyone will harm him.

Although the Greeks furnished us no proof that they were treacherous, I believe that they would not have exhibited such unremitting servitude if they had had good intentions. Actually, they were concealing the wrongs which were to be avenged after we crossed the Arm. However, it was not held against the Greeks that they closed the city gates to the throng, since it had burned many of their houses and olive trees, either for want of wood or by reason of arrogance and the drunkenness of fools. The king frequently punished offenders by cutting off their ears, hands, and feet, yet he could not thus check the folly of the whole group. Indeed, one of two things was necessary, either to kill many thousands at one time or to put up with their numerous evil deeds. As I was saying, a ship supplied us an ample market, and in front of the palace and even in the tents we had a rate of exchange which would have

been adequate if it had lasted; namely, less than two denarii for one staminae and a mark for thirty stamina (three solidi). But after we had traveled three days beyond the city we paid five or six denarii for one stamina and lost a mark on twelve soldi.

Now while the king was awaiting the forces coming from Apulia, when they were crossing between Brindisi and Durazzo, the feast of St. Denis [patron saint of France] occurred, and he celebrated it with proper veneration. Since the Greeks celebrate this feast, the emperor knew of it, and he sent over to the king a carefully selected group of his clergy, each of whom he had equipped with a large taper decorated elaborately with gold and a great variety of colors; and thus he increased the glory of the ceremony. These clergy certainly differed from ours as to words and order of service, but they made a favorable impression because of their sweet chanting; for the mingling of voices, the heavier with the light, the eunuch's, namely, with the manly voice (for many of them were eunuchs), softened the hearts of the Franks. Also, they gave the onlookers pleasure by their graceful bearing and gentle clapping of hands and genuflexions. We recall these favors on the part of the emperor so that there may be manifest the treachery of him who simulated the friendship which we are accustomed to show only to our most intimate friends, while he harbored a feeling which we could not have appeased save by our very death. Surely no one could understand the Greeks without having had experience of them or without being endowed with prophetic inspiration.

FOCUS QUESTIONS

1. Why were the Franks so suspicious of the Byzantines even after they had received their hospitality?

2. What accounts for the religious tensions between the Byzantines and the Franks, both of whom were Christian?

3. Was there anything about Byzantium and the Byzantines that Odo admired?

4. Do you think there was anything that the emperor could have done to remedy the situation, or was hostility between the Greeks and the Franks culturally inevitable?

57

Memoirs (after 1175 C.E.)

USAMA IBN MUNQIDH

Following their capture of Antioch in 1098 and Jerusalem in 1099, the crusaders established several Christian states in Palestine and Syria. Although the new crusading rulers encouraged immigration from western Europe, the bulk of their new subjects remained native Muslim. Fortunately, we can see something of how these Muslims viewed the Franks, thanks to the memoirs of Usama ibn Manqidh (1095–1188). Usama, a prominent Syrian nobleman, frequently fought against the crusaders, but he also had extensive commercial and personal dealings with them. Though the Franks alternatively angered and amused him, they also fascinated him.

Near the end of his long life, Usama recorded a series of short vignettes about his recollections of the Franks, and the following selections from his memoirs reveal the clash of cultures that resounded throughout the Middle East in the twelfth century. One deals with Usama's experience traveling on a safe-conduct pass from Baldwin III, the Christian King of Jerusalem; another records his astonishment of the lack of common sense displayed by a Frankish knight; and the last group illustrates the difference between new and old Christian residents of the Holy Land and between Christian monks and Muslim sufis.

I entered the, service of the just King Nur ad Din—God have mercy on him!—and he wrote to al-Malik as-Salih asking him to send my household and my sons out to me; they were in Egypt, under his patronage. Al-Malik as-Salih wrote back that he was unable to comply because he feared that they might fall into Frankish hands. He invited me instead to return to Egypt myself: "You know," he wrote, "how strong the friendship is between us. If you have reason to mistrust the Palace, you could go to Mecca, and I would send you the appointment to the governorship of Aswan and the means to combat the Abyssinians. Aswan is on the frontier of the Islamic empire. I would send your household and your sons to you there." I spoke to Nur ad-Din about this, and asked his advice, which was that he would certainly not choose to return to Egypt once he had extricated himself. "Life is too short!" he

said. "It would be better if I sent to the Frankish King for a safe-conduct for your family, and gave them an escort to bring them here safely." This he did—God have mercy on him!—and the Frankish King gave him his cross, which ensures the bearer's safety by land and sea. I sent it by a young slave of mine, together with letters to al-Malik as-Salih from Nur ad-Din and myself. My family were dispatched for Damietta on a ship of the vizier's private fleet, under his protection and provided with everything they might need.

At Damietta they transferred to a Frankish ship and set sail, but when they neared Acre, where the Frankish King was—God punish him for his sins—he sent out a boatload of men to break up the ship with hatchets before the eyes of my family, while he rode down to the beach and claimed everything that came ashore as booty. My young slave swam ashore with the safe-conduct, and said: "My Lord King, is not this your safe-conduct?" "Indeed it is," he replied, "But surely it is a Muslim custom that when a ship is wrecked close to land the local people pillage it?" "So you are going to make us your captives?" "Certainly not." He had my family escorted to a house, and the women searched. Everything they had was taken; the ship had been loaded with women's trinkets, clothes, jewels, swords and other arms, and gold and silver to the value of about 30,000 *dinar*. The King took it all, and then handed five hundred *dinar* back to them and said: "Make your arrangements to continue your journey with this money." And there were fifty of them altogether! At the time I was with Nur ad-Din in the realm of Kin Mas 'ud, at Ru'ban and Kaisun; compared with the safety of my sons, my brother and our women, the loss of the rest meant little to me, except for my books. There had been 4,000 fine volumes on board, and their destruction has been a cruel loss to me for the rest of my life.

Among the Franks—God damn them!—no quality is more highly esteemed in a man than military prowess. The knights have a monopoly of the positions of honour and importance among them, and no one else has any prestige in their eyes. They are the men who give counsel, pass judgment and command the armies. On one occasion I went to law with one of them about some herds that the Prince of Baniyas seized in a wood; this was at a time when there was a truce between us, and I was living in Damascus. I said to King Fulk, the son of Fulk. "This man attacked and seized my herd. This is the season when the cows are in calf; their young died at birth, and he has returned the herd to me completely ruined." The King turned to six or seven of his knights and said: "Come, give a judgment on this man's case." They retired from the audience chamber and discussed the matter until they all agreed. Then they returned to the King's presence and said: "We have decided that the Prince of Baniyas should indemnify this man for the cattle that he has ruined." The King ordered that the indemnity should be paid, but such was the pressure put on me and the courtesy shown

me that in the end I accepted four hundred *dinar* from the Prince. Once the knights have given their judgment neither the King nor any other commander can alter or annul it, so great an influence do their knights have in their society. On this occasion the King swore to me that he had been made very happy the day before. When I asked him what had made him happy he said: "They told me that you were a great knight, but I did not believe that you would be chivalrous." "Your Majesty," I replied, "I am a knight of my race and my people." When a knight is tall and well-built they admire him all the more.

A very important Frankish knight was staying in the camp of King Fulk, the son of Fulk. He had come on a pilgrimage and was going home again. We got to know one another, and became firm friends. He called me "brother" and an affectionate friendship grew up between us. When he was due to embark for the return journey he said to me: "My brother, as I am about to return home, I should be happy if you would send your son with me," (the boy, who was about fourteen years old, was beside me at the time), "so that he could meet the noblemen of the realm and learn the arts of politics and chivalry. On his return home he would be a truly cultivated man." A truly cultivated man would never be guilty of such a suggestion; my son might as well be taken prisoner as go off into the land of the Franks. I turned to my friend and said: "I assure you that I could desire nothing better for my son, but unfortunately the boy's grandmother, my mother, is very attached to him, and she would not even let him come away with me without extracting a promise from me that I would bring him back to her." "Your mother is still alive?" "Yes." "Then she must have her way."

This is an example of Frankish barbarism, God damn them! When I was in Jerusalem I used to go to the Masjid al-Aqsa, beside which is a small oratory which the Franks have made into a church. Whenever I went into the Mosque, which was in the hands of Templars who were friends of mine, they would put the little oratory at my disposal, so that I could say my prayers there. One day I had gone in, said the *Allah akhbar* and risen to begin my prayers, when a Frank threw himself on me from behind, lifted me up and turned me so that I was facing east. "That is the way to pray!" he said. Some Templars at once intervened, seized the man and took him out of my way while I resumed my prayer. But the moment they stopped watching him he seized me again and forced me to face east, repeating that this was the way to pray. Again the Templars intervened and took him away. They apologized to me and said: "He is a foreigner who has just arrived today from his homeland in the north, and he has never seen anyone pray facing any other direction than east." I have finished my prayers," I said, and left, stupefied by the fanatic who had been so perturbed and upset to see someone praying facing Mecca.

I paid a visit to the tomb of John the son of Zechariah—God's blessing on both of them—in the village of Sebastea in the province of Nablus. After saying my prayers, I came out into the square that was bounded on one side by the Holy Precinct. I found a half-closed gate, opened it and entered a church. Inside were about ten old men, their bare heads as white as combed cotton. They were facing the east, and wore (embroidered?) on their breasts staves ending in crossbars turned up like the rear of a saddle. They took their oath on this sign, and gave hospitality to those who needed it. The sight of their piety touched my heart, but at the same time it displeased and saddened me, for I had never seen such zeal and devotion among the Muslims. For some time I brooded on this experience, until one day, as Mu'in ad-Din and I were passing the Peacock House, he said to me: "I want to dismount here and visit the Old Men (the ascetics)." "Certainly," I replied, and we dismounted and went into a long building set at an angle to the road. For the moment I thought there was no one there. Then I saw about a hundred prayer-mats, and on each a sufi, his face expressing peaceful serenity, and his body humble devotion. This was a reassuring sight, and I gave thanks to Almighty God that there were among the Muslims men of even more zealous devotion than those Christian priests. Before I had never seen sufis in their monastery, and was ignorant of the way they lived.

FOCUS QUESTIONS

1. Quite plainly, Usama's views of Christian knights were mixed. What did he admire about the crusaders and what baffled him about them?

2. Many Muslim kings particularly despised the Templars, a Christian order of fighting monks whom they often executed immediately on their capture. Why was Usama friendly with them?

3. Discuss the differences in the notions of honor among Christian knights and Usama's Muslim warriors.

4. Was there anything Usama admired in the Christian practice of their religion?

58

The Dissipator of Anxieties (1250 C.E.)

JAMAL AD-DIN IBN WASIL

By the middle of the thirteenth century, the Muslims had driven the Franks out of almost all of their former possessions in Palestine. Desperate to reverse these losses, King Louis IX of France launched the West's last major crusade in 1250. Marshaling a formidable army and fleet, he attempted to capture a series of Egyptian towns, which he hoped to ransom in exchange for Jerusalem. The crusaders managed to seize Damietta, the Egyptian Delta, before their plans went awry when the Moslems cut off Louis's army from its base in Damietta and forced the king of the Franks to surrender.

In a later history of thirteenth-century Egypt, ibn Wasil (1233–1293), a prominent Muslim diplomat and administrator, presented an eyewitness account of this great victory and of Louis's negotiations for his own ransom. The verses that Jamal ad-Din ibn Wasil composed on this occasion, taunting Louis for his humiliation, stand as an epitaph for the first attempt by a Western power to exert its influence outside of Europe.

While the Franks stabilized their positions, re-inforcements were reaching them from further up the Nile, from Damietta. The Muslims took some ships on camel-back up to the Bahr al-Mahalla, and there launched them and embarked troops. There was water at that time from the flooding of the Nile, stagnant, but communicating with the Nile itself. When the Frankish vessels coming upstream from Damietta passed close to the Bahr al-Mahalla the Muslims, who were lying in wait, fell on them and gave battle. The Muslim squadron from al-Mansura came downstream to join the fight and they surrounded the Franks and captured them and their ships. Fifty-two Frankish men-of-war were taken, with about a thousand men on board and all the provisions they were carrying. The prisoners were taken on camels to the Muslim camp. For the Franks the defeat broke their supply-line and seriously weakened their position. They found themselves very short of provisions and blockaded without the means either of staying put

or of leaving their position. The Muslims had the upper hand, and now nourished plans to attack.

On 1 dhu l-hijja/7 March 1250 the Franks took seven Muslim fire-ships on the Bahr al-Mahalla, but the Muslims escaped with their gear. On the second, al-Malik al-Mu'azzam ordered the amir Husam ad-Din to enter Cairo and take up residence in the vizier's palace and to perform all the usual functions of the Sultan's viceroy. The Qadi Jamal ad-Din ibn Wasil, the author, says: The Sultan gave robes of honour to me and also to a group of lawyers who presented themselves to do him homage. Al-Malik al-Mu'azzam's liberality extended in this way to anyone who presented himself at his gate. So I entered Cairo with the amir Husam ad-Din. On Monday 9 dhu l-hijja, the day of 'Arafa, Muslim galleys attacked the Frankish supply-ships. The encounter took place near the Mosque of Victory and the Muslims took thirty-two vessels from the Franks, of which seven were galleys. This weakened the Franks even more, and supplies in the camp were even scarcer. Then the

Franks opened negotiations for a truce with the Muslims. Their ambassadors arrived and went into consultation with the amir Zain ad-Din, a *jamdar* amir, and the Grand Qadi Badr ad-Din. The Franks wanted to exchange Damietta for Jerusalem and a part of the Syrian coast, but this was not acceptable. On Friday 26 dhu l-hijja the Franks burnt all their encampments, sparing only the ships, and decided to take refuge in Damietta. At the end of the year (647) they were still in the same position, facing the Muslims.

On the night before Wednesday 3 muharram 648/7 April 1250, the resplendent night that disclosed a great victory and a stupendous triumph, the Franks marched out with all their forces towards Damietta, which they counted on to defend them, and their ships began to move downstream in convoy.

When the Muslims heard the news they set out after them, crossed to the Frankish bank of the river and were soon at their heels. As Wednesday dawned the Muslims had surrounded the Franks and were slaughtering them, dealing out death and captivity. Not one escaped. It is said that the dead numbered 30,000. In the battle the Bahrite mamluks of al-Malik as-Salih distinguished themselves by their courage and audacity: they caused the Franks terrible losses and played the major part in the victory. They fought furiously: it was they who flung themselves into the pursuit of the enemy: they were Islam's Templars. The accursed King of France and the great Frankish princes retreated to the hill of Munya, where they surrendered and begged for their lives. They were given assurances by the eunuch Jamal ad-Din Muhsin as-Salihi, on the strength of which they surrendered. They were all taken to Mansura, where chains were put on the feet of the King of France and his companions. They were imprisoned in the house where the secretary Fakhr ad-Din ibn Luqman was living, and the eunuch Sabih al-Mu'azzami, a servant of al-Malik al-Mu'azzam Turanshah, son of al-Malik as-Salih Najm ad-Din Ayyub, was set to guard them; he had come with his master from Hisn Kaifa and had been promoted and shown great honour.

The amir Husam ad-Din told me: "The King of France was an extremely wise and intelligent man. In one of our conversations I said to him: 'How did Your Majesty ever conceive the idea, a man of your character and wisdom and good sense, of going on board ship and riding the back of this sea and coming to a land so full of Muslims and soldiers, thinking that you could conquer it and become its ruler? This undertaking is the greatest risk to which you could possibly expose yourself and your subjects.' The King laughed but did not reply. 'In our land,' I added, 'when a man travels by sea on several occasions, exposing himself and his possessions to such a risk, his testimony is not accepted as evidence by a Court of Law.' 'Why not?' 'Because such behaviour suggests to us that he lacks sense, and a man who lacks sense is not fit to give evidence.' The King laughed and said: 'By God, whoever said that was right, and whoever made that ruling did not err.' "

Referring to this episode, the imprisonment of the King of France in Fakhr ad-Din ibn Luqman's house, and the appointment of the eunuch Sabih to look after him, Jamal ad-Din ibn Yahya ibn Matrub wrote:

Speak to the Frenchman, if you visit him, a
true word from a good counsellor:
"God requite you for what has happened,
the slaughter of the Messiah's adorers!
You came to the East boasting of
conquest, believing our martial drum-roll
to be a mere breath of wind.
And your stupidity has brought you to a
place where your eyes can no longer see in
the broad plain any way of escape.
And of all your company, whom you
commanded so well that you led them into
the tomb's embrace,
Of fifty thousand not one can be seen that
is not dead, or wounded and a prisoner.
God help you to other similar adventures:
who knows that in the end Jesus will not
breathe freely (of your impious worship)!"

If your Pope is content with this, how
often is a statesman guilty of deceit!
And say to them, if they ever think of
returning to take their revenge, or for
any other reason:

"The house of Ibn Luqman is always ready
here, and the chain and the eunuch Sabih
are still here."

FOCUS QUESTIONS

1. Why did Louis have to surrender?

2. In the negotiations for his release, why did
   King Louis agree that his testimony should not
   be accepted in a court of law?

3. Use Jamal ad-Din's poem to discuss the Muslim
   attitude to Christianity.

4. What did the poet mean when he concluded,
   "the house of Ibn Luqam is always ready"?

The Italian Renaissance

A Modern View of St. Peter's in Rome.

59

On the Family (1435–1444 C.E.)

LEON BATTISTA ALBERTI

Leon Battista Alberti (1404–1472) was one of the great virtuosi of the Renaissance. The illegitimate son of one of the wealthiest Florentine merchants, Alberti was an outstanding athlete and man of action as well as an influential writer. After having studied law and entered the service of the church, he achieved his greatest fame as an architect, designing a number of exquisite private mansions. His writings include classic works on the principles of painting and architecture.

On the Family is an exploration of the duties, obligations, and benefits of family life. Alberti uses the popular dialogue form to elaborate on the themes of parental responsibility, love, marriage, and the management of the household. He views the family from a variety of perspectives: as a kinship group, an economic unit, and a political body.

In our discussion we may establish four general precepts as sound and firm foundation for all the other points to be developed or added. I shall name them. In the family the number of men must not diminish but augment; possessions must not grow less, but more; all forms of disgrace are to be shunned—a good name and fine reputation is precious and worth pursuing; hatreds, enmities, rancor must be carefully avoided, while good will, numerous acquaintances, and friendships are something to look for, augment, and cultivate.

We shall take up these four points of wisdom in order to see how men become rich, good, and well-beloved. First we must begin by seeing how a family becomes, as we may say, populous. We shall give some thought to the reasons for a decline in numbers. Then we shall turn to the second point. I am delighted to find that by some providential chance we happened to begin our talk with a kind of prelude to all this, in which I urged you to avoid all lust and lascivious greed. Did I not intend to be brief in this matter, as before so in what is to come? Perhaps I would

show you more clearly how in all four things that remain to our consideration, sensual pleasure and lascivious love are the most destructive cause of total ruin. Another time and place for this discussion may arise, while you, I know, need no persuasion to make you keep to your education, your noble pursuits, and your studies, and avoid idleness and less than honorable desires. So let us return to our subject. There we shall speak as lucidly and simply as we can, without any elegant and very polished rhetoric. I think among ourselves good thoughts are far more important than a pretty style. Listen to me.

Families increase in population no differently than do countries, regions, and the whole world. As anyone who uses his imagination will quickly realize, the number of mortal men has grown from a small number to the present almost infinite multitude through the procreation and rearing of children. And, for the procreation of children, no one can deny that man requires woman. Since a child comes into the world as a tender and delicate creature, he needs someone to whose care and devotion he comes as a cherished trust. This person must nourish him with diligence and love and must defend him from harm. Too much cold or too much sun, rain, and the wild blowing of a storm are harmful to children. Woman, therefore, did first find a roof under which to nourish and protect herself and her offspring. There she remained, busy in the shadow, nourishing and caring for her children. And since woman was busy guarding and taking care of the heir, she was not in a position to go out and find what she and her children required for the maintenance of their life. Man, however, was by nature more energetic and industrious, and he went out to find things and bring what seemed to him necessary. Sometimes the man remained away from home and did not return as soon as his family expected. Because of this, when he came back laden, the woman learned to save things up in order to make sure that if in the future her husband stayed away for a time, neither she nor her children would suffer. In this way it seems clear to me that nature and human reason taught mankind the necessity of having a spouse, both to increase and continue generations and to nourish and preserve those already born. It also became clear that careful gathering and diligent preserving were essential to the maintenance of human life in the married state.

Nature showed, further, that this relationship could not be permitted with more than one wife at a time, since man was by no means able to provide and bring home more than was needed for himself and one wife and children. Had he wished to find food and to gather goods for more wives and families, one or another of them would certainly sometimes have lacked some of the necessities. And the woman who found herself lacking what are or ought to be the necessities of life, would she not have had sufficient reason even to abandon her offspring in order to preserve her own life? Perhaps under pressure of such need she would even have had the right to seek out another companion. Marriage, therefore, was instituted by nature, our most excellent and divine teacher of all things, with the provision that there should be

one constant life's companion for a man, and one only. With her he should dwell under one roof, her he should not forget or leave all alone, but to her return, bearing things with him and ordering matters so that his family might have all that was necessary and sufficient. The wife was to preserve in the house the things he brought to her. To satisfy nature, then, a man need only choose a woman with whom he can dwell in tranquillity under one roof all his life.

Young people, however, very often do not cherish the good of the family enough to do this. Marriage, perhaps, seems to them to take away their present liberty and freedom. It may be, as the comic poets like to tell us, that they are held back and dissuaded by some mistress. Sometimes, too, young men find it hard enough to manage one life, and fear as an excessive and undesirable burden the task of supporting a wife and children besides. They may doubt their capacity to maintain in honorable estate a family which grows in needs from day to day. Viewing the conjugal bed as a troublesome responsibility, they then avoid the legitimate and honorable path to the increase of a family.

If a family is not to fall for these reasons into what we have described as the most unfortunate condition of decline, but is to grow, instead, in fame and in the prosperous multitude of its youth, we must persuade our young men to take wives. We must use every argument for this purpose, offer incentive, promise reward, employ all our wit, persistence, and cunning. A most appropriate reason for taking a wife may be found in what we were saying before, about the evil of sensual indulgence, for the condemnation of such things may lead young men to desire honorable satisfactions. As other incentives, we may also speak to them of the delights of this primary and natural companionship of marriage. Children act as pledges and securities of marital love and kindness. At the same time they offer a focus for all a man's hopes and desires. Sad, indeed, is the man who has labored to get wealth and power and lands, and then has no true heir and perpetuator of his memory. No one can be more suited than a man's true and legitimate sons to gain advantages by virtue of his character, position, and authority, and to enjoy the fruits and rewards of his labor. If a man leaves such heirs, furthermore, he need not consider himself wholly dead and gone. His children keep his own position and his true image in the family.

It will serve our purpose, also, to remind the young of the dignity conferred on the father in the ancient world. Fathers of families wore precious jewels and were given other tokens of dignity forbidden to any who had not added by his progeny to the population of the republic. It may also help to recall to young men how often profligates and hopeless prodigals have been restored to a better life by the presence of a wife in the house. Add to this what a great help sons can be as hands to get work done—how they give zealous and loyal aid and support when fortune is hard and men unkind—and how your sons more than anyone spring to your defense and are ready to avenge the injury and harm inflicted upon you by evil and outrageous men. Likewise, our children are our comfort and are apt at every age to make us happy and give us great joys and satisfactions. These things it is good to tell them. It also helps to point out how much children come to mean in old age, when we live under the pressure of various needs.

Let it be the responsibility of the whole house to see that once they have the desire they have also the ability honorably to establish a family. Let the entire family contribute, as if to purchase its own growth, and let them all join by gathering something from each member to put up a sufficient sum for a fund which will support those who shall be born. In this way an expense which would have been disastrously heavy for one alone shall be shared among many and become merely a light obligatory payment. It seems to me that in a family where good customs prevail, no one would be unwilling to pay any amount to ransom back from slavery a humble member, not even of his own family but of his country and language. No attempt should be made, therefore, to evade the light expense which might restore a greater number to one's own blood and to one's family. Year after

year you give wages to strangers, to various outsiders. You feed and clothe both foreigners and slaves, not so much to enjoy the fruit of their labor as to have a large company in your household. To contribute to a single charity which would support your own kinsmen would cost you far less. The company of your own relatives will yield you more honor and more pleasure than that of strangers. Cherished and faithful kinsmen will do more useful work and suit your household better than the workers you have taken into your service, whose loyalty you have merely bought. One should show such kindness and charity toward one's family, then, so that a father may be sure his children need never want for the necessities of life.

Perhaps it will help to put our young people under some compulsion like this: fathers could say in their wills, "If you do not marry when you reach the appropriate age, you are no heir of mine." As to what is the appropriate time of life to take a wife, to relate all the ancient opinions on this matter would take a long time. Hesiod would have a man marry at thirty; Lycurgus wanted fatherhood to begin at thirty-seven; to our modern minds it seems to be practical for a man to marry at twenty-five. Everyone at least agrees that to give this kind of responsibility to the willful and ardent youth under twenty-five is dangerous. A man of that age spends his fire and force better in establishing and strengthening his own position than in procreating. The youthful seed, moreover, seems faulty and frail and less full of vigor than that which is ripened. Let men wait for solid maturity.

When, by the urging and counsel of their elders and of the whole family, young men have arrived at the point of marriage, their mothers and other female relatives and friends, who have known the virgins of the neighborhood from earliest childhood and know the way their upbringing has formed them, should select all the well-born and well-brought-up girls and present that list to the new groom-to-be. He can then choose the one who suits him best. The elders of the house and all of the family shall reject no daughter-in-law unless she is tainted with the breath of scandal or bad reputation. Aside from that, let the man who will have to satisfy her satisfy himself. He should act as do wise heads of families before they acquire some property—they like to look it over several times before they actually sign a contract. It is good in the case of any purchase and contract to inform oneself fully and to take counsel. One should consult a good number of persons and be very careful in order to avoid belated regrets. The man who has decided to marry must be still more cautious. I recommend that he examine and anticipate in every way, and consider for many days, what sort of person it is he is to live with for all his years as husband and companion. Let him be minded to marry for two purposes: first to perpetuate himself in his children, and second to have a steady and constant companion all his life. A woman is needed, therefore, who is likely to bear children and who is desirable as a perpetual mate.

They say that in choosing a wife one looks for beauty, parentage, and riches. The beauty of a man accustomed to arms, it seems to me, lies in his having a presence betokening pride, limbs full of strength, and the gestures of one who is skilled and adept in all forms of exercise. The beauty of an old man, I think, lies in his prudence, his amiability, and the reasoned judgment which permeates all his words and his counsel. Whatever else may be thought beautiful in an old man, certainly it differs sharply from what constitutes beauty in a young cavalier. I think that beauty in a woman, likewise, must be judged not only by the charm and refinement of her face, but still more by the grace of her person and her aptitude for bearing and giving birth to many fine children.

Among the most essential criteria of beauty in a woman is an honorable manner. Even a wild, prodigal, greasy, drunken woman may be beautiful of feature, but no one would call her a beautiful wife. A woman worthy of praise must show first of all in her conduct, modesty, and purity. Marius, the illustrious Roman, said in that first speech of his to the Roman people: "Of women we require purity, of men labor." And I certainly agree. There is nothing more disgusting than a coarse and dirty woman. Who is stupid enough not to see clearly that a woman who does not care for neatness and cleanliness in her appearance, not only in her dress and body but in all her behavior and language, is by no means well mannered? How can it be anything but obvious that a bad mannered woman is also rarely virtuous? We shall consider elsewhere the harm that comes to a family from women who lack virtue, for I myself do not know which is the worse fate for a family, total celibacy or a single dishonored woman. In a bride, therefore, a man must first seek beauty of mind, that is, good conduct and virtue.

In her body he must seek not only loveliness, grace, and charm but must also choose a woman who is well made for bearing children, with the kind of constitution that promises to make them strong and big. There's an old proverb, "When you pick your wife, you choose your children." All her virtues will in fact shine brighter still in beautiful children. It is a well-known saying among poets: "Beautiful character dwells in a beautiful body." The natural philosophers require that a woman be neither thin nor very fat. Those laden with fat are subject to coldness and constipation and slow to conceive. They say that a woman should have a joyful nature, fresh and lively in her blood and her whole being. They have no objections to a dark girl. They do reject girls with a frowning black visage, however. They have no liking for either the undersized or the overlarge and lean. They find that a woman is most suited to bear children if she is fairly big and has limbs of ample length. They always have a preference for youth, based on a number of arguments which I need not expound here, but particularly on the point that a young girl has a more adaptable mind. Young girls are pure by virtue of their age and have not developed any spitefulness. They are by nature modest and free of vice. They quickly learn to accept affectionately and unresistingly the habits and wishes of their husbands.

Now we have spoken of beauty. Let us next consider parentage, and what are the qualities to look for there. I think the first problem in choosing a family is to investigate closely the customs and habits of one's new relatives. Many marriages have ruined the family, as one may hear and read every day, because they involved union with a litigious, quarrelsome, arrogant, and malevolent set of men. For brevity's sake I cite no examples here. I think that no one is so great a fool that he would not rather remain unmarried than burden himself with terrible relatives. Sometimes the links of family have proved a trouble and disaster to the man, who has had to support both his own family and that of the girl he married. Not infrequently it happens that the new family, because they feel unable to manage their own affairs or because they really are so unfortunate, all settle down in the house of their new kinsman. As the new husband you cannot keep them without harm to yourself, nor can you send them away without incurring censure.

To sum up this whole subject in a few words, for I want above all to be brief on this point, let a man get himself new kinsmen of better than plebeian blood, of a fortune more than diminutive of a decent occupation, and of modest and respectable habits. Let them not be too far above himself, lest their greatness overshadow his own honor and position. Too high a family may disturb his own and his family's peace and tranquility, and also, if one of them falls, you cannot help to support him without collapsing or wearing yourself out as you stagger under a weight too great for your arms and your strength. I also do not want the new relatives to rank too low, for while the first error puts you in a position of servitude, the second causes expense. Let them be equals, then, and, to repeat, modest and respectable people.

The matter of dowry is next, which I would like to see middling in size, certain and prompt rather than large, vague, or promised for an indefinite future. I know not why everyone, as if corrupted by a common vice, takes advantage of delay to grow lazy in paying debts. Sometimes, in cases of marriage, people are further tempted because they hope to evade payment altogether. As your wife spends her first year in your house, it seems impossible not to reinforce the new bonds of kinship by frequent visiting and parties. But it will be thought rude if, in the middle of a gathering of kinsmen, you put yourself forward to insist and complain. If, as new husbands usually do, you don't want to lose their still precarious favor, you may ask your in-laws in restrained and casual words. Then you are forced to accept any little excuse they may offer. If you make a more forthright demand for what is your own, they will explain to you their many obligations, will complain of fortune, blame the conditions of the time, complain of other men, and say that they hope to be able to ask much of you in greater difficulties. As long as they can, in fact, they will promise you bounteous repayment at an ever-receding date. They will beg you, and overwhelm you, nor will it seem possible for you to spurn the prayers of people you have accepted as your own family. Finally, you will be put in a position where you must either suffer the loss in silence or enter upon expensive litigation and create enmity.

What is more, it will seem that you can never put an end to the pressure from your wife on this point. She will weep many tears, and the pleadings and insistent prayers of a new love that has just begun are apt to have a certain force. However hard and twisted your temperament you can hardly impose silence on someone who pleads with an outsider, thus softly and tear-fully, for the sake of her own father and brothers. Then imagine how impossible for you to turn a deaf ear on your own wife doing so in your own house, in your own room. You are bound, in the end, to suffer either financial loss or loss of affection. This is why the dowry should be precisely set, promptly paid, and not too high. The larger the payments are to be and the longer they are to be carried, the more discussion you will be forced into, the more reluctantly you will be paid, and the more obliged you will feel to spend inordinate sums for all sorts of things. There will be indescribable bitterness and often totally ruinous results in setting dowries very high. We have said now how a wife is to be selected from outside and how she is to be received into the house. It remains to be seen how she is to be treated once she is within.

FOCUS QUESTIONS

1. Many historians view the Renaissance as a period of increasing secularization. How does Alberti's work reflect this trend?

2. How did Alberti define the role of the father in a family? Where does he get his examples?

3. In what ways is the family like a state?

4. How, according to Alberti, does nature shape the role of women in the family?

5. What are the qualities of a good wife? Why do you think Alberti has nothing to say about the qualifications of a good husband?

60

The Life of Leonardo da Vinci (1550 C.E.)

GIORGIO VASARI

Giorgio Vasari (1511–1574) celebrated the achievements of hundreds of artists in his Lives of the Most Eminent Italian Architects, Painters, and Sculptors, *which he published first in 1550 and then in an enlarged edition eighteen years later. Vasari undertook his project not as a historian or biographer, but as an artist. He believed that only a creative artist could understand the momentous accomplishments of the Renaissance.*

Vasari's father was a potter; his uncle, with whom he lived as a teenager, was a painter. Apprenticed at an early age, Giorgio studied for a time in Michelangelo's studio. He secured the backing of powerful patrons and was soon in demand throughout the Italian peninsula. As he traveled, he collected materials for his Lives. *His biography of Leonardo is one of the best known and shows Vasari's concern for detail, anecdote, and instruction.*

LIFE OF LEONARDO DA VINCI

Painter and Sculptor of Florence

The greatest gifts are often seen, in the course of nature, rained by celestial influences on human creatures; and sometimes, in supernatural fashion, beauty, grace, and talent are united beyond measure in one single person, in a manner that to whatever such an one turns his attention, his every action is so divine, that, surpassing all other men, it makes itself clearly known as a thing bestowed by God (as it is), and not acquired by human art. This was seen by all mankind in Leonardo da Vinci, in whom, besides a beauty of body never sufficiently extolled, there was an infinite grace in all his actions; and so great was his genius, and such its growth, that to whatever difficulties he turned his mind, he solved them with ease. In him was great bodily strength, joined to dexterity, with a spirit and courage ever royal and magnanimous; and the fame of his name so increased, that not only in his lifetime was he held in esteem, but his reputation became even greater among posterity after his death.

Truly marvellous and celestial was Leonardo, the son of Ser Piero da Vinci; and in learning and in the rudiments of letters he would have made great proficience, if he had not been so variable and unstable, for he set himself to learn many things, and then, after having begun them, abandoned them. Thus, in arithmetic, during the few months that he studied it, he made so much progress, that, by continually suggesting doubts and difficulties to the master who was teaching him, he would very often bewilder him. He gave some little attention to music, and quickly resolved to learn to play the lyre, as one who had by nature a spirit most lofty and full of refinement: wherefore he sang divinely to that instrument, improvising upon it. Nevertheless, although he occupied himself with such a variety of things, he never ceased drawing and working in relief, pursuits which suited his fancy more than any other. Ser Piero, having observed this, and having considered the loftiness of his intellect, one day took some of his drawings and carried them to Andrea del Verrocchio, who was much his friend, and besought him straitly [*sic*] to tell him whether Leonardo, by devoting himself to drawing, would make any proficience. Andrea was astonished to see the extraordinary beginnings of Leonardo, and urged Ser Piero that he should make him study it; wherefore he arranged with Leonardo that he should enter the workshop of Andrea, which Leonardo did with the greatest willingness in the world. And he practised not one branch of art only, but all those in which drawing played a part; and having an intellect so divine and marvellous that he was also an excellent geometrician, he not only worked in sculpture, making in his youth, in clay, some heads of women that are smiling, of which plaster casts are still taken, and likewise some heads of boys which appeared to have issued from the hand of a master; but in architecture, also, he made many drawings both of ground-plans and of other designs of buildings; and he was the first, although but a youth, who suggested the plan of reducing the river Arno to a navigable canal from Pisa to Florence. He made designs of flour-mills, fulling-mills, and engines, which might be driven by the force of water; and

since he wished that his profession should be painting, he studied much in drawing after nature, and sometimes in making models of figures in clay, over which he would lay soft pieces of cloth dipped in clay, and then set himself patiently to draw them on a certain kind of very fine Rheims cloth, or prepared linen; and he executed them in black and white with the point of his brush, so that it was a marvel, as some of them by his hand, which I have in our book of drawings, still bear witness; besides which, he drew on paper with such diligence and so well, that there is no one who has ever equalled him in perfection of finish; and I have one, a head drawn with the style in chiaroscuro, which is divine.

And there was infused in that brain such grace from God, and a power of expression in such sublime accord with the intellect and memory that served it, and he knew so well how to express his conceptions by draughtmanship, that he vanquished with his discourse, and confuted with his reasoning, every valiant wit. And he was continually making models and designs to show men how to remove mountains with ease, and how to bore them in order to pass from one level to another; and by means of levers, windlasses, and screws, he showed the way to raise and draw great weights, together with methods for emptying harbours, and pumps for removing water from low places, things which his brain never ceased from devising.

It is clear that Leonardo, through his comprehension of art, began many things and never finished one of them, since it seemed to him that the hand was not able to attain to the perfection of art in carrying out the things which he imagined; for the reason that he conceived in idea difficulties so subtle and so marvellous, that they could never be expressed by the hands, be they ever so excellent. And so many were his caprices, that, philosophizing of natural things, he set himself to seek out the properties of herbs, going on even to observe the motions of the heavens, the path of the moon, and the courses of the sun....

...

He also painted in Milan, for the Friars of S. Dominic, at S. Maria dell Grazie, a Last Supper,

Leonardo da Vinci, *The Last Supper*. Leonardo da Vinci was the impetus behind the High Renaissance concern for the idealization of nature, moving from a realistic portrayal of the human figure to an idealized form. Evident in Leonardo's *Last Supper* is his effort to depict a person's character and inner nature by the use of gesture and movement. Unfortunately, Leonardo used an experimental technique in this fresco, which soon led to its physical deterioration.

a most beautiful and marvellous thing; and to the heads of the Apostles he gave such majesty and beauty, that he left the head of Christ unfinished, not believing that he was able to give it that divine air which is essential to the image of Christ. This work, remaining thus all but finished, has ever been held by the Milanese in the greatest veneration, and also by strangers as well; for Leonardo imagined and succeeded in expressing that anxiety which had seized the Apostles in wishing to know who should betray their Master. For which reason in all their faces are seen love, fear, and wrath, or rather, sorrow, at not being able to understand the meaning of Christ; which thing excites no less marvel than the sight, in contrast to it, of obstinacy, hatred, and treachery in Judas; not to mention that every least part of the work displays an incredible diligence, seeing that even in the tablecloth the texture of the stuff is counterfeited in such a manner that linen itself could not seem more real.

It is said that the Prior of that place kept pressing Leonardo, in a most importunate manner, to finish the work; for it seemed strange to him to see Leonardo sometimes stand half a day at a time, lost in contemplation, and he would have liked him to go on like the labourers hoeing in his garden, without ever stopping his brush. And not content with this, he complained of it to the Duke, and that so warmly, that he was constrained to send for Leonardo and delicately urged him to work, contriving nevertheless to show him that he was doing all this because of the importunity of the Prior. Leonardo, knowing that the intellect of that Prince was acute and discerning, was pleased to discourse at large with the Duke on the subject, a thing which he had never done with the Prior: and he reasoned much with him about art, and made him understand that men of lofty genius sometimes accomplish the most when they work the least, seeking out inventions with the mind, and forming those perfect ideas which the hands afterwards express and reproduce from the images already conceived in the brain. And he added that two heads were still wanting for him to paint; that of Christ, which he did not wish to seek on earth; and he could not think that it was possible to conceive in the imagination that beauty and heavenly grace which should be the mark of God incarnate. Next, there was wanting that of Judas, which was also troubling him, not thinking himself capable of imagining features that should represent the countenance of him who, after so many benefits received, had a mind so cruel as to resolve to betray his Lord, the Creator of the world. However, he would seek out a model for the latter; but if in the end he could not find a better, he should not want that of the importunate and tactless Prior. This thing moved the Duke wondrously to laughter, and he said that Leonardo had a thousand reasons on his side. And so the poor Prior, in confusion, confined himself to urging on the work in the garden, and left Leonardo in peace, who finished only the head of Judas, which seems the very embodiment of treachery and inhumanity; but that of Christ, as has been said, remained unfinished.

Leonardo undertook to execute, for Francesco del Giocondo, the portrait of Mona Lisa, his wife; and after toiling over it for four years, he left it unfinished; and the work is now in the collection of King Frances of France, at Fontainebleau. In this head, whoever wished to see how closely art could imitate nature, was able to comprehend it with ease; for in it were counterfeited all the minutenesses that with subtlety are able to be painted, seeing that the eyes had that lustre and watery sheen which are always seen in life, and around them were all those rosy and pearly tints, as well as the lashes, which cannot be represented without the greatest subtlety. The eyebrows, through his having shown the manner in which the hairs spring from the flesh, here more close and here more scanty, and curve according to the pores of the skin, could not be more natural. The nose, with its beautiful nostrils, rosy and tender, appeared to be alive. The mouth, with its opening, and with its ends united by the red of the lips to

the flesh-tints of the face, seemed, in truth, to be not colours but flesh. In the pit of the throat, if one gazed upon it intently, could be seen the beating of the pulse. And, indeed, it may be said that it was painted in such a manner as to make every valiant craftsman, be he who he may, tremble and lose heart. He made use, also, of this device: Mona Lisa being very beautiful, he always employed, while he was painting her portrait, persons to play or sing, and jesters, who might make her remain merry, in order to take away that melancholy which painters are often wont to give to the portraits that they paint. And in this work of Leonardo's there was a smile so pleasing, that it was a thing more divine than human to behold; and it was held to be something marvellous, since the reality was not more alive....

…

There was very great disdain between Michelangelo Buonarroti and him, on account of which Michelangelo departed from Florence, with the excuse of Duke Giuliano, having been summoned by the Pope to the competition for the façade of S. Lorenzo. Leonardo, understanding this, departed and went into France, where the King, having had works by his hand, bore him great affection; and he desired that he should colour the cartoon of S. Anne, but Leonardo, according to his custom, put him off for a long time with words.

Finally, having grown old, he remained ill many months, and, feeling himself near to death, asked to have himself diligently informed of the teaching of the Catholic faith, and of the good way and holy Christian religion; and then, with many moans, he confessed and was penitent; and although he could not raise himself well on his feet, supporting himself on the arms of his friends and servants, he was pleased to take devoutly the most holy Sacrament, out of his bed. The King, who was wont often and lovingly to visit him, then came into the room; wherefore he, out of reverence, having raised himself to sit upon the bed, giving him an account of his sickness and the circumstances of it, showed withal how much he had offended God and mankind in not having worked at his art as he should have done. Thereupon he was seized by a paroxysm, the messenger of death; for which reason the King having risen and having taken his head, in order to assist him and show him favour, to the end that he might alleviate his pain, his spirit, which was divine, knowing that it could not have any greater honour, expired in the arms of the King, in the seventy-fifth year of his age.

FOCUS QUESTIONS

1. If Leonardo is the classic example of the "Renaissance Man," how would you define the term?

2. What flaws does Vasari identify in Leonardo?

3. What might you deduce from Vasari's *Life* about the social position of the artist in Renaissance Italy?

4. Why was Leonardo such a successful painter?

5. How did the famous artists of Leonardo's time get along with one another?

61

The Prince (1513 c.e.)

NICCOLÒ MACHIAVELLI

Niccolò Machiavelli (1469–1527) was born in Florence, the son of a struggling lawyer. Marked from his youth as a brilliant student, he received a sound humanist education, which he put to use in the service of the state. At the age of 25, Machiavelli entered the service of the Republic of Florence as a diplomat and political advisor. His career brought him into contact with many of the most powerful figures of his age, but it was abruptly cut short in 1512 when the Republic was overthrown. Machiavelli was jailed and tortured before being sent into exile.

Forced into retirement, Machiavelli studied ancient history and began to write. In 1513 he finished The Prince, *which remains one of the classics of Western political theory. A distillation of his experience in government and colored by his own cynical view of human nature,* The Prince *is a treatise on the art of governing successfully. Machiavelli wrote it in hopes of being allowed to return to government service, and it reflects his passionate desire for the restoration of political stability in Florence.*

NICCOLÒ MACHIAVELLI TO THE MAGNIFICENT LORENZO DE' MEDICI

It is a frequent custom for those who seek the favor of a prince to make him presents of those things they value most highly or which they know are most pleasing to him. Hence one often sees gifts consisting of horses, weapons, cloth of gold, precious stones, and similar ornaments suitable for men of noble rank. I too would like to commend myself to Your Magnificence with some token of my readiness to serve you; and I have not found among my belongings anything I prize so much or value so highly as my knowledge of the actions of men, acquired through long experience of contemporary affairs and extended reading in those of antiquity. For a long time I have thought carefully about these matters and examined them minutely; now I have condensed my thoughts into a little volume, and send it to Your Magnificence. My book is not stuffed with pompous phrases or elaborate, magnificent words, neither is it decorated with any form of extrinsic rhetorical embroidery, such as many authors use to present or adorn their materials. I wanted my book to be absolutely plain, or at least distinguished only by the variety of the examples and the importance of the subject.

I hope it will not be thought presumptuous if a man of low social rank undertakes to discuss the rule of princes and lay down principles for them. When painters want to represent landscapes, they stand on low ground to get a true view of the mountains and hills; they climb to the tops of the mountains to get a panorama over the valleys. Similarly, to know the people well one must be a prince, and to know princes well one must be, oneself, of the people.

ON DIFFERENT KINDS OF TROOPS, ESPECIALLY MERCENARIES

I said before that a prince must lay strong foundations, otherwise he is bound to come to grief. The chief foundations on which all states rest, whether they are new, old, or mixed, are good laws and good arms. And since there cannot be good laws where there are not good arms, and where there are good arms there are bound to be good laws, I shall set aside the topic of laws and talk about arms.

Let me say, then, that the armies with which a prince defends his state are either his own or are mercenaries, auxiliaries, or mixed. Mercenaries and auxiliaries are useless and dangerous. Any man who founds his state on mercenaries can never be safe or secure. The reason is that they have no other passions or incentives to hold the field, except their desire for a bit of money, and that is not enough to make them die for you.

MILITARY DUTIES OF THE PRINCE

A prince, therefore, should have no other object, no other thought, no other subject of study, than war, its rules and disciplines; this is the only art for a man who commands, and it is of such value [*virtù*] that it not only keeps born princes in place, but often raises men from private citizens to princely fortune. On the other hand, it is clear that when princes have thought more about the refinements of life than about war, they have lost their positions. The quickest way to lose a state is to neglect this art; the quickest way to get one is to study it. Because he was a soldier, Francesco Sforza raised himself from private citizen to duke of Milan; his successors, who tried to avoid the hardships of warfare, became private citizens after being dukes. Apart from the other evils it brings with it, being defenseless makes you contemptible. This is one of the disgraces from which a prince must guard himself, as we shall see later. Between a man with arms and a man without them there is no proportion at all. It is not reasonable to expect an armed man to obey one who is unarmed, nor an unarmed man to be safe among armed servants; because, what with the contempt of the former and the mistrust of the latter, there's no living together. Thus a prince who knows nothing of warfare, apart from his other troubles already described, can't hope for respect from his soldiers or put any trust in them.

ON THE REASONS WHY MEN ARE PRAISED OR BLAMED— ESPECIALLY PRINCES

It remains now to be seen what style and principles a prince ought to adopt in dealing with his subjects and friends. I know the subject has been treated frequently before, and I'm afraid people will think me rash for trying to do so again, especially since I intend to differ in this discussion from what others have said. But since I intend to write something useful to an understanding reader, it seemed better to go after the real truth of the matter than to repeat what people have imagined. A great many men have imagined states and princedoms such as nobody ever saw or knew in the real world, for there's such a difference between the way we really live and the way we ought to live that the man who neglects the real to study the ideal will learn how to accomplish his ruin, not his salvation. Any man who tries to be good all the time is bound to come to ruin among the great number who are not good. Hence a prince who wants to keep his post must learn how not to be good, and use that knowledge, or refrain from using it, as necessity requires.

Putting aside, then, all the imaginary things that are said about princes, and getting down to the truth, let me say that whenever men are discussed (and especially princes because they are prominent), there are certain qualities that bring them either praise or blame. Thus some are considered generous, others stingy; some are givers, others grabbers; some cruel, others merciful; one man is treacherous, another faithful; one is feeble and effeminate, another fierce and spirited; one humane, another proud; one lustful, another chaste; one straightforward, another sly; one harsh, another gentle; one serious, another playful; one religious, another skeptical, and so on. I know everyone will agree that among these many qualities a prince certainly ought to have all those that are considered good. But since it is impossible to have and exercise them all, because the conditions of human life simply do not allow it, a prince must be shrewd enough to avoid the public disgrace of those vices that would lose him his state. If he possibly can, he should also guard against vices that will not lose him his state; but if he cannot prevent them, he should not be too worried about indulging them. And furthermore, he should not be too worried about incurring blame for any vice without which he would find it hard to save his state. For if you look at matters carefully, you will see that something resembling virtue, if you follow it, may be your ruin, while something else resembling vice will lead, if you follow it, to your security and well-being.

ON CRUELTY AND CLEMENCY— WHETHER IT IS BETTER TO BE LOVED OR FEARED

The question arises: is it better to be loved than feared, or vice versa? I don't doubt that every prince would like to be both; but since it is hard to accommodate these qualities, if you have to make a choice, to be feared is much safer than to be loved. For it is a good general rule about men, that they are ungrateful, fickle, liars and deceivers, fearful of danger and greedy for gain. While you serve their welfare, they are all yours, but when the danger is close at hand, they turn against you. People are less concerned with offending a man who makes himself loved than one who makes himself feared: the reason is that love is a link of obligation which men, because they are rotten, will break any time they think doing so serves their advantage; but fear involves dread of punishment, from which they can never escape.

Still, a prince should make himself feared in such a way that, even if he gets no love, he gets no hate either; because it is perfectly possible to be feared and not hated, and this will be the result if only the prince will keep his hands off the property of his subjects or citizens, and off their women. When he does have to shed blood, he should be sure to have a strong justification and manifest cause; but above all, he should not confiscate people's property, because men are quicker to forget the death of a father than the loss of a patrimony.

Returning to the question of being feared or loved, I conclude that since men love at their own inclination but can be made to fear at the inclination of the prince, a shrewd prince will lay his foundations on what is under his own control, not on what is controlled by others. He should simply take pains not to be hated, as I said.

THE WAY PRINCES SHOULD KEEP THEIR WORD

How praiseworthy it is for a prince to keep his word and live with integrity rather than by craftiness, everyone understands; yet we see from recent experience that those princes have accomplished most who paid little heed to keeping their promises, but who knew how craftily to manipulate the minds of men. In the end, they won out over those who tried to act honestly.

You should consider then, that there are two ways of fighting, one with laws and the other with force. The first is properly a human method, the second belongs to beasts. But as the first method does not always suffice, you sometimes have to turn to the second. Thus a prince must know how to make good use of both the beast and the man. Ancient writers made subtle note of this fact when they wrote that Achilles and many other princes of antiquity were sent to be reared by Chiron the centaur, who trained them in his discipline. Having a teacher who is half man and half beast can only mean that a prince must know how to use both these two natures, and that one without the other has no lasting effect.

Since a prince must know how to use the character of beasts, he should pick for imitation the fox and the lion. As the lion cannot protect himself from traps, and the fox cannot defend himself from wolves, you have to be a fox in order to be wary of traps, and a lion to overawe the wolves. Those who try to live by the lion alone are badly mistaken. Thus a prudent prince cannot and should not keep

his word when to do so would go against his interest, or when the reasons that made him pledge it no longer apply. Doubtless if all men were good, this rule would be bad; but since they are a sad lot, and keep no faith with you, you in your turn are under no obligation to keep it with them.

HOW A PRINCE SHOULD ACT TO ACQUIRE REPUTATION

Nothing gives a prince more prestige than undertaking great enterprises and setting a splendid example for his people.

A prince ought to show himself an admirer of talent, giving recognition to men of ability and honoring those who excel in a particular art. Moreover, he should encourage his citizens to ply their callings in peace, whether in commerce, agriculture, or in any other business. The man who improves his holdings should not be made to fear that they will be taken away from him; the man who opens up a branch of trade should not have to fear that he will be taxed out of existence. Instead, the prince should bestow prizes on the men who do these things, and on anyone else who takes the pains to enrich the city or state in some special way. He should also, at fitting times of the year, entertain his people with festivals and spectacles.

THE INFLUENCE OF LUCK ON HUMAN AFFAIRS AND THE WAYS TO COUNTER IT

I realize that many people have thought, and still do think, that events are so governed in this world that the wisdom of men cannot possibly avail against them, indeed is altogether useless. On this basis, you might say that there is no point in sweating over anything, we should simply leave all matters to fate. This opinion has been the more popular in our own times because of the tremendous change in things during our lifetime, that actually is still going on today, beyond what anyone could have imagined. Indeed, sometimes when I think of it, I incline toward this opinion myself. Still, rather than give up on our free will altogether, I think it may be true that Fortune governs half of our actions, but that even so she leaves the other half more or less, in our power to control.

I conclude, then, that so long as Fortune varies and men stand still, they will prosper while they suit the times, and fail when they do not. But I do feel this: that it is better to be rash than timid, for Fortune is a woman, and the man who wants to hold her down must beat and bully her. We see that she yields more often to men of this stripe than to those who come coldly toward her. Like a woman, too, she is always a friend of the young, because they are less timid, more brutal, and take charge of her more recklessly.

FOCUS QUESTIONS

1. Why does Machiavelli think that he is fit to offer advice to princes?

2. How important is force in the rule of states?

3. What seems to be Machiavelli's view of human nature?

4. Machiavelli addressed his book to a prince. How do you think this fact shaped the book?

5. Many people believed *The Prince* was immoral, and yet it was very widely read. How do you think it might have been useful?

6. Contemporaries saw Machiavelli as a dangerous man. Does *The Prince* offer any ground for this opinion?

62

The Book of the City of Ladies
(ca. 1400 c.e.)

CHRISTINE DE PIZAN

Christine de Pizan (1364–ca.1430) was one of the first explicitly feminist writers in European history. She was born in Italy but raised at the court of Charles V of France where her father was a physician and astrologer. Her father insisted that Christine be given the education received by young men and she was taught languages, music, and moral and natural philosophy and spent much time reading classical literature. From early on, Christine was a trailblazer: she wrote in the vernacular, Middle French, instead of the high language of learning, Latin. She married early but was widowed by the age of 24 and spent the rest of her life in literary pursuits. She wrote poetry, political tracts, a flattering biography of Charles V, and several works on moral philosophy of which the most famous was The Book of the City of Ladies *(1405). Despite her avowed feminism, Christine enjoyed the financial support of noble male patrons until she entered a convent in 1418. She died there around 1430.*

Using traditional forms of debate, such as questions and answers, and characters that are personifications of certain ideals (here Reason, Justice, and Rectitude), she argues against the stereotypes of women prevalent in her medieval society. As was typical in this time period, Christine's book opens with a justification of its writing. The Book of the City of Ladies *(1405) reflects Christine's wide reading in classical authors as well as her deep commitment to Christianity. The work takes the form of a dialogue between Christine and Reason in the first part and Christine and Rectitude in the second.*

1. *Here begins the* Book of the City of Ladies, *the first chapter of which explains why and for what purpose the book was written.*

One day, I was sitting in my study surrounded by many books of different kinds, for it has long been my habit to engage in the pursuit of knowledge. My mind had grown weary as I had spent the day struggling with the weighty tomes of various authors whom I had been studying for some time. I looked up from my book and decided that, for once, I would put aside these difficult texts and find instead something amusing and easy to read from the works of the poets. As I searched around for some little book, I happened to chance upon a work which did not belong to me but was amongst a pile of others that had been placed in my safe-keeping. I opened it up and saw from the title that it was by Matheolus. With a smile, I made my choice. Although I had never read it, I knew that, unlike many other works, this one was said to be written in praise of women. Yet I had scarcely begun to read it when my dear mother called me down to supper, for it was time to eat. I put the book to one side, resolving to go back to it the following day.

The next morning, seated once more in my study as is my usual custom, I remembered my previous desire to have a look at this book by Matheolus. I picked it up again and read on a little. But, seeing the kind of immoral language and ideas it contained, the content seemed to me likely to appeal only to those who enjoy reading works of slander and to be of no use whatsoever to anyone who wished to pursue virtue or to improve their

moral standards. I therefore leafed through it, read the ending, and decided to switch to some more worthy and profitable work. Yet, having looked at this book, which I considered to be of no authority, an extraordinary thought became planted in my mind which made me wonder why on earth it was that so many men, both clerks and others, have said and continue to say and write such awful, damning things about women and their ways. I was at a loss as to how to explain it. It is not just a handful of writers who do this, nor only this Matheolus whose book is neither regarded as authoritative nor intended to be taken seriously. It is all manner of philosophers, poets and orators too numerous to mention, who all seem to speak with one voice and are unanimous in their view that female nature is wholly given up to vice.

As I mulled these ideas over in my mind again and again, I began to examine myself and my own behaviour as an example of womankind. In order to judge in all fairness and without prejudice whether what so many famous men have said about us is true, I also thought about other women I know, the many princesses and countless ladies of all different social ranks who have shared their private and personal thoughts with me. No matter which way I looked at it and no matter how much I turned the question over in my mind, I could find no evidence from my own experience to bear out such a negative view of female nature and habits. Even so, given that I could scarcely find a moral work by any author which didn't devote some chapter or paragraph to attacking the female sex, I had to accept their unfavorable opinion of women since it was unlikely that so many learned men, who seemed to be endowed with such great intelligence and insight into all things, could possibly have lied on so many different occasions. It was on the basis of this one simple argument that I was forced to conclude that, although my understanding was too crude and ill-informed to recognize the great flaws in myself and other women, these men had to be in the right. Thus I preferred to give more weight to what others said than to trust my own judgment and experience.

I dwelt on these thoughts at such length that it was as if I had sunk into a deep trance. My mind became flooded with an endless stream of names as I recalled all the authors who had written on this subject. I came to the conclusion that God had surely created a vile thing when He created woman. Indeed, I was astounded that such a fine craftsman could have wished to make such an appalling object which, as these writers would have it, is like a vessel in which all the sin and evil of the world has been collected and preserved. This thought inspired such a great sense of disgust and sadness in me that I began to despise myself and the whole of my sex as an aberration in nature.

With a deep sigh, I called out to God: 'Oh Lord, how can this be? Unless I commit an error of faith, I cannot doubt that you, in your infinite wisdom and perfect goodness, could make anything that wasn't good. Didn't you yourself create woman especially and then endow her with all the qualities that you wished her to have? How could you possibly have made a mistake in anything? Yet here stand women not simply accused, but already judged, sentenced and condemned! I just cannot understand this contradiction. If it is true, dear Lord God, that women are guilty of such horrors as so many men seem to say, and as you yourself have said that the testimony of two or more witnesses is conclusive,[1] how can I doubt their word? Oh God, why wasn't I born a male so that my every desire would be to serve you, to do right in all things, and to be as perfect a creature as man claims to be? Since you chose not to show such grace to me, please pardon and forgive me, dear Lord, if I fail to serve you as well as I should,

for the servant who receives fewer rewards from his lord is less obligated to him in his service.'

Sick at heart, in my lament to God I uttered these and many other foolish words since I thought myself very unfortunate that He had given me a female form.

2. *Christine tells how three ladies appeared to her, and how the first of them spoke to her and comforted her in her distress.*

Sunk in these unhappy thoughts, my head bowed as if in shame and my eyes full of tears, I sat slumped against the arm of my chair with my cheek resting on my hand. All of a sudden, I saw a beam of light, like the rays of the sun, shine down into my lap. Since it was too dark as that time of day for the sun to come into my study, I woke with a start as if from a deep sleep. I looked up to see where the light had come from and all at once saw before me three ladies, crowned and of majestic appearance, whose faces shone with a brightness that lit up me and everything else in the place. As you can imagine, I was full of amazement that they had managed to enter a room whose doors and windows were all closed. Terrified at the thought that it might be some kind of apparition come to tempt me, I quickly made the sign of the cross on my forehead.

With a smile on her face, the lady who stood at the front of the three addressed me first: 'My dear daughter, don't be afraid, for we have not come to do you any harm, but rather, out of pity on your distress, we are here to comfort you. Our aim is to help you get rid of those misconceptions which have clouded your mind and made you reject what you know and believe in fact to be the truth just because so many other people have come out with the opposite opinion. You're acting like that fool in the joke who falls asleep in the mill and whose friends play a trick on him by dressing him up in women's clothing. When he wakes up, they manage to convince him that he is a woman despite all evidence to the contrary! My dear girl, what has happened to your sense? Have you forgotten that it is in the furnace that gold is refined, increasing in value the more it is beaten and fashioned into different shapes? Don't you know that it's the very finest things which are the subject of the most intense discussion? Now, if you turn your mind to the very highest realm of all, the realm of abstract ideas, think for a moment whether or not those philosophers whose views against women you've been citing have ever been proven wrong. In Fact, they are all constantly correcting each other's opinions, as you yourself should know from reading Aristotle's *Metaphysics* where he discusses and refutes both their views and those of Plato and other philosophers. Don't forget the Doctors of the Church either, and Saint Augustine in particular, who all took issue with Aristotle himself on certain matters, even though he is considered to be the greatest of all authorities on both moral and natural philosophy. You seem to have accepted the philosophers' views as articles of faith and thus as irrefutable on every point.

'As for the poets you mention, you must realize that they sometimes wrote in the manner of fables which you have to rake as saying the opposite of what they appear to say. You should therefore read such texts according to the grammatical rule of *antiphrasis*,[2] which consists of interpreting something that is negative in a positive light, or vice versa. My advice to you is to read those passages where they criticize women in this way and to turn them to your advantage, no matter what the author's original intention was. It could be that Matheolus is also meant to be read like this because there are some passages in his book which, if taken literally, are just out-and-out heresy. As for what these authors—not just Matheolus but also the more authoritative writer of the *Romance of the Rose*—say about the God-given, holy state of matrimony, experience should tell you that they are completely wrong when they say that marriage is insufferable thanks to women. What husband ever gave his wife the power over him to utter the kind of insults and obscenities which these authors claim that women do? Believe me, despite what you've read in books, you've never actually *seen* such a thing because it's all a pack of outrageous lies. My dear friend, I have to say that it is your naivety which has led you to take what they come out with as the truth. Return to your senses and stop worrying your head about such foolishness. Let me tell you that those who speak ill of women do more harm to themselves than they do to the women they actually slander.'

FOCUS QUESTIONS

1. Why does Christine de Pizan believe she needs to write this book?

2. Who do you think was Christine's intended audience?

3. Do you think we are meant to take Christine's vision literally?

4. What is the relationship between God and philosophy in this text?

China and Japan
in the Middle Ages

Werner Forman/Art Resource, NY

Samurai. During the Kamakura period, painters began to depict the adventures of the new warrior class. Here is an imposing mounted samurai warrior, the Japanese equivalent of the medieval knight in feudal Europe. Like his European counterpart, the samurai was supposed to live by a strict moral code and was expected to maintain an unquestioning loyalty to his liege lord. Above all, a samurai's life was one of simplicity and self-sacrifice.

FOCUS QUESTIONS

1. This painting of a samurai warrior is an example of Kamakura art, a Japanese movement associated with increased realism. Do you think this painting looks realistic?

2. Why are the samurai and his horse depicted looking behind them?

3. Notice that this image was painted on a coarse-grain wood. Why might the painter have chosen that material?

4. Behind the samurai, there is no background but the grain of the wood. Why did the artist choose to allow the material to serve as background?

63

The Hojo Code (1232 c.e.)

Feudalism in thirteenth-century Japan resulted from the breakup of central authority and the rise of military commanders, known as shoguns. The head of the Hojo family attained this office at the beginning of the thirteenth century and wrote a code to establish relations between lords and vassals as well as to define civil and criminal laws. Like other feudal systems, the crucial relationships were hierarchical, with lords owning and vassals serving. The Hojo Code covers all forms of public conduct from religious observances to personal behavior. One striking difference between feudalism in the West and in Japan involves the property rights of women.

INSTITUTES OF JUDICATURE

1.—The Shrines of the gods must be kept in repair; and their worship performed with the greatest attention.

The majesty of the gods is augmented by the veneration of men, and the fortunes of men are fulfilled by the virtue of the gods. Therefore the established sacrifices to them must not be allowed to deteriorate; and there must be no remissness in paying ceremonial honours to them as if they were present. Accordingly throughout the provinces of the Kwanto Dominion and likewise in the Manors, the Land Reeves, the *Kannushi* (Shinto) priests and others concerned must each bear this in mind, and carefully carry out this duty. Moreover, in the case of shrines which have been enfeoffed (endowed with benefices) the deed of grant must be confirmed each generation, and minor repairs executed from time to time as prescribed therein. If serious damage should happen to a shrine a full report of the circumstances is to be made, and such directions will be given (from Kamakura) as the exigencies of the case may require.

2.—(Buddhist) Temples and pagodas must be kept in repair and the Buddhist services diligently celebrated.

Although (Buddhist) temples are different from (Shinto) shrines, both are alike as regards worship and veneration. Therefore the merit of maintaining them both in good order and the duty of keeping up the established services, as provided in the foregoing article is the same in both cases. Let no one bring trouble on himself through negligence herein.

In case the incumbent does what he pleases with the income of the temple benefice or covetously misappropriates it, or if the duties of the clergy be not diligently fulfilled by him, the offender shall be promptly dismissed, and another incumbent appointed.

3.—Of the duties devolving on Protectors in the Provinces.

In the time of the august Right General's House it was settled that those duties should be the calling out and dispatching of the Grand Guard for service at the capital, the suppression of conspiracies and rebellion and the punishment of murder and violence (which included night attacks on houses, robbery, dacoity and piracy). Of late years, however, Official Substitutes (*Daikwan*) have been taken on and distributed over the countries and townships and these have been imposing public burdens (corvée) on the villages. Not being Governors of the provinces they yet hinder the (Agricultural) work of the province: not being Land-Reeves they are yet greedy of the profits of the land. Such proceedings and schemes are utterly unprincipled.

Be it noted that no person, even if his family were for generations vassals of the August House (of the Minamoto) is competent to impress for military service unless he has an investiture of the present date.

On the other hand again, it is reported that inferior managers and village officials in various places make use of the name of vassals of the August House as a pretext for opposing the orders of the Governor of the provinces or of the lord of the Manor. Such persons, even if they are desirous of being taken into the ser-vice of the Protectors, must not under any circumstances be included in the enrollment for service in the Guards. In short, conformably to the precedents of the time of the August General's House, the Protectors must cease altogether from giving directions in matters outside of the hurrying-up of the Grand Guards and the suppression of plots, rebellion, murder and violence.

In the event of a Protector disobeying this article and intermeddling in other affairs than those herein named, if a complaint is instituted against him by the Governor of the Province or the lord of a Manor, or if the Land-Reeve or the folk aggrieved petition for redress, his downright lawlessness being thus brought to light, he shall be divested of his office and a person of gentle character appointed in his stead. Again, as regards Delegates (*Daikwan*) not more than one is to be appointed by a Protector.

4.—Of Protectors omitting to report cases of crime and confiscating the successions to fiefs, on account of offences.

When persons are found committing serious offences, the Protectors should make a detailed report of the case (to Kamakura) and follow such directions as may be given them in relation thereto; yet there are some who, without ascertaining the truth or falsehood of an accusation, or investigating whether the offence committed was serious or trifling, arbitrarily pronounce the escheat of the criminal's heridaments, and selfishly cause them to be confiscated. Such unjust judgments are a nefarious artifice for the indulgence of license. Let a report be promptly made to us of the circumstances of each case and our decision upon the matter be respectfully asked for, any further persistence in transgressions of this kind will be dealt with criminally.

In the next place, with regard to a culprit's rice-fields and other fields, his dwelling-house, his wife and children, his utensils and other articles of property. In serious cases, the offenders are to be taken in charge by the Protector's office; but it is not necessary to take in charge their farms, houses, wives, children and miscellaneous gear along with them.

Furthermore, even if the criminal should in his statement implicate others as being accomplices or accessories, such are not to be included in the scope of the Protector's judgment, unless they are found in possession of the booty (or other substantial evidence of guilt be forthcoming).

5.—Of Land-Reeves in the provinces detaining a part of the assessed amounts of the rice-tax.

If a plaint is instituted by the lord of the Manor alleging that a Land-Reeve is withholding the land-tax payable to him, a statement of account will be at once taken, and the plaintiff shall receive a certificate of the balance that may be found to be due to him. If the Land-Reeve be adjudged to be in default, and has no valid plea to urge in justification, he will be required to make compensation in full. If the amount is small, judgment will be given for immediate payment. If the amount be greater than he is able to pay at once, he will be allowed three years within which to completely discharge his liability. Any Land-Reeve who, after such delay granted, shall make further delays and difficulties, contrary to the intention of this article, shall be deprived of his post.

6.—Governors of provinces and Manorial Houses may exercise their normal jurisdiction without referring to the Kwanto (authorities).

In cases where jurisdiction has heretofore been exercised by the Governor's Yamens, by lords of Manors, by Shinto Shrines or by Buddhist Temples on the footing of lords of Manors, it will not be necessary for us now to introduce interference. Even if they wish to refer a matter to us for advice, they are not permitted to do so.

In the next place, as regards the bringing of suits before us direct, without producing a letter of recommendation from the local tribunal.

The proper procedure in bringing a suit is for the parties to come provided with letters of recommendation from their own tribunal, whether it be that of a Provincial Governor, a manor, a shrine, or a temple. Hence persons who come unprovided with such letters have already committed a breach of propriety and henceforth their suits will not be received injudicature.

7.—Whether the fiefs which have been granted since the time of Yoritomo by the successive *Shogun's* and by Her Ladyship the Dowager (Masako) are to be revoked or exchanged in consequence of suits being brought by the original owners.

Such fiefs having been granted as rewards for distinguished merit in the field, or for valuable services in official employment, have not been acquired without just title. And if judgment were to be given in favour of some one who alleged that such was originally the fief of his ancestors, though the one face might beam with joy, the many comrades could assuredly feel no sense of security. A stop must be put to persons bringing such unsettling suits.

In case, however, one of the grantees of the present epoch should commit a crime, and the original owner, watching his opportunity should thereupon bring a suit for recovery of possession, he cannot well be prohibited from doing so.

In the next place, as regards attempts that may be made to disturb tenures by occasion of the *Shogun's* judicature having through failure of heirs come to an end.

Whereas some persons who, in consequence of not having right on their side, were formerly nonsuited are found scheming, after allowing an interval of years to elapse, to bring suit a second time, the mere framing of such an intention is an offence of no light criminality. Hence-forward should any persons, disregarding the adjudications of the *Shogun* and his successors, wantonly institute suits of disturbance, in every such case the grounds of the invalidity of the claim are to be endorsed at full length upon the title-deeds in his possession.

8.—Of fiefs which, though deeds of investiture are held, have not been had in possession through a series of years.

With respect to the above, if more than twenty years have elapsed since the present holder was in possession his title is not to be enquired into and no change can be made: following herein the precedent of the time of the Yoritomo house. And if any one falsely alleging himself to be in possession, obtains by deceit a deed of grant, even though he may have the document in his possession it is not to be recognized as having validity.

9.—Of plotters of treason.

The purport of the provision relating to such persons cannot well be settled beforehand. In some cases, precedent is to be followed; in others, such action should be taken as the particular circumstances may require.

10.—Of the crimes of killing, maiming and wounding: furthermore, whether parents and children are to be held mutually responsible for each other's guilt.

A person who is guilty of killing or maiming, unless he acted without premeditation, as in a chance altercation or in the intoxication of a festive party, shall be punished in his own person by death or else by banishment or by confiscation of his investiture; but his father, or his son, unless they have actually been accomplices, shall not be held responsible.

Next, the offence of cutting or wounding must be dealt with in the same way, the culprit alone being responsible.

Next, in case a son or a grandson slays the enemy of his father or grand-father, the father or grand-father, even if they were not privy to the offence, are nevertheless to be punished for it. The reason is that the gratification of the father's or grand-father's rage was the motive prompting to the sudden execution of a cherished purpose.

Next, in case a man's son, without his knowledge, is guilty of killing or maiming another, or attempting to do so, for the purpose of appropriating that other's post or seizing his property or valuables, if the fact of the father's non-connivance is clearly proven by the evidence, he is not to be held responsible.

11.—Whether in consequence of a husband's crime the estate of the wife is to be confiscated or not.

In cases of serious crime, treason, murder and maiming, also dacoity, piracy, night-attacks, robbery and the like, the guilt of the husband extends to the wife also. In cases of murder and maiming, cutting and wounding, arising out of a sudden dispute, however, she is not to be held responsible.

12.—Of abusive language.

Quarrels and murders have their origin in abusive and insulting language. In grave cases the offender shall be sent into banishment, in minor cases, ordered into confinement. If during the course of a judicial hearing one of the parties gives vent to abuse or insults, the matter in dispute shall be decided in favour of the other party. If the other party however has not right on his side, some other fief of the offender shall be confiscated. If he has no fief he shall be punished by being sent into banishment.

13.—Of the offence of striking (or beating) a person.

In such cases the person who receives the beating is sure to want to kill or maim the other in order to wipe out the insult; so the offence of beating a person is by no means a trivial one. Accordingly, if the offender be a *Samurai*, his fief shall be confiscated; if he has no fief he shall be sent into banishment: persons of lower rank, servants, pages and under, shall be placed in confinement.

14.—When a crime or offence is committed by Deputies, whether the principals are responsible.

When a Deputy is guilty of murder or any lesser one of the serious crimes, if his principal arrests and sends him on for trial, the master shall not be held responsible. But if the master in order to shield the Deputy reports that the latter is not to blame, and the truth is afterwards found out, incriminating him, the former cannot escape responsibility and accordingly his fief shall be confiscated. In such cases the Deputy shall be imprisoned (in order to be tried and dealt with).

Again, if a Deputy either detains the rice-tax payable to the lord of the Manor or contravenes the laws and precedents even though the action is that of the Deputy alone, his principal shall nevertheless be responsible.

Moreover, whenever, either in consequence of a suit instituted by the lord of a Manor, or in connection with matters of fact alleged in a plaintiff's petition, a Deputy receives a summons from the Kwanto or is sent for from Rokuhara, and instead of making up his mind to come at once, shilly-shallies and delays, his principal's investiture shall in like manner be revoked. Extenuating circumstances may, however, be taken into consideration.

15.—Of the crime of forgery.

If a *Samurai* commits the above, his fief shall be confiscated; if he has no investiture he shall be sent into exile. If one of the lower class commits it, he shall be branded in the face by burning. The amanuensis shall receive the same punishment.

Next, in suits if it is persistently alleged that the title-deed in the defendant's possession is a forgery and when the document is opened and inspected, if it is found to be indeed a forgery then the punishment shall be as above provided; but if it be found to be without flaw, then a fine propordonate to his position shall be inflicted on the false accuser, to be paid into the fund for the repairing of Shrines and temples. If he have not means wherewith to pay the fine he shall be deported.

...

19.—Of kinsmen, whether near or distant, who having been reared and supported, afterwards turn their backs on the descendants of their original masters.

Of persons who were dependent on a kinsman for their upbringing some were treated on a footing of affectionate intimacy as if they were sons; and where that was not so (owing to their belonging to a lower rank in life) they were maintained as if they were vassals. When persons so circumstanced rendered some loyal service to their masters, the latter, in their abounding appreciation of the spirit so displayed have in some cases handed them an allocation-note and in other cases have granted them a deed of enfeoffment. Yet they pretend that those grants were merely free-will gifts and take a view of things opposite to that taken by the sons or grandsons of their first master, with the result that the tenor of the relations to each other becomes very different from what it ought to be. For a time they act coquettishly, and those who were on the footing of sonship keep it up whilst the others observe the etiquette proper to vassalship; and then after a period of shilly-shallying some of them avail themselves of (literally, borrow) the badge of somebody who is not related to them, whilst the others go the length of taking up the opposite way of thinking. When such persons forge all at once the predecessors benefaction and act in opposition to his son or grandson the fiefs which were so assigned to them are to be taken from them and given back to the descendant of the original holder.

20.—Of the succession to a fief when the child, after getting the deed of assignment, predeceases the parents.

Even when the child is alive, what is to hinder the parents from revoking the assignment? How much more, then, are they free to dispose of the fief after the child has died; the thing must be left entirely to the discretion of the father or grandfather.

21.—Whether when a wife or concubine, after getting an assignment from the husband, has been divorced, she can retain the tenure of the fief or not.

If the wife in question has been repudiated in consequence of having committed some serious transgression. Even if she holds a written promise of the by-gone days she may not hold the fief of her former husband. On the other hand, if the wife in question had a virtuous record and was innocent of any fault and was discarded by reason of the husband's preference for novelty, the fief which had been assigned to her cannot be revoked.

22.—Of parents who when making a disposition of their fief pass over a grown up son whose relationship has not been severed.

When parents have brought up their son to man's estate and he has shown himself to be diligent and deserving then, either in consequence of a step-mother's slanders or out of favouritism to the son of a concubine although the son's relationship has not been severed, suddenly to leave him out and without rhyme or reason make no grant to him, would be the very extreme of arbitrariness. Accordingly,

for the wife's son who has now arrived at manhood one fifth of the fief must be cut off and assigned as his share to any older brother who is without sufficient means. However this grant should be made to depend upon proofs given, no matter whether the recipient be the son of the wife or the son of a concubine, and however small the amount of the share may be. Even if he be the son of the wife but has no service to show he does not come within the scope of the rule; neither, on the other hand, do persons who have been unfilial (even though they have rendered service).

23.—Of the adoption of heirs by women.

Although the spirit of the (ancient) laws does not allow of adoption by females, yet since the time of the General of the Right (Yoritomo) down to the present day it has been the invariable rule to allow women who had no children of their own to adopt an heir and transmit the fief to him. And not only that, but all over the country, in the capital as well as in the rural districts there are abundant evidences of the existence of the same practice. It is needless to enumerate the cases. Besides, after full consideration and discussion, its validity has been recognized, and it is hereby confirmed.

24.—Whether a widow who has succeeded to her husband's fief and who marries again should continue to hold it.

Widows who have succeeded to the fief of their deceased husband should give up everything else and devote themselves to their husbands' welfare in the after-world and those who disregard that observance cannot be held blameless. Hence if any such, soon forgetting their conjugal constancy marry again, the fief held by their late husband is to be granted to the husband's son. If the deceased husband had no son, the fief should be disposed of in some other way.

…

33.—Of robbing and theft; also of incendiaries. For the two kinds of stealing the punishment (death) is already established by precedents. Can there be hesitation or reconsideration on that point? Next as regards the man who sets on fire (a house, etc.) he is to be regarded in the same light as a brigand and it is right that he should be outlawed.

34.—Of illicit intercourse with another person's wife.

Whoever embraces another person's wife is to be deprived of half of his fief, and to be inhibited from rendering service any more, regardless of whether it was a case of rape or adultery. If he have no investiture he must be sent into banishment. A woman who commits adultery shall in like manner be deprived of her fief, and if she have none she must also be sent into banishment.
...

41.—Of Slaves and unclassed persons.

(In cases of dispute respecting the ownership of such persons) the precedent established by the late *Shogun's* House must be adhered to; that is to say, if more than ten years have elapsed without the former owner having asserted his claim, there shall be no discussion as to the merits of the case and the possession of the present owner is not to be interfered with.

42.—Of inflicting loss and ruin on absconding farmers under the pretext of smashing runaways.

When people living in the provinces run away and escape, the lord of the fief and others, proclaiming that runaways must be smashed up, detain their wives and children, and confiscate their property. Such a mode of procedure is quite the reverse of benevolent government. Henceforth such must be referred (to Kamakura) for adjudication, and if it is found that the farmer is in arrear as regards payment of his land tax and levies, he shall be compelled to make good the deficiency. If he is found not to be so in arrear, the property seized from him shall be forthwith restored to him. And it shall be entirely at the option of the farmer himself whether he shall continue to live in the fief or go elsewhere.

FOCUS QUESTIONS

1. What is the relationship between lords and vassals in *The Hojo Code?*

2. What is the place of agriculture in medieval Japan? How is it regulated in the *Code?*

3. Do women have the same legal rights as men?

4. Why was kinship so important in Japanese society?

5. Why did it seem important to codify laws in the early thirteenth century?

64

A Chronicle of Gods and Sovereigns (1339–1343 C.E.)

KITABATAKE CHIKAFUSA

Kitabatake Chikafusa (1292–1354) was descended from a branch of the Japanese imperial family. He became its head at the age of 13 when his father took Buddhist vows. Most of Kitabatake's life was spent at the Imperial court, where he held important posts as a counselor and as head of the academies that trained the children of other courtiers. He was personally responsible for the education of one of the Imperial princes. He lived through a long period of civil war and governmental instability and twice fled the capital. It was during his second period of voluntary exile that he wrote A Chronicle of Gods and Sovereigns.*

The Chronicle *is an expression of the divine origins of Japan and a celebration of the Imperial dynasty, which Kitabatake claims has descended unbroken from its creation by the goddess of the sun. This succession is what makes Japan the greatest of all nations in Kitabatake's account.*

Japan is the divine country. The heavenly ancestor it was who first laid its foundations, and the Sun Goddess left her descendants to reign over it forever and ever. This is true only of our country, and nothing similar may be found in foreign lands. That is why it is called the divine country.

THE NAMES OF JAPAN

In the Age of the Gods, Japan was known as the "ever-fruitful land of reed-covered plains and luxuriant ricefields." This name has existed since the creation of heaven and earth. It appeared in the command given by the heavenly ancestor Kunito-kotachi to the Male Deity and the Female Deity. Again, when the Great Goddess Amaterasu bequeathed the land to her grandchild, that name was used; it may thus be considered the primal name of Japan. It is also called the

country of the great eight islands. This name was given because eight islands were produced when the Male Deity and the Female Deity begot Japan. It is also called Yamato, which is the name of the central part of the eight islands. The eighth offspring of the deities was the god Heavenly-August-Sky-Luxuriant-Dragon-fly-Lord Youth [and the land he incarnated] was called Oyamato, Luxuriant-Dragon-fly-Island. It is now divided into forty-eight provinces. Besides being the central island, Yamato has been the site of the capital through all the ages since Jimmu's conquest of the east. That must be why the other seven islands are called Yamato. The same is true of China, where All-Under-Heaven was at one time called Chou because the dynasty had its origins in the state of Chou, and where All-Within-the-Seas was called Han when the dynasty arose in the territory of Han.

The word Yamato means "footprints on the mountain." Of old, when heaven and earth were divided, the soil was still muddy and not yet dry, and people passing back and forth over the mountains left many footprints; thus it was called Yamato—"mountain footprint." Some say that in ancient Japanese *to* meant "dwelling" and that because people dwelt in the mountains, the country was known to Yama-to—"mountain dwelling."

In writing the name of the country, the Chinese characters Dai-Nippon and Dai-Wa have both been used. The reason is that, when Chinese writing was introduced to this country, the characters for Dai-Nippon were chosen to represent the name of the country, but they were pronounced as "Yamato." This choice may have been guided by the fact that Japan is the Land of the Sun Goddess, or it may have thus been called because it is near the place where the sun rises....

The creation of heaven and earth must everywhere have been the same, for it occurred within the same universe, but the Indian, Chinese, and Japanese traditions are each different. According to the Indian version, the beginning of the world is called the "inception of the kalpas." (A kalpa has four stages—growth, settlement, decline, and extinction—each with twenty rises and falls. One rise and fall is called a minor kalpa; twenty minor kalpas constitute a middle kalpa, and four middle kalpas constitute a major kalpa.) A heavenly host called "Light-Sound" spread golden clouds in the sky which filled the entire Brahmaloka. Then they caused great rains to fall, which accumulated on the circle of wind to form the circle of water. It expanded and rose to the sky, where a great wind blew from it foam which it cast into the void; this crystallized into the palace of Brahma. The water gradually receding formed the palaces of the realm of desire, Mount Sumeru, the four continents, and the Iron Enclosing Mountain. Thus the countless millions of worlds came into existence at the same time. This was the kalpa of creation. (These countless millions of worlds are called the three-thousand-great-thousand worlds.)

The heavenly host of Light-Sound came down, were born, and lived. This was the kalpa of settlement. During the kalpa of settlement there were twenty rises and falls. In the initial stage, people's bodies shone with a far-reaching effulgence, and they could fly about at will. Joy was their nourishment. No distinction existed between the sexes. Later, sweet water, tasting like cream and honey, sprang from the earth. (It was also called earth-savor.) One sip of it engendered a craving for its taste. Thus were lost the godlike ways, and thus also was the light extinguished, leaving the wide world to darkness. In retribution for the actions of living creatures, black winds blew over the oceans, bearing before them on the waves the sun and the moon, to come to rest half-way up Mount Sumeru, there to shine forth on the four continents under the heavens. From that time on there were the day and the night, the months, and the seasons. Indulgence in the sweet waters caused men's faces to grow pale and thin. Then the sweet waters vanished, and vegetable food (also called earth-rind) appeared, which all creatures ate. Then the vegetable food also vanished, and wild rice of multiple tastes was provided them. Cut in the morning, it ripened by evening. The eating of the rice left dregs in the body, and thus the two orifices were created. Male and female came to differ, and this led to sexual desire. They called each other husband and wife, built houses, and lived together. Beings from the Light-Sound Heaven who were later to be born entered women's wombs, and once born became living creatures.

Later, the wild rice ceased to grow, to the dismay of all creatures. They divided the land and planted cereals, which they made their food. Then there were those who stole other people's crops, and fighting ensued. As there was no one to decide such cases, men got together and established a Judge-King whom they called kshatriya (which means landowner). The first king bore the title of People's Lord [*Minshu*]. He enjoyed the love and respect of the people because he ruled the country with laws which embodied the ten virtues. The realm of Jambu was prosperous and peaceful with no sickness or extremes of cold or heat. Men lived so long that their years were almost without number. Successive descendants of People's Lord ruled the land for many years, but as the good laws gradually fell into abeyance, the life-span decreased until it was only 84,000 years. People were eighty feet tall. During this period there was a king, the wheels of whose chariot rolled everywhere without hindrance. First the precious Golden Wheel came down from heaven and appeared before the king. Whenever the king went abroad, the wheel rolled ahead of him, and the lesser rulers evinced their welcome and homage. No one dared do otherwise. He reigned over the four continents and enjoyed all treasures—elephants, horses, pearls, women, lay-Buddhists, and military heroes. He who is possessed of these Seven Treasures is called a Sovereign of the Golden Wheel. There followed in succession [sovereigns of] Silver, Copper, and Iron Wheels. Because of the inequality of their merits, the rewards also gradually diminished. The life-span also decreased by one year each century, and human stature was similarly reduced by one foot a century. It was when the life-span had dropped to 120 years that Shakya Buddha appeared. (Some authorities say that it was when the life-span was 100 years. Before him three Buddhas had appeared.)

When the life-span has been reduced to a bare ten years, the so-called Three Disasters will ensue, and the human species will disappear almost entirely, leaving a mere 10,000 people. These people will practice good deeds, and the life-span will then increase and the rewards improve. By the time that a life-span of 20,000 years is reached, a King of the Iron Wheel will appear and rule over the southern continent. When the life-span reaches 40,000 years, a King of the Copper Wheel will appear and rule over the eastern and southern continents. When the life-span reaches 60,000 years, a King of the Silver Wheel will appear and rule over three continents, the eastern, western, and southern. When the life-span reaches 84,000 years, a King of the Golden Wheel will appear and rule over all four continents. The rewards in his reign will be those mentioned above. In his time a decline will again set in, followed by the appearance of Maitreya Buddha. There are then to follow eighteen other rises and falls....

In China, nothing positive is stated concerning the creation of the world even though China is a country which accords special importance to the keeping of records. In the Confucian books nothing antedates King Fu-hsi. In other works they speak of heaven, earth, and man as having begun in an unformed, undivided state, much as in the accounts of our Age of the Gods. There is also the legend of King P'an-ku, whose eyes were said to have turned into the sun and the moon, and whose hair turned into grasses and trees. There were afterwards sovereigns of Heaven, sovereigns of Earth, and sovereigns of Man, and the Five Dragons, followed by many kings over a period of 10,000 years.

The beginnings of Japan in some ways resemble the Indian descriptions, telling as it does of the world's creation from the seed of the heavenly gods. However, whereas in our country the succession to the throne has followed a single undeviating line since the first divine ancestor, nothing of the kind has existed in India. After their first ruler, King People's Lord, had been chosen and raised to power by the populace, his dynasty succeeded, but in later times most of his descendants perished, and men of inferior genealogy who had powerful forces became the rulers, some of them even controlling the whole of India. China is also a country of notorious disorders. Even in ancient times, when life was simple and conduct was proper, the throne was offered to wise men, and no single lineage was established. Later, in times of disorder, men fought for control of the country. Thus some of the rulers rose from the ranks of the plebeians, and there were even some of barbarian origin who usurped power. Or, some families after generations of service as ministers surpassed their princes and eventually supplanted them. There have already been thirty-six changes of dynasty since Fu-hsi, and unspeakable disorders have occurred.

Only in our country has the succession remained inviolate, from the beginning of heaven and earth to the present. It has been maintained within a single lineage, and even when, as inevitably has happened, the succession has been transmitted collaterally, it has returned to the true line. This is due to the ever-renewed Divine Oath, and makes Japan unlike all other countries.

It is true that the Way of the Gods should not be revealed without circumspection, but it may happen that ignorance of the origins of things may result in disorder. In order to prevent that disaster, I have recorded something of the facts, confining myself to a description of how the succession has legitimately been transmitted from the Age of the Gods. I have not included information known to everyone.

Then the Great Sun Goddess conferred with Takami-musubi and sent her grandchild to the world below. Eighty million deities obeyed the divine decree to accompany and serve him. Among them were thirty-two principal deities, including the gods of the Five Guilds—Amieno Koyane (the first ancestor of the Nakatomi family), Ameno Futodama (the first ancestor of the Imbe family), Ameno Uzume (the first ancestor of the Sarume family), Ishikoridome (the first ancestor of the mirrormakers), and Tamaya (the first ancestor of the jewel-makers). Two of these deities, those of the Nakatomi and the Imbe, received a divine decree specially instructing them to aid and protect the divine grandchild. The Sun Goddess, on bestowing the three divine treasures on her grandchild, uttered these words of command, "The reed-plain-of-one-thousand-five-hundred-autumns-fair-rice-ear land is where my descendants shall reign. Thou, my illustrious grandchild, proceed thither and govern the land. Go, and may prosperity attend thy dynasty, and may it, like Heaven and Earth, endure forever."

Then the Great Goddess, taking in her own hand the precious mirror, gave it to her grandchild, saying, "When thou, my grandchild, lookst on this mirror, it will be as though thou lookst at myself. Keep it with thee, in the same bed, under the same roof, as thy holy mirror." She then added the curved jewel of increasing prosperity and the sword of gathered clouds, thus completing the three regalia. She again spoke, "Illumine all the world with brightness like this mirror. Reign over the world with the wonderful sway of this jewel. Subdue those who will not obey thee by brandishing this divine sword." It may indeed be understood from these commands why Japan is a divine country and has been ruled by a single imperial line following in legitimate succession. The Imperial Regalia have been transmitted [within Japan] just as the sun, moon, and stars remain in the heavens. The mirror has the form of the sun; the jewel contains the essence of the moon; and the sword has the substance of the stars. There must be a profound significance attached to them.

The precious mirror is the mirror made by Ishikoridome, as is above recorded. The jewel is the curved bead of increasing prosperity made by Tamanoya, and the sword is the sword of gathered clouds, obtained by the god Susa-no-o and offered by him to the Great Goddess. The goddess's commands on the Three Regalia must indicate the proper methods of governing the country. The mirror does not possess anything of its own, but without selfish desires reflects all things, showing their true qualities. Its virtue lies in its response to these qualities, and as such represents the source of all honesty. The virtue of the jewel lies in its gentleness and submissiveness; it is the source of compassion. The virtue of the sword lies in its strength and resolution; it is the source of wisdom. Unless these three virtues are joined in a ruler, he will find it difficult indeed to govern the country. The divine commands are clear; their words are concise, but their import is far-reaching. Is it not an awe-inspiring thing that they are embodied in the imperial regalia?

The mirror stands first in importance among the regalia, and is revered as the true substance of ancestor-worship. The mirror has brightness as its form: the enlightened mind possesses both compassion and decision. As it also gives a true reflection of the Great Goddess, she must have given her profound care to the mirror. There is nothing brighter in heaven than the sun and the moon. That is why, when the Chinese characters were devised, the symbols for sun and for moon were joined to express the idea of brightness. Because our Great Goddess is the spirit of the sun, she illuminates with a bright virtue which is incomprehensible in all its aspects, but dependable alike in the realm of the visible and invisible. All sovereigns and ministers have inherited the bright seeds of the divine light, or they are the descendants of the deities who received personal instruction from the Great Goddess. Who would not stand in reverence before this fact? The highest object of all teachings, Buddhist and Confucian included, consists in realizing this fact and obeying in perfect consonance its principles. It has been the power of the dissemination of the Buddhist and Confucian texts which has spread these principles. It is just the same as the fact that a single mesh of a net suffices to catch a fish, but you cannot catch one unless the net has many meshes. Since the reign of the Emperor Ojin, the Confucian writings have been disseminated, and since Prince Shotoku's time Buddhism has flourished in Japan. Both these men were sages incarnate, and it must have been their intention to spread a knowledge of the way of our country, in accordance with the wishes of the Great Sun Goddess.

FOCUS QUESTIONS

1. Why does Kitabatake believe that Japan is a divine country?

2. What is Kitabatake's attitude toward other countries?

3. What is significant about Kitabatake's interpretation of the meaning of the three sacred regalia of the Imperial family?

4. Why, in the fourteenth century, does someone feel it is necessary to tell the story of the creation of Japan?

65

Kadensho (1440–1442 C.E.)

ZEAMI MOTOKIYO

Zeami Motokiyo (1363–1443) was the greatest of the early Japanese dramatists and the cofounder, with his father, Kan'ami, of No drama. He was first an actor who became the favorite of the Shogun Ashikaga Yoshimitsu. Zeami then became a playwright and composed over a hundred No dramas, many of which are still performed. Father and son both fell out of favor with the accession of a new shogun, and in 1422 Zeami became a Zen monk.

Along with his literary creations, Zeami wrote a series of instructional manuals for No actors. The Kadensho established the underlying philosophy of No as well as prescribing training rituals for the complex singing, dancing, miming, and acting that was required. The following selection presents some of the philosophy and ritual of No drama.

ON ATTAINING THE STAGE
OF YUGEN

Yugen is considered to be the mark of supreme attainment in all of the arts and accomplishments. In the art of the No in particular the manifestation of *yugen* is of the first importance. In general, a display of *yugen* in the No is apparent to the eye, and it is the one thing which audiences most admire, but actors who possess *yugen* are few and far between. This is because they do not in fact know the true meaning of *yugen*. There are thus none who reach that stage.

In what sort of place, then, is the stage of *yugen* actually to be found? Let us begin by examining the various classes of people on the basis of the appearance that they make in society. May we not say of the courtiers, whose behavior is distinguished and whose appearance far surpasses that of other men, that theirs is the stage of *yugen*? From this we may see that the essence of *yugen* lies in a true state of beauty and gentleness. Tranquility and elegance make for *yugen* in personal appearance. In the same way, the *yugen* of discourse lies in a grace of language and a complete mastery of the speech of the nobility and gentry, so that even the most casual utterance will be graceful. With respect to a musical performance, it may be said to possess *yugen* when the melody flows beautifully and sounds smooth and sensitive. In the dance there will be *yugen* when the discipline has been thoroughly mastered and the audience is delighted by the beauty of the performer's movements and by his serene appearance. In acting, there will be *yugen* when the performance of the Three Roles is beautiful. If the characterization calls for a display of anger or for the representation of a devil, the actions may be somewhat forceful, but as long as the actor never loses sight of the beauty of the effect and bears in mind always the correct balance between his mental and physical actions and between the movements of his body and feet, his appearance will be so beautiful that it may be called "the *yugen* of a devil."

All these aspects of *yugen* must be kept in mind and made a part of the actor's body, so that whatever part he may be playing *yugen* will never be absent. Whether the character he portrays be of high or low birth, man or woman, priest, peasant, rustic, beggar, or outcast, he should think of each of them as crowned with a wreath of flowers. Although their positions in society differ, the fact that they can all appreciate the beauty of flowers makes flowers of all of them. Their particular flower is shown by their outward appearance. An actor, by the use of his intelligence, makes his presentation seem beautiful. It is through the use of intelligence that the above principles are thoroughly grasped; that poetry is learned so as to impart *yugen* to his discourse; that the most elegant costuming is studied so as to impart *yugen* to his bearing: though the characterization varies according to the different parts, the actor should realize that the ability to appear beautiful is the seed of *yugen*. It is all too apt to happen that an actor, believing that once he has mastered the characterization of the various parts he has attained the highest stage of excellence, forgets his appearances and therefore is unable to enter the realm of *yugen*. Unless an actor enters the realm of *yugen* he will not attain the highest achievements. If he fails to attain the highest achievements, he will not become a celebrated master. That is why there are so few masters. The actor must consider *yugen* as the most important aspect of his art and study to perfect his understanding of it.

The "highest achievement" of which I have spoken refers to beauty of form and manners. The most careful attention must therefore be given to the appearance presented. Accordingly, when we thoroughly examine the principles of *yugen* we see that when the form is beautiful, whether in dancing, singing, or in any type of characterization, it may properly be called the "highest achievement." When the form is poor, the performance will be inferior. The actor should realize that *yugen* is attained when all of the different forms of visual or aural expression are beautiful. It is when the actor himself has worked out these principles and made himself their master that he may be said to have entered the realm of *yugen*. If he fails to work out these principles for himself, he will not master them, and however much he may aspire to attain *yugen*, he will never in all his life do so.

Portrait of a Zen Master. Reflecting the chaos of the fourteenth century, the art of portraiture flourished, and artists produced a full gallery of warriors and holy men in startlingly realistic detail. This painting of a Zen master, complete with crooked mouth, stubble, and worry lines, is an unflattering one. Nevertheless, with economy of line, the artist has managed to convey the master's spiritual and mental intensity.

ON THE ONE MIND LINKING ALL POWERS

Sometimes spectators of the No say, "The moments of 'no-action' are the most enjoyable." This is an art which the actor keeps secret. Dancing and singing, movements and the different types of miming are all acts performed by the body. Moments of "no-action" occur in between. When we examine why such moments without actions are enjoyable, we find that it is due to the underlying spiritual strength of the actor which unremittingly holds the attention. He does not relax the tension when the dancing or singing come to an end or at intervals between the dialogue and the different types of miming, but maintains an unwavering inner strength. This feeling of inner strength will faintly reveal itself and bring enjoyment. However, it is undesirable for the actor to permit this inner strength to become obvious to the audience. If it

is obvious, it becomes an act, and is no longer "no-action." The actions before and after an interval of "no-action" must be linked by entering the state of mindlessness in which one conceals even from oneself one's intent. This, then, is the faculty of moving audiences, by linking all the artistic powers with one mind.

> Life and death, past and present—
> Marionettes on a toy stage.
> When the strings are broken,
> Behold the broken pieces.

This is a metaphor describing human life as it transmigrates between life and death. Marionettes on a stage appear to move in various ways, but in fact it is not they who really move—they are manipulated by strings. When these strings are broken, the marionettes fall and are dashed to pieces. In the art of the No too, the different sorts of miming are artificial things. What holds the parts together is the mind. This mind must not be disclosed to the audience. If it is seen, it is just as if a marionette's strings were visible. The mind must be made the strings which hold together all the powers of the arts. If this is done the actor's talent will endure. This resolution must not be confined to the times when the actor is appearing on the stage. Day or night, wherever he may be, whatever he may be doing, he should not forget this resolution, but should make it his constant guide, uniting all his powers. If he unremittingly works at this his talent will steadily grow. This article is the most secret of the secret teachings.

THE NINE STAGES OF THE NO IN ORDER

The Higher Three Stages

1. The flower of the miraculous
"At midnight in Silla the sun is bright."
The miraculous transcends the power of speech and is where the workings of the mind are defeated. And does "the sun at midnight" lie within the

realm of speech? Thus, in the art of the No, before the *yugen* of a master-actor all praise fails, admiration transcends the comprehension of the mind, and all attempts at classification and grading are made impossible. The art which excites such a reaction on the part of the audience may be called the flower of the miraculous.

2. The flower of supreme profundity

"Snow covers the thousand mountains—why does one lonely peak remain unwhitened?"

A man of old once said, "Mount Fuji is so high that the snow never melts." A Chinese disagreed, saying, "Mount Fuji is so deep...." What is extremely high is deep. Height has limits but depth is not to be measured. Thus the profound mystery of a landscape in which a solitary peak stands unwhitened amidst a thousand snow-covered mountains may represent the art of supreme profundity.

3. The flower of stillness

"Snow piled in a silver bowl."

When snow is piled in a silver bowl, the purity of its white light appears lambent indeed. May this not represent the flower of stillness?

The Middle Three Stages

1. The flower of truth

"The sun sinks in the bright mist, the myriad mountains are crimson."

A distant view of hills and mountains bathed in the light of the sun in a cloudless sky represents the flower of truth. It is superior to the art of versatility and exactness, and is already a first step towards the acquisition of the flowers of the art.

2. The art of versatility and exactness

"To tell everything—of the nature of clouds on the mountains, of moonlight on the sea."

To describe completely the nature of clouds on the mountains and of moonlight on the sea, of the whole expanse of green mountains that fills the eyes, this is indeed desirable in acquiring the art of versatility and exactness. Here is the dividing point from which one may go upward or downward.

3. The art of untutored beauty

"The Way of ways is not the usual way."

One may learn the Way of ways by traveling along the usual way. This means that the display of beauty should begin at the stage of the beginner. Thus the art of untutored beauty is considered the introduction to the mastery of the nine stages.

The Lower Three Stages

1. The art of strength and delicacy

"The metal hammer flashes as it moves, the glint of the precious sword is cold."

The movement of the metal hammer represents the art of strong action. The cold glint of the precious sword suggests the unadorned style of singing and dancing. It will stand up to detailed observation.

2. The art of strength and crudity

"Three days after its birth the tiger is disposed to devour an ox."

That the tiger cub only three days after its birth has such audacity shows its strength; but to devour an ox is crude.

3. The art of crudity and inexactness

"The squirrel's five talents."

Confucius said, "The squirrel can do five things. He can climb a tree, swim in the water, dig a hole, jump, and run: all of these are within its capacities but it does none well." When art lacks delicacy it becomes crude and inexact.

In the attainment of art through the nine stages, the actor begins with the middle group, follows with the upper group, and finally learns the lower three. When the beginner first enters the art of the No, he practices the various elements of dancing and singing. This represents the stage of untutored beauty. As the result of persistent training, his untutored style will develop into greater artistry, constantly improving until, before he is aware of it, it reaches the stage of versatility and exactness. At this stage if the actor's training is comprehensive and he expands his art in versatility and magnitude until he attains full competence, he will be at the stage of the flower of truth. The above are the stages from the learning of the Two Disciplines to the mastery of the Three Roles.

Next the actor progresses to the stage of calm and the flower that arouses admiration. It is the point where it becomes apparent whether or not he has realized the flower of the art. From this height the actor can examine with insight the preceding stages. He occupies a place of high achievement in the art of calm and the realization of the flower. This stage is thus called the flower of stillness.

Rising still higher, the actor achieves the ultimate degree of *yugen* in his performance, and reveals a degree of artistry which is of that middle ground where being and nonbeing meet. This is the flower of supreme profundity.

Above this stage, words fail before the revelation of the absolute miracle of the actor's interpretation. This is the flower of the miraculous. It is the end of the road to the higher mysteries of the art.

It should be noted that the origin of all these stages of the art may be found in the art of versatility and exactness. It is the foundation of the art of the No, for it is the point where are displayed the breadth and detail of performance which are the seeds of the flowers of the highest forms of the art. The stage of versatility and exactness is also the dividing line where is determined the actor's future. If he succeeds here in obtaining the flower of the art he will rise to the flower of truth; otherwise he will sink to the lower three stages.

The lower three stages are the turbulent waters of the No. They are easily understood and it is no special problem to learn them. It may happen, however, that an actor who has gone from the middle three stages to the upper three stages, having mastered the art of calmness and the flower of the miraculous, will purposely descend and indulge in the lower three stages. Then the special qualities of these stages will be blended with his art. However, many of the excellent actors of the past who had mounted to the upper three stages of the art refused to descend to the lower three. They were like the elephant of the story who refused to follow in the tracks of a rabbit. There has been only one instance of an actor who mastered all the stages— the middle, then the upper, and then the lower: this was the art of my late father. Many of the heads of theatres have been trained only up to the art of versatility and exactness and, without having risen to the flower of truth, have descended to the lower three stages, thus failing in the end to achieve success. Nowadays there are even actors who begin their training with the lower three stages and perform with such a background. This is not the proper order. It is therefore no wonder that many actors fail even to enter the nine stages.

There are three ways of entering the lower three stages. In the case of a great master who has entered the art by way of the middle stages, ascended to the upper stages of the art, and then descended to the lower stages, it is quite possible to give a superb performance even within the lower stages. Actors who have dropped to the lower stages from the level of versatility and exactness will be capable only of parts which call for strength with delicacy or crudity. Those actors who have willfully entered the art from the lower three stages have neither art nor fame and cannot be said even to be within the nine stages. Although they have taken the lower three stages as their goal, they fail even in this, to say nothing of reaching the middle three stages.

FOCUS QUESTIONS

1. What is *yugen?*
2. What is the role of beauty in No drama?
3. What makes good No actors?
4. How is No drama influenced by religion?

66

All Men Are Brothers (14th century C.E.)

SHIH NAI-AN

All Men Are Brothers, *a classic of Chinese literature, is a loosely connected novel composed of stories that had been part of an oral tradition before it was first written down in the fourteenth century. Very little is known of its supposed author, Shih Nai-an, and scholars continue to dispute whether this obscure bureaucrat did indeed codify the stories. The novel revolves around the activities of a group of bandits whose bravery and daring in the face of a corrupt government gain the support of the common people. The bandits live by their own code, expose official corruption, and deal out a form of rough justice.* All Men Are Brothers, *a very loose translation of its actual title, was so popular that it was banned in the seventeenth century and an Imperial decree was made to destroy all existing copies of the work.*

The story here involves Wu Sung, "the wounded star," who avenges his brother's murder by himself killing his brother's wife and her lover. He throws himself upon the mercy of the local court. The work is graphically and gratuitously violent.

It is said: So—Wu Sung told these four neighbors, "I, this humble one, swore I would revenge my brother's death and it was meet that I should commit this crime and although I die I shall not repent. Yet when I killed my sister-in-law I frightened you, Honorable Neighbors. Yet now when I go forth I cannot say whether it is to death or to life and so will I at this moment burn the tablet of my elder brother. As for all these household goods, I pray you to sell them for me that I may have silver wherewith to plead my case at court and to use in my need. Today I will go myself to the court and make report, and you are not to take on yourselves the task of judging whether my sin be light or heavy. Only be true witnesses for me."

Straightway then he burned the spirit tablet and the paper money. There were two boxes upstairs which he brought down and he opened them to see what was there and he gave all to the neighbors to sell for him. Then guarding the old woman Wang he drove her forth before him and taking up the two heads he went straight to the magistrate's court. By now he had aroused the whole city of Yang Ku and the people on the street to see him were beyond counting.

Now the magistrate had heard the report from one who came to tell it and first he was afraid and he went at once to his Hall Of Audience.

Thither did Wu Sung come still guarding that old woman Wang and he came and knelt in that hall before the magistrate and he placed there the dagger with which he had committed the fierce deed and he laid the two heads there. Then Wu Sung knelt at the right side and the old woman knelt in the center and the four neighbors knelt at the left, and Wu Sung drew out of his bosom the paper that the man Hu had written and he read it out from first to last. The magistrate commanded his assistants first to inquire into the old woman Wang's story and they all told the same tale. The witness of the four neighbors was equally clear. Then Ho and Yün Ko told their stories clearly and they also gave clear witness.

After this the magistrate called for those who were this day appointed to examine into wounds and causes of death and the like and he appointed one in charge of all and all these were sent under guard to the Street Of Purple Stone and there they examined carefully the body of the murdered woman, and below the Bridge Of The Lions in front of the wine shop they found also the body of Hsi Men Ch'ing. And they wrote down all they found, who these were who had been so killed and how old they were and all concerning them, and they returned to the court and placed their report there. Then the magistrate commanded long racks to be brought made of wood and these were fastened upon the necks of Wu Sung and the old woman and they were locked into gaol. As for the other common folk, they were put into the gatehouse.

Now the magistrate himself thought that Wu Sung was a very honorable, fearless fellow and he remembered the time when he had sent him to the capital city and he meditated in his heart upon all the goodness of Wu Sung and so he called to his presence the one in control of such matters as these and he said, "We must also remember that Wu Sung is a good fellow and we must change somewhat the stories that have been written down about him, and we will say that the matter came about because Wu Sung was about to sacrifice to his brother Wu The Elder and his sister-in-law would not let him and so because of this they struggled together. The woman pushed over the spirit tablet and Wu Sung because he would protect the box where the tablet stood and the spirit therein, in his anger killed her. Then Hsi Men Ch'ing, because he before this had evil intercourse with this woman, forced his way forward to protect her and so there was a struggle and neither could win over the other and thus struggling they fought their way to the Bridge Of The Lions and there Wu Sung killed him."

When this was written it was read to Wu Sung and he heard it and the magistrate wrote his explanation and sent all to the governor who was above him and he sent messengers to this governor and besought him to manage the affair.

Now although this city of Yang Ku was but a small county seat yet there were honorable and just men there who were of families of noble people, and these were all ready to help Wu Sung with silver and there were those who sent to him gifts of wine and food and money and rice. And Wu Sung went to the rooms where he lived and he took his possessions and gave them to a soldier and he took out some twelve or thirteen ounces of silver and gave these to Yün Ko's old father. Of all the soldiers who were under Wu Sung's command more than half made haste to send wines and meats and one appointed to it took the report of all these things and the proofs, the silver that Ho had kept, the bones, the confession the neighbor had written down from the murdered woman, and the knife with which Wu Sung had killed the pair. All these various men went also and they all set forth on the road toward the city called Tung P'ing, where the higher governor was.

All these men then gathered in front of this governor's court and all the onlookers crowded about the gates. When the governor, who was named Ch'en Wen Chao, heard what was come about he immediately went into his Hall Of Justice. Now this governor was a wise man and a man clever to examine into matters and he had already heard about this affair. So he commanded that all these persons be brought forward and there in the hall he looked first and read this report from the city of Yang Ku. Then he read all that had been written of what people had witnessed, and when this was done he questioned every man again himself and all the proofs, the silver, the bones, the knife, he took and wrapped up and he set his seal upon the parcel and he entrusted it to the keeper of such things in the court.

After this he took off the heavy rack that Wu Sung wore and put on his neck a light one in its place and put him in the gaol. As for the old woman, he had a heavy rack put upon her neck and cast her in that part of the gaol which was for those condemned to die. Then he called the representative of the magistrate at Yang Ku and he gave him an answering letter and he commanded Ho and Win Ko and the four neighbors, these six, to return first to the county seat and remain in their homes, and if they were summoned, to come quickly.

Among these who had come from the city of Yang Ku was the wife of Hsi Men Ch'ing and this one the governor ordered to remain in his court until later when judgment was come down from above and this matter might be decided.

Then Ho and Yün Ko and the four neighbors led all those who had come thither from the county seat and they returned again. Wu Sung was locked in the gaol and he had but a few soldiers to bring him food.

Now let it be told how the governor Ch'en pitied Wu Sung. He saw that Wu Sung was a righteous, brave man and he sent men to the gaol to see to him and because of this the gaol keepers and those who were in charge of the prisoners did not dare to ask Wu Sung for any money but they gave him wine and food to eat. The governor Ch'en corrected clearly all the reports and accusations that had been sent him of the matter and sent them all to the one who was yet above him and he sent a secret letter by one whom he trusted to go by day and by night to the capital to manage the affair rightly for him there.

Now that one who controlled the laws was a friend of the governor Ch'en's, and he reported this matter to the highest official and the degree of each crime was fixed thus; as for the old woman Wang she was the one who roused the evil desire between Hsi Men Ch'ing and the woman who was Wu The Elder's wife and she had deceived the woman and led her into evil with the man. Nor did the woman plan at first to kill her husband but the old woman bid her do it so that in the end she even poisoned her own husband. Moreover, it was this old hag who led this woman to drive out Wu Sung and prevent him from making sacrifice to his elder brother, and for this murder was done. Thus by enticing the woman and enticing the man she enticed them to violate a sacred relationship. According to the law, therefore, the old woman ought to die by the slicing of her flesh from her bones, bit by bit.

As for Wu Sung, although it was meet that he should revenge his brother's death and although he

did quarrel and kill Hsi Men Ch'ing, and although he went himself and reported his deed to the magistrate, yet his crime could not be forgiven and he must be branded on his face and exiled to some place many hundreds of miles away. As for the two who were adulterers, they were dead and it was not necessary to fix their sentence. As for all these other persons, they were to be released and restored to their homes.

When this judgment came it was to be carried out at once. When the governor Ch'en saw the answer that had come he wrote straightway a special proclamation and he bade Ho and Yün Ko and the four neighbors brought again to him and Hsi Men Ch'ing's wife also, the whole group of them, and they all went before the governor to hear the judgment. And Wu Sung was brought out of the jail and before all these the judgment was read aloud.

Then the rack was taken from Wu Sung's neck and his back was beaten forty strokes. But high and low they all protected Wu Sung and of these forty strokes only five or seven touched his flesh and a new rack was put upon his neck to hold his hands fast also as he went into exile, and upon his face were branded the two lines of gold letters, and after this he was sent step by step to Meng Chou. As for these other persons, all was done to them according to the judgment and each was allowed to go home.

But out of the great gaol the old woman Wang was brought and she stood alone before them all to hear her sentence. When it had been read to her, her crime was written down upon a placard and she set her own mark there. Then this old woman was laid across a rack of wood, a beam set upon four posts, and four long nails were pinned through her and three ropes also bound her fast and a sign was written upon her that she was to be sliced to strips. Then the rack was carried through the city and upon broken drums and gongs a great noise was made. In front of her a banner was held high telling of her crime and behind her came guards with poles who urged them on, and they held aloft two sharp-pointed knives, from which waved bunches of paper flowers. The procession was led to the part of the city that was most crowded and there the old woman was sliced.

FOCUS QUESTIONS

1. What does Wu Sung expect will happen to him after he murders his sister-in-law?
2. What is the role of the four neighbors?
3. Why is the old woman made the victim?
4. What is the basis for the way Wu Sung is judged?
5. Why would the story of Wu Sung be popular? What lessons would it teach?

67

The Yangzhou Massacre (1645 C.E.)

ANONYMOUS

The fall of the Ming Dynasty left China in political and economic chaos. Civil wars raged throughout the land of self-appointed peasant leaders, who gathered marauding armies that plundered the countryside. Hundreds of thousands died when the dikes of the Yellow River were cut in 1642. By the early 1640s, there was a power struggle taking place between Ming loyalists and supporters of the Manchu, who made clear their desire to become emperors. Several bloody battles ensued before full-scale resistance to the Manchu was organized in the city of Yangzhou on the Yellow River. After a brief siege, the city was taken and in retaliation for its opposition its inhabitants were put to the sword. Contemporary estimates put the death toll at tens of thousands, some say hundreds of thousands, and the fate of Yangzhou became a warning of the fate that awaited other opponents of the Manchu.

This anonymous account survived by chance, the manuscript making its way to Japan. Though it is a harrowing account told in first person by a terrified survivor, it allows us to glimpse the nature of warfare at the end of China's long period of civil disturbances. While the Yangzhou Massacre was not the worst of atrocities committed against the Chinese people, it is a particularly well-documented one.

On the 14th of the fourth month of 1645, Commandant Shi Kefa gave up the defense of Boyanghe and retreated to Yangzhou. Ordering the city gates closed, he prepared for a siege. Up to the 24th, the city remained unconquered and our soldiers held all of the gates. My house was in the eastern part of the new city, where a general named Yang was in command. His officers and soldiers stood around like chessmen....

Early in the afternoon the next day, my wife's relatives came from Guazhou to take refuge from the Earl of Xingping's fleeing soldiers. My wife, not having seen the family for a long time, was greatly cheered. By then one or two people had already told me that a large force of enemy soldiers was about to enter the city. I rushed out to ask people about it. Someone said, "They're our reinforcements from Huang Degong, Marquis of Qingnan."

I noticed that the guards on the wall were still quiet and orderly but that people in the streets were getting excited. Crowds of barefoot and disheveled refugees were flocking into the city. When questioned, they were too distraught to reply. At that point dozens of mounted soldiers in confused waves came surging south looking as though they had given up all hope. Along them appeared a man who turned out to be the commandant himself. It seems he had intended to leave by the east gate but could not because the enemy soldiers outside the wall were drawing too near; he was therefore forced to cut across this part of town to reach the south gate. This is how we first learned for sure that the enemy troops would enter the city.

Just then a mounted soldier with slackened reins rode slowly north, his face upturned, wailing. Two soldiers walked in front of his horse, not willing to let go of the reins. This image is still vivid in my memory, and I wish I had learned the man's name. When the rider was still some way off, the panicky guards on the city walls began to jump, discarding their helmets and spears, some breaking their legs or even their necks. By the time I looked back at the guard tower on the city wall, it was empty.

The commandant had seen that the city wall was too narrow for the cannon to be set up there and so had ordered a platform to be erected, one side resting on the footpath on the wall and the other against the houses opposite. This way more space was available for deploying the cannon. Yet before this work could be finished, the enemy soldiers had scaled the wall, swords in hand, and begun the carnage. This caused those defending the wall to flee in such disorder that they clogged the exits. Many of them ran to the cannon platforms which had been set up and climbed on their hands and knees in an attempt to cross over to the houses behind. The platforms were not stable and collapsed as soon as the weight of the people became too great; people fell like leaves, eight or nine out of ten dashed to death. Those who reached the houses shattered the roof tiles as they trampled on them, making a noise which reverberated in all directions and sounded like the clash of swords or

severe hail. The people inside the houses, in their terror and confusion, poured out by the hundreds. At the same time every room and courtyard, even bedrooms, was invaded by those who had jumped from the roofs in their frantic search for hiding places. The owners were powerless to prevent it. In my neighborhood all the doors were tightly fastened, everyone holding his or her breath.

My house backed against the city wall, and peeping through the chinks in my window, I saw the soldiers on the wall marching south then west, solemn and in step. Although the rain was beating down, it did not seem to disturb them. This reassured me because I gathered that they were well-disciplined units.

Then I heard urgent knocking at my door, which turned out to be my neighbors. They had agreed to try to placate and welcome the "royal army." As a sign of submission, they wanted to set up tables and place burning incense on them. I knew that nothing much could help, but having no other way to calm them, I tentatively agreed. Thereupon I changed my clothes and stuck out my head to watch and wait. For a long time no one came. I retreated again to the back window and found that the regiment on the wall had broken ranks; some soldiers were walking about, others standing still.

All of a sudden I saw some soldiers escorting a group of women dressed in Yangzhou fashion. This was my first real shock. Back in the house, I said to my wife, "Should things go badly when the soldiers enter the city, you may need to end your life."

"Yes," she replied, "Whatever silver we have you should keep. I think we women can stop thinking about life in this world." She gave me all the silver, unable to control her crying.

At this point a townsman came rushing in and shouted, "They've come! They've come!" I dashed out and saw a few mounted soldiers coming from the north, riding slowly with reins in hand. As soon as they reached the group who were welcoming the royal army, they lowered their heads as if to consult with each other. Each of us was looking out for himself and not talking to the others, even though we were only an arm's length apart.

As the soldiers grew nearer I discovered that they were going from door to door demanding money. They were not extravagant in their demands, however, leaving as soon as they were given a little. In cases where they failed to get any, they waved their swords about but did not strike anyone. Finally they came to my door. One mounted soldier pointed to me and yelled to another behind him, "Search the man in blue for me." But before the man had dropped his reins, I had run away. He did not try to pursue me, but remounted and rode off.

I thought to myself, "I am wearing rough clothes and look like a commoner. Why did he pick on me?" Soon my younger brother arrived, then my two older brothers. We discussed the situation and I said, "The people who live in our neighborhood are all rich merchants. It will be disastrous if they think we are rich too." I then urged my brothers to brave the rain and quickly take the women by the back route to my older brother's house. His home was situated behind Mr. He's graveyard and was surrounded by the huts of poor families. I stayed behind alone to see what was going to happen. A long time passed as I nervously waited for my eldest brother to return. I could find "no way up to Heaven nor any door down to earth." Besides, it rained in torrents.

Finally, my eldest brother reappeared and said, "People are being killed in the streets! What are we waiting for here? It doesn't matter so much whether we live or die, as long as we brothers stay together." Immediately I gathered together our ancestral tablets and went with him to our second brother's house. There ten people in all (my one younger and two elder brothers, my elder brother's wife, a nephew, my own wife and son, my wife's younger brother and sister, and I) took refuge.

As it grew darker, we could hear soldiers butchering people outside our door. As a temporary refuge, we climbed to the roof. In the downpour we ten squatted together covered only by a rug, our tangled hair soaked through. The bitter cries, resounding through the air, pierced my ears and wrenched my soul. Not until very late that night did we have the courage to come down from the roof and start a fire to cook some rice. By then fires

had broken out everywhere in the city. More than a dozen places close by were ablaze, as were innumerable ones further off. The red glow flashed like lightning or a sunset as the crackling ceaselessly thundered in our ears. We could hear the faint sounds of people being beaten. Even the wind wailed with an inexpressible bitterness.

When the rice was cooked, we stared at each other, so overcome with grief that we were unable to raise our chopsticks to eat. We were equally unable to think of a plan. My wife took the silver she had given me and divided it into four shares. Each of us brothers hid one share so that our clothes, hats, shoes, and belts were all stuffed. My wife also found a ragged coat and worn-out pair of shoes for me to change into. That done, we lay awake with our eyes wide open until dawn. During the night there seemed to be a bird in the air, twittering like a reed organ or sobbing like a child, hovering somewhere not too high above our heads. Everyone reported having heard it.

The 26th. After a while, the fires began to abate and the day gradually brightened. Once more we climbed up to the roof to hide but found that a lot of people had already sought refuge there by the rain gutters.

Without any warning a man from the building east of us began to scramble up our wall. A soldier with his sword drawn was running after him. But when he saw our group, he abandoned the chase and made directly for us. In alarm I sneaked down as fast as I could. My brothers followed immediately, none of us stopping until we had run over a hundred paces. In our escape I lost track of my wife and son and did not know whether they had been killed.

The cunning soldiers, suspecting that many people were still hidden, tried to entice them out by posting a placard promising clemency. About fifty to sixty people, half of them women, emerged. My elder brother said, "We four by ourselves will never survive if we run into these vicious soldiers, so we had better join the crowd. Since there are so many of them, escape will be easier. Even if things do not turn out well, as long as we are together, we will have no cause for regret." In our bewilderment we could think of no other way to save our lives. Thus agreed, we went to join the group.

The leaders were three Manchu soldiers. They searched my brothers and found all the silver they were carrying, but left me untouched. At that point some women appeared, two of whom called out to me. I recognized them as the concubines of my friend Mr. Zhu Shu and stopped them anxiously. They were disheveled and partly naked, their feet bare and covered with mud up to the ankles. One was holding a girl whom the soldiers hit with a whip and threw into the mud. Then we were immediately driven on. One soldier, sword in hand, took the lead; another drove us from behind with a long spear; and a third walked along on our right and left flanks alternately, making sure no one escaped. In groups of twenty or thirty we were herded along like sheep and cattle. If we faltered we were struck, and some people were even killed on the spot. The women were tied together with long chains around their necks, like a clumsy string of pearls. Stumbling at every step, they were soon covered with mud. Here and there on the ground lay babies, trampled by people or horses. Blood and gore soaked the fields, which were filled with the sound of sobbing. We passed gutters and ponds piled high with corpses; the blood had turned the water to a deep greenish-red color and filled the ponds to the brim.

We arrived at the house of the jailer, Yao Yongyan. Entering through the back door, we passed through many rooms and found bodies everywhere. I supposed that this was where we would die. We went through several rooms until we came to the street door. We then entered the house of the Shanxi merchant, Jiao Chengwang, which had been taken over by the three soldiers. Another soldier was already there. He had seized several attractive women and was rifling their trunks for fancy silks, which he piled in a heap. Seeing the three soldiers arrive, he laughed and pushed several dozen of us into the back hall. The women he led into a side chamber.

In that room there were two square tables at which three tailors and a middle-aged woman were making clothes. The woman was a local resident. Her face was heavily made up and she was wearing brightly colored clothes. She laughed and flirted, seeming to be in high spirits. Whenever she came across anything fine, she shamelessly tried to wheedle it away from the soldiers. The soldiers often said to people, "When we conquered Korea, we captured tens of thousands of women, and yet not one of them lost her chastity. How can there be so little shame in a great country like China?"

The three soldiers stripped the women of their wet clothing all the way to their underwear, then ordered the seamstress to measure them and give them new garments. The women, thus coerced, had to expose themselves and stand naked. What shame they endured! Once they had changed, the soldiers grabbed them and forced them to join them in eating and drinking, then did whatever they pleased with them, without any regard for decency.

One soldier suddenly jumped up, his sword drawn, and cried out, "Come on, you southern Barbarians!" Several of those standing in the front had already been tied up, my eldest brother among them. Saying to me, "What alternative do we have?" he took my hand and ran forward. My younger brother also followed. The fifty-odd men who were bound were so scared that they could not move, even when the soldiers raised their swords and shouted. Right behind my eldest brother, I rushed out of the hall, but soon discovered that the slaughter was going on outside as well as inside. Outside a group of people were standing in a row awaiting their fate. At first I thought of submitting, but suddenly my heart took a leap, and, as if helped by some spirit, I sprang away quickly and returned to the back hall without attracting the attention of any of the bound men.

The western section of the building, where many old women still remained, was not a safe place for me to hide, and so I slipped out back. It was impossible for me to walk through that area, though, because it was filled with horses and camels. Trembling, I dropped to the floor and crawled under the bellies of these beasts. If the slightest thing had startled them, I would have been trampled into the mud.

After passing through several courtyards, I could locate no way out except a side alley leading to the back door. But this door was fastened tightly with an iron lock. Once more I headed out to the front along the lane, but hearing people being killed in the front panicked me. I looked back, and on the left side I saw four people in the kitchen. It seemed they had been captured and forced to do the cooking. I begged them to let me attend the fire or draw water for them so that I could save myself. But they adamantly refused, "Whenever we four are ordered to work, they call the roll. If they find more people next time, they will surely suspect some trick, and our lives will be in jeopardy." I appealed to them plaintively, but this made them even more angry and they threatened to hand me over. With this I left, more anxious than ever.

Not very far from the house I saw some steps and a platform on which a jar had been placed. I climbed up the platform, but no sooner had I touched the jar than I fell off. The jar had been empty, and I had inadvertently used too much force. Seeing no alternatives, once more I ran to the door at the end of the lane. Using both hands I shook the lock a hundred times but failed to make it move. I struck it with stones, but the sound was loud enough to reach the outer courtyard and I was afraid of being heard. So I reverted to shaking the lock, my fingers aching and bleeding. Then unexpectedly the lock turned! I pulled at it with all my strength and soon had it off. Next I tried the bolt which was made of hibiscus wood. Water-logged from the rain, it was swollen and twice as solid as the lock. I pulled on the bolt with all my might. Instead of the bolt loosening, the hinges ripped off, the door fell flat, and the wall collapsed with a sound like a thunderclap.

I leapt over it as if flying. Where such strength came from I have no idea. With all possible speed, I ran out the back door and found myself at the base of the city wall. Foot soldiers and horsemen were everywhere, making it impossible to go forward. Therefore I turned at the back door of a house to the left of the Jiaos' residence and elbowed my way in. Any place that was safe was full of people who did not want to let any more in. This house was divided, back to front, into five rooms, all of which were crowded like this. I made my way straight to the front gate. Because it was close to the street where soldiers were endlessly streaming by, it was considered a dangerous spot and deserted. Entering quickly, I found a bed with a wooden canopy. I climbed on top of it by way of the pillars and crouched to conceal myself.

Scarcely had I regained my breath when I heard the sound of my younger brother wailing, coming from the other side of the wall. Then I heard the blows of the sword. After three blows there was silence. A few moments later I heard my elder brother implore, "I have silver in the cellar at home. Release me and I will go and fetch it for you." There was one blow, then silence again. For a time my spirit was wrenched out of my body; my heart was boiling, my eyes tearless, my innards torn. No longer in control of myself, all I wanted was to die.

Later on a soldier brought a woman in and wanted her to sleep with him in the bed below me. Despite her refusal, he forced her to yield. "This is too near the street. It is not a good place to stay," the woman said. I was almost discovered, but after a time the soldier departed with the woman.

The room had a ceiling which seemed to be made of matting. It was not strong enough to sustain the weight of a man, but if I could creep across it, I could reach the beam. I climbed up by holding the rafters with both hands and resting my foot on the projecting roof pole. Inside it was pitch black, since the mat was underneath. Every time the soldiers came in they would thrust upward through the matting with their spears and, finding it empty, conclude that no one was up there. Thus I managed to end the day without encountering any more soldiers. But I have no idea how many were slaughtered underneath me. Every time a few mounted soldiers passed along the street, dozens of men and women, loudly lamenting, would be trailing behind them. As the day was cloudy, I could not judge this time. A long time passed, then mounted soldiers came less and less frequently until only the incessant weeping of the people could be heard from the outside.

I thought of my brothers, two of whom were already dead. I did not know the fate of my eldest brother or the whereabouts of my son and wife. I wanted to find them and see them again. Therefore I slowly climbed down from my hiding place by holding onto the beam and furtively made my way to the front street. The heads of the corpses in the street were piled up on each other like pillows, and as it grew dark, it was impossible to recognize them. I bent over several corpses and called out, but received no answer. To the south I saw the torches of a confused crowd approaching and quickly got out of their way. As I walked along the foot of the city wall, I constantly stumbled against dead bodies. Whenever I heard something I dropped to the ground and pretended to be a corpse myself. After a long while I reached a path. In the darkness people could not see each other and often collided. But the main street was lit by torches and was as bright as day. Walking from seven to nine in the evening, I finally reached my elder brother's house.

I found the door closed and was afraid to knock. Then I heard my sister-in-law's voice. I knocked gently a few times, and my wife came to answer. My eldest brother had come back earlier, and both my wife and son were there. I wept with my eldest brother but did not dare to tell him of the deaths of our other brothers. My sister-in-law questioned me, but I gave her only vague replies....

When dawn brought in the 29th, five days had passed since the 25th, and I was beginning to imagine that by some stroke of fortune we might be spared. But then I heard some garbled stories about a planned wholesale slaughter of the population. It seemed that over half of those who had survived so far had decided to risk their lives in an attempt to flee by climbing over the city walls with ropes, but so many were killed that the moat became as flat as a road from the corpses, and suffering reached a new height. Those who did escape had to face the bandits who at night waited stealthily in groups by the moat and robbed the refugees of their gold and silver.

With the danger so great and my eldest brother unwilling to be separated from us, we decided not to try escape. But I worried all night; our old hiding place was no longer safe, and my wife had already had to plead pregnancy to survive. Finally we decided I would hide in the dense weeds by the pond and my wife and [son] Penger would lie on top. Though the soldiers repeatedly forced them to come out of hiding, they were able to induce them to go away by offering money.

At length, however, there came a soldier of the "Wolf Men" tribe, a vicious-looking man with a head like a mouse and eyes like a hawk. He attempted to abduct my wife. She was obliged to creep forward on all fours, pleading as she had with the others, but to no avail. When he insisted that she stand up, she rolled on the ground and refused. He then beat her so savagely with the flat of his sword that the blood flowed out in streams, totally soaking her clothes. Because my wife had once admonished me, "If I am unlucky I will die no matter what; do not plead for me as a husband or you will get caught too," I acted as if I did not know she was being beaten and hid far away in the grass, convinced she was about to die. Yet the depraved soldier did not step there; he grabbed her by the hair, cursed her, struck her cruelly, and then dragged her away by the leg. There was a small path about an arrow's shot in length winding out from the field to the main street. The soldier dragged my wife along this and every few steps would hit her again. Just then they ran into a body of mounted soldiers. One of them said a few words to the soldier in Manchu. At this he dropped my wife and departed with them. Barely able to crawl back, she let out a loud sob, every part of her body injured.

Suddenly the whole city was ablaze. The thatched huts surrounding He's graveyard were quickly reduced to ashes. Only one or two houses, a little separated from the others, were fortunate enough to escape. Those hidden in the houses now were forced out by the fire, and ninety-nine in a hundred were killed as they showed themselves. Those who stayed inside, sometimes up to a hundred people in a single house, were cremated; their numbers now will never be known.

At this point it was no longer possible to hide. If caught, whether we offered money or not, we would be killed. The only recourse left was to go to the roadsides and lie among the corpses so that no one could distinguish us from the dead. My son, my wife, and I went and lay among the graves, so dirty and muddy from head to foot we did not look at all human.

As time passed the fire raged fiercer. The lofty trees around the graves caught fire; it glowed like lightning and roared like a landslide. The violence of the wind made the fire burn so brilliantly that the sun seemed to turn pale. To us it looked as though countless demons were driving hundreds and thousands of people into hell. Many times we fainted with fright, hardly sure whether we were still among the living. Then, startled by the sound of loud footsteps and terrible screams, I spotted my eldest brother some way off, standing beside a wall struggling with a soldier who had caught him. Since he was very strong, he succeeded in throwing off the soldier and began to run away, but was instantly pursued. The soldier I recognized as the man who the previous day had abducted and then released my wife. By midday my brother had not returned and my heart began to pound.

Finally he came running, with no clothes on and his hair undone, driven along by the soldier. Out of desperation he asked me for silver to save his life. I had only one ingot left, but I took it out and offered it to the soldier. Seeing it made him so angry that he struck my brother with his sword. The latter rolled to the ground, his body bathed in blood. Penger, only five years old, pulled at the soldier and cried for him to stop. The man then wiped the blood from his sword on my son's clothes. Had he delivered one more blow, my brother would surely have died. Next the soldier grabbed me by the hair and demanded more silver, hitting me over and over again with the back of his sword. I apologized for having no more silver and said, "If you insist on silver, then I am afraid I shall die, but there are other things I can give you." Without letting go of my hair, he went with me to Mrs. Hong's house. On the steps I poured out the contents of two earthenware jars full of my wife's possessions and let the soldier take what he wanted. He grabbed all my wife's gold and pearl jewelry and the best of her clothes. Seeing the silver locket around my son's neck, he took his sword and cut it off. When he left he turned and said, "Even though I did not kill you, someone else will." I then knew it was true that the city was to be razed; our death seemed inevitable.

After leaving our son at the house, my wife and I quickly went out to look for my brother. We found that his neck had a gash an inch deep on both the front and the back, and his chest had even worse wounds. We helped him to Mrs. Hong's house, where he lay confused and half insensible to the pain. After attending to him, we went back to hide in our old place.

Our neighbors were all hidden among the rushes. Someone yelled to me, "Tomorrow the city will be razed and no one will be spared. You had better abandon your wife and flee with me." My wife also advised me to go, but I kept thinking of the danger my brother was in. How could I bear to leave him? So far I had relied on my supply of silver; now that it was gone I realized we could not survive. Brooding on this, I lost consciousness.

It took a long time before I came to my senses. I saw that fires in the city were gradually dying down, and I heard a cannon fired three times in the distance. The soldiers on patrol were decreasing in number. My wife clutched our boy as we sat together in a manure pit....

Unexpectedly there appeared a handsome-looking man of less than thirty, a double-edged sword hung by his side, dressed in Manchu-style hat, red coat, and a pair of black boots. His follower, in a yellow jacket, was also very gallant in appearance. Immediately behind them were several residents of Yangzhou. The young man in red, inspecting me closely, said, "I would judge from your appearance that you are not one of these people. Tell me honestly, what class of person are you?"

I remembered that some people had obtained pardons and others had lost their lives the moment they said that they were poor scholars. So I did not dare come out at once with the truth and instead concocted a story. He pointed to my wife and son and asked who they were, and I told him the truth. "Tomorrow the prince will order that all swords be sheathed and all of you will be spared," he said and then commanded his followers to give us some clothes and an ingot of silver. He also asked me, "How many days have you been without food?"

"Five days," I replied.

"Then come with me," he commanded. Although we only half trusted him, we were afraid to disobey. He led us to a well-stocked house, full of rice, fish, and other provisions. "Treat these four people well," he said to a woman in the house and then left.

By this time night had already fallen. We learned that my wife's brother had been carried off by the soldiers. Now knowing whether he was dead or alive, my wife was in a state of grief. A few moments later the old woman brought some boiled rice and fish for us to eat. Since we were not very far from Mrs. Hong's house, I took some food to my eldest brother, but he could not eat more than a few mouthfuls because his throat was too sore to swallow. I wiped his hair and washed his wounds, my heart rent by his condition. However, knowing of the order to end the slaughter in the city made us all feel somewhat comforted.

The next day was the last of the fifth month. Killing and pillaging continued, although not on the previous scale. Still the mansions of the rich were thoroughly looted, and almost all the teenage girls were abducted. On this day the Earl of Xingping reentered Yangzhou, and every grain of rice, every inch of silk now entered these tigers' mouths. The resulting devastation is beyond description.

The 2nd. Civil administration was established in all the prefectures and counties; proclamations were issued aimed at calming the people, and monks from each temple were ordered to burn corpses. The temples themselves were clogged with women who had taken refuge, many of whom had died of fright or starvation. The "List of Corpses Burned" records more than eight hundred thousand, and this list does not include those who jumped into wells, threw themselves into the river, hanged themselves, were burned to death inside houses, or were carried away by the soldiers.

The 3rd. Distribution of food was announced. I went with old Mrs. Hong to the Juekou Gate to get some rice. This rice, heaped as high as a mound, was part of what the commandant had stored as rations for his troops. Several thousand bushels soon disappeared. The people lined up for food had scorched hair, smashed heads, broken legs and arms, and sword cuts all over their faces which resembled streams of wax pouring down from a candle. In the struggle for rice, even friends and relatives ignored each other. The strong got some and then returned for more, while the old, weak, or severely wounded were not able to get a single ration all day long.

The 4th. As the sky was clear, the sun shone hot, and the bodies began to smell. Everywhere around us the dead were being burned; the smoke gathered like a mist, and the stench permeated the area. On the day I burned some cotton along with some bones of the dead and used the ashes as a salve for my brother's wounds. Unable to speak, he could only nod to me through silent tears.

The 5th. By now those who had remained hidden were beginning to reappear. Upon meeting one another, people would cry but were at a loss for words.

We five, although less apprehensive than before, still did not dare to stay home. Early in the morning we got up and, after eating a little food, went out to a deserted field. We dressed in the same fashion as before because of the hundreds of foragers roving about. Although they carried no swords, they intimidated people with clubs and seized their possessions. Anyone who tried to resist them was clubbed to death, and any woman they encountered was molested. At first we did not know whether they were Manchu soldiers, our own guards, or commoners-turned-bandits.

That day my brother's wounds festered, broke open, and he died. Words cannot express my grief.

When this calamity began there had been eight of us: my two elder brothers, my younger brother, my elder brother's wife, their son, my wife, my son, and myself. Now only three of us survived for sure, though the fate of my wife's brother and sister-in-law was not yet known.

From the 25th of the fourth month to the 5th of the fifth month was a period of ten days. I have described here only what I actually experienced or saw with my own eyes; I have not recorded anything I picked up from rumors or hearsay. The younger generation is now fortunate enough to enjoy the blessing of peace and has grown lax. Reading this account should wake them up.

FOCUS QUESTIONS

1. How did the siege of Yangzhou take place? Why were the attackers more successful than the defenders?

2. What was the first priority of those attempting to save their lives?

3. What honor did the marauders display in making and keeping promises?

4. Which were the atrocities that especially held the attention of the author? What does this say about his values and his fears?

European Encounters

Spaniard Kicking American Indian. The Spanis attitude toward the native inhabitants of their colonies is ex-emplified by this sixteenth-century drawing of a spurred Spaniard kicking an already kneeling, service native.

FOCUS QUESTIONS

1. Why is there a mule in the picture?

2. The Spaniard has a mustache, but the native man is clean-faced. What could this mean?

3. Why is the Spaniard kicking the American Indian in the throat?

4. The American Indian's hands are reaching toward the flat of the Spaniard's sword. What does this signify?

68

The History of the Great and Mightie Kingdom of China (1585 C.E.)

JUAN GONZALEZ DE MENDOZA

Juan Gonzalez de Mendoza was a Spanish missionary who spent most of his early life abroad. He went first to Mexico City, where he was involved with the earliest missions from Spanish America to the Philippines. His interest in missionary work in Asia led to his return to Spain and to an audience with King Philip II. Although Mendoza hoped to be appointed to a second mission to the Philippines, instead he remained in Madrid to process the reports sent back from the Asian missions. In 1580 he was appointed one of the heads of a new mission to China, but by the time he reached Spanish America the mission had been postponed. Mendoza returned to Europe and was called to Rome and commissioned by the Pope to collect all of the information that was known about China. The result was The History of the Great and Mightie Kingdom of China *(1585), one of the most popular books of the sixteenth century, going through forty-six editions in fifteen years.*

Mendoza compiled his history from the few eyewitness accounts of early Portuguese ambassadors and from the dispatches of Christian missionaries. He read everything that had previously been written about China and synthesized it in a lively and direct style. His work is notable for its description of the political structure of Ming rule as well as for its description of social customs. The following selection includes his famous description of the custom of footbinding.

Both men and women of this countrie are of a good disposition of their bodies, well proportioned and gallant men, somewhat tall: they are all for the most part brode faced, little eyes and flat noses, and without bearde save only upon the ball of the chinne: but yet there be some that have great eyes and goodly beardes, and their faces well proportioned, yet of these sorts (in respect of the others) are verie few: and it is to bee beleeved that these kinde of people doo proceede of some strange nation, who in times past when it was lawfull to deale out of that countrie, did joyne one with another.

Those of the province of Canton (which is a hot country) be browne of colour like to the Moores: but those that be farther within the countrie be like unto Almaines, Italians and Spanyardes, white and redde, and somewhat swart. All of them do suffer their nailes of their left hande to grow very long, but the right hand they do cut: they have long haire, and esteeme it very much and maintaine it with curiositie: of both they make a superstition, for that they say thereby they shall be carried into heaven. They do binde their haire up to the crowne of their heade, in calles of golde verie curious, and with pinnes of the same.

The garments which the nobles and principals do use, bee of silke of different colours, of the which they have excellent good and verie perfite: the common and poore people doo apparell themselves with another kinde of silke more courser, and with linnen, serge, and cotton: of all the which there is great abundance. And for that the countrie for the most part is temperate, they may suffer this kinde of apparell, which is the heaviest that they doo use: for in all the whole kingdome they have no cloth, neither doo they suffer it to be made, although they have great aboundance of woolle, and very good cheape: they do use their coates according unto our old use of antiquities with long skirts and full of plaites, and a flappe over the brest to be made fast under the left side, the sleeves verie bigge and wide: upon their coates they doo use cassockes or long garments according unto the possibilitie of either of them, made according as wee doo use, but only their sleeves are more wider. They of royall bloode and such as are constituted unto dignitie, do differ in their apparell from the other ordinarie gentlemen: for that the first have their garments laide on with gold and silver downe to the waste, and the others alonely garnished on the edges, or hem: they do use hose verie well made and stitched, shoes and buskins of velvet, verie curious. In the winter (although it be not very colde,) they have their garments furred with beasts skins, but in especiall with Martas Cevellinas, of the which they have great aboundance (as aforesaid) and generally they do use them at all times about their necks. They that be not married doo differ from them that be married, in that they do kirrle their haire on their foreheade, and wear higher hattes. Their women do apparell themselves verie curiouslie, much after the fashion of Spaine: they use many jewels of gold and precious stones: their gownes have wide sleeves; that wherewith they do apparel themselves is of cloath of gold and silver and divers sortes of silkes, whereof they have great plentie, as aforesaid, and excellent good, and good cheape: and the poore folkes doo apparell themselves with velvet, unshorne velvet and serge. They have verie faire haire, and doo combe it with great care and diligence, as do the women of Genouay, and do binde it about their heade with a broad silke lace, set full of pearles and precious stones, and they say it doth become them verie well: they doo use to paint themselves, and in some place in excesse.

Amongst them they account it for gentilitie and a gallant thing to have little feete, and therefore from their youth they so swadell and binde them verie straight, and do suffer it with patience: for that she who hath the least feete is accounted the gallantest dame. They say that the men hath induced them unto this custome, for to binde their feete so harde, that almost they doo loose the forme of them, and remaine halfe lame, so that their going is verie ill, and with great travell: which is the occasion that they goe but little abroad, and fewe times doo rise up from their worke that they do; and was invented onely for the same intent. This custome hath indured manie yeares, and will indure many more, for that it is stablished for a law: and that woman which doth breake it, and not use it with her children, shalbe counted as evill, yea shalbe punished for the same. They are very secreat and honest, in such sort that you shall not see at any time a woman at her window nor at her doores: and if her husband doo invite any person to dinner, she is never seene nor eateth not at the table, except the gest be a kinsman or a very friende: when they go abroade to visite their father, mother, or any other kinsfolkes, they are carried in a little chaire by foure men, the which is made close, and with lattises rounde about made of golde wyre and with silver, and curteines of silke; that although they doo see them that be in the streete, yet they cannot be seene. They have many servants waiting on them. So that it is a great marvell when that you shall meete a principall woman in the streete, yea you will thinke that there are none in the citie, their keeping in is such: the lameness of their feet is a great helpe thereunto. The women as well as the men be ingenious; they doo use drawne workes and carved works, excellent painters of flowers, birds and beasts, as it is to be seene upon beddes and bords that is brought from thence. I did see my selfe, one that was brought unto Lysborne in the yeare 1582, by Captaine Ribera, chiefe sergant of

Manilla, that it was to be wondred at the excellencie thereof: it caused the kings majestie to have admyration, and he is a person that little wondreth at things. All the people did wonder at it: yea the famous imbroiderers did marvaile at the curiousnesse thereof. They are great inventers of things, that although they have amongst them many coches and wagons that goe with sailes, and made with such industrie and policie that they do governe them with great ease: this is crediblie informed by many that have seen it: besides that, there be many in the Indies, and in Portugall, that have seene them painted upon clothes, and on their earthen vessell that is brought from thence to be solde: so that it is a signe that their painting hath some foundation. In their buying and selling they are verie subtill, in such sort that they will depart a haire. Such merchants as do keepe shoppes (of whom in every citie there is a great number) they have a table or signe hanging at their doore, whereon is written all such merchandise as is within to be sold.

That which is commonly sold in their shops is cloth of golde and silver, cloth of tissue, silkes of divers sorts and excellent colours: others there be of poorer sort that selleth serges, peeces of cotton, linnen and fustian of all colours; yet both the one and the other is verie goode cheape, for that there is great aboundance, and many workemen that do make it. The apothecarie that selleth simples, hath the like table: there be also shops full of earthen vessels of divers making, redde, greene, yellow, and gilt; it is so good cheape that for foure rials of plate they give fiftie peeces: very strong earth, the which they doo breake all to peeces and grinde it, and put it into sesternes with water, made of lime and stone; and after that they have well tumbled and tossed it in the water, of the creame that is upon it they make the finest sort of them, and the lower they go, spending that substance that is the courser: they make them after the forme and fashion as they do here, and afterward they do gild them, and make them of what colour they please, the which will never be lost: then they put them into their killes and burne them. This hath beene seene and is of a truth, as appeareth in a booke set foorth in the Italian toonge, by Duardo Banbosa, that they do make them of periwinkle shelles of the sea: the which they do grinde and put them under the ground to refine them, whereas they lie 100 years: and many other things he doth treat of to this effect. But if that were true, they should not make so great a number of them as is made in that kingdome, and is brought into Portugall, and carried into the Peru, and Nova Espania, and into other parts of the world: which is a sufficient proofe for that which is said. And the Chinos do agree for this to be true. The finest sort of this is never carried out of the countries for that it is spent in the service of the king, and his governours, and is so fine and deere, that it seemeth to be of fine and perfite cristal: that which is made in the province of Saxii is the best and finest. Artificers and mechanicall officers doo dwell in streets appointed, whereas none do dwell amongst them, but such as be of the same occupation or arte: in such sort that if you doo come at the beginning of the street, looke what craft or art they are there, it is to be understood that all that streete are of that occupation. It is ordayned by a law and statute, that the sonne shall inherite his fathers occupation, and shall not use any other without licence of the justice: if one of them bee verie rich and will not worke, yet he cannot let but have in his shop men that must worke of his occupation. Therefore they that do use it, by reason that they are brought up in it from their youth, they are famous and verie curious in that which they do worke, as it is plainelie seene in that which is brought from thence to Manilla, and into the Indies, and unto Portugall. Their currant monie of that kingdome is made of golde and silver, without any signe or print, but goeth by waight: so that all men carrieth a ballances with them, and little peeces of silver and golde, for to buy such things as they have neede of. And for things of a greater quantitie they have bigger ballances in their houses, and waights, that are sealed, for to give to every man that which is theirs: for therein the justices have great care. In the government of Chincheo they have copper monie coyned, but it is nothing woorth out of that province.

FOCUS QUESTIONS

1. To whom does Mendoza compare the Chinese people? Why?

2. What does the passage tell us about the position of women in Chinese society?

3. What does he think about the custom of footbinding?

4. Why do you think Mendoza's *History* was so popular in the sixteenth century?

69

Journals (1583–1610 C.E.)

MATTEO RICCI

Matteo Ricci (1552–1610) was born into a noble Italian family. At the age of 16 he was sent to Rome to study law but became more interested in the new science that was sweeping Western Europe. He studied mathematics and astronomy and then petitioned to join the Jesuits. He was sent on a Jesuit mission to the Far East and studied for the priesthood in east India. He was assigned the difficult task of organizing a mission to China, a task at which earlier Jesuit missionaries had failed. Ricci learned the Chinese language with such proficiency that he persuaded officials to allow him into the country, where he taught Chinese intellectuals about mathematics and science and published the first six books of Euclid's Elements *in Chinese. After a long delay, he was finally allowed to enter the closed City of Peking in 1601, where he stayed for the rest of his life teaching science, mathematics, and Christianity to Chinese intellectuals.*

Ricci's most important published work was his History of the Introduction of Christianity into China. *But the journals that he kept and edited for publication allow one of the few glimpses of an outsider's view of Chinese society and government during a period when China was closed to foreign visitors. In this selection Ricci describes Chinese government.*

We shall touch upon this subject only insofar as it has to do with the purpose of our narrative. It would require a number of chapters, if not of whole books, to treat this matter in full detail.... Chinese imperial power passes on from father to son, or to other royal kin, as does our own. Two or three of the more ancient kings are known to have bequeathed the throne to successors without royal relationship rather than to their sons, whom they judged to be unfitted to rule. More than once, however, it has happened that the people, growing weary of an inept ruler, have stripped him of his authority and replaced him with someone preeminent for character and courage whom they henceforth recognized as their legitimate King. It may be said in praise of the Chinese that ordinarily they would prefer to die an honorable death rather than swear allegiance to a usurping monarch. In fact, there is a proverb extant among their philosophers, which reads: "No woman is moral who has two husbands, nor any vassal faithful to two lords."

There are no ancient laws in China under which the republic is governed in perpetuum, such as our laws of the twelve tables and the Code of Caesar. Whoever succeeds in getting possession of the throne, regardless of his ancestry, makes new laws according to his own way of thinking. His successors on the throne are obliged to enforce the laws which he promulgated as founder of the dynasty, and these laws cannot be changed without good reason.... The extent of their kingdom is so vast, its borders so distant, and their utter lack of knowledge of a transmaritime world is so complete that the Chinese imagine the whole world as included in their kingdom. Even now, as from time beyond recording, they call their Emperor, Thiencu, the Son of Heaven, and because they worship Heaven as the Supreme Being, the Son of Heaven and the Son of God are one and the same. In ordinary speech, he is referred to as Hoamsi, meaning supreme ruler or monarch, while other and subordinate rulers are called by the much inferior title of Guam.

Only such as have earned a doctor's degree or that of licentiate are admitted to take part in the government of the kingdom, and due to the interest of the magistrates and of the King himself there is no lack of such candidates. Every public office is therefore fortified with and dependent upon the attested science, prudence, and diplomacy of the person assigned to it, whether he be taking office for the first time or is already experienced in the conduct of civil life. This integrity of life is prescribed by ... law ..., and for the most part it is lived up to, save in the case of such as are prone to violate the dictates of justice from human weakness and from lack of religious training among the gentiles. All magistrates, whether they belong to the military or to the civil congress, are called Quon-fu, meaning commander or president, though their honorary or unofficial title is Lau-ye or Lau-sie, signifying lord or

father. The Portuguese call the Chinese magistrates, mandarins, probably from mandando, mando mandare, to order or command, and they are now generally known by this title in Europe.

Though we have already stated that the Chinese form of government is monarchical, it must be evident from what has been said, and it will be made clearer by what is to come, that it is to some extent an aristocracy. Although all legal statutes inaugurated by magistrates must be confirmed by the King in writing on the written petition presented to him, the King himself makes no final decision in important matters of state without consulting the magistrates or considering their advice....

Tax returns, impost, and other tribute, which undoubtedly exceed a hundred and fifty million a year, as is commonly said, do not go into the Imperial Exchequer, nor can the King dispose of this income as he pleases. The silver, which is the common currency, is placed in the public treasury, and the returns paid in rice are placed in the warehouses belonging to the government. The generous allowance made for the support of the royal family and their relatives, for the palace eunuchs and the royal household, is drawn from this national treasury. In keeping with the regal splendor and dignity of the crown, these annuities are large, but each individual account is determined and regulated by law. Civil and military accounts and the expenses of all government departments are paid out of this national treasury, and the size of the national budget is far in excess of what Europeans might imagine. Public buildings, the palaces of the King and of his relations, the upkeep of city prisons and fortresses, and the renewal of all kinds of war supplies must be met by the national treasury, and in a kingdom of such vast dimensions the program of building and of restoration is continuous. One would scarcely believe that at times even these enormous revenues are not sufficient to meet the expenses. When this happens, new taxes are imposed to balance the national budget.

Relative to the magistrates in general, there are two distinct orders or grades. The first and superior order is made up of the magistrates who govern the various courts of the royal palace, which is considered to be a model for the rule of the entire realm. The second order includes all provincial magistrates or governors who rule a province or a city. For each of these orders of magistrates, there are five or six large books containing the governmental roster of the entire country. These books are for sale throughout the kingdom. They are being continually revised, and the revision, which is dated twice a month in the royal city of Pekin, is not very difficult because of the singular typographical arrangement in which they are printed. The entire contents of these books consist of nothing other than the current lists of the names, addresses, and grades of the court officers of the entire government, and the frequent revision is necessary if the roster is to be kept up to date. In addition to the daily changes, occasioned by deaths, demotions, and dismissals in such an incredibly long list of names, there are the frequent departures of some to visit their homes at stated periods. We shall say more later on of this last instance, which is occasioned by the custom requiring every magistrate to lay aside his official duties and return to his home for three full years, on the death of his father or his mother. One result of these numerous changes is that there are always a great many in the city of Pekin awaiting the good fortune of being appointed to fill the vacancies thus created.

Besides the classes or orders of the magistrates already described and many others which we shall pass over because they differ but little from our own, there are two special orders never heard of among our people. These are the Choli and the Zauli, each consisting of sixty or more chosen philosophers, all prudent men and tried, who have already given exceptional proof of their fidelity to the King and to the realm. These two orders are reserved by the King for business of greater moment pertaining to the royal court or to the provinces, and by him they are entrusted with great responsibility, carrying with it both respect and authority. They correspond in some manner to what we would call keepers of the public conscience, inasmuch as they inform the King as often as they see fit, of any infraction of the law in any part of the entire kingdom. No one is spared from their scrutiny,

even the highest magistrates, as they do not hesitate to speak, even though it concerns the King himself or his household. If they had the power of doing something more than talking, or rather of writing, and if they were not wholly dependent upon the King whom they admonish, their particular office would correspond to that of the Lacedemonian Ephors. And yet they do their duty so thoroughly that they are a source of wonder to outsiders and a good example for imitation. Neither King nor magistrates can escape their courage and frankness, and even when they arouse the royal wrath to such an extent that the King becomes severely angry with them, they will never desist from their admonitions and criticism until some remedy has been applied to the public evil against which they are inveighing. In fact, when the grievance is particularly acute, they are sure to put a sting into their complaints and to show no partiality where the crown or the courts are concerned. This same privilege of offering written criticism is also granted by law to any magistrate and even to a private citizen, but for the most part it is exercised only by those to whose particular office it pertains. Numerous copies are made of all such written documents submitted to the crown and of the answers made to them. In this way, what goes on in the royal headquarters is quickly communicated to every corner of the country. These documents are also compiled in book form, and whatever of their content is deemed worthy of handing down to posterity is transcribed into the annals of the King's regime.

Besides the regular magistrates there are in the royal palace various other organizations, instituted for particular purposes. The most exalted of these is what is known as the Han-lin-yuen, made up of selected doctors of philosophy and chosen by examination. Members of this cabinet have nothing to do with public administration but outrank all public officials in dignity of office. Ambition for a place in this select body means no end of labor and of sacrifice. These are the King's secretaries, who do both his writing and his composing. They edit and compile the royal annals and publish the laws and statutes of the land. The tutors of kings and princes are chosen from their number. They are entirely devoted to study and there are grades within the cabinet which are determined by the publications of its members. Hence, they are honored with the highest dignity within the regal court, but not beyond it....

The Chinese can distinguish between their magistrates by the parasols they use as protection against the sun when they go out in public. Some of these are blue and others yellow. Sometimes for effect they will have two or three of these sunshades, but only one if their rank does not permit of more. They may also be recognized by their mode of transportation in public. The lower ranks ride on horseback, the higher are carried about on the shoulders of their servants in gestatorial chairs. The number of carriers also has a significance of rank; some are allowed only four, others may have eight. There are other ways also of distinguishing the magistracy and the rank of dignity therein; by banners and pennants, chains and censer cups, and by the number of the guards who give orders to make way for the passage of the dignitary. The escort itself is held in such high esteem by the public that no one would question their orders. Even in a crowded city everyone gives way at the sound of their voices with a spontaneity that corresponds to the rank of the approaching celebrity.

Before closing this chapter on Chinese public administration, it would seem to be quite worthwhile recording a few more things in which this people differ from Europeans. To begin with, it seems to be quite remarkable when we stop to consider it, that in a kingdom of almost limitless expanse and innumerable population, and abounding in copious supplies of every description, though they have a well-equipped army and navy that could easily conquer the neighboring nations, neither the King nor his people ever think of waging a war of aggression. They are quite content with what they have and are not ambitious of conquest. In this respect they are much different from the people of Europe, who are frequently discontent with their own governments and covetous of what others enjoy. While the nations of the West seem to be entirely consumed with the idea of supreme domination, they cannot even preserve what their ancestors have bequeathed them, as the Chinese have done through a period of some thousands of years....

Another remarkable fact and quite worthy of note as marking a difference from the West, is that the entire kingdom is administered by the Order of the Learned, commonly known as The Philosophers. The responsibility for orderly management of the entire realm is wholly and completely committed to their charge and care. The army, both officers and soldiers, hold them in high respect and show them the promptest obedience and deference, and not infrequently the military are disciplined by them as a schoolboy might be punished by his master. Policies of war are formulated and military questions are decided by the Philosophers only, and their advice and counsel has more weight with the King than that of the military leaders. In fact very few of these, and only on rare occasions, are admitted to war consultations. Hence it follows that those who aspire to be cultured frown upon war and would prefer the lowest rank in the philosophical order to the highest in the military, realizing that the Philosophers far excel military leaders in the good will and the respect of the people and in opportunities of acquiring wealth.

FOCUS QUESTIONS

1. What is the relationship between emperor and magistrate in Ricci's account of Chinese administration?

2. What characteristics of Chinese government does Ricci most admire?

3. What is the role of the Choli and the Zauli?

4. Why did Ricci write the *Journals?* Who was his intended audience?

5. Do you think that Ricci's description of Chinese government is accurate?

70

Chronicle of Guinea (1453 C.E.)

GOMES EANES DE ZURARA

Gomes Eanes de Zurara (1410?–1474) was an historian and biographer who is one of the principal sources for the life of Prince Henry the Navigator. Little is known for certain about his early life. Probably the son of a priest, he learned to read and write, though it was said that he did not have the benefit of much formal education. His early life might have been spent in the military. He became a member of the Order of Christ, one of the more important of the lay religious societies in Portugal and one that would have enabled him to make the acquaintance of many powerful patrons. He obtained preferment of a position in the Royal Library and by 1452 appears to have become the Royal Chronicler, an official position at court. He was commissioned by King Alfonso V to collect all of the extant information concerning the life of Prince Henry, and much of it is contained in the Chronicle of Guinea *that was presented to the king in 1453.*

The Chronicle of Guinea *celebrates Portuguese exploration of the coast of Africa under the direction of Prince Henry. It is now recognized that Zurara freely embellished his account both of Henry's role in these events and of his character and conduct. Nevertheless, he provides much rich detail of the exploration of Africa from the point of view of those Europeans who first arrived there. In this section of the work, Zurara recounts the capture of Africans he calls "Moors" and their enslavement. This is the first reliable account of how the Portuguese captured African villagers, assigned them as chattel to the various royal and naval authorities (Prince Henry is here identified as the Infant), and then sold them. Throughout the account he is sympathetic to the plight of the natives, but from a distinctly Christian point of view.*

CHAPTER XXIV

How the caravels arrived at Lagos, and of the account that Lançarote gave to the Infant.

The caravels arrived at Lagos, whence they had set out, having excellent weather for their voyage, for fortune was not less gracious to them in the serenity of the weather than it had been to them before in the capture of their booty.

And from Lagos the news reached the Infant, who happened to have arrived there a few hours before, from other parts where he had been for some days. And as you see that people are desirous of knowledge, some endeavoured to get near the shore; and others put themselves into the boats they found moored along the beach, and went to welcome their relations and friends; so that in a short time the news of their good fortune was well known, and all were much rejoiced at it. And for that day it sufficed for those who had led the enterprize to kiss the hand of the Infant their Lord, and to give him a short account of their exploits: after which they took their rest, as men who had come to their fatherland and their own homes; and you may guess what would be their joy among their wives and children.

And next day Lançarote, as he who had taken the main charge of the expedition, said to the Infant: "My Lord, your grace well knoweth that you have to receive the fifth of these Moors, and of all that we have gained in that land, whither you sent us for the service of God and of yourself.

"And now these Moors, because of the long time we have been at sea; as well as for the great sorrow that you must consider they have at heart, at seeing themselves away from the land of their birth, and placed in captivity, without having any understanding of what their end is to be;—and moreover because they have not been accustomed to a life on shipboard—for all these reasons are poorly and out of condition; wherefore it seemeth to me that it would be well to order them to be taken out of the caravels at dawn, and to be placed in that field which lies outside the city gate, and there to be divided into five parts, according to custom; and that your Grace should come there and choose one of these parts, whichever you prefer."

The Infant said that he was well pleased, and on the next day very early, Lançarote bade the masters of the caravels that they should put out the captives, and take them to that field, where they were to make the divisions, as he had said already. But before they did anything else in that matter, they took as an offering the best of those Moors to the Church of that place, and another little Moor, who afterwards became a friar of St. Francis, they sent to St. Vincent do Cabo, where he lived ever after as a Catholic Christian, without having understanding or perception of any other law than that true and holy law in which all we Christians hope for our salvation. And the Moors of that capture were in number 235.

CHAPTER XXV

Wherein the Author reasoneth somewhat concerning the pity inspired by the captives, and of how the division was made.

O, Thou heavenly Father—who with Thy powerful hand, without alteration of Thy divine essence, governest all the infinite company of Thy Holy City, and controllest all the revolutions of higher worlds, divided into nine spheres, making the duration of ages long or short according as it pleaseth Thee—I pray Thee that my tears may not wrong my conscience; for it is not their religion but their humanity that maketh mine to weep in pity for their sufferings. And if the brute animals, with their bestial feelings, by a natural instinct understand the sufferings of their own kind, what wouldst Thou have my human nature to do on seeing before my eyes that miserable company, and remembering that they too are of the generation of the sons of Adam?

On the next day, which was the 8th of the month of August, very early in the morning, by reason of the heat, the seamen began to make ready their boats, and to take out those captives, and carry them on shore, as they were commanded. And these, placed all together in that field, were a marvellous sight; for amongst them were some white enough, fair to look upon, and well proportioned; others were less white like mulattoes; others again were as black as Ethiops, and so ugly, both in features and in body, as almost to appear (to those who saw them) the images of a lower hemisphere. But what heart could be so hard as not to be pierced with piteous feeling to see that company? For some kept their heads low and their faces bathed in tears, looking one upon another; others stood groaning very dolorously, looking up to the height of heaven, fixing their eyes upon it, crying out loudly, as if asking help of the Father of Nature; others struck their faces with the palms of their hands, throwing themselves at full length upon the ground; others made their lamentations in the manner of a dirge, after the custom of their country. And though we could not understand the words of their language, the sound of it right well accorded with the measure of their sadness. But to increase their sufferings still more, there now arrived those who had charge of the division of the captives, and who began to separate one from another, in order to make an equal partition of the fifths; and then was it needful to part fathers from sons, husbands from wives, brothers from brothers.

No respect was shewn either to friends or relations, but each fell where his lot took him.

O powerful fortune, that with thy wheels doest and undoest, compassing the matters of this world as pleaseth thee, do thou at least put before the eyes of that miserable race some understanding of matters to come; that they may receive some consolation in the midst of their great sorrow. And you who are so busy in making that division of the captives, look with pity upon so much misery; and see how they cling one to the other, so that you can hardly separate them.

And who could finish that partition without very great toil? for as often as they had placed them in one part the sons, seeing their fathers in another, rose with great energy and rushed over to them; the mothers clasped their other children in their arms, and threw themselves flat on the ground with them, receiving blows with little pity for their own flesh, if only they might not be torn from them.

And so troublously they finished the partition; for besides the toil they had with the captives, the field was quite full of people, both from the town and from the surrounding villages and districts, who for that day gave rest to their hands (in which lay their power to get their living) for the sole purpose of beholding this novelty. And with what they saw, while some were weeping and others separating the captives, they caused such a tumult as greatly to confuse those who directed the partition.

The Infant was there, mounted upon a powerful steed, and accompanied by his retinue, making distribution of his favours, as a man who sought to gain but small treasure from his share; for of the forty-six souls that fell to him as his fifth, he made a very speedy partition of these; for his chief riches lay in his purpose; for he reflected with great pleasure upon the salvation of those souls that before were lost.

And certainly his expectation was not in vain; for, as we said before, as soon as they understood our language they turned Christians with very little ado; and I who put together this history into this volume, saw in the town of Lagos boys and girls (the children and grandchildren of those first captives, born in this land) as good and true Christians as if they had directly descended, from the beginning of the dispensation of Christ, from those who were first baptised.

CHAPTER XXVI

How the Infant Don Henry made Lançarote a Knight.

Although the sorrow of those captives was for the present very great, especially after the partition was finished and each one took his own share aside (while some sold their captives, the which they took to other districts); and although it chanced that among the prisoners the father often remained in Lagos, while the mother was taken to Lisbon, and the children to another part (in which partition their sorrow doubled the first grief)—yet this sorrow was less felt among those who happened to remain in company. For as saith the text, the wretched find a consolation in having comrades in misfortune. But from this time forth they began to acquire some knowledge of our country; in which they found great abundance, and our men began to treat them with great favour. For as our people did not find them hardened in the belief of the other Moors; and saw how they came in unto the law of Christ with a good will; they make no difference between them and their free servants, born in our own country; but those whom they took while still young, they caused to be instructed in mechanical arts, and those whom they saw fitted for managing property; they set free and married to women who were natives of the land; making with them a division of their property, as if they had been bestowed on those who married them by the will of their own fathers, and for the merits of their service they were bound to act in a like manner. Yea, and some widows of good family who bought some of these female slaves, either adopted them or left them a portion of their estate by will; so that in the future they married right well; treating them as entirely free. Suffice it that I never saw one of these slaves put in irons like other captives, and scarcely any one who did not turn Christian and was not very gently treated.

And I have been asked by their lords to the baptisms and marriages of such, at which they, whose slaves they were before, made no less solemnity than if they had been their children or relations.

And so their lot was now quite the contrary of what it had been; since before they had lived in perdition of soul and body; of their souls, in that they were yet pagans, without the clearness and the light of the holy faith; and of their bodies, in that they lived like beasts, without any custom of reasonable beings—for they had no knowledge of bread or wine, and they were without the covering of clothes, or the lodgment of houses; and worse than all, through the great ignorance that was in them, in that they had no understanding of good, but only knew how to live in a bestial sloth.

But as soon as they began to come to this land, and men gave them prepared food and coverings for their bodies, their bellies began to swell, and for a time they were ill; until they were accustomed to the nature of the country; but some of them were so made that they were not able to endure it and died, but as Christians.

Now there were four things in these captives that were very different from the condition of the other Moors who were taken prisoners from this part. First, that after they had come to this land of Portugal, they never more tried to fly, but rather in time forgot all about their own country, as soon as they began to taste the good things of this one; secondly, that they were very loyal and obedient servants, without malice; thirdly, that they were not so inclined to lechery as the others; fourthly, that after they began to use clothing they were for the most part very fond of display, so that they took great delight in robes of showy colours, and such was their love of finery, that they picked up the rags that fell from the coats of the other people of the country and sewed them on to their garments, taking great pleasure in these, as though it were matter of some greater perfection. And what was still better, as I have already said, they turned themselves with a good will into the path of the true belief, and in this same they died. And now reflect what a guerdon should be that of the Infant in the presence of the Lord God; for thus bringing to true salvation, not only those, but many others, whom you will find in this history later on.

FOCUS QUESTIONS

1. How were the captive Moors divided? What was the share of Prince Henry (the Infant)?

2. What about the Moors moved de Zurara?

3. What is de Zurara's attitude to race?

4. What was the experience of the Moors in Portugual?

71

Journal of the First Voyage
of Vasco da Gama (1497–1499 C.E.)

Vasco da Gama (ca. 1460–1524) was the greatest of the Portuguese explorers and sea captains. Little is known about his childhood. His father was also a sea captain and had been given command of the voyage that da Gama ultimately undertook. He must have studied mathematics and navigation, for his first public employment was in command of a squadron of ships. After his father's death in 1496, da Gama was commissioned to explore further the eastern coast of Africa, which had been opened when the Portuguese sailed around the Cape of Good Hope. Da Gama rounded the continent, discovered Mozambique, and then, with the aid of an African navigator crossed the Indian Ocean. When he returned two years later laden with Eastern spices he was hailed as a hero. Da Gama made two more voyages to India and was ultimately appointed Portuguese viceroy.

The anonymous Journal of the First Voyage of Vasco da Gama *is an eyewitness account of da Gama's path-breaking journey. The selections here describe what the Portuguese found when they landed in West Africa.*

On Wednesday, April 4 [1498], we made sail to the north-west, and before noon we sighted an extensive country, and two islands close to it, surrounded with shoals. And when we were near enough for the pilots to recognize these islands, they told us that we had left three leagues behind us an island inhabited by Christians. We manoeuvred all day in the hope of fetching this island, but in vain, for the wind was too strong for us. After this we thought it best to bear away for a city called Mombasa, reported to be four days ahead of us.

The above island was one of those which we had come to discover, for our pilots said it was inhabited by Christians.

When we bore away for the north it was already late, and the wind was high. At nightfall we perceived a large island, which remained to the north of us. Our pilot told us that there were two towns on this island, one of Christians and the other of Moors.

That night we stood out to sea, and in the morning (5 April) we no longer saw the land. We then steered to the north-west, and in the evening we again beheld the land. During the following night we bore awry to the N. by W., and during the morning-watch we changed our course to the north-north-west. Sailing thus before a favourable wind, the *S. Raphael*, two hours before the break of day (6 April), ran aground on a shoal, about two leagues from the land. Immediately the *Raphael* touched bottom, the vessels following her were warned by shouts, and these were no sooner heard than they cast anchor about the distance of a gunshot from the stranded vessel, and lowered their boats. When the tide fell the *Raphael* lay high and dry. With the help of the boats many anchors were laid out, and when the tide rose again, in the course of the day, the vessel floated and there was much rejoicing.

On the mainland, facing these shoals, there rises a lofty range of mountains, beautiful of aspect. These mountains we called Serras de Sao Raphael, and we gave the same name to the shoals.

When the vessel was high and dry, two *almadias* approached us. One was laden with fine oranges, better than those of Portugal. Two of the Moors remained on board, and accompanied us next day to Mombasa.

On Saturday morning, the 7th of the month, and eve of Palm Sunday, we ran along the coast and saw some of the islands at a distance of fifteen leagues from the mainland, and about six leagues in extent. They supply the vessels of the country with masts. All are inhabited by Moors.

On Saturday (7 April) we cast anchor off Mombasa, but did not enter the port. No sooner had we been perceived than a *zavra* [small boat] manned by Moors came out to us: in front of the city there lay numerous vessels all dressed in flags. And we, anxious not to be outdone, also dressed our ships, and we actually surpassed their show, for we wanted in nothing but men, even a few whom we had being very ill. We anchored here with much pleasure, for we confidently hoped that on the following day we might go on land and hear mass jointly with the Christians reported to live there under their own *alcaide* in a quarter separate from that of the Moors.

The pilots who had come with us told us there resided both Moors and Christians in this city; that these latter lived apart under their own lords, and that on our arrival they would receive us with much honour and take us to their houses. But they said this for a purpose of their own, for it was not true. At midnight there approached us a *zavra* with about 100 men, all armed with cutlasses and bucklers. When they came to the vessel of the captain-major they attempted to board her, armed as they were, but this was not permitted, only four or five of the most distinguished men among them being allowed on board. They remained about a couple of hours, and it seemed to us that they paid us this visit merely to find out whether they might not capture one or the other of our vessels.

On Palm Sunday (8 April) the King of Mombasa sent the captain-major a sheep and large quantities of oranges, lemons and sugarcane, together with a ring, as a pledge of safety, letting him know that in case of his entering the port he would be supplied with all he stood in need of. This present was conveyed to us by two men, almost white,

who said they were Christians, which appeared to be the fact. The captain-major sent the king a string of coral-beads as a return present, and let him know that he purposed entering the port on the following day. On the same day the captain-major's vessel was visited by four Moors of distinction.

Two men were sent by the captain-major to the king, still further to confirm these peaceful assurances. When these landed they were followed by a crowd as far as the gates of the palace. Before reaching the king they passed through four doors, each guarded by a doorkeeper with a drawn cutlass. The king received them hospitably, and ordered that they should be shown over the city. They stopped on their way at the house of two Christian merchants, who showed them a paper, an object of their adoration, on which was a sketch of the Holy Ghost. When they had seen all, the king sent them back with samples of cloves, pepper and corn, with which articles he would allow us to load our ships.

On Tuesday (10 April), when weighing anchor to enter the port, the captain-major's vessel would not pay off, and struck the vessel which followed astern. We therefore again cast anchor. When the Moors who were in our ship saw that we did not go on, they scrambled into a *zavra* attached to our stern; whilst the two pilots whom we had brought from Mozambique jumped into the water, and were picked up by the men in the *zavra*. At night the captain-major questioned two Moors (from Mozambique) whom we had on board, by dropping boiling oil upon their skin, so that they might confess any treachery intended against us. They said that orders had been given to capture us as soon as we entered the port, and thus to avenge what we had done at Mozambique. And when the torture was being applied a second time, one of the Moors, although his hands were tied, threw himself into the sea, whilst the other did so during the morning watch.

About midnight two *almadias*, with many men in them, approached. The *almadias* stood off whilst the men entered the water, some swimming in the direction of the *Berrio*, others in that of the *Raphael*. Those who swam to the *Berrio* began to cut the cable. The men on watch thought at first that they were tunny fish, but when they perceived their mistake they shouted to the other vessels. The other swimmers had already got hold of the rigging of the mizzenmast. Seeing themselves discovered, they silently slipped down and fled. These and other wicked tricks were practised upon us by these dogs, but our Lord did not allow them to succeed, because they were unbelievers.

Mombasa is a large city seated upon an eminence washed by the sea. Its port is entered daily by numerous vessels. At its entrance stands a pillar, and by the sea a low-lying fortress. Those who had gone on shore told us that in the town they had seen many men in irons; and it seemed to us that these must be Christians, as the Christians in that country are at war with the Moors.

The Christian merchants in the town are only temporary residents, and are held in much subjection, they not being allowed to do anything except by the order of the Moorish king.

It pleased God in his mercy that on arriving at this city all our sick recovered their health, for the climate of this place is very good.

After the malice and treachery planned by these dogs had been discovered, we still remained on Wednesday and Thursday (11 and 12 April).

We left in the morning (13 April), the wind being light, and anchored about eight leagues from Mombasa, close to the shore. At the break of day (14 April) we saw two boats about three leagues to the leeward, in the open sea, and at once gave chase, with the intention of capturing them, for we wanted to secure a pilot who would guide us to where we wanted to go. At vespertime we came up with one of them, and captured it, the other escaping towards the land. In the one we took we found seventeen men, besides gold, silver, and an abundance of maize and other provisions; as also a young woman, who was the wife of an old Moor of distinction, who was a passenger. When we came up with the boat they all threw themselves into the water, but we picked them up from our boats.

That same day (14 April) at sunset, we cast anchor off a place called Milinde, which is thirty leagues from Mombasa. The following places are

between Mombasa and Milinde, viz. Benapa, Toca, and Nuguoquioniete.

On Easter Sunday (15 April) the Moors whom we had taken in the boat told us that there were at this city of Melinde four vessels belonging to Christians from India, and that if it pleased us to take them there, they would provide us, instead of them, Christian pilots and all we stood in need of, including water, wood and other things. The captain-major much desired to have pilots from the country, and having discussed the matter with his Moorish prisoners, he cast anchor off the town, at a distance of about half a league from the mainland. The inhabitants of the town did not venture to come aboard our ships, for they had already learnt that we had captured a vessel and made her occupants prisoners.

On Monday morning (16 April) the captain major had the old Moor taken to a sandbank in front of the town, where he was picked up by an *almadia*. The Moor explained to the king the wishes of the captain-major, and how much he desired to make peace with him. After dinner the Moor came back in a *zavra*, accompanied by one of the king's cavaliers and a Sharif: he also brought three sheep. These messengers told the captain-general that the king would rejoice to make peace with him, and to enter into friendly relations; that he would willingly grant to the captain-major all his country afforded, whether pilots or anything else. The captain-major upon this sent word that he proposed to enter the port on the following day, and forwarded by the king's messengers a present consisting of a *balandrau* [a tunic worn by the Brothers of Mercy in Portugal], two strings of coral, three wash-hand basins, a hat, little bells and two pieces of lambel [striped cotton stuff].

Consequently, on Tuesday (17 April) we approached nearer to the town. The king sent the captain-major six sheep, besides quantities of cloves, cumin, ginger, nutmeg, and pepper, as also a message, telling him that if he desired to have an interview with him he (the king) would come out in his *zavra*, when the captain-major could meet him in a boat.

On Wednesday (18 April), after dinner, when the king came up close to the ships in a *zavra*, the captain-major at once entered one of his boats, which had been well furnished, and many friendly words were exchanged when they lay side by side. The king having invited the captain-major to come to his house to rest, after which he (the king) would visit him on board his ship, the captain-major said that he was not permitted by his master to go on land, and if he were to do so a bad report would be given of him. The king wanted to know what would be said of himself by his people if he were to visit the ships, and what account could he render them? He then asked for the name of our king, which was written down for him, and said that on our return he would send an ambassador with us, or a letter.

When both had said all they desired, the captain-major sent for the Moors whom he had taken prisoner, and surrendered them all. This gave much satisfaction to the king, who said he valued this act more highly than if he had been presented with a town. And the king, much pleased, made the circuit of our ships, the bombards of which fired a salute. About three hours were spent in this way. When the king went away he left in the ship one of his sons and a Sharif, and took two of us away with him, to whom he desired to show his palace. He, moreover, told the captain that as he would not go ashore he would himself return on the following day to the beach, and would order his horsemen to go through some exercises.

The king wore a robe (royal cloak) of damask trimmed with green satin, and a rich *touca* (turban). He was seated on two cushioned chairs of bronze, beneath a round sunshade of crimson satin attached to a pole. An old man, who attended him as a page, carried a short sword in a silver sheath. There were many players on *anafils*, and two trumpets of ivory, richly carved, and of the size of a man, which were blown from a hole in the side, and made sweet harmony with the *anafils*.

On Thursday (19 April) the captain-major and Nicolau Coelho rowed along the front of the town, bombards having been placed in the poops of their long-boats. Many people were along the shore, and among them two horsemen, who appeared to take much delight in a sham fight. The king was carried in a palanquin from the stone steps of his palace to the side of the captain-major's boats. He again begged the captain to come ashore, as he had a helpless father who wanted to see him, and that he and his sons would go on board the ships as hostages. The captain, however, excused himself.

We found here four vessels belonging to Indian Christians. When they came for the first time on board Paulo da Gama's ship, the captain-major being there at the time, they were shown an altarpiece representing Our Lady at the foot of the cross, with Jesus Christ in her arms and the apostles round her. When the Indians saw this picture they prostrated themselves, and as long as we were there they came to say their prayers in front of it, bringing offerings of cloves, pepper, and other things.

These Indians are tawny men; they wear but little clothing and have long beards and long hair, which they braid. They told us that they ate no beef. Their language differs from that of the Arabs, but some of them know a little of it, as they hold much intercourse with them.

On the day on which the captain-major went up to the town in the boats, these Christian Indians fired off many bombards from their vessels, and when they saw him pass they raised their hands and shouted lustily, *Christ! Christ!*

That same night they asked the king's permission to give us a night-fête. And when night came they fired off many bombards, sent up rockets, and raised loud shouts.

These Indians warned the captain-major against going on shore, and told him not to trust to their "fanfares," as they neither came from their hearts nor from their goodwill.

On the following Sunday, 22 April, the king's *zavra* brought on board one of his confidential servants, and as two days had passed without any visitors, the captain-major had this man seized, and sent word to the king that he required the pilots whom he had promised. The king, when he received this message, sent a Christian pilot, and the captain-major allowed the gentlemen, whom he had retained in his vessel, to go away.

We were much pleased with the Christian pilot whom the king had sent us. We learnt from him that the island of which we heard at Moçambique as being inhabited by Christians was in reality an island subject to this same King of Moçambique; that half of it belonged to the Moors and the other half to the Christians; that many pearls were to be found there, and that it was called Quylee [Kilwa]. This is the island the Moorish pilots wanted to take us to, and we also wished to go there, for we believed that what they said was true.

The town of Malindi lies in a bay and extends along the shore. It may be likened to Alcouchette. Its houses are lofty and well whitewashed, and have many windows; on the land side are palm-groves, and all around it maize and vegetables are being cultivated.

We remained in front of this town during nine days, and all this time we had fêtes, sham fights, and musical performances ("fanfares").

FOCUS QUESTIONS

1. Why did da Gama and his crew stop in so many African ports?

2. Why does the king of Mombasa send da Gama sheep, fruit, and a ring?

3. Why does the author compare Malindi to Alcouchette?

4. Why is it important to the author to identify people as Christians when he encounters them in Africa?

72

Letter from the First Voyage (1493 C.E.)

CHRISTOPHER COLUMBUS

The Italian Christopher Columbus (1451–1506) dreamed of making his fortune in the spice trade. As a young mariner he had worked with a mapmaker and became obsessed with the idea of reaching the Spice Islands via a western route. This was as much a practical as a theoretical idea—Muslim conquests had disrupted the traditional Mediterranean trade, and the Portuguese had to make the long journey around Africa in stages. Columbus lobbied for his plan in both Portugal and Spain before convincing Queen Isabella of Castile to provide limited financial backing in return for a hefty share of any profits from the voyage. In 1492, Columbus sailed west in command of three ships from the Canary Islands and landed in the Caribbean, which he believed was a string of islands off the China mainland.

This letter is one of Columbus's early communications, though it was written nearly six months after his discovery. It was obviously composed for public consumption and was one of the most widely printed documents from the voyages of discovery.

A Letter addressed to the noble Lord Raphael Sanchez, Treasurer to their most invincible Majesties, Ferdinand and Isabella, King and Queen of Spain, by Christopher Columbus, to whom our age is greatly indebted, treating of the islands of India recently discovered beyond the Ganges, to explore which he had been sent eight months before under the auspices and at the expense of their said Majesties.

Knowing that it will afford you pleasure to learn that I have brought my undertaking to a successful termination, I have decided upon writing you this letter to acquaint you with all the events which have occurred in my voyage, and the discoveries which have resulted from it. Thirty-three days after my departure from Cadiz I reached the Indian sea, where I discovered many islands, thickly peopled, of which I took possession without resistance in the name of our most illustrious Monarch, by public proclamation and with unfurled banners. To the first of these islands, which is called by the Indians Guanahani, I gave the name of the blessed Saviour (San Salvador), relying upon whose protection I had reached this as well as the other islands; to each of these I also gave a name. In the meantime I had learned from some Indians whom I had seized, that that country was certainly an island: and therefore I sailed towards the east, coasting to the distance of three hundred and twenty-two miles, which brought us to the extremity of it; from this point I saw lying eastwards another island, fifty-four miles distant from Juana, to which I gave the name of Española: I went thither, and steered my course eastward as I had done at Juana, even to the distance of five hundred and sixty-four miles along the north coast. This said island of Juana is exceedingly fertile, as indeed are all the others; it is surrounded with many bays, spacious, very secure, and surpassing any that I have ever seen; numerous large and healthful rivers intersect it, and it also contains many very lofty mountains. All these islands are very beautiful, and distinguished by a diversity of scenery; they are filled with a great variety of trees of immense height, and which I believe to retain their foliage in all seasons; for when I saw them they were as verdant and luxuriant as they usually

are in Spain in the month of May—some of them were blossoming, some bearing fruit, and all flourishing in the greatest perfection, according to their respective stages of growth, and the nature and quality of each: yet the islands are not so thickly wooded as to be impassable. The nightingale and various birds were singing in countless numbers, and that in November, the month in which I arrived there. There are besides in the same island of Juana seven or eight kinds of palm trees, which, like all the other trees, herbs, and fruits, considerably surpass ours in height and beauty. The pines also are very handsome, and there are very extensive fields and meadows, a variety of birds, different kinds of honey, and many sorts of metals, but no iron. In that island also which I have before said we named Española, there are mountains of very great size and beauty, vast plains, groves, and very fruitful fields, admirably adapted for tillage, pasture, and habitation. The inhabitants of both sexes in this island, and in all the others which I have seen, or of which I have received information, go always naked as they were born, with the exception of some of the women, who use the covering of a leaf, or small bough, or an apron of cotton which they prepare for that purpose. None of them are possessed of any iron, neither have they weapons, being unacquainted with, and indeed incompetent to use them, not from any deformity of body (for they are well-formed), but because they are timid and full of fear.

They carry however in lieu of arms, canes dried in the sun, on the ends of which they fix heads of dried wood sharpened to a point, and even these they dare not use habitually; for it has often occurred when I have sent two or three of my men to any of the villages to speak with the natives, that they have come out in a disorderly troop, and have fled in such haste at the approach of our men, that the fathers forsook their children and the children their fathers. This timidity did not arise from any loss or injury that they had received from us; for, on the contrary, I gave to all I approached whatever articles I had about me, such as cloth and many other things, taking nothing of theirs in return: but they are naturally timid and fearful. As soon however as they see that they are safe, and have laid aside all fear, they are very simple and honest, and exceedingly liberal with all they have; none of them refusing any thing he may possess when he is asked for it, but on the contrary inviting us to ask them. They exhibit great love towards all others in preference to themselves: they also give objects of great value for trifles, and content themselves with very little or nothing in return.

I however forbad that these trifles and articles of no value (such as pieces of dishes, plates, and glass, keys, and leather straps) should be given to them, although if they could obtain them, they imagined themselves to be possessed of the most beautiful trinkets in the world. It even happened that a sailor received for a leather strap as much gold as was worth three golden nobles, and for things of more trifling value offered by our men, especially newly coined blancas, or any gold coins, the Indians would give whatever the seller required: as, for instance, an ounce and a half or two ounces of gold, or thirty or forty pounds of cotton, with which commodity they were already acquainted. Thus they bartered, like idiots, cotton and gold for fragments of bows, glasses, bottles, and jars; which I forbade as being unjust, and myself gave them many beautiful and acceptable articles which I had brought with me, taking nothing from them in return; I did this in order that I might the more easily conciliate them, that they might be led to become Christians, and be inclined to entertain a regard for the King and Queen, our Princes and all Spaniards, and that I might induce them to take an interest in seeking out, and collecting, and delivering to us such things as they possessed in abundance, but which we greatly needed.

They practise no kind of idolatry, but have a firm belief that all strength and power, and indeed all good things, are in heaven, and that I had descended from thence with these ships and sailors, and under this impression was I received after they had thrown aside their fears. Nor are they slow or stupid, but of very clear understanding; and those men who have crossed to the neighbouring islands give an admirable description of everything they observed; but they never saw any people clothed, nor any ships like ours.

In all these islands there is no difference of physiognomy, of manners, or of language, but they all clearly understand each other, a circumstance very propitious for the realization of what I conceive to be the principal wish of our most serene King, namely, the conversion of these people to the holy faith of Christ, to which indeed, as far as I can judge, they are very favourable and well-disposed. There was one large town in Española of which especially I took possession, situated in a remarkably favourable spot, and in every way convenient for the purposes of gain and commerce. To this town I gave the name of Navidad del Señor, and ordered a fortress to be built there, which must by this time be completed, in which I left as many men as I thought necessary, with all sorts of arms, and enough provisions for more than a year. I also left them one caravel, and skilful workmen both in ship-building and other arts, and engaged the favor and friendship of the King of the island in their behalf, to a degree that would not be believed, for these people are so amiable and friendly that even the King took a pride in calling me his brother. But supposing their feelings should become changed, and they should wish to injure those who have remained in the fortress, they could not do so, for they have no arms, they go naked, and are moreover too cowardly; so that those who hold the said fortress, can easily keep the whole island in check, without any pressing danger to themselves, provided they do not transgress the directions and regulations which I have given them.

As far as I have learned, every man throughout these islands is united to but one wife, with the exception of the kings and princes, who are allowed to have twenty: the women seem to work more than the men. I could not clearly understand whether the people possess any private property, for I observed that one man had the charge of distributing various things to the rest, but especially meat and provisions and the like. I did not find, as some of us had expected, any cannibals amongst them, but on the contrary men of great deference and kindness. Neither are they black, like the

Ethiopians: their hair is smooth and straight: for they do not dwell where the rays of the sun strike most vividly, and the sun has intense power there, the distance from the equinoctial line being, it appears, but six-and-twenty degrees. On the tops of the mountains the cold is very great, but the effect of this upon the Indians is lessened by their being accustomed to the climate, and by their frequently indulging in the use of very hot meats and drinks.

Finally, to compress into few words the entire summary of my voyage and speedy return, and of the advantages derivable therefrom, I promise, that with a little assistance afforded me by our most invincible sovereigns, I will procure them as much gold as they need, as great a quantity of spices, of cotton, and of mastic (which is only found in Chios), and as many men for the service of the navy as their Majesties may require. I promise also rhubarb and other sorts of drugs, which I am persuaded the men whom I have left in the aforesaid fortress have found already and will continue to find; for I myself have tarried no where longer than I was compelled to do by the winds, except in the city of Navidad, while I provided for the building of the fortress, and took the necessary precautions for the perfect security of the men I left there. Although all I have related may appear to be wonderful and unheard of, yet the results of my voyage would have been more astonishing if I had had at my disposal such ships as I required.

But these great and marvellous results are not to be attributed to any merit of mine, but to the holy Christian faith, and to the piety and religion of our Sovereigns; for that which the unaided intellect of man could not compass, the spirit of God has granted to human exertions, for God is wont to hear the prayers of his servants who love his precepts even to the performance of apparent impossibilities. Thus it has happened to me in the present instance, who have accomplished a task to which the powers of mortal men had never hitherto attained; for if there have been those who have anywhere written or spoken of these islands, they have done so with doubts and conjectures, and no one has ever asserted that he has seen them, on which account their writings have been looked upon as little else than fables. Therefore let the king and queen, our princes and their most happy kingdoms, and all the other provinces of Christendom, render thanks to our Lord and Savior Jesus Christ, who has granted us so great a victory and such prosperity. Let processions be made, and sacred feasts be held, and the temples be adorned with festive boughs. Let Christ rejoice on earth, as he rejoices in heaven in the prospect of the salvation of the souls of so many nations hitherto lost. Let us also rejoice, as well on account of the exaltation of our faith, as on account of the increase of our temporal prosperity, of which not only Spain, but all Christendom will be partakers.

Such are the events which I have briefly described. Farewell.

Lisbon, the 14th of March.

CHRISTOPHER COLUMBUS,
Admiral of the Fleet of the Ocean.

FOCUS QUESTIONS

1. What was Columbus's purpose when he wrote this letter?

2. Columbus found the islands he explored to be "thickly peopled." What seems to be his attitude toward the inhabitants of the islands?

3. The Europeans engaged in trade with the Indians and prided themselves upon getting a good deal. How did the trade work? Do you think the Indians felt the same way?

4. What appear to be the overall goals of the Spanish explorers?

5. Can you make some generalizations about fifteenth-century European views of alien cultures?

73

The True History of the Conquest of New Spain (1552–1568 C.E.)

BERNAL DÍAZ

Bernal Díaz del Castillo (ca. 1492–1581) was one of the soldiers who accompanied Hernán Cortés on the conquest of the Aztecs. Díaz left Spain for the New World at the age of 18 and had explored both Cuba and the Yucatán Peninsula before he joined the Cortés expedition. After the conquest of Mexico, Díaz accompanied Cortés on his unsuccessful expedition into Honduras. He remained in Central America for most of his life, settling in what is now Guatemala, where his papers, including the manuscript copy of his True History, *remain.*

Díaz wrote The True History of the Conquest of New Spain *to refute what he regarded as inaccurate accounts of the conquest. Although he was an eyewitness and participant, his history was not written until many years later and was undoubtedly colored by his polemical purpose. Nevertheless, his description of Tenochtitlán, capital of Montezuma's empire, remains compelling.*

As we had already been in Mexico for four days and none of us had left our quarters except to go to the houses and gardens, Cortés told us it would be a good idea to go to the main plaza and see the great temple of their Uichilobos....

Many of Montezuma's chiefs were sent to accompany us, and when we arrived at the great square we were struck by the throngs of people and the amount of merchandise they displayed, at the efficiency and administration of everything.

The chiefs who accompanied us showed us how each kind of merchandise was kept separate and had its place marked out. Let us start with the dealers in gold, silver, and precious stones, feathers, cloth, and embroidered goods, and other merchandise in the form of men and women to be sold as slaves. There were as many here as the Negroes brought from Guinea by the Portuguese. Some were tied to long poles with collars around their necks so they couldn't escape, and others were left free. Then there were merchants who sold home-spun clothing, cotton, and thread, and others who sold cacao, so that one could see every sort of goods that is to be found in all of New Spain, set out the way it's done where I come from, Medina del Campo, during fair time....

I wonder why I waste all these words in telling what they sold in that great square, for I shall never finish describing everything in detail. But I must mention the paper, which is called *amal*, the little pipes scented with liquidambar and filled with tobacco, and the yellow ointments and other things of the same sort, all sold separately. Cochineal was sold under the arcades, and herbs and many other kinds of goods. There were buildings where three judges sat, and magistrates who inspected the merchandise.... I wish I could get through with telling all the things they sold there, but only to finish looking and inquiring about everything in that great square filled with people would have taken two days, and then you wouldn't have seen everything.

When we climbed to the top of the great *cu* there was a kind of platform, with huge stones where they put the poor Indians to be sacrificed, and an image like a dragon and other evil figures, with a great deal of blood that had been shed that day. Montezuma, accompanied by two priests, came out from an oratory dedicated to the worship of his cursed idols at the top of the *cu*, and said with great deference toward all of us, "You must be tired, Señor Malinche, after climbing up this great temple of ours." Through our interpreters, who went with us, Cortés replied that neither he nor the rest of us ever got tired from anything. Then Montezuma took him by the hand and bade him look at his great city and at all the other cities rising from the water, and the many towns around the lake; and if he had not seen the market place well, he said, he could see it from here much better.

There we stood looking, for that large and evil temple was so high that it towered over everything. From there we could see all three of the causeways that led into Mexico: the road from Iztapalapa, by which we had entered four days earlier; the Tacuba road, by which we fled the night of our great rout; and the road from Tepeaquilla.

We saw the fresh water that came from Chapultepec, which supplied the city, and the bridges on the three causeways, built at certain intervals so the water could go from one part of the lake to another, and a multitude of canoes, some arriving with provisions and others leaving with merchandise. We saw that every house in this great city and in the others built on the water could be reached only by wooden drawbridges or by canoe. We saw temples built like towers and fortresses in these cities, all whitewashed; it was a sight to see. We could look down on the flat-roofed houses and other little towers and temples like fortresses along the causeways.

After taking a good look and considering all that we had seen, we looked again at the great square and the throngs of people, some buying and others selling. The buzzing of their voices could be heard more than a league away. There were soldiers among us who had been in many parts of the world, in Constantinople and Rome and all over Italy, who said that they had never before seen a market place so large and so well laid out and so filled with people.

Then Cortés said to Montezuma, through Doña Marina, "Your Highness is indeed a great prince, and it has delighted us to see your cities. Now that we are here in your temple, will you show us your gods?"

Montezuma replied that he would first have to consult with his priests. After he had spoken with them, he bade us enter a small tower room, a kind of hall where there were two altars with very richly painted planks on the ceiling. On each altar there were two giant figures, their bodies very tall and stout. The first one, to the right, they said was Uichilobos, their god of war. It had a very broad face with monstrous, horrible eyes, and the whole body was covered with precious stones, gold, and pearls that were stuck on with a paste they make in this country out of roots. The body was circled with great snakes made of gold and precious stones, and in one hand he held a bow and in the other some arrows. A small idol standing by him they said was his page; he held a short lance and a shield rich with gold and precious stones. Around the neck of Uichilobos were silver Indian faces and things that we took to be the hearts of these Indians, made of gold and decorated with many precious blue stones. There were braziers with copal incense, and they were burning in them the hearts of three Indians they had sacrificed that day. All the walls and floor were black with crusted blood, and the whole place stank.

To the left stood another great figure, the height of Uichilobos, with the face of a bear and glittering eyes made of their mirrors, which they call *tezcal*. It was decorated with precious stones the same as Uichilobos, for they said that the two were brothers. This Tezcatepuca was the god of hell and had charge of the souls of the Mexicans. His body was girded with figures like little devils, with snakelike tails. The walls were so crusted with blood and the floor was so bathed in it that in the slaughterhouses of Castile there was no such stink. They had offered to this idol five hearts from the day's sacrifices.

In the highest part of the *cu* there was another recess, the wood of which was very richly carved, where there was another figure, half man and half lizard, covered with precious stones and with a mantle over half of it. They said that its body was filled with all the seeds there are in all the world. It was the god of sowing and ripening, but I do not remember its name. Everything was covered with blood, the walls as well as the altar, and it stank so much that we couldn't get out fast enough.

Our captain said to Montezuma, half laughingly, "Lord Montezuma, I do not understand how such a great prince and wise man as yourself can have failed to come to the conclusion that these idols of yours are not gods, but evil things—devils is the term for them. So that you and your priests may see it clearly, do me a favor: Let us put a cross on top of this tower, and in one part of these oratories, where your Uichilobos and Tezcatepuca are, we will set up an image of Our Lady [an image that Montezuma had already seen], and you will see

how afraid of it these idols that have deceived you are."

The two priests with Montezuma looked hostile, and Montezuma replied with annoyance, "Señor Malinche if I had thought that you would so insult my gods, I would not have shown them to you. We think they are very good, for they give us health, water, good seed-times and weather, and all the victories we desire. We must worship and make sacrifices to them. Please do not say another word to their dishonor."

When our captain heard this and saw how changed Montezuma was, he didn't argue with him any more, but smiled and said, "It is time for Your Highness and ourselves to go."

Montezuma agreed, but he said that before he left he had to pray and make certain offerings to atone for the great sin he had committed in permitting us to climb the great *cu* and see his gods, and for being the cause of the dishonor that we had done them by speaking ill of them.

FOCUS QUESTIONS

1. What impressed Díaz most about the city? Is his list of the merchandise he saw for sale random or ordered?

2. Why does Díaz describe the Aztec gods as devils?

3. How does the fact that the Aztecs sacrificed humans color Díaz's account of their religion?

4. Who do you have more sympathy for, Cortés or Montezuma? How does Díaz manipulate your sympathies?

74

An Aztec Account of the Conquest of Mexico (1528 C.E.)

There are several surviving accounts of the conquest of Mexico written by indigenous tribesmen. They tell the story of the fall of Tenochtitlán and the suffering of the tribesmen who defended it. One of these accounts is cast in a narrative form not unlike that of Bernal

Díaz. It relates the experience of the warriors of Tlatelolca in attempting to defend their city and the suffering they experienced during the Spanish siege.

The manuscript of this anonymous account has been preserved in Paris. It was written in 1528 in the Nahuatl language, perhaps by more than one author. Whoever composed it was clearly an eyewitness to the events being described. "The Captain" referred to is Corte and "The Sun" is Don Pedro de Alvarado, one of Cortés's lieutenants.

Year 1—Canestalk. The Spaniards came to the palace at Tlayacac. When the Captain arrived at the palace, Motecuhzoma sent the Cuetlaxteca to greet him and to bring him two suns as gifts. One of these suns was made of the yellow metal, the other of the white. The Cuetlaxteca also brought him a mirror to be hung on his person, a gold collar, a great gold pitcher, fans and ornaments of quetzal feathers and a shield inlaid with mother-of-pearl.

The envoys made sacrifices in front of the Captain. At this, he grew very angry. When they offered him blood in an "eagle dish," he shouted at the man who offered it and struck him with his sword. The envoys departed at once.

Then the Captain marched to Tenochtitlán. He arrived here during the month called Bird, under the sign of the day 8-Wind. When he entered the city, we gave him chickens, eggs, corn, tortillas and drink. We also gave him firewood, and fodder for his "deer." Some of these gifts were sent by the lord of Tenochtitlán, the rest by the lord of Tlatelolco.

During this time, the people asked Motecuhzoma how they should celebrate their god's fiesta. He said: "Dress him in all his finery, in all his sacred ornaments."

During this same time, The Sun commanded that Motecuhzoma and Itzcohuatzin, the military chief of Tlatelolco, be made prisoners. The Spaniards hanged a chief from Acolhuacan named Nezahualquentzin. They also murdered the king of Nauhtla, Cohualpopocatzin, by wounding him with arrows and then burning him alive.

For this reason, our warriors were on guard at the Eagle Gate. The sentries from Tenochtitlán stood at one side of the gate, and the sentries from Tlatelolco at the other. But messengers came to tell them to dress the figure of Huitzilopochtli. They left their posts and went to dress him in his sacred finery: his ornaments and his paper clothing.

When this had been done, the celebrants began to sing their songs. That is how they celebrated the first day of the fiesta. On the second day they began to sing again, but without warning they were all put to death. The dancers and singers were completely unarmed. They brought only their embroidered cloaks, their turquoises, their lip plugs, their necklaces, their clusters of heron feathers, their trinkets made of deer hooves. Those who played the drums, the old men, had brought their gourds of snuff and their timbrels.

The Spaniards attacked the musicians first, slashing at their hands and faces until they had killed all of them. The singers—and even the spectators—were also killed. This slaughter in the Sacred Patio went on for three hours. Then the Spaniards burst into the rooms of the temple to kill the others: those who were carrying water, or bringing fodder for the horses, or grinding meal, or sweeping, or standing watch over this work.

The king Motecuhzoma, who was accompanied by Itzcohuatzin and by those who had brought food for the Spaniards, protested: "Our lords, that is enough! What are you doing? These people are not carrying shields or *macanas* Our lords, they are completely unarmed!"

The Sun treacherously murdered our people on the twentieth day after the Captain left for the coast. We allowed the Captain to return to the city in peace. But on the following day we attacked him with all our might, and that was the beginning of the war.

Now the Spaniards began to wage war against us. They attacked us by land for ten days, and then

Quetzalcoatl. Quetzalcoatl was a favorite deity of the Central American peoples. His visage of a plumed serpent, as shown here, was prominent in the royal capital of Teotihuacán. According to legend, Quetzalcoatl, the leader of the Toltecs, was tricked into drunkenness and humiliated by a rival god. In disgrace, he left his homeland but promised to return. In 1519, the Aztec monarch Montezuma welcomed Herna Cortés, the leader of the Spanish expedition, believing he was a representative of Quetzalcoatl.

their ships appeared. Twenty days later, they gathered all their ships together near Nonohualco, off the place called Mazatzintamalco. The allies from Tlaxcala and Huexotzinco set up camp on either side of the road.

Our warriors from Tlatelolco immediately leaped into their canoes and set out for Mazatzintamalco and the Nonohualco road. But no one set out from Tenochtitlán to assist us: only the Tlatelolcas were ready when the Spaniards arrived in their ships. On the following day, the ships sailed to Xoloco.

The fighting at Xoloco and Huitzillan lasted for two days. While the battle was under way, the warriors from Tenochtitlán began to mutiny. They said: "Where are our chiefs? They have fired scarcely a single arrow! Do they think they have fought like men?" Then they seized four of their own leaders and put them to death. The victims were two captains, Cuauhnochtli and Cuapan, and the priests of Amantlan and Tlalocan. This was the second time that the people of Tenochtitlán killed their own leaders.

THE FLIGHT TO TLATELOLCO

The Spaniards set up two cannons in the middle of the road and aimed them at the city. When they fired them, one of the shots struck the Eagle Gate. The people of the city were so terrified that they began to flee to Tlatelolco. They brought their idol Huitzilopochtli with them, setting it up in the House of the Young Men. Their king Cuauhtemoc also abandoned Tenochtitlán. Their chiefs said: "Mexicanos! Tlatelolcas! All is not lost! We can still defend our houses. We can prevent them from capturing our storehouses and the produce of our lands. We can save the sustenance of life, our stores of corn. We can also save our weapons and insignia, our clusters of rich feathers, our gold earrings and precious stones. Do not be discouraged; do not lose heart. We are Mexicanos! We are Tlatelolcas!"

During the whole time we were fighting, the warriors of Tenochtitlán were nowhere to be seen. The battles at Yacacolco, Atezcapan, Coatlan, Nonohualco, Xoxohuitlan, Tepeyacac and elsewhere were all fought by ourselves, by Tlatelolcas. In the same way, the canals were defended solely by Tlatelolcas.

The captains from Tenochtitlán cut their hair short, and so did those of lesser rank. The Otomies and the other ranks that usually wore headdresses did not wear them during all the time we were fighting. The Tlatelolcas surrounded the most important captains and their women taunted them: "Why are you hanging back? Have you no shame? No woman will ever paint her face for you again!" The wives of the men from Tenochtitlán wept and begged for pity.

When the warriors of Tlatelolco heard what was happening, they began to shout, but still the brave captains of Tenochtitlán hung back. As for the Tlatelolcas, their humblest warriors died fighting as bravely as their captains.

The Spaniards made ready to attack us, and the war broke out again. They assembled their forces in Cuepopan and Cozcacuahco. A vast number of our warriors were killed by their metal darts. Their ships sailed to Texopan, and the battle there lasted three days. When they had forced us to retreat, they entered the Sacred Patio, where there was a four-day battle. Then they reached Yacacolco.

The Tlatelolcas set up three racks of heads in three different places. The first rack was in the Sacred Patio of Tlilancalco [Black House], where we strung up the heads of our lords the Spaniards. The second was in Acacolco, where we strung up Spanish heads and the heads of two of their horses. The third was in Zacatla, in front of the temple of the earth-goddess Cihuacoatl, where we strung up the heads of Tlaxcaltecas.

The women of Tlatelolco joined in the fighting. They struck at the enemy and shot arrows at them; they tucked up their skirts and dressed in the regalia of war.

The Spaniards forced us to retreat. Then they occupied the market place. The Tlatelolcas—the Jaguar Knights, the Eagle Knights, the great warriors—were defeated, and this was the end of the battle. It had lasted five days, and two thousand Tlatelolcas were killed in action. During the battle, the Spaniards set up a canopy for the Captain in the market place. They also mounted a catapult on the temple platform.

EPIC DESCRIPTION OF THE
BESIEGED CITY

And all these misfortunes befell us. We saw them and wondered at them; we suffered this unhappy fate.

> Broken spears lie in the roads;
> we have torn our hair in our grief.
> The houses are roofless now, and their walls
>   are red with blood.
> Worms are swarming in the streets and plazas,
>   and the walls are splattered with gore.
> The water has turned red, as if it were dyed,
> and when we drink it,
> it has the taste of brine.
> We have pounded our hands in despair against
>   the adobe walls,
> for our inheritance, our city, is lost and dead.

The shields of our warriors were its defense,
  but they could not save it.
We have chewed dry twigs and salt grasses;
we have filled our mouths with dust and bits
  of adobe;
we have eaten lizards, rats and worms....
When we had meat, we ate it almost raw. It
was scarcely on the fire before we snatched it and
gobbled it down.

They set a price on all of us: on the young
men, the priests, the boys and girls. The price of a
poor man was only two handfuls of corn, or ten
cakes made from mosses or twenty cakes of salty
couch-grass. Gold, jade, rich cloths, quetzal feathers—everything that once was precious was now
considered worthless.

FOCUS QUESTIONS

1. How were the Spaniards greeted when they
first arrived? How was the offering of blood
understood by the natives? How was it understood by the Spaniards?

2. How did the war begin? Why does the author
believe that it was the natives who started it?

3. What was the nature of Montezuma's army?
Did he command a single state?

4. How did the Tlatelolcas taunt their own allies?
What values are implicit in their insults?

75

History of the Inca Empire (1653 C.E.)

BERNABE COBO

*Bernabe Cobo (1580–1657), a Jesuit missionary, was one of the great historians of the
civilizations of South America. He left his home in southern Spain as a teenager to travel
to the New World. He spent most of his life in Peru, where he worked to convert
Incas to Western religion and agricultural practices. Little is known of his life, but it is clear
that he spent many years diligently collecting materials for his history and, as a result,
preserved many oral accounts of the nature of Incan life before the coming of the Spanish.*

The portion of the History of the Inca Empire *that has survived is more a
sociological and anthropological account of pre-Columbian South American culture
than a conventional history. Cobo collected the legends of the founding of the Incas and
recorded the oral traditions surrounding the monarchy, but he was most interested in
customs and social organization.*

OF THE LAWS AND PUNISHMENTS WITH WHICH THE INCAS GOVERNED THEIR KINGDOM

Since the Indians lacked writing, they had no written laws, but the ones that their kings had established were preserved by tradition, use, and observance. I will record here the most important laws that were most prominent in their memories.

Where the Inca was present, he alone was the judge, and before him all offenses committed were tried; and where he was not present, his governors and caciques administered justice. They were selected to serve as judges according to the nature of the case.

When someone committed an offense that was deserving of punishment, he was apprehended and put in jail, and in order to bring his case to trial, he was taken out of jail and brought before the Inca or the presiding judge and *curaca*. During the trial, witnesses were brought out and confronted the accused. Each one told what he knew about the case against the accused, and in this way they convinced the judge. After the case was heard, without other proceedings, time limit, or delay, the Inca or judge pronounced the sentence and ordered that the delinquent be punished in accordance with his guilt.

He that killed another in order to rob him received the death penalty, and before it was executed, the guilty person was tortured in jail to increase the punishment, and after being tortured, he was killed.

He that killed by treachery was put to death publicly and insultingly, even though he was a nobleman and the dead man was of much lesser station.

He that killed by casting spells received the death penalty. This punishment was executed with much publicity, bringing together the people of the surrounding towns so that they would be present at the execution, and likewise all of his household and family were killed because it was presumed that they all knew that craft.

If someone was killed in a quarrel, first it was determined who caused it; if the dead man did, the killer was given a light punishment at the discretion of the Inca; if the one who caused the fight was the slayer, he received the death penalty, or at the very best, he was exiled to the provinces of the Andes, a sick and unhealthy land for the Indians of the sierra; there he would serve for his whole life, as on the galleys, in the Inca's *chacaras* of coca.

The cacique that killed one of his subjects without permission from the Inca was punished in public by being given certain blows on the back with a stone (this was called stone punishment, and it was a great insult). It was done even though the Indian may have been guilty of some act of disobedience against the cacique in question. If after the cacique was reprehended and punished, he repeated the same offense, he died for it; and if this punishment was not executed, due to pleas and intercessions, the Inca took the offender's cacicazgo away from him and gave it to another.

The husband that killed his wife for adultery was set free without punishment, but if he killed her due to anger and passion, he received the death penalty if he was an ordinary man, but if he was an important gentleman who commanded respect, he did not die, but he was given another punishment.

The woman that killed her husband received the death penalty, and it was executed in this way: she was hung up by the feet in some public place, and she was left like this until she died, without anyone daring to take her down.

The pregnant woman that took potions in order to kill her baby received the death penalty, and the same punishment was given to the person that gave her the potions or maliciously made her abort by striking her or some other mistreatment.

He that forced a single woman was given the stone punishment for the first time, and the second time, the death penalty.

He that forcibly corrupted some maiden received the death penalty if she was a noble woman, and if she was not, the first time, he was given a certain torture that was used, and the second time, he died.

He that committed adultery with another man's wife who was not of the nobility was tortured, but if she was of the nobility, he received the death penalty and she died also.

He that took the daughter from her father against his will got no punishment at all, if the daughter consented and was not forced and both were from the same town; however, the father could punish her if he wished for having taken a husband without his consent, but the Inca would order that they be apprehended and separated because nobody could take a wife without his permission.

When someone was found in the house of another with his daughter, if the father made a complaint, the delinquent was punished at the discretion of the Inca and his governor.

He that scaled the walls of the house or retreat of the *mamaconas* was killed; he was hung by the feet and left that way within the very house where he committed the offense, and if any of the *mamaconas* let him inside and sinned with him, she was given the same punishment.

In certain cases marriage was prohibited, and fornication in the cases in which marriage was prohibited was punishable with the death penalty, and this punishment was executed without remission, if the guilty party was not a noble, because a noble got only a public reprimand.

He that robbed without reason, besides paying for the stolen item if he had the resources, was exiled to the Andes, nor would he dare to return without the Inca's permission.

He that stole things to eat from necessity was reprimanded and given no other punishment than being warned to work and that if he did it again he would be punished by being struck on the back with a stone in public.

He that stole some fruit from the fields or orchards by necessity while traveling was killed for it if the property belonged to the Inca; if the property belonged to someone else, the man was pardoned.

When one of the Indians that served in the *tambos* did not turn over the load that he was carrying to the proprietor, the town that the Indian in question was from had to pay for it because the town was responsible for the service of that tambo, and the Indian was punished.

He that stole the water with which the *chacaras* were irrigated and brought it to his *chacara* before it was his turn was punished with an arbitrary penalty.

He that insulted another was given an arbitrary punishment, but he that had provoked the words was given a greater penalty.

He that injured another or caused some similar harm was punished with an arbitrary penalty, and if it was done treacherously, he was tortured.

He that maimed another in a quarrel to such an extent that the injured party could not do ordinary work was obliged to support the injured party from his own property, apart from the punishment that was given to him for the offense, and if he had no property, the Inca fed the injured party from his property, and the delinquent was given a greater punishment.

He that maliciously burned a bridge received the death penalty, and it was executed without fail.

The Indian that was disobedient to his cacique for the first time was given the punishment that the Inca deemed appropriate: the second time he did it, he was given the stone punishment, and the third time, death.

The *mitima* Indian that left the place where he had been put by the Inca to serve as *mitima* was tortured the first time, and the second, he was killed.

He that changed the dress and insignia of the province where he was born committed a great offense against the Inca, against his nation, and against the province whose dress he adopted, and thus he was accused by all of them and punished with rigor.

He that removed the stone boundary markers or entered into the land or property of another was given the stone punishment for the first time, and the second time, he received the death penalty.

He that hunted without permission on any land where trespassing was prohibited was castigated by being struck on the back with a stone and tortured.

If someone's livestock damaged someone else's property, the owner of the property could take as much of the livestock as the damage was worth, and they had established how many feet of maize equaled a certain unit of measurement, by which they assigned a specific penalty that was paid in proportion to the amount of damage done.

When travelers had something stolen from them in a *tambo*, first of all the cacique in charge of the *tambo* was punished, and afterward the latter punished the rest of his subjects for negligence and not having been watchful.

The Indian that did not show the proper respect for the Inca and lords was put in jail, where he was left for a long time, and if, in addition to this, they found him to be guilty of something else, he was killed.

He that was a liar and perjurer was tortured as a punishment, and if he was very addicted to this vice and did not mend his ways with this punishment, he was killed in public.

If a governor failed to administer justice or covered up anything for reasons of bribery or because he was so inclined, the Inca himself punished him, taking his *cacicazgo* and post away from him and denying him the right to have others, and if the injustice involved something serious, the Inca ordered that the offender be killed.

The Incas had two prisons in Cuzco. One of them was half a league away from the city, in front of the parish of San Sebastian, which used to be called Arauaya, and was located in a place named Umpillay; here thieves and other criminals were punished with the death penalty, which was executed by hanging the wrongdoers upside down and leaving them hanging there until they died. The other prison was underground within the city; in it they had enclosed lions [pumas], bears, tigers [jaguars], and serpents; and the people who committed the most atrocious offenses, such as treason against the king and the like, were thrown to these wild beasts and eaten by them. These Indians had many other laws which were very beneficial for governing their republic well. True it is that some of them were too rigorous, such as those that required the death penalty and other exorbitant punishments for light offenses. Also it should be known that justice was not uniform and equal among them; although they prided themselves on being just and punishing all offenses, they always gave different penalties to the nobles and the wealthy than they gave to the humble and poor. This was due to an illusion that they had which was to say

that a public reprimand was a far greater punishment for an Inca of noble blood than the death penalty for a plebeian. They justified their follies as well as their lofty positions on the assumption that they were children of the Sun and the first ones to found the religion and sacrifices of the Sun. Therefore, in the enforcement of their laws, they paid careful attention to these privileges, and thus the punishments were different according to the social status of the person that broke the laws. It turned out that for the same offenses that a common person would get the death penalty, nobles of Inca lineage would get no other punishment than a public reprimand; but this reprimand was so feared that the Indians affirm that it has happened only a few times, and very rarely has a noble been executed.

HOW THE INCAS ADMINISTERED NEWLY CONQUERED LANDS

Although it was very extensive and composed of many and very different nations, the entire empire of the Incas was a single republic, governed by the same laws, privileges, and customs, and it was observant of the same religion, rites, and ceremonies; however, before being brought under Inca rule, the several nations had their own common law and a different way of living and governing themselves. This union and uniformity was maintained everywhere; and it must be understood that what we say here that the Incas introduced into the nations that they subjugated was the same type of government that they maintained at the Inca court and where they ruled before.

The first thing that these kings did when they won a province was to take out of it six or seven thousand families (more or less, according to what seemed fitting to them, judging by the number and disposition of the people they found) and send them to other parts of the quiet and peaceful provinces, distributing them throughout a number of towns; and in exchange for them they put the same number of other people, who were made to leave the places where the first were settled, or from wherever the Incas wished, and among them were many *orejones* of noble blood. These individuals who settled in new lands were called *mitimaes*, which is the same as to say "newcomers" or "outsiders" in contrast to the natives; this name referred to the new vassals as well as to the old ones who were exchanged for them; in fact, both went from their own lands to strange lands; and even today we use the word in this way, calling all of the newcomers who are settled in all the provinces of this kingdom *mitimaes*. Care was taken in this transmigration that those who were transferred, the recently conquered as well as the others, did not move to just any land, in a haphazard way, but to the places that were of the same climate and qualities or very similar to those they were leaving and in which they were raised. Therefore, those who were native to cold lands were taken to cold lands and those from hot lands to hot lands, so that in this way they would not regret moving from their natural home so much and they would be healthier in the new lands, without falling ill from the change, which would be the case if they were taken to lands of the opposite climate of their homeland. The people who were moved by the Inca in this way were relieved from obedience to their former caciques, and they were ordered to submit to the rule of the caciques of the lands where they were placed; and there it was ordered that both types of *mitimaes* be given places to build homes and lands in which to prepare their *chacaras* and plant their crops, and they were to remain there as perpetual residents of the towns where they were placed; and they were to follow the practices and way of life of the local people, except that they retained the dress, emblems, and symbols of the people from their nation or province; moreover, this custom has been preserved up to the present time, for even now on the basis of the aforementioned things, we can distinguish between the natives of each town and the *mitimaes*.

The Inca introduced this change of residence in order to keep his dominion quiet and safe. The city of Cuzco, capital of the kingdom where the Inca had his court and residence, was far away from the most remote provinces in which there were many nations of barbaric and warlike people; therefore, the Inca felt that he could not maintain peace and obedience in any other way, and since this was the main reason why this measure was taken, the Inca ordered that the majority of the *mitimaes* who were made to go to recently subjugated towns settle in the provincial capitals so that they could serve as a garrison and presidio—not for a salary or for a limited time; rather, the *mitimaes* and their descendants would remain perpetually. And, as would be the case with warriors, they were given some privileges so they would appear to be more noble, and the Inca commanded that they always be very obedient and do whatever their captains and governors might order. With this skillful plan, as long as these *mitimaes* were loyal to the governors, if the natives rebelled, soon they would be reduced to obeying the Inca, and if the *mitimaes* made a disturbance and started an uprising, they would be repressed and punished by the natives; and thus, by means of this resolution to make the majority of their people reestablish themselves by shifting some to the places of others, the king kept his states secure from rebellion. Moreover, trade and commerce between provinces was more frequent and all the land better supplied with what was needed. Furthermore, with this transfer of their vassals from one place to another, the Incas aimed to achieve throughout their kingdom similarity and uniformity in matters pertaining to religion and political government, and they expected all of the nations of the kingdom to learn the language of Cuzco, which in this way came to be the general language of all Peru. With this shuffling of domiciles, the newly conquered, who were transferred within the kingdom, learned all this in a short time and without suffering or compulsion, and the old vassals who settled as *mitimaes* in the newly pacified areas taught the natives; great care was taken in this and the natives were compelled to learn, for the Incas obliged everyone to accept their language, laws, and religion, along with all of the opinions related to these matters that were established in Cuzco. The Incas eliminated, either completely or partially, the practices and rites that the conquered people had before Inca ways were imposed. In order to introduce and establish these things more effectively, besides the aforementioned conversion of the people, upon conquering a province, the Incas had the people's main idol taken away and placed in Cuzco with the same services and cult that it used to have in the province of its origin, and the natives were obliged to take care of all this, exactly as had been done when the aforementioned idol or *guaca* was in their province. For that reason Indians from all the provinces of the kingdom resided in Cuzco. These Indians were occupied in the care and ministry of their idols, and there they learned the practices and customs of the courtiers. Since they took turns by their *mitas* and assigned time for service, after returning to their own province they maintained the practices they had seen and learned in the court, and they taught all this to their people.

In the process of moving the *mitimaes*, no thought was given to the distance that there was from their lands to where they were ordered to go, even though it was very great. On the contrary, not infrequently, it happened that they were transplanted from one end of the kingdom to the other; other times they were moved three or four hundred leagues, more or less, as the prince deemed fitting; for this reason, today in the provinces of Collao there are *mitimaes* who are natives originally from the provinces of Chinchaysuyu, and in the latter provinces there are many Indians from the former. It is a proven fact that the Indians of different provinces were so mixed and thrown together that there is hardly a valley or town throughout Peru where some *ayllo* and tribal group of *mitimaes* would not be found. Mainly, the Inca took two things into consideration when moving his subjects. The first one was (as has been stated) that they not go to a climate that was contrary to their nature, and the other, that all the provinces of his empire be well populated and well supplied with food and everything necessary for human life. For this reason, he put people from elsewhere in the sparsely populated areas, and from the places that had more people than could be comfortably supported, the Inca took colonies to settle in the less populous ones; and these people who by order of the king left their own land and the jurisdiction of their caciques and

settled in strange lands, giving obedience at the same time to the local caciques, are the ones who were actually called *mitimaes* during the time of the Incas. But after the Spaniards occupied this land, this name has been extended to others who were not actually *mitimaes* formerly; in fact, the word was extended to include the Indians who, by order of their caciques and with their permission or that of the Inca, lived away from their towns and provinces of origin in the districts of other caciques, although they were not under the jurisdiction of the latter, but under the caciques of the province from whence they came or where they were born. For an explanation of this, it is necessary to presuppose the existence of an ancient custom of these people, and it is that when some province did not produce certain foods, especially none of their bread, which was *maize*, but was suitable for other uses, special arrangements were made. For example, due to the extreme cold, the provinces of Collao do not produce maize or other seeds or fruits of temperate lands, but they are very abundant in pasture lands and most appropriate for raising livestock and producing *papas* [potatoes], from which *chuño*, their substitute for bread, is made, as well as some other roots. For the inhabitants of these provinces, the Inca had picked out lands which lie in the hot valleys of the seacoast on one side and on the other side of the mountains toward the Andes; in these temperate valleys they plant the crops that they lack in their own lands; and since these valleys were from twenty, thirty, and more leagues away from their land and they could not come to cultivate them as a community group the way they do in the rest of the kingdom, the caciques took care to send, at the appropriate times, people to farm there, and after the crops were harvested, these people returned to their own towns. Apart from this, by order of the Inca, on the outskirts of each town there were a certain number of Indians with their women and houses; they resided permanently with their children and descendants in the aforementioned valleys, in order to care for and cultivate the *chacaras* of their caciques and their communities. These people, although they lived in the land of others, were under the jurisdiction of their own caciques, and not those of the land where they resided; but after the Spaniards entered into this kingdom, at the time that the land was visited for the first time in order to parcel it out and entrust it to the settlers, these Indians who were found in the aforementioned valleys, put there by their caciques for the reason just stated, were counted and assigned in repartimiento along with the natives of the district where they were living. They were also relieved from obedience to their former caciques, and they were put under the control of the caciques in whose jurisdiction and land they were living. Consequently, they were entrusted to the same encomendero to whom the district in question was parceled out and not to the encomendero of the *cacicazgo* of which they were natives. To all of these people who, in the aforementioned manner, had remained in the lands where we find them, we also give now the name of *mitimaes*, without distinguishing them from the first ones, the only people that were *mitimaes* at the time of the Incas.

FOCUS QUESTIONS

1. Characterize the Inca nation before the Spanish arrived.

2. How did Cobo's background influence his interpretation of Incan culture?

3. How did Cobo get his information? Why is his work written in the past tense?

4. Why was illicit intercourse with a noble woman punished more harshly than if committed with a common woman?

76

Apologetic History of the Indies (1566 C.E.)

BARTOLOMÉ DE LAS CASAS

Bartolomé de las Casas (1474–1566) was a Dominican friar, a bishop in the New World, and the Spanish government's unofficial "Protector of the Indians." Born in the bustling port of Seville, Las Casas witnessed Columbus's triumphant return from his first voyage. The exotic goods and the exotic tales with which the mariners returned fired the young friar's imagination. In 1498 Las Casas was presented with an Indian for use as a personal servant, and he was entranced by the simplicity and gentle nature of the Native Americans; he thereupon decided to devote his life to their salvation.

Arriving in the New World in 1502, Las Casas set about his mission, preaching among the Indians and baptizing those that he converted. He was appalled by the harsh treatment some Spaniards meted out to these innocent people. He returned to Spain in

1515 and launched a vigorous campaign to ensure the Indians' protection. The Apologetic History(1566) was a reflection of Las Casas's belief in the inherent goodness of the Native Americans, and of his conviction that all of humanity were God's children.

APOLOGETIC AND SUMMARY HISTORY TREATING THE QUALITIES, DISPOSITION, DESCRIPTION, SKIES AND SOIL OF THESE LANDS; AND THE NATURAL CONDITIONS, GOVERNANCE, NATIONS, WAYS OF LIFE AND CUSTOMS OF THE PEOPLES OF THESE WESTERN AND SOUTHERN INDIES, WHOSE SOVEREIGN REALM BELONGS TO THE MONARCHS OF CASTILE

Argument of the Work

The ultimate cause for writing this work was to gain knowledge of all the many nations of this vast new world. They had been defamed by persons who feared neither God nor the charge, so grievous before divine judgment, of defaming even a single man and causing him to lose his esteem and honor. From such slander can come great harm and terrible calamity, particularly when large numbers of men are concerned and, even more so, a whole new world. It has been written that these peoples of the Indies, lacking human governance and order nations, did not have the power of reason to govern themselves—which was inferred only from their having been found to be gentle, patient and humble. It has been implied that God became careless in creating so immense a number of rational souls and let human nature, which He so largely determined and provided for, go astray in the almost infinitesimal part of the human lineage which they comprise. From this it follows that they have all proven themselves unsocial and therefore monstrous, contrary to the natural bent of all peoples of the world; and that He did not allow any other species of corruptible creature to err in this way, excepting a strange and occasional case. In order to demonstrate the truth, which is the opposite, this book brings together and compiles certain natural, special and accidental causes which are specified below.... Not only have [the Indians] shown themselves to be very wise peoples and possessed of lively and marked understanding, prudently governing and providing for their nations (as much as they can be nations, without faith in or knowledge of the true God) and making them prosper injustice; but they have equalled many diverse nations of the world, past and present, that have been praised for their governance, politics and customs, and exceed by no small measure the wisest of all these, such as the Greeks and Romans, in adherence to the rules of natural reason. This advantage and superiority, along with everything said above, will appear quite clearly when, if it please God, the peoples are compared one with another. This history has been written with the aforesaid aim in mind by Fray Bartolomé de Las Casas, or Casaus, a monk of the Dominican Order and sometime bishop of Chiapa, who promises before the divine word that everything said and referred to is the truth, and that nothing of an untruthful nature appears to the best of his knowledge.

CHAPTER CXXVII. THE INDIANS POSSESSED MORE ENLIGHTENMENT AND NATURAL KNOWLEDGE OF GOD THAN THE GREEKS AND ROMANS

... These Indian peoples surpassed the Greeks and Romans in selecting for their gods, not sinful and criminal men noted for their great baseness, but virtuous ones—to the extent that virtue exists among people who lack the knowledge of the true God that is gained by faith…. The following argument can be formed for the proof of the above: The Indian nations seem to show themselves to be or to have been of better rational judgment and more prudent and upright in what they considered God to be. For nations which have reached the knowledge that there is a God hold in common the natural concept that God is the best of all things that can be imagined. Therefore the nation which has elected virtuous men as God or gods, though it might have erred in not selecting the true God, has a better concept and estimation of God and more natural purity than one which has selected and accepted for God or gods men known to be sinful and criminal. The latter was the case of the Greek and Roman states, which the former is that of all these Indian nations…. It seems probable that none of these Indian peoples will be more difficult of conversion than the ancient idolaters. First, because, as we have proved and are still proving, all these peoples are of good reason. Second, because they show less duplicity and more simplicity of heart than others. Third, because they are in their natural persons better adjusted, as has been proved above—a quality characteristic of men who may more easily be persuaded of the truth. Fourth, because an infinite number in their midst have already been converted (although some with certain difficulty, namely, those who worshiped many gods; for it is not possible except by a great miracle for a religion so aged, mellowed and time-honored to be abandoned suddenly, in a short time or with ease—as proven by all of the world's past and ancient idolaters)….

CHAPTER CCLXII. FROM ALL THAT HAS BEEN SAID IT IS INFERRED THAT THE INDIAN NATIONS EQUALLED AND EVEN SURPASSED ALL THE ANCIENT ONES IN GOOD LAWS AND CUSTOMS

… Let us compare [the ancients] with the people of the realms of Peru as concerns women, marriage and chastity. The [Peruvian] kings honored and favored marriages with their presence and performed them themselves or through their proconsuls and delegates. They themselves exhorted the newlyweds to live happily, and in this these people were superior to all nations. They were certainly superior to the Assyrians and Babylonians, … even to our own Spaniards of Cantabria, … more especially to the renowned isle of England … and to many others…. To whom were they not superior in the election and succession of kings and those who were to govern the country? They always chose the wisest, most virtuous and most worthy of ruling, those who had subordinated all natural and sensual affection and were free and clean of repugnant ambition and all private interests.

They were likewise more than moderate in exacting tribute of vassals and, so that the people should not be molested, in levying the costs of war. Their industries existed so that nations might communicate among each other and all live in peace. They had a frequent and meticulous census of all deaths and births and of the exact number of people in all estates of the realms. All persons had professions, and each one busied himself and worked to gain his necessary livelihood. They possessed abundant deposits of provisions which met all the necessities of their warriors, reduced the burden and trouble for the subjects and were distributed in the lean years…. Who of the peoples and kings of the world ever kept the men of their armies under such discipline that they would not dare to touch even a single fruit hanging over the road from a tree behind a wall? Not the Greeks, nor Alexander, nor the Romans, nor even our own Christian monarchs. Has anyone read of soldiers who, no matter where they were marching when not in battle, were as well commanded, trained, sober and orderly as good friars in a procession? They established order and laws for the obedience which vassals must show toward their immediate lords and for reverence between each other, the humble to the humble and the mighty to the mighty. The rearing of children, in which parents inculcate the obedience and faithfulness owed to superiors—where is it surpassed? … Has anyone read of any prince in the world among the ancient unbelievers of the past or subsequently among Christians, excepting St. Louis of France, who so attentively assisted and provided for the poor among his vassals—those not only of his own village or city but of all his large and extensive realms? They issued public edicts and personal commands to all nobles and provincial governors, of whom there were many, that all poor, widows and orphans in each province should be provided for from their own royal rents and riches, and that alms should be given according to the need, poverty and desert of each person. Where and among what people or nation was there a prince endowed with such piety and beneficence that he never dined unless three or four poor people ate from his plate and at his table? … Then, there is that miracle— such it may be called for being the most remarkable, singular and skilful construction of its kind, I believe, in the world—of the two highways … across the mountains and along the coast. The finer and more admirable of these extends for at least six and perhaps eight hundred leagues and is said to reach the provinces of Chile…. In Spain and Italy I have seen portions of the highway said to have been built by the Romans from Spain to Italy, but it is quite crude in comparison with the one built by these peoples….

CHAPTER CCLXIII. THE INDIANS ARE AS CAPABLE AS ANY OTHER NATIONS TO RECEIVE THE GOSPEL

Thus it remains stated, demonstrated and openly concluded … throughout this book that all these peoples of the Indies possessed—as far as it possible through natural and human means and without the light of faith—nations, towns, villages and cities, most fully and abundantly provided for. With a few exceptions in varying degrees they lacked nothing, and some were endowed in full perfection for political and social life and for attaining and enjoying that civic happiness which in this world any good, rational, well provided and happy republic wishes to have and enjoy; for all are by nature of very subtle, lively, clear and most capable understanding. This they received (after the will of God, Who wished to create them in this way) from the favorable influence of the heavens, the gentle attributes of the regions which God gave them to inhabit, the clement and soft weather; from the composition of their limbs and internal and external sensory organs; from the quality and sobriety of their diet; from the fine disposition and healthfulness of the lands, towns and local winds; from their temperance and moderation in food and drink; from the tranquility, calmness and quiescence of their sensual desires; from their lack of concern and worry over the worldly matters that stir the passions of the soul, these being joy, love, wrath, grief and the rest; and also, *a posteriori*, from the works they accomplished and the effects of these. From all these causes, universal and superior, particular and inferior, natural and accidental, it followed, first by nature and then by their industry and experience, that they were endowed with the three types of prudence: the monastic, by which man knows how to rule himself; the economic, which teaches him to rule his house; and the political, which sets forth and ordains the rule of his cities. As for the divisions of this last type (which presupposes the first two types of prudence to be perfect) into workers, artisans, warriors, rich men, religion (temples, priests and sacrifices), judges and magistrates, governors, customs and into everything which concerns acts of understanding and will, … they were equal to many nations of the world outstanding and famous for being politic and reasonable…. We have, then, but slight occasion to be surprised at defects and uncouth and immoderate customs which we might find among our Indian peoples and to disparage them for these; for many and perhaps all other peoples of the world have been much more perverse, irrational and corrupted by depravity, and in their governments and in many virtues and moral qualities much less temperate and orderly. Our own forbears were much worse, as revealed in irrationality and confused government and in vices and brutish customs throughout the length and breadth of this our Spain, which has been shown in many places above. Let us, then, finish this book and give immense thanks to God for having given us enough life, strength and help to see it finished.

FOCUS QUESTIONS

1. Las Casas wrote at nearly the same time as Columbus. Do their views of Native Americans differ? How? In what ways do they operate from the same assumptions?

2. How did some Europeans justify the mistreatment of Native Americans? How does Las Casas refute those arguments?

3. In his letter, Columbus depicted a simple, almost primitive society. Does Las Casas find this to be the case?

4. Why, according to Las Casas, were the Native Americans a more admirable people than the ancient Greeks and Romans?

77

Description of Lima, Peru (ca. 1600 C.E.)

PEDRO DE LEÓN PORTOCARRERO

After the conquest of the Incas by Francisco de Pizarro, the Spaniards set about creating a new capital for their Peruvian empire. Where the center of Inca life was in the highlands, Pizarro decided to create a new city along the coast. Originally called the City of Kings after its erection in 1535, it soon came to be known as Lima. It served as the administrative capital of the Habsburg's South American empire and drew thousands of fortune hunters, priests, and aspirants to government service. It was also a basin for African slaves whose labor was needed in the silver mines of Potosí but who made their first landing at Lima. By the beginning of the seventeenth century Lima had a population of around 25,000, composed predominantly of Africans and Spaniards. Lima was considered a phenomenon of Spanish empire building, and a number of missionaries used it as a subject for their concerns about the treatment of native people, the corruption of the conquistadors, and the destruction of the environment. Pedro León Portocarrero seems to have written his account for a different purpose. A converso, *or Jew who had converted to Christianity, he had been subjected to the Inquisition in his native Toledo before secretly immigrating to New Spain in 1600. He lived in Peru for fifteen years, ten of them in Lima; and he may have been a spy for the Dutch, who had designs on Spain's Peruvian settlements.*

The Description of Lima *is a remarkably detailed account of a city that had literally grown out of the fields in the sixteenth century. Pedro de León Portocarrero takes special pride in the number and beauty of the city's churches, the orderly grid pattern by which its main streets were laid out, and the strength and placement of its fortifications. It is this emphasis that has led historians to speculate about Portocarrero's loyalty.*

The eight most important streets of Lima converge in the city's *plaza mayor* [central square, or *plaza de armas*], with two entering at [and leaving from] each corner. These streets are very straight, and all of them carry on into the open country. First there is the Street of the Plaza Mayor next to the [viceregal] palace and between the arsenal and the houses of the municipal council. This street runs directly north, crossing the river [Rímac] by a bridge, into the neighborhood of San Lázaro [Saint Lazarus]. Turning left from here, one goes along a very grand street, the Royal Highway of the Plains, which passes along the Caraballo River, and through the cultivated plots of land and countryside, to Chancay by way of the Arena mountain range. Four leagues [about 14 miles] on is Caraballo, an Indian community. Returning to Lima's bridge [over the Rímac], the street goes straight to the church and hospital of San Lázaro, into which anyone who is afflicted with Saint Lazarus's illness [blindness] is taken. Turning to the right, one arrives opposite the wooded park in between San Lázaro and the Hill of San Cristóbal. It features a great variety of trees, such as cedars and poplars, as well as trees bearing oranges, lemons, olives, apples, and other fruits. It has eight rows of trees interspersed with four fountains whose waters fall into stone basins, and are connected to channels from the river which are used to irrigate. All of these rows run directly to the monastery of the Barefoot Franciscan friars that stands at the foot of the Hill of San Cristóbal. These friars have a well-built house and garden. Upstream near the Hill of San Cristóbal is the road to Lurigancho, an Indian community which lies beyond the hill, one league [about 31/2 miles] from Lima. Out here there are many cultivated fields as the road leads up to the mountains.

Another street leaves [the *plaza mayor*] from the east side of the palace and approaches the slaughterhouses, coming out in a square that is next to the Franciscans' monastery, a large and very rich house. Including its garden, it takes up two blocks right next to the river. From there, the street passes by the church of San Pedro and reaches [another] large and rich convent, that of Santa Clara. Next to these nuns' abode, running from north to south, is the city's principal water aqueduct. The street then passes the northern part of the walled district [the Cercado] of the Indians. From this point a road begins that extends straight to the reservoir, the source of much of the water that courses through pipes into the city's fountains in the squares, in the palace, and in the monasteries and houses of the nobility. This is the water that the people of this city drink, finding it better than the water from the river. This reservoir is in the middle of a green meadow, and [leaving from it] the road passes through many cultivated fields, heading to the Valley of Santa Inés, a beautiful valley bursting with fruit and water. Out here there are many Indians, and the road continues toward the mountains.

Another street leaves from the palace and the houses of the archbishop and proceeds straight to the east, passing the College of Santo Toribio and the houses of the main postal office, and continuing to the square of the Inquisition, some three blocks east from the plaza mayor. The secret jails and their prisoners are here, and her, [too,] the inquisitors live and have their chapel, taking up an entire block on the south side [of the square]. On the east side of this square is the church and House of Charity, in which poor sick women are treated and many poor maidens are sheltered until they leave to be married, and [also] where women who live indecently are taken in. Near to this charitable house, on the north side [of the square of the Inquisition], is the College of the King. From here the street leads into the square of Santana (Santa Ana), in which there is the convent of the Barefoot nuns and the hospital and parish church of Santa Ana. This is the hospital for Indians in which all their illnesses are treated. Its income from rent is 30,000 assayed pesos [monetary unit of 12 reales in value]. The street continues along next to the church of the Barefoot nuns, by the drilled rock and on to the church of the Prado, right next to the gate into the Indians' Cercado. Next to this entrance lies Dr. Franco's small farm, once owned by the author of this account. The road [then] runs perfectly straight to the east, through fields of wheat and alfalfa. To its right, two leagues [about 7 miles] from Lima, sits Late, an Indian town. And from here another road stretches toward Santa Inés and the mountains. Turning back to the Royal Highway, it passes through the area of Late (*la rinconada de Lata*), where cucumbers, sweet potatoes, maize fields, and vegetable gardens flourish. [A trip along this road] is a delightful excursion for the people of Lima. The road [the Royal Highway] goes to la Seneguilla, where it resumes its course.

Another street leaves the plaza mayor next to the cathedral and leads to the monastery of the Conception, which houses nuns and is rich and pleasant. It carries on to the hospital of San Andrés, a large and excellent house in which Spaniards are treated when they are ill. It crosses the plaza of Santa Ana and joins the main road that heads to the mountains. Turning back, next to the church of Santa Ana, on its right side, this street proceeds to the lime and brick ovens. The owner of these works is Alonso Sánchez, a lime processor who, in my time there, employed four hundred Black slaves. This road carries on to the open country and to the Royal Highway of the coastal plains, [while] another turns to the east and comes out at the guaquilla of Santa Ana [probably a small mound of pre-Hispanic remains or a shrine to Saint Anne, and possibly both]. Here, there is a large field all around, filled with irrigated gardens adjacent to a large water channel. And from here a road heads southeast to the gunpowder works, where much powder is ground very fine. Here is their watermill where the work is done, and [also] a separate house where the powder is locked up. This powder house

is a quarter of a league from the city, and its road passes on through the fields and the valley of la Seneguilla.

Another street leaves [the *plaza mayor*] by the Clothiers' Street. These shops [more than twenty, according to Salinas] stock clothing for Blacks. This street goes straight south and passes by the side of the Mercedarian friars' monastery and leads directly to the convent of the nuns of the Incarnation, the most renowned [religious] house in Lima, in which there are more than four hundred professed nuns. Many of the rich nobles' daughters come [to stay in this house] to learn good manners, and they leave it [ready] to marry. In this convent there are splendid and intelligent women, endowed with a thousand graces, and all of them, both nuns and [pious] lay women, have Black women slaves to serve them. They [the nuns] make preserves and assortments of sweets of various kinds, and they are so good that one cannot imagine a greater treat. They have a large and comfortable garden, and this convent and its garden extend for two blocks in length and one in width. For any woman who wishes to enter a convent in Lima, the cost of her admission and necessities alone is 6,000 pesos, while for a nun who wants a separate cell, a Black woman to serve her, and 100 pesos of income, the endowment required is 12,000 pesos; for others the cost is [still] more, set in accordance with their wealth: but even they never quite get the best [of everything]. Continuing on from this convent, one arrives at the monastery of the Conventual Dominican friars and heads into the open country and the coastal plains road.

Another street leaves by the main one, [and] that is the Merchants' Street, along which there are always at least forty shops [but Salinas claimed more than twenty warehouses and at least two hundred shops] packed full of assorted merchandise, whatever riches the world has to offer. Here is where all of the important business in Peru transpires, because there are merchants in Lima whose estates are valued at 1 million pesos, with many more at 500,000 or 200,000, and at 100,000 pesos there are very many. Among the ranks of these rich [merchants], few operate shops. [Rather,] they put their money to work in Spain, in Mexico, and in other places. And there are some who have dealings in the great China, and many merchants [also] invest in rent-producing property. Here [on this street], they sell merchandise on credit for at least a year, and, if the orders are large, for two and three years, receiving their payment [in installments] three times a year.

Commerce in Lima is the most true, fair, and worry free that one can find in the world because the order of buying and selling is that which has been practiced for many years, an order set down by "the Corsican" [Don Nicolás Vargas]. He was the principal merchant and the richest man Peru has ever seen. His sons are the marquises of Santillana, both of Seville. "The Corsican" established a scale of value for all goods made anywhere in the world, and all are obliged to pay those prices. On some commodities he set [the estimated price] very high and on others very low, in accordance with their value at the time. And the brokers [even now] follow his practice on merchandise that was produced and named after his time; and this method of appraisal has been preserved up to today.

The order that the merchants observe in buying their goods is that they take the [manifests of] the merchandise that the transporters give them in order to [start with] the same prices they would in Spain or Mexico. Then, they immediately revise the prices of items, with the prices of some goods rising and others falling, according to the current demand and value of the merchandise locally. Thus, the setting of the price is up to date, with each kind [of goods] given the value at which one can sell it at the time of its purchase. And the reckoning and the repricing is made in assayed pesos, and by this the value is determined, and it is made also with [attention to] the running account. These [become] the prices because [at them] the given merchandise can be sold, reflecting the sum of the one account and the other, with both accounts governed by current [financial] conditions. Then one can begin to see if one profits or loses, and the men who sell them set their own refixed prices and accounts; and thus the price rises and falls accordingly, and they buy these goods at so much

percent, more or less, of the cost. Later, as they come from Spain, once all is in order, they send the cargo to the buyers' house, supplying everything correctly and accompanied by an account.

In merchandising one must always take into account the damaged goods and additions. "Damaged goods" are things that are broken, stained, or that have become damp or rotten. An "addition" occurs with the kinds of merchandise that one sells of different qualities; for example, saying it is from one master craftsman's shop when it turns out to be from another's, or saying that a piece of cloth is twenty-four [in size] when it is twenty-two, or not to have the advertised brand, and such things. This is what one means by damages and additions; and in order that they be accounted for, a third of each part is chosen and scrutinized. And the ones [who do this] are always merchants of good conscience who remove what they should and discount the value of the merchandise. Because of this [wise and honest practice] the goods are never returned, litigation and grief are avoided, others buy at the current estimated price, and [still] others at so much percent above the cost in Castile or Mexico. And sometimes they buy a variety of loose goods; but with the assorted large shipments, some of which are worth 100,000 pesos, the sales are always by the rate [method].

All the merchants are exceedingly skillful in their buying. A merchant will collect all the manifests of shipments brought to the plaza for sale, and quickly refix their prices, and from there choose and buy whatever seems best to him. This gives an idea of the merchants of Lima. [Everyone] is involved, from the viceroy to the archbishop; all have dealings and everyone is a merchant, even if it is through a third party or on the sly.

Continuing on with [the description of] this sixth street, one reaches the immense and wealthy monastery of the Mercedarian friars, and then passes to the parish church of San Diego, [also] a hospital for convalescents recovering after treatments of their illnesses in the hospital of San Andrés. When their health returns and they can move about, they are sent to this convalescent hospital. There, they receive all they need until they are sufficiently fit to go back to work. From here, the road meets a little square and the Conventual Mercedarians, and goes directly to the countryside and the sea to the south, about three-quarters of a league from Lima passing the Indian community of Magdalena.

From among the arcades [on the *plaza mayor*] where there are four streets and the Merchants' Street [already described], another street leaves, beginning with the Street of the Mantas [cloaks and coverings of coarse cotton cloth], which is also lined with merchants' shops. This street, like the Merchants' Street, takes up its own block. Along this entire street, proceeding directly west, there are many shops with different specialties: chandlers, confectioners, boilermakers who work with a lot of copper, blacksmiths, and other craftsmen. And it passes next to the Espíritu Santo hospital for sailors who are gathered there and cured when they are ill, [then] under the arch and on to the church of Monserrat. The street heading south from there goes straight toward the road to [Lima's port of] Callao....

The last of the eight streets that leaves the square departs from beside the arsenal in the palace, the houses of the municipal council, and the house of Don Alonso de Carabajal, because in all of the intersections of the plaza there are three corners. This street proceeds straight to the monastery of the Dominican friars, the most wealthy and outstanding [of the male religious houses] in Lima, the north walls of which are washed by the river. And here, in a bit of space not occupied by the friars, sits the theater. The compound consists of two blocks of houses, with seven patios. This street carries on straight to the river. For anyone going south, by turning left from any of these last streets [I have described], one can reach Callao.

One [other] street [worth mentioning, the better to understand the design of Lima], two blocks from the east side of the plaza mayor and running north to south, goes by the church of San Francisco to the house [and church] of the Jesuit fathers, the richest and most powerful residence [of all religious] in Lima. Even the facings of the altars [in the Jesuits' church] are made of finely worked and thick silver. Its memorials they put up during the week of

mourning [Holy Week] are all of crimson velvet, all adorned on top in solid silver, with a thousand bows, intricately worked by an artist's chisel, so high that they reach the church's ceiling and so wide that they stretch across high pillars and arches from one wall to the other. They have infinite riches in this monastery and residence.

On another street that runs behind the Jesuits' establishment is the College of San Martín, also belonging to the Society of Jesus; it has more than five hundred students, the sons of notables throughout the kingdom [of Peru] who send them there to study, and who pay the Jesuits an annual fee of 150 ordinary pesos for each one, from which sum the students are fed [as well as instructed]. These Jesuits offer a very elaborate course of studies incorporating many branches of learning. As it continues, the street passes next to the monastery of the Trinity for nuns, and then arrives at the parish church and house for orphans, children abandoned by mothers who did not want their parents to know of their ruinous acts and [thus] gave birth to the children without parental knowledge. Farther along one comes upon another Jesuit convent and house of no small amount of wealth. It was built when I was living in Lima with a gift of 300,000 pesos from the secretary to the Inquisition, Antonio Correa. From such choice morsels many in Peru stuff themselves without choking, because they have the stomach for everything. They [the Jesuits] keep a lovely garden and also have many riches in this house, so that no Jesuit suffers want. The street [then] carries on to Guadalupe, a monastery of the Franciscan friars. Here, the Royal Highway of the coastal plains heads south, the ocean on its right, straight to Pachacama [formerly the site of the great pre-Hispanic divinity, Pacha Camac], an Indian community four leagues from the city.

Extending from east to west, another street passes close to the Jesuits' church and into the Street of the Silversmiths [with more than forty public shops, says Salinas, and over two hundred people trained to work in silver and gold], which runs from the corner of the Street of the Mantas [with more than thirty shops selling clothing mostly to native Andeans] to the corner of the Merchants'

Street. Off this Street of the Silversmiths is the Hatters' Alley, [which] leads to the church of San Agustín. In this block there are a great number of apothecaries, and all of them are not more than a block from the [central] plaza. San Agustín is the rich house and the church of the Augustinian friars. The street passes to the great and sumptuous parish church of San Sebastián and continues up to the mills of Montserrat, to which a large channel provides water for the milling and irrigation of gardens, turning left for the port of Callao.

Another two streets, heading from east to west, leave from beside the [convent of the] Incarnation and San Diego and pass near to San Marcelo, the principal parish church in Lima. Here, taking up a space on the left side, is the [monastery] of the Conventual Augustinians. Both of these streets lead straight to the road bound for Callao.

These are the highlights of Lima. The city has many other streets, but the ones described here have all the monasteries, churches, and squares, and all that is best about the city, something that the others do not have for our purpose.

FOCUS QUESTIONS

1. What are the qualities of the streets of Lima that Portocarrero praises? Why are these especially noteworthy?

2. What social institutions did the Spanish transplant to the New World?

3. What is Portocarrero's attitude toward slavery?

4. How is commerce conducted in Lima?

The Golden Age of Islam

Islamic Unity. Persian Satavid ruler Shah Abbas
and Indian Mughal emperor Jahangir never
met, but were united in a hope that their two
great Islamic empires would cooperate and
benefit the larger world. Their hopes were ar-
ticulated in allegorical artwork like this, depicting the rulers embracing as they stand on
symbols of peace on a globe of the earth.

78

The Perfection of Faith (11th century c.e.)

'ABD UL-HAQQ AL DIHLAWI AL-BUKHARI

'Abd ul-Haqq al Dihlawi al-Bukhari (Shaykh Abdul Haqq Dehlvi, 1551–1642) was one of the most significant interpreters of Muslim texts in late medieval India. Though he was born and died in Delhi, 'Abd ul-Haqq traveled across the Muslim world and made his pilgrimage to Mecca in 1587, where he also studied Sunni doctrine, then out of favor in Mughal India. He returned to his homeland and became a teacher, translator, and writer. For more than half a century his seminary at Delhi was the center of Muslim religious learning in India. He composed biographies of the Prophet Mohammed and of Muslim saints and even authored a brief history of India that stressed the introduction of Muslim monotheism into the country. He is credited with having written over one hundred books.

The Perfection of Faith was his most important statement of the Sunni belief in divine revelation through the orthodox texts of Sarī'a as well as through the Koran. Though regarded as mystics, the Sunnis preached and taught what they believed to be the pure form of Muslim teaching and opposed the tenets of Sufism that gained in popularity among newly converted Hindus.

THE ATTRIBUTES OF GOD

In truth, the creation and the proper ordering of the world will not come right except with one creator and one governor.... The Nourisher of the World is alive, is wise and powerful, and a free agent. Whatever He does is by His own intent and choice and not under compulsion and necessity. Without these attributes such a strange and wonderful world quite certainly would not appear or be conceivable. Such a world is not possible from a dead, ignorant, powerless, or unfree agent. These attributes [of life, wisdom, power, and freedom] appear in created things. If they are not in God, from whence do they appear? He is a speaker of speech, a hearer of hearing, and a seer of seeing, because to be dumb, deaf, and blind is to be deficient and deficiencies are not proper to God. The Holy Qur'an is eloquent as to that. It is impossible to comprehend the reality of these attributes, indeed of the totality of divine attributes by analogy and reason. But God has created a likeness of those in the essence of humankind, which he has interpenetrated in some way or other with His own attributes. But in truth, the attributes of man do not survive as God's attributes survive. "God's eternal attributes remain."

The attributes of God are eternal and are of equal duration with His essence.

Whatever He possesses—perfection and reality—is constant in eternity; because the location of accidents was created, it does not become eternal. Except in a body there is neither limitation, cause, nor time; the creator of the world is not body and substance. That is to say, He is not a body and an attribute, that is to say, with the bodily qualities that the body has, like blackness and whiteness. He is not formed so that He has bodily shape and He is not compounded so that He is joined together repeatedly. He is not numbered so that it is possible to count Him. He is not limited so that he has a limit and He is not in a direction, that is to say, He is not above or below, before or after, left or right. He is not in a place and not in a moment, because all these are attributes of the world and the Nourisher of the World is not subject to worldly attributes and His purposes are not subject to time. Time does not include or circumscribe Him. His existence is not dependent upon time. For in that condition when there was not time, there was He. Now also there is time and He exists. Therefore, He is not in time.

THE TRANSCENDENCE OF GOD

Whatever exists, except God's essence and attributes, is created, that is to say, it comes into existence from nonexistence and is not eternal. As proof, the tradition of the Prophet, "There was God and there was nothing besides Him." As proof too, the world changes and is a place of many vicissitudes. Whatever is of this description is not eternal, and whatever is eternal does not change. We know that there is one real mode of existence—that of God's essence and attributes and there is no way for change in that mode.... And Almighty God is capable of extinguishing the world. After existence it passes away. As the Word of God says: "Everything perishes except the mode [Him]." Thus the angels, paradise, hell, and such like things to whose lastingness a tradition has testified, also are perishable.... Although God can annihilate in the twinkling of an eye, those who do not die will know that God is the creator of the world who has brought it into existence from nonexistence because, since the world is not eternal, the meaning of creation is that it was not and then it was. Whatever was of that order must have had a creator to bring it from nonexistence into existence because if it was created from itself it must always have been. Since it did not always exist, it was not created by itself but by another. The Nourisher of the World must be eternal. If He were not eternal He would be created. He would be of the world, not the self-existent Nourisher of the World. That is to say that the world's existence is by reason of its own essence and not by reason of something

other than itself. But the world needs something other than itself and whatever needs something other than itself is not fit for lordship. The meaning of God's own words is future, that is, He Himself is coming into existence Himself. Certainly it must be that the end of the chain of existences is in one essence which is from itself. Otherwise it will continue in the same way endlessly and this is not reasonable.

FREE WILL

First it is necessary to understand the meaning of compulsion and choice so that the essence of this problem may become clear. Man's actions are of two kinds. One, when he conceives something, and, if that thing is desired by and is agreeable to his nature, a great desire and passion for it wells up from within him, and he follows that passion and moves after it. Or, if the thing is contrary and repugnant to him, dislike and abhorrence for it wells up within him and he shuns it. His relation to the action and to stopping the action before the appearance of the desire and the loathing were on a par. It was possible that he might act or not act, whether at the stage of conception when the power to act was near, or before conceiving the idea when he was farther from acting. This motion of man is called an optional motion and the action that results from that motion is called an optional action. The other kind of action is when there is no conception, arousing of desire and wish, but motion occurs and then desire, like the trembling of a leaf. This motion is called compulsory and obligatory. If the meaning of desire and intention (as distinct from choice) is as stated, it may be objected: "Who says that man is not discerning and is not perspicacious? The creation of man occurred by choice, and such is the composition of his nature. Who says that all human motions and actions are compulsory? To say this is to deny virtue. No intelligent person will agree to this."

But there are difficulties in this conclusion. For, if, after comprehension and conversance with the eternal knowledge, intentions, decree, and ordination of God, it is conceived that it is not (really) man who brings actions into existence, that conclusion will be reached because it is realized that if God knew from all eternity that a particular action must be performed by a particular individual, that action must therefore be so performed, whether without that individual's choice, as in compulsory motion, or with his choice. If the action was optional (in form), the individual did not (really) have choice either in his decision or in his action. Furthermore, although the individual may have had choice in his action, yet he did not have any choice in its first beginnings.

For example, when an eye opens and does not see, there is no image before it. If after seeing and observing visible objects, they are desired, a rousing of passion and desire is compulsory and the existence of motion toward them is also obligatory. Thereafter, although this action occurs through the human being's choice, yet in fact this choice is obligatory and compulsory upon him. Obligation and necessity are contrary to the reality of choice. Man has choice but he has not choice in his choice; or to put it another way, he has choice in appearance, but in fact he is acting under compulsion…. Imám Ja'far Sádiq, who is a master of the people of the Sufi way and a chief of the people of Truth, says that there is no compulsion or freedom. But he lays down that the truth is to be found between compulsion and freedom. The Jabarites are those who say that fundamentally man has no choice and his motions are like those of inanimate nature. The Qadariya are those who say that man has choice and that man is independent in his transactions. His actions are his own creations. Imám Ja'far says that both these two schools of thought are false and go to extremes. The true school of thought is to be found between them but reason is at a loss and confounded in the comprehension of this middle way; in truth this confusion is found among people of a disputatious and contending sort who wish to found articles of faith upon reason, and who will not acknowledge anything as true and believe in it unless it pleases their reason and falls within their understanding. But for believers, the short proof of this is what is put forward in the Sharī'a and the Qur'ān, in which it is written that God has both power and will and, notwithstanding that, He charges obedience and disobedience to His servants. And He says, God never commits injustice but men have inflicted injustice upon themselves. "God was not one to wrong them but they did wrong themselves."

In this verse He establishes two things. He has imputed creation to Himself and action to men. Therefore we must of necessity believe that both are true and must be believed—that creation is from God and action from man. Although we do not reach to the end of this problem and as the proof of the Sharī'a and what is commanded and forbidden is itself a consequence of choice, then it is necessary to believe that. The problem of divine power and ordination and the problem of man's choice become known to us by the traditions of the right path [Sharī'a]. Since both are known from the Sharī'a, what is the controversy and the disputing about? One must believe in both. In this matter faith in the middle way is necessary. In truth, deep thought into this problem is among the indications of idleness and ignorance because no action and no truth is affected by controversy about it. One has to act. The real truth of the matter is that which is with God.

FOCUS QUESTIONS

1. What is the proof of the existence of one God?

2. What are the attributes of God?

3. What sources does 'Abd ul-Haqq use to prove his assertions?

4. Why is the question of free will central to Muslim beliefs?

79

The Ruba'iyat (11th century C.E.)

OMAR KHAYYÁM

Omar Khayyám (ca. 1048–1131) was a mathematician, astronomer, and philosopher whose fame rests on his poetry. He was born in Nishapour, Iran, one of the greatest cities of the Middle East before its destruction during the thirteenth century. Nishapour was famed for its schools, and Omar Khayyám studied mathematics and philosophy there. He wrote a treatise on algebra that gained him recognition and patronage. He was appointed to head a commission to make astronomical observations and to reform the Eastern calendar. His efforts resulted in the Jalali Calendar, which many regard as more accurate than those used in the West.

The Ruba'iyat *consists of 1,200 individual quatrains, that is, sets of four lines in which the first, second, and fourth rhyme. They are not connected to each other and seem to have been composed over many years. They reveal Omar Khayyám's philosophical and scientific interests as well as his personality. The* Ruba'iyat *went unpublished for 700 years until a chance discovery of a manuscript by an English professor. By the end of the nineteenth century,* Ruba'iyat *had become some of the best-loved poetry in the world.*

I

Awake! for Morning in the Bowl of Night
Has flung the Stone that puts the Stars to
    Flight:
And Lo! the Hunter of the East has caught
The Sultán's Turret in a Noose of Light.

VII

Come, fill the Cup, and in the Fire of
    Spring
The Winter Garment of Repentance fling:
The Bird of Time has but a little way
To fly—and Lo! the Bird is on the Wing.

VI

And David's Lips are lock't; but in divine
High piping Pehleví, with "Wine! Wine!
    Wine!
Red Wine!"—the Nightingale cries to the
    Rose
That yellow Cheek of hers to incarnadine.

IX

But come with old Khayyám, and leave the
    Lot
Of Kaikobád and Kaikhosrú forgot:
Let Rustum lay about him as he will,
Or Hátim Tai cry Supper—heed
    them not.

XVI

Think, in this batter'd Caravanserai
Whose Doorways are alternate Night and
    Day,
How Sultán after Sultán with his Pomp
Abode his Hour or two, and went his way.

XVII

They say the Lion and the Lizard keep
The Courts where Jamsh yd gloried and drank
    deep;
And Bahrám, that great Hunter—the Wild
    Ass
Stamps o'er his Head, and he lies fast asleep.

XVIII

I sometimes think that never blows so red
The Rose as where some buried Caesar bled;
That every Hyacinth the Garden wears
Dropt in its Lap from some once lovely Head.

XXI

Lo! some we loved, the loveliest and the best
That Time and Fate of all their Vintage prest,
Have drunk their Cup a Round or two
    before,
And one by one crept silently to Rest.

XXXII

There was a Door to which I found no Key:
There was a Veil past which I could not see:
Some little Talk awhile of Me and Thee
There seem'd—and then no more of Thee
    and Me.

XLI

For "Is" and "Is-not" though *with* Rule and
    Line
And "Up-and-down" *without*, I could define,
I yet in all I only cared to know,
Was never deep in anything but—Wine.

XLIX

'Tis all a Chequer-board of Nights and Days
Where Destiny with Men for Pieces plays:
Hither and thither moves, and mates, and
    slays,
And one by one back in the Closet lays.

LXVIII

That ev'n my buried Ashes such a Snare
Of Perfume shall fling up into the Air,
As not a True Believer passing by
But shall be overtaken unaware.

LXXII

Alas, that Spring should vanish with the Rose!
That Youth's sweet-scented Manuscript
    should close!
The Nightingale that in the Branches sang,
Ah, whence, and whither flown again, who
    knows!

LXXVII

For let Philosopher and Doctor preach
Of what they will, and what they will not—
    each
Is but one Link in an eternal Chain
That none can slip, nor break, nor overreach.

LXXXV

What! from his helpless Creature be repaid
Pure Gold for what he lent us dross-allay'd
Such for a Debt we never did contract,
And cannot answer—Oh, the sorry trade!

XCVI

"Well," said another, "Whoso will, let try,
My Clay with long oblivion is gone dry:
But fill me with the old familiar Juice,
Methinks I might recover by-and-by!"

FOCUS QUESTIONS

1. What is Khayyám's attitude toward wine? Love? Life? Death?

2. Does Khayyám's expertise in math and science influence his poems?

3. What do Khayyám's quatrains tell us about the state of religion in eleventh- and twelfth-century Persia?

4. Why is the *Ruba'iyat* so popular in the West? Why do you think that it has been frequently banned in Muslim countries?

80

The History of Mehmed the Conqueror (1453 C.E.)

KRITOVOULOS

Mehmed II (1432–1481) was one of the great military geniuses of world history. He consolidated the expansion of the Ottoman Empire in Asia Minor, and in 1453 organized the siege of Constantinople. He personally directed the combined land and naval assault and brilliantly improvised the tactics that led to the fall of the city. The fall of Constantinople to the Ottomans was a watershed. No longer could the West assume military superiority over the East. Ottoman dominance of Asia Minor and its threat to the lands of the Holy Roman Empire continued for nearly two centuries.

Kritovoulos was a Greek who entered the service of Mehmed II, probably after the siege. Nothing is known of his personal life. Although he was not an eyewitness of the fall of Constantinople, he gathered numerous accounts together in composing his history. He was a servant and admirer of the Ottoman Sultan; however, he was also a Greek who mourned the collapse of the center of the Greek Orthodox Church and the inheritor of the Eastern Empire.

To the Supreme Emperor, King of Kings, Mehmed, the fortunate, the victor, the winner of trophies, the triumphant, the invincible, Lord of land and sea, by the will of God, Kritovoulos the Islander, servant of thy servants.

Seeing that you are the author of many great deeds, O most mighty Emperor, and in the belief that the many great achievements of generals and kings of old, nor merely of Persians and Greeks, are not worthy to be compared in glory and bravery and martial valor with yours, I do not think it just that they and their deeds and accomplishments, as set forth in the Greek historians and their writings from contemporary times and up to the present, should be celebrated and admired by all, and that these should enjoy everlasting remembrance, while you, so great and powerful a man, possessing almost all the lands under the sun, and glorious in your great and brilliant exploits, should have no witness, for the future, of your valor and the greatest and best of your deeds, like one of the unknown and inglorious ones who are till now unworthy of any memorial or record in Greek; or that the deeds of others, petty as they are in comparison to yours, should be better known and more famed before men because done by Greeks and in Greek history, while your accomplishments, vast as they are, and in no way inferior to those of Alexander the Macedonian, or of the generals and kings of his rank, should not be set forth in Greek to the Greeks, nor passed on to posterity for the undying praise and glory of your deeds.

Sultan Mehmed considered it necessary in preparation for his next move to get possession of the harbor and open the Horn for his own ships to sail in. So, since every effort and device of his had failed to force the entrance, he made a wise decision, and one worthy of his intellect and power. It succeeded in accomplishing his purpose and in putting an end to all uncertainties.

He ordered the commanders of the vessels to construct as quickly as possible glideways leading from the outer sea to the inner sea, that is, from the harbor to the Horn, near the place called Diplokion, and to cover them with beams. This road, measured from sea to sea, is just about eight stadia. It is very steep for more than half the way, until you reach the summit of the hill, and from there again it descends to the inner sea of the Horn. And as the glideways were completed sooner than expected, because of the large number of workers, he brought up the ships and placed large cradles under them, with stays against each of their sides to hold them up. And having under-girded them well with ropes, he fastened long cables to the corners and gave them to the soldiers to drag, some of them by hand, and others by certain machines and capstans.

So the ships were dragged along very swiftly. And their crews, as they followed them, rejoiced at the event and boasted of it. Then they manned the ships on the land as if they were on the sea. Some of them hoisted the sails with a shout, as if they were setting sail, and the breeze caught the sails and bellied them out. Others seated themselves on the benches, holding the oars in their hands and moving them as if rowing. And the commanders, running along by the sockets of the masts with whistlings and shouting, and with their whips beating the oarsmen on the benches, ordered them to row. The ships, borne along over the land as if on the sea, were some of them being pulled up the ascent to the top of the hill while others were being hauled down the slope into the harbor, lowering the sails with shouting and great noise.

It was a strange spectacle, and unbelievable in the telling except to those who actually did see it—the sight of ships borne along on the mainland as if sailing on the sea, with their crews and their sails and all their equipment. I believe this was a much greater feat than the cutting of a canal across at Athos by Xerxes, and much stranger to see and to hear about....

Thus, then, there assembled in the bay called Cold Waters, a little beyond Galata, a respectable fleet of some sixty-seven vessels. They were moored there.

The Romans, when they saw such an unheard-of thing actually happen, and warships lying at anchor in the Horn—which they never would have suspected—were astounded at the impossibility of the spectacle, and were overcome by the greatest consternation and perplexity. They did not know what to do now, but were in despair. In fact they had left unguarded the walls along the Horn for a distance of about thirty stadia, and even so they did not have enough men for the rest of the walls, either for defense or for attack, whether citizens or men from elsewhere. Instead, two or even three battlements had but a single defender.

And now, when this sea-wall also became open to attack and had to be guarded, they were compelled to strip the other battlements and bring men there. This constituted a manifest danger, since the defenders were taken away from the rest of the wall while those remaining were not enough to guard it, being so few.

Then, with fine insight, the Sultan summoned the shield-bearers, heavy infantry and other troops and said: "Go to it, friends and children mine! It is time now to show yourselves good fighters!" They immediately crossed the moat, with shouts and fearful yells, and attacked the outer wall. All of it, however, had been demolished by the cannon. There were only stockades of great beams instead of a wall, and bundles of vine-branches, and jars full of earth. At that point a fierce battle ensued close in and with the weapons of hand-to-hand fighting. The heavy infantry and shield-bearers fought to overcome the defenders and get over the stockade, while the Romans and Italians tried to fight these off and to guard the stockade. At times the infantry did get over the wall and the stockade, pressing forward bravely and unhesitatingly. And at times they were stoutly forced back and driven off.

The Sultan followed them up, as they struggled bravely, and encouraged them. He ordered those in charge of the cannon to put the match to the cannon. And these, being set off, fired their stone balls against the defenders and worked no little destruction on both sides, among those in the near vicinity.

So, then, the two sides struggled and fought bravely and vigorously. Most of the night passed, and the Romans were successful and prevailed not a little. Also, Giustinianni and his men kept their positions stubbornly, and guarded the stockade and defended themselves bravely against the aggressors....

Sultan Mehmed saw that the attacking divisions were very much worn out by the battle and had not made any progress worth mentioning, and that the Romans and Italians were not only fighting stoutly but were prevailing in the battle. He was very indignant at this, considering that it ought not to be endured any longer. Immediately he brought up the divisions which he had been reserving for later on, men who were extremely well armed, daring and brave, and far in advance of the rest in experience and valor. They were the elite of the army: heavy infantry, bowmen, and lancers, and his own bodyguard, and along with them those of the division called Janissaries.

Calling to them and urging them to prove themselves now as heroes, he led the attack against the wall, himself at the head until they reached the moat. There he ordered the bowmen, stingers, and musketeers to stand at a distance and fire to the right, against the defenders on the palisade and on the battered wall. They were to keep up so heavy a fire that those defenders would be unable to fight, or to expose themselves because of the cloud of arrows and other projectiles falling like snowflakes.

To all the rest, the heavy infantry and the shieldbearers, the Sultan gave orders to cross the moat swiftly and attack the palisade. With a loud and terrifying war-cry and with fierce impetuosity and wrath, they advanced as if mad. Being young and strong and full of daring, and especially because they were fighting in the Sultan's presence, their valor exceeded every expectation. They attacked the palisade and fought bravely without any hesitation.

Needing no further orders, they knocked down the turrets which had been built out in front, broke the yardarms, scattered the materials that had been gathered, and forced the defenders back inside the palisade.

… The Romans in that section fought bravely with lances, axes, pikes, javelins, and other weapons of offense. It was a hand-to-hand encounter, and they stopped the attackers and prevented them from getting inside the palisade. There was much shouting on both sides—the mingled sounds of blasphemy, insults, threats, attackers, defenders, shooters, those shot at, killers and dying, of those who in anger and wrath did all sorts of terrible things. And it was a sight to see there: a hard fight going on hand-to-hand with great determination and for the greatest rewards, heroes fighting valiantly, the one party struggling with all their might to force back the defenders, get possession of the wall, enter the City, and fall upon the children and women and the treasures, the other party bravely agonizing to drive them off and guard their possessions, even if they were not to succeed in prevailing and in keeping them.

Instead, the hapless Romans were destined finally to be brought under the yoke of servitude and to suffer its horrors. For although they battled bravely.... They abandoned the palisade and wall where they had been fighting, and thought of only one thing—how they could get away safe themselves.

But the Emperor Constantine besought them earnestly, and made promises to them if they would wait a little while, till the fighting should subside. They would not consent, however, but taking up their leader and all their armor, they boarded the galleons in haste and with all speed, giving no consideration to the other defenders.

The Emperor Constantine forbade the others to follow. Then, though he had no idea what to do next—for he had no other reserves to fill the places thus left vacant, the ranks of those who had so suddenly deserted, and meantime the battle raged fiercely and all had to see to their own ranks and places and fight there—still, with his remaining Romans and his bodyguard, which was so few as to be easily counted, he took his stand in front of the palisade and fought bravely.

Sultan Mehmed, who happened to be fighting quite nearby, saw that the palisade and the other part of the wall that had been destroyed were now empty of men and deserted by the defenders. He noted that men were slipping away secretly and that those who remained were fighting feebly because they were so few. Realizing from this that the defenders had fled and that the wall was deserted, he shouted out: "Friends, we have the City! We have it! They are already fleeing from us! They can't stand it any longer! The wall is bare of defenders! It needs just a little more effort and the City is taken! Don't weaken, but on with the work with all your might, and be men and I am with you!"

So saying, he led them himself. And they, with a shout on the run and with a fearsome yell, went on ahead of the Sultan, pressing on up to the palisade. After a long and bitter struggle they hurled back the Romans from there and climbed by force up the palisade. They dashed some of their foe down into the ditch between the great wall and the palisade, which was deep and hard to get out of, and they killed them there. The rest they drove back to the gate.

He had opened this gate in the great wall, so as to go easily over to the palisade. Now there was a great struggle there and great slaughter among those stationed there, for they were attacked by the heavy infantry and not a few others in irregular formation, who had been attracted from many points by the shouting. There the Emperor Constantine, with all who were with him, fell in gallant combat.

The heavy infantry were already streaming through the little gate into the City, and others had rushed in through the breach in the great wall. Then all the rest of the army, with a rush and a roar, poured in brilliantly and scattered all over the City. And the Sultan stood before the great wall, where the standard also was and the ensigns, and watched the proceedings. The day was already breaking.

Then a great slaughter occurred of those who happened to be there: some of them were on the streets, for they had already left the houses and were running toward the tumult when they fell unexpectedly on the swords of the soldiers; others were in their own homes and fell victims to the violence of the Janissaries and other soldiers, without any rhyme or reason; others were resisting, relying on their own courage; still others were fleeing to the churches and making supplication—men, women, and children, everyone, for there was no quarter given.

The soldiers fell on them with anger and great wrath. For one thing, they were actuated by the hardships of the siege. For another, some foolish people had hurled taunts and curses at them from the battlements all through the siege.

Now, in general they killed so as to frighten all the City, and to terrorize and enslave all by the slaughter.

When they had had enough of murder, and the City was reduced to slavery, some of the troops turned to the mansions of the mighty, by bands and companies and divisions, for plunder and spoil. Others went to the robbing of churches, and others dispersed to the simple homes of the common people, stealing, robbing, plundering, killing, insulting, taking and enslaving men, women, and children, old and young, priests, monks—in short, every age and class.

And the desecrating and plundering and robbing of the churches—how can one describe it in words? Some things they threw in dishonor on the ground—ikons and reliquaries and other objects from the churches. The crowd snatched some of these, and some were given over to the fire while others were torn to shreds and scattered at the crossroads. The last resting places of the blessed men of old were opened, and their remains were taken out and disgracefully torn to pieces, even to shreds, and made the sport of the wind while others were thrown on the streets.

Chalices and goblets and vessels to hold the holy sacrifice, some of them were used for drinking and carousing, and others were broken up or melted down and sold. Holy vessels and costly robes richly embroidered with much gold or brilliant with precious stones and pearls were some of them given to the most wicked men for no good use, while others were consigned to the fire and melted down for gold.

After this the Sultan entered the City and looked about to see its great size, its situation, its grandeur and beauty, its teeming population, its loveliness, and the costliness of its churches and public buildings and of the private houses and community houses and of those of the officials. He also saw the setting of the harbor and of the arsenals, and how skilfully and ingeniously they had everything arranged in the City—in a word, all the construction and adornment of it. When he saw what a large number had been killed, and the ruin of the buildings, and the wholesale ruin and destruction of the City, he was filled with compassion and repented not a little at the destruction and plundering. Tears fell from his eyes as he groaned deeply and passionately: "What a city we have given over to plunder and destruction!"

Thus he suffered in spirit. And indeed this was a great blow to us, in this one city, a disaster the like of which had occurred in no one of the great renowned cities of history, whether one speaks of the size of the captured City or of the bitterness and harshness of the deed. And no less did it astound all others than it did those who went through it and suffered, through the unreasonable and unusual character of the event and through the overwhelming and unheard-of horror of it.

FOCUS QUESTIONS

1. What is the author's attitude toward Mehmed?

2. Why should Mehmed be compared to Alexander the Great and other ancients?

3. What was warfare like in the middle of the fifteenth century?

Does Kritovoulos glorify it or treat it critically?

4. Why did Kritovoulos write his history? What lessons did he wish to convey?

81

Letters Between Sultan Selîm I and Shah Ismâ'îl (ca. 1514 C.E.)

The Ottoman Empire did not only expand at the expense of the Christian West. By the sixteenth century, Ottomans were invading the territory of other Muslim states and taking tribute where they could. In 1502 a conflict began between the Ottomans and the Safavids, a powerful and rival Muslim family that contested the legitimacy of Ottoman rule over their territory. Ismâ'îl, head of the Safavid family, proclaimed himself shah and attempted to drive the Ottomans from his lands. Sultan Selîm I responded with a reign of terror against Safavid communities. Matters came to a head in 1514 when armies of the two Muslim states fought at Chaldirân. The Ottomans won decisively.

In the months before the war, the shah and sultan conducted an unusual form of personal diplomacy by sending each other letters setting out their respective positions. They provide a unique glimpse into the attitudes of sixteenth-century Muslim rulers.

SELÎM TO ISMÂ'ÎL

(UNDATED, CA. 1514)

It is from Solomon and it is: 'In the Name of God, the Merciful, the Compassionate. Rise not up against me, but come to me in surrender.'

[Qur'ân XXVII: 30–31]

God's blessings upon the best of his creatures, Muhammad, his family, and his companions all.

This is a Scripture We have sent down, blessed; so follow it, and be godfearing; haply so you will find mercy.

[Qur'ân VI: 156]

This missive which is stamped with the seal of victory and which is, like inspiration descending from the heavens, witness to the verse "We never chastise until We send forth a Messenger" [Qur'ân XVII:15] has been graciously issued by our most glorious majesty—we who are the Caliph of God Most High in this world, far and wide; the proof of

the verse "And what profits men abides in the earth" [Qur'ân XIII:17] the Solomon of Splendor, the Alexander of eminence; haloed in victory, Far-idûn[1] triumphant; slayer of the wicked and the infidel, guardian of the noble and the pious; the warrior in the Path, the defender of the Faith; the champion, the conqueror; the lion, son and grandson of the lion; standard-bearer of justice and righteousness, Sultân Selîm Shâh, son of Sultân Bayezîd, son of Sultân Muhammad Khân—and is addressed to the ruler of the kingdom of the Persians, the possessor of the land of tyranny and perversion, the captain of the vicious, the chief of the malicious, the usurping Darius of the time, the malevolent Zahhâk of the age, the peer of Cain, Prince Ismâ'il.

As the Pen of Destiny has drawn up the rescript "Thou givest the kingdom to whom Thou wilt" [Qur'ân III:26] in our sublime name and has signed it with the verse "Whatsoever mercy God opens to men, none can withhold" [Qur'ân XXXV:2], it is manifest in the Court of Glory and the Presence of

---

1. An ancient and celebrated king of Persia, who began to reign about 750 B.C.E.

Deity that we, the instrument of Divine Will, shall hold in force upon the earth both the commandments and prohibitions of Divine Law as well as the provisions of royal proclamations. "That is the bounty of God; he gives it unto whomsoever He will" [Qur'ân LVII:21].

It has been heard repeatedly that you have subjected the upright community of Muhammad (Prayers and salutations upon its founder!) to your devious will, that you have undermined the firm foundation of the Faith, that you have unfurled the banner of oppression in the cause of aggression, that you no longer uphold the commandments and prohibitions of the Divine Law, that you have incited your abominable Shî'î faction to unsanctified sexual union and to the shedding of innocent blood, that like they "Who listen to falsehood and consume the unlawful" [Qur'ân V:42] you have given ear to idle deceitful words and have eaten that which is forbidden:

> He has laid waste to mosques, as it is said,
> Constructing idol temples in their stead,

that you have rent the noble stuff of Islâm with the hand of tyranny, and that you have called the Glorious Qur'ân the myths of the Ancients. The rumor of these abominations has caused your name to become like that of Hârith deceived by Satan.[2]

Indeed, as both the *fatwas* of distinguished *'ulamâ'*[3] who base their opinion on reason and tradition alike and the consensus of the Sunî[4] community agree that the ancient obligation of extirpation, extermination, and expulsion of evil innovation must be the aim of our exalted aspiration, for "Religious zeal is a victory for the Faith of God the Beneficent"; then, in accordance with the words of the Prophet (Peace upon him!) "Whosoever introduces evil innovation into our order must be expelled" and "Whosoever does aught against our order must be expelled," action has become necessary and exigent. Thus, when the Divine Decree of Eternal Destiny commended the eradication of the infamously wicked infidels into our capable hands, we set out for their lands like ineluctable fate itself to enforce the order "Leave not upon the earth of the Unbelievers even one" [Qur'ân LXXI:26]. If God almighty wills, the lightning of our conquering sword shall uproot the untamed bramble grown to great heights in the path of the refulgent Divine Law and shall cast them down upon the dust of abjectness to be trampled under the hooves of our legions, for "They make the mightiest of its inhabitants abased. Even so they too will do" [Qur'ân XXVII:34]; the thunder of our avenging mace shall dash out the muddled brains of the enemies of the Faith as rations for the lionhearted *ghâzîs*. "And those who do wrong shall surely know by what overthrowing they will be overthrown" [Qur'ân XXVI:227].

> When I the sharp-edged sword draw from its
>   sheath,
> Then shall I raise up doomsday on the earth.
> Then shall I roast the hearts of lion-hearted
>   men,
> And toast the morning with a goblet of their
>   blood.
> My crow-feathered arrow will fix the eagle in
>   his flight;
> My naked blade will make the sun's heart
>   tremble.
> Inquire of the sun about the dazzle of my rein;
> Seek news of Mars about the brilliance of my
>   arms.
> Although a Sûfî[5] crown you wear, I bear a
>   trenchant sword:

---

2. *Hârith:* possibly a reference to Hârith ibn Suwayd, who pretended to convert to Islâm in Muhammad's time, apostasized, and was ordered executed by Muhammad when he tried to rejoin the young Muslim community. Selîm is alluding to parallels between Hârith's and Ismâ'îl's career.

3. *Fatwas:* legal opinions, *'ulamâ':* learned men.

4. *Sunî community:* those who follow the practice of Muhammad, i.e., not those like Shî'ites who followed 'Alî.

5. Allusion to Safavî origins as mystical order. The "crown" was their special headgear.

The owner of the sword will soon possess the
crown.
O Mighty Fortune, pray grant this my single
wish:
Pray let me take both crown and power from
the foe.

But "Religion is Counsel," and should you
turn the countenance of submission to the *qibla*
of bliss and the *Ka'ba*[6] of hope—our angelic
threshold, the refuge of the noble moreover,
should you lift up the hand of oppression from
the heads of your subjects ruined by tyranny and
sedition, should you take up a course of repentance, become like one blameless and return to
the sublime straight path of the Sunna[7] of
Muhammad (Prayers and salutations upon him
and God's satisfaction upon his immaculate family
and his rightly-guided companions all!). For "My
companions are like the stars: whomever you
choose to follow, you will be guided aright" and
finally should you consider your lands and their
people part of the well-protected Ottoman state,
then shall you be granted our royal favor and our
imperial patronage.

He whose face touches the dust of my
    threshold in submission
Will be enveloped in the shadow of my favor
    and my justice.
How great the happiness of him who complies
    with this!
On the other hand, if your evil, seditious
    habits have become a part of your nature,
    that which has become essential can never
    again be accidental.
What avail sermons to the black-hearted?

Then, with the support and assistance of God, I
will crown the head of every gallows tree with the
head of a crown-wearing Sûfî and clear that faction
from the face of the earth—"The party of God,
they are the victors" [Qur'ân V:56]; I will break
the oppressors' grip with the power of the

miraculous white hand of Moses, for "God's hand
is over their hands" [Qur'ân XLVIII:10]. Let them
remove the cotton of negligence from the ears of
their intelligence and, with their shrouds on their
shoulders, prepare themselves for "Surely that
which you are promised will come to pass" [Qur'ân
VI:134]. The triumphant troops "As though they
were a building well-compacted" [Qur'ân LXI:4]
crying out like fate evoked "When their term
comes they shall not put it back a single hour nor
put it forward" [Qur'ân VII:34] and maneuvering
in accordance with "Slay them wherever you find
them" [Qur'ân IV:89], will wreak ruin upon you
and drive you from that land. "To God belongs
the command before and after, and on that day the
believers shall rejoice" [Qur'ân XX:4]. "So the last
roots of the people who did evil were cut off.
Praise be to God, the Lord of the Worlds" [Qur'ân
VI:45].

ISMA'IL TO SELÎM (UNDATED, CA. 1514)

May his godly majesty, the refuge of Isâm, the
might of the kingdom, he upon whom God looks
with favor, the champion of the sultanate and of the
state, the hero of the faith and of the earth, Sultân
Selîm Shâh (God grant him immortal state and
eternal happiness!) accept this affectionate greeting
and this friendly letter, considering it a token of our
good will.

Now to begin: Your honored letters have arrived one after another, for "No sooner has a thing
doubled than it has tripled." Their contents, although indicative of hostility, are stated with boldness and vigor. The latter gives us much enjoyment
and pleasure, but we are ignorant of the reason for
the former. In the time of your late blessed father
(May God enlighten his proof!) when our royal
troops passed through the lands of Rûm to chastise

---

6. *Qibla*: direction of prayer for Muslims, i.e., the K'ba or holy building in Mecca.

7. *Sunna*: practice, example, custom.

the impudence of Alâ' al-Dawla Dhûl) Qadr,[8] complete concord and friendship was shown on both sides. Moreover, when your majesty was governor at Trebizond [i.e., before his accession] there existed perfect mutual understanding. Thus, now, the cause of your resentment and displeasure yet remains unknown. If political necessity has compelled you on this course, then may your problems soon be solved.

> Dispute may fire words to such a heat
> That ancient houses be consumed in flames.

The intention of our inaction in this regard is twofold:

1. Most of the inhabitants of the land of Rûm are followers of our forefathers (May God the All-Forgiving King have mercy upon them!).

2. We have always loved the *ghâzî*-titled[9] Ottoman house and we do not wish the outbreak of sedition and turmoil once again as in the time of Tîmûr.

> Why should we then take umbrage at these provocations? We shall not.
> The mutual hostility of kings is verily an ancient rite.
> Should one hold the bride of worldly rule too close,
> His lips those of the radiant sword will kiss.

Nevertheless, there is no cause for improper words: indeed, those vain, heretical imputations are the mere fabrications of the opium-clouded minds of certain secretaries and scribes. We therefore think that our delayed reply was not completely without cause for we have now dispatched our honored personal companion and servant Shâh Qulî Aghâ (May he be sustained!) with a golden casket stamped with the royal seal and filled with a special preparation for their use should they deem it necessary. May he soon arrive so that with assistance from above the mysteries concealed behind the veil of fate might be disclosed. But one should always exercise free judgment not bound solely by the words of others and always keep in view that in the end regrets avail him naught.

At this writing we were engaged upon the hunt near Isfahân; we now prepare provisions and our troops for the coming campaign. In all friendship we say do what you will.

> Bitter experience has taught that in this world of trial
> He who falls upon the house of 'Alî[10] always falls.

Kindly give our ambassador leave to travel unmolested. "No soul laden bears the load of another" [Qur'ân VI:164; LIII:38].

When war becomes inevitable, hesitation and delay must be set aside, and one must think on that which is to come. Farewell.

FOCUS QUESTIONS

1. Why does Selîm quote the Koran (Qur'ân) so often in his letter?

2. What is Selîm's self-conception?

3. What is Ismâ'îl's attitude toward Selîm? What does he mean when he says, "In all friendship we say do what you will do"?

4. What purpose do you think these letters served?

---

8. *Alâ al-Dawla Dhûl-Qadr:* ruler of partially Shî'ite Dhûl-Qadr Turkomans in Elbistan and Mar'ash, buffer state between Ottomans and Safavids. Ismâ'îl had attacked them for the faith.

9. An allusion to the Ottoman origin as frontier warriors for the faith.

10. House of 'Alî, i.e., the Shî'ites.

82

The History and Description of Africa (1550 C.E.)

LEO AFRICANUS

Leo Africanus (ca. 1485–1554), whose Arabic name was al-Hassan ibn-Mohammed al-Wazzan, was born in Granada to a prominent Moorish family. After the expulsion of the Moors from Spain in 1492, his family left Granada, and Leo was raised in Morocco, where he studied under the tutelage of Arabic scholars. Ultimately, Leo Africanus became a merchant and traveled throughout northern Africa and the Arabian Middle East. In 1517, during a voyage to Constantinople, he was captured by pirates. Because he was obviously an educated man, Leo Africanus was taken to Rome and presented to Pope Leo X, who personally instructed him in both Latin letters and Christianity. He was baptized John Leo, in honor of the Pope, and spent the next decade living in Rome.

Leo Africanus wrote a number of works that introduced Europeans to the achievements of Arabic science and philosophy; he also composed an Arabic-Spanish dictionary. He was chiefly known for his History and Description of Africa, *which was written first in Arabic and then rewritten in Italian by Leo himself.* History and Description of Africa *was first published in 1550 and was the principal source of European knowledge about the peoples of northern Africa.*

ABASSIA, OR THE EMPIRE
OF PRETE IANNI

The Abassins are a people subject to *Prete Ianni*, whose empire (if we consider the stile which he useth in his letters) hath most ample confines. For he intituleth himselfe emperour of the great and higher Ethiopia, king of Goiame, which (as *Botera* supposeth) is situate betweene Nilus and Zaire; of Vangue a kingdome beyond Zaire; of Damut which confineth with the land of the Anzichi; and towards the south he is called king of Cafate and Bagamidri, two provinces bordering upon the first great lake, which is the originall fountains of Nilus; as likewise of the kingdomes of Xoa, Fatigar, Angote, Baru, Baaliganze, Adea, Amara, Ambea,

Vague, Tigremahon, Sabaim, where the Queene of Saba governed, and lastly of Barnagaes, and lorde as farre as Nubia, which bordereth upon Egypt. But at this present the center or midst of his Empire (as *John Barros* writeth) is the lake of Barcena. For it extendeth eastward towarde the Red sea, as farre as Suaquen, the space of two hundred twentie and two leagues. Howbeit betweene the sea and his dominions runneth a ridge of mountaines inhabited by Moores, who are masters of al the seacoast along, except the porte of Ercoco, which belongeth to the *Prete*. And likewise on the west, his empire is restrained by another mountainous ridge stretching along the river of Nilus, where are founde most rich mines of golde; amongst which are the mines of Damut and of Sinassij, wholie in the possession of Gentiles which pay tribute unto the *Prete*.

Northward it is bounded by an imaginarie line supposed to be drawn from Suachen to the beginning of the isle Meroe above mentioned; which line extendeth an hundred and five and twentie leagues. From thence the Abassin borders trend south somewhat crookedly in manner of abowe, as farre as the kingdome of Adea (from the mountaines whereof springeth a river called by *Ptolemey* Raptus which falleth into the sea about Melinde) for the space of two hundred and fiftie nine leagues; next unto the which borders, inhabite certaine Gentiles of blacke colour, with curled haire. And heere the saide empire is limited by the kingdome of Adel, the head citie whereof called Arar, standeth in the latitude nine degrees. So that all this great empire may containe in compasse six hundred threescore and two leagues, little more or lesse. It is refreshed and watered by two mightie rivers which convey their streames into Nilus, called by *Ptolemey* Astaboras and Astapus, and by the naturall inhabitants Abagni and Tagassi; the first whereof taketh his originall from the lake of Barcena, and the second from the lake of Colve. Barcena lieth in seven degrees of north latitude; & Colve under the verie Equinoctiall. The first (besides Abagni) ingendereth also the river of Zeila: and the second (besides Tagassi) giveth effence to the river of Quilimanci. Between Abagni and the Red sea lieth the province of Barnagasso: betwene Abagni and Tagassi are the kingdomes of Angote and Fatigar; and more towards the bay of Barbarians, the provinces of Adea and of Baru: and somewhat lower, that of Amara. In briefe, beyond the river of Tagassi ly the regions of Bileguanzi, and of Tigremahon.

The Abassins have no great knowledge of Nilus by reason of the mountaines which devide them from it; for which cause they call Abagni, the father of rivers. Howbeit they say that upon Nilus do inhabite two great and populous nations; one of Iewes towards the west, under the government of a mightie king; the other more southerly, consisting of Amazones or warlike women; whereof wee will speake more at large in our relation of Monomotapa.

Throughout all the dominion of the *Prete* there is not any one city of importance, either for multitude of inhabitantes, for magnificent buildings, or for any other respect. For the greatest townes there, containe not above two thousand housholds; the houses being (cottage-like) reared up with clay and covered with straw, or such like base matter. Also *Ptolemey* entreating of these partes, maketh mention but of three or foure cities onely, which he appointeth to the south of the Isle Meroe. Howbeit in some places upon the frontiers of Abassia there are certaine townes verie fairely built, and much frequented for traffique. The Portugales in their travailes throughout the empire have often declared unto the Abassins, how much better it were, for avoiding of the outrageous injuries and losses daily inflicted by the Moores and Mahumetans both upon their goods and persons, if the emperour would build cities and castles stronglie walled and fortified. Whereunto they made answere, that the power of their Neguz, or emperour, consisted not in stone-walles, but in the armes of his people. They use not ordinarily any lime or stone, but onely for the building of churches (saying, that so it becommeth us to make a difference between the houses of men, and churches dedicated to God) and of their Beteneguz or houses of the emperour, wherein the governours of provinces are placed to execute justice. These Beteneguz stand continually open, and yet in the governours, absence no man dare enter into them, under paine of being punished as a traytour. Moreover in the city of Axuma (esteemed by them to have beene the seate of the Queene of *Saba*) stand certaine ruinous buildings like unto pyramides; which by reason of their greatness, remaine even til this present, notwithstanding their many yeeres antiquitie. Likewise there are in this countrie divers churches and oratories hewen out of the hard rocke, consisting but of one onely stone, some sixtie, some fortie, and some thirtie fathomes long, being full of windowes, and engraven with strange and unknowne characters. Three such churches there are of twelve fathomes broade and eightie in length.

The Abassins which are subject to the *Prete*, hold opinion, that their prince deriveth his petigree from *Melich* the sonne of *Salomon*, which (as they say) he begot of the Queene of *Saba;* and that themselves are descended from the officers and attendants which *Salomon* appointed unto this his sonne when he sent him home unto his mother: which seemeth not altogether unlikely, if you consider the Jewish ceremonies of circumcision, observing of the sabaoth, & such like, which they use untill this present: likewise they abhorre swines flesh and certaine other meates, which they call uncleane. The *Prete* absolutely governeth in all matters, except it be in administring of the sacraments, and ordaining of priests. Hee giveth and taketh away benefices at his pleasure; and in punishing offenders, maketh no difference betweene his clergie and laitie. The administration of their sacraments is wholie referred to the Abuna or Patriarke. The *Prete* is lorde and owner of all the lands and possessions in his empire, except those of the church; which are in number infinite; for the monasteries of saint *Antonie* (besides which there are none of any other order) and the colleges of the Canons and of the Hermites, to-gither with the parishes, are innumerable. They are all provided by the king, both of revenewes and of ornaments.

They have two winters and two summers; which they discerne not by colde and heate, but by rainie and faire weather. They begin their yeere upon the 26 of August, and divide it into twelve moneths, each moneth containing thirtie daies, whereunto they adde every common yeere five daies, and in the leape yeere sixe, which odde daies they call Pagomen, that is, The end of the yeere. Their ordinaire journeies in travelling are twelve miles a day. The common harlots dwell without their townes, and have wages allowed them out of the common purse: neither may they enter into any cities, nor apparell themselves, but only in yellow.

The soil of Abassia aboundeth generally with graine, and in especiall with barly and all kindes of Pulse, but not so much with wheate; they have sugar likewise (not knowing how to refine it) and hony, and cotton-wooll, orenges, cedars, and limons, grow naturally there. They have neither melons, citrons, nor rape-roots: but many plants & herbes different from ours. Their drinke is made of barley and millet: neither have they any wine made of grapes, but onely in the houses of the emperour, and the Abuna. They are not destitute of Elephants, mules, lions, tygres, ounces, and deere. Their owne countrey horses are but of a small size: howbeit they have also of the Arabian and the Egyptian breed, the coltes whereof within fower daies after they be foled, they use to suckle with kine. They have great and terrible apes; and infinite sorts of birds; but neither cuckowes nor Pies, so farre as ever could bee learned. Heere are likewise great store of mines of gold, silver, iron, and copper; but they know not how to digge and refine the same: for the people of this countrey are so rude and ignorant, that they have no knowledge nor use of any arte or occupation. Insomuch as they esteeme the carpenters or smithes craft for an unlawful and diabolicall kinde of science; and such as exercise the same, live among them like infamous persons; neither are they permitted to enter into any of their churches. In the kingdome of Bagamidri are founde most excellent mines of silver, which they knowe none other way how to take from the ore, but onely by melting it with fire into thinne plates. Goiame aboundeth with base gold. In the kingdome of Damut they digge and refine it somewhat better. They have neither the arte of making cloth (for which cause the greater part of them go clad in beasts skins) nor yet the manner of hauking, fowling, or hunting; so that their countries swarme with partridges, quailes, fesants, cranes, geese, hens, hares, deere, and other like creatures: neither knowe they how to make any full use nor benefite of the fruitefulness of their countrey, or of the commoditie of rivers. They sowe mill for the most parte, sometimes in one place, and sometimes in another, according as the raine giveth them opportunitie. In summe, they shew no wit nor dexterity in any thing so much as in robbery and warre; unto both which they have a kind of naturall inclination. Which is occasioned (as I suppose) by the continuall voyages made by the *Prete*, and by their usuall living in the wide fields, and that in divers and sundry places. For to travaile continually, and remaine in the fields without any stable or firme habitation, compelleth men as it were, of necessitie, to lay holde on all that comes next to hande, be it their owne, or belonging to others.

They are much subject to tempests; but to an inconvenience far more intollerable, namely to innumerable swarmes of locusts, which bring such desolation upon them, as is most dreadfull to consider: for they consume whole provinces, leaving them quite destitute of succour both for man and beast. They use no stamped coine in all this empire, but insteede thereof certaine rude pieces of golde, and little balls of iron, especially in Angote; as likewise salt and pepper, which are the greatest riches that they can enjoy.

Hence it is, that the tributes which are payed to the prince, consist onely of such things as his owne dominions do naturally afforde; as namely of salt, gold, silver, corne, hides, elephants teeth, the horne of the Rhinoceros, with slaves, and such like. Which forme of tribute (being most agreeable to nature) is used also in other parts of Africa. Their salt is taken out of a certaine great mountains in the province of Balgada, and is made into square pieces.

The most populous place in all Abassia is the court of the *Prete*, wheresoever it resideth; and there are erected five or six thousand tents of cotton of divers colours, with so notable a distinction of streetes, lanes, market-places, and Tribunals; that even in a moment every man knoweth his owne station and the place where he is to doe his business. A man may conjecture the greatnes of this courte, if he doe but consider, that (according to the report of some who have there bin personally present)

besides the camels which carry the tents, the mules of carriage exceede the number of fiftie thousand. Their mules serve them to carry burthens, and to ride upon: but their horses are onely for the warres. The Mahumetans have now brought this prince to great extremity: but heretofore while he was in his flourishing estate, he lived so majestically, that he never spake but by an interpreter; nor would be seene to his subjects, but onely upon solemne dayes. At other times it was held as a great favour, if he did shew but the halfe part of his feete to ambassadours, and to his favorites. And no marvel: for amongst the Ethiopians it hath beene an ancient custome (as *Strabo* writeth) to adore their kinges like gods, who for the most part live enclosed at home. This so strange and stately kinde of government, did exceedingly abase his subjects, whom the *Prete* used like slaves; so that upon the smallest occasions that might be, he would deprive them of all honour and dignity, were they never so great. Abassia containeth many large plaines, and very high mountaines, all fruitfull. In some places you shall have most extreame coulde and frostie weather: but not any snowe throughout the whole empire, no not in the mountaines.

The *Prete* hath many moores in his dominions, and upon his borders; but the most populous of all others are the Moores called Dobas, who are bound by a law never to marry, till they can bring most evident testimony, that each of them hath slaine twelve Christians. Wherefore the Abassin merchants passe not by their country, but with most strong guardes.

FOCUS QUESTIONS

1. What do the Ethiopians believe to be the source of their emperor's power?

2. What were the symbols of the prince's greatness?

3. What threatened the well-being of the Ethiopians?

4. What aspects of Ethiopia does Leo Africanus think are important to describe? What does he leave out?

83

Travels in the Mughal Empire (1656–1668 C.E.)

FRANÇOIS BERNIER

François Bernier (1620–1688) was a Frenchman who spent most of his life traveling in the East. He came from humble origins—his father leased a farm—but was successful academically. Bernier studied medicine and for a time was a companion to Gassendi, one of the great French philosophers. In 1656 Bernier began a long journey to the East that brought him first to Egypt and then to the Indian subcontinent. During a ten-year exploration of India and Persia, he kept a journal and wrote a number of books. The most important of these, The History of the Late Rebellion in the States of the Great Mogol, *was an instant success throughout Europe, where it was translated into English, Dutch, German, and Italian. The exotic civilizations described in Bernier's work captured the imagination of Europeans.*

Bernier's descriptive accounts of the cities he visited in the East are remarkable for their detail. They are the best surviving records of everyday life in the Mughal Empire, even though they are unabashedly Eurocentric in outlook.

It is about forty years ago that *Chah-Jehan*, father of the present *Great Mogol, Aureng-Zebe*, conceived the design of immortalising his name by the erection of a city near the site of the ancient *Dehli*.... Here he resolved to fix his court, alleging as the reason for its removal from *Agra*, that the excessive heat to which that city is exposed during summer rendered it unfit for the residence of a monarch....

Dehli, then, is an entirely new city, situated in a flat country, on the banks of the *Gemna*, a river which may be compared to the *Loire*, and built on one bank only in such a manner that it terminates in this place very much in the form of a crescent, having but one bridge of boats to cross to the country. Excepting the side where it is defended by the river, the city is encompassed by walls of brick.

... The walls of the citadel, as to their antique and round towers, resemble those of the city, but being partly of brick, and partly of a red stone which resembles marble, they have a better appearance. The walls of the fortress likewise excel those of the town in height, strength, and thickness, being capable of admitting small field-pieces, which are pointed toward the city. Except on the side of the river, the citadel is defended by a deep ditch faced with hewn stone, filled with water, and stocked with fish....

Adjoining the ditch is a large garden, filled at all times with flowers and green shrubs, which, contrasted with the stupendous red walls, produce a beautiful effect.

Next to the garden is the great royal square, faced on one side by the gates of the fortress, and on the opposite side of which terminate the two most considerable streets of the city.

The tents of such *Rajas* as are in the King's pay, and whose weekly turn it is to mount guard, are pitched in this square; those petty sovereigns having an insuperable objection to be enclosed within walls. The guard within the fortress is mounted by the *Omrahs* and *Mansebdars*.

In this place also at break of day they exercise the royal horses, which are kept in a spacious stable not far distant....

Here too is held a *bazar* or market for an endless variety of things; which like the *Pont-neuf* at *Paris*, is the rendezvous for all sorts of mountebanks and jugglers. Hither, likewise, the astrologers resort, both *Mahometan* and *Gentile*. These wise doctors remain seated in the sun, on a dusty piece of carpet, handling some old mathematical instruments, and having open before them a large book which represents the signs of the zodiac. In this way they attract the attention of the passengers, and impose upon the people, by whom they are considered as so many infallible oracles. They tell a poor person his fortune for a *payssa* (which is worth about one sol); and after examining the hand and face of the applicant, turning over the leaves of the large book, and pretending to make certain calculations, these impostors decide upon the *Sahet* or propitious moment of commencing the business he may have in hand. Silly women, wrapping themselves in a white cloth from head to foot, flock to the astrologers, whisper to them all the transactions of their lives, and disclose every secret with no more reserve than is practised by a scrupulous penitent in the presence of her confessor. The ignorant and infatuated people really believe that the stars have an influence which the astrologers can control.

I am speaking only of the poor *bazar-astrologers*. Those who frequent the court of the grandees are considered by them eminent doctors, and become wealthy. The whole of *Asia* is degraded by the same superstition. Kings and nobles grant large salaries to these crafty diviners, and never engage in the most trifling transaction without consulting them. They read whatever is written in heaven; fix upon the *Sahet*, and solve every doubt by opening the *Koran*.

Of the numberless streets which cross each other, many have arcades....

Amid these streets are dispersed the habitations of *Mansebdars*, or petty *Omrahs*, officers of justice, rich merchants, and others; many of which have a tolerable appearance. Very few are built entirely of brick or stone, and several are made only of clay and straw, yet they are airy and pleasant, most of them having courts and gardens, being commodious inside and containing good furniture. The thatched roof is supported by a layer of long, handsome, and strong canes, and the clay walls are covered with a fine white lime.

Intermixed with these different houses is an immense number of small ones, built of mud and thatched with straw, in which lodge the common troopers, and all that vast multitude of servants and camp-followers who follow the court and the army.

It is owing to these thatched cottages that *Dehli* is subject to such frequent conflagrations. More than sixty thousand roofs were consumed this last year by three fires, during the prevalence of certain impetuous winds which blow generally in summer. So rapid were the flames that several camels and horses were burnt. Many of the inmates of the seraglio also fell victims to the devouring element; for these poor women are so bashful and helpless that they can do nothing but hide their faces at the sight of strangers, and those who perished possessed not sufficient energy to fly from the danger.

That which so much contributes to the beauty of European towns, the brilliant appearance of the shops, is wanting in *Dehli*. For though this city be the seat of a powerful and magnificent court, where an infinite quantity of the richest commodities is necessarily collected, yet there are no streets like ours of *S. Denis*, which has not perhaps its equal in any part of *Asia*. Here the costly merchandise is generally kept in warehouses, and the shops are seldom decked with rich or showy articles. For one that makes a display of beautiful and fine cloths, silk, and other stuffs striped with gold and silver, turbans embroidered with gold, and brocades, there are at least five-and-twenty where nothing is seen but pots of oil or butter, piles of baskets filled with rice, barley, chick-peas, wheat, and an endless variety of other grain and pulse, the ordinary aliment not only of the *Gentiles*, who never eat meat, but of the lower class of *Mahometans*, and a considerable portion of the military.

There is, indeed, a fruit-market that makes some show....

There are many confectioners' shops in the town, but the sweetmeats are badly made, and full of dust and flies....

Bakers also are numerous, but the ovens are unlike our own, and very defective....

In the *bazars* there are shops where meat is sold roasted and dressed in a variety of ways. But there is no trusting to their dishes, composed, for aught I know, of the flesh of camels, horses, or perhaps oxen which have died of disease. Indeed no food can be considered wholesome which is not dressed at home.

Meat is sold in every part of the city; but instead of goats' flesh that of mutton is often palmed upon the buyer; an imposition which ought to be guarded against, because mutton and beef, but particularly the former, though not unpleasant to the taste, are heating, flatulent, and difficult of digestion. Kid is the best food, but being rarely sold in quarters, it must be purchased alive, which is very inconvenient, as the meat will not keep from morning to night, and is generally lean and without flavour. The goats' flesh found in quarters at the butchers' shops is frequently that of the she-goat, which is lean and tough.

But it would be unreasonable in me to complain; because since I have been familiarised with the manners of the people, it seldom happens that I find fault either with my meat or my bread.

FOCUS QUESTIONS

1. What is Bernier's attitude toward Dehli and its inhabitants?

2. Why was a new Dehli built in the seventeenth century?

3. What was life like for a merchant in seventeenth-century Dehli? What was it like for a peasant?

4. What role did astrologers play in the Mughal Empire?

The Reform of Christianity

Fishing for Souls. Painted in the midst of the Protestant reformation, Catholic counter-reformation, and wars of religion, this allegorical representation pictures groups of Protestants (left) and Catholics (right) on opposite sides of a river, fishing for the souls of Christians.

FOCUS QUESTIONS

1. Why are the people in the water naked?

2. What does the rainbow uniting the two sides of the river mean?

3. Why is there a small animal in the foreground on the left bank?

4. Why are the trees on the right leafy in contrast to the bare trees on the left?

84

In Praise of Folly (1509 C.E.)

DESIDERIUS ERASMUS

Desiderius Erasmus (ca. 1466–1536) was the leading intellectual light of the early sixteenth century. An orphan, Erasmus was educated in a monastery and became a monk. His intellectual gifts were so great that he was allowed to travel throughout the continent searching for ancient manuscripts and perfecting his skills as a linguist, philologist, and writer. His principal scholarly achievements, an edition of the Greek New Testament and of the Writings of Saint Jerome, were both published in 1516. But Erasmus was better known for his popular writings, especially his Adages *and the satirical* In Praise of Folly.*

In Praise of Folly was written for Sir Thomas More, with whom Erasmus had made friends on his first trip to England. It is a spoof, in which Folly demands praise for all of the ways of the world. It is under Folly's influence that people behave as they do and that institutions are organized with an upside-down logic. Erasmus was particularly scathing in his description of the state of religion and of the Catholic Church. Historians are fond of saying that Erasmus laid the egg that Luther hatched.

The next to be placed among the regiment of fools are such as make a trade of telling or inquiring after incredible stories of miracles and prodigies: never doubting that a lie will choke them, they will muster up a thousand several strange relations of spirits, ghosts, apparitions, raising of the devil, and such like bugbears of superstition, which the farther they are from being probably true, the more greedily they are swallowed, and the more devoutly believed. And these absurdities do not only bring an empty pleasure, and cheap divertisement, but they are a good trade, and procure a comfortable income to such priests and friars as by this craft get their gain. To these again are nearly related such others as attribute strange virtues to the shrines and images of saints and martyrs, and so would make their credulous proselytes believe, that if they pay their devotion to St. Christopher in the morning, they shall be guarded and secured the day following from all dangers and misfortunes: if soldiers, when they first take arms, shall come and mumble over such a set prayer before the picture of St. Barbara, they shall return safe from all engagements: or if any pray to Erasmus on such particular holidays, with the ceremony of wax candles, and other fopperies, he shall in a short time be rewarded with a plentiful increase of wealth and riches.

The next to these are another sort of brainsick fools, who style themselves monks and of religious orders, though they assume both sides very unjustly: for as to the last, they have very little religion in them; and as to the former, the etymology of the word monk implies a solitariness, or being alone; whereas they are so thick abroad that we cannot pass any street or alley without meeting them. Now I cannot imagine what one degree of men would be more hopelessly wretched, if I did not stand their friend, and buoy them up in that lake of misery, which by the engagements of a holy vow they have voluntarily immerged themselves in. But when this sort of men are so unwelcome to others, as that the very sight of them is thought ominous, I yet make them highly in love with themselves, and fond admirers of their own happiness. The first step whereunto they esteem a profound ignorance, thinking carnal knowledge a great enemy to their spiritual welfare, and seem confident of becoming greater proficients in divine mysteries the less they are poisoned with any human learning. They imagine that they bear a sweet consort with the heavenly choir, when they tone out their daily tally of psalms, which they rehearse only by rote, without permitting their understanding or affections to go along with their voice.

Among these some make a good profitable trade of beggary, going about from house to house, not like the apostles, to break, but to beg, their bread; nay, thrust into all public-houses, come aboard the passage-boats, get into the travelling waggons, and omit no opportunity of time or place for the craving people's charity; doing a great deal of injury to common highway beggars by interloping in their traffic of alms. And when they are thus voluntarily poor, destitute, not provided with two coats, nor with any money in their purse, they have the impudence to pretend that they imitate the first disciples, whom their master expressly sent out in such an equipage.

It is pretty to observe how they regulate all their actions as it were by weight and measure to so exact a proportion, as if the whole loss of their religion depended upon the omission of the least punctilio. Thus they must be very critical in the precise number of knots to the tying on of their sandals: what distinct colours their respective habits, and what stuff made of, how broad and long their girdles: how big, and in what fashion, their hoods; whether their bald crowns be to a hair's-breadth of the right cut; how many hours they must sleep, at what minute rise to prayers, and so on. And these several customs are altered according to the humours of different persons and places. While they are sworn to the superstitious observance of these trifles, they do not only despise all others, but are very inclinable to fall out among themselves; for though they make profession of an apostolic

charity, yet they will pick a quarrel, and be implacably passionate for such poor provocations, as the girting on a coat the wrong way, for the wearing of clothes a little too darkish coloured or any such nicety not worth the speaking of.

Some are so obstinately superstitious that they will wear their upper garment of some coarse dog's hair stuff, and that next their skin as soft as silk: but others on the contrary will have linen frocks outermost, and their shirts of wool, or hair. Some again will not touch a piece of money, though they make no scruple of the sin of drunkenness, and the lust of the flesh. All their several orders are mindful of nothing more than of their being distinguished from each other by their different customs and habits. They seem indeed not so careful of becoming like Christ, and of being known to be his disciples, as the being unlike to one another, and distinguishable for followers of their several founders.

Most of them place their greatest stress for salvation on a strict conformity to their foppish ceremonies, and a belief of their legendary traditions; wherein they fancy to have acquitted themselves with so much of supererogation, that one heaven can never be a condign reward for their meritorious life; little thinking that the Judge of all the earth at the last day shall put them off, with a who hath required these things at your hands; and call them to account only for the stewardship of his legacy, which was the precept of love and charity. It will be pretty to hear their pleas before the great tribunal: one will brag how he mortified his carnal appetite by feeding only upon fish: another will urge that he spent most of his time on earth in the divine exercise of singing psalms: a third will tell how many days he fasted, and what severe penance he imposed on himself for the bringing his body into subjection: another shall produce in his own behalf as many ceremonies as would load a fleet of merchant-men: a fifth shall plead that in threescore years he never so much as touched a piece of money, except he fingered it through a thick pair of gloves: a sixth, to testify his former humility, shall bring along with him his sacred hood, so old and nasty, that any seaman had rather stand bare headed on the deck, than put it on to defend his ears in the sharpest storms: the next that comes to answer for himself shall plead, that for fifty years together, he had lived like a sponge upon the same place, and was content never to change his homely habitation: another shall whisper softly, and tell the judge he has lost his voice by a continual singing of holy hymns and anthems: the next shall confess how he fell into a lethargy by a strict, reserved, and sedentary life: and the last shall intimate that he has forgot to speak, by having always kept silence, in obedience to the injunction of taking heed lest he should have offended with his tongue.

Now as to the popes of Rome, who pretend themselves Christ's vicars, if they would but imitate his exemplary life, in the being employed in an unintermitted course of preaching; in the being attended with poverty, nakedness, hunger, and a contempt of this world; if they did but consider the import of the word pope, which signifies a father; or if they did but practice their surname of most holy, what order or degrees of men would be in a worse condition? There would be then no such vigorous making of parties, and buying of votes, in the conclave upon a vacancy of that see: and those who by bribery, or other indirect courses, should get themselves elected, would never secure their sitting firm in the chair by pistol, poison, force, and violence.

How much of their pleasure would be abated if they were but endowed with one dram of wisdom? Wisdom, did I say? Nay, with one grain of that salt which our Saviour bid them not lose the savour of. All their riches, all their honour, their jurisdictions, their Peter's patrimony, their offices, their dispensations, their licenses, their indulgences, their long train and attendants (see in how short a compass I have abbreviated all their marketing of religion); in a word, all their perquisites would be forfeited and lost; and in their room would succeed watchings, fastings, tears, prayers, sermons, hard studies, repenting sighs, and a thousand such like severe penalties: nay, what's yet more deplorable, it would then follow, that all their clerks, amanuenses, notaries, advocates, proctors, secretaries, the offices of grooms, ostlers, serving-men, pimps (and somewhat else, which for modesty's sake I shall not mention);

in short, all these troops of attendants, which depend on his holiness, would all lose their several employments. This indeed would be hard, but what yet remains would be more dreadful: the very Head of the Church, the spiritual prince, would then be brought from all his splendour to the poor equipage of a scrip and staff.

But all this is upon the supposition only that they understood what circumstances they are placed in; whereas now, by a wholesome neglect of thinking, they live as well as heart can wish: whatever of toil and drudgery belongs to their office that they assign over to St. Peter, or St. Paul, who have time enough to mind it; but if there be any thing of pleasure and grandeur, that they assume to themselves, as being hereunto called: so that by my influence no sort of people live more to their own ease and content. They think to satisfy that Master they pretend to serve, our Lord and Saviour, with their great state and magnificence, with the ceremonies of instalments, with the titles of reverence and holiness, and with exercising their episcopal function only in blessing and cursing. The working of miracles is old and out-dated; to teach the people is too laborious; to interpret scripture is to invade the prerogative of the schoolmen; to pray is too idle; to shed tears is cowardly and unmanly; to fast is too mean and sordid; to be easy and familiar is beneath the grandeur of him, who, without being sued to and entreated, will scarce give princes the honour of kissing his toe; finally, to die for religion is too self-denying; and to be crucified as their Lord of Life, is base and ignominious.

Their only weapons ought to be those of the Spirit; and of these indeed they are mighty liberal, as of their interdicts, their suspensions, their denunciations, their aggravations, their greater and lesser excommunications, and their roaring bulls, that fright whomever they are thundered against; and these most holy fathers never issue them out more frequently than against those, who, at the instigation of the devil, and not having the fear of God before their eyes, do feloniously and maliciously attempt to lessen and impair St. Peter's patrimony: and though that apostle tells our Saviour in the gospel, in the name of all the other disciples, we have left all, and followed you, yet they challenge as his inheritance, fields, towns, treasures, and large dominions; for the defending whereof, inflamed with a holy zeal, they fight with fire and sword, to the great loss and effusion of Christian blood, thinking they are apostolical maintainers of Christ's spouse, the church, when they have murdered all such as they call her enemies; though indeed the church has no enemies more bloody and tyrannical than such impious popes, who give dispensations for the not preaching of Christ; evacuate the main effect and design of our redemption by their pecuniary bribes and sales; adulterate the gospel by their forced interpretations, and undermining traditions; and lastly, by their lusts and wickedness grieve the Holy Spirit, and make their Saviour's wounds to bleed anew.

FOCUS QUESTIONS

1. How has superstition affected the message of the Church, according to Erasmus?

2. What is wrong with most members of religious orders?

3. The papacy, Erasmus says, is also corrupt. How? How might it be reformed?

4. Erasmus identifies many serious failings in the Church. Why do you think people allowed them to continue? What purpose was the Church serving?

5. The Church comes in for a great deal of criticism from Erasmus. Do you think he contributed to the origins of the Reformation? How might the scope of his criticism have been limited by his choice of forum?

85

The Freedom of a Christian (1520 C.E.)
Of Marriage and Celibacy (1566 C.E.)

MARTIN LUTHER

Martin Luther (1483–1546) was undoubtedly the central figure of the sixteenth century. Trained for the law, he underwent a spiritual crisis that led him to enter an Augustinian monastery. There his extraordinary gifts were recognized, and he quickly distinguished himself as a scholar, teacher, and pastor. In 1517 he protested against the sale of indulgences and found himself at the center of a political and religious controversy. Luther refused to recant his views and was condemned by both the pope and the Holy Roman emperor. He broke from the Roman Catholic Church and founded his own religious movement, first called Protestantism and later Lutheranism.

Throughout his political struggles, Luther wrote incessantly. The spread of his message and his movement was aided by the invention of printing and by the increase of literacy. He translated parts of the Bible into German, prepared a new church service, and even wrote hymns. But his most important works were the explanations of his faith. The Freedom of a Christian *is one of the central statements of Luther's theology.*

Among the many church reforms that Luther undertook was permitting clergy to marry. In his later years he took a wife, a former nun from a dissolved monastery. Luther's views on marriage, however, were not part of his systematic theology. They were collected in The Table Talk, *a work complied by his followers after his death.*

THE FREEDOM OF A CHRISTIAN

Many people have considered Christian faith an easy thing, and not a few have given it a place among the virtues. They do this because they have not experienced it and have never tasted the great strength there is in faith. It is impossible to write well about it or to understand what has been written about it unless one has at one time or another experienced the courage which faith gives a man when trials oppress him. But he who has had even a faint taste of it can never write, speak, meditate, or hear enough concerning it. It is a living "spring of water welling up to eternal life," as Christ calls it in John 4 [:14].

As for me, although I have no wealth of faith to boast of and know how scant my supply is, I nevertheless hope that I have attained to a little faith, even though I have been assailed by great and various temptations; and I hope that I can discuss it, if not more elegantly, certainly more to the point, than those literalists and subtile disputants have previously done, who have not even understood what they have written.

To make the way smoother for the unlearned—for only them do I serve—I shall set down the following two propositions concerning the freedom and the bondage of the spirit:

A Christian is a perfectly free lord of all, subject to none.

A Christian is a perfectly dutiful servant of all, subject to all.

These two theses seem to contradict each other. If, however, they should be found to fit together they would serve our purpose beautifully.

Both are Paul's own statements, who says in I Cor. 9 [:19], "For though I am free from all men, I have made myself a slave to all," and in Rom. 13 [:8], "Owe no one anything, except to love one another." Love by its very nature is ready to serve and be subject to him who is loved. So Christ, although he was Lord of all, was "born of woman, born under the law" [Gal. 4:4], and therefore was at the same time a free man and a servant, "in the form of God" and "of a servant" [Phil. 2:6–7].

Let us start, however, with something more remote from our subject, but more obvious. Man has a twofold nature, a spiritual and a bodily one. According to the spiritual nature, which men refer to as the soul, he is called a spiritual, inner, or new man. According to the bodily nature, which men refer to as flesh, he is called a carnal, outward, or old man. Because of this diversity of nature the Scriptures assert contradictory things concerning the same man, since these two men in the same man contradict each other, "for the desires of the flesh are against the Spirit, and the desires of the Spirit are against the flesh," according to Gal. 5 [:17].

First, let us consider the inner man to see how a righteous, free, and pious Christian, that is, a spiritual, new, and inner man becomes what he is. It is evident that no external thing has any influence in producing Christian righteousness or freedom, or in producing unrighteousness or servitude. A simple argument will furnish the proof of this statement. What can it profit the soul if the body is well, free, and active, and eats, drinks, and does as it pleases? For in these respects even the most godless slaves of vice may prosper. On the other hand, how will poor health or imprisonment or hunger or thirst or any other external misfortune harm the soul?

One thing, and only one thing, is necessary for Christian life, righteousness, and freedom. That one thing is the most holy Word of God, the gospel of Christ, as Christ says, John 11 [:25], "I am the resurrection and the life; he who believes in me, though he die, yet shall he live"; and John 8 [:36], "So if the Son makes you free, you will be free indeed"; and Matt. 4 [:4], "Man shall not live by bread alone, but by every word that proceeds from the mouth of God." Let us then consider it certain and firmly established that the soul can do without anything except the Word of God and that where the Word of God is missing there is no help at all for the soul. If it has the Word of God it is rich and lacks nothing since it is the Word of life, truth, light, peace, righteousness, salvation, joy, liberty, wisdom, power, grace, glory, and of every incalculable blessing.

You may ask, "What then is the Word of God, and how shall it be used, since there are so many words of God?" I answer: The Apostle explains this in Romans 1. The Word is the gospel of God concerning his Son, who was made flesh, suffered, rose from the dead, and was glorified through the Spirit who sanctifies. Faith alone is the saving and efficacious use of the Word of God, according to Rom. 10 [:9]: "If you confess with your lips that Jesus is Lord and believe in your heart that God raised him from the dead, you will be saved." Furthermore, "Christ is the end of the law, that every one who has faith may be justified" [Rom. 10:4]. Again, in Rom. 1 [:17], "He who through faith is righteous shall live." The Word of God cannot be received and cherished by any works whatever but only by faith. Therefore it is clear that, as the soul needs only the Word of God for its life and righteousness, so it is justified by faith alone and not any works; for if it could be justified by anything else, it would not need the Word, and consequently it would not need faith.

Should you ask how it happens that faith alone justifies and offers us such a treasure of great benefits without works in view of the fact that so many works, ceremonies, and laws are prescribed in the Scriptures, I answer: First of all, remember what has been said, namely, that faith alone, without works, justifies, frees, and saves; we shall make this clearer later on. Here we must point out that the entire Scripture of God is divided into two parts: commandments and promises. Although the commandments teach things that are good, the things taught are not done as soon as they are taught, for the commandments show us what we ought to do but do not give us the power to do it. They are intended to teach man to know himself, that through them he may recognize his inability to do good and may despair of his own ability. That is why they are called the Old Testament and constitute the Old Testament. For example, the commandment, "You shall not covet" [Exod. 20:17], is a command which proves us all to be sinners, for no one can avoid coveting no matter how much he may struggle against it. Therefore, in order not to covet and to fulfil the commandment, man is compelled to despair of himself, to seek the help which he does not find in himself elsewhere and from someone else, as stated in Hosea [13:9]: "Destruction is your own, O Israel: your help is only in me." As we fare with respect to one commandment, so we fare with all, for it is equally impossible for us to keep any one of them.

Now when a man has learned through the commandments to recognize his helplessness and is distressed about how he might satisfy the law—since the law must be fulfilled so that not a jot or tittle shall be lost, otherwise man will be condemned without hope—then, being truly humbled and reduced to nothing in his own eyes, he finds in himself nothing whereby he may be justified and saved. Here the second part of Scripture comes to our aid, namely, the promises of God which declare the glory of God, saying, "If you wish to fulfil the law and not covet, as the law demands, come, believe in Christ in whom grace, righteousness, peace, liberty, and all things are promised you. If you believe, you shall have all things; if you do not believe, you shall lack all things."

The following statements are therefore true: "Good works do not make a good man, but a good man does good works: evil works do not make a wicked man, but a wicked man does evil works." Consequently it is always necessary that the substance or person himself be good before there can be any good works, and that good works follow and proceed from the good person, as Christ also says, "A good tree cannot bear evil fruit, nor can a bad tree bear good fruit" [Matt. 7:18]. It is clear that the fruits do not bear the tree and that the tree does not grow the fruits, also that, on the contrary, the trees bear the fruits and the fruits grow on the trees. As it is necessary, therefore, that the trees exist before their fruits and the fruits do not make trees either good or bad, but rather as the trees are, so are the fruits they bear; so a man must first be good or wicked before he does a good or wicked work, and his works do not make him good or wicked, but he himself makes his works either good or wicked.

Illustrations of the same truth can be seen in all trades. A good or bad house does not make a good or a bad builder; but a good or a bad builder makes a good or a bad house. And in general, the work never makes the workman like itself, but the workman makes the work like himself. So it is with the works of man. As the man is, whether believer or unbeliever, so also is his work—good if it was done in faith, wicked if it was done in unbelief. But the converse is not true, that the work makes the man either a believer or an unbeliever. As works do not make a man a believer, so also they do not make him righteous. But as faith makes a man a believer and righteous, so faith does good works. Since, then, works justify no one, and a man must be righteous before he does a good work, it is very evident that it is faith alone which, because of the pure mercy of God through Christ and in his Word, worthily and sufficiently justifies and saves the person. A Christian has no need of any work or law in order to be saved since through faith he is free from every law and does everything out of pure liberty and freely. He seeks neither benefit nor salvation since he already abounds in all things and is saved through the grace of God because in his faith he now seeks only to please God.

So a Christian, like Christ his head, is filled and made rich by faith and should be content with this form of God which he has obtained by faith; only, as I have said, he should increase this faith until it is made perfect. For this faith is his life, his righteousness, and his salvation: it saves him and makes him acceptable, and bestows upon him all things that are Christ's, as has been said above, and as Paul asserts in Gal. 2 [:20] when he says, "And the life I now live in the flesh I live by faith in the Son of God." Although the Christian is thus free from all works, he ought in this liberty to empty himself, take upon himself the form of a servant, be made in the likeness of men, be found in human form, and to serve, help, and in every way deal with his neighbor as he sees that God through Christ has dealt and still deals with him. This he should do freely, having regard for nothing but divine approval.

He ought to think: "Although I am an unworthy and condemned man, my God has given me in Christ all the riches of righteousness and salvation without any merit on my part, out of pure, free mercy, so that from now on I need nothing except faith which believes that this is true. Why should I not therefore freely, joyfully, with all my heart, and with an eager will do all things which I know are pleasing and acceptable to such a Father who has overwhelmed me with his inestimable riches? I will therefore give myself as a Christ to my neighbor, just as Christ offered himself to me; I will do nothing in this life except what I see is necessary, profitable, and salutary to my neighbor, since through faith I have an abundance of all good things in Christ."

Behold, from faith thus flow forth love and joy in the Lord, and from love a joyful, willing, and free mind that serves one's neighbor willingly and takes no account of gratitude or ingratitude, of praise or blame, of gain or loss. For a man does not serve that he may put men under obligations. He does not distinguish between friends and enemies or anticipate their thankfulness or unthankfulness, but he most freely and most willingly spends himself and all that he has, whether he wastes all on the thankless or whether he gains a reward. As his Father does, distributing all things to all men richly and freely, making "his sun rise on the evil and on the good" [Matt. 5:45], so also the son does all things and suffers all things with that freely bestowing joy which is his delight when through Christ he sees it in God, the dispenser of such great benefits.

Therefore, if we recognize the great and precious things which are given us, as Paul says [Rom. 5:5], our hearts will be filled by the Holy Spirit with the love which makes us free, joyful, almighty workers and conquerors over all tribulations, servants of our neighbors, and yet lords of all. For those who do not recognize the gifts bestowed upon them through Christ, however, Christ has been born in vain; they go their way with their works and shall never come to taste or feel those things. Just as our neighbor is in need and lacks that in which we abound, so we were in need before God and lacked his mercy. Hence, as our heavenly Father has in Christ freely come to our aid, we also ought freely to help our neighbor through our body and it works, each one should become as it were a Christ to the other that we may be Christs to one another and Christ may be the same in all, that is, that we may be truly Christians.

OF MARRIAGE AND CELIBACY

DCCXV

A preacher of the gospel, being regularly called, ought, above all things, first, to purify himself before he teaches others. Is he able, with a good conscience, to remain unmarried? Let him so remain; but if he cannot abstain living chastely, then let him take a wife; God has made that plaster for that sore.

DCCXVI

It is written in the first book of Moses, concerning matrimony: God created a man and woman and blessed them. Now, although this sentence was chiefly spoken of human creatures, yet we may apply it to all the creatures of the world—to the fowls of the air, the fish in the waters, and the beasts of the field, wherein we find a male and a female consorting together, engendering and increasing. In all these, God has placed before our eyes the state of matrimony. We have its image, also, even in the trees and earth.

DCCXVII

Between husband and wife there should be no question as to *meum* and *tuum*. All things should be in common between them, without any distinction or means of distinguishing.

DCCXVIII

St. Augustine said, finely: A marriage without children is the world without the sun.

DCCXIX

Maternity is a glorious thing, since all mankind have been conceived, born, and nourished of women. All human laws should encourage the multiplication of families.

DCCXX

The world regards not, nor comprehends the works of God. Who can sufficiently admire the state of conjugal union, which God has instituted and founded, and whence all human creatures, yea, all states proceed. Where were we, if it existed not? But neither God's ordinance, nor the gracious presence of children, the fruit of matrimony, moves the ungodly world, which beholds only the temporal difficulties and troubles of matrimony, but sees not the great treasure that is hid therein. We were all born of women—emperors, kings, princes, yea, Christ himself, the Son of God, did not disdain to be born of a virgin. Let the contemners and rejecters of matrimony go hang, the Anabaptists and

Adamites, who recognise not marriage, but live all together like animals, and the papists, who reject married life, and yet have strumpets; if they must needs contemn matrimony, let them be consistent and keep no concubines.

DCCXXI

The state of matrimony is the chief in the world after religion: but people shun it because of its inconveniences, like one who, running out of the rain, falls into the river. We ought herein to have more regard to God's command and ordinance, for the sake of the generation, and the bringing up of children, than to our untoward humours and cogitations; and further, we should consider that it is a physic against sin and unchastity. None indeed, should be compelled to marry; the matter should be left to each man's conscience, for bride-love may not be forced. God has said, "It is not good that the man should be alone;" and St. Paul compares the church to a spouse, or bride and a bridegroom. But let us ever take heed that, in marrying, we esteem neither money nor wealth, great descent, nobility, nor lasciviousness.

DCCXXII

The Lord has never changed the rules he imposed on marriage, but in the case of the conception of his Son Jesus Christ. The Turks, however, are of opinion that 'tis no uncommon thing for a virgin to bear a child. I would by no means introduce this belief into my family.

DCCXXV

Men have broad and large chests, and small narrow hips, and more understanding than the women, who have but small and narrow breasts, and broad hips, to the end they should remain at home, sit still, keep house, and bear and bring up children.

DCCXXVI

Marrying cannot be without women, nor can the world subsist without them. To marry is physic against incontinence. A woman is, or at least should be, a friendly, courteous, and merry companion in life, whence they are named, by the Holy Ghost, house-honours, the honour and ornament of the house, and inclined to tenderness, for thereunto are they chiefly created, to bear children, and be the pleasure, joy, and solace of their husbands.

DCCXXVII

Dr. Luther said one day to his wife: You make me do what you will; you have full sovereignty here, and I award you, with all my heart, the command in all household matters, reserving my rights in other points. Never any good came out of female domination. God created Adam master and lord of living creatures, but Eve spoilt all, when she persuaded him to set himself above God's will. 'Tis you women, with your tricks and artifices, that lead men into error.

FOCUS QUESTIONS

1. What role does faith play in Luther's thought?

2. How important is the "Word of God"? What is it, according to Luther?

3. Luther believes that faith offers more hope for salvation than good works do. Why is this?

4. *Of Marriage and Celibacy* is composed of words spoken by Luther, taken down by his followers. How does this make it different from *The Freedom of a Christian*?

5. Why does Luther think clergy should be allowed to marry?

6. Why is matrimony important?

7. What is Luther's view of women? What does he see as their role in marriage, and how does he think they should be treated?

8. Luther spent most of his early adulthood as a celibate monk. How do you think this might have affected his views of marriage?

86

Institutes of the Christian Religion (1534 C.E.)

JOHN CALVIN

John Calvin (1509–1564) was the seminal thinker among the post-Luther generation of religious reformers. French by birth and a lawyer by training, Calvin found himself the leader of the Reformation in the Swiss city of Geneva. There he helped establish a new form of church, government that depended not upon a hierarchy of priests and bishops as in the Catholic Church, but instead gave power to individual congregations of believers. Calvin's principal theological contribution was to emphasize the doctrine of predestination as the foundation of individual salvation.

The Institutes of the Christian Religion *was first written for the purpose of gaining acceptance for Protestantism in France. Through successive editions, Calvin expanded and refined his theology.*

KNOWLEDGE OF GOD INVOLVES TRUST AND REVERENCE

What is God? Men who pose this question are merely toying with idle speculations. It is far better for us to inquire, "What is his nature?" and to know what is consistent with his nature. What good is it to profess with Epicurus some sort of God who has cast aside the care of the world only to amuse himself in idleness? What help is it, in short, to know a God with whom we have nothing to do? Rather, our knowledge should serve first to teach us fear and reverence; secondly, with it as our guide and teacher, we should learn to seek every good from him, and having received it, to credit it to his account. For how can the thought of God penetrate your mind without your realizing immediately that, since you are his handiwork, you have been made over and bound to his command by right of creation, that you owe your life to him?—that whatever you undertake, whatever you do, ought to be ascribed to him? If this be so, it now assuredly follows that your life is wickedly corrupt unless it be disposed to his service, seeing that his will ought for us to be the law by which we live. Again, you cannot behold him clearly unless you acknowledge him to be the fountain-head and source of every good. From this too would arise the desire to cleave to him and trust in him, but for the fact that man's depravity seduces his mind from rightly seeking him.

Because it acknowledges him as Lord and Father, the pious mind also deems it meet and right to observe his authority in all things, reverence his majesty, take care to advance his glory, and obey his commandments. Because it sees him to be a righteous judge, armed with severity to punish wickedness, it ever holds his judgment seat before its gaze, and through fear of him restrains itself from provoking his anger. And yet it is not so terrified by the awareness of his judgment as to wish to withdraw, even if some way of escape were open. But it embraces him no less as punisher of the wicked than as benefactor of the pious. For the pious mind realizes that the punishment of the impious and wicked and the reward of life eternal for the righteous equally pertain to God's glory. Besides, this mind restrains itself from sinning, not out of dread of punishment alone; but, because it loves and reveres God as Father, it worships and adores him as Lord. Even if there were no hell, it would still shudder at offending him alone.

Here indeed is pure and real religion; faith so joined with an earnest fear of God that this fear also embraces willing reverence, and carries with it such legitimate worship as is prescribed in the law. And we ought to note this fact even more diligently: all men have a vague general veneration for God, but very few really reverence him; and wherever there is great ostentation in ceremonies, sincerity of heart is rare indeed.

SUPERSTITION

Experience teaches that the seed of religion has been divinely planted in all men. But barely one man in a hundred can be found who nourishes in his own heart what he has conceived; and not even one in whom it matures, much less bears fruit in its season (cf. Ps. 1:3). Now some lose themselves in their own superstition, while others of their own evil intention revolt from God, yet all fall away from true knowledge of him. As a result, no real piety remains in the world. But as to my statement that some erroneously slip into superstition, I do

not mean by this that their ingenuousness should free them from blame. For the blindness under which they labor is almost always mixed with proud vanity and obstinacy. Indeed, vanity joined with pride can be detected in the fact that, in seeking God, miserable men do not rise above themselves as they should, but measure him by the yardstick of their own carnal stupidity, and neglect sound investigation; thus out of curiosity they fly off into empty speculations. They do not therefore apprehend God as he offers himself, but imagine him as they have fashioned him in their own presumption. When this gulf opens, in whatever direction they move their feet, they cannot but plunge headlong into ruin. Indeed, whatever they afterward attempt by way of worship or service of God, they cannot bring as tribute to him, for they are worshiping not God but a figment and a dream of their own heart. Paul eloquently notes this wickedness: "Striving to be wise, they make fools of themselves" (Rom. 1:22f.). He had said before that "they became futile in their thinking" (Rom. 1:21). In order, however, that no one might excuse their guilt, he adds that they are justly blinded. For not content with sobriety but claiming for themselves more than is right, they wantonly bring darkness upon themselves—in fact, they become fools in their empty and perverse haughtiness. From this it follows that their stupidity is not excusable, since it is caused not only by vain curiosity but by an inordinate desire to know more than is fitting, joined with a false confidence.

THE DIVINE WISDOM DISPLAYED
FOR ALL TO SEE

There are innumerable evidences both in heaven and on earth that declare his wonderful wisdom; not only those more recondite matters for the closer observation of which astronomy, medicine, and all natural science are intended, but also those which thrust themselves upon the sight of even the most untutored and ignorant persons, so that they cannot open their eyes without being compelled to witness them. Indeed, men who have either quaffed or even tasted the liberal arts penetrate with their aid far more deeply into the secrets of the divine wisdom. Yet ignorance of them prevents no one from seeing more than enough of God's workmanship in his creation to lead him to break forth in admiration of the Artificer. To be sure, there is need of art and of more exacting toil in order to investigate the motion of the stars, to determine their assigned stations, to measure their intervals, to note their properties. As God's providence shows itself more explicitly when one observes these, so the mind must rise to a somewhat higher level to look upon his glory. Even the common folk and the most untutored, who have been taught only by the aid of the eyes, cannot be unaware of the excellence of divine art, for it reveals itself in this innumerable and yet distinct and well-ordered variety of the heavenly host. It is, accordingly, clear that there is no one to whom the Lord does not abundantly show his wisdom. Likewise, in regard to the structure of the human body one must have the greatest keenness in order to weigh, with Galen's skill, its articulation, symmetry, beauty, and use. But yet, as all acknowledge, the human body shows itself to be a composition so ingenious that its Artificer is rightly judged a wonder-worker.

MAN AS THE LOFTIEST PROOF OF DIVINE WISDOM

Certain philosophers, accordingly, long ago not ineptly called a man a microcosm because he is a rare example of God's power, goodness, and wisdom, and contains within himself enough miracles to occupy our minds, if only we are not irked at paying attention to them. Paul, having stated that the blind can find God by feeling after him, immediately adds that he ought not to be sought afar off (Acts 17:27). For each one undoubtedly feels within the heavenly grace that quickens him. Indeed, if there is no need to go outside ourselves to comprehend God, what pardon will the indolence of that man deserve who is loath to descend within himself to find God?

For the same reason, David, when he has briefly praised the admirable name and glory of God, which shine everywhere, immediately exclaims: "What is man that thou art mindful of him?" (Ps. 8:4). Likewise, "Out of the mouths of babes and sucklings thou hast established strength" (Ps. 8:2). Indeed, he not only declares that a clear mirror of God's works is in humankind, but that infants, while they nurse at their mother's breasts, have tongues so eloquent to preach his glory that there is no need at all of other orators. Consequently, also, he does not hesitate to bring their infant speech into the debate, as if they were thoroughly instructed, to refute the madness of those who might desire to extinguish God's name in favor of their own devilish pride. Consequently, too, there comes in that which Paul quotes from Aratus, that we are God's offspring (Acts 17:28), because by adorning us with such great excellence he testifies that he is our Father. In the same way the secular poets, out of a common feeling and, as it were, at the dictation of experience, called him "the Father of men." Indeed, no one gives himself freely and willingly to God's service unless, having tasted his fatherly love, he is drawn to love and worship him in return.

GOD BESTOWS THE ACTUAL KNOWLEDGE OF HIMSELF UPON US ONLY IN THE SCRIPTURES

That brightness which is borne in upon the eyes of all men both in heaven and on earth is more than enough to withdraw all support from men's ingratitude—just as God, to involve the human race in the same guilt, sets forth to all without exception his presence portrayed in his creatures. Despite this, it is needful that another and better help be added to direct us aright to the very Creator of the universe. It was not in vain, then, that he added the light of his Word by which to become known unto salvation; and he regarded as worthy of this privilege those whom he pleased to gather more closely and intimately to himself. For because he saw the minds of all men tossed and agitated, after he chose the Jews as his very own flock, he fenced them about that they might not sink into oblivion as others had. With good reason he holds us by the same means in the pure knowledge of himself, since otherwise even those who seem to stand firm before all others would soon melt away. Just as old or bleary-eyed men and those with weak vision, if you thrust before them a most beautiful volume, even if they recognize it to be some sort of writing, yet can scarcely construe two words, but with the aid of spectacles will begin to read distinctly; so Scripture, gathering up the otherwise confused knowledge of God in our minds, having dispersed our dullness, clearly shows us the true God.

THE WORD OF GOD AS HOLY SCRIPTURE

But whether God became known to the patriarchs through oracles and visions or by the work and ministry of men, he put into their minds what they should then hand down to their posterity. At any rate, there is no doubt that firm certainty of doctrine was engraved in their hearts, so that they were convinced and understood that what they had learned proceeded from God. For by his Word, God rendered faith unambiguous forever, a faith that should be superior to all opinion. Finally, in order that truth might abide forever in the world with a continuing succession of teaching and survive through all ages, the same oracles he had given to the patriarchs it was his pleasure to have recorded, as it were, on public tablets. With this intent the law was published, and the prophets afterward added as its interpreters. For even though the use of the law was manifold, as will be seen more clearly in its place, it was especially committed to Moses and all the prophets to teach the way of reconciliation between God and men, whence also Paul calls "Christ the end of the law" (Rom. 10:4). Yet I repeat once more: besides the specific doctrine of faith and repentance that sets forth Christ as Mediator, Scripture adorns with unmistakable marks and tokens the one true God, in that he has created and governs the universe, in order that he may not be mixed up with the throng of false gods.

Therefore, however fitting it may be for man seriously to turn his eyes to contemplate God's works, since he has been placed in this most glorious theater to be a spectator of them, it is fitting that he prick up his ears to the Word, the better to profit. And it is therefore no wonder that those who were born in darkness become more and more hardened in their insensibility; for there are very few who, to contain themselves within bounds, apply themselves teachably to God's Word, but they rather exult in their own vanity. Now, in order that true religion may shine upon us, we ought to hold that it must take its beginning from heavenly doctrine and that no one can get even the slightest taste of right and sound doctrine unless he be a pupil of Scripture. Hence, there also emerges the beginning of true understanding when we reverently embrace what it pleases God there to witness of himself. But not only faith, perfect and in every way complete, but all right knowledge of God is born of obedience. And surely in this respect God has, by his singular providence, taken thought for mortals through all ages.

FAITH RESTS UPON GOD'S WORD

This, then, is the true knowledge of Christ, if we receive him as he is offered by the Father: namely, clothed with his gospel. For just as he has been appointed as the goal of our faith, so we cannot take the right road to him unless the gospel goes before us. And there, surely, the treasures of grace are opened to us; for if they had been closed, Christ would have benefited us little. Thus Paul yokes faith to teaching, as an inseparable companion, with these words: "You did not so learn Christ if indeed you were taught what is the truth in Christ" (Eph. 4:20–21 p.).

Yet I do not so restrict faith to the gospel without confessing that what sufficed for building it up had been handed down by Moses and the prophets. But because a fuller manifestation of Christ has been revealed in the gospel, Paul justly calls it the "doctrine of faith" (cf. I Tim. 4:6). For this reason, he says in another passage that by the coming of faith the law was abolished (Rom. 10:4; cf. Gal.

3:25). He understands by this term the new and extraordinary kind of teaching by which Christ, after he became our teacher, has more clearly set forth the mercy of the Father, and has more surely testified to our salvation.

Yet it will be an easier and more suitable method if we descend by degrees from general to particular. First, we must be reminded that there is a permanent relationship between faith and the Word. He could not separate one from the other any more than we could separate the rays from the sun from which they come. For this reason, God exclaims in The Book of Isaiah: "Hear me and your soul shall live" (ch 55:3). And John shows this same wellspring of faith in these words: "These things have been written that you may believe" (John 20:31). The prophet, also, desiring to exhort the people to faith, says: "Today if you will hear his voice" (Ps. 95:7; 94:8, Vg.). "To hear" is generally understood as meaning to believe. In short, it is not without reason that in The Book of Isaiah, God distinguishes the children of the church from outsiders by this mark: he will teach all his children (Isa. 54:13; John 6:45) that they may learn of him (cf. John 6:45). For if benefits were indiscriminately given, why would he have directed his Word to a few? To this corresponds the fact that the Evangelists commonly use the words "believers" and "disciples" as synonyms. This is especially Luke's usage in The Acts of the Apostles: indeed he extends this title even to a woman in Acts 9:36.

Therefore if faith turns away even in the slightest degree from this goal toward which it should aim, it does not keep its own nature, but becomes uncertain credulity and vague error of mind. The same Word is the basis whereby faith is supported and sustained; if it turns away from the Word, it falls. Therefore, take away the Word and no faith will then remain.

We are not here discussing whether a human ministry is necessary for the sowing of God's Word, from which faith may be conceived. This we shall discuss in another place. But we say that the Word itself, however it be imparted to us, is like a mirror in which faith may contemplate God. Whether, therefore, God makes use of man's help in this or works by his own power alone, he always represents himself through his Word to those whom he wills to draw to himself. And for this reason, Paul defines faith as that obedience which is given to the gospel (Rom. 1:5), and elsewhere praises allegiance to faith in Philippians (Phil. 1:3–5; cf. I Thess. 2:13). In understanding faith it is not merely a question of knowing that God exists, but also—and this especially—of knowing what is his will toward us. For it is not so much our concern to know who he is in himself, as what he wills to be toward us.

Now, therefore, we hold faith to be a knowledge of God's will toward us, perceived from his Word. But the foundation of this is a preconceived conviction of God's truth. As for its certainty, so long as your mind is at war with itself, the Word will be of doubtful and weak authority, or rather of none. And it is not even enough to believe that God is trustworthy (cf. Rom. 3:3), who can neither deceive nor lie (cf. Titus 1:2), unless you hold to be beyond doubt that whatever proceeds from him is sacred and inviolable truth.

FOCUS QUESTIONS

1. What seems to be Calvin's view of human nature?

2. How, according to Calvin, does God reveal himself?

3. Historians have often noted the importance of Scripture in Protestant thought. What is Calvin's view? What do you think the practical effect of this might have been for society?

4. How does Calvin's background as a lawyer and literate member of the professional class affect his work?

5. Both Calvin and Luther were Protestants, but they had very different theological views. Can you detect some of these differences in their writings?

87

Letter from India (1543 C.E.)

FRANCIS XAVIER

Francis Xavier (1506–1552) was born in the mountain kingdom of Navarre that straddled the warring states of France and Spain. During his childhood, this Basque country was ruled by the kings of Spain to whom his father served as president of the council. Francis grew up in privileged circumstances, his ancestral home was a hilltop castle, and it was expected that he would receive the best education possible. In 1525 he was sent to the University of Paris, then the leading center of intellectual life in France. While at university, he fell in with another Basque countryman also studying in Paris, Ignatius Loyola. Loyola had recently experienced a profound religious conversion and had pledged to live his life in imitation of Jesus. After much persuasion, he convinced Francis Xavier to do the same, and they became founding members of the Society of Jesus. Xavier left his studies to enter the service of the pope; his first assignment was under the direction of the king of Portugal, whose eastern empire included many non-Christians. Francis Xavier arrived in India in 1542 to establish a mission there. He lived amongst the poorest populations and by translating a catechism into native dialect was able to bring the message of Christianity to the villagers. He baptized and converted thousands. He traveled widely throughout Asia, making a mission to the savage Spice Islands and visiting Japan, whose people he much admired. His final objective was to reach China and establish a mission there, but he died in 1552 before he could fulfill this dream.

Throughout his time in Asia, Francis Xavier reported his experiences to his Jesuit colleagues who remained at home. Many of his letters were private documents, but some were thought so important to the cause of the counter-reformation that they were published and widely distributed. Only two of his letters from the interior of India have survived. In the letter reprinted here, he tells of his experiences among the native peoples whom he calls the Paravas.

We have in these parts a class of men among the pagans who are called Brahmins. They keep up the worship of the gods, the superstitious rites of religion, frequenting the temples and taking care of the idols. They are as perverse and wicked a set as can anywhere be found, and I always apply to them the words of holy David, *"from an unholy race and a wicked and crafty man deliver me, O Lord."* They are liars and cheats to the very backbone. Their whole study is, how to deceive most cunningly the simplicity and ignorance of the people. They give out publicly that the gods command certain offerings to be made to their temples, which offerings are simply the things that the Brahmins themselves wish for, for their own maintenance and that of their wives, children, and servants. Thus they make the poor folk believe that the images of their gods eat and drink, dine and sup like men, and some devout persons are found who really offer to the idol twice a day, before dinner and supper, a certain sum of money. The Brahmins eat sumptuous meals to the sound of drums, and make the ignorant believe that the gods are banqueting. When they are in need of any supplies, and even before, they give out to the people that the gods are angry because the things they have asked for have not been sent, and that if the people do not take care, the gods will punish them by slaughter, disease, and the assaults of the devils. And the poor ignorant creatures, with the fear of the gods before them, obey them implicitly. These Brahmins have barely a tincture of literature, but they make up for their poverty in learning by cunning and malice. Those who belong to these parts are very indignant with me for exposing their tricks. Whenever they talk to me with no one by to hear them they acknowledge that they have no other patrimony but the idols, by their lies about which they procure their support from the people. They say that I, poor creature as I am, know more than all of them put together. They often send me a civil message and presents, and make a great complaint when I send them all back again. Their object is to bribe me to connive at their evil deeds. So they declare that they are convinced that there is only one God, and that they will pray to Him for me. And I, to return the favour, answer whatever occurs to me, and then lay bare, as far as I can, to the ignorant people whose blind superstitions have made them their slaves, their imposture and tricks, and this has induced many to leave the worship of the false gods, and eagerly become Christians. If it were not for the opposition of the Brahmins, we should have them all embracing the religion of Jesus Christ.

The heathen inhabitants of the country are commonly ignorant of letters, but by no means ignorant of wickedness. All the time I have been here in this country I have only converted one Brahmin, a virtuous young man, who has now undertaken to teach the Catechism to children. As I go through the Christian villages, I often pass by the temples of the Brahmins, which they call pagodas. One day lately, I happened to enter a pagoda where there were about two hundred of them, and most of them came to meet me. We had a long conversation, after which I asked them what their gods enjoined them in order to obtain the life of the blessed. There was a long discussion amongst them as to who should answer me. At last, by common consent, the commission was given to one of them, of greater age and experience than the rest, an old man, of more than eighty years. He asked me in return, what commands the God of the Christians laid on them. I saw the old man's perversity, and I refused to speak a word till he had first answered my question. So he was obliged to expose his ignorance, and replied that their gods required two duties of those who desired to go to them hereafter, one of which was to abstain from killing cows, because under that form the gods were adored; the other was to show kindness to the Brahmins, who were the worshippers of the gods. This answer moved my indignation, for I could not but grieve intensely at the thought of the devils being worshipped instead of God by these blind heathen, and I asked them to listen to me in turn. Then I, in a loud voice, repeated the Apostles' Creed and the Ten Commandments. After this I gave in their own language a short explanation, and told them what Paradise is, and what Hell is, and also who they are who go to Heaven to join the company of the blessed, and who are to be sent to the eternal punishments of hell. Upon hearing these things they all rose up and vied with one another in embracing me, and in confessing that the God of the Christians is the true God, as His laws are so agreeable to reason. Then they asked me if the souls of men like those of other animals perished together with the body. God put into my mouth arguments of such a sort, and so suited to their ways of thinking, that to their great joy I was able to prove to them the immortality of the soul. I find, by the way, that the arguments which are to convince these ignorant people must by no means be subtle, such as those which are found in the books of learned schoolmen, but must be such as their minds can understand. They asked me again how the soul of a dying person goes out of the body, how it was, whether it was as happens to us in dreams, when we seem to be conversing with our friends and acquaintance? (Ah, how often this happens to me, dearest brothers, when I am dreaming of you!) Was this because the soul then leaves the body? And again, whether God was black or white? For as there is so great a variety of colour among men, and the Indians being black themselves, consider their own colour the best, they believe that their gods are black. On this account the great majority of their idols are as black as black can be, and moreover are generally so rubbed over with oil as to smell detestably, and seem to be as dirty as they are ugly and horrible to look at. To all these questions I was able to reply so as to satisfy them entirely. But when I came to the point at last, and urged them to embrace the religion which they felt to be true, they made that same objection which we hear from many Christians when urged to change their life,—that they would set men talking about them if they altered their ways and their religion, and besides, they said that they should be afraid that, if they did so, they would have nothing to live on and support themselves by.

I have found just one Brahmin and no more in all this coast who is a man of learning: he is said to have studied in a very famous Academy. Knowing this, I took measures to converse with him alone. He then told me at last, as a great secret, that the students of this Academy are at the outset made by their masters to take an oath not to reveal their mysteries, but that, out of friendship for me, he would disclose them to me. One of these mysteries was that there only exists one God, the Creator and Lord of heaven and earth, whom men are bound to worship, for the idols are simply images of devils. The Brahmins have certain books of sacred literature which contain, as they say, the laws of God. The masters teach in a learned tongue, as we do in Latin. He also explained to me these divine precepts one by one; but it would be a long business to write out his commentary, and indeed not worth the trouble. Their sages keep as a feast our Sunday. On this day they repeat at different hours this one prayer: "I adore Thee, O God; and I implore Thy help for ever." They are bound by oath to repeat this prayer frequently, and in a low voice. My

friend added, that the law of nature permitted them to have more wives than one, and their sacred books predicted that the time would come when all men should embrace the same religion. After all this he asked me in my turn to explain the principal mysteries of the Christian religion, promising to keep them secret. I replied, that I would not tell him a word about them unless he promised beforehand to publish abroad what I should tell him of the religion of Jesus Christ. He made the promise, and then I carefully explained to him those words of Jesus Christ in which our religion is summed up: "He who believes and is baptized shall be saved." This text, with my commentary on it, which embraced the whole of the Apostles' Creed, he wrote down carefully, as well as the Commandments, on account of their close connection with the Creed. He told me also that one night he had dreamt that he had been made a Christian to his immense delight, and that he had become my brother and companion. He ended by begging me to make him a Christian secretly. But as he made certain conditions opposed to right and justice, I put off his baptism. I don't doubt but that by God's mercy he will one day be a Christian. I charged him to teach the ignorant and unlearned that there is only one God, Creator of heaven and earth; but he pleaded the obligation of his oath, and said he could not do so, especially as he was much afraid that if he did it he should become possessed by an evil spirit.

And now I have nothing more to tell you except that so great is the intensity and abundance of the joy which God is accustomed to bestow upon those workmen of His vineyard who labour diligently in cultivating this barbarous part of the same, that for my part I do really believe that if there is in this life any true and solid happiness, it is here. It often happens to me to hear one whose lot it is to labour in this field cry out, *"O Lord, I beseech Thee overwhelm me not now in this life with so much delight, or at least, since in Thy boundless goodness and mercy Thou dost so overwhelm me, take me away to the abode of the blessed. For any one who has once known what it is to taste in his soul Thy ineffable sweetness must of necessity think it very bitter to live any longer without seeing Thee face to face."*

It is one of my greatest consolations, dearest brethren, to think often of you, and to call to mind that sweet and tender intercourse with you which God of His immense goodness vouchsafed to me of old. At the same time it makes me think over and feel very keenly, how much precious time I then spent uselessly, and gathered so little fruit from your holy example and conversation, and from your knowledge of the things of God. However, I owe it to your prayers for me that God has given me the blessing, absent as I am from you in the body, of having, by means of your care and intercession for me, the infinite number of my sins shown to me from God, and of having courage and strength given me to cultivate with all diligence the soil of heathendom. Endless thanks to God's goodness, and to your charity!

Among the many great blessings of my life past and present, and for which I have to thank the mercy of God, I count it as the greatest that I have heard the tidings of the approbation and confirmation of our Institute by the Holy Father. I give God endless thanks that He has now at last ordained to be publicly ratified by His Vicar, so as to be remembered by posterity for ever, that same rule of life which He Himself laid down in secret to His servant our Father Ignatius.

Here, then, I will leave off writing, begging of God that since in His goodness He has united us in a common way of life, and then has separated us so widely for the good of the Christian religion, so also He will be pleased to bring us together again in the abode and home of the Blessed. That He may grant us this grace, let us, if you will, plead the prayers, among others, of the infants and children whom I have baptized with my own hand, here, and whom God has called away to His mansions in heaven before they had lost their robe of innocence. They are, I think, more than a thousand in number, and I pray to them over and over again, begging that they will obtain for us from God that for what remains of this life, or rather of this time of exile, He will teach us to do His will, and to do it so completely as to accomplish all that He requires of us exactly as He Himself desires it to be done.

FOCUS QUESTIONS

1. What is Xavier's opinion of the Brahmins?
2. Why can't Xavier convert the Brahmin?
3. What was France Xavier's reaction to questions about the race of God?

4. Do you believe Xavier's account of how he converted the Paravas?

88

The Life of St. Teresa (1611 C.E.)

TERESA OF AVILA

One of the most remarkable women of her age, Teresa de Cepeda (1515–1582) was born at Avila into a prosperous Spanish family. From childhood she was extremely pious and believed that she had been singled out for some special service to the Lord. Over her father's objections, she entered a Carmelite convent at the age of 21. There she undertook a rigorous spiritual regimen that ultimately broke her health. During this period, she had visions and became convinced that her mission was to travel throughout Spain founding new monasteries and convents. Despite objections by leaders of her order, Teresa followed this spiritual guidance. A prolific author of devotional works, she was widely revered during her lifetime and was canonized as Saint Teresa of Avila in 1622.

In her autobiography, which was published after her death, Teresa describes her intensely personal and mystical relationship with God. Her writings had a profound impact upon ordinary men and women, who identified with the new spiritual rebirth of Spanish Catholicism.

I was one day in prayer, when I found myself in a moment, without knowing how, plunged apparently into hell. I understood that it was our Lord's will I should see the place which the devils kept in readiness for me, and which I had deserved by my sins. It was but a moment, but it seems to me impossible I should ever forget it even if I were to live many years.

The entrance seemed to be by a long and narrow pass, like a furnace, very low, dark, and close. The ground seemed to be saturated with water, mere mud, exceedingly foul, sending forth pestilential odours, and covered with loathsome vermin. At the end was a hollow place in the wall, like a closet, and in that I saw myself confined. All this was even pleasant to behold in comparison with what I felt there. There is no exaggeration in what I am saying.

But as to what I then felt, I do not know where to begin, if I were to describe it; it is utterly inexplicable. I felt a fire in my soul. I cannot see how it is possible to describe it. My bodily sufferings were unendurable. I have undergone most painful sufferings in this life, and, as the physicians say, the greatest that can be borne, such as the contraction of my sinews when I was paralysed, without speaking of others of different kinds, yea, even those of which I have also spoken, inflicted on me by Satan; yet all these were as nothing in comparison with what I felt then, especially when I saw that there would be no intermission, nor any end to them.

These sufferings were nothing in comparison with the anguish of my soul, a sense of oppression, of stifling, and of pain so keen, accompanied by so hopeless and cruel an infliction, that I know not how to speak of it. If I said that the soul is continually being torn from the body, it would be nothing, for that implies the destruction of life by the hands of another; but here it is the soul itself that is tearing itself in pieces. I cannot describe that inward fire or that despair, surpassing all torments and all pain. I did not see who it was that tormented me, but I felt myself on fire, and torn to pieces, as it seemed to me; and, I repeat it, this inward fire and despair are the greatest torments of all.

Left in that pestilential place, and utterly without the power to hope for comfort, I could neither sit nor lie down; there was no room. I was placed as it were in a hole in the wall; and those walls, terrible to look on of themselves, hemmed me in on every side. I could not breathe. There was no light, but all was thick darkness. I do not understand how it is; though there was no light, yet everything that can give pain by being seen was visible.

I know not how it was, but I understood distinctly that it was a great mercy that our Lord would have me see with mine own eyes the very place from which His compassion saved me. I have listened to people speaking of these things, and I have at other times dwelt on the various torments of hell, though not often, because my soul made no progress by the way of fear; and I have read of the divers tortures, and how the devils tear the flesh with red-hot pincers. But all is as nothing before this; it is a wholly different matter. In short, the one is a reality, the other a picture; and all burning here in this life is as nothing in comparison with the fire that is there.

Ever since that time, as I was saying, everything seems endurable in comparison with one instant of sufferings such as those I had then to bear in hell. I am filled with fear when I see that, after frequently reading books which describe in some manner the pains of hell, I was not afraid of them, nor made any account of them. Where was I? How could I possibly take any pleasure in those things which led me directly to so dreadful a place? Blessed forever be Thou, O my God! and oh, how manifest is it that Thou didst love me much more than I did love Thee! How, often, O Lord, didst Thou save me from that fearful prison! and how I used to get back to it contrary to Thy will!

It was that vision that filled me with the very great distress which I feel at the sight of so many lost souls, especially of the Lutherans—for they were once members of the Church by baptism—and also gave me the most vehement desires for the salvation of souls; for certainly I believe that, to save even one from those overwhelming torments, I would most willingly endure many deaths. If here on earth we see one whom we specially love in great trouble or pain, our very nature seems to bid us compassionate him; and if those pains be great, we are troubled ourselves. What, then, must it be to see a soul in danger of pain, the most grievous of all pains, forever? Who can endure it? It is a thought no heart can bear without great anguish. Here we know that pain ends with life at last, and that there are limits to it; yet the sight of it moves our compassion so greatly. That other pain has no ending; and I know not how we can be calm, when we see Satan carry so many souls daily away.

THE EFFECTS OF THE DIVINE GRACES IN THE SOUL—THE INESTIMABLE GREATNESS OF ONE DEGREE OF GLORY

It is painful to me to recount more of the graces which our Lord gave me than these already spoken of; and they are so many, that nobody can believe they were ever given to one so wicked: but in obedience to our Lord, who has commanded me to do it, and you, my fathers, I will speak of some of them to His glory. May it please His Majesty it may be to the profit of some soul! For if our Lord has been thus gracious to so miserable a thing as myself, what will He be to those who shall serve Him truly? Let all people resolve to please His Majesty, seeing that He gives such pledges as these even in this life.

My love of, and trust in, our Lord, after I had seen Him in a vision, began to grow, for my converse with Him was so continual. I saw that, though He was God, He was man also; that He is not surprised at the frailties of men; that He understands our miserable nature, liable to fall continually, because of the first sin, for the reparation of which He had come. I could speak to Him as a friend, though He is my Lord, because I do not consider Him as one of our earthly lords, who affect a power they do not possess, who give audience at fixed hours, and to whom only certain persons may speak. If a poor man have any business with these, it will cost him many goings and comings, and currying favour with others, together with much pain and labour before he can speak to them. Ah, if such a one has business with a king! Poor people, not of gentle blood, cannot approach him, for they must apply to those who are his friends; and certainly these are not persons who tread the world under their feet; for they who do this speak the truth, fear nothing, and ought to fear nothing; they are not courtiers, because it is not the custom of a court, where they must be silent about those things they dislike, must not even dare to think about them, lest they should fall into disgrace.

O my Lord! O my King! who can describe Thy Majesty? It is impossible not to see that Thou art Thyself the great Ruler of all, that the beholding of Thy Majesty fills men with awe. But I am filled with greater awe, O my Lord, when I consider Thy humility, and the love Thou hast for such as I am. We can converse and speak with Thee about everything whenever we will; and when we lose our first fear and awe at the vision of Thy Majesty, we have a greater dread of offending Thee—not arising out of the fear of punishment, O my Lord, for that is as nothing in comparison with the loss of Thee!

I am not yet fifty, and yet I have seen so many changes during my life, that I do not know how to live. What will they do who are only just born, and who may live many years? Certainly I am sorry for those spiritual people who, for certain holy purposes, are obliged to live in the world; the cross they have to carry is a dreadful one.

CERTAIN HEAVENLY SECRETS, VISIONS, AND REVELATIONS

One night I was so unwell that I thought I might be excused making my prayer; so I took my rosary, that I might employ myself in vocal prayer, trying not to be recollected in my understanding, though outwardly I was recollected, being in my oratory. These little precautions are of no use when our Lord will have it otherwise. I remained there but a few moments thus, when I was rapt in spirit with such violence that I could make no resistance whatever. It seemed to me that I was taken up to heaven; and the first persons I saw there were my father and my mother. I saw other things also; but the time was no longer than that in which the *Ave Maria* might be said, and I was amazed at it, looking on it all as too great a grace for me. But as to the shortness of the time, it might have been longer, only it was all done in a very short space.

It happened, also, as time went on, and it happens now from time to time, that our Lord showed me still greater secrets. The soul, even if it would, has neither the means nor the power to see more than what He shows it; and so, each time, I saw nothing more than what our Lord was pleased to let me see. But such was the vision, that the least part of it was enough to make my soul amazed, and to raise it so high that it esteems and counts as nothing all the things of this life. I wish I could describe in some measure, the smallest portion of what I saw; but when I think of doing it, I find it impossible; for the mere difference alone between the light we have here below, and that which is seen in a vision—both being light—is so great, that there is no comparison between them; the brightness of the sun itself seems to be something exceedingly loathsome. In a word, the imagination, however strong it may be, can neither conceive nor picture to itself this light, nor any one of the things which our Lord showed me in a joy so supreme that it cannot be described; for then all the senses exult so deeply and so sweetly, that no description is possible.

I was in this state once for more than an hour, our Lord showing me wonderful things. He seemed as if He would not leave me. He said to me: "See, My daughter, what they lose who are against Me; do not fail to tell them of it." Ah, my Lord, how little good my words will do them, who are made blind by their own conduct, if Thy Majesty will not give them light! Some, to whom Thou hast given it, there are, who have profited by the knowledge of Thy greatness; but as they see it revealed to one so wicked and base as I am, I look upon it as a great thing if there should be any found to believe me. Blessed be Thy name, and blessed be Thy compassion; for I can trace, at least in my own soul, a visible improvement. Afterwards I wished I had continued in that trance for ever, and that I had not returned to consciousness.

FOCUS QUESTIONS

1. How does Teresa's gender affect her account of her life? Can you note any differences from male religious writers of the period?

2. What, according to Teresa's vision, was hell like?

3. What sort of relationship did Teresa have with God?

4. Judging from Teresa's work, what sort of generalizations might you make about contemporary views of heaven and hell?

5. Why do you think Teresa wrote about her experiences? How do you think society responded to her?

Literary Credits

Thomas Wright, editor. The Travels of Marco Polo: The Venetian. (London: George Bell & Sons, 1880), pp. B, 171–179.

1. From *The Huarochiri Manuscript: A Testament of Ancient and Colonial Andean Religion*, translated and edited by Frank Salomon and Gelrge L. Urioste, Copyright 1991. By permission of the University of Texas Press.

2. *The Creation Epic.* Morris Jastrow. *The Civilization of Babylonia and Assyria.* (Philadelphia: J.B. Lippincott, 1915), pp. 428–441.

3. *The Book of Genesis.* From *The Holy Bible*, King James Version.

4. From *Japan: A Documentary History*, ed. David J. Lu (Armonk, NY: M.E. Sharpe, 1997): 37–39. English translation copyright © 1997 by David J. Lu. Reprinted with permission of M.E. Sharpe, Inc. All Rights Reserved. Not for Reproduction.

5. From *Gilgamesh*, translated by William Ellery Leonard, Copyright 1934 by William Ellery Leonard, renewed © 1962 by Barbara A. Hayward. Used by permission of Viking Penguin, a division of Penguin Books, USA, Inc.

6. Pritchard, James B.; *Ancient Near Eastern Texts Relating to the Old Testament.* Copyright 1950 Princeton University Press © renewed 1978 renewed, 2nd. Edition 1955, 1983 renewed PUP Reprinted by permission of Princeton University Press.

7. Pritchard, James B.; *Ancient Near Eastern Texts Relating to the Old Testament.* Copyright 1950 Princeton University Press © renewed 1978 renewed, 2nd. Edition 1955, 1983 renewed PUP Reprinted by permission of Princeton University Press.

8. *Instructions in Letter Writing by an Egyptian Scribe.* From Mirlam Lichthelm. *Ancient Egyptian Literature*, Three Volumes. Copyright © 1973–1980 by the Regents of the University of California. Reprinted by permission of the publisher.

9. Excerpts from the *Book of Exodus* from the Revised Standard Version of the *Bible*. Copyright 1946, 1952, 1971 by the Division of Christian Education of the National Council of the Churches of Christ of USA.

10. Homer, *The Iliad*, translated by William Cullen Bryant, (Boston: Houghton Mifflin, 1898), pp. 259–267, 269–274.

11. Herodotus, *Description of Africa.* G.C. Macaulay, *The History of Herodotus* (London, 1904) Vol. 1, pp. 359–369. Macmillan and Co., Limited. New York: The Macmillan Company.

12. Plato, *The Apology.* From *The Best Known Works of Plato*, translated by B. Jowett, M.A. (Garden City, NY: Blue Ribbon Books, 1942).

13. Plato, *The Republic.* From *The Dialogues of Plato, Volume 3*, translated by B. Jowett. (Oxford: Clarendon Press, 1892), pp. 42–50.

14. Aristotle, *The Politics*. From *The Politics and Economics of Aristotle*, translated by Edward Walford. (London: Bell & Daldy, 1866), pp. 239–243, 245–250.

15. *The Upanishads*. Epiphanius Wilson, *Sacred Books of the East*, Revised Edition. (London: The Colonial Press, 1900), pp. 158, 160–161, 168–169, 171–172.

16. *The Buddha*. Edward Conze, editor, *Buddhist Texts Through the Ages*. (Oxford: Bruno Cassirer Publishers, Ltd., 1954).

17. *The Bhagavad-Gita*. Lionel D. Barnett, translator, *The Bhagavad-Gita*. (London: J.M. Dent & Sons, Ltd., 1905 (pp. 84–91, 127–131. Reprinted by permission of Everyman's Library.

18. Confucius, *Analects*. From *The Analects of Confucius*, translated and annotated by Arthur Waley. Reprinted by permission of Taylor & Francis Publishers, Ltd.

19. From *Lao-Tzu: Tao-Te Ching* by Lao-Tzu, translated by Robert G Henricks, translation copyright © 1989 by Robert G. Henricks. Used by permission of Ballantine Books, a Division of Random House, Inc.

20. Sun Tzu, *The Art of War*, edited with a foreword by James Clavell. (New York: Delacorte Press, 1983, pp. 9–20.

21. Selected songs from *The Book of Songs*, edited and translated by Arthur Waley. Copyright 1937 by Arthur Waley. Used by permission of Grove/Atlantic, Inc.

22. From *Records of the Grand Historian of China*, translated from the *Shih chi of Ssu-Ma Ch'ien* by Burton Watson, Vol. II. Copyright © 1961 Columbia University Press. Reprinted by permission of the publisher.

23. From Han Fei Tzu, *Memorials* in *The Complete Works of Han Fei Tzu, A Classic of Chinese Legalism*. Reprinted by permission of Arthur Prubsthain, London, England.

24. Cicero, *On the Laws*. From *The Treatise of M.T. Cicero*, translated by C.D. Yonge. (London: Henry G. Bohn, 1853), pp. 406–413, 416–417, 419.

25. From Virgil, *The Aeneid*, translated by T.C. Williams. (Boston: Houghton Mifflin, 1910), pp. 1–2, 8–14.

26. Suetonius, "Life of Augustus," in *The Lives of the Twelve Caesars*, translated by Alexander Thomson, revised by T. Forester. (London: George Bell & Sons, 1909), pp. 87–92, 96–97, 115–116, 129–130, 145–146.

27. Excerpts from *The Sermon on the Mount* from the Revised Standard Version of the *Bible*. Copyright 1946, 1952, 1972 by the Division of Christian Education of the National Council of the Churches of Christ in the USA.

28. Justinian, *Code*. From *The Digest of Justinian*, Latin text ed. by T. Mommsen with the aid of Paul Krueger, English translation edited by Alan Watson, Vol. II. Copyright © 1985 by the University of Pennsylvania Press. Reprinted with permission of the University of Pennsylvania Press.

29. From *Secret History* by Procopius, translated by Richard Atwater. Reprinted by permission of the University of Michigan Press.

30. *The Koran*. Reprinted by permission from *The Short Koran*, edited by George M. Lamsa. Copyright © 1949, Ziff-Davis Publishing Co.

31. Ibn Ishaq, *The Life of Muhamnmed*. From www.faithfreedom.org/Articles/sira/03.htm taken from translation made by Edward Rehatsek in the 19th Century.

32. (pp. 147–153) from *The Book of Contemplation: Islam and the Crusades* by Usama Ibn Munqidh translated by Paul M. Cobb (Penguin Books, 2008). Copyright © Paul M. Cobb, 2008. Reproduced by permission of Penguin Books Ltd.

33. Ibn Said, *Book of the Maghrib*. From Ahmed ibn Mohammed al-Makkari, *The History of the Mohammedan Dynasties in Spain*, translated by Pascual de Gayangos (London: Oriental Translation Fund, 1840), pp. 1, 95–102.

34. Khaldun, Ibn; *The Muqaddimah*. © 2005 by Princeton University Press. Reprinted by permission of Princeton University Press.

35. Ibn Battuta, *Travels in Africa*. From *Corpus of Early Arabic Sources for West African History*, translated by J.F.P. Hopkins, edited and annotated by N. Levtzion and J.F.P. Hopkins, pp. 282–7, 296–7. Copyright © University of Ghana, International Acade. Reprinted with the permission of Cambridge University Press.

36. Joao Dos Santos, *Ethiopia Oriental. Hakluytus Posthumus or Purchas His Pilgrimes* (Vol. IX,

J. Maclehose, Glasgow, 1905), pp. 241–245, 253–255.

37. Pan Chao, *Lessons for Women*. From Nancy Lee Swann, *Pan Chao: Foremost Woman Scholar of China* (New York: The Century Company, 1932), pp. 82–90.

38. Fa-hsien, *A Record of Buddhistic Kingdoms*, translated and annotated by James Legge, (Oxford: Clarendon Press, 1886), pp. 34–38, 42–43, 51–52, 57–60.

39. From *Japan: A Documentary History*, ed. David J. Lu (Armonk, NY: M.E. Sharpe, 1997), pp. 23–26. English translation copyright © 1997 by David J. Lu. Reprinted with permission of M.E. Sharpe, Inc.

40. Form of Acknowledgement: Reprinted with permission of The Free Press, a Division of Simon & Schuster, Inc., from *Chinese Civilization: A Sourcebook*, Second Edition, Revised and Enlarged by Patricia Buckley Ebrey. Copyright © 1993 by Patricia Buckley Ebrey. Copyright 1981 by The Free Press. All rights reserved.

41. *The Lotus of the Wonderful Law*. David J. Lu, *Sources of Japanese History*, Vol. I, (New York: McGraw-Hill, 1974), pp. 52–54.

42. Lady Murasaki, *The Tale of Genji*. From *The Tale of Genji* by Lady Murasaki, translated from the Japanese by Arthur Waley, 1926. Houghton Mifflin Company.

43. Form of Acknowledgement: Reprinted with permission of The Free Press, a Division of Simon & Schuster, Inc., from *Chinese Civilization: A Sourcebook*, Second Edition, Revised and Enlarged by Patricia Buckley Ebrey. Copyright © 1993 by Patricia Buckley Ebrey. Copyright 1981 by The Free Press. All rights reserved.

44. (pp. 12–16) from *The Laws of Manu* translated with an introduction and notes by Wendy Doniger with Brian K. Smith (Penguin Classics, 1991). Copyright © Wendy Doniger and Brian K. Smith, 1991. Reproduced by permission of Penguin Books Ltd.

45. Tacitus, *The Germania*, The Oxford Translation, Revised. (New York: Arthur Hinds & Co., n.d.), pp. 3, 11–13, 15–16, 19–26.

46. From *The Burgundian Code*, translated by Katherine Fischer. Copyright © 1949 by the University of Pennsylvania Press. Reprinted with permission of the University of Pennsylvania Press.

47. Einhard, *Life of Charlemagne*. From *Early Lives of Charlemagne* by Einhard & The Monk of St. Gall; translated and edited by Professor A.J. Grant. New York: Cooper Square Publishers, Inc., 1966.

48. *Magna Carta*. From Boyd C. Barrington, editor, *Magna Carta*, (Philadelphia: Wm. J. Campbell, 1900), pp. 228–234, 237–240, 244, 246–250.

49. (pp. 57–60) from *NJAL'S SAGA* translated with an introduction and notes by Robert Cook (Penguin Press, 2001). Copyright © Leifer Erikisson Publishing Ltd., 1997. Reproduced by permission of Penguin Books Ltd.

50. Reprinted by permission of of the publishers and the Trustees of the Loeb Classical Library from St. Augustine: Volume I, LCL 411, translated by G.E. McCracken, 1957, St. Augustine: Volume II, LCL 412, translated by W.M. Green, 1963, St. Augustine: Volume IV, LCL 414, translated by Philip Levine, 1966, St. Augustine: Volume VII, LCL 417, translated by W.M. Green, 1972, Loeb Classical Library, Cambridge, Mass.: Harvard University Press by the President and Fellows of Harvard College. Loeb Classical Library is a registered trademark of the President and Fellows of Harvard College.

51. St. Benedict of Nursia, *The Rule*, translated by Dom Justin McCann, (Latrobe, PA: Archabbey Press, 1950), p. 63ff. Reprinted by permission.

52. St. Francis of Assisi. *Admonitions*. From *The Admonitions of St. Francis of Assisi* by Lothar Hardick O.F.M., translated by David Smith. Reprinted by permission of the Franciscan Press of Quincy University.

53. St. Thomas Aquinas, *Summa Theologica*. From *Summa Theologica* by St. Thomas Aquinas, translated by Fathers of the English Dominican Province. Copyright © 1948 Benziger Bros., Inc. Reprinted with permission from McGraw-Hill.

54. (pp. 66–9) from *The Letters of Abelard and Heloise translated* and introduced by Betty Radice (Penguin Classics, 1974). Copyright © Betty Radice, 1974. Reproduced by permission of Penguin Books Ltd.

55. *The Alexiad*. From *The Alexiad of Princess Anna Comnena*, pp. 248, 262–264, translated by Elizabeth A.S. Dawes. Copyright © 1967 by Routledge &